**DOMESDAY BOOK**

Devon

*History from the Sources*

# DOMESDAY BOOK

A Survey of the Counties of England

*LIBER DE WINTONIA*

Compiled by direction of

# KING WILLIAM I

Winchester
1086

# DOMESDAY BOOK

general editor

JOHN MORRIS

9

# Devon

edited by
Caroline and Frank Thorn

*from a draft translation prepared by*
Caroline Thorn and Agnes O'Driscoll

(Part Two)

PHILLIMORE
Chichester
1985

1985
Published by
PHILLIMORE & CO. LTD.
London and Chichester
*Head Office*: Shopwyke Hall,
Chichester, Sussex, England

© Mrs. Susan Morris, 1985

ISBN 0 85033 491 8 (case)
ISBN 0 85033 492 6 (limp)

*Printed in Great Britain by*
*The Cromwell Press*
*Trowbridge*
*Wilts*

# DEVON

(Part One)
Introduction
The Exeter Domesday (Introduction)
DB and Exon. Extracts

## The Domesday Survey of Devon

**Bibliography, Abbreviations and Acknowledgements**

(Part Two)
Introductory Notes
General Notes
Exon. Extra Information and Discrepancies with DB
(including an Introduction)
Lordship and Villagers' Table ('L')
Details Table ('D')
Appendix
Persons Index
Places Indices
Maps and Map Keys
Technical Terms
Systems of Reference

# Note 1

## INTRODUCTORY NOTES

### 1. PLACES

In the text of the south-western counties, neither the Exchequer Domesday nor the Exon. Book includes the Hundred rubrication that is an important aid to the identification of places. This absence is particularly important in a large county such as Devonshire, where a number of places are named only from the rivers on which they lie, such as *Clist* from the river Clyst, *Lonmele* or *Lonmine* from the river Lowman, *Colum* or *Colun* from the Culm, *Teigne* or *Taigne* from the Teign, *Otri* and variants from the river Otter, and *Limet* or *Nimete* from the old name of the two Yeo rivers (see Introductory Note 2). Moreover, a single DB form can represent two or more places in different Hundreds or in widely separated parts of the County. Thus DB *Wiche* will be one of several places called Wick, Week or Wyke; there are two Allers represented by *Alra*, two Bickleighs by *Bichelie*; Sampford Courtenay and Sampford Spiney are both represented by DB *Sanford* and there are many places represented by *Bere* or *Bera*, *Bocheland*, *Lege*, *Cumba*, *Hele* and *Stoche*. Only occasionally does DB differentiate places of the same basic name: *Bovi* and *Adonebovi* (3;8. 17,22); *Racheneforde* and *Litel Racheneford* (16,148. 23,13); *Torilande* and *Liteltorelande* (15,16. 34,9); *Lonmine* and *Oplomie* (25,19. 35,16) and *Niresse* and *Ulpesse* (3,69-70). All place-names need to be treated with care: thus Alphington and West Alvington happen to have different DB forms, but they have the same origin and other evidence, apart from the DB form, is needed to distinguish them.

The absence of Hundred information can in part be made good from the evidence of the Exon. Book Tax Returns for Devon (folios 65a-71a), printed by Ellis in DB3, translated in the Devonshire Association Volume (see Bibliography) and tabulated and discussed, Hundred by Hundred, in the articles of O. J. Reichel; there is a brief discussion below and in the Appendix to this volume, but the present editors hope to publish their fuller analysis separately at a later date.

The Tax Return for each Hundred gives the total hidage for the Hundred, the amount of tax the King receives on how many hides, then the amount of (exempt) lordship land (in total and in detail), followed by details of holdings for which tax is owed. Place-names are rarely included (those that do appear are included in Places Index 1 of this volume), but when the personal-names and the extents of lands given in the Returns are compared with DB and the corresponding Exon., most entries can be satisfactorily identified and located. A very clear resumé of the problems of dating the Tax Returns is given in VCH Dorset iii pp. 117-118.

In this county volume it is not intended to incorporate all the information recoverable from the Tax Returns but only that which is needed to support discussion of the text of DB and then only when the information is reasonably certain. Since the Tax Returns give the total hidage for each Hundred, it is sometimes possible to deduce all the constituent villages of a Hundred simply by adding together the hidage of places considered likely to be in the Hundred, then adjusting the list until the correct total is obtained. But this argument based on totals only, when there are many discrepancies between the Tax Returns and DB and when many villages have the same hidage figures, must be regarded as an unreliable procedure. This is the method adopted by Eyton in his analyses for Somerset and Dorset (see Bibliography). It is wisely avoided by Reichel, but even so he is sometimes careless, sometimes excessively ingenious, and sometimes he employs mere guesswork in his identification of hidage figures with places. References to the Tax Return Hundreds are given in Roman numerals; the relation of the Tax Return Hundreds to the 'modern' (that is mid-nineteenth century) Hundreds is given at the beginning of the Appendix and that of the 'modern' Hundreds to those of the Tax Returns is given at the head of the Map Keys.

A secondary source of place-name identification from within the Exchequer DB and Exon. Domesday returns themselves is the order in which places are entered in each fief. In some counties where the text of DB has full Hundredal rubrication, lands are found to be entered in a consistent order of Hundreds within each chapter, probably as the scribe rearranged into fiefs information that was first returned, or later checked, by Hundreds; see Sawyer (2) in the Bibliography. Among the south-west counties, Cornwall, Devon and Somerset show a consistent sequence of Hundreds within each chapter in the order in which material is arranged in the Exon. Domesday. Moreover, in Somerset, the sequence is the same as that of a list of Hundreds included among the folios of the

# Note 1

Exon. Book (folios 64a,b, see DB Somerset Appendix I); similarly, in Devon the sequence is that of the second list found on folio 63a, with the proviso that Hundreds are sometimes entered in groups rather than one following another in strict order (see the Appendix).

Where the order of Exon. differs from that of Exchequer DB, as for example in Chapters 1, 3, 15 and 52 or in the treatment of Chapters 8–13a, it is the Exon. order that clearly preserves a standard sequence of Hundreds. The process of condensing Exon. into Exchequer DB afforded the chance to rearrange some material: thus Chapters 1 and 15 were reconstructed on different lines (see Chs. 1 and 15 notes); Chapter 52 was rearranged by subtenants; the lands of Walter of Claville were separated from those of Gotshelm to form the separate chapters 24–25; the 'Lands of the Churches that have been given to the Saints in Alms' (Chs. 8–13a), the Lands of the French Men-at-Arms (Ch. 22 note), of the King's Servants (Ch. 51 note) and of the English Thanes (Ch. 52 note) were completely reorganised and this destroyed or distorted the original Hundredal sequence.

In the notes which follow it is thus the order of Exon. that is cited to indicate the Hundred in which a place lay in 1086; in most chapters the sequence is given in an introductory note. Although the order is not without occasional obscurities (see Chs. 19, 34), if a place apparently belonging to one Hundred falls within a group of places belonging to another, there is a strong presumption that either the place has been incorrectly identified or that a minor adjustment has been made to the boundary of the Hundred since 1086; such cases are examined in individual notes and an overall summary given in the Appendix.

Total and secure identification of places, which is so vital for any serious study of the text of Domesday, is a long and complex task. First the editor must satisfy himself that the evolution of the place-name from the DB form to its modern-day form is credible and that there are enough intermediate forms to prove it. Then the 1086 Hundred must be established in order to distinguish this place from others of the same name, elsewhere in the County. Then the identification must be clinched by a study of genealogy and manorial descent: thus a place held by Baldwin the Sheriff in 1086 should later be found held by the Honour of Okehampton; a place held by Bretel under the Count of Mortain should reappear in the Honour of Ashill. Study of later documents will often confirm the 1086 Hundred and give the extent and the sub-manors of the DB holding. Lastly, the details of DB, such as lands added or taken away, mills, fisheries, salt-workings, etc., must be harmonised with the identification.

Much of this task is outside the scope of this edition and must await the work of other scholars: a full revision of the elderly and unreliable EPNS volumes would be needed in order to eradicate the many errors and omissions and allow a modern treatment of major names, and a fuller treatment of minor, and field, names; it is to be hoped that some day the indices of the Book of Fees and of the Feudal Aids will be revised, and the appearance of further VCH volumes studying the County Hundred by Hundred and manor by manor will trace the descent of each DB holding, give greater exactness to old identifications and correct others. An editor for this County feels less secure using the tools currently available to him than one who has to hand the Dorset place-name volumes of A. D. Mills or the Somerset VCH volumes of Dr. Dunning.

Nonetheless, the publication of VCH volume i for Devon in 1906 marked an important stage in the identification of Domesday places. The Devonshire Association had published between 1884 and 1892 an extended text of Exon. Domesday and of the Tax Returns, together with a translation, the former unfortunately rearranged to follow Exchequer Book order; this had stimulated a number of Devonshire scholars and antiquarians, among them R. N. Worth, the Reverend T. W. Whale and the Reverend O. J. Reichel, to study a number of aspects of the Book, including the place-names. Worth's superficial study (1893) provoked Whale and Reichel to analyse the Hundredal arrangement of the Exon. Book and to publish articles on the Hundreds, the identifications of many places and on some of the major documents needed to follow the descent of Domesday manors during the next centuries. Reichel included Whale's identifications in his VCH volume, where there was disagreement, but the former is more usually correct and it is to him that are due all the durable identifications of DB places. Although the Domesday Gazetteer (1975) made a number of new proposals, there has been no full-scale study of the place-names since the publication of the VCH volume, the EPNS volumes being largely based on Reichel's work.

# Note 1

Reichel continued to publish articles reconstructing the 1086 Hundreds and following the history of manors, and also prepared a number of surveys that the Devonshire Association had not the means to publish during his lifetime; these appeared as ten supplementary volumes plus a cumulative index after his death, surveying eighteen Hundreds in great detail and with a sound command of his material.

Reichel's work is formidable in bulk and in detail and is still regarded as an authoritative source. But it must be used with caution. Some of his theories about the making of Domesday have been superseded and the work on individual identifications is very uneven: the early studies (for example those of Hartland and North Tawton and Witheridge Hundreds) use unreliable secondary sources, are poor in detail and method, and were never revised; but later work is often based on this insecure material. Throughout Reichel's work, his handling of place-name forms is frequently careless and unsound, with the result that many of his identifications cannot in fact be derived from the DB forms which he cites. Assumption and assertion, rather than conclusive evidence, play a major part in some of his identifications, especially of the unnamed subdivisions of DB holdings; moreover, in attempting to identify every entry in the Book of Fees with a named DB counterpart, he ignores the fact that many represent unnamed subdivisions of named DB lands or are later subinfeudations; and that many DB lands are not later held by knight-service and so do not appear in feudal lists. This leads him to over-hasty identifications where other evidence is lacking.

Much work remains to be done to trace the evolution of place-names and the descent of manors in Devon. Meanwhile, the notes to this volume, while they do not claim to be exhaustive, are intended to offer enough later information from selected sources to support identifications that might reasonably have been questioned, and to show where further research is needed.

A number of adjacent modern settlements in Devon, now distinguished by affixes such as 'East' and 'West', 'Upper' and 'Lower', share the same DB place-name form. The existence of separate, but nearby, villages is rarely evidenced in Devon DB and such places are not normally distinguished in the translation and the Indices of this volume, the grid reference referring to the larger village. Where later evidence enables these modern separate villages to be traced from individual DB holdings, this fact is recorded in the notes below.

On the other hand, to avoid confusion, affixes are included where two places of the same basic name are in different parts of the County, or in different Hundreds. Thus South Milton appears in order to distinguish it from the distant Milton Abbot and Milton Damerel; East Putford and West Putford are adjacent but distinguished because they lie in different Hundreds, but the adjacent villages of East and West Hagginton appear simply as Hagginton.

A number of identifications in this edition differ from those of VCH or DG. For convenience, the major discrepancies are set out below in a table. Differentiation of adjacent places of the same basic name is ignored, as are variant spellings and alternative forms. Moreover, only identifications that actually conflict are noticed; where one identification is more precise than another, but still in the same parish, it is usually ignored. Places within inverted commas are identifiable, but now lost, or not precisely identified and located (as explained in the Introduction to the Indices of Places).

| DB column | Chapter and Section | DB Form | VCH | DG | This edition |
|---|---|---|---|---|---|
| 100b | 1,6 | *Ringedone* | ?Frenchstone | Ringdon in George Nympton | *Ringedone* |
| 100b | 1,11 | *Cherletone* | Charton | as VCH | 'Charlton' |
| 100d | 1,31 | *Toritone* | Little Torrington (TWW). Upcot in Sheepwash (OJR) | Little Torrington | as DG |

# Note 1

| DB column | Chapter and Section | DB Form | VCH | DG | This edition |
|---|---|---|---|---|---|
| 101a | 1,41 | *Blachepole* | Blackpool in Chittlehampton (OJR). Blackpool in South Molton (TWW) | Blackpool in South Molton | as DG |
| 101a | 1,41 | *Nimete* | Warkleigh in South Molton (OJR) Twitchin (TWW) | George Nympton | *Nimete* |
| 101a | 1,47 | *Hamistone* | Little Hempston (OJR), Broad Hempston (TWW) | Broad and Little Hempston | Littlehempston |
| 101c | 1,71 | *Aisbertone* | Washburton in Ashprington | Ashprington | as DG |
| 101c | 1,72 | *Vlwardesdone* | ?in Down St. Mary | Wolfin | ?Down St. Mary |
| 102b | 3,8 | *Brungarstone* | ?Bawtor in Hennock | as VCH (Bottor) | *Brungarstone* |
| 102b | 3,15 | *Beldrendiland* | West Barlington in Roborough | Brandize | as VCH (Barlington) |
| 102c | 3,24 | *Pillande* | Pilland (TWW) Pulcress manor in Pilton (OJR) | Pilland | as DG |
| 102c | 3,27 | *Hagintone* | Kings Heanton | as VCH | Hagginton |
| 102d | 3,45 | *Brai* | Bray in South Molton (OJR) Little Bray in Charles (TWW) | High and Little Bray | (East) Bray in South Molton |
| 102d | 3,46 | *Norcote* | Northcote in Braunton | Northcote in East Down | as DG |
| 102d | 3,53 | *Stodlei* | Stoly in Shirwell | Stoodleigh in West Buckland | as DG |
| 103a | 3,73 | *Morceth* | Rowlstone in Morchard Bishop | Cruwys Morchard | as DG |
| 103a | 3,76 | *Celvertesberie* | ?Colston in Templeton | as VCH | *Celvertesberie* |
| 103b | 3,85 | *Farewei* | Farway in Colyton | Farway (parish) | as DG |
| 103c | 3,96 | *Cheletone* | Charlton Luggeston in Upottery (OJR) Charlton in Axmouth (TWW) | Charton | 'Charlton' |
| 104a | 6,6 | *Aiserstone* | in Ashburton | Sherberton | Ashton |
| 104a | 6,7 | *Aisse* | Abbots Ash *alias* Ashford in Aveton Giffard | Ashford | 'Abbots Ash' |

Note 1

| DB column | Chapter and Section | DB Form | VCH | DG | This edition |
|---|---|---|---|---|---|
| 104c | 14,4 | Landeshers | ?Houndbear (OJR) or Hawkerland (TWW) | (unidentified) | Landeshers |
| 104c | 15,2 | Stochelie | 'Stockleigh' (unlocated) in Hayridge Hundred | Leigh in Silverton | Stochelie |
| 104c | 15,6 | Stochelie | Stockleigh in Highampton (OJR) Lee in Hartland (TWW) | Stockleigh in Highampton | as DG |
| 104d | 15,16 | Liteltorelande | ?Woodland in Little Torrington | as VCH | Little Torrington |
| 104d | 15,17 | Stochelie | South Stockleigh alias Sutton Satchville | Stockleigh Pomeroy | 'Stockleigh' |
| 104d | 15,18 | Stochelie | Stockleigh Luccombe alias Little Stockleigh | Stockleigh English | 'Stockleigh' |
| 104d | 15,20 | Colebroch | Holbrook | Colebrook | as VCH |
| 104d | 15,22 | Rochebere | Rockbear alias Hockland in Colyton Raleigh | Rockbeare Parish | as DG |
| 104d | 15,25 | Lege | Northleigh | Northleigh, Southleigh and Brimley | as VCH |
| 104d | 15,28 | Hewis | ?Yedmerston in Modbury | North Huish | Hewis |
| 105a | 15,43 | Hamistone | Broadhempston (OJR). Little Hempston (TWW) | Broad and Little Hempston | Broadhempston |
| 105b | 15,47 | Hele | Hele Satchvil in Buckland Brewer (OJR). Littleham (TWW) | Hele in Petrockstowe | Hele in Meeth and Petrockstowe |
| 105b | 15,50 | Tori | ?Ridge in Plympton St. Mary (OJR) ?Torr in Newton Ferrers (TWW) | Torridge | as DG |
| 105b | 15,57 | Alwinestone | Little Bampton alias Petton in Bampton | (unidentified) | Alwinestone |
| 105c | 15,63 | Cherletone | Charlton in Plymtree | Cheriton in Payhembury | as DG |
| 105c | 15,66 | Holescome | Luscombe alias Halwells Combe alias Jeclescombe alias Julescombe in Bigbury | Hollowcombe (in Ermington) | as DG |

# Note 1

| DB column | Chapter and Section | DB Form | VCH | DG | This edition |
|---|---|---|---|---|---|
| 106a | 16,22 | *Cacheberge* | Kigbear in Okehampton | Cookbury | as VCH |
| 106b | 16,28 | *Mildecote* | Middlecot in Ashwater (OJR) or in Broadwood Kelly (TWW) | Middlecott in Broadwood Kelly | as DG |
| 106b | 16,30 | *Mildelcote* | Corston in Broadwood Kelly | Middlecott in Broadwood Kelly | as DG |
| 106c | 16,42 | *Helescane* | ?Hele Poure in Meeth (OJR) 'Henshaw' or Huntshaw Wood (TWW) | Hele (in Meeth) | *Helescane* |
| 106c | 16,46 | *Liege* | Rowland's Leigh *alias* Rashleigh in Wembworthy (OJR) Leigh in Coldridge (TWW) | Rashleigh | Leigh |
| 106c | 16,47 | *Bera* | Cherrybear in Dolton | as VCH | Great Beere |
| 107a | 16,79 | *Ringedone* | ?Fraynes and Westacot in Chittlehampton | Ringdon in West Anstey | as DG (Ringcombe), see note |
| 107a | 16,88 | *Smidelie* | Snedleigh *alias* Stoodleigh in West Buckland | Snydles | as DG |
| 107b | 16,104 | *Colun* | Collumpton or Hele in Bradninch | Combe Sackville | 'Monk Culm' |
| 107c | 16,105 | *Bernardesmore* | East Culm with Longmoor (OJR) Dunmore in Silverton (TWW) | (unidentified) | 'Bernardsmoor' |
| 108a | 16,139 | *Petecote* | Pennycot in Shobrooke | Patcott | *Petecote* |
| 108a | 16,146 | *Welingedinge* | (unidentified) | Wilson (in Worlington) | Wilson (in Witheridge) |
| 108b | 16,160 | *Magnetone* | Manaton | *Magnetone* | as VCH |
| 108c | 16,167 | *Alreford* | Allerford in Axminster or Rosamundford in East Budleigh | Aller | *Alreford* |
| 108c | 16,176 | *Prenla* | West Prawle in Portlemouth | East Prawle | as VCH |
| 109a | 17,18 | *Lidemore* | ?More Killatree in Pyworthy | (unidentified) | *Lidemore* |
| 109a | 17,23 | *Cumbe* | Combe Fishacre | Longcombe | as VCH |

# Note 1

| DB column | Chapter and Section | DB Form | VCH | DG | This edition |
|---|---|---|---|---|---|
| 109a | 17,24 | Cumbe | Longcombe (OJR) Combe Fishacre (TWW) | Combe Fishacre | as DG |
| 109a | 17,25 | Hamestone | Hempston Chatard *alias* Uphempston in Little Hempston | Broad and Little Hempston | Littlehempston |
| 109b | 17,46 | Hewis | North Huish | South Huish | as VCH |
| 109b | 17,50 | Lege | East and West Leigh *alias* Thurisleigh in Harberton | Leigh in Harberton | as DG |
| 109d | 17,72 | Leuricestone | Leigham in Eggbuckland (OJR) Laira Green (TWW) | Laira | *Leuricestone* |
| 110a | 17,93 | Waliforde | 'Walford' *alias* Collaford or Collard in Shaugh Prior | *Waliforde* lost in Plympton St. Mary | as DG ('Walford') |
| 110b | 19,2 | Fereurde | Alfardisworthy in Bradworthy | Virworthy | as DG |
| 110b | 19,10 | Hacome | Nether Haccombe *alias* Netherton in Combe-in-Teignhead | Haccombe in Exeter St. Thomas | Haccombe in Combein Teignhead |
| 110c | 19,22 | Hewise | ?Orway in Kentisbeare | Hays Park | *Hewise* |
| 110d | 19,29 | Racumbe | Higher Rocombe (TWW). Horridge in Ilsington (OJR) | Rocombe | as DG |
| 110d | 19,32 | Horescome | 'Awlescombe' probably Owlacombe or Garland Hayes in Bradninch | Buckerell | Awliscombe |
| 110d | 19,33 | Ædelstan | Yardlestone in Tiverton (OJR) Healstone *alias* Yowleston in Puddington (TWW) | Yowlestone | as DG |
| 110d | 19,36 | Madescame | Woodscombe in Cruwys Morchard | (unidentified) | Mackham |
| 110d | 19,36 | Orescome | Awlescombe | Buckerell | as VCH |
| 110d | 19,40 | Toredone | Down in Witheridge | Thorn | *Toredone* |
| 110d | 19,42 | Otri | ?Ivedon | Waringstone and Deer Park | Ivedon |
| 110d | 19,43 | Otri | On the Otter | Hembury | Ivedon |
| 110d | 19,43 | Holescome | Awlescombe | Buckerell | as VCH |

# Note 1

| DB column | Chapter and Section | DB Form | VCH | DG | This edition |
|---|---|---|---|---|---|
| 111a | 19,46 | *Lege* | Southleigh | Northleigh, Southleigh and Brimley | as VCH |
| 111a | 20,2 | *Ferse* | Foss *alias* Fairlinch in Braunton | Furzehill in Lynton | Furze in West Buckland |
| 111a | 20,5 | *Bere* | Bar *alias* Beare in East Worlington | Beara in Kings Nympton | 'Beare' |
| 111a | 20,6 | *Waford* | Little Washford, now Stewarton (OJR). Washford Moor (TWW) | Washford Pyne | as DG |
| 111a | 20,8 | *Bradeford* | Bradford in Cruwys Morchard | Bradford in Witheridge | as DG |
| 111b | 20,15 | *Loscume* | Luscombe *alias* West Combe in Dartington | Luscombe in Rattery | as DG |
| 111b | 21,6 | *Derte* | ?Wellton in Cadeleigh (OJR) Dart Farm, Silverton (TWW) | Dart in Cadeleigh | as DG |
| 111b | 21,11 | *Assecote* | ?Wood, outlier of East Worlington | (unidentified) | *Assecote* |
| 111c | 21,15 | *Forhode* | ?Fardown, outlier of Colyton | Farwood | as DG |
| 111c | 23,1 | *Holecome* | Hollacombe in Kentisbury (OJR) Holcombe, Bampton (TWW) | Hollacombe in Kentisbury | as DG |
| 111d | 23,4 | *Stotlege* | ?In Berrynarbor or Stoodleigh in Witheridge Hundred | Stoodleigh in West Buckland | as DG(?) |
| 111d | 23,7 | *Hocheorde* | Hockford | as VCH | Hockworthy |
| 111d | 23,15 | *Sutreworde* | Unidentified, apparently Lustleigh | Southbrook | as VCH |
| 112a | 23,16 | *Godrintone* | Gurrington *alias* Goodrington in Woodland | Goodrington in Paignton | as DG |
| 112a | 23,17 | *Hetfelle* | ?Holditch in Thorncombe | Heathfield in Honiton | *Hetfelle* |
| 112a | 23,24 | *Wodicome* | Widdecombe in Stockenham, Coleridge Hundred | as VCH | ?Woodcombe in Chivelstone |
| 112b | 24,4 | *Ratdone* | Raddon i.e. West Yeo in Witheridge (OJR). West Raddon in Shobrook (TWW) | West Raddon | as DG |

# Note 1

| DB column | Chapter and Section | DB Form | VCH | DG | This edition |
|---|---|---|---|---|---|
| 112b | 24,17 | Bere | ?Netherton in Farway | as VCH | Bere |
| 112c | 24,27 | Chetelescote | Gilscot in Colridge | as VCH | Chetelescote |
| 112c | 24,28 | Nimet | Wolfin | Nymet | as VCH |
| 112c | 24,32 | Fereordin | Farworthy, an outlier of Sutcombe | Virworthy | as DG |
| 112d | 25,7 | Brigeford | Brushford in Winkleigh | Brushford (parish) | as DG |
| 112d | 25,16 | Lonmine | Childlowman (Chieflowman) | Chieflowman and Craze Lowman | Uplowman |
| 112d | 25,18 | Loteland | (unidentified) | Littleland | Loteland |
| 113a | 25,27 | Vlestanecote | Ulverstone in Awlescombe (OJR) Wilson in Cheriton (TWW) | Woolston in Staverton | Vlestanecote |
| 113a | 25,28 | Herstanhaia | Cliston Hayes alias Bluehayes in Broadclist | Bluehayes | Herstanhaia |
| 113b | 28,12 | Bevleie | Beenleigh in Harbertonford (OJR). Beenleigh in Diptford (TWW) | Beenleigh in Diptford | as DG |
| 113c | 29,4 | Dunestanetone | Dunstone in Stockenham | as VCH | Dunstone in Yealmpton |
| 113c | 29,9 | Metwi | Lovaton Bastard in Meavy | (unidentified) | Meavy |
| 113c | 29,10 | Terra Sancti Petri de Plintone | at Sutton Prior | Sutton Prior | (Not a place-name) |
| 113d | 32,5 | Cageford | Chagford in Throwleigh | Chagford Parish | as DG |
| 113d | 32,8 | Tovretone | Little Tiverton alias West Exe | Tiverton | as DG |
| 113d | 32,9 | Wasfelte | Little Washfield in Washfield, Witheridge Hundred | Washfield | 'Little Washfield' |
| 113d | 34,1 | Wiche | South Week | Germansweek and Southweek | as VCH |
| 114a | 34,4 | Alwineclancavele | ?East Yeowelston in Bradworthy | as VCH | Alwineclancavele |
| 114a | 34,9 | Torilande | Yelland or Kingscot next Dodscot in St. Giles in the Wood | Torilande | ?Great Torrington |
| 114a | 34,13 | Bolewis | ?Moulish | Bowlish | Mowlish |

# Note 1

| DB column | Chapter and Section | DB Form | VCH | DG | This edition |
|---|---|---|---|---|---|
| 114a | 34,17 | *Standone* | Unidentified (OJR) Eastanton Down (TWW) | Eastanton | *Standone* |
| 114b | 34,23 | *Orescome* | Old Awliscombe now Buckerell | Buckerell | Awliscombe |
| 114b | 34,26 | *Orescome* | Awliscombe Giffard (OJR). Harcombe, Buckerel (TWW) | Buckerell | Awliscombe |
| 114c | 34,34 | *Heppastebe* | ?Oxeton *alias* Hill and Exton in Faringdon | (unidentified) | *Heppastebe* |
| 114c | 34,37 | *Credie* | Merrifield (OJR) Upper Creedy (TWW) | Lower Creedy | as DG |
| 114c | 34,42 | *Odeordi* | Woodford in Thelbridge | Adworthy | as DG |
| 114c | 34,45 | *Otrie* | Buckerell | Waringstone and Deer Park | Ivedon |
| 114c | 34,45 | *Holescumbe* | Old Awlescombe | Buckerell | Awliscombe |
| 114c | 34,47 | *Otri* | ?Ivedon (OJR) Hembury Fort (TWW) | Hembury Fort | Ivedon |
| 114d | 35,3 | *Wenford* | West Wanford in Milton Damarel | Wonford in Thornbury | as DG |
| 114d | 35,5 | *Tamerlande* | Luffincott | Lost in Luffincott | *Tamerlande* |
| 115a | 35,17 | *Lovecote* | Lovecot in Buckland Filleigh | Lovacott in Shebbear | as DG |
| 115b | 35,27 | *Alfelmestone* | Yealmstone | as VCH | Train |
| 115b | 35,30 | *Macheswelle* | Unidentified (OJR) Maker (TWW) | (unidentified) | Monkswell |
| 115d | 36,24 | *Dertre* | Queen Dart | as VCH | 'Dart' |
| 115d | 36,25 | *Restone* | Rifton in Stoodleigh (OJR) Reston in Cheldon (TWW) | Rifton | as DG |
| 115d | 39,3 | *Ferding* | ?Beardon, member of Willsworthy | (unidentified) | *Ferding* |
| 116a | 39,8 | *Hiele* | Hele in Collumpton (OJR). Hele in Meeth (TWW) | Hele in Bradninch | Hele in Petrockstowe and Meeth |
| 116a | 39,9 | *Radewei* | Redway in Rewe | as VCH | ?Roadway in Mortehoe |
| 116b | 40,2 | *Toritone* | ?Whitsleigh in St. Giles in the Wood | Great Torrington | as DG |

# Note 1

| DB column | Chapter and Section | DB Form | VCH | DG | This edition |
|---|---|---|---|---|---|
| 116b | 41,2 | Lege | Leigh Boty alias Besley | Besley | Westleigh |
| 116d | 42,20 | Derte | Dart Tracy alias East Dart in Witheridge | Dart Raffe | 'Dart' |
| 116d | 43,1 | Patford | Parford in Drewsteignton (OJR). Batworthy, Gidleigh (TWW) | Parford | as DG |
| 117a | 45,1 | Scapelie | Shapleigh in South Tawton Hundred | Shapley in North Bovey | ?Shapley in Chagford |
| 117a | 46,2 | Nochecote | Noggacot alias Northcote in Tiverton | (unidentified) | Nutcott |
| 117b | 47,14 | Lewendone | Livaton alias Lounston Peverel in Ilsington | Lowton in Bridford | Lowton in Moretonhampsted |
| 117c | 48,12 | Lege | Bramlelgh (OJR) Whitleigh (TWW) | Northleigh, Southleigh and Brimley | ?Northleigh |
| 117c | 49,4 | Colun | Culm Vale in Stoke Canon or Whiteheathfield in Collumpton (OJR). Culm John (TWW) | Culm Vale | as DG |
| 117c | 50,4 | Cumbe | (?Thorn) Combe in Cruwys Morchard | Coombe in Cruwys Morchard | as DG(?) |
| 117c | 51,2 | Tavelande | 'Tawland' probably Cocktree in Taw Green | Taw Green | as DG |
| 118a | 52,3 | Coltesworde | Coltsworthy in Clawton | Culsworthy in Abbots Bickington | as DG |
| 118a | 52,6 | Alesland | Alesland alias Hasland in Buckland Filleigh (OJR). in Petrockstowe (TWW) | Allisland in Petrockstowe | as DG |
| 118a | 52,7 | Hame | Chilsdon in Petrockstowe (TWW) Embury in Buckland Filleigh (OJR) | Embury | Hame |
| 118a | 52,9 | Limete | ?Natson in Bow | 'Nymet' | as VCH |
| 118a | 52,15 | Cume | Comberew in Drewsteignton | Coombe in Drewsteignton | as DG |
| 118a | 52,19 | Dune | Down Umfravil alias Charton | Rousdon and Down Ralph | 'Down Umfraville' |

# Notes 1 - 2

| DB column | Chapter and Section | DB Form | VCH | DG | This edition |
|---|---|---|---|---|---|
| 118b | 52,22 | *Henberie* | Broadhembury or Payhembury | as VCH | Payhembury |
| 118b | 52,23 | *Codeford* | Codford in Payhembury | Coddiford in Cheriton Fitzpaine | as DG |
| 118b | 52,26 | *Wiche* | Northweek in Thornbury (OJR) Week in Peters Marland (TWW) | Northwick | ?Week in Thornbury |
| 118b | 52,29 | *Colsovenescote* | Kismilton in West Putford | Colscott in West Putford | as DG |
| 118b | 52,36 | *Brai* | West Bray in Chittlehampton (OJR). South Bray (TWW) | South Bray in Chittlehampton | Bray in South Molton |
| 118c | 52,37 | *Midelcote* | Middlecot in Chagford (OJR) Middle Blackpole, Chittlehampton (TWW) | Middlecott in Chagford | as DG |
| *Terrae Occupatae* 501 b1 = Ch. 44 note | | *Esseorda* | Exeworthy | Exworthy | *Esseorda* |

## 2. PLACES NAMED FROM RIVERS

Many places in Devonshire are named from the rivers on whose banks they stand; among places mentioned in DB are those called after the Axe, the Bovey, the Clyst, the Coly, the Creedy, the Culm, the Dart and Little Dart, the Exe, the Lyme, the Lowman, the Lyd, the Meavy, the Otter, the Plym, the Sid, the Tamar, the Tavy, the Taw, the Teign, the Torridge and the two rivers called 'Nymet', now the Mole and the Yeo, tributary to the Taw. Where places had at first the same basic name, a process of differentiation by prefix, suffix and the addition of separate names from people, churches and other nearby places produces the modern distinct forms. This process had already begun in 1086: thus *Alseministre* or *Axeministre* distinguishes Axminster from *Alsemude,* Axmouth; *Adonebovi,* now Little Bovey, separates one place from two simply called *Bovi*; *Colitone* (Cullompton) and *Culmestoche* (Culmstock) stand out from several places simply called *Colun* or *Colum*; *Sideberie* and *Sedemude* are distinguished from each other, as is *Oplomie* (Uplowman) from places called *Lonmele, Lonmine*; *Taincome* (Teigncombe) stands apart from two places called *Teintone* or *Tantone* and several called *Teigne* or *Taigne*.

This process continued after DB, producing North Bovey and Bovey Tracey, Culm Davy and Culm Pyne, Mary Tavy and Peter Tavy, North, South and Bishops Tawton, Teigngrace and Teignharvey as well as Kings and Bishops Teignton, Black, Great and Little Torrington and Uplyme (DB *Lim*) to distinguish it from Lyme Regis at the river mouth in Dorset. In some cases, completely different forms have displaced the original river names; thus besides Godameavy and Hoo Meavy, Gratton and Lovaton appear to have been named from the river Meavy in 1086 (17,79-82 and 29,9 notes).

In the case of four rivers the problems of identification are made more complex by the large numbers of places that had the same DB form. There are similar examples in DB Wiltshire, and especially in Dorset:

### River Clyst
The Clyst rises near Broadhembury in Hayridge Hundred (15), passes through Cliston Hundred (20), touches Wonford (19), then reaches the estuary of the Exe through (East) Budleigh Hundred (14). Domesday Book itself distinguishes *Clistone*, now Broad Clyst, and *Clisewic*, now Clyst St. George, but the other 'Clists' have to be identified from Hundred order and later evidence. The upper reach of the river is marked by Clyst William (form OE *aēwielm* 'river-spring') in Plymtree parish, Hayridge Hundred. In Cliston Hundred the river passes through Clyst Hydon, Clyst St. Lawrence, Clyst Gerred, Ashclyst, Broad Clyst and West Clyst, which last lay in Wonford Hundred in 1086. Sowton, also in Wonford Hundred, was formerly called Clyst Fomison. In Budleigh Hundred, the river flows through Clyst St. Mary, then through Clyst St. George.

### River Nymet, now the Yeo and Mole
This Yeo is a tributary of the Mole and the Mole of the Taw: both the former seem to have been called 'Nymet' in 1086. DB appears to distinguish two places called *Nimetone* (now Bishops Nympton and Kings Nympton) from two called *Nimete*; but Bishops Nympton continued to be called *Bysshopes Nymet* from time to time and Kings Nympton shows the same alternation of forms. The Nymptons lie south of the river in Witheridge Hundred (7); on the north side in South Molton Hundred (6) George Nympton was *Nimete* in 1086, and *Nymet Sancti Georgii* or *Nymet Georgii* until the 14th century. The name *Nimete* or *Limet* also appears to have applied to a portion of Satterleigh and Warkleigh parishes where other names have now replaced that of the river (1,41 note).

### River Nymet, now the Yeo
Another Yeo feeds into the Taw and DB records ten places, all simply *Limet* or *Nimet* from its former name. They present some difficulties of identification since all lay in the same Hundred, (North) Tawton (12), and four are held by the same man, Baldwin. It seems likely that apart from Broadnymett, Nichols Nymet, Nymet Rowland and Nymet Tracey (*alias* Bow) which preserve the name, Burston, Hampson, Natson, Walson, Wolfin and Zeal Monachorum were also called from the river in 1086.

### River Otter
This river rises on the southern side of the Blackdown Hills where Churchstanton parish (formerly in Devon) abuts Otterford (in Somerset). It passes through the Hundreds of Axminster (17), Hemyock (16), Ottery St. Mary (21) and (East) Budleigh (14). With the exception of *Otritone* (Otterton), all twelve places were called plain *Otri, Otrit* or *Oteri* in 1086. Names of different origins have replaced several; thus in Axminster Hundred the river passes through Upottery, Mohuns Ottery and Combe Raleigh (*Otri*, see 23,21); next comes Ivedon (a detached part of Tiverton Hundred), Weston or Waringstone (in Hemyock Hundred) named from the 1086 holder *Warin* and Rapshays (in (East) Budleigh Hundred) which were all 'Ottery' in 1086. The river then passes through the ecclesiastical Hundred named from Ottery St. Mary, then descends through Dotton and Otterton, both in (East) Budleigh Hundred, to the sea.

A masterly discussion of the Devon river-names is to be found in Ekwall (ERN).

### 3. UNNAMED AND OMITTED HOLDINGS
The few main holdings for which place-names have not been included by DB are listed in Places Index 2, but it is evident that DB does not include all the places that existed in the County in 1086. Its normal practice is to name one manor, large or small, and leave the individual members, villages, hamlets, sub-manors or sub-holdings unspecified, their resources and values being included under the main holding. Thus, as explained in the notes, holdings such as 1,34 Chillington, 7 hides, 2,2 Crediton, 15 hides, and 5,1 Tavistock, 3½ hides, included a number of other places which later evidence can often identify. (Conversely some DB named 'manors' are in practice so small that they can scarcely have been independent units; later evidence often shows them as part of larger manors.)

Where documents survive that represent stages of the Domesday enquiry earlier than Exon., they suggest that considerably more detail, including the names of sub-manors and lower levels of subtenancies, was collected than was actually used in the finished volumes (see Appendices III-V to the Worcester volume in this series). Sometimes this information seems to have escaped the process of revision and pruning, as in 3,8 Bovey Tracey, where Exchequer DB names nine added lands. In two cases, Exon. Domesday includes this information although it has been eliminated by the abbreviation which produced Exchequer DB. Thus Battishill, Combebowe, Ebsworthy, Fernworthy, Kersford and Way are named as added to Bridestowe (16,7), and Burntown, Warne and Wringworthy to Mary Tavy (17,13). Exon. also names Boode, part of Braunton (3,32), and includes two whole entries omitted from DB. That for Werrington entered under Tavistock Abbey (Ch. 5 note; see Exon. Notes after 5,5) may have been excluded as the land had been awarded to the King by the Domesday Commissioners (1,50 note), but *Sotrebroc* ('Shutbrook' or 'Floyers Hayes') seems to have been missed when the complex section called 'Lands of the French Men-at-Arms in Devonshire' was divided into individual fiefs (Ch. 22 note; see Exon. Notes to Ch. 22). Both Exon. DB and the *Terrae Occupatae* sometimes notice a customary due which Exchequer DB passes over, and the *Terrae Occupatae* names a few places otherwise unrecorded: *Esseorda* added to Silverton (Ch. 44 and 1,7 notes), Chaffcombe (2,2 note), Widefield (39,6 note) and Whitley (Ch. 44 note), and refers to an unnamed 1 furlong (*ferdinus*) in *Moltona* Hundred which is waste and claimed by no one (500 a 4; see the end of the Exon. Notes). Neither Exon. nor Exchequer DB is entirely complete. Just as, in Somerset, a holding of Shaftesbury Abbey evidenced in the Somerset Tax Returns is nowhere to be found in DB, so the Devon Tax Returns and later evidence suggest that the fief of the wife of Hervey of Helléan was more extensive than recorded in DB (Ch. 44 note) and that the Priests of Exminster held ½ hide in Exminster Hundred (1,4 note).

Finally, neither Exmoor nor Dartmoor is mentioned in DB. The latter was appurtenant to Lydford (1,2 note) for administrative purposes and its presence can be felt in the references to wild mares and to moor, or waste, on the manors that lay around its perimeter.

## 4. THE COUNTY BOUNDARY

The border of the 1086 County has not remained unchanged until the 20th century, even if the 1974 county reorganisation (ignored in this series) is laid aside. Churchstanton (37,1) was transferred to Somerset in 1896 and Thorncombe (16,165), long a detached part of Axminster Hundred (17) entirely surrounded by Dorset, was transferred to that County in 1844. Stockland (ED 2) was brought into Dorset in 1832 and Chardstock (ED 1) in 1896; on the same boundary Hawkchurch and Dalwood, not separately mentioned in DB Dorset (but see ED note here and 1,4. 11,1 and 17,1 notes there), were taken into Devon in 1896 and 1832 respectively.

The position on the border with Cornwall, well-marked for much of its length by the river Tamar, was more complex. Until recent times parts of the Cornish parishes of Whitstone, Launcells, Kilkhampton and North Tamerton, though east of the Tamar, have lain in that County and parts of the Devonshire parishes of Bridgerule, Pancrasweek, Luffincott and Northcott lay west of the Tamar. These, however, are of no significance for Domesday and the major examples, the transfer of 1015 acres of West Bridgerule to Devon (bringing Borough and Tackbeare (EC 1-2) into the County) and of 1043 acres of North Tamerton to Cornwall, only date from 1844.

Other changes are of greater moment. Celtic Cornwall had been penetrated from Saxon Devon and a number of Cornish lands had at first been dependent on Devonshire manors. Traces of this arrangement are found in DB where Landinner and Trebeigh are said to have been dependent on Lifton (1,25) before 1066 and Maker on Walkhampton (1,20-22 note). Landinner and Trebeigh were already fully in Cornwall by 1086, but although Maker was held in that County by the Count of Mortain in 1086, part at least was returned to Devon and only reunited with the portion that remained in Cornwall in 1844.

The history of Werrington (including North Petherwin and lying west of the Tamar) is more complex: in 1086 it had apparently just been incorporated in Devon as it had been awarded to the King against the Abbot of Tavistock. It remained in Devon until 1966 when it was returned to Cornwall. See 1,50 note.

Lundy Island was and is a part of Devonshire; it is not mentioned in DB, but was probably surveyed as part of Hartland (RH i pp. 73b, 89b).

# GENERAL NOTES

Users of these Notes should bear in mind the following:

These Notes follow the correct order of the text, ignoring displacements in the MS; thus the notes for 49,7 follow those for 49,6 rather than those for 51,2. The chapter numbers are those of the translation, rather than those of the Landholders' List which is defective in a couple of places (see notes to L 25 and Ch. 41 below).

References to other DB counties are to the Chapters and Sections of the editions in the present series.

Because Record type (as in Farley) could not be used in the Notes for this edition, in quotations as many as possible of the abbreviation signs have been inserted by hand as they appear in the DB and Exon. MSS (e.g. in *car͗, uɨtti, dim̄, p͗ti*), especially where it is thought they are of vital importance; elsewhere either an apostrophe has had to be used, as in *geld'* (for MS *gelð*), or brackets round the extended portion (e.g. Radulf(lus) for MS Radulf', or, when there is no reasonable doubt, the Latin is fully extended. The runic ⁊ which the Exchequer scribe uses all the time for *et* ('and'), and either the ⁊ or the & of the Exon. MS, have always been reproduced.
Also for reasons of production, the Anglo-Saxon *þ* and *ð* are reproduced as *th*, except in the note on *ferling* at 1,4 and in 15,18 note.

In the Notes below, Roman numerals refer to the Tax Return Hundreds and Arabic to the 'modern' Hundred. An introductory note to each chapter gives the presumed 1086 Hundreds with their late 11th century names in two columns reading left before right but the Hundreds given in individual notes are the 'modern' ones in which lie the parishes that contain the DB places. The correspondence between the 'modern' and the late 11th century Hundreds is tabulated in the Appendix and at the beginning of the Map Keys.

Details from the Tax Returns for Devon (Exon. 65a to 71a, see Introductory Note 1 and the Appendix) have only been given in the General Notes and Exon. Notes in the following instances: where they support a place-name identification; where they supply or suggest a byname for a holder given only a simple name in DB; where they record tax unpaid in cases where the identification of the holding is fairly certain. Not included are conjectural identifications, nor exact identifications where the Return adds no information to DB, nor where there are large discrepancies in the lordship land.

**The Manuscript** is written on either side of leaves, or folios, of parchment (sheepskin) measuring about 15 by 11 ins. (38 by 28 cms.). On each side, or page, are two columns, making four to each folio. The folios were numbered in the 17th century and the four columns of each are here lettered a, b, c, d. The Manuscript emphasises words and usually distinguishes chapters and sections by the use of red ink. Underlining in the MS indicates deletion.

**A study of the MS** has shown that on the whole Devon is a neatly executed county, particularly when it is compared with Herefordshire for example. The parchment is generally thick and of good quality and, with the exception of the first three folios, is 'whiter' than the yellow, greasy-looking parchment of counties such as Hertfordshire and Buckinghamshire. Both these aspects are reflected in the fewness of Farley's errors relative to the size of the County (22 major ones, compared with more than a dozen in Dorset which is only just over half the size of Devon). Finn (LE p. 156) enumerates only three postscripts at the foot of columns, two marginal additions and a few misplacements, but in fact there are five postscripts (1,45. 3,19. 3,55. 3,75. and 49,7) and four important marginal additions (1,50. 3,6. 16,65. and 48,12) and three minor ones (1,57. 17,9. and 23,6). The Exchequer scribe also completely omitted the manor of *Sotrebroc* held by Flohere which is detailed in the large Exon. section 'Lands of French Men-at-Arms in Devonshire' (see Ch. 22

# C

note below and Exon. Notes Ch. 22), and the entry on Werrington (see Exon. Notes after 5,5). Apart from these, there are numerous neatly-executed minor corrections and interlineations of numbers and letters, most of which were done at once (judging by the colour of ink) and which are easily identified in the MS. Due to lack of space in the Notes below, attention is usually only drawn to those occasions when a correction in Exchequer DB is paralleled by a similar one in the Exon. MS. Some entries are inevitably worse than others, e.g. 3,54. 15,62 (see notes) and 39,15. Some of the corrections and additions (e.g. see notes to 16,5. 34,46. 48,12 and 49,7) and the marginal *par's* (see 15,47-52 note) are done in much paler ink, probably at a later stage and perhaps as a result of checking the Exon. MS (this is likely to have been the case with 49,7; see note). In some cases entries were corrected in two stages (e.g. see notes to 15,79 and 17,13). There are a few gaps left in entries for information not to hand at the time of writing (e.g. 16,175. 35,6. 52,26;30 and perhaps also 15,7) and a certain amount of space is left at the end of some chapters for additional manors to be detailed if necessary (see notes to 1,72 and 13a,3), as well as after the account of Exeter (see C 7 note).

Despite the general clarity of the scribe's work on the County, the facsimile fails to reproduce, or reproduces incorrectly, some letters and signs, sometimes because they are fainter than usual or have become mixed up with the rubrication, but also on many occasions for no apparent reason; these are indicated in the notes below (see L 11 note).

With one exception (see below), Devon has four vertical scorings, one down each edge of the two columns, delimiting them, though it is not always possible in the present binding to see the side one on the inner edges of folios. There are only two horizontal scorings, marking the top and bottom, which are generally visible, but within them the number of lines per column varies, even between the two columns on one side of the folio; the average number of lines for Devon, however, is 60, which makes it one of the densest packed counties in DB. As the scribe generally used all the space between the two horizontal rulings, the appearance of anything below the bottom marginal ruling indicates that it was a later addition; similarly with the vertical scoring.

The exception to this ruling is on the first folio of the County where the bottom half of col. 100a is ruled horizontally for the Landholders' List and where there are four extra vertical scorings, one after the first letter of the landholders in the left column, one before the Chapter numbers in the right-hand landholders' column and two enclosing the first letters of each of the names in this right-hand column. The normal left-hand score falls between the Chapter numbers and the first letters of the landholders in the left column (the Chapter numbers 1-26 being in the margin); there may have been a fifth extra vertical score before the Chapter numbers to match the one before those in the right column, but the binding now obscures it. This additional vertical scoring begins five lines above the top of the List. At the end of the County, col. 118d is scored, though blank, and the whole of folio 119 is blank and not ruled at all.

**DEVON.** *Devenescire* is written in red capitals across the top of both columns on each side of folios 100a,b to 118c,d inclusive. The form *Devenescire* also appears at the head of the Landholders' List on 100a.

C 1   EXETER. The other boroughs in Devon are Barnstaple, Lydford and Totnes, the chief entries for which are 1,1. 1,2 and 17,1 respectively. Okehampton (16,3; see note), like Wimborne Minster in Dorset (Dorset General Notes B), appears also to have been a borough, judging by its burgesses, castle and market, although DB does not give it this title. See the last note under C 7.

300 HOUSES, LESS 15. This series keeps to the exact translation here and elsewhere with *minus*, rather than translating here as 285 houses, because sometimes the reason for the abstraction is noted; e.g. the 'less 30d' of the value of the main manor of Bovey Tracey, 3,8, is explained in the £4 30d value of the added lands (cf. also in DB Wilts. 2,1 '100 hides, less 3', where the removal of the 3 hides is explained). Exon. has the same phrase using *minus*. Details of other houses in Exeter appear under the fiefs of the holders, usually at the beginnings or ends of the chapters; see 3,1 note.

HOUSES .... CUSTOMARY DUES. The rate of payment of customary dues for a house in Exeter appears to be 8d; see 3,2. 5,15. 9,2. 17,2. 19,1. 23,27(Exon. Notes). 30,4.

C

36,27. 39,22. 43,6. 47,15. For a destroyed house (*domus uastata*) in Barnstaple the rate is given as 2d in (28,17) (see note), in 16,2 a payment was made by 6 destroyed houses in Exeter (see Exon. Notes there) and cf. 3,1, though in many counties in DB destroyed or vacant houses paid no tax (e.g. Oxfords. B 4, col. 154a, and cf. 3,3 here where there is no mention of payment for the 7 destroyed houses in Barnstaple nor is there for the 2 houses in Exeter (2,1) destroyed by fire). See notes to 2,1. 32,6 and 34,58 for possible exceptions to this rate of payment. According to VCH p. 396 this customary due was the 'ground-rent from tenements belonging to the King and rented by the burgesses, the house or land gavel'. See also Maitland DBB p. 204.

C 2    THIS (CITY) PAYS £18. The revenues of a City or Borough included the house rents, ground rents, market tolls, profits of the court, the mint, the King's mill, etc.; see Tait p. 141 and Round in EHR xxxiv (1919) pp. 62-64. DB Herefords. C 12 (col. 179a) states that the customary dues detailed 'above' (i.e. C 2-11) formed (part of) the revenues (of Hereford).
£18 .... B(ALDWIN) .... £6 .... COLWIN £12 .... QUEEN EDITH. There are several examples in DB of this division of a City's or Borough's total revenues between the King (or Queen in this instance) and the Sheriff (or, more often, the Earl) at a rate of two-thirds to one-third, particularly before 1066. See 1,1 and 1,55 (and notes) and Herefords. C 12 (col. 179a), Staffs. B 12 (col. 246a), Glos. B 1 (col. 162c), Cheshire C 2;22 (cols. 262 c,d), Kent D 1 (col. 1a), Shrops. C 12 (col. 252a), etc. See Tait Ch. VII. (This 'third penny' is not to be confused with the third penny of a Hundred; see 1,41 note and the articles cited there.)
   Exeter was long associated with the Queens of England; see J. M. Kemble *Anglo-Saxons in England* (London 1876) ii App. C p. 555. It would seem that King Edward's grant of his two-thirds from Exeter to his wife Queen Edith was repeated by his successors, for in a register of Holy Trinity Priory, London, are some charters of a gift by Queen Maud, Henry I's wife, of £25 being two-thirds of the revenues of Exeter (British Library Lansdowne MS 114, folio 50 (No. 15); see J. H. Round *The Commune of London*, London 1899, p. 85 and OJR in TDA 29 p. 455 and note 3). Even after Queen Edith's death in 1075 Colwin continued to receive the £12 for administering her estate, although it was now technically in King William's hands. See notes below.
B(ALDWIN) THE SHERIFF. Of Devon; see Ch. 16 note.
WEIGHED AND ASSAYED .... AT FACE VALUE. *ad pensum et arsuram* .... *ad numerum*; other forms of the Latin for the first part appear elsewhere in DB as *ad pondus et (ad) arsuram/combustionem*, and *ad pensam et (ad) arsuram*. The money was weighed to avoid losses due to the clipping of coins or wear, and assayed, that is tested by fire for the presence of alloy, a similar process to blanching (see DB Dorset General Notes 1,1). Any deficiency was then made good. Sometimes the coins were not actually melted down, but an extra number of pence were required to be paid in compensation for any loss; this was achieved by using an *ora* of 20d instead of the normal *ora* of 16d (see 1,28 note). Payment made in coin that had been subjected to these methods was the opposite of payment 'at face value'. See *Dialogus de Scaccario* p. xxxviii ff. and S. Harvey 'Royal Revenue and Domesday Terminology' in EcHR (2nd series) xx (1967) pp. 221-228.
COLWIN. Colwin here and in several other instances in DB Devon is probably Colwin the reeve, a thane (see notes to 42,3 and 52,1), and the £12 is his payment for administering Queen Edith's property in Exeter. He appears to have transferred his services to the King, see 1,25 where the Exon. states that he 'farmed' Lifton, one of Queen Edith's lands that passed to King William. See also Exon. 97 b 3 (after the Exon. Notes to 1,55). According to PNDB p. 218 note 4 all the entries in Devon for Colwin refer to the same man.
FROM THE ADMINISTRATION OF (THE PROPERTY OF) QUEEN EDITH. DB *in ministeriis Eddid reginae*. Latin *ministerium* 'service, administration, office' is derived from *ministro* 'I serve, I administer' and *minister* 'slave, servant, assistant'. The phrase literally means 'in the services' or 'in the administrations of Queen Edith' and some other noun such as 'land' or 'property' is implied. Queen Edith had a large share of Exeter's revenues (see four notes above) and it seems as if her property there continued to be administered after her death by Colwin (her reeve).
QUEEN EDITH. Daughter of Earl Godwin and husband of Edward the Confessor. She died in 1075.

C 3    48 HOUSES HAVE BEEN DESTROYED. There is a difference of opinion as to the reason for the destruction of the houses here. Freeman iv p. 162 suggests that, like the

# C

C 3 (cont'd.)   houses in Warwicks. B 2 (col. 238a), in Glos. G 4 (col. 162a) and in Cambs. B 1 (col. 189a), these were destroyed to make room for the castle (although one is not recorded in DB, see Ch. 16 note), and that the houses in Barnstaple (1,1) and Lydford (1,2) were destroyed because these towns resisted King William. Round in FE p. 431 ff. disagrees. According to DGSW pp. 280, 282-283, 289, the reference to devastated houses here and for Barnstaple and Lydford suggests the presence of a castle in these places; in other words that the houses were destroyed to make room for castles. Cf. DB Dorset General Notes B 1 on destroyed houses in Boroughs in that county.

DESTROYED. *uastatae sunt.* In DB *uasta* and *uastata* are applied both to buildings and to land. There should be a distinction between them, *uasta* (adjective) describing land that is 'waste' or 'unproductive' or a house that is 'decaying', 'ruinous' or 'unoccupied', and *uastata* (past participle passive) meaning land that has been 'wasted' or 'laid waste' or 'ravaged' (for example by an army, cf. the Exon. addition at the end of 17,41) or a house that has been 'damaged', 'demolished' or 'destroyed'. With the verb *esse* 'to be' past participles can be used adjectivally (e.g. *territus sum* — 'I am frightened') or strictly as participles to form the perfect tense (e.g. *territus sum* — 'I have been frightened'). Thus *uastata est* could mean 'it is damaged' or 'it has been damaged' and *uastata erat* 'it was damaged' or 'it had been damaged'. This distinction is not always clear in DB; moreover, that between *uasta* and *uastata* is unreal, since Exon. sometimes has one where DB, for the corresponding entry, has the other: thus in 1,2 and 3,34 DB has *uasta(e)* and Exon. *uastata(e)*. Moreover, *uastata* is sometimes used of land in contexts where the reference cannot be to destruction but to natural sterility. Thus in the case of 19,18 'Badgworthy' (on the edge of Exmoor), Exon. says *erat uastata*, where the sense should be 'it was waste'. In the case of *Ferse* [*Furze* 20,2] the very place-name suggests unproductive land, although DB has *est uastata* 'laid waste' and Exon. *est penitus uastata* 'completely laid waste'. In view of these uncertainties, in this edition *uasta* and *uastata* are treated as interchangeable and translated according to the context. The DB Latin can be read from the facing Latin text, the Exon., where it is discrepant, is given in the Exon. Notes.

C 4   BEFORE 1066. *T.R.E.* = *tempore regis Edwardi* 'in the time of King Edward' i.e. 1043-1066. The same phrase is used in Exon. here, though the formula regularly used there is *ea die qua rex eduuardus fuit vivus et mortuus* 'on the day on which King Edward was alive and dead', actually 5th January 1066. Cf. *T.R.W.* in 2,2.

½ SILVER MARK. That is 6s 8d. In DB Dorset B 2 (col. 75a) ½ silver mark for 5 hides was paid for the upkeep of the guards (cf. 1 silver mark for 10 hides in Dorset B 1;3 and 2 silver marks for 20 hides in B 4), suggesting that the rate was 1 silver mark for every 10 hides.

FOR THE USE OF THE MEN-AT-ARMS. *ad opus militum.* The meaning of the fairly common DB phrase *ad opus* varies with the context: here the ½ silver mark is for the upkeep of the men-at-arms. In Herefords. 1,2 *opus* is translated 'use' where a contrast is implied between money going to the King and what the Sheriff receives for administering the land. Sometimes *opus* means 'benefit', as in Worcs. H 2-3 in Worcs. App. V, and as apparently in the Exon. for 15,67 here, although the word is not really necessary there and it is interesting that the Exchequer scribe changes the phrase. Exon. sometimes has, for example, 'value for the Abbot's use' where DB has 'value to the Abbot' (see Exon. Notes 5,1;4 and for the reverse see Somerset General Notes 6,1) and see Dorset Exon. Notes 11,1 for a correspondence between 'lordship' and 'use' in the value statement. The predominant Latin meaning of *opus*, however, is 'work' and there are occasions in DB where this is the appropriate rendering.

C 5   GAVE (AS MUCH) SERVICE AS 5 HIDES OF LAND. That is, one man. DB Wilts. B 5 (col. 64c) states that if the King went on an expedition on land or sea, the King had one man for each Honour of 5 hides; similarly in Berks. B 10 (col. 56c) with the addition that each hide paid 4s for his supplies or pay for 2 months.

C 6   BARNSTAPLE .... CITY. See 17,1 note.

C 7   LAND FOR 12 PLOUGHS. That is, 12 carucates of land; see 1,2 and note.

AFTER THIS ENTRY there is almost one third of a column blank before the Landholders' List. It is possible that the scribe left the space deliberately for the later inclusion of details of the other Boroughs in Devon (Barnstaple, Lydford, Totnes, ?Okehampton; some of the information on Barnstaple seems to have arrived late, see 3,6 note). But it is more likely, as seems to be the case in some other counties, that he wrote the Landholders' List first on col. 100a (probably after the main body of the text; see

C, L, 1

L 25 note), guessing how much room he would need for the Boroughs, which in the event turned out to be too much. Perhaps he decided later that the details of the Boroughs other than the 'county borough' (see Ballard p. 4 ff.) would be better dealt with in the chapters of the landholders who held them (e.g. Totnes held by Iudhael in 17,1). The colour of the ink used in the Exeter details is the same as that used for the Landholders' List and Ch. 1 on 100a,b.

L 11    MONT ST. MICHEL. In the MS and Farley *Michael*, but the *l* is only partially reproduced in the facsimile, perhaps because of its closeness to the rubricated numbers in the next column, or possibly because it falls on one of the vertical scorings (see above), though the *R* of *MAR'* in the line above, similarly written on the scoring, appears clearly in the facsimile. Cf. notes to 1,2. 3,94. 13,1. 15,62. 16,17;39;121. 17,50. 19,34. 20,6. 33,2. 34,56. 39,15 and 52,30 for other examples of poor reproduction in the facsimile; see also 1,63 note for place-names reproduced incorrectly.

L 19    WILLIAM CHEEVER. In the MS *Chieure* clearly; Farley misprints *Cieure*.

L 25    WALTER. It would seem that the gap of a line after 24,21 and the larger than usual *Walterius* in 24,22 (see note) suggested to the scribe making the Landholders' List at the end, that the subject was another Walter, not Walter of Claville, so he allocated him a separate line, and the rubricator duly gave this superfluous Walter a chapter number, with the result that the numbers in the Landholders' List do not tally with the chapter numbers in the main text until Ch. 41 (see Ch. [40] note).

L 37    IN THE MS *xxxvi* with an additional *i* interlined over the *v* (not over the *i* as in Farley; the *T* of *Tetbald'* prevents its being written there, indicating that the numbers – in red ink – were added after the text had been written). The scribe of the text had obviously not left sufficient room for the *xxxvii* to be written altogether. Similarly for the interlined *i* in L 48.

L 48    IN THE MS *xlvii* with an *i* added over the first *i* (not over the second *i*, as in Farley); see L 37 note.

Ch. [1]  THE RUBRICATOR OF THE MS has omitted the *I* beside the first chapter heading, as in several counties in DB, probably in error.

Ch. 1   LAND OF THE KING. There are several differences between the arrangement of the King's land in the Exchequer and Exon. Domesdays, as is also the case in Dorset. Exon. arranges the material by the 1086 holder and then, within each grouping, by Hundred, whereas Exchequer DB arranges it by 1066 holder.

Lands in Exon. are grouped under the following heads:
*Dominicatus Regis ad Regnum Pertinens* ('The King's Lordship belonging to the Throne') = DB 1,3-14;23-24;15-22;1-2. C. The great majority of these manors name the 1086 Hundreds (see Appendix).
*Dominicatus Regis* ('The King's Lordship'; see Exon. Notes 1,25-56) = DB 1,36;25;29; 37-38;30;39;31;51;40;26-27;41-42;56;28;52;43-44;32;45;33;46-48;53-54;34;55;49;35;50.
*Terra Mahillis Reginae* ('Land of Queen Matilda') = DB 1,57-66;72;67-69;35 (the last a duplicate of land at Tiverton entered in the previous group; see Exon. Notes 1,35); 70-71. Within each group, lands are entered in the normal order of Hundreds (see the Appendix and individual notes below).

Exchequer DB treats the order differently: details of Exeter (C) are put at the head of the County and the two other Boroughs belonging to the King, Barnstaple and Lydford, form 1,1-2. The order then proceeds:

1,3–22   King Edward's former Lordship, belonging to the Crown.
1,23–34  Two crown manors acquired by exchange with Walter of Douai for Bampton (23,5).
1,25–28  Lands of Queen Edith.
1,29–35  Lands of Gytha.
1,36–49  Lands of 'Earl' Harold.
1,50     A misplaced entry held by Gytha in 1066; see note.
1,51–55  Lands of Earl Leofwin.
1,56     An odd manor, held by Ordwulf in 1066.
1,57–70  Lands held by Brictric then Queen Matilda.
1,71     A manor held by Iudhael in 1066.
1,72     A manor held by Boia in 1066.

It will be seen that in using Exon. for Devon, the Exchequer scribe rearranged the material more than he had for the other south-west counties, adding sub-headings at the end of 1,22 and before 1,25;29;36;51;57, whereas there are only three sub-headings in Dorset DB for Ch. 1, and in Somerset Ch. 1 only two, with two together in Cornwall Ch. 1 and none in Wilts. Ch. 1.

**1,1** BARNSTAPLE. On the descent of Barnstaple, see OJR H8 p. 408 ff.
BURGESSES .... 9 OUTSIDE THE BOROUGH. This probably means that they held land outside the Borough walls; see DB Herefords. C 1 (col. 179a) "103 men dwelling inside and outside the wall (*murum*)" and also C 6 there. Cf. 1,2 below where the burgesses have 2 carucates of land outside the Borough, and 17,1 where 15 burgesses outside the Borough of Totnes work the land. It is possible, however, that it means that, though the burgesses lived in Barnstaple, they were attached to other manors; cf. DB Warwicks. B 2 (col. 238a) where the dwellings of various landholders detailed in the Borough of Warwick "belong to the lands which these barons hold outside the Borough and are there assessed". Dwellings (i.e. town houses) seem to imply burgesses; in 16,1 Baldwin the Sheriff has 12 houses in Exeter that belong(ed) to his manor of Kenn and 16,58 (Kenn) states that 11 burgesses in Exeter are attached to the manor (see 16,1 note). However, elsewhere in Devon 18 burgesses are recorded for Barnstaple: 17 in entries mentioning only the Borough itself and not the rural manor to which (apparently) the burgesses were attached (3,3 and 16,2) and one in the description of the manor of Fremington.
  On the whole subject of burgesses within and without a Borough and his view of the meaning of the latter, see Finberg *Tavistock Abbey* pp. 73–75.
PAY 40s. DB uses the old English currency system which lasted for a thousand years until 1971. The pound contained 20 shillings, each of 12 pence, abbreviated respectively as £(ibrae), s(olidi) and d(enarii). DB often expresses sums above a shilling in pence (as 15d and 30d, instead of 1s 3d and 2s 6d respectively, in 1,11) and above a pound in shillings (as here, instead of £2).
BY WEIGHT .... AT FACE VALUE. See C 2 notes above on these methods of payment and the two-thirds to one-third division of the Borough's revenues.
20s TO THE BISHOP OF COUTANCES. See 3,3. Other examples in DB of a bishop receiving a third of a borough's revenues are in Worcs. 2,49 (Bishop of Worcester of the Borough of Worcester) and Kent 7,10 (Bishop Odo of the Borough of Fordwich, though he had granted it to St. Augustine's, Canterbury; see *Regesta* i nos. 99, 100). See second note under C 2 on the third penny of a borough. On the origin of the episcopal share in the borough's revenues, see Tait p. 20.
23 HOUSES DESTROYED .... See first note under C 3.

**1,2** LYDFORD. A Borough with an associated parish which was a part of Lifton Hundred (18). The Forest of Dartmoor was appurtenant to it; see RH i pp. 76a, 92a, Fees pp. 757, 1371, 1425, FA i p. 385 and OJR in TDA 46 p. 217. See also 34,3 where Roger holds ½ furlong ('ferling') in Lydford from Ralph of Pomeroy.
BURGESSES .... 41 OUTSIDE. See 1,1 note. No burgesses are recorded elsewhere in Devon as being in Lydford. According to Finberg *Tavistock Abbey* p. 74 three of these 41 'can be identified as inhabitants of Fernworthy, 8 miles away on the other side of Dartmoor'.
CARUCATES OF LAND. *carucatae* here and elsewhere in the south-west counties, in Glos. and Herefords. and occasionally elsewhere in DB, are not the carucates of the former Danish areas (which are equivalent to the hide), but are the same as 'land for y ploughs'. That the two terms were synonymous is proved by the fact that on several occasions DB uses the term *carucatae terrae* where Exon. has *terra est ... car*, as here (see Exon. Notes), and vice versa (as in Somerset, see Exon. Notes 2,1 there). Carucates also appear in Exon. in the lordship land holding for 1,3;5 and 52,10 and are to be compared with Exon.'s 'land for ... ploughs' for the lordship and villagers' land holding in 23,5. In both DB and Exon. carucates of land are recorded for 34,56 and 'land for ... ploughs' in C 7.
  Land was usually measured in carucates when it had not been hidated; it did not pay tax (see 23,5). However, in the Exon. for Devon 1,3;5 and 52,10 carucates are used for the lordship land, although the lands were hidated, and see also in DB Dorset 49,12. In DB Herefords. there is a distinction between the newly conquered lands measured still in carucates and the older acquisitions assessed in hides.
40 HOUSES DESTROYED ... See first note under C 3.
EXPEDITION. In the MS and Farley *expeditio*; the facsimile fails to reproduce all of the ascender of the *d*, the middle of which is rather faint in the MS. See L 11 note.
(THE BOROUGH) PAYS AS MUCH SERVICE .... The subject of *redd'* is not given, but from the statement in C 6 it has been taken to be Lydford understood. In Exon. however, the *reddī* should probably be extended to *reddunt* as the burgesses are the subject of the preceding sentence there on the 2 carucates. See C 5 note on the likely amount of service required. Cf. 17,1 note 'Totnes, Barnstaple and Lydford ....'.

| | |
|---|---|
| 1,2 (cont'd.) | AFTER THIS ENTRY in the MS a space has been left equivalent to about 3 lines (there are no horizontal rulings, except for the top and bottom ones), perhaps for some more details of this Borough. It is interesting that in Exon. there is a gap of 7 lines (amounting to the rest of the folio) after 87 b 2 (= 1,2), though there is also a 3-line space after 87 b1 (= 1,1). Farley does not print the space after 1,2, though he does print the spaces left either side of 51,13. 51,14 and 51,15. |
| 1,3 | THE KING HOLDS. Repeated at the beginning of 1,3–21 inclusive. |

(NORTH) TAWTON. DB *Tauuetone*. A parish and *caput* of North Tawton Hundred. This entry can be distinguished from South Tawton (1,29) because the latter can be identified from its dependency, Ash. It passed to the Honour of Plympton, being held by Joel *de Valletorta* in Fees p. 787; see RH i p. 75b, FA i pp. 370, 422, Cal. Inq. PM vol. i no. 564. It included *Seleda* [Slade GR SS 6701] in Fees p. 1263, *Stoddon* according to Fees p. 787 or *Stoddone* and *Wyke* in Cal. Inq. PM vol. iv (o.s.) no. 63 (= TDA 38 p. 324) [Staddon SS 6702 and Week SS 6501] and *Alfeton* or *Affeton* [?Affeton in East Worlington, SS 7513] in Fees p. 787; see 21,9–12 note and OJR in TDA 29 p. 246. The church was granted to St. Nicholas', Exeter, *Regesta* ii p. 59 no. 779.

TAX FOR ½ VIRGATE. Although North Tawton is a fairly large and valuable manor, the tax assessment is seen to be low. Cf. 2,12 and note. It is possible that manors in Devon were 'under-rated' as they were in Cornwall (where the tax assessment of a manor is very often half the hidage given for it). The reason for this is not known but may be due to the poverty of these counties (which is suggested by the under-stocking of plough-teams, see next note) or to the later subjection and hidation of the area known as 'West Wales'; see Maitland DBB pp. 463, 467 and Round FE p. 93. However, the low level of tax assessment of the Devon manor often seems to have little relation to the size of its population, resources and value; see the table in DGSW p. 238. Moreover, in Devon there is a great deal of evidence that the manor paid tax on all its land, i.e. that the geld-hide was the same as the manorial hide; see 1,4 note on the hide. It is certainly true that in Devon DB there is a high proportion of minute holdings, many of them no more than a furlong ('ferling'; see fourth note under 1,4) in extent (one-sixteenth of a hide), almost certainly too small to have existed independently and in fact later evidence shows many of them combined or part of larger holdings.

LAND FOR 30 PLOUGHS. This estimate of the ploughlands, very common in the south-west counties and elsewhere in DB, though rare in Gloucestershire, Worcestershire and Herefordshire, is a convenient way of giving the true arable extent without the complexities associated with the hide (see 1,4 note on it). A check has been made here on the occurrence of the phrase in Devon and as to whether the actual ploughs recorded on the lordship and villagers' land correspond with this estimate. Devon (like Cornwall to an even greater extent) is remarkable in the 'understocking' of plough-teams: in almost 66% of the entries for which all the details are given (Exon. included) the number of ploughs recorded falls below the assessment, by as much as 65 ploughs in 1,30 and 53 ploughs in 1,27;50. The reason for this may be the method of agriculture used or the poverty of the County; see Maitland DBB p. 425. Meanwhile, in about 28% the figures tally (as here) and there are some 60 entries (= *c*. 6%) where there are more ploughs recorded than in the estimate (as many as 21 ploughs in excess in 11,1). In about a quarter of these latter the Exchequer scribe has drawn attention to this fact by the use of *tamen* with the ploughs on the land, generally when he has not given the details of lordship and villagers' ploughs (e.g. in 17,74). However, there are over 70 entries where no details of ploughs on the land are given, though there is a plough estimate and the entries are otherwise full (e.g. 2,10. 3,12), and 8 entries (e.g. 6,13. 9,1) where ploughs are recorded but there is no estimate. Finally, there are some 30 short entries, many of them on the tenure of houses in Exeter, where, as expected, no details whatsoever are given. On the frequent artificiality of the numbers in the plough assessment, see R. Welldon Finn p. 97 ff. of "The Teamland of the Domesday Inquest" in EHR lxxxiii (1968). See also J. S. Moore "The Domesday Teamland: a reconsideration" in TRHS 5th ser. xiv (1964) pp. 109–130.

IN LORDSHIP .... 3 SLAVES. After Gloucestershire and Cornwall (see DB Glos. W 9 note) Devon has the highest proportion of slaves to other categories of population recorded in DB – about one in five. They are more numerous in certain fiefs than in others, e.g. in that of Buckfast Abbey they form over a quarter of the population, and almost as high a proportion on royal land that had belonged to Queen Matilda (1,57–71 inclusive). The slave came at the bottom end of the social scale: he belonged to his

1,3 (cont'd.) master utterly, providing most of the labour on his land, he could be bought and sold, had almost no rights and rarely any share in the villagers' land and ploughs (see below); see Finberg *Tavistock Abbey* p. 36 ff. and pp. 60-61. Despite this, it should be noted that neither DB nor Exon. for Devon definitely state that the slaves were in lordship. Although in Devon DB they are regularly listed immediately after the lordship ploughs before the rest of the population, the punctuation is ambiguous (but see 2,19 note). The necessity in this edition of not adding the lordship land given in Exon. immediately after the lordship ploughs, but after the slaves as well, might mislead the reader into believing that according to DB the slaves were also in lordship. In Exon. (see sample at the front of this edition) the slaves are almost invariably listed after the other 'villagers', quite separate from the statement of the lordship land and ploughs. When the Exchequer scribe gives no details of lordship ploughs (and occasionally when he does, see, for example, 2,21 and 3,67) he regularly lists the slaves after the villagers and smallholders and in at least 20 entries (e.g. 1,9;19;35 etc.) the phrase "with *y* ploughs" ends the list, and, in several more (e.g. 43,1. 44,1 etc.), the phrase is varied to "*z* villagers .... with 1 slave have *y* ploughs". It is hard to tell in such cases whether the scribe meant that there the slaves shared the other villagers' ploughs. There are some entries where this does appear to be the meaning, e.g. in 28,16 (see note) and in 29,4 where, despite a lordship plough being given, the slaves are listed with the villagers "with 2 ploughs". Cf. DB Herefordshire 1,10a. However, in listing the slaves at the end of the list of 'villagers', the Exchequer scribe may merely be guilty of copying the Exon. too closely, rather than be making a point.

Normally in Exon. the villagers' land and ploughs are stated after the lordship land and ploughs, and it is not clear what categories of population were covered by the word *villani*, whether just villagers and smallholders etc. or whether the slaves were included (cf. Exon. Notes 1,26 and 3,63). When only slaves, or slaves and 1 villager, are listed and the Exon. has in full *villani ... y carr̄*, as for 3,79. 5,9. 16,6. 28,16, etc. (and cf. Exon. Note 34,56), it would seem clear proof that the slaves were counted as 'villagers'. Moreover, there are numerous cases (e.g. for 3,53;55. 19,18 etc.) where the Exon. scribe wrote *villt̄* which could be extended either to *villanus*, referring only to the 1 villager recorded or to *villani*, covering the slaves and the 1 villager (or smallholder as in 19,9). However, in all these cases the Exon. scribe may merely be using the word *villt̄* or *villani* in a set formula with no regard as to what classes of inhabitants the manor included; it should be remembered here that the details of villagers' land and ploughs precede the list of population.

Sometimes in Exon. the villagers' ploughs are given in a different formula, e.g. for 6,13 "The Abbot has 1 smith and 10 slaves who have 2 ploughs" (Exchequer DB has the same here), which definitely implies by the use of the plural *qui habent* that the slaves shared the ploughs. The case for slaves with ploughs is even stronger in the Exon. entry for 28,5 "(Gilbert has) 2 villagers and 2 slaves who have another plough", though in DB the slaves are listed after the lordship plough. But again, in some of this last-mentioned type of entry, Exon. definitely excludes the slaves from a share in the ploughs, e.g. for 1,29 "The King has 6 villagers and they have 3 ploughs; the King has 1 slave" (and here DB implies that the villagers and the slaves had the ploughs). Similarly at 15,40 and 15,99, in Exon. the slaves are clearly excluded from the ploughs, but the opposite appears in DB. Even within Exon. there is a difference in the treatment of slaves of the same manor, e.g. in the summary of Glastonbury Abbey's fief in Devon (527 b 7) which refers to its only holding in that county (DB 4,1) the phrase is "16 villagers and 4 smallholders and 4 slaves who have 5 ploughs", whereas in the main Exon. entry (161 a 1) it is the *vill(ani)* as a class who hold the ploughs.

The evidence for and against slaves having a share in the villagers' land holding is equally dubious. As Exchequer DB for Devon never mentions the villagers' land holding, this evidence only comes from Exon. and the same problems occur as to whether slaves are included in the word *vill(ani)* as are detailed above; see, for example, Exon. Notes to 16,6. 16,145-146. 19,9 and 35,5. However, in the Exon. for 34,13 the slaves, as well as the villagers, have 1 furlong ('ferling') (but DB, by substituting 'smallholders' for 'slaves' may be correcting an Exon. mistake). In the Exon. for Somerset 21,55 there can be no doubt about the 6 slaves of that manor holding 1 virgate. Cf. also Somerset Exon. Notes to 21,71 and 45,7. Finally, in Exon. a slave is stated to live on a furlong ('ferling') at East Buckland and, apparently, 2 slaves shared with the other 'villagers' the payment of £8 in revenue for Lympstone; see Devon Exon. Notes 3,54 and 26,1. It may be relevant

| | |
|---|---|
| 1,3 (cont'd.) | that DB Middlesex, which lists the land holdings of various 'villagers' (men-at-arms, Frenchmen, villagers, smallholders and cottagers; see the Appendix there), makes no mention of slaves with land.<br>31 VILLAGERS. *xxxi uill(anu)s*. The singular occurs regularly in DB with 21,31 etc., but the plural is used occasionally (e.g. 16,3 *xxi uill(an)i* and cf. 2,24 note on Cottagers). In Exon. both singular (e.g. for 1,13. 52,34) and plural (e.g. for 15,8. 16,107) are used, but in the entry for 5,6 *xxi uillanos* has been corrected to *uillanū* singular.<br>SMALLHOLDERS. *Bordarii*, apparently from *borda* 'a wooden hut' (perhaps Frankish *\*bord(e)* < common Germanic *bord* 'plank'). Unlike the slave (see note above) the smallholder had a hut of his own to live in; Finberg *Tavistock Abbey* p. 62. Although not as numerous as in DB Dorset and Cornwall, the smallholders in Devon formed more than a quarter of the recorded population. Most of the time in DB Devon they are listed after the villagers (but see 17,56 note) and before the cottagers (*cotarii*) who, though very similar in many respects (see 15,21 note), seem to have been poorer. However, in 14,1-2 (see note) they appear after the slaves. Smallholders may have been very similar to, if not sometimes identical with, Cottagers (*coscez*); see 2,24 note. In the Exon. for 20,6, 3 smallholders are stated to have 1 furlong ('ferling'), and no doubt elsewhere they share the land holding ascribed to the *villani* as a class in Exon., as well as the ploughs (see Exon. Note 3,63). Smallholders sometimes paid dues and probably owed their lords some form of labour service (see DB Dorset General Notes 1,1 and Herefordshire 19,1 and note). See DB Middlesex Appendix on a summary of the land holdings of smallholders, among other classes, in that county, and R. Lennard "The Economic Position of the Bordars and Cottars of Domesday Book" pp. 342-371 of The Economic Journal vol. lxi (June 1951).<br>ACRES. DB *acra*, Exon. *agra, ager*, is used mostly as a square measure, though it can also be used as a linear measure, as in 7,2. 28,2 and 32,4 (and see DB Dorset General Notes 1,1). On the number of acres in a hide, see 1,4 note on the hide, and on the linking of the acre with the furlong in the measurement of pasture, see 1,53 note. The acre was occasionally used in tax assessment; see 6,6 note.<br>IT PAYS. *Reddit* is regularly used here in Ch. 1; see 1,32 note for the possible reason for its use rather than that of *Valet*.<br>CATTLE. *animalia*, commonly called *animalia otiosa* "idle animals" elsewhere (e.g. Exon. 174 b 4 = Somerset 2,7), i.e. beef or dairy cattle (see 7,4 note on cows), in contrast to ploughing oxen, although occasionally in Exon. they seem to be oxen (see 17,26;38; 77 and Exon. Notes for 17,28;39;53; also Somerset Exon. Notes 25,41 and Cornwall Exon. Notes 4,23). Cattle and other animals were generally omitted from Exchequer DB, though sometimes they were mistakenly not eliminated when the original returns were abstracted (see Glos. 3,7 and note), and sometimes, as probably in Worcs. 19,9 and possibly in Kent 5,85 and Northants. 48,13, they took the place of the plough-team statement. Sometimes, too, they may have been included to make a particular point, as probably in Herts. 31,8 where a catalogue of livestock etc. is given for land wrongfully appropriated by Bishop Odo. Cf. 1,41 note on the moorland pasture dues from *animalia*, though it is possible that these included sheep as well. |
| 1,4 | EXMINSTER. A parish and the chief manor of Exminster Hundred (24). It passed to the Honour of Plympton and its sub-manors included *Breynton'* [Brenton GR SX 9086], *Holleham* [unidentified] and later *Suthwod'* [Southwood, see 2,4-6 note]; see Fees pp. 264, 790, FA i pp. 346-347, 389, Cal. Inq. PM vol. ii no. 539, iv no. 44, viii no. 273 and OJR in TDA 47 pp. 210-212. The advowson went to Plympton Priory; see TE p. 143b. ½ hide of lordship, held by the priests of Exminster, is mentioned in the Tax Return for Exminster Hundred (xxiii), though neither DB nor the main Exon. records this.<br>Exminster was one of several manors in Devon bequeathed by King Alfred to his younger son (BCS no. 553 = KCD ii p. 112 no. 314 = ECDC p. 9 no. 16 = Sawyer (1) no. 1507). Besides *Exanmynster* these places included *Heortigtun* [Hartland 1,30], *Axanmutha* [Axmouth 1,14], *Branecescumbe* [Branscombe 2,22], *Columtun* [Cullompton 9,1], *Twyfyrde* [Tiverton 1,35] and *Liwtune* [Lifton, 1,25].<br>IT ANSWERED FOR. *defendebat se pro*, a common phrase in other DB counties (e.g. Sussex, Bucks., Beds., Herts.) where it means the same as *geldabat pro* "paid tax for". See Exon. Notes 16,15 where Exon. has 'answered for' for DB's 'paid tax for'. For both here and 1,5;28 (where the phrase occurs again), Exon. has the same wording, but for DB's *geldabat pro* of 16,74 Exon. has *defendebat se* interlined above *reddidit Gildum* which is then marked for deletion (possibly because the former is the phrase used in the |

# 1

**1,4**  Exon. for Braunton (1,5), of which 16,74 was a part).
(cont'd.) HIDE. The hide is a unit of land measurement, either of productivity, of extent or of tax liability, and contained 4 virgates. Administrators attempted to standardize the hide at 120 acres, but incomplete revision and special local reductions left hides of widely differing extents in different areas. See Dr. John Morris in DB Sussex Appendix. There is some evidence that there were smaller hides in the south-west. A 40-acre geld-hide may be implied in the Wiltshire Tax Return for Calne Hundred, where one of the versions (Exon. 13 a 5) has two parts of a virgate and the third part of a virgate while the other two versions (Exon. 1 a 4 and 7 b 1) have 7 acres and 3 acres (the virgate was always a quarter of a hide). A 40-acre hide is also suggested in the details given in DB Dorset 36,4 (see General Notes there). Another 'small hide' of 48 acres for tax purposes has also been postulated; see Eyton *Dorset* p. 14 ff. This latter might be afforded credence in view of the frequent division of the virgate into thirds and quarters: a 40-acre hide — i.e. a 10-acre virgate — is not easily divisible by either 3 or 4, nor is a 30-acre virgate (120-acre hide) by 4, and similarly with one-third of a furlong ('ferling', see next note). However, there is apparently evidence against a 48-acre hide in 6,6 (see note), where it does not seem likely that only 3 acres formed a furlong ('ferling'). See J. Tait "Large Hides and Small Hides" in EHR xvii (1902); Finn LE pp. 122-123; DGSW pp. 80-81; VCH Wilts. ii p. 182. A hide of 12 acres has also been suggested for Cornwall; see Cornwall General and Exon. Notes 1,1.

It will be noticed that in this entry the details of lordship and villagers' land and the sub-holdings do not add up to the taxed hides. Although lordship land did not in fact pay tax (see Exon. Notes 2,11; DB Herefords. 8,2 and Glos. 39,6, and the evidence of the Tax Returns), on 94% of the Devon entries for which all the land details are given (in Exon.) — and similarly for Somerset and Dorset — the lordship land does add up with the villagers' land holding (and usually with the sub-holdings, if any, see below) to the amount of land which paid tax in 1066. This is because the taxed land was regularly the same as the size of the holding (except for Cornwall; see 1,3 note above): e.g. 20,15 sub-holding "Ansketel holds 1 furlong of this land .... It paid tax for as much" (see also the 20,10 sub-holding). Cf. the common formula in DB Shrops., Worcs., Herefords. etc. "*y* hides (there) which pay tax". Very often what in DB is given as the amount of land that paid tax is given in Exon. as the size of the holding, e.g. for 34,11 and 36,9 and in the summary of Glastonbury Abbey's Devon land compared to 4,1, and in the T.O. entry for 15,12; the reverse occurs in 40,4 (see Exon. Notes to all these). What the details show is how the total holding was apportioned and one would expect these details to add up to the total. However, in about 4% — some 32 entries — the details total less than the land taxed (as here) and in 2% or 15 entries (as e.g. 1,38. 3,96. 15,58) the details exceed it. In these reckonings 4 furlongs ('ferlings') have been taken to form 1 virgate, but see note below on the *ferling*. Scribal error may have caused some of these apparent discrepancies, as perhaps at 28,8 (see note), or the composition of the holdings may have changed — more land being cultivated, without the tax being altered from the 1066 figure (in this case the taxed land would differ from the size of the holding). Cf. 1,57 note on cases where it is the alteration in the tax figure in Exon. which has led to the total of details no longer agreeing with it. Moreover, it is not always clear whether the hidage of sub-holdings is to be taken into account when working out whether the sum of the details tallies with the tax given; see 1,12 note and cf. 1,18 note.

There are about 60 manors for which no villagers' land holding is given for some reason, and about a further 170 where no details are given or the land is not hidated. It is interesting that for a group of manors in Lifton Hundred (16,7-13) either all details of land holding are omitted or just the lordship land is stated, although the plough-teams are included and the entries are otherwise complete. However, this omission of villagers' land is not restricted to one Hundred or one part of the County, though over a third relate to manors in Wonford Hundred (as in 3,65-68 and 52,11-14). According to Finn MDeD p. 109 the scribe he calls 'G' was responsible for the frequent omission of the amount of villagers' land; this seems true of the majority of entries in Devon, though the scribe he calls 'A' was responsible for the group 16,7-13. See Dorset Exon. Notes 1,18 on the lack of villagers' land holding in the Exon. for Dorset. The entries for which no Exon. survives cannot of course be checked, because only in 2,2 and 7,1 does Exchequer DB state the lordship land and it never gives the villagers' holding.

See 10,2 note on the hide being used as a measurement of woodland and pasture. See also 1,3 note and the Appendix on the possible low level of tax assessment in Devon.

1,4         LORDSHIP .... 1 FURLONG. DB *ferling* (plural *ferlings*), Exon. *ferlinus, ferdinus,*
(cont'd.) *fertinus,* from OE *feorðling, feording,* ME *ferling, ferthing,* 'a fourth a quarter'. In DB Hunts. B 1 ;7;9-12 the *ferling* is a quarter in the sense 'a ward or precinct' in a town; in Kent 5,188 a mill in Dover pays 48 measures (*ferlingels*) of corn; elsewhere the word is used as a term of measurement of extent. 'Ferling' appears in the OED (though now only in historical use and with a reference to farthing), but John Morris decided to translate it as 'furlong' like the furlong or 'furrow-length' (DB *quarentena,* Exon. *quadragenaria,* see note below) which was used to measure woodland, pasture, etc.; DGSW uses the words ferlings, ferdings and fertings. Because the translation 'furlong' has already occurred in DB Cornwall and Somerset in this series, it has been thought best to keep to it in Devon, both in the text and in the Notes. (In DB Hants. NF 10,4 it was translated 'quarter', i.e. of a virgate). *Ferling* appears regularly in both Exon. and DB for Devon, Somerset and Cornwall in the record of tax assessment of the manor and of the lordship and villagers' holding there (but see Devon 47,6 where it is used to measure underwood, see note). That it mainly occurs in these three counties (and not in Dorset and Wiltshire) may be due to the generally small size of holdings in them, or possibly to the fact that Devon, Somerset and Cornwall were treated in Exon. as a separate group from the other two counties.
As to the size of the *ferling,* the name suggests that there were 4 to a virgate, 16 to a hide, and this equation fits the great majority of entries where the details of lordship and villagers' land add up to the land taxed. However, in 15,25. 21,14. 23,23;26. 35,7 and 52,4 there would need to be only 2 *ferlings* to a virgate for the total of the details to agree with the tax, and in 16,118, 8 *ferlings* to a virgate might seem to be correct. But there are many entries where there is a discrepancy between the taxed hides and the sum of the lordship and villagers' land and these may be among them; see above in the note on the hide. The occurrence in 5,10 (Details Table), 15,15-16 and 17,98 of third parts of a 'furlong' might suggest that there were 3 acres to a 'furlong': 48 acres to a hide, rather than 120 acres (which would be 7½ acres to the 'furlong') and than 40 acres (i.e. 2½ acres to the 'furlong'); see note above. But in 3,46 and 16,144 fourth parts of a 'furlong' are mentioned which are not so easily divisible in terms of acres, neither with the hide of 40, 48 nor 120 acres. In Fees ii p. 1308 there is mention of 16 acres forming one *ferling* on Henry of Pomeroy's manor of Berry in 1293, but this would mean a hide of 256 acres. See Finberg *Tavistock Abbey* pp. 39-40 on the various numbers of acres that could form the *ferling.*
FISHERY. Fisheries (DB *piscaria*; Exon. *piscatoria, piscatio, piscatura, pescaria, piscatia*) are mentioned for 13 places in DB Devon (here and in 1,60;71. 12,1. 16,69. 17,32;48; 105. 19,10. 21,19-20. 29,6 and 35,10) and in the Exon. for 28,13. The existence of a fishery is suggested at 20,15 where, according to Exon., 2 fishermen paid 80 salmon, and also perhaps at 36,9 where 3 salt-workers paid a packload of fish as well as their salt and money renders (see 1,23 note). (It is interesting that in 5 of the entries containing fisheries — 1,71. 12,1. 17,105. 19,10 and 21,20 — salt-houses are also mentioned.) All the places with fisheries were on the lower reaches of rivers; DGSW p. 269. Fisheries were not just areas where fishing was done, but were fixed contrivances for catching fish, whether weirs (as presumably at Weare Giffard 35,10) or 'stake-nets' or 'draw-nets' or hatches etc.; see Lennard p. 248 and Round in VCH Essex i pp. 424-425. With the exception of the two fisheries in 1,71 and the ones at 17,105 and 19,10 and in the Exon. for 28,13, all these Devon fisheries paid rents of some kind, either so many salmon as at 17,32;48 or, more often, commuted money rents. Some fisheries recorded elsewhere in DB paid no rents for some reason, as the one at Marden in Herefords. 1,4 or the two at Oare in Kent 5,141. Sometimes they were reserved for the supply of the lord's hall, as in Kent 13,1 and Hants. 16,5 and 35,4, or were rented by the villagers, as would seem to be the case in Shrops. 4,18,2. See 35,10 note for the ½ fishery at Weare Giffard.
LEAGUES. The *leuga* (sometimes spelled *leuua, leuuede*) was a measure of length, usually of woodland and pasture, though a few meadows are measured in leagues in Devon. It was traditionally reckoned at a mile and a half; but if so, some stretches of woodland etc., will have been of immense length (see Round in VCH Northants. i p. 280 and DB Worcs. 1,1c note). The league is used regularly as a linear measure, both measurements being given for the land, as in 1,8. In a great number of instances, however, only one dimension is given, as in 1,27 "meadow, 2 leagues". It has been thought that the league was here being used as a square measure (so Eyton *Dorset* i p. 31 ff.), but it would seem that by this phrase the scribe meant that the meadow, for example, measured 2

# 1

1,4
(cont'd.)
leagues in length and 2 in breadth (i.e. 4 square leagues). Many examples in the Exon. for Devon (and for Dorset; see General Notes 1,2 there) prove this by giving two measurements for DB's one, e.g. "pasture, ½ league in length and in width" for DB 17,20's "pasture, ½ league" (see also Exon. Notes to 17,15–16;81. 20,11. 25,1. 33,1 and 38,1). For the proof that when the scribe writes e.g. "1 league in (both) length and (in) width" (as here with "3½"), he means "1 league in length and 1 league in width"; see note below to 1,28 and cf. Exon. Notes 1,49. It would seem from these correspondences that all these phrases involving the so-called 'areal' league were interchangeable and were often used when both measurements of a piece of land were the same (but see 1,29;37). The furlong is used similarly; see next note.

12 FURLONGS. DB *quarentina*, Exon. *quadragenaria*, a twelfth of the league (see above note), reckoned at 220 yards, an eighth of a mile. In Devon the largest number of furlongs recorded in one dimension is in "pasture, 30 furlongs" in 2,7. In a great number of cases in DB the furlong is used linearly, both measurements of the land being given, as here. In many other instances, however, only one measurement is given, as in "woodland, 8 furlongs" in 1,8. Eyton *Dorset* p. 31 ff. thought that this meant that the furlong, like the league (see above), was being used as a square measure (e.g. in 1,8 the woodland would measure 8 by 1 furlongs or 4 by 2 furlongs, etc., making 8 square furlongs). However, there are numerous instances where the Exon. for Devon (and Dorset; see General Notes 1,1 there) gives two dimensions for DB's one, e.g. DB 23,15 "pasture, 10 furlongs", Exon. "pasture 10 furlongs in both length and width", that is, 10 furlongs by 10 furlongs = 100 square furlongs; see also Exon. Notes to 17,85. 24,20. 35,3. For the proof that when the scribe writes, for example, "2 furlongs in (both) length and width" he means "2 furlongs in length and 2 furlongs in width", see the examples quoted in the preceding note on leagues. It would thus seem that when the length and breadth of a piece of land were the same, the scribe used these two phrases indifferently. See 1,53 note on furlongs and acres being combined in measurements.

WOODLAND. Woodland is omitted about a dozen times in Exchequer DB, when it is nevertheless in Exon. Only for three of these is there a possible reason for the omission; see notes to 3,81. 16,164 and 32,5. However, the fact that the Exchequer scribe transferred the woodland details from the head of the list in Exon. to the end (perhaps because woodland was of less importance than meadow and pasture), may be a reason for this number of omissions — having written down the details of meadow and pasture he forgot to go back to the beginning of the Exon. list for the woodland.

WHEN B(ALDWIN) ACQUIRED IT. Probably when he acquired the 'farming' of the manor for the King; see 1,5 note on 'holds it at a revenue ....' and Exon. Notes 1,5 (second note). This meaning of *recepit* is different from cases where Exon. gives the value of a manor as when the tenant-in-chief 'acquired it' (received it from King William) which regularly corresponds to DB's 'Value was' formula.

WILLIAM OF EU .... ½ VIRGATE. It has been added to his manor of Powderham 22,1, where a plough is also recorded on the ½ virgate.

REEVE. The functions of the reeve (*praepositus, praefectus*) as a subordinate of the Sheriff and as a local official in the manor and in the village were probably varied; see Lennard p. 272 ff. and Morris pp. 157–8. See also DB Herefords. 1,3 note. From the statement in the Exon. for 15,67 (see Exon. Notes) it would seem that the reeve helped to collect the royal revenue.

1 FURLONG .... MONKS OF BATTLE. This furlong ('ferling') lay at Kenbury [GR SX 9287], first granted by Edward the Confessor in 1063 to SS. Mary, Thomas and Olaf in Exeter as ½ virgate and ½ *ferling* at *Kenbiri* (ECDC p. 15 no. 70 = KCD no. 814 = Sawyer (1) no. 1037). It passed to the monks of Battle together with the Church of St. Olaf, see *Regesta* i p. 15 no. 58 (and nos. 59, 62, 401, pp. 16, 101) and Ch. 9 note, also OJR in TDA 30 p. 288, 33 p. 607, 36 p. 379, 47 p. 212 and Oliver *Mon.* p. 117. It is curious that there is no cross-reference to this furlong ('ferling') under the fief of Battle Church (Ch. 9) although there is one for the ½ virgate that was removed from Exminster (see above note).

½ PLOUGH CAN PLOUGH IT. The fact that this information appears at the end of the statement in Exon. (which the Exchequer scribe had rearranged and which began with the monks of Battle holding the furlong ('ferling') may be the reason for its omission in DB. However, the Exchequer scribe may have deliberately excluded it as unimportant; cf. the omitted plough estimate in the Landinner and Trebeigh statement in 1,25 and in the added holding in 3,76. On numerous occasions information in sub-holdings given in

Exon. seems to have been 'pruned out' by the Exchequer scribe. See fifth note under 1,34.

1,5 BRAUNTON. DB *Brantone*. Apparently from OE *brōm — tūn* 'farm where the broom grows', but *Branctona* (the form used in Hundred List I; see Appendix), and other forms with -c- given below, suggest derivation from St. Branoc, there being a St. Brannocks Well in the parish; see DEPN s.n. and EPNS i p. 32. Braunton is now a parish and was the chief manor of Braunton Hundred. The land had been held by Saxon kings and 10 hides at *Brannocminster* were granted by King AEthelbald of Wessex to Glastonbury Abbey between 855 and 860 (ECDC no. 13 p. 9 = Sawyer (1) no. 1695). *Brancminstre* was later exchanged by King Edgar for 7 *mansiunculae* at High Ham in Somerset (ECDC no. 40 p. 12 = BCS no. 1294 = Sawyer (1) no. 791); see Ch. 4 note. By 1086 a portion of the manor had already been granted out to Algar the priest (13a,3); later it probably formed the manor of Braunton Dean. The rest of Braunton was later divided, Braunton Abbot being granted to the Abbey of Cleeve in Somerset by Henry III, Mon. Ang. v p. 133; see Fees p. 1427 and FA i p. 360. Braunton Gorges was a grant to Robert *de Siccavilla* in 1202, later held by the Gorges family, while the Church of Braunton was held by St. Mary and St. Peter in Exeter (*Regesta* ii pp. 72, 185, nos. 841, 1391, iii p. 106 no. 284). On the whole manor see Fees pp. 97, 265, 782, FA i pp. 360, 375, 415, Cal. Inq. PM vol. i no. 799, vi no. 508, x no. 46, xv no. 499 and OJR H8 pp. 408-418.

HOLDS IT AT A REVENUE FROM THE KING. Exon. *tenet eam ad firmam de rege*; that is, he 'farmed' the land. However, see Exon. Notes here for Lennard's view that Baldwin did not 'farm' Braunton himself, but merely had charge of it from the King and let it out to someone else to 'farm' (rather like the Sheriff of Glos. in DB Glos. 1,62 let out Hempsted at a fixed rent of 60s at face value [the translation in the Glos. volume is incorrect here]). Although Sheriffs regularly did 'farm' royal land (in Exon. Baldwin is said to 'farm' Bradstone 1,36), manors were also 'farmed' by others, such as Colwin in 1,25 and Gotshelm in 1,61;64-65, whom there is no reason to suspect were ever Sheriffs — Colwin was probably the reeve of that name in C 2 (see note). It was not, of course, just royal land that could be 'farmed'; e.g. two manors of Roger of Ivry in Glos. 41,2-3 and the Abbey of Fécamp's manor of Steyning in Sussex 5,2 are said to be 'at a revenue'. Occasionally, the villagers themselves 'farmed' a manor; see 25,28 and 26,1, and 6,6 note. Under this system the *firmarius* or 'farmer' agreed to pay a fixed sum of money to the King, the lord of the manor or the Sheriff, which he hoped he would more than recover from the rents and dues he received from that manor as well as from the profits of the lordship. See Lennard Chs. V and VI on the practice of 'farming'. See next note but one, and cf. the Exon. for 15,23, for *firma* being used in a slightly different sense, and see 1,21 note on the term 'one night's revenue' (*firma unius noctis*).

1 VIRGATE .... TAKEN AWAY. It lay at Blakewell, 16,74. A further virgate removed from Braunton (but returned) is mentioned in 3,32.

PAID 20s IN KING'S REVENUE. *reddebat .... in firma regis. firma* here represents the whole revenue the King received for Braunton, to which the alienated virgate contributed 20s. Cf. the T.O. rendering for the similar DB phrase in 1,15 (see Exon. Notes there). Or perhaps the phrase could be translated 'in(to) the King's revenue', where *firma* would be used more in the sense of 'treasury'; cf. 1,55, and also the Exon. for the same DB phrase of *in firma* in 1,49 (see Exon. Notes there).

ROBERT OF PONT-CHARDON. DB *de Pont cardon*, Exon. *de ponte cardonis*. Pont-Chardon is in the département of Orne, France; OEB p. 108. Heanton Punchardon (16,69) is named after him or his successors.

ADDED VIRGATE .... BELONGED .... TO FILLEIGH. This added land is called Lobb; see 16,80 where more details are given.

1,6 SOUTH MOLTON. A parish and the chief manor in South Molton Hundred (6). It was afterwards given to the Earl of Gloucester; see FA i p. 325, RH i p. 80b, Cal. Inq. PM vol. iii no. 371, v no. 538, vi no. 710, viii nos. 396-397, ix no. 428, xvi no. 538 and OJR H3 pp. 77-79.

1½ VIRGATES OF LAND. An unusual formula for Devon: normally a manor is said to have 'paid tax for' so many hides/virgates, or the 1086 holder is said to have so many hides/virgates 'in the manor'; both these phrases appear to mean the same, see 1,4 note on the hide. It is interesting that the same wording occurs in Exon.

12 PIGMEN. There are far more pigmen (*porcarii*) recorded for Devon than for any other DB county (according to DGSW p. 352 the Devon pigmen formed 70% of the total entries of them in DB). It is very odd that the Exchequer scribe when using Exon. omitted

|1,6|pigmen from over a third of the entries — 25 occurrences. The reason for this is hard to
(cont'd.) find, as the omissions are not confined to particular areas or fiefs; for example, pigmen
are recorded in DB for 16,44 but not for 16,43;45-46, although in Exon. these entries
run consecutively; similarly they are entered in DB 16,141 though not in 16,140, the
preceding entry in Exon. too. However, see notes to 15,12 and 16,23 for possible
reasons for the omission of the pigmen there. It is unlikely that the Exchequer scribe
omitted so many pigmen from Exon. because he misread *porcarii* for *porci*, which latter
he was excluding (see Lennard p. 258 note 4): the only dubious reading is that at 17,16
(see Exon. Notes).

These pigmen, who so often appear in groups, seem to have been independent pig-farmers, paying rent, rather than herdsmen for the villagers' pigs; Lennard p. 258. It is interesting that the Exchequer scribe seems to have changed the 1 villager and 1 pigman recorded for the added furlong ('ferling') in the Exon. for 17,17 to "2 villagers". In DB Worcs. 10,4 pigmen are equated with *rustici* "countrymen" (see note there). In some 45 out of the 68 entries (DB and Exon. combined), the pigmen are said to pay so many pigs, a payment which is stated to be annual on several occasions in Exon. (e.g. for 1,67. 2,2;4; 11 etc.) and on two occasions (1,26 and 10,1) these are commuted to money-rents (as also in DB Somerset 1,11 and 2,1). Pigmen are regularly entered in both DB and Exon. after the slaves, villagers and smallholders, but they appear before the slaves (though still after the villagers and smallholders) in 5 entries, and, very unusually, before the villagers and smallholders in 1,66. In 23,9 and 42,6 they are entered after the resources, possibly because originally omitted (see notes). It is not possible to tell whether pigmen had a share in the villagers' ploughs (as apparently in 1,9;66 and 16,44); in DB Herefords. 1,42 and perhaps also here in 16,10 (see note), they had ploughs of their own; for the Exon. evidence, see Exon. Notes 1,26. For the majority of manors in DB, however, the pigmen are entered after the other inhabitants and their ploughs (and land). See 1,18 note on pigs.

RINGEDONE. OJR (in TDA 33 p. 608 and H3 p. 68) gratuitously identifies this place, added to South Molton, as Frenchstone in George Nympton. He is followed by DG which maps 'Ringdon' where Frenchstone lies; but no place called 'Ringdon' has been recorded in George Nympton parish. There is another 'Ringdon' (now Ringcombe in West Anstey) in the same Hundred (see 16,79 note), but it is probably too remote to have been part of South Molton in 1086.

1,7   SILVERTON. A parish, head of the Tax Return Hundred of Silverton, now Hayridge (15). Silverton itself was granted by Henry II to the Earl of Devon and was held of his Honour of Plympton by the Vautort and Corbet families then by the Beauchamps; see RH i pp. 70b, 95a, FA i pp. 321, 382, Cal. Inq. PM vol. iii no. 156, vi no. 318, ix no. 109, xi no. 35.

This large 1086 manor will have contained: (1) *Torverton'* [Thorverton GR SS 9202, now a separate parish] given to the monastery of Marmoutier at Tours by Henry III (or by William I according to Fees p. 96; see RH i p. 70b, Cal. Inq. PM vol. ii no. 265); (2) part of Cullompton (the rest had been granted by William I to Battle Church, 9,1 note) given in 1291 to the Abbey of Buckland Monachorum by Isabella Countess of Devon (Fees p. 264, RH i p. 70b, FA i p. 368, Oliver *Mon.* p. 383, VE ii p. 378); and (3) *Childetun'* [Chilton in Thorverton, SS 9205]; see Fees pp. 96, 782, FA i p. 425, Cal. Inq. PM vol. vi no. 101, vii nos. 416, 663, xvi no. 126. Smaller subdivisions of the manor were *Paddekebrok'* [Padbrook ST 0106], Fees p. 789, FA i p. 368 and *Suthwod'* and *Niweland'* ['Southwood', unidentified, and Newland in Cullompton, ST 0407], Fees p. 789, FA i p. 425. On the whole manor see OJR in TDA 33 p. 608, 37 pp. 416, 426, 42 pp. 229-231.

½ furlong ('ferling') had been added to this manor from the manor of *Esseorda* held by the wife of Hervey of Helléan. This information is not recorded in the main Exon. returns nor in DB, but appears in the T.O. (see Exon. Notes to Ch. 44).

IT NEVER PAYS TAX. *geld'* may here abbreviate the perfect *geldavit* 'it has never paid tax', as in 1,11;14. Exon. has *redd' gild'*. In DB and Exon. *geld'* and *redd' gildum* can be the abbreviations for both the present and imperfect/perfect tenses, though generally with the addition of *T.R.E.*, and its Exon. equivalent, if the past is meant, as in 1,9. 3,95 etc. Cf. notes to 2,2 and 9,2 and Exon. Notes 23,1.

WITH ALL THAT BELONGS THERE. DB *cum omnibus ibi pertinentibus*; Exon. *cum omnibus quae ibi pertinent* (not ....*qui*.... (= 'all who') as DGSW p. 239 note 2 transcribes the $\bar{q}$ in the MS), extending into the right margin but with no sign that it was added. A very unusual phrase in DB for the south-west counties, though it occurs regularly in

| | |
|---|---|
| 1,7 (cont'd.) | charters, grants and other documents of the period (e.g. *Regesta* i App. nos. ix, xi etc., Oliver *Mon*. p. 116 no. 1 etc.). If it refers, as in these documents, to other manorial details such as mills, meadows, etc., then it is unnecessary. If it does not, then one would expect the phrase to occur regularly in Exon. and DB.
It is just possible that in the original returns from which Exon. was taken, some mention might have been made of this manor paying one night's revenue (on which, see 1,21 note), because a phrase which occurs regularly in connection with the night's revenue resembles this unusual phrase: e.g. Wilts. 1,1-2 *cum omnibus consuetudinibus*, Dorset 1,2 *cum suis appendiciis et consuetudinibus* and 1,21 below *cum suis apendiciis*. Such information would be expected of this manor, though it would normally occur near the end of the entry with the present value. Possibly the original returns at this point were damaged in some way and the Exon. scribe in perplexity jotted down what remained of a phrase such as *Hoc manerium reddebat (dimidiam) firmam unius noctis cum omnibus consuetudinibus quae ibi pertinent*. As on several other occasions (see the Introduction to the Exon. Notes) the Exchequer scribe seems merely to have copied the Exon. (though not quite word for word here) without bothering about the meaning.
3 MILLS. The mills that DB records are of course water-mills, not windmills, which latter did not appear in Britain for another century. Far fewer mills are recorded in DB Devon than are in Somerset and Dorset, for example. Their render, said on numerous occasions in Exon. to be *per annum*, is usually given; but see notes to 5,1 and 23,22. See also notes to 34,23 and 16,45. |
| 1,8 | HEMYOCK. A parish, formerly the chief manor of Hemyock Hundred (16). The church went to Torre Abbey (VE ii p. 362), the manor to the Honour of Plympton (Fees p. 1368, Cal. Inq. PM vol. ii no. 590, x no. 384, see OJR H2 p. 39). The manor later contained *Madisheue* or *Madescay*, granted out by Henry I, Fees p. 342, RBE ii p. 452; it appears to have belonged to William Cheever [Mackham, 19,36 note] in 1086; see OJR in TDA 37 pp. 423, 440. |
| 1,9 | (EAST) BUDLEIGH. A parish, *caput* of the single Hundred of Budleigh (14), later divided into East and West. Besides the Budleigh given by Henry I to the Abbey of Mont St. Michel (Fees p. 95), and Budleigh Salterton, this complex manor contained: (1) 1 hide at *Fenoteri* [Venn Ottery GR SY 0791], held in Fees p. 95 by Philip *de Fornell'* (Furneaux) as a serjeanty, see RBE ii p. 560, Fees pp. 264, 764, 1368, RH i pp. 66b, 92b, Cal. Inq. PM vol. iii no. 508, v no. 27, vii no. 441 and FA i pp. 325, 365; (2) *Bradeham* [Bradham SY 0181 in Withycombe Raleigh], given in 1205 by King John to the Church of St. Nicholas in Exeter, Fees pp. 95, 764, 1424, TE p. 152a, RH i p. 66a, FA i p. 365, VE ii p. 313, Oliver *Mon*. p. 125, Ch. 9 note; (3) *Hulle* [Hill in Withycombe Raleigh, SY 0081], formerly part of Bradham, Fees p. 342, RH i p. 66b; (4) *Harpeford* [Harpford parish SY 0990] given to Oliver *de Dinant* and by him to the Priory at Dinan; it is called *Ortiland* ['Otterland'] in RBE ii p. 560; see Fees pp. 96, 764, RH i p. 66a, FA i pp. 325, 365, Cal. Inq. PM vol. iii no. 532, iv no. 44, vii no. 462, xi no. 374 (see 11,1 and 52,35 notes); (5) *Langelegh'* [Langley SS 9109, now in Cadeleigh parish, Hayridge Hundred (EPNS ii p. 560); earlier in (West) Budleigh Hundred], held with *Braderig'* [Broadridge, see 35,24 note] by Ralph *de Welinthon'* of the Honour of Plympton, Fees pp. 761, 1424, RH i p. 93a, FA i pp. 364, 426; (6) *Blakebergh'* [Blackberry in Bicton, SY 0686], held by Roger *le Poer* of the Honour of Plympton in Fees pp. 762, 790; see FA i pp. 364, 426, Cal. Inq. PM vol. iv (o.s.) no. 63 (= TDA 38 p. 325); this was perhaps a part of Bicton (51,1). And (7) *Yetematon'* and *Daledich'* [Yettington in Bicton, SY 0585, and Dalditch in East Budleigh, SY 0483], held by the Honour of Okehampton with *La Shete* [Shute, see 16,139 note] in Fees pp. 762, 787; see FA i pp. 364, 426. On the manor as a whole see OJR in TDA 35 pp. 280, 287-288, 297-298, 301. |
| 1,10 | KINGSTEIGNTON. DB *Teintone*. Now a parish, formerly the chief manor of Teignton, now Teignbridge, Hundred (23). It remained in royal hands until given to Peter *Burdun* by Henry III; see Fees pp. 98, 782, RH i p. 81b, FA i pp. 339, 390, and Cal. Inq. PM vol. iv no. 20, vii no. 708, xi no. 236, xvi no. 1085. The holding included *Teyngewyk* [Highweek parish GR SX 8471] given by Henry III to Theobald *de Englissevile*, RH i p. 81b; see RH i p. 90a, Fees pp. 264, 612, 1372, 1426, Cal. Inq. PM vol. i no. 714, x no. 488 and OJR in TDA 29 p. 226. Part of Newton Abbot (*Novelevile* in RH i p. 82b, see EPNS ii p. 473) belonged to *Teyngewyk*, part to Wolborough; see 16,163 note. |
| 1,11 | AXMINSTER. A parish and head of Axminster Hundred (17). It remained royal land until granted by King John to William *Briwere* from whom it passed via his fourth |

1,11       daughter to Reginald *de Mohun* who gave the manor for the foundation of Newenham
(cont'd.)  Abbey (at GR SY 2897 in the parish); see Fees pp. 97, 264, 797, 1263, 1307, RBE ii
           p. 558, Oliver *Mon.* pp. 357-369 and Davis MCGB p. 78.
              In Fees p. 788 John *Capy* and William *de Aqua* (from Latin 'water'; probably the
           toponymic surname here means 'at the source' or 'at the spring') hold in *Membyr'*
           [Membury] from the Honour of Plympton. This appears to have been granted out of
           the manor of Axminster and to be represented in FA i p. 366 by *Capieheghes* [Casehayes
           in Membury, EPNS ii p. 644, *Memburye Capye* in Cal. Inq. PM vol. iv (o.s.) no. 63 =
           TDA 38 p. 326] and *La Watere* [Waterhouse farm in Membury, ST 2603]; see FA i
           p. 429. On the whole manor see OJR H4 p. 144.
              HOW MANY HIDES ARE THERE. *quot hidae sint ibi*; *sint* is subjunctive. In 1,7;14, the
           other entries in which the formula is used, the form is *sī* which could abbreviate *sint* or
           the indicative *sunt*. Exon. has *sī* here and for 1,14 and *s̄* for 1,7 (Ellis misprints *S*). This
           formula also occurs in the first chapters of Somerset, Wiltshire and Dorset. In Dorset and
           Wiltshire the verb is either *sint* or *sī*; in Somerset *sint* and *sī* are used in DB, but *sunt* or *s̄*
           in all the corresponding Exon. entries except for one (*sint*). The subjunctive and
           indicative are interchangeable in indirect questions in Medieval Latin. But see Round
           FE p. 109.
              TO THIS MANOR ARE OWED.... For 'Charlton', see 3,96; Honiton, 15,23; Smallridge,
           34,51; Membury, 19,44; Rawridge, 10,2. There is no mention in any of these entries of
           the unpaid customary dues, though for the similar list in 1,23 (see note), there is a cross-
           reference for Fardel in 15,67.
              'DENEWORTHY'. A place now lost, lying in Membury parish; see EPNS ii p. 645.
              ALRIC. See PNDB pp. 150-151 s.n. *Alric* and 17,88-89 note below.
              UNDERCLEAVE. DB *Odesclive*. The DB form does not evolve to the modern one, but
           both forms may represent the same place; see EPNS ii p. 636 and OJR H4 p. 149.
              EDRIC THE CRIPPLE. *Manc(us)* in DB and Exon.; see OEB p. 322 and cf. Asgar the
           Cramped (1,23-24 note).
              EDWARD SON OF EDRIC. That is, Edric the Cripple, as the *filius eiusdem Eddrici* of
           Exon. makes clear.
              THIS MANOR'S CHURCH. The Church of Axminster (not Underclteave, as Exon.
           makes clear); it was granted to St. Peter's, York, by Edward the Confessor; see Harmer
           no. 120 (= ECDC no. 71 p. 15), Oliver *Mon.* p. 317 and OJR H4 p. 146.

1,12       KINGSKERSWELL. DB *Carsewelle*. Now a parish in Haytor Hundred (29), to which it
           formerly gave its name, Kerswell. RH i p. 71b records that its first holder after 1086 was
           John *le Droun*. It was granted out successively by Henry II and King John, then by
           Henry III to Nicholas *de Molis* who held it in 1242 as *Karswill'* with *Depeford* [Diptford
           1,15]; see RBE ii p. 559, RH i p. 89a, Fees pp. 265, 769, 1372, FA i pp. 318, 349, 392,
           Cal. Inq. PM vol. iii no. 283, v nos. 202, 603, viii no. 139, ix no. 427, xi no. 309, xii no.
           333, xvi no. 1085, and OJR in TDA 40 p. 126, 50 p. 328.
              TAX .... 1½ HIDES .... CHURCH .... ½ VIRGATE. Here it would seem that the ½ virgate
           belonging to the church is needed to combine with the lordship and villagers' land to
           reach the tax of 1½ hides (which in Devon is the same as the size of the holding; see 1,4
           note on the hide). However, in the next entry, almost identical in form, the church's ½
           virgate seems to be additional to the hide of tax because of the 1 virgate in lordship and
           3 virgates of villagers' holding. As it is also additional in 1,18 and 1,33 (see notes), it
           would seem that in this entry either there was an error in the lordship or villagers' land,
           or, as in some other entries, these did not add up to the tax, or perhaps the church land
           here had been taken out of the lordship or villagers' holding, though not stated; (cf. 1,70
           where Gotshelm's virgate is said in Exon. to be 'of the villagers' land').

1,13       COLYTON. A parish and the chief manor of Colyton Hundred (22). It was granted by
           Henry II to Robert *de Dunstanvil'* in 1159. In 1242 (Fees p. 782) Reginald *de Valle Torta*
           and Alice *Basseth'* hold in *Culiton'* from Walter *de Dunstanvil'*. The land then passed to
           William *de Courtenay* and his successors on the remarriage of Joan *Bassett* who had been
           wife of Reginald *de Valle Torta*; see Fees p. 1367, RH i p. 68b, Cal. Inq. PM vol. iii
           no. 31, xiv no. 325, FA i p. 329 and OJR H7 p. 342. The church was later held by St.
           Mary and St. Peter, Exeter, *Regesta* ii p. 72 no. 841, p. 185 no. 1391, iii p. 106 no. 284.
              Sub-manors of Colyton, all held by the Courtenays, were: (1) *Monketon* [Monkton
           parish GR ST 1803, see EPNS ii p. 627] in HD p. 56, FA i p. 329, Cal. Inq. PM vol. ii
           nos. 306, 436, 593, iii no. 415, vi no. 478, vii no. 297, xi no. 300, xii no. 436; (2)
           *Whytewell* [Whitwell SY 2392] in FA i p. 329; (3) *Policumbe* [Colcombe SY 2494] in

| | |
|---|---|
| 1,13 (cont'd.) | FA i p. 330 and (4) *Coliford* [Colyford SY 2592] in RH i pp. 68a, 94b, Cal. Inq. PM vol. ii no. 71. A further manor was the *Culint'* [Colyton] granted by Henry III to the nuns of Polsloe Priory; see Fees p. 96, FA i p. 330, Oliver *Mon.* p. 168 and OJR H7 p. 345. TAX FOR 1 HIDE .... CHURCH LIES ½ VIRGATE. See 1,12 note. |
| 1,14 | AXMOUTH. A parish and formerly chief manor of Axmouth Hundred which later merged with Axminster (17). It had been one of the manors given by King Alfred in his will to his younger son (1,4 note) and according to RH i p. 63a it had been a possession of King Athelstan (*c.* 924–939). It was given at an unknown date to Richard *de Redvers* who gave it to the Abbey of Montebourg; see FA i p. 328, Round CDF p. 314 no. 879, *Regesta* ii p. 67 no. 825 and OJR H4 p. 178. BECAUSE. In the MS $\dot{q}a$, the usual abbreviation for *quia*; Farley misprints $\dot{q}$ (= *qui* 'who'). 16 GOATS. *caprae*, she-goats, important for their milk. |
| 1,15 | DIPTFORD. A parish in Stanborough Hundred (28); it gave its name to the corresponding Tax Return Hundred (xxvi) in which it can be identified. It followed much the same manorial descent as Kingskerswell (1,12 note) with which it is often associated in later records, coming to Nicholas *de Molis* in 1230; see Fees pp. 769, 782, 794, 1372, FA i pp. 323, 395, Cal. Inq. PM vol. iii no. 283, v no. 603, viii no. 139. Members of Diptford were *Horn'e* [Horner GR SX 7654], *Asswelle* [Ashwell SX 7655] and *Tuveton* [Tennaton SX 7455] in RH i p. 79a; see RH i p. 91a, Fees pp. 1371, 1386, Cal. Inq. PM vol. xii no. 333, and, on the whole manor, OJR in TDA 45 pp. 198–199. FARLEIGH. This added land seems to have descended with Diptford, being held by John *de Meolys* in FA i p. 351 and appears there to have been counted as a part of Langford (1,55). *Fernlegh'* is there also associated with *Wagelond* [Wagland GR SX 7654], *Lappelond* [Lapland, EPNS i p. 300] and *Wrangeton* [Wrangaton in Ugborough, SX 6757, see 1,55 note]. This last is held by the prior of Plympton; see FA i pp. 395, 397 and OJR in TDA 45 p. 201. IN THE TIME OF WILLIAM OF VAUVILLE. He appears to have been in charge of at least some of the King's manors here, with the ability to transfer land; see 3,32. He may have been Baldwin's predecessor as Sheriff; Finn MDeD p. 95 note 1. See the phrase 'Before Baldwin('s time)' in the past value of 1,30;33, and cf. DB Herefords. 1,72 where 'in Earl William's time' Roger of Pîtres (the Sheriff then) transferred 2½ hides to Gloucestershire. Vauville is near Beaumont-Hague in the département of Manche, France; OEB p. 119. But there is also a Vauville in Calvados, south of Deauville. A THANE HELD IT FREELY BEFORE 1066. Exon. "a thane held it jointly in 1066; he could go to whomever he would"; see Exon. Notes. A check has been made, both in Exon. and in DB for the south-west counties and in particular for Devon, on the occurrences of the phrases 'held it freely (*libere*)'; 'held it jointly (*pariter/in paragio*)', and also 'held it as one/two manors (*pro uno manerio/duobus maneriis*)', which almost invariably occur as descriptions of the 1066 tenure of a manor, often relating, as here, to tenure by thanes. In the details that follow the evidence of the T.O. has been largely discounted, as it is not clear whether this document was used by either the Exon. or Exchequer scribes. These phrases appear to be interchangeable: for example, in Devon 1,32. 3,22. 15,26–27;79. 28,16. 36,23, etc., DB has 'freely' while the corresponding Exon. entries have only 'jointly'. Again, in 1,29. 5,2;8 the TRE holders in DB are stated to have held the land 'as a manor' or 'as two manors', whereas in Exon. they are said to have held 'jointly'; in 15,12 DB similarly has the 1066 tenant holding the land 'as one manor', while Exon. states that he 'could go to whichever lord he would'. For the examples in Somerset of *pro manerio* in DB corresponding to *pariter* in Exon., see Exon. Notes there to 1,6 (third note), 5,2 (last note), 5,9-10;15 etc., and for *libere* in DB corresponding to *pariter* in Exon. see the Exon. Notes to 35,4. 36,7 (twice);13. 37,6;12. 45,5. 46,2;14, etc. In a great many entries in DB there is no description of the type of 1066 tenure of manors, while Exon. regularly states that the manor in question was held 'jointly' by the TRE tenant or that the latter 'could go where he would'; see Exon. Notes to Devon and Somerset *passim*. In Devon these DB entries are predominantly in the first part of the County, suggesting that at some time in the writing out a decision was made to include details of previous tenure. The later addition of so many *pariter*'s and *in paragio*'s in the margin and interlined, also points to this; see 15,47–52 note. It was very important to know the way in which a manor had been held in 1066, when so many lands were |

**1,15 (cont'd.)** acquired unlawfully and their ownership contested. For example, note the number of instances in Ch. 15 of the word 'freely' and the stress laid on the fact that many of the TRE holders there had been free, but (despite this) their lands had been 'added' to those of Edmer Ator or Ordwulf (see 15,31 and note and Exon. Notes to it); the Count of Mortain was notorious for his 'thefts' of land (cf. Dorset General Notes 26,1). In 15,53, Exon. states that the TRE holder held his land 'jointly and now it has been added to Ordwulf's land'; here 'jointly' is being used in exactly the same way as 'freely' in 15,31. Also in 34,5 the fact that Ledmer, who held in 1066, was a free man is set against the seizure (testified in court) of his land by Ralph of Pomeroy; in the T.O. for this entry he is said to have held it 'jointly' in 1066 and Ralph appropriated it. Very often it is the 1066 tenure of an *added* land that is described in such a manner; for example, the added ½ virgates of 1,46 and 1,49 had been held freely in 1066, and *Nimete* had been wrongfully joined to Molland (1,41) and it had been held jointly by two brothers according to Exon., while Blackpool, also joined to Molland, had been held 'as a manor' before 1066.

The phrase 'could go to whichever lord he would (with this land)', which in the Exon. for Devon is more common than 'freely', meant that the holder was free to choose whichever lord he wanted as his patron and protector of his land; he was not 'bound' to anyone in particular.

The words *in paragio* and *pariter* are more complicated to explain, but they would seem to imply a form of land tenure whereby a man's estate was not physically divided among his heirs, but enjoyed equally by them, with one heir being responsible to the lord and King for the services due from the land and the other heirs being answerable only to the first. These heirs were often the deceased's children, as probably in 1,41 and 3,40 (see Exon. Notes to there), and in Dorset 26,37 and 30,3; but the 6 thanes who according to Exon. held jointly the added land of 16,7 do not appear to be related at all. This type of tenure had the important advantage of preserving the unity of the manor; see VCH Dorset iii pp. 34-35 for other advantages. See Vinogradoff pp. 245-249 and Maitland DBB pp. 145-146. However, there are a great many examples of the 1066 tenants, though holding 'jointly', having separate pieces of land for which they presumably paid tax individually, which would mean that the 'joint tenure' referred only to the services due from the lands. Land held in parage was very often equally divided among the heirs, e.g. in Somerset 5,10. 19,64. 22,28. 24,10, etc., where of two thanes who had held jointly, one had held one half of the land and the other the other half (see Exon. Notes there). See also Devon Exon. Notes 15,52 where each of the 4 thanes held 1 furlong. However, there are numerous cases of land being held jointly that was not partitioned equally, as in 35,9 where Exon. states that West Putford had been held jointly in 1066 by 2 thanes, one of whom had ½ hide, the other ½ virgate. Likewise in Somerset 5,9 two thanes had held East Harptree jointly, one holding 3 hides, the other 2 hides; also Somerset 5,47 where three thanes had held Radstock jointly, but their holdings were of 6 hides, 1 hide and 3 virgates; similarly for Somerset 5,59;61-62; 64-65. 19,13-14;29;32;72. 21,63;65;73;85. 25,27;43. 28,1. 37,8;11. 45,7 and many more (see the Exon. Notes to these).

In a great many entries only one person (very often a thane) is said to have held the manor 'jointly' in 1066, e.g. in 16,144. 17,17. 19,40. 28,16. 34,55;57, etc. (and see Dorset General Notes 26,1 and Somerset Exon. Notes *passim* for examples there). According to Vinogradoff p. 245 ff. this meant either that the deceased only had one son, but tenure in parage would continue as that son would probably have more than one child, or that the heir held responsible for the whole holding was the only one mentioned. However, Finn (LE pp. 88-89), discussing the large number of occurrences of the phrase 'a thane held it jointly' in the T.O. entries concerning manors that had been combined in 1086, believed that *pariter* there meant that the added land had been held in the same way as the manor to which it had been joined, that is it had been held 'as a manor', this view being borne out by the Exchequer DB's frequent substitution of *pro manerio* for *pariter*. But it seems more likely that the T.O. scribe in making the point that of two manors combined in 1086 one had been held 'jointly' — or that its holder 'could go where he would' — was implying that the 1086 holder had been wrong to add land that had been thus held; this would explain the presence in the T.O. (= 'Seized Lands') of so many entries on manors that had merely been combined.

Thus it would seem that 'joint' tenure implied free tenure and the land so held had the status of a 'manor', and that the scribes of Exon. and DB saw no real difference in meaning in the phrases *libere, pariter, pro manerio*.

1,16 See DB Dorset General Notes 26,1 and Somerset Exon. Notes Introduction p. 310. See also Devon Exon. Notes 45,1 and 1,32 note below on thanes.

1,16 (WEST) ALVINGTON. A parish in Stanborough Hundred (28) and identifiable in the Tax Return for Diptford (Stanborough) Hundred (xxvi). It is 'West' probably by reference to Alphington (1,43) and was held from the Crown under Henry II by the *Daubengny* family. Oliver *Daubengny's* holding escheated to the King and was given to Alice *de Ryvers*. On her death it was given to William *de Feritate*, then to Patrick *de Chawrth*, then to Matthew *Besille*; see RH i p. 79a, Fees pp. 99, 264, 766, FA i p. 323, Cal. Inq. PM vol. i no. 718, viii no. 139, xi no. 26 and OJR in TDA 45 pp. 195–196.

The advowson of the church was held by the canons of Salisbury *de antiquis temporibus* 'from ancient times' (RH i p. 79a), implying a dedication before 909 when the great diocese of Sherborne was subdivided between Sherborne, Wells and Crediton; see Fees pp. 1264, 1371, 1425–1426. The see of Sherborne had united with that of Ramsbury in 1058 and the episcopal seat was transferred to Salisbury between 1075 and 1078.

1,17 PLYMPTON. *Caput* of Plympton Hundred (26) and involving both the parishes of Plympton St. Mary and Plympton Erle (or St. Maurice). The estate was crown land until Henry I gave it to Richard *de Redvers*. It then became head of the Plympton Barony, the seat of the Earls of Devon; see RH i p. 77a, FA i p. 401, Cal. Inq. PM vol. i no. 564, iii no. 156, xvi no. 214, OJR H6 pp. 279-282 and Ch. 21 note.

A sub-manor was *Radeford* [Radford in Plymstock, GR SX 5052], held from the Honour of Plympton in FA i p. 335. The church of Plympton was later granted to St. Mary and St. Peter in Exeter, see *Regesta* ii p. 72 no. 841 and p. 185 no. 1391, iii no. 284 p. 106.

CANONS .... HOLD 2 HIDES. In Exon. these men are described as the Canons of St. Peter's of Plympton and the Tax Return for Plympton Hundred (xxviii) states that St. Peter's of *Plintona* has 2 hides of lordship land. St. Peter's of Plympton was apparently a secular college founded before 909 for a dean and 4 prebends. It was suppressed and refounded for Augustinian canons in 1121 and dedicated to SS. Peter and Paul; see Knowles in MRH pp. 338, 150 and in HRH p. 181, also Mon. Ang. vi p. 51. This priory had probably been the centre of a large ecclesiastical estate. Edward the Elder had, between 899 and 909, exchanged the minster at *Plymentun'* for 23 hides in Somerset (at Wellington, Bishops Lydeard and West Buckland) with Asser, Bishop of Sherborne, these latter lands forming the basis of the possessions of the Bishops of Wells (see ECDC p. 9 no. 17 = Sawyer (1) no. 380). William the Conqueror, however, gave the church of Plympton to the Bishop of Exeter with 2 hides of land, lying in Wembury [GR SX 5148], Boringdon [SX 5358] and Colebrook [SX 5457]. These lands were later held by the Priory of Plympton and included *Rigweye* ['Ridgeway' SX 5356, EPNS i p. 255] and *Apeldreslade* [Applethorn Slade, EPNS i p. 254] both in Plympton St. Mary parish; see *Regesta* ii p. 211 no. 1515, TE p. 153, VE ii p. 375, Oliver *Mon.* pp. 129, 134–135, 145 and OJR in TDA 30 pp. 290, 308, 33 p. 588, H6 pp. 281-282.

1,18 YEALMPTON. A parish in Plympton Hundred (26). For the descent, see FA i pp. 353, 380, 401, Cal. Inq. PM vol. v no. 213, viii no. 280, xvi no. 875 and OJR H6 pp. 297–298. A member of the manor was *Cokflute* [Cofflete SX 5451 in Brixton], FA i p. 334.

CLERGY OF THIS VILLAGE ... 1 HIDE. This hide appears to be additional to the 2½ hides given in the tax assessment; see 1,12 note on another instance (in 1,13) of a sub-holding being treated separately and see also 1,33 note.

The land was at *Linham* [Lyneham GR SX 5753] in Yealmpton (see FA i p. 334), the mother church being Salisbury. In saying that 'the King assigned it to them in alms' DB implies that the grant was made by the Conqueror; in fact it may have been a confirmation, the grant dating from before the partition of the diocese of Sherborne (1,16 note); see OJR in TDA 30 pp. 287, 310, 33 p. 612 and H6 p. 299. For the Tax Return evidence see the Exon. Notes here.

10 PIGS. Without doubt there were a great many more pigs in Devon than Exon. records, as only those pigs which formed part of the lordship are given, whereas according to Lennard p. 255 ff. the pigs were largely the responsibility of the special pig-farmers (*porcarii*; see 1,6 note on pigmen) or the 'villagers' themselves. The fact that in half the entries where pigmen are recorded (DB and Exon. combined) there is no mention of pigs in the list of livestock, supports the view that the herds of pigs that the pigmen were farming are not recorded at all in Devon.

1,19 WALKHAMPTON. A parish in Roborough Hundred (25), formerly named Walkhampton

Hundred from this royal estate. Sutton, Kings Tamerton and Maker (1,20-22), although itemised separately, belonged to it (1,22 note). Walkhampton was granted to the Redvers family of whom Baldwin was created the first Earl of Devon in 1141; see Cal. Inq. PM vol. i no. 564. Isabella *de Fortibus*, Countess of Devon, gave it together with Buckland (Monachorum) and Bickleigh (21,19-20) to her mother Amice and in 1278 the latter gave all three lands, together with a part of Cullompton (1,7 note) to found the Abbey of Buckland Monachorum; see Oliver *Mon.* p. 383, VE ii p. 378 and OJR H3 p. 117. The Abbot of Buckland holds *Waltamton* in FA i p. 341; see TE p. 149b.

1,20-22   SUTTON. (KINGS) TAMERTON. MAKER. All were in Roborough Hundred (25). Sutton lay in the parish of St. Andrews, Plymouth, and was the basis of the modern town of Plymouth. By the 14th century there were three manors of the name: Sutton Ralph, Sutton Vautort and Sutton Prior, the last being held by Plympton Priory (see 1,17 note) and described as *Sutton Prior' alias Plymouth* in VE ii p. 375; see TE p. 153, EPNS i p. 236, Oliver *Mon.* p. 135, C. W. Bracken in TDA 74 and Hoskins *Devon* p. 454.

Kings Tamerton is in St. Budeaux parish. Maker has, since 1844, been wholly in Cornwall. It lies west of the Tamar river and 5 hides there (at *Macuir*) had been given to Sherborne Abbey by King Geraint *c*. 705 (ECDC p. 16 no. 72) together with 12 hides at *Kelk* [Kilkhampton, DB Cornwall 1,5] and land at *Ros* [Roseland]. It may have passed into royal hands when Plympton was exchanged by the King with Sherborne Church (1,17 note) and since that time Maker, or rather that part known as Vaultersholme tithing (including Mount Edgecumbe), was regarded as part of the Devonshire Hundred of Roborough. In 1086 Maker had been temporarily removed from Walkhampton (1,22) and it may be the 1 tax-paying virgate of Maker held in DB Cornwall (5,2,14) by Reginald (of Vautortes) from the Count of Mortain, although the details of ploughs and the values do not tally. Part of Maker appears to have been restored to Devon before the end of the 13th century and to have remained there until 1844 when both parts of Maker were reunited; see Hoskins and Finberg DS p. 26.

After the Conquest all three estates, which had been part of Walkhampton, were treated as a unit and later given to the Vautort family. They descended together, being held of the Honour of Trematon; in 1285 *Sutton, Makerton and Kingestamerton* were held by John *Vautord* of the Earl of Cornwall, Honour of Trematon, FA i p. 340; see Fees pp. 99, 797, Cal. Inq. PM vol. iii no. 604, vi no. 157 and OJR H3 pp. 110-111.

1,21   THESE THREE MANORS PAID .... That is, Walkhampton, Sutton and Kings Tamerton. This statement appears in Exon. after the details of the main manor of Kings Tamerton and before the description of Maker's removal from Walkhampton.

ONE NIGHT'S REVENUE. *firma unius noctis*: here *firma* represents OE *feorm* 'a food rent'; see OED *farm* sb.i. 1,5 notes on other meanings of *firma*. Many royal manors, especially in the south-west, had to pay this revenue which generally took the place of the normal tax payment, the manors not usually being assessed in hides (though these here and those in DB Herefords. 1,1 and Glos. 1,9;11;13 were hidated). Originally this fixed rent meant the amount of food needed to support the King and his household for one night; see *Dialogus de Scaccario* pp. 40-41 and DB Cambs. 1,1 where before 1066 the manor of Soham paid '3 days' revenue in corn, honey and malt and everything else'. However, by the 11th century these food rents were generally commuted to money payments. From examples in Somerset and Hampshire £80 appears to have been a probable figure before 1066, and £100 after, for one night's revenue. See Poole p. 29 and Round FE p. 110 ff. In Wilts. 1,5;7 also, figures appear of £110 and £100 for the present value of manors which paid one night's revenue [*redd*' in these entries is probably to be translated 'paid', rather than 'pays' as given in the volumes in this series]. Here in Devon, however, as in Northants. B 36, col. 219a, the combined 1086 payments of these three manors fell far short of the £100 figure. It would seem that in some cases (e.g. in DB Dorset 1,2-4, Glos. 1,9;11;13 and Wilts. 1,2-4) these food rents were not commuted, the manors continuing to pay the night's revenue in 1086. See also Beds. 1,1;3 where Leighton Buzzard and Houghton Regis still in 1086 paid half a day's revenue in 'wheat, honey and other things'.

In DB Somerset and Dorset, as here, there are several instances of manors combining to provide this rent; see Somerset General Notes 1,2;10 and Dorset General Notes B 1 and 1,5. This is the only reference in Devon to the night's revenue, though one would have expected some mention of it for the unhidated, non-tax-paying manors of 1,7;11; 14 (however, see 1,7 note on the phrase 'with all that belongs there'). There is no apparent reason why the Exchequer scribe omitted in 1,21 such an important statement which is in Exon.

| | |
|---|---|
| 1,21 (cont'd.) | WITH THEIR DEPENDENCIES. *cum suis apendiciis*, a difficult phrase which occurs several times in DB. Sometimes it seems to refer to sub-holdings of a manor or lands that were added to a manor, as in 23,5 where DB's "Value of the whole of Bampton with its dependencies" appears in Exon. as "Value of Bampton with this land", referring to the 1 hide attached to Bampton. Likewise in DB Wilts. 12,4 where the unidentified *Alvestone* attached to Bradford on Avon appears to be the dependency mentioned in the Value statement. The phrase is common in DB Wilts. Ch. 1: in 1,3;5 the manors of Amesbury and Chippenham, like these three here in Devon, with their dependencies pay one night's revenue with the addition of the phrase "with all customary dues"; likewise in 1,11 Corsham "with its dependencies pays £30 by weight", and in 1,12 Melksham "paid tax for 84 hides with its dependencies". Similarly in Dorset 1,2 a group of manors pays one night's revenue "with its dependencies and customary dues", and also in Somerset 1,2 and in the Exon. for Somerset 1,9. In Devon, 16,3 DB's "Value of the whole" (of Okehampton) appears in Exon. as "value of this manor with its dependencies", see 16,3 note for the lands that were members of Okehampton manor. However, in Somerset 1,10 "the whole of Milborne (Port) with the said dependencies pays ....", the "said dependencies" are those of the market entered in the preceding statement and probably refer to tolls, stallage rents, etc. |
| 1,22 | THIS ENTRY is not really a separate section, but a misplaced piece of information added at the end of the King's lands that came directly from King Edward. In Exon. it is also misplaced, being tacked onto the details of Kings Tamerton (with no gallows sign before it), due to the scribe's first belief that Maker had been removed from Kings Tamerton (see Exon. Notes here); it should, of course, have been added on the preceding folio after the details of Walkhampton. The Exon. scribe does not change during these two folios. THESE THREE MANORS BELONG TO WALKHAMPTON. Either Maker must be included with Sutton and Kings Tamerton, although it is no longer part of Walkhampton, or the Exon. scribe wrote the present *apendunt* for the past *appenderunt* 'belonged' and the Exchequer scribe copied the mistake (though correcting the *p* to *pp*), or the Exon. scribe wrote *iii mans* for *ii* (i.e. Sutton and Kings Tamerton) because of the *iii mans* which paid one night's revenue five lines above, and the Exchequer scribe similarly perpetuated the error. The use of *mansiones* in DB, as in Exon., instead of the more usual Exchequer form *maneria* (pl.), also suggests a too close following of the original (cf. 34,2;4 note). NINETEEN MANORS. That is, 1,3-21 inclusive. AND BELONG TO THE KING. It is possible that *ptin'* abbreviates the past *pertinuit* rather than *pertinet*, meaning 'and belonged to the King', that is to King Edward. |
| 1,23-24 | ASGAR THE CRAMPED. DB *Asgar*, Exon. *Ansgerus contractus*. The forms *Anser* and *Asgar* represent the same name: ON *Asgeirr* (anglicized *Ansger*), ODan *Esger* and OG *Anger*. DB also has the form *Asgar* where Exon. has *Ansger* in 23,16;22-24;27 (see Exon. Notes to these). Cf. *Osgot/Ansgot* (3,90 note). *Contractus* is the past participle of the Latin verb *contrahere* 'to draw together, contract' and presumably refers to Ansger/Asgar's physical condition. The translations of VCH ('the hunch-back'), RMLWL ('the Cripple') and OEB p. 306 ('mutilated, maimed') appear to limit *contractus* too much: there is no knowing which of these (if any) described his state. Cf. Edric the Cripple in 1,11 and Ralph Crooked Hands in DB Somerset (see General Notes 6,9 there). |
| 1,23 | ERMINGTON. Chief manor of Ermington Hundred (27) and now a parish. Ermington was not royal land before 1066, having been acquired by William (together with Blackawton 1,24) in exchange for Bampton (23,5) which King Edward had held. Thereafter, Ermington named the Hundred that had previously been called *Alleriga*. Ermington continued to be a King's holding until Henry I gave it to Matilda *Peverel* (who gave the Church of *Ermintone* to Montacute; MC nos. 141-142, 150 pp. 171-172, 177). She was sister of William *Peverel* of Essex and this land appears to have passed from him to Hugh *Peverel* of Sampford Peverell (27,1). In Fees p. 789 Hugh *Peverel* holds *Erminton' cum membris* and Fees p. 771 gives the manor as *Erminton'* with the members of (1) *Kingeston'* [Kingston parish GR SX 6347], see Cal. Inq. PM vol. ii no. 440; (2) *Habothun'* (or *Holboghton*, HD p. 56) [Holbeton parish SX 6150], see FA i p. 352, Cal. Inq. PM vol. ii nos. 306, 593, vii no. 297, and (3) *Killebyre* [?Kilbury in Buckfastleigh, SX 749658], see 6,13 note. FA i p. 352 includes the above and adds *Halswill* [lost, but there was an Isabel *de Halleswill'* in Ermington parish in 1332 (LSR p. 96], *La Clyve* [Cleeve SX 6355] and *Swyneston* [Swainstone SX 6054] held by the prior of Plympton; see FA i p. 399 and on the manor as a whole RH i pp. 69a, 91a, Cal. Inq. PM vol. vi no. 486, viii no. 230, x no. 192 and OJR H6 pp. 320-324. |

1

1,23 (cont'd.) 1 SALT-HOUSE. The term *salina* comprehends all kinds of salt-workings from the coastal pans (as in Devon) to the boilers of Worcs. and Cheshire, with their associated sheds and buildings; 'salt-house' is the most comprehensive term. See DB Worcs. 1,3a note on salt-extraction. There are 69 salt-houses recorded in Devon (including the one at Lobb in 35,20 which is only in Exon.) for 23 places; most manors only had a single salt-house, though Bishopsteignton (2,4) had 24 and Seaton (7,3) had 11. Salt-workers are mentioned for a further five places (1,26. 11,1. 15,23. 34,11 and 36,9). Most of the manors for which salt-houses and salt-workers are recorded lie on the estuaries of the south coast, though there is a group round the Taw-Torridge estuary in the north. See notes to 7,4 and 10,1 for inland manors with salt-workings recorded. Except for nine entries, the payments of the salt-houses are given; these are said several times in Exon. to be *per annum*. These payments are mostly in money, but the 4 salt-houses in 15,66 also paid 2 packloads of salt.

THESE CUSTOMARY DUES. The places mentioned are Fardel (15,67), Dinnaton (15,70) although only one holding is recorded (see next note but one), Broadaford (15,69) and Ludbrook (15,26, see note). With the exception of Fardel, there are no cross-references in Ch. 15 to these withheld dues. Cf. 1,11.

FARDEL .... CUSTOMARY DUES OF THE HUNDRED. In 15,67 (Fardel) this is rendered 'customary dues from pleas (*consuetudines placitorum*)', that is in the Hundred Courts.

AND FROM THE OTHER DINNATON. In the MS the *de* is interlined above and between 7 and *altera*, though with no omission sign; Farley prints it above the 7 which is less clear. The Latin is *altera Dunitone* (*altera*, feminine, apparently agreeing with an understood *mansio*), which probably means "the other (holding in) Dinnaton" (cf. the use of *alia*, see 17,92 note) rather than "the other (place called) Dinnaton" (cf. in 15,26;45 notes), as there is only one modern place called Dinnaton and only one in Fees and FA. Moreover, both DB and Exon. mention only one holding at Dinnaton, that of Reginald from the Count of Mortain (15,70). It is therefore possible that the Exon. scribe, writing in the margin of the MS, inadvertently copied the same piece of information down twice (though with slightly different phrasing; see Exon. Notes) and the Exchequer scribe assumed that there were two holdings in Dinnaton, hence the use of *altera*. It is unlikely that the folio in Exon. containing details of this second Dinnaton manor has been lost, as there is no sign of omissions elsewhere in the Count's lands and in any case it is improbable that the folio was already lost when the Exon. MS was used at Winchester. Another possibility is that the Exon. scribe wrote 'Dinnaton' once for 'Ludbrook', because there were two holdings in Ludbrook, 15,26;72 (held by different people TRE but by one in 1086) or perhaps two places called Ludbrook (see 15,26 note). The Exchequer scribe then perpetuated the mistake when abbreviating the entries.

COUNT OF MORTAIN'S MEN. Godfrey holds Fardel and Reginald the other manors; see Exon. Notes. However, in 15,67 Reginald is said to hold Fardel; see note there. Reginald is probably Reginald of Vautortes; see 15,26-30 note.

1,24 BLACKAWTON. DB *Avetone*. A parish in Coleridge Hundred (30), and identifiable in the Tax Return for Chillington (Coleridge) Hundred (xxvii). It had, like Ermington (1,23), come to the King by exchange with Bampton (23,5). Blackawton went to the Honour of Plympton, *Aveton'* being held with *Stokes* [Stockenham, part of Chillington (1,34) in 1086] in 1242 (Fees p. 790) by Herbert son of Matthew. This latter place is *Stoke in la Hamme* held with *Blake Aueton* in Cal. Inq. PM vol. iv (o.s.) no. 63 (= TDA 38 p. 322). Peter son of Matthew gave *Blakaueton* to Torre Abbey, the Abbot and Convent holding it in FA i p. 332. See FA i pp. 349, 393, Cal. Inq. PM vol. iii no. 156, TE p. 153a, VE ii p. 361, Oliver *Mon*. p. 169 and OJR in TDA 43 pp. 202-203.

1,25-56 ENTERED IN HUNDRED ORDER in Exon. as follows:

| | | | |
|---|---|---|---|
| 1,36;25 | Lifton | 1,56 | Cliston |
| 1,29 | (South Tawton), see note | 1,28;52; 43-44 | Wonford |
| 1,37-38 | Torrington | | |
| 1,30 | Hartland | 1,32 | Witheridge |
| 1,39;31;51 | Merton | 1,45 | Teignton |
| 1,40 | Fremington | 1,33;46 | Budleigh |
| 1,26 | Exminster | 1,47-48 | Kerswell |
| 1,27 | (North Molton) | 1,53 | Axminster |
| 1,41 | (Molland) | 1,54 | Colyton |
| 1,42 | Bampton | 1,34 | Chillington |

1,55   *Alleriga*        1,35   Tiverton
1,49   Witheridge        1,50   Torrington

1,25  UNDERMENTIONED LANDS. That is, 1,25-28 inclusive.
LIFTON. Now a parish, *caput* of Lifton Hundred (18). For the descent of the manor see RBE ii p. 453, Fees pp. 342, 757, 1262, 1371, RH i p. 74b, FA i p. 320, Cal. Inq. PM vol. iii no. 604, viii no. 45, x no. 46, OJR in TDA 46 p. 216 and Alexander (1931).
   For details of a customary due owed to Lifton by a holding of Iudhael and Alfred in *Bradeoda* [Broadwoodwidger 17,5, see note], see the last note under Exon. Notes for this entry.
COLWIN HOLDS IT AT A REVENUE. Probably Colwin the reeve, see C 2 note. Exchequer DB also omits from Exon. details of manors being 'farmed' at 1,5;36;57-59; 61;64-65. 25,28 and 26,1. These can be found either in the Exon. additions in the translation or in the Exon. Notes. The Exchequer scribe in Devon does not usually include such information.
LANDINNER AND TREBEIGH. Exon. has *Lamliner* (not *Laniliner* as Ellis prints) and *Trebichen*. In King Alfred's will (see 1,4 note), among other lands, Lifton 'and the lands that are administered by it, namely all that I have among the [West] Welsh [in Cornwall], except *Triconscire* [Trigg]' was granted out to his younger son and these two manors were probably among its dependencies (see Hoskins and Finberg DS p. 24). In Cornwall (DB 5,1,14;20) Landinner had been held TRE by (Queen) Edith and Trebeigh by Oswulf, but both were in the hands of the Count of Mortain in 1086. According to Exon. for Cornwall 3,7 (181 b 2) and the T.O. for Cornwall (508 a 7) Trebeigh and three other manors (cf. last note under 1,50) had been purchased by Abbot Sihtric of Tavistock in 1066 and Abbot (Geoffrey) was claiming it and the others from the Count.
COUNT HAS (1)½ VIRGATES. In the Exon. MS *habet comes virgam et dimidiam*; *i* is omitted before *virgam*, perhaps in error, though it is often thus omitted, especially, as here, when there is a fraction after it, both in Exon. (e.g. for 3,66-67;92. 6,7. 15,68. 16,69. 17,41. 28,10. 34,18. 42,10) and in DB (e.g. in 15,36 and 17,102). Cf. Dorset General Notes 12,16.

1,26  KENTON. A parish in Exminster Hundred (24). It continued to be a royal possession until Henry III granted it to Richard, Earl of Cornwall, *c.* 1222. It seems to have included a remote dependency *Suthteyng* ['South Teign'] which appears to have lain in Chagford on the river South Teign; see LSR (1332) p. 124 and EPNS ii p. 425 (under Teigncombe). In Cal. Inq. PM vol. iii no. 604 (of Edmund, Earl of Cornwall) *Suthteng* is said to be a hamlet pertaining to *Wyk* [Great Weeke GR SX 7187 in Chagford] and includes rent for a water course to the mill of *Shilstone* [?Shilstone in Drewsteignton, SX 7090; see 43,3]. There were other outlying parts of Exminster Hundred in the same parish; see 16,61-62; 64 note. For the manor as a whole, see Fees pp. 97, 264, RH i pp. 74b, 89a, 96b, FA i p. 378, Cal. Inq. PM vol. viii no. 29, x no. 46 and OJR in TDA 47 p. 217.
4 PIGMEN WHO PAY 20s. This appears to be a commuted rent (as also in 10,1); see 1,6 note.

1,27  NORTH MOLTON. Now a parish in South Molton Hundred (6); but in 1086 it appears to have constituted a Hundred in its own right, at least for some purposes (see 1,41 note and the Appendix). But its hidage, together with that of Molland (1,41) and South Molton (1,6), appears to be needed to account for the King's land given in the Tax Return for South Molton Hundred (vii). The manor was given by King John to Roger *la Zouche* some time before 1220; see RBE ii p. 559, Fees pp. 99, 797, FA i pp. 376, 418, Cal. Inq. PM vol. v no. 458, x no. 606, xi no. 187, xii no. 191, xiv no. 81 and OJR H9 pp. 523-525.
4 SMITHS. DB *ferrarios*, Exon. *ferrarios*, either 'blacksmiths' or 'ironworkers', see Exon. Notes here. VCH p. 409 translates the Exon. as ironworkers, which is how DGSW pp. 247, 251 translates the DB form. Cf. *faber* 'smith' in 6,13 and 19,35. The DB form *ferrarios*, accusative instead of the usual nominative as in *vill(an)i* etc., is no doubt the result of direct copying of the Exon., where all the population are in the accusative after *habet Rex*; cf. 23,15 note on beekeepers.
PASTURE, AS MUCH. That is, as much as the meadow (2 leagues), as Exon. states. There are many entries in DB where the formulae *tantundem, totidem* are used when two 'resources' have the same measurements and succeed each other. Attention is not drawn again in these notes to this.
WOODLAND, 1 LEAGUE IN LENGTH AND WIDTH. That is, the length and the width each measured 1 league; see 1,28 note.

1,28 WONFORD. Formerly the chief manor that named the Hundred (19); now in Heavitree parish. *Wonford*, including *Halsford* [now Halsfordwood GR SX 8793 in Whitestone parish], was given to Geoffrey *de Mandevil'* by Henry I; see Fees pp. 96, 612, RH i p. 85a, FA i pp. 313, 377, Cal. Inq. PM vol. ii nos 154, 265 and OJR in TDA 44 p. 315.

An outlying portion of this manor appears to have been at Drascombe [GR SX 7092] and Budbrooke [SX 7592] in Drewsteignton parish: ½ virgate in *Droscomb'* had been given by William I to the predecessors of Richard *de Droscumb'* for the service of carrying a bow and three arrows behind the King when he came to hunt in Dartmoor Forest, Fees p. 96; see RBE ii pp. 452, 559, Fees pp. 264, 342, 1188, 1250, 1370, RH i p. 85a, FA i p. 312 and OJR in TDA 44 p. 313. *Boggebrok* was part of Drascombe and held by the same service; see RH i p. 85a, FA i p. 312, Cal. Inq. PM vol. ii nos. 95, 171, 448, v no. 244, vi no. 238 and OJR in TDA 44 p. 314.

PASTURE ½ LEAGUE IN LENGTH AND WIDTH. That is, both the length and the width of the pasture measured ½ league, as is made clear by the Exon. 'pasture, ½ league in length and as much (*tantundem*) in width'. The phrase 'in both length and width' also meant the same. See 1,4 note 'leagues' on the so-called 'areal' league.

£18 OF PENCE AT 20 TO THE *ORA*. An *ora* was literally an ounce; a unit of currency still in use in Scandinavia. It was reckoned at either 16d or 20d. The 16d was the normal rate; the 20d rate was primarily a unit of account, found on estates in the King's hands, and was payment 'at face value'. For every 16d due in revenue, 20d was collected, the result being equivalent to a payment in assayed or 'blanched' money (see DB Glos. 1,58 'they pay £40 of blanched money at 20 (pence) to the *ora*'). See C 2 note above on assaying and the references cited there.

1,29 GYTHA, MOTHER OF EARL HAROLD.... Countess Gytha, sister of the Danish Earl Ulf and wife of Earl Godwin. She is also designated 'Earl Harold's mother' in DB Dorset 1,14. After the 'fall' of Exeter she escaped to either Steep Holme or Flat Holme in the Bristol Channel, and thence, probably in 1069, to St. Omer in Flanders. She held 1,29-35 inclusive and the misplaced 1,50 (see note).

(SOUTH) TAWTON. Now a parish in Wonford Hundred (19), but in 1086 it seems to have formed a separate 'Hundred' for some purposes, like North Molton and Molland (1,27;41) and to have administered a number of manors that later lay in Wonford Hundred (19), that is Patford (43,1), ?Shapley (45,1) and Taw Green (51,2), which owed, but had not paid, customary dues to South Tawton; see also 15,7 Gidleigh (note).

South Tawton was royal land until Henry I gave it, as *Suthtaut'*, to Rozelin *de Bello Monte*; see Fees p. 98, Cal. Inq. PM vol. i no. 588, v nos. 198, 615 and OJR in TDA 44 pp. 346-348. The church of the manor was granted to St. Nicholas', Exeter, (*Regesta* ii p. 59 no. 779) and the manor itself included *Wike* [West Wyke, East Week etc. GR SX 6592, 6692] and *Ailricheston* or *Aderichescote* [Addiscott in South Tawton, SX 6693, EPNS ii p. 448], Fees p. 98; see RBE ii p. 560 and OJR in TDA 44 p. 336.

6 VILLAGERS WITH 1 SLAVE HAVE THEM THERE. The Latin *has* refers to the ploughs, not to the 1½ virgates. The phrase '*y* villagers have it/them there' occurs about 14 times in DB Devon; the *hanc* or *has* generally refers to the ploughs in the plough assessment as being the last-mentioned feminine noun (cf. 1,11 "Land for 1 plough, which 2 villagers and 1 smallholder have there", where the *quam* refers to the plough). Exon. with its fuller wording also makes this clear. But occasionally, as in 22,2 (see note; perhaps an error) the *hanc* refers to the land. See also notes to 24,11 and 25,28 and DB Dorset General Notes 3,14.

In this entry Exon. states that the villagers had the ploughs, but it definitely excludes the slaves from a share in them (see 1,3 note on slaves).

1,30 HARTLAND. DB *Hertitone*, see EPNS i p. 71. A parish and formerly the principal manor of Hartland Hundred (3). It was long a possession of the Dinham family, Geoffrey *Dynanth'* holding *Hertiland'* in chief from the King in Fees p. 782. The manor included *Thorry* [Tower GR SS 2225], Cal. Inq. PM vol. v no. 29, viii no. 238. For the history of the manor see 1,4 note, RH i p. 73b, Cal. Inq. PM vol. iii no. 532, iv no. 44, vii nos. 141, 462, xv no. 746, FA i pp. 341, 371, 410 and the article by R. Pearse Chope.

BEFORE BALDWIN ('S TIME). Presumably the Exchequer scribe meant by *Ante Balduin* here and in 1,33 the time before Baldwin acquired the management (or perhaps the 'farming') of this royal manor. See Exon. Notes here and cf. 1,15 note 'in the time of William of Vauville'.

1,31 (LITTLE) TORRINGTON. DB *Toritone*. It lies in a group of Shebbear Hundred places (4) in the order of the Exon. Book (1,39;31;51) and is therefore unlikely to be Great

1,32 Torrington, which lay in Fremington Hundred (5), despite the fact that the form *Liteltorelande* (for Little Torrington) appears in DB (see notes to 15,16. 16,34 and 34,9). This manor (despite the assertion of OJR in H10 p. 553) seems to have gone to the Honour of Plympton, Richard *de Crues* holding in *Parva Toriton'* in Fees p. 788; see FA i pp. 329, 358, 411 and Cal. Inq. PM vol. i no. 564, xiv no. 325. *Little Toriton* included *Tadyeport* [Taddiport GR SS 4818] in Cal. Inq. PM vol. v no. 244.

WITHERIDGE. A parish and former *caput* of Witheridge Hundred (7). The land passed to the Honour of Plympton, *Wyrig'* being held thence in Fees p. 758 by Roger *Filius Pagani* (Fitzpaine) from the heirs of William *Brywerre* and by them from the Earl of Devon; see Fees p. 787, RH i pp. 87b, 92a, FA i pp. 342, 419 and Cal. Inq. PM vol. v no. 607, xi no. 118. The land also seems to have included *Odethon'* [Woodington in Thelbridge, GR SS 8112], Fees pp. 760, 787, which is coupled with *Hegsteford* [Henceford in Thelbridge, SS 8211] in FA i p. 343; see HD p. 56, Cal. Inq. PM vol. vii no. 297, xvi no. 1085.

VALUE £6. With the exception of here and in 1,35;56;66 the word used in the Value statement of the main manors (i.e. not sub-holdings or added lands) in Ch. 1 is *reddit* 'pays'. Although *valet* and *reddit* normally appear to be interchangeable, it is possible that the overwhelming use of *reddit* in Ch. 1 (as also in DB Somerset and Cornwall Ch. 1) means that the manors were being 'farmed' and the payment was by the 'farmer' to the King; see 2,2 note on 'Value' and Exon. Notes here.

VALUE WHEN HE (SHE?) ACQUIRED IT. Exon. *q(uan)do recep' val(ebat); recep'* no doubt abbreviates *recepit*, which is often written in full in this phrase. It is not clear who is the subject of the verb; it could be either Gytha, the value being when she originally acquired the manor, or, more likely, the King, the value being when her lands passed to him (either in 1066 or after her escape from Exeter in 1068; see 1,29 note). See Exon. Notes 2,14 on this phrase.

THANES .... HELD FREELY. Thanes were generally free to choose their lord (e.g. in 16,5. 17,13. 24,14. 42,4) unless they held church land (see 5,1). However, according to Exon. the thanes who held land as subtenants in 15,39 and 17,33 could not separate themselves from their tenants-in-chief. See also DB Somerset Exon. Notes 25,9. Almost every time in Devon that a thane is recorded as having held land, he is said to have held it freely and/or jointly (see 1,15 note on these terms). See 52,50-53 note on women being classed as 'thanes'. See Maitland DBB p. 161 ff. and Vinogradoff p. 79 ff. on thanes generally and Exon. Notes here on their land being called 'thaneland' in the T.O.

IT PAYS 5s. Or perhaps 'they pay 5s', referring to the villagers; see Exon. Notes here.

1,33 WOODBURY. In (East) Budleigh Hundred (14), followed in the order of Exon. by Colaton Raleigh (1,46), also in that Hundred. *Wdebir'* was given to the predecessors of Geoffrey *de Alba Mara* by Henry I (Fees p. 95) and long continued to be held by the family; see Fees pp. 763, 782, 1189, 1250, 1424, RH i pp. 66ab, 92b, Cal. Inq. PM vol. vi no. 271, vii no. 672, xi nos. 272-273, FA i pp. 325, 427 OJR in TDA 35 p. 288 and 11,1 note.

Land here called *Grendel* [Greendale and Greendale Barton, GR SY 0089 on the Grindle Brook in Woodbury and Clyst St. Mary parishes] was given to Torre Abbey at its foundation by Reginald *de Alba Mara*, TE p. 153a, Oliver *Mon.* p. 169. It included *Grendon Salt'ton* [Woodbury Salterton SY 0189], VE ii p. 361.

(MONT) ST. MICHEL. The scribe probably omitted the *de Monte* because of lack of space in the central margin (see next note); it is in the Exon. (cf. Exon. Notes 16,93 where 'Mont' is similarly omitted, though it is in DB) VCH p. 410 translates as 'St. Michael of the Mount', perhaps meaning the cell in Cornwall of Mont St. Michel.

HOLDS THIS MANOR'S CHURCH. Written over an erasure in the MS, presumably of something shorter, hence the need to write *Eccta S̄ Michael* in the central margin, though there are signs of an erasure also in the margin.

MANOR'S CHURCH, WITH 1 HIDE, 1 VIRGATE AND ½ FURLONG. As in 1,13 and 1,18, the church land here appears additional to the 10 hides on which tax was paid. See 1,12 note. This land was given by the Abbot of Mont St. Michel in 1205 to the Bishop of Exeter and by him to Exeter Cathedral; see OJR in TDA 33 p. 620 and in 35 p. 300. It is not cross-referenced under the fief of Mont St. Michel (Ch. 11).

1,34 CHILLINGTON. In Stockenham parish, Coleridge Hundred (30). This royal holding originally named the Hundred and can be identified in the Tax Return (xxvii). Coleridge lies in the same parish. Chillington will have included the later parishes of Stokenham [GR SX 8042] and Harberton [SX 7758] and other lands in adjacent parishes in 1086.

| | |
|---|---|
| 1,34 (cont'd.) | Of these, Harberton was the first part to be granted out, by Henry I to Roger *de Nonant*. It descended to the Vautort family and became *caput* of the Barony of Hurberton which received half the lands that had been held in 1086 by Iudhael of Totnes (Ch. 17 note). The individual members of the manor of Harberton or other grants to the Vautorts out of Chillington are given in FA i p. 331 as *Hurberton, Polkeston* [Poulston in Halwell, SX 7754, of which another part lay in Stanborough Hundred (see 17,43)], *Bothon* (*Bodeton* in RH i p. 89b, *Boghedon* in FA i p. 394) [Bowden in Totnes, SX 8058], *Stancumb, Alinton* and *Burge* [see 17,53 note], *Hurberneford* [Harbertonford in Harberton, SX 7856], *Wasseburn* [Washbourne in Halwell, SX 7954; see 25,24], *Colton* [Collaton in Halwell, SX 7952], *Croketon* [Crockadon in Halwell, SX 7753], *Sopcome* [Sharpham in Ashprington, SX 8158], *Holne Buzun* [part of Holne parish, Stanborough Hundred, SX 7069, see EPNS i p. 301 and 20,11 note], *Thuresleg(h)* [Dorsley SX 7760, see 17,50 note] and *Hele* [Bosomzeal in Dittisham, SX 8554]. Fees pp. 777-778 has most of the above together with a separate holding at *Houne Erguileys*, part of Holne above, held by the Abbot of Buckfast in FA i p. 349, probably the *Sutholm* ['South Holne'] of RH i p. 89b. FA i p. 393 specifies three Washbourne manors, *Wasseburn Bausen, Wyet* and *Dorant* and adds *Scoriaton* [Scorriton in Buckfastleigh, SX 7068] and *Hosefenne* [Hawson Court in Buckfastleigh, SX 7168]. On all this see Fees p. 98, HD pp. 39, 41, FA i p. 349, TE p. 149b, Cal. Inq. PM vol. ii no. 165, vi no. 183, viii no. 280, xi no. 35, xii nos. 119, 163, xiii no. 99, xvi no. 875 and OJR in TDA 43 pp. 203-209.
 Chillington and Stokenham were for a time retained by the King after the grant of Harberton, then Stokenham was granted to a predecessor of Herbert son of Matthew, following the same descent as Blackawton (1,24) except that it was not granted to Torre Abbey. *Aveton'* is held with *Stokes* in Fees p. 790 (Honour of Plympton) by Herbert son of Matthew. It is *Stok in Hamme* in FA i p. 331; see FA i p. 392, RH i p. 90a, Cal. Inq. PM vol. v no. 213, viii no. 250 and OJR in TDA 43 pp. 203-204.
 Stancombe in Sherford, held as *Stancumb'* by Henry Prior in Fees p. 790 and called *Stauncomb Prioris* in FA i p. 394 (Honour of Plympton), was probably part of this land; see FA i p. 350 and OJR in TDA 43 p. 226.
 VILLAGERS .... 36 PLOUGHS. No obvious reason emerges from a study of the Exon. MS why the Exchequer scribe should have omitted the villagers' ploughs here. They are also omitted in 3,83. 15,68. 16,162. 25,4;20. 40,4. 41,1 and 48,5, for all of which the reason appears to be merely carelessness, caused perhaps by the speed with which the Exon. MS no doubt had to be excerpted. There are some 14 other entries where Exon. has a small number of oxen (or cattle!) forming (part of) the villagers' ploughs and these are discounted by the Exchequer scribe; see 3,44 note.
 SHERFORD. A parish in Coleridge Hundred (30). *Scireford* was granted by Countess Gytha *c.* 1050 to the Church of St. Olaf in Exeter (ECDC p. 15 no. 68 = KCD no. 926 = Sawyer (1) no. 1236), passing thence to the monks of Battle and to St. Nicholas' Priory; see Mon. Ang. iii p. 377, TE p. 152a, VE ii p. 315 and Ch. 9 note.
 ABBOT OF BATTLE HOLDS IT. Gausbert, Abbot of Battle *c.* 1076-1095 (Knowles HRH p. 29). There is no cross-reference to this holding under the Abbey's fief (Ch. 9).
 IN LORDSHIP .... 1 PLOUGH. The Exchequer scribe may have intentionally omitted the lordship plough, because Sherford no longer belonged to Chillington. However, he includes the other manorial details for it. Moreover, the lordship ploughs are omitted from some dozen other manors, though they are recorded perfectly clearly in the Exon. See also Exon. Notes 16,167.
 4 VILLAGERS, 11 SMALLHOLDERS AND 2 SLAVES. All in the accusative case after *habet*. The Exon. addition obscures this in translation. |
| 1,35 | TIVERTON. A parish, formerly the chief manor in Tiverton Hundred (9); it can be identified in the Tiverton Hundred Tax Return (xi). Exon. accidentally duplicates the details for the manor at 98 a 2 and 110 b 2; see Exon. Notes here. This large and important holding had belonged to King Alfred (1,4 note) and was given by Henry I to Richard *de Redvers*. Thence it descended with the lands of the Earls of Devon in their Honour of Plympton; see Fees p. 264, RH i p. 83b, Cal. Inq. PM vol. i no. 63, ii no. 539 and OJR H1 pp. 12-14. The church of the manor was given by Baldwin *de Redvers* to the Priory of St. Martin des Champs in Paris; see Oliver *Mon.* p. 193a and Round CDF p. 462 no. 1276.
 Subdivisions of this holding lay in *La Kove* [Cove GR SS 9519] and *Mere* [East Mere SS 9516], in a second *La Mere* (*West Mere* in FA i p. 432) [West Mere SS 9915] and at *Leuerlegh'* [Lurley SS 9214] in Fees p. 789; see Cal. Inq. PM vol. iii no. 309 and FA i |

1,35    pp. 319, 369, 432-433. *La Pole* [Pool Anthony SS 9712] may have been part of the
(cont'd.)   royal manor or represent 46,1 West Manley; see Cal. Inq. PM vol. v no. 527, xiv no. 325
and 46,1 note. On these subdivisions see OJR H1 pp. 17-19.
COMMON PASTURE. Common pasture is also recorded in 1,33 (in Exon. only; see
note), and in 2,9-10. 5,8. 16,37;39. 19,45. 24,27. 25,3. 42,21 and 50,2. See 2,9-10 note
and Exon. Notes 25,3.
WOODLAND, 4 FURLONGS; [........] 1 LEAGUE IN LENGTH .... WIDTH. Both
versions of the Exon. (see Exon. Notes) have the same odd phrasing: *i leugam in
longitudine 7 vi quadragenarias 7 dimidiam in latitudine 7 iiii quadragenarias nemoris*.
It is possible that the Exon. scribe omitted whatever measured 1 league in length and 6½
furlongs in width, as occurs several times in the Exon. for Devon (see Exon. Notes 1,46),
and the Exchequer scribe was unable to supply the missing noun; it may have been
*nemusculus* "underwood", though that normally comes after woodland in Exon.
However, DGSW p. 258 suggests that there were two stretches of wood (one measuring
4 furlongs (by 4 furlongs), the other 1 league by 6½ furlongs), a meaning to which the
Exon. word order inclines. See 1,53 note and also Exon. Notes 28,2 for other possible
examples of two areas of woodland in one manor.
THE SIGN IN THE LEFT MARGIN opposite the last line in this entry corresponds to
the marginal sign beside the manor of Werrington, 1,50, and indicates the correct position
of that entry in the schedule of the King's lands. See 1,50 note.

1,36    EARL HAROLD. Son of Earl Godwin and Countess Gytha and brother of Queen Edith;
King of England from 6th January to 14th October 1066. William the Conqueror did not
recognise his title to the crown, hence the persistent use in DB of 'Earl' instead of 'King'.
Harold was Earl of East Anglia (1045), received half of Swein's earldom (1046), was Earl
of the West Saxons on his father's death in 1053, and Earl of Hereford (1058).
BRADSTONE. A parish in Lifton Hundred (18). It was later held of the Honour of
Plympton; see Fees pp. 756, 789, FA i pp. 320, 355, 405 and OJR in TDA 46 p. 202.
BALDWIN THE SHERIFF ACQUIRED IT AT A REVENUE. That is, he 'farmed' it;
see second note under 1,5 on the practice of 'farming'.

1,37    (BLACK) TORRINGTON. A parish and the chief manor of (Black) Torrington Hundred
(11). It is placed in Exon. order next to Holsworthy (1,38) lying in the same Hundred,
and is thus distinguished from Little Torrington (in Shebbear Hundred) and Great
Torrington (in Fremington Hundred). The manor was given with Kings Nympton (1,49)
to Joel *de Meduana* by Henry I, to Geoffrey *de Luscy* by King John (Fees p. 97), then
by Henry III to Roger *La Zouche* who holds *Blaketorrintun'* in Fees p. 265; see Fees
pp. 612, 1369, 1426, RH i p. 64b, Cal. Inq. PM vol. ii no. 165, v no. 458, x no. 606,
FA i p. 327, OJR H5 pp. 208-209. Part of the manor was at *Whiteleye* [Higher Whiteleigh
GR SS 4202], Cal. Inq. PM vol. iv no. 416, vii no. 641.
(WEST) PUTFORD PAYS. A manor belonging to Ralph of Pomeroy, 34,7, although
there is no reference to a customary due there. According to the T.O. entry (see Exon.
Notes), West Putford paid 30d, but since he acquired the land Ralph has withheld the
due. Although the DB *redd'* can abbreviate the past *reddebat* (like *geld'*, see 1,7 note),
the main Exon. entry has *reddit* in full. Possibly new information had come to light
between the writing of the main Exon. and the compilation of the T.O.

1,38    HOLSWORTHY. A parish in (Black) Torrington Hundred (11). The early descent of
*Hallesworth* is given in RH i p. 65a. It was granted by Henry II to Fulk *Paynel* until he
should recover his land in Normandy, but instead of being returned to the King it
descended to Payne *de Chaworth* then to his son Patrick before being purchased by
Henry *Tracy* and passing on his death to Geoffrey *de Camvill*. See Fees p. 1264, FA i
p. 327, Cal. Inq. PM vol. v nos. 143, 527, vi no. 710, viii nos. 396-397, xi nos. 118, 299
and OJR H5 pp. 189-190, 209-210.

1,39    SHEBBEAR. A parish, formerly the chief manor of Shebbear (earlier Merton) Hundred
(4). The church, together with the chapelry of Sheepwash (see below), was given to the
Abbey of Torre by King John (see Fees p. 1427 and VE ii p. 362); the manor itself was
granted to various royal followers, escheating several times to the Crown; see Fees p. 265,
Cal. Inq. PM vol. x no. 46 and OJR H10 p. 549.
Newton St. Petrock (51,16) had originally belonged to Shebbear (RH i p. 78a). *Sepewass*
[Sheepwash GR SS 4806], held with *Childeton* [Chilton in Thorverton, see 1,7 note]
and said to have been granted to the predecessors of Henry *de Fornell'*, Nicholas *Avenell'*
and Jacob son of Gerard by William I (Fees p. 96), was a sub-manor of Shebbear; see
Fees p. 782, Cal. Inq. PM vol. ii no. 165, FA i p. 329 and OJR H10 p. 550.

1,40 TAWSTOCK. A parish in Fremington Hundred (5). It was given by King Henry I to Iudhael of Totnes and passed to his grandson William *de Braose* being held of him by Philip then by Richard *de Chartrai*. It passed via William's daughter to the Earls of Leicester. Later Tawstock was divided, one third going to Buckland Priory (Somerset) for the support of the sisters of the Order of St. John of Jerusalem, two-thirds to Matilda, wife of Henry *de Tracy*, then to Geoffrey *de Camvill*, being held of his Honour of Barnstaple; see Fees pp. 97, 265, RH i p. 70a, Cal. Inq. PM vol. ii no. 76, v no. 143, vi no. 710, x no. 494, Mon. Ang. vi p. 671 and OJR H8 pp. 503-506.

 Tithes from Tawstock were given by Iudhael to his priory of St. Mary Magdalene in Barnstaple (Oliver *Mon*. pp. 196-198; see Round CDF p. 460 no. 1272 and 3,3 note). *Hengestecot'* [Hiscott in Tawstock, GR SS 5426] held by Richard *de Hydon'* from Henry *de Tracy*'s Honour of Barnstaple, will have been part of this land; see Fees p. 773.
LANGLEY .... (HIGH) BICKINGTON. See 1,67.

1,41 MOLLAND. A parish near West Anstey, now in South Molton Hundred (see 3,61 note). Like North Molton (1,27) and South Tawton (1,29), it may have formed a quasi-Hundred in 1086, although its 1 hide lordship seems to account for part of the lordship assigned to the King in the South Molton Hundred Tax Return (vii). Fees p. 96 records that William the Conqueror gave *Mouland* to the predecessors of William *de Beumeis* from whom William *de Boterell'* purchased it (whence Bottreaux Mill GR SS 8226). It descended in the family, being held in Fees p. 783 by the heirs of William *de Boterellis* from Ralph *de Mortemer*; see FA i p. 376, Cal. Inq. PM vol. ii no. 47, iv no. 95 and OJR H9 p. 530.

 The church was at one time held by Troarn Abbey (*Regesta* iii p. 328 no. 902) and later by Hartland Abbey (VE ii p. 333 and Oliver *Mon*. pp. 204, 207).
BLACKPOOL .... *NIMETE*. Blackpool (DB *Blachepole*) is probably in South Molton parish although there is another Blackpool in Chittlehampton parish (GR SS 6224). Both Blackpools are in South Molton Hundred (6), remote from Molland, but in 1086 *Blachepole* was a dependency of it. *Nimete* is some place, probably close by, named from the river Mole (formerly 'Nymet', see Introductory Note 2). Blackpool went to the Honour of Stogursey (Somerset) and it is likely that *Nimete* represents parts of Satterleigh and Warkleigh parishes held of the same Honour: in Fees p. 794 (Fees of John *de Nevil'*) are *Wauerkelegh'* [Warkleigh SS 6522], *Westbray* [Bray in South Molton, GR SS 6726, 6926, see EPNS ii p. 346 and notes to 3,45 and 52,36] and *Sudbray* [South Bray in Chittlehampton, SS 6624] coupled with *Blakepole*; see FA i p. 326. FA i p. 418 includes these and adds *Stone* and *Doune* (*Stevenedon* in FA i p. 362) [unidentified], *Poggyslegh* [Pugsley SS 6423], *Grenedon* [Greendown SS 6524] and *Prusteton* [?Preston SS 6522]; see OJR H3 pp. 92-94.
ALWARD. The forms in Devon of this name are *Eluuard(us)*, *Aluuard(us)*, *Ailuuard(us)* in DB and *Eluuard(us)*, *Aluuard(us)*, *Aluard(us)*, *Ailuuard(us)*, *Ailuard(us)* in Exon. They are common reductions for OE *Aelfweard* or *Aethelweard* (the latter especially in the case of *Ailuuardus*; see 3,45 note); see PNDB §§ 109, 111 and pp. 155-157 s.n. *Al-weard* and pp. 188-189 s.n. *Aethelweard*. As it is often impossible to discern whether *Aelf*- or *Aethel*- is intended, the present editors on the advice of JMcND have decided to keep to the base form *Al-ward*. In previous volumes in this series the forms 'Alfward' and 'Aethelward' have been used.
THIRD PENNY OF .... HUNDREDS. This is the third penny of the revenue from the pleas of these Hundreds (only a small portion of a Hundred's revenues), to which Harold had been entitled as Earl and which passed to the King with the manor it was attached to. See also in 1,45 and in DB Herefords. 19,2;10, Hants. 1,19 and Shrops. 4,1,1. Cf. 15,67 'the customary dues from the pleas'. This third penny is the same as the third penny of the pleas of the shire (see Warwicks. 1,6 and Dorset 1,8), but is quite different from the third penny of the total revenues of a Borough (see second note under C 2 above). See Round GM Appendix H pp. 287-296 and in EHR xxxiv (1919) pp. 62-64. Cf. *Dialogus de Scaccario* i xvii (not ii xvii, as Round GM p. 293), pp. 64-65 of Johnson's edition.
NORTH MOLTON, BAMPTON AND BRAUNTON HUNDREDS. Bampton (8) and Braunton (1) survived until recent times; for North Molton, see 1,27 note and the Appendix.
THE (DUES FROM EVERY) THIRD ANIMAL. Molland received a third of the dues payable for the overnight pasturing of cattle on the moorland (probably Exmoor). The King received the remaining two-thirds of the dues. Cattle from everywhere in Devon, except from the Boroughs of Totnes and Barnstaple, were allowed to pasture freely

during the day in the 'forest'; VCH p. 399 and p. 409 note 10. For the only other reference to moor in Devon, see 17,83.

1,42 MOREBATH. A parish in Bampton Hundred (8). It was first granted out by Henry I as *Morba* to Bretel *de Ambreres*. Under King John it was held by Geoffrey *de Luscy*, then by the prior *de Berliz* [Barlinch in Somerset]; see Fees p. 97, RH i p. 64a, FA i pp. 369, 381 and OJR in TDA 30 p. 441.

1,43 ALPHINGTON. A parish in Wonford Hundred (19). In FA i p. 318 it was held by John *de Nuvile* (Neville) from Hugh *de Cortenay*, but not as an Okehampton Honour fee; see RH i p. 84a, Cal. Inq. PM vol. ii no. 438 and OJR in TDA 44 p. 322. In Fees p. 264 *Alfinton'* is associated with *Ken* [Kenn 16,58] held by Hawisia *de Curtenay*. Part of this land appears to have been in *Matford* [Matford GR SX 9289], held in Fees p. 785 by Ralph *de Bosco* and in FA i p. 345 by the heir of Oliver *Deneham* from the Honour of Okehampton and stated to be in Wonford Hundred; see FA i pp. 363, 385, Cal. Inq. PM vol. iv (o.s.) no. 63 (= TDA 38 p. 327), iii (n.s.) no. 532, iv no. 44, vii no. 462. The rest of Matford (15,55. 19,9) lay just over the border in Exminster Hundred (24).
1 COB. *Roncinus*, probably a pack-horse. However, see DB Somerset Exon. Notes 8,5 where *roncinos* is glossed above *caballos*, which is ordinarily to be translated 'riding horses', 'war horses', but in that case ML *caballus* may be reflecting OE *capel*, ON *kapall* ('a nag'), which is its meaning in CL.

1,44 TOPSHAM. A parish in Wonford Hundred (19). This was alienated church land, having been granted by King Athelstan to St. Mary's, Exeter, in 937 as 1 *mansa* called *Toppesham* (ECDC p. 10 no. 21 = BCS nos. 721-722 = Sawyer (1) no. 433) and taken away by Earl Harold; see Ch. 2 note.
It was granted to the Earl of Devon by Henry III and became a part of his Honour of Plympton; see RH i p. 84a, Cal. Inq. PM vol. ii no. 539, iii no. 156. Isabella, Countess of Devon, is recalled in Countess Wear [SX 9490] in the parish. Sub-manors given in FA i p. 345 were *Rohorne* [Rowhorne in Whitestone, SX 8794], *Saghe* (*Sege* by *Toppesham* in Cal. Inq. PM vol. xiv no. 325) ['Sedge', EPNS ii p. 455] and *La Clyve* [unidentified, but apparently represented by *Hyncton in Toppysham* — a lost 'Hinton' — in Cal. Inq. PM vol. iv (o.s.) no. 63 = TDA 38 p. 321]; see FA i p. 386, 43,3 note and OJR in TDA 44 pp. 316-317. Baldwin *de Redvers*, Earl of Devon, granted to the Priory of St. James in Exeter ½ fishery at Topsham and the right to erect mills between *Scutebroca* ['Floyers Hayes', Ch. 22 note] and *Toppesham*, Oliver *Mon.* p. 191.

1,45 MORETONHAMPSTEAD. DB *Mortone*. A parish in Teignbridge Hundred (23). For the descent, see RH i pp. 82a, 90a, FA i p. 378, Cal. Inq. PM vol. ii no. 153, iii no. 422 and OJR in TDA 29 p. 226. In 1346 (FA i p. 391) *Morton* was held by Hugh *de Cortenay*. A sub-manor of Moretonhampstead may well have been *Hugheton Sawte* [Howton GR SX 7487], held in FA i p. 339 by Ralph *le Buttiller* from Walter *de Furneaus* and by him from the Countess of Devon.
TO THE MANOR OF MORETONHAMPSTEAD....HUNDRED. This is written below the bottom marginal ruling with a thinner pen and in much paler ink than the main entry. It is similar in ink colour and style to the additions at the foot of cols. 102b (3,19) and 103a (3,75), suggesting that they were done at the same time; none of these is rubricated, which often points to a late addition, though the rubricator occasionally missed entries (e.g. 20,13). The transposition signs are as in the translation, not the 'hands' that Farley prints, though the sign at the end of 1,45 is not executed as well as the one at the foot of the column. This statement may have been originally omitted from DB because in Exon. it appears on the reverse of the folio, preceded only by the past value of the manor which the Exchequer scribe also did not record, as was often his habit. The omission was probably found when a check of Exon. was made.

1,46 COLATON (RALEIGH). A parish in (East) Budleigh Hundred (14). Fees p. 96 records that *Coletun* was given to Nicholas *de Meriet* by Henry I in exchange for Topsham (1,44). In Fees p. 762 *Colethon'* is held from the same man and Patrick *de Chaworces* by the Abbot of Dunkeswell (whence a portion is sometimes called *Colaton Abbot*, VE ii p. 304), Wimund *de Ralegh'* and Ralph *Springham*; see Fees p. 783, FA i pp. 364, 426, Cal. Inq. PM vol. xi nos. 118, 299 and OJR in TDA 35 p. 286.
Part of the manor lay at *Boystok'* [Bystock GR SY 0283], held from Nicholas *de Meryeth* in Fees p. 763. It went to Polsloe Priory; see FA i pp. 365, 427, TE p. 152b and OJR in TDA 35 p. 291.
WILD MARES. *equas siluestras* (a scribal error for *siluestres*). *Siluestres* is from Latin *silua* 'wood', but here it has the same meaning as *saluaticum, siluaticum* 'savage, wild';

cf. 24,9 note on Walter the Wild. There are 170 wild mares recorded on 12 manors in the Exon. for Devon (DGSW pp. 285-286 omits the 8 at Wadham, 52,40). Although 72 are recorded for the double holding of Lynton and Ilkerton (19,16), which is near Exmoor, and a further 16 are on manors near Exmoor and Dartmoor, the remainder (almost half) belong to manors distant from these moors. These *equae siluestres* may be the same as the *equae indomitae* 'unbroken mares' (see 15,36 note); certainly they never occur together on a manor. Both were recorded in even greater numbers in the Exon. for Cornwall and Somerset.

1,47 LITTLEHEMPSTON. A parish in Haytor Hundred (29), identifiable in the Tax Return for Kerswell (Haytor) Hundred (xxv); it is a smaller holding than the Count of Mortain's Broadhempston (15,43). It was given by Henry I to Reginald, Earl of Cornwall, and held under him by the Arundel family: in Fees p. 769 John *de Arundel* holds *Hemmeston' Bubba* from the Earl of Cornwall; see FA i p. 318, Cal. Inq. PM vol. v no. 462, x no. 242, xvi no. 1027, OJR in TDA 36 pp. 369-370, 40 p. 129, 50 p. 364, also 15,43 and 17,25 notes.

1,48 SPITCHWICK. It lies in Widecombe in the Moor parish in the detached part of Haytor Hundred (29) and, like the previous entry, can be identified in the Tax Return for Kerswell (Haytor) Hundred (xxv). The manor passed to the Honour of Stoke Curcy (Stogursey); see 1,41 note. In Fees p. 768 Michael *de Spichewik'* holds 1 fee in *Spychewik'* from John *de Nova Villa* (Neville) from the Honour of *Stok Curcy*; see FA i pp. 318-319, 348, Cal. Inq. PM vol. iv no. 289, and OJR in TDA 40 p. 118, 50 p. 374. There is a grant of *unum hospitem* in *Espicewic* to Troarn Abbey in *Regesta* iii p. 328 no. 902.

1,49 (KINGS) NYMPTON. A parish in Witheridge Hundred (7). It had the same descent as (Black) Torrington (1,37), *Nimet'* being given to Joel of Mayne by Henry I (Fees p. 97), and later, as *Nimieton'*, by King Henry III to Roger *la Zouche* (Fees p. 612); see Fees pp. 761, 1370, 1427, RH i pp. 87b, 92a, FA i p. 344, RBE ii p. 560, Cal. Inq. PM vol. iv no. 221, v no. 458, xii no. 12 and OJR in TDA 30 p. 412. The adjacent Queens Nympton in South Molton parish and Hundred is named from Queen Victoria, EPNS ii pp. xiii and 346.

1,50 THIS ENTRY was originally omitted from the list of lands Gytha held in 1066, either by mistake or because of the problems of its ownership (see Exon. Notes after 5,5). In Exon. it appears after Gytha's manor of Tiverton (= 1,35) as the last entry under the King's lordship lands in Devon, apparently as an afterthought because it is not with the other royal manors in its Hundred (Black Torrington, 11); see Exon. Notes here on the state of the entry. The sign in the left margin of the DB MS, level with the first line of the entry, corresponds to the sign in the left margin at the end of 1,35 and indicates the correct position of 1,50 in the schedule.

WERRINGTON. A Devonshire parish with a complex early history, in (Black) Torrington Hundred (11), but lying west of the Tamar, finally incorporated in Cornwall in 1966. In the Tax Return for Torrington Hundred (iii) there is interlined at the end of the details of lordship land in this Hundred the phrase *Rex dim̄ hid' ī oluritona* ('The King (has in lordship?) ½ hide in Werrington'); cf. the interlined detail of Northlew 1,57 (see note). (This ½ hide seems to be in addition to the 3½ hides lordship assigned to the King at the beginning of this Return.) It is possible that this ½ hide is that said by DB to have been removed by the Count of Mortain (see note below), in which case it will have been removed after the compilation of the Tax Return. (It is unlikely that the fact that this information is interlined points to the ½ hide's having been returned to the King after the returns were compiled, since there is no change of scribe or colour of ink.) It is more likely, however, that this ½ hide is half of the lordship of Werrington, since the ½ hide removed by the Count of Mortain seems to have lain in Boyton (west of the Tamar) and is recorded in the Cornish *Terrae Occupatae* (508 a 5; see Exon. Notes 1,50), see below.

These complications are due to Werrington's lying astride the Devon/Cornwall border (with parts of the manor on both sides of the Tamar), to the fact that it was alienated church land in disputed ownership and because the land seems only to have been confirmed as a royal holding at the very moment of the DB enquiry.

DB Werrington included the parishes of North Petherwin and Werrington, west of the Tamar, and St. Giles in the Heath east of it. In the early 11th century, the Tamar was probably the county boundary and North Petherwin and Werrington lay in the Cornish Hundred of Stratton, St. Giles in the Heath in (Black) Torrington Hundred, Devon. This large manor of Werrington appears to have been royal land since the time of King Egbert (802-839), then a holding of Countess Gytha and to have been granted by her to Abbot

1,50
(cont'd.)
Sihtric of Tavistock between 1066 and 1068. Apparently, proof of this grant was lacking and the DB Commissioners treated Werrington as rightly belonging to the King, together with many of Gytha's other lands, although the Abbot's counterclaim is entered in Exon. 178 b 2 (see Exon. Notes after 5,5). It is possible that the Tax Return for the Cornish Hundred of Stratton (72 b 1), in allowing the Abbot 1 hide 1 virgate of lordship land, was continuing to account for some or all of Werrington's lordship as lying in Cornwall and belonging to Tavistock while the Torrington Tax Return gave part of the lordship to the King. On restoration to the Crown, Werrington was joined to Gytha's other estates (see previous note) and appears to have been administered fully as a part of Devon. This was necessary since her Cornish estates were in the hands of the Count of Mortain. As Werrington straddled the Devon-Cornwall border, it seems that the Cornish part (except Boyton, see below) was taken into Devon.

Werrington was restored to Tavistock Abbey in 1096 (Mon. Ang. ii p. 497, *Regesta* i p. 97 no. 378) and the Abbot continued to hold it until the Dissolution; see FA i p. 327 and VE ii p. 381. The holding in later times included *Hauekedon'* [Haukadon GR SX 3689], *Panneston'* [Panson, see Ch. 5 and 35,4 notes] and *Kary* [Carey SX 3691] in Fees p. 781; see FA i p. 409 and OJR H5 pp. 217-218. On the whole question see Hoskins and Finberg in DS, and Finberg in DCNQ vol. 23 pp. 104-107 and in EHR lix (1944) pp. 237-251 and J. J. Alexander in DCNQ vol. 14 pp. 273-276.

FREEDMEN. DB *coliberti*, Exon. *quoliberti*; former slaves. A continental term, not otherwise found in England; used in DB to render a native term, stated on three occasions to be *(ge)bur* (Worcs. 8,10a and Hants. 1,10;23). The *coliberti* are found mainly in the counties in Wessex and western Mercia, particularly in Wiltshire and Somerset. In Devon only 32 are recorded (the 25 here and 7 in 1,56), on each occasion in DB being listed after the slaves and before the rest of the villagers, but in Exon. they appear between the smallholders and slaves here and between the villagers and smallholders for 1,56, though this may not be significant. It is not clear, therefore, from their position whether they helped work the lordship or the villagers' ploughs. In other counties in DB some held land (Somerset 2,1 etc.) and paid dues (Herefordshire 1,6; Worcestershire 8,7 etc.). See Vinogradoff pp. 468-469, Maitland DBB pp. 36-37, 328-330, and also 5,8 note below and DB Oxfordshire 1,6 note on boors.

COUNT OF MORTAIN HOLDS ½ HIDE .... 1066. This sentence is written completely in the right margin of the MS in the same colour ink as the rest of the entry, though perhaps with a thinner pen. In Exon. it appears at the end of the entry for Werrington, but there is no sign that it was a particularly late addition (though see first note under Exon. Notes 1,50 for the state of the whole entry). The ½ hide was probably Boyton [GR SX 3191], just over the border in Cornwall; see DB Cornwall 3,7 and 5,5,4. Like Werrington itself, Boyton had belonged to Tavistock Abbey and, together with three other manors (cf. 1,25 note on Landinner and Trebeigh), was claimed by Abbot Geoffrey from the Count as having been bought by Abbot Sihtric 'with the Church's goods (*de bonis aecclesiae*)' in 1066 (see Cornwall Exon. Notes 3,7). See Finberg *Tavistock Abbey* p. 6. The identification of the ½ hide with land detailed in Cornwall DB would explain why there is no cross-reference to it under the Count's fief here (Ch. 15), whereas, for example, Walter's subtenancy in 1,63 is cross-referenced in his fief.

1,51
EARL LEOFWIN. Brother of Earl (King) Harold and governor and probably Earl of Kent and the Home Counties from 1057. He was killed at the Battle of Hastings. See Freeman ii p. 583 (3rd edition, 1877), and iii p. 484 (2nd edition, 1875).

BEAFORD. DB *Baverdone*; see EPNS i p. 86. It is a parish lying in Shebbear Hundred (4) and was given to Baldwin *de Redvers*, first Earl of Devon, descending in the Honour of Plympton. Ralph *de Wylinton'* holds *Beuford* in Fees p. 788 from that Honour; see RH pp. 78a, 93b, FA i pp. 329, 412, Cal. Inq. PM vol. viii no. 177, ix no. 103, xv nos. 154, 866 and OJR H10 p. 554 and 36,7 note.

1,52
PINHOE. DB *Pinnoch*, Exon. *Pinnoc* (Ellis misprints *Pinnoe*), is a parish in Wonford Hundred (19). It appears to have been given by Henry III to Robert *de Vallibus* being held by his widow Matilda in Fees p. 1371; see FA i p. 311, Cal. Inq. PM vol. xvi no. 1027 and OJR in TDA 44 p. 316.

BATTLE ABBEY .... 1 VIRGATE. Probably at Monkerton [GR SX 9693]; see OJR in TDA 33 p. 618, 44 p. 289 and EPNS ii p. 443. This virgate is not entered in the Abbey's fief (Ch. 9).

1,53
KILMINGTON. A parish in Axminster Hundred (17). It passed to the Honour of Plympton, *Kilmeton* being held in FA i p. 319 from the Countess of Devon; see FA i

1,53 pp. 366, 429, Cal. Inq. PM vol. i no. 798, iii no. 519, vi no. 710, viii nos. 396–397, xv
(cont'd.) no. 524 and OJR H4 p. 150.
PASTURE, 12 FURLONGS AND 12 ACRES. In the MS the scribe originally wrote
7 *xii* *ac̄* only, but then corrected it in slightly paler ink and with a scratchy pen to
7 *xii* *q̄Rent*' 7 *xii* *ac̄*; he employed the unusual (for this county) abbreviation for
*quarentina* (normally *q̄*) in order to cover the *ac̄*, and the 7 *xii* *ac̄* are added in the
margin. Either when copying Exon. his eye slipped from the first *xii* to the second, or
he was at first unsure about the mixture of furlongs and acres with only pasture (see also
in Exon. Notes 22,1). It is possible that the Exon. scribe omitted *nemusculi* "underwood"
after the "12 furlongs", as perhaps also at 28,2 (see Exon. Notes to these). On several
occasions the Exon. scribe has omitted a noun but included its measurement and the
Exchequer scribe has supplied one, probably correctly, relying on the fact that in Exon.
the resources are regularly recorded in a set order of woodland, underwood, meadow,
pasture (see the sample at the front of this edition, though no underwood is in fact
recorded for that entry). See Exon. Notes 1,46 for examples of these omissions.
However, there are other examples of acres and furlongs being combined in measurements, e.g. see Dorset General Notes 5,1 and perhaps Devon Exon. Notes to 28,2, and
of acres and leagues combined, e.g. in 32,4 and see Exon. Notes to 21,19 and 22,1. The
most likely interpretation, though, is that in Kilmington there were two stretches of
pasture, one of 12 furlongs (by 12 furlongs) and the other of 12 acres; see 1,35 note and
cf. Exon. Notes 28,2 and DB Dorset 36,2 and 55,29 for mention of pasture in two
places in one manor, and cf. Dorset 3,13.

1,54 WHITFORD. In Shute parish, Colyton Hundred (22); in 1086 it no doubt accounted
for Shute as well. Whitford was given by King John to Thomas *Basset*. Through the
remarriage of Alice Bassett it passed to the *Saundford* family, then to the Courtenays;
see Fees pp. 96, 782, RH i p. 68b, FA i pp. 330, 428, Cal. Inq. PM vol. iii no. 510,
x no. 91 and OJR H7 pp. 345–348.

1,55 LANGFORD. In Ugborough parish, Ermington Hundred (27). It was given by Henry II
to Peter *de Orivallo* and by King John to William *Briwere*, passing to Reginald *de Mohun*
on his marriage to Alice, daughter of William *Briwere*. It was sometimes called *Langeford
Lestre* from William *de Atrio*, gallicised as William *del Estre* (from Lestre in the
département of Manche; an earlier William of Lestre was a subtenant of the Count of
Mortain in Devon and Somerset). This later William held from William *de Mohun* in Fees
pp. 769, 782; see Fees p. 97, RH i pp. 69a, 90b, RBE ii p. 558, HD p. 56, Cal. Inq. PM
vol. ii nos. 306, 593, iii no. 283, v no. 603, vii no. 297, viii no. 139, ix no. 427, xvi
no. 1085, and OJR H6 p. 308. In 1303 (FA i p. 351) Langford was held with Farleigh,
Wagland, Lapland and Wrangaton (this last lying in Langford parish); see FA i p. 397
and 1,15 note.
BOROUGH OF TOTNES PAID 20s.... This is the third penny of Totnes which had been
attached to Earl Leofwin's manor here. As King William had already given his two-thirds
share in Totnes to Iudhael (17,1), he handed over the Earl's third which was now also in
his hands. See second note under C 2 above on the third penny of a Borough's total
revenues.

1,56 BROADCLYST ... ORDWULF HELD IT. Although Ordwulf probably had no connection
with the House of Godwin whose lands are described in 1,25–55, this manor was probably
included here rather than at the end of Ch. 1 with 1,72, the other manor held in 1066
by a 'commoner' (except for 1,23–24 which had been exchanged), because in Exon. it
was in the section of King's lordship lands which covers 1,25–56 (see Exon. Notes) and
in the correct place for a holding in Cliston Hundred (20).
The Hundred, of which this place was *caput*, was named from the DB form *Clistone*;
for the later name, Broadclyst, see EPNS ii p. 573, which cites *Clyston alias Brodeclyst*
(1413). The place can be identified in the Cliston Hundred Tax Return (xii). The manor
of Cliston was granted by Henry I to Roger *de Nunant* (Fees p. 98) and appears to have
been held by his family of the Vautort Honour of Hurberton (see Ch. 17 note). This
large holding had a number of members which Fees p. 777 lists as *Kildringthon'*
[Killerton GR SS 9701], *Suthwymple* [South Whimple SY 0094], *Brokhille* [Brockhill
SX 9895], *Lymbyr'* [Lymbury SX 9898], *Bere* [Beare SS 9800], *Sudthbrok*
[Southbrook SY 0296], *Craneford'* [Crannaford SS 0196] and *Kynewardesbergh'*
[unidentified]. In FA i pp. 332–333, 433 the above are repeated and *Breysteston* is
added [a 'Brightston' in Cliston Hundred, see 43,2 note, apparently distinct from 2,17
'Brightston' in Budleigh Hundred]. *Craneford* is there coupled with *Holewill* [Nether
Holwells SS 015965]; that *Langacre* ['Longacre', lost, see EPNS ii p. 576] was part of

the manor is clear from Cal. Inq. PM vol. vi no. 710. The manor's church was given by Roger II *de Nonant* to the monastery of SS. Sergius and Bacchus in Angers, mother church of St. Mary of Totnes, *Regesta* ii p. 50 no. 735a. On the whole manor see Cal. Inq. PM vol. ii no. 165, iii no. 532, iv no. 44, xii no. 119 and OJR H7 pp. 368-375.

1,57-72    IN THE ORDER OF EXON. these entries (together with 1,35) form the 'Land of Queen Matilda in Devonshire' and are in the following Hundredal arrangement:

        1,57-58         Torrington             1,69    Wonford
        1,59            Hartland               1,35    Tiverton (see note)
        1,60-63         Merton                 1,70    Halberton
        1,64-66;72;67-68  Tawton               1,71    Chillington

Most of these estates pass to the Honour of Gloucester; see Ch. 24 note.

1,57    BRICTRIC HELD .... LATER QUEEN MATILDA. That is, 1,57-71 inclusive. In view of the statement that Queen Matilda acquired his lands, it is almost certain that Brictric is Brictric son of Algar, on whom see 24,21 note. In DB Cornwall 1,13 an almost identical heading is given and in Dorset 1,15-17 Brictric and Matilda are linked together as previous holders of the King's land. Queen Matilda apparently held these lands until her death in 1083 when they passed to her husband, King William.
NORTHLEW. DB *Leuia*. The modern form distinguishes the name from Lewtrenchard (16,9) which has the same origin. It is a parish in (Black) Torrington Hundred (11), and appears in the Tax Return for Torrington Hundred (iii), where the King's (lordship?) holding of 1 virgate in *Leuua* is interlined (cf. the interlineation of the '½ hide in Werrington', immediately preceding this; see 1,50 note). Like other of Queen Matilda's estates, it was given (probably by William II) to Robert Fitz Hamon and passed to Robert, created Earl of Gloucester, with Mabel, Fitz-Hamon's daughter, being thenceforth held of the Honour of Gloucester. Halwill (1,58) had the same descent, both being held in Fees p. 778 as *Lyu* and *Huleghewill*' of the Honour of Gloucester 'from the part of Earl Richard'; see FA i pp. 327, 357, 408, Cal. Inq. PM vol. ii no. 76, iii nos. 371, 519, iv no. 434, vi no. 710, viii no. 390, xv no. 524, xvi no. 538, OJR H5 pp. 228-229 and 1,66 note.
TAX FOR 1 HIDE, 1 VIRGATE OF LAND AND 1 FURLONG. The *7 uno ferling* is written in the right margin, slightly above the level of the rest of the line and in paler ink with no sign as to where it belongs, though it obviously fits with the tax. It is interesting that in Exon. the furlong (*ferlino*, abl.) is interlined, perhaps later (though by the same scribe and in the same colour ink), and that the details of the lordship and villagers' land total only 1 hide and 1 virgate. This suggests that the existence of the furlong was discovered after the tax and details had been written, and when he added it the Exon. scribe failed to assign it to the lordship or the villagers' land holding. See 1,4 note on the hide for other discrepancies in tax and holdings, and cf. notes to 12,1. 15,10;13. 16,96 and 34,10 on other alterations to the tax resulting in the details total not agreeing with it.
PASTURE, 8 FURLONGS LONG.... Or perhaps 'pastures 8 furlongs ....' as *pasturae* can be either genitive singular or nominative plural. Although the genitive is not normally used in this phrase (though compare 35,25), it seems more likely that the measurements of only one pasture were being given. Exon. has the genitive singular (*viii quadragenariae pascuae in longitudine et iiii in latitudine*), so the Exchequer scribe may have taken the case from there by mistake or omitted *in* before *lg*. Cf. DB Dorset General Notes 5,2.

1,58    HALWILL. A parish in (Black) Torrington Hundred (11). It had the same descent as Northlew; see 1,57 note.

1,59    CLOVELLY. A parish in Hartland Hundred (3). It passed to the Honour of Gloucester, Roger *Giffard* holding *Clovely* in Fees p. 780 'from the part of Earl Richard' from that Honour; see RH i p. 73b, FA i pp. 342, 410 and Cal. Inq. PM vol. iii no. 371, ix no. 90, x no. 596, xvi no. 538.

1,60    BIDEFORD. A parish in Shebbear Hundred (4). Like other of Matilda's estates (1,57 note) it came to the Honour of Gloucester. The heir of Richard *de Greinvill*' holds *Bydeford*' in Fees p. 778 'from the part of Earl Richard'; see FA i pp. 328, 358, 410, RH i p. 78a, Cal. Inq. PM vol. iii no. 371, v no. 538, ix no. 428, xvi no. 538 and OJR H10 p. 559.
WITH 20 PLOUGHS. In the MS there is an erasure of some figures after the *xx*. Farley's treatment of such erasures varies: he leaves a gap for them here and in 15,62;74 and 50,2, but not in 1,61. 3,12. 15,12. 17,84 and 19,4;6. In the Exon. MS the *xx carr̄* is clear and neat.
A FISHERY .... It is interesting that in Exon. this statement is also added at the end of

the entry in two lines (one interlined) after the value, though by the same scribe as the rest of the entry. Presumably the fishery was still there in 1086, as Exon. has *reddit* in full for the payment.

1,61 LITTLEHAM. A parish in Shebbear Hundred (4). For the descent, see OJR H10 p. 560. IN LORDSHIP 1 PLOUGH. *In dñio st una ē car̄*: "In lordship are is 1 plough". The *st* is superfluous and appears in the MS in paler ink, as if the scribe had tried to erase it; Farley presumably did not think it was erased because he prints it. The parchment also appears to be rubbed — or there is an erasure — after the *ē*, resulting in a small gap (not shown by Farley; see 1,60 note).
GOTSHELM HOLDS .... AT A REVENUE. That is, he 'farms' them; see second note under 1,5 on 'farming'.

1,62 LANGTREE. A parish in Shebbear Hundred (4). The DB estate was in later times held of the Honour of Gloucester; in Fees p. 779 Earl Richard held *Langetre* in lordship through default of service from the heirs of William of Torrington; see RH i pp. 78a, 94a, FA i pp. 328, 375, 411, Cal. Inq. PM vol. i no. 798, iii no. 371, iv no. 434, v no. 538, ix no. 428, xiv no. 209 and OJR H10 p. 561.

1,63 IDDESLEIGH. A parish in Shebbear Hundred (4). Like other of Matilda's lands it passed to the Honour of Gloucester, being held under it in the 13th century by the *de Reini* or *de Reigny* family (see Ashreigney 1,65). In Fees p. 779 John *de Reyngny* holds in *Edwislegh'* and in *Uppecoth'* of the Honour of Gloucester 'from the part of Earl Richard' (see 1,57 note). *Uppecoth'* is probably Upcott in Dowland, (North) Tawton Hundred, GR SS 5709, probably the 2½ virgates of Iddesleigh which are said by DB to lie in (North) Tawton Hundred (see note below), rather than Upcott in Bideford (OJR H10 p. 560). See FA i pp. 328, 411 and Cal. Inq. PM vol. iii no. 371, v no. 538, ix no. 428, xvi no. 538. *Esse* and *La Hille* [Ash SS 5706 and Hill SS 5806 in the south of the parish], held in Fees p. 779 by Luke *Tremeneth'* and Richard *de Speckoth'* were no doubt part of this holding; see FA i pp. 359, 412, and OJR H10 p. 562.
WALTER HOLDS 1 VIRGATE. Walter of Claville; this land is referred to, but not named, in 24,22.
ALWARE PET. DB *Aluuare*; Exon. *Aluuatet*. Probably OE *Alwaru*, fem., considering the form and the Exon. byname, but see PNDB p. 154 for alternatives. The Exon. form has loss of *r* (see PNDB § 70) and the suffix *-tet* is ODan or ContGerm *Tet* 'pet, darling' (see PNDB p. 153 s.n. *Altet* and note 3 and p. 382 s.n. *Teitr*; Redin p. 70 s.nn. *Taebba, Taetwa*). The TRE tenant of the same piece of land is given in 24,22 as *Aleuesdef* 'Aelfeva Thief', a totally different name (see note). It is very unlikely that the names could have become confused by any usual process of mishearing or miswriting. (JMcND)
SHE COULD NOT BE SEPARATED FROM HIM. That is, she was bound to Brictric as her lord and the protector of her land; she could not choose another patron, nor sell the land without his permission. See 1,15 note on 'freely' on the opposite phrase 'could go where he would'.
2½ VIRGATES .... IN (NORTH) TAWTON HUNDRED. Despite the capital *I* for *In* and the capitals for *Tavetone Hund'* which is rubricated, the phrase 'In (North) Tawton' belongs with the 2½ virgates and is not an isolated Hundred head. See Exon. Notes here. Cf. the use of capitals for Teignbridge Hundred in 1,47 and the rubricated capitals in Dorset 1,30 and 37,13 in phrases concerning Buckland and Purbeck Hundreds.
IN (NORTH) TAWTON HUNDRED. In the MS and Farley *TAVETONE*; the facsimile fails to reproduce all the *A*, some of which is rather faint in the MS and also the rubrication obscures it, so that it resembles *TIVETONE*. Other examples of place-names being incorrectly reproduced in the facsimile include those in 6,8. 14,4. 19,4. 25,21. 29,7 and 42,16; see notes to these and cf. L 11 note.
Iddesleigh parish, although in Shebbear Hundred (4), lies east of the river Torridge which for much of its course divides Shebbear from North Tawton Hundred (12). Brimblecombe (40,3), now in the parish, apparently lay in North Tawton Hundred in 1086 and Upcott in Dowland (see above) seems to have been a member of Iddesleigh although in North Tawton Hundred.

1,64 WINKLEIGH. Now a parish in (North) Tawton Hundred (12). It was *caput* of a small Hundred in the 13th century and later (see Anderson pp. 85-86), but there is no evidence that it was a separate Hundred in 1086; indeed, this and the following entries in the Exon. Book (1,64-66;72;67-68) form a (North) Tawton group, and 1,64-68 with a total lordship of 3½ hides probably account for the 3½ hides lordship recorded for the King in the Tawton Hundred Tax Return (ix). The same Tax Return records ½ hide lying in

| | |
|---|---|
| 1,64 (cont'd.) | the royal manor of *UUincileia*, for which the King has not had tax; this could refer to part of the villagers' 3½ hides and perhaps to Norman Parker's sub-holding of 1½ virgates as well.
This royal manor, with its various members, passed to the Honour of Gloucester. In FA i p. 424 its members are given as *Wynklegh, Holecomb'* [Hollocombe GR SS 6311], *Byrch* [Birch in Coldridge, SS 7005], *Coleton* (or *Calecoth'* in Fees p. 778) [Collacott SS 6511], *Losbere* [probably Loosebeare in Zeal Monachorum, held by Cranborne Abbey in 1086 (8,1)], *Toytirton* ['Titterton' in Coldridge, SS 6605; see 25,7;13 notes] and *Southcote* [Southcott SS 6306]. See Fees pp. 264, 778, RH i p. 87a, Cal. Inq. PM vol. iii no. 371, iv no. 434, v nos. 29, 538, vi no. 710, vii no. 141, viii no. 238, ix no. 428, xvi nos. 258, 538.
PARK FOR BEASTS. *parcus bestiarum*. Cf. DB Cambs. 14,78 and 41,1 *parcus bestiarum siluaticarum* and Herefords. 1,41 *parcus ferarum*. *Parcus* was usually an area of woodland reserved for hunting within the bounds of the manor (though see Herefords. 1,41 note), contrasting with *foresta*, land outside.
NORMAN PARKER. Exon. *Normann(us) custos parci*; probably the keeper of the 'park for beasts', so perhaps the byname had not yet ceased to describe the individual's occupation and 'the Park-keeper' should be the translation. Cf. 51,1 William the Porter and Ch. 48 Nicholas the Bowman. See OEB pp. 248, 263 and cf. Ansketel Parker in DB Somerset 46,17-19. |
| 1,65 | LEVEL WITH THE FIRST LINE of this entry in the MS in the left margin is a rather misshapen *o* mark, not reproduced by Farley. Similar signs occur beside other manors called *AISSE* (3,4. 6,2;7 and 34,5, but not 16,143 nor the addition to 1,29), probably a contemporary checking mark. No further attention is drawn in these notes to these marks. Cf. the marks beside the *OTRI* manors and their treatment in this edition; 10,1 note. See also notes to 34,1 and 16,58.
ASHREIGNEY. A parish in (North) Tawton Hundred (12); see 1,64 note. It passed to the Honour of Gloucester, *Esse* being held by John *de Reyngny* in Fees p. 778; see FA i p. 422 and Cal. Inq. PM vol. v no. 538, ix no. 428, xvi no. 538. If this holding had originally been 2 hides, the ½ virgate referred to in the tax statement as not there, may well be that held in 1086 by Alward Mart as a gift from the Queen in alms; see 52,30 and note. OJR in TDA 29 p. 246 and in VCH p. 413 note 8 also ascribes the 'missing ½ virgate' to Alward Mart's land, but he is referring to the difference of ½ virgate between the tax assessment and the total of lordship and villagers' land; however, there are many instances of such 'discrepancies' in Devon, see 1,4 note on the hide. |
| 1,66 | LAPFORD. A parish in (North) Tawton Hundred (12); see 1,64 note. It passed to the Honour of Gloucester; see FA i pp. 340, 423, and Cal. Inq. PM vol. i no. 798, iii no. 371, xvi no. 538. In Cal. Inq. PM vol. v no. 538 and ix no. 428 it is held with *Northliu* and *Doune* [Northlew 1,57 and ?Down St. Mary 1,72].
IRISHCOMBE. In Meshaw parish, Witheridge Hundred (7); but apparently assessed with Lapford in 1086. |
| 1,67 | (HIGH) BICKINGTON. A parish in (North) Tawton Hundred (12); see 1,64 note. It passed to the Honour of Gloucester, *Bukinthon'* being held of that Honour in Fees. p. 778; there were later two manors *Bukyngton Loges* and *Bukyngton Clavyle*, FA i p. 423. See OJR in TDA 33 p. 626 and 34 p. 727.
LANGLEY. DB *Bichenelie*. It now lies partly in Yarnscombe parish, Hartland Hundred (3), partly in Atherington parish, (North) Tawton Hundred (12); see EPNS i p. 83, ii p. 357. The first element of the DB form appears to be the OE personal name *Beocca* as in High Bickington on which *Bichenelie* was dependent.
TAWSTOCK. See 1,40 and Exon. Notes to 1,40. |
| 1,68 | MORCHARD (BISHOP). DB *Morchet*. Later a parish in Crediton Hundred (13). In 1086 many parts of the later parish were included under the Bishop of Exeter's great manor of Crediton, but Morchard itself, not purchased by the Bishop until 1165 (Hoskins *Devon* p. 439; see TE p. 151a, VE ii pp. 289-290), was a secular holding, and so in (North) Tawton Hundred (12); see 1,64 note and OJR in TDA 29 p. 247. |
| 1,69 | HOLCOMBE (BURNELL). A parish in Wonford Hundred (19). It was later held of the Honour of Gloucester, Ralph son of Bernard (whence Burnell) holding in Fees p. 779; see RH i p. 84, FA i pp. 315, 386, Cal. Inq. PM vol. iii no. 371, xiii no. 18 and OJR in TDA 44 pp. 290, 333. Kingsford and Kingswell [GR SX 8391, 8592] in the parish probably preserve the memory of the royal holding here; see EPNS ii p. 442.
WOODLAND, 110 ACRES. The *cx* is written over an erasure and the *c* is very blurred. In Exon. the acreage of the woodland is written in words for some reason (as are the |

numbers of population and animals and the value) and the whole entry is written over an erasure.

1,70 HALBERTON. A parish, *caput* of Halberton Hundred (10). The King's 1½ hides of lordship land are recorded in the Tax Return for Halberton (xvii), but some of the royal manor lay in Tiverton Hundred, since the Tax Return for it (xi) records 3 virgates attached to the royal manor of *Halbertone* as failing to pay tax. The manor went to the Honour of Gloucester, and contained also *Woberneford'* [Oburnford GR SS 9809] and *Chyldelomen* [Chieflowman ST 0015 in Uplowman, in Tiverton Hundred in the Middle Ages]; see Fees pp. 264, 612, 780, FA i pp. 337–338, 432, Cal. Inq. PM vol. i no. 548, iii no. 371, v no. 538, ix nos. 288, 428, xvi no. 538 and OJR in TDA 33 p. 627 and H2 pp. 54–57.
GOTSHELM .... 1 VIRGATE .... OF THE VILLAGERS' LAND. That is, of the 3½ hides recorded for the villagers; the T.O. entry states that Gotshelm appropriated the land (see Exon. Notes here). Cf. Exon. Notes 15,49.

1,71 ASHPRINGTON. DB *Aisbertone*. A parish in Coleridge Hundred (30), the DB holding being identifiable in the Tax Return for Chillington (Coleridge) Hundred (xxvii). The manor was held by Iudhael (of Totnes) of the Queen and the church was given by him to Totnes Priory, a dependency of SS. Sergius and Bacchus in Angers; see *Regesta* ii p. 50 no. 735a, FA i p. 378, VE ii p. 367, Oliver *Mon.* p. 238 ff. and OJR in TDA 43 p. 203. For the form see TE p. 149b (*Aspirton* or *App'ngtone*) and EPNS i p. 314.
IUDHAEL. DB *Juhel*, Exon. *Iuhellus*; see PNDB §103 for the loss of *d*.

1,72 ?DOWN (ST. MARY) .... BOIA HELD IT. Although in Exon. this manor appears under the heading of 'Land of Queen Matilda in Devonshire' (see Exon. Notes 1,57–72), it does not appear to have any connection with her or with her predecessor Brictric. Cf. note to 1,56, another manor included in Exon. in a section to which it did not belong.
In the order of the Exon. Book *Oluuardesdona* (DB *Vluardesdone*) lies among a group of holdings in (North) Tawton Hundred (12). Reichel (in TDA 29 pp. 247, 262), followed by DG, identifies it as Wolfin, but this cannot be a corruption of 'Wulfweard's *dūn*' since Wolfin is *Wolvysnymet* named from a family called *Lupus* or *Le Lou*; see 24,28 note. OJR's later identification with Bradaford in Down St. Mary (TDA 33 p. 626, 36 p. 356) is an unsupported conjecture, but it is possible that part of Down St. Mary itself was the DB manor (see 6,4 note). A place called *Doune* has the same later descent as Northlew and Lapford (1,57 and 1,66 notes) but this would imply that the OE name Wulfweard was dropped as an element in the place-name, DB *Vluardesdone* (OE *Wulfweardes Done* 'Wulfweard's (estate at) Downe') being replaced by a name derived from the dedication of the church to St. Mary.
BOIA. Possibly Boia, the priest of Bodmin, who holds 1 hide in Pendavey in Cornwall from the Count of Mortain (DB Cornwall 1,6), which had been part of the King's land. On this name see PNDB p. 205 and OEB pp. 238–239 s.n. *Boga*.
AFTER THIS ENTRY the rest of col. 101c, room for some 15 lines, has been left blank in the MS, probably in case more of the King's manors in Devon should be revealed later on. The DB scribe left spaces after the first chapters in several counties, e.g. one-fifth of a col. and a whole folio in Notts., ½ col. in Kent and see Worcs. 1,7 note and cf. Dorset General Notes 1,30. Cf. 13a,3 note below.

Ch. 2 BISHOP OF EXETER. Bishop Osbern 1072–1103, brother of William FitzOsbern, Earl of Hereford. He came over to England from Normandy in King Edward's time and probably became that king's chaplain. See Exon. Notes 2,7 for his predecessor Bishop Leofric, who is only named in Exon. This chapter records the Devon holdings of St. Peter's, Exeter, as Exon. states, rather than the private fief of Bishop Osbern; the opposite is true of Ch. 3 (see note).
A document drawn up between 1069 and 1072 and found in several versions (see Mon. Ang. ii p. 527, KCD no. 940, Robertson pp. 226–229 (text) and pp. 473–477 (notes)) lists lands that were given or restored to St. Peter's minster at Exeter by Bishop Leofric. They include the alienated Devonshire estates of *Culmstoke* [Culmstock 2,12], *Brancescumbe* [Branscombe 2,22], *Sealtecumbe* [Salcombe 2,16], land at *Sce Maria circean* [St. Marychurch 2,8], *Stofordtune* [Staverton 2,7], *Spearcanwille* [Sparkwell GR SX 7865, probably part of Staverton 2,7; see 16,162 note], *Morcheslige* [Marshall farm near Ide, SX 8888, probably part of Ide 2,6], *Sidefullan Huuisc* [a holding of St. Sidwell's, presumably in the parish of Exeter St. Sidwells, EPNS ii p. 437], *Brightricesstane* ['Brightston' 2,17], *Toppeshamme* ('which Harold unjustly took away') [Topsham, 1,44 note], *Stoce* [Stoke Canon 2,13], *Sydebirig* [Sidbury 2,15], *Niwantune*

[Newton St. Cyres 2,2], *Northtune* [perhaps Norton, a tithing of Crediton Hundred; see 2,2 note], *Clist* [unidentified unless it is part of 'Brightston', 2,17 note]. Leofric also gave lands of his own in Devon, at *Doflisc* [Dawlish 2,5], *Holacumbe* [Holcombe in Dawlish, 2,5 note], and *Suthwuda* [Southwood, 2,5 note]. The document adds that when Leofric took over the minster, the only land that it controlled was an estate of 2 hides at *Ide* [Ide 2,6].
Other lists of Exeter Church lands are found in TE p. 151 and VE ii pp. 289-294.
THE EXON. ORDER of this chapter, with the probable 1086 Hundreds is:

| | | | |
|---|---|---|---|
| 2,3 | ?Tawton | 2,15-17 | Budleigh |
| 2,2 | Crediton | 2,18 | Kerswell |
| 2,4-6 | Exminster | 2,19-20 | Teignton |
| 2,9-10 | Braunton | 2,21 | Witheridge |
| 2,11 | South Molton | 2,7-8 | Kerswell |
| 2,12 | Hemyock | 2,22 | Colyton |
| 2,13 | Wonford | 2,23-24 | Chillington |
| 2,14 | Silverton | 2,1 | Borough of Exeter |

2,1    1 CHURCH. St. Stephen's Church, the head of the Bishop's fief, granted to him by the Conqueror; Oliver *Mon.* p. 134. Three other churches in Exeter are recorded in DB Devon: St. Peter's (i.e. the Cathedral, see 2,2 note), St. Olaf's held by Battle Abbey (see 9,2 note) and one held by the Count of Mortain in 15,1 (see note). See also 16,89-92 note on St. Mary's. See OJR in TDA 30 pp. 258-315.
1 SILVER MARK. 13s 4d; see C 4 note above.
47 HOUSES PAY 10s 10d. With the exception of the 6 Exeter houses of Ralph of Pomeroy's paying 3s 4d in 34,58 (perhaps a scribal error, see note) and possibly the house in 32,6 (see note), the regular customary payment of a house in Exeter is given in DB as 8d (see C 1 note above). The payment of 47 would thus be 31s 4d, while 47 houses paying 10s 10d works out at almost exactly 2¾d a house. In Exon., however, the Bishop is stated to have 48 houses, of which ten pay 10s 10d (i.e. 13d a house). Although a different payment could have been intended, it is more likely that the entries in both Exon. and Exchequer DB are corrupt (the Exon. entry is untidy and corrected, see Exon. Notes); the rest of the entry is unusual as well (see next note). On the houses in Exeter held by various landholders, see 3,1 note.
2½ ACRES .... [AND] BELONG. In the MS *ii ac tr̃ẹ 7 dimid'* .... *q̇* .... *pertinent*. The *q̇* (= *qui*, masculine nominative plural) grammatically refers to the burgesses, but it is highly unlikely that the burgesses 'belonged' to the church. One would expect *quae* (feminine nom. plural) to agree with the 2½ acres. The Exchequer scribe seems to have been following his Exon. copy too closely, for there the Bishop "has .... 2½ acres of land (*agros*, masculine) which (*q̇*) lie with the burgesses' land [and] which (*q̇*) belong to the church"; he ought to have changed the *q̇* of the Exon. to *quae* when he substituted *ac(rae)* for Exon.'s *agros*.

2,2    THE BISHOP HIMSELF HOLDS. Repeated at the beginning of 2,2-13 inclusive.
CREDITON. The chief manor of Crediton Hundred (13), which was almost entirely ecclesiastical; see the Appendix. Crediton had originally been part of the great see of Sherborne, then from 909 to 1050 was itself a bishop's seat until Leofric removed it to Exeter. By a charter of 739, King Æthelheard had granted to Forthhere, Bishop of Sherborne, 20 *cassati* at *Cridie* (Crawford I-III = ECDC no. 2 p. 8 = Sawyer (1) no. 255) and this holding was amplified in 930 by a grant of 3 *cassatae* at *Sandforda* [Sandford GR SS 8202] by King Athelstan to Eadulf, Bishop of Crediton (Crawford IV = ECDC no. 18 p. 9 = Sawyer (1) no. 405; see ECDC no. 44 p. 13 = Sawyer (1) no. 890). An adjacent grant was *Munceatun* ['Monkton' lost in Shobrooke and Thorverton], also by King Athelstan (BCS no. 726 = ECDC no. 24 p. 10 = Sawyer (1) no. 387).
The Hundred has its own Tax Return (viii) in which Bishop Osbern is recorded as having 4½ hides lordship land. In later times the Hundred of Crediton, which was largely co-extensive with the DB manor, consisted of the tithings of *Norton'* [Norton GR SX 8899], *Smalbrok'* [Smallbrook SY 8698], *Forde* [Ford SX 7997], *Youford'* [Yeoford SX 7899], *Youweton'* [Uton or Yeoton SX 8298], *Rigge Episcopi* [Rudge SS 7407], *Criditon', Kynewardlegh'* [Kennerleigh SS 8107], *Rolueston'* [Rolstone Barton SS 7905], *Wolmereston'* [Whelmstone Barton SS 7500], *Colbrok'* [Colebrooke SS 7700], *Southcote* [Southcott SS 7505], *Rigge Arundel* [Rudge SX 8597], *Wodelond* [Woodland SX 7797], *Knolle* [Knowle SS 7801], *Pideslegh'* [Pidsley SS 8105], *Dodderigge* [Doddridge SS 8405], and *Hengstehill'* [Henstill SS 8003]; see LSR (1334) pp. 54-55.

**2,2**  In FA i p. 337 the members of Crediton are *Yeweton* [Uton, see above], *Waddon*
**(cont'd.)** [?Waddon in Chudleigh, part of 2,4 Bishopsteignton; see 2,4-6 note], *Tetteburn* [Venny
Tedburn SX 8297 in Crediton Hamlets], *Colbrok'* [Colebrooke, see above], *Yewe*
['Yeo', an *Amiora de Youwe* is found in LSR (1332) p. 32 and a *Robert atte Yo* p. 34;
see Fees p. 399 and Cal. Inq. PM vol. iv (o.s.) no. 63 (= TDA 38 p. 331), vol. v (n.s.)
no. 527 and vol. xi nos. 118, 299], *Pachescot* [Paschoe SS 7501 in Colebrooke],
*Troiburgg* [Trobridge SX 8397 in Crediton], *Wolmereston* [Whelmstone, see above],
*Talaton* [probably 2,14 Talaton], *Stocklegh'* [now Priorton SS 8304 in Sandford,
*Stokeley Prieton* on Donn's map of 1765; see Oliver *Mon.* pp. 137-138 and TE p. 153],
*Hocweye* [Hookway SX 8598 in Crediton Hamlets], *Cnizteston* [Knightstone SS 7806
in Morchard Bishop, *Knyttheton* in Cal. Inq. PM vol. v no. 35] and *La Femme* [Venn
SS 7705 in Morchard Bishop]. Colebrooke will have included *Paynston alias Colbroke*
[Penstone SS 7700], VE ii pp. 293-294.

Part of Down St. Mary was in this Hundred in 1086 (6,4 note), but not all of Morchard
Bishop parish was; see 1,68 and 24,29 notes. There is, however, a Bishopsleigh at SS 7809
in the parish. Sandford parish was part of the holding of Crediton and it is probable that
*Comb* [Combe Lancey SS 8101], *Sakynton* [unidentified] and *Dourysch* [Dowrich
SS 8205] — in later times held by the Honour of Bradninch — were alienations from it;
FA i pp. 337, 356, 423, Cal. Inq. PM vol. iii no. 604. On the constituents of this Hundred
see FA i pp. 356, 373, 423, VE ii pp. 324-326 and OJR in TDA 33 pp. 627-628 and in
TDA 54 pp. 146-181.

In addition to the details given in DB, the T.O. names *Chefecoma* [Chaffcombe in
Down St. Mary, EPNS ii p. 368] as held by the Canons of Exeter; see Exon. Notes.
OF WHICH 6 HIDES ARE IN LORDSHIP. The *ea* in *de ea* (literally 'of it') refers to
*terra* 'land'. The only other instance in Exchequer DB for Devon of the lordship land
being stated is in 7,1 (see note), although it was often given in DB Somerset, Wiltshire
and Dorset and in Cornwall Ch. 1. The surviving portion of Exon. states the lordship and
villagers' land holdings regularly for all the south-west counties.
VALUE. *Valet (valebat, valuit*, past tenses) normally means the amount due to lords
from their lands (e.g. "Value ... to the Abbot ... to the men-at-arms" in 5,1;4 and "Value
to Gerald" in 45,3, that is to the 1086 holders, and see the Exon. for these). Cf. "Value of
the Bishop's lordship" in Dorset 2,2. For DB's plain past tense, or when there is no past
value given in DB, Exon. regularly has "Value when he acquired it", 'he' being very often
named as the tenant-in-chief and the date being when he was given the manor by King
William (see Exon. Notes to 2,14 and 16,88). DB also occasionally has this formula; see
2,11;18-19. 11,1. 16,3. Once in the T.O. entry referring to 34,5 DB's "[Value] formerly
20s" is given as "Value when he appropriated it, 20s", 'he' being Ralph of Pomeroy.
Exon. regularly has *per annum* with the value statements, as also does DB 45,3.

For evidence that DB's simple *valet* sometimes concealed the fact that a manor was
being held at a revenue (was being 'farmed') either by an individual not resident on the
estate or by the villagers themselves, see Hoyt's article and Lennard Ch. V. See also 6,6
note below and Exon. Notes to 25,28 and 26,1.

*reddit, reddebat/reddidit* "pays, paid", would seem to have a similar meaning to *valet,
valebat/valuit.* The two verbs appear to be interchangeable, especially in Exon. For
example in 395 a 1-2 and 395 b 2 (= DB 24,11-12;16) *reddit* is used, but in 395 a 3-4 and
395 b1;3 (= 24,13-15;17) *valet* is the verb; all these entries are by the same scribe. And
in the Exon. for 16,29 the scribe has in the 1086 value interlined in the same colour ink
ℓ̄ (= *vel* "or") *valet* above *reddit* (which is not underlined for deletion), but for the past
value he has plain *valebat.* Moreover, Exon. often has *reddit* for DB's *valet* (e.g. for
11,2-3. 15,3. 24,11;16 etc.) or vice versa (e.g. in 1,7) both in the main 'Value' statement
and in the payment of mills etc. (as in 15,57). In several entries the two terms occur in
the same sentence, as in the Exon. for this entry; in 1086 Crediton *valet*, but when the
Bishop acquired it, *reddebat*, whereas DB has *valebat* and *valet* understood. Similarly in
the Exon. for 3,4 Ashwater "pays", but when the Bishop acquired it, the "value was".
See also 3,82 note. However, there is a belief that when *reddit* is used, it means that the
manor was being 'farmed' (see Hoyt and Lennard Ch. V and cf. 1,32 note and Exon.
Notes 25,28) and that Exon.'s frequent interlineations of *reddit* above *valet* (e.g. for
1,27;41-42. 32,4) and vice versa, possibly in correction (although there is a singular lack
of underlining for deletion), are intended to draw the distinction between the two terms
(but see Lennard's reservation on p. 123). In 1,26 DB has *reddit*, but the Exon. has *valet*
which would be odd for a manor that seems to have been 'farmed' by Jocelyn (see Exon.

2,2
(cont'd.)
Notes 1,55), unless in fact there was no difference in meaning in the two terms. The present editors feel sure that to the Exon. scribe, as to the Exchequer scribe, *valet* meant the same as *reddit*, hence no mention is made in the Exon. Notes of DB's having *valet* for Exon.'s *reddit* and vice versa. Sometimes, however, DB's *reddit* seems to be an error; see notes to 3,82. 15,53 and 24,18.

BISHOP ALSO HOLDS .... NEWTON (ST. CYRES) .... DUNN HOLDS IT. Despite the apparently successful claim by Bishop Osbern that these 3 hides in Newton St. Cyres were his and part of Crediton, the same land appears with all its manorial details (though valued at twice the amount) in 52,34, as held by Dunn from King Edward and then from King William (or so Dunn stated) with no mention of St. Peter's or Bishop Osbern. The position seems to have been that Newton St. Cyres originally belonged to St. Peter's, Exeter, but that some time during King Edward's reign (note that the *cartae* only state that the church had it *before* he came to the throne, see note below) Dunn got possession of the manor, legally or illegally; then Bishop Osbern (on behalf of St. Peter's) tried to recover the land, although Dunn remained as subtenant (or tenant-in-chief from the evidence of 52,34). See Galbraith p. 121 on the probable reason for the two entries.

It is interesting that in the Exon. for 2,2 the scribe originally wrote 'With this manor the Bishop claims a manor....', but then the same scribe (in the same colour ink as the rest of the entry) underlined *clamat* and wrote *habet* 'has' above. The fact that this correction was obviously an early one — and anyway was seen by the Exchequer scribe — cannot be the reason for the land being ascribed to Dunn in 52,34, which is the view of Finn 'The Exeter Domesday and its Construction' in BJRL xli (1959) p. 385. It is also noteworthy that there is no mention of any dispute over the land in the T.O. Cf. the case of Werrington (1,50 and in the Exon. Notes after 5,5) which also does not appear in the T.O. This may be because these cases had already come before the shire court (Finn MDeD p. 96 note 3), though the removal of the virgate from Braunton (1,5) which seems to have been heard in court (see 16,74 note) is nevertheless detailed in the T.O.

NEWTON (ST. CYRES). In Crediton Hundred (13); 'St. Cyres' from the dedication of the church to St. Ciricius, EPNS ii p. 410.

PAYS TAX FOR 3 HIDES. Or perhaps 'paid tax', as *geld̄* can also abbreviate *geldabat* (see 1,7 note). Exon. has the past tense, as also have both DB and Exon. in the corresponding 52,34. See Exon. Notes. Cf. 51,16 and note.

TITLE DEEDS. *Cartas*, often translated 'charters' or 'documents'.

TESTIFY. *testantur*, deponent, as also in Exon. The normal form of the verb also occurs regularly in DB. Both forms (*testare* and *testari*) were common in Medieval Latin.

ST. PETER'S CHURCH. Dedicated to the Blessed Virgin Mary and St. Peter, it was originally founded as a monastery for Benedictine monks by King Athelstan in 932, was restored by King Edgar in 968, then after the devastation caused by the Danes under Swein in 1003 the monks were brought back and their lands confirmed by King Canute in 1019. When the see of St. German's and Crediton was transferred to Exeter in 1050, the monks were sent to Winchester and secular canons were placed by Bishop Leofric (1046-1072) in what was now called the 'Cathedral'. See Mon. Ang. ii p. 513.

BEFORE THE REIGN OF KING EDWARD. Literally 'before King Edward ruled', both in DB and in Exon., that is, before 1043.

AFTER 1066. *T(empore) R(egis) Will(elm)i* 'in the time of King William' (1066-1087), but translated as 'after 1066' in this series in line with *T.R.E.*, see C 4 note above.

KING'S BARONS. 'Frenchmen (*francigeni*)' in the Exon., although the French only formed part of the jurors in the shire court who heard pleas such as this (see 34,5 note); but according to Freeman v p. 766 *francigeni* here may mean no more than 'free men'. Cf. 16,74 where 'the men of the Hundred' state that Blakewell is part of Braunton, and 15,67 where the reeves and King's men ('Hundred men (*hundremani*) and King's reeve' in Exon.) are connected with claims. The 'King's barons' also appear as performing a similar function in the Werrington dispute; see Exon. Notes after 5,5.

2,3
BURY. In Lapford parish, now (North) Tawton Hundred (12). The identity is not quite certain, but this entry in Exon. is in the correct position for a Tawton Hundred place, or for one in Crediton Hundred; see EPNS ii p. 369 and OJR in TDA 29 p. 259, 36 p. 356.

2,4-6
BISHOPSTEIGNTON. DAWLISH. IDE. Parishes in Exminster Hundred (24); their combined lordship accounts for the Bishop's 7 hides lordship in the Tax Return for Exminster Hundred (xxiii). *Teygton Episcopi* and *Ide Sancti Petri* are coupled in FA i p. 378 with *Chuddelegh* [Chudleigh GR SX 8797, part of Bishopsteignton]; see RH i p. 89b. Bishopsteignton also included *Teyngmue* [Teignmouth SX 9373], *Nethir Rixstinole* [Lower Rixtail SX 9477], *La Fenne* [Venn SX 9275], *Waddon* [Waddon

SX 8879, see 2,2 note] and *Lunaton* [Luton SX 9076] in FA i pp. 347, 389. Teignmouth is *Westeyngmouth* and *Estteyngmouth* in VE ii pp. 289-293 and part had been alienated to the Honour of Okehampton, see Fees p. 787, Cal. Inq. PM vol. xiv no. 325.
Dawlish was granted by Edward the Confessor to Leofric his Chaplain as 7 *mansi* at *Doflisc* (ECDC no. 60 p. 14 = Sawyer (1) no. 1003); Leofric bequeathed it in 1069 to Exeter Church. It included *Suthwod'* [Southwood SX 9375] alienated to the Honour of Plympton (Fees p. 790; see FA i p. 389) and *Holcomb'* [Holcombe in Dawlish, SX 9574] granted in 1069 to Bishop Leofric by the Conqueror (*Regesta* i p. 8 no. 28). The bounds of Holcombe correspond roughly to East Teignmouth. Ide may have included Marshall farm; see Ch. 2 note and on all three manors see OJR in TDA 33 p. 628 and in TDA 47 pp. 220-223.

2,5-8   IN THE LEFT MARGIN OF THE MS beside the first line of each of these entries is written *c* in the same colour ink and style as the entries themselves, denoting that the manors were for the canons' supplies (see 2,8 note).

2,6   IN THE MS *Ipsę* (Farley *Ipsae*), in error for *Ipse* in the phrase *Ipsę eps teñ* 'The Bishop himself holds'. In this instance Farley does not correct the scribe's obvious error, though that is often his practice (see 28,1 note).

2,7-8   STAVERTON. ST. MARYCHURCH. Two parishes in Haytor Hundred (29). The Dean and Chapter of Exeter Church hold *Staverthon'* in Fees p. 769 and *Stavertone* and *Seynte Marie Churche* in FA i p. 378; see FA i p. 318, TE pp. 145a, 151b and VE ii pp. 293-294. Fees p. 769 also records *Pafford'* [Combe Pafford GR SX 9166] as held by the Church. This appears to have been a sub-manor of St. Marychurch and is *Comb Pafford alias Seyntemarychurch* in VE ii p. 293; see OJR in TDA 40 p. 131. Staverton probably included Sparkwell (Ch. 2 note) as well as *Metherell* ['Metherell'] (VE ii pp. 292-293), a lost place in the parish (EPNS ii p. xiv).

2,8   THESE 4 VILLAGES, MARKED ABOVE, .... CANONS' SUPPLIES. *Supra notatae:* marked with the marginal *c*'s (see 2,5-8 note). The revenues from these 4 manors were devoted to supplying the canons with provisions, and perhaps clothing as in DB Dorset 12,14. According to VCH p. 390 the phrase is important as it implies that "these estates, being held in alms, were free from the claims of military tenure".

2,9-10   HAXTON. BENTON. In Bratton Fleming parish, Braunton Hundred (1). This 'exchange' with the Count of Mortain was not long in the hands of the Church, but passed to the Honour of Bradninch (see Ch. 19 note), *Hakeston'* and *Duntingthon'* (for *Buntinthon'*, see EPNS i p. 30) being held in Fees p. 792 by Baldwin *le Flemeng* with *Esse* [Ash 19,14]; see FA i pp. 360, 415, 439, Cal. Inq. PM vol. xv no. 351, OJR H8 pp. 392, 448 and notes to 15,40-41 and 19,14.
COMMON PASTURE WITH BRATTON (FLEMING). That is, the pasture land was shared with the Count of Mortain's adjacent manor of Bratton Fleming (15,40), with which Haxton and Benton had presumably once been combined, being originally held by the Count. *Braton(a)e* is probably in the dative case (after *communis*) or in the locative case. See 1,35 note.

2,10   ADDED TO THE ABOVE VILLAGE. Benton was combined with Haxton; see Exon. Notes.
COUNT OF MORTAIN GAVE .... IN EXCHANGE. As usual the Count got the better bargain in his exchange here: Haxton and Benton paid tax for 3 virgates and were worth £1 10s in 1086, whereas Launceston, where his castle was, had a hide of land and paid tax for only 1 virgate and its value was £4. Cf. DB Dorset 56,36 and note.
A CASTLE IN CORNWALL. That is Launceston (DB Cornwall 5,1,22). This had originally been Sherborne land, part of *Landwithan* [Lawhitton, DB Cornwall 2,9], granted to Sherborne Church by King Egbert (815-839), ECDC p. 17 no. 76 = Crawford VII = Sawyer (1) no. 1296. On the creation of the see of Crediton (2,2 note) it passed to that Church and then to Exeter. It appears to have been seized by Harold, then 'exchanged' by the Count of Mortain; see Finberg in DCNQ 23 p. 123.

2,11   (BISHOPS) TAWTON. A parish in South Molton Hundred (6) and identifiable in its Tax Return (vii); see next note. It is *Tauton Episcopi* in FA i p. 376; see RH i p. 80b. The 12 hides will have contained a number of villages (lying in the parishes of Bishops Tawton, Landkey and Swimbridge) of which FA i p. 326 names *Brodehertford* [part of Harford GR SS 6031], *Brunescote* [Broomscott SS 6231], *Parva Herpford* [part of Harford, see above], *Londekey* [Landkey SS 5931; see Cal. Inq. PM vol. xvi no. 258], *Westecote* [Westacott SS 5832], *Ackot* [Accott SS 6432], *Stafford* [Stowford SS 6226, see Cal. Inq. PM vol. iii no. 604, vi no. 297], *Dinington* (*Dynenthon'* in Fees p. 767) and *La*

| | |
|---|---|
| 2,11 (cont'd.) | *Wodelond* [Dennington and Dinnaton, both SS 6228, with Woodland SS 6126], *Hernesburgh* (or *Yernesburgh* in FA i p. 418) [Irishborough or Ernsborough in Swimbridge SS 6328] and *Halgmerston* [Halmpstone SS 5928]. In FA i p. 362 Accott is coupled with *Newelond* [Landkey Newland and Swimbridge Newland, SS 6030] and *Bovystok* [unidentified]; see FA i p. 419 and OJR H3 pp. 68, 81.<br>12 HIDES; 3 .... HAVE NEVER PAID TAX .... 9 HAVE. The Tax Return for South Molton Hundred (vii) states that the King had no tax from 3 hides which the men of the Bishop of Exeter hold; these 3 hides must have been part of the 9 hides which paid tax, for the lordship 3 hides never paid tax anyway (see Exon. Notes). These 9 hides would either have been held by the villagers (Exon. does not give their holding) or have been sub-infeudated, though this is not mentioned here.<br>WHEN HE ACQUIRED IT. When Bishop Osbern acquired it; see 2,2 note on 'value' and Exon. Notes to 2,14 and 16,88. |
| 2,12 | CULMSTOCK. A parish in Hemyock Hundred (16), identifiable in its Tax Return (xiv). Although taxed for 5 hides, its 15 ploughlands suggest a larger holding. It appears originally to have been a grant of 11 hides at *Culum* [Culmstock] and 3 at *Cumbe* [DB *Cumbe* – now Culm Davy, see 36,18] by Sulca, *ancilla Christi*, to Glastonbury Abbey (ECDC no. 6 p. 8 = Sawyer (1) no. 1691; see Ch. 4 note). Later (ECDC p. 10 no. 23 = BCS no. 724 = Sawyer (1) no. 386), King Athelstan granted to SS. Mary and Peter in Exeter 5 *cassati* at *Culumstocc*. The bounds included part of Uffculme (see 9,1). In FA i p. 383, the Dean and Chapter of the Blessed Peter of Exeter hold *Colmpstoke*; see TE p. 151. |
| 2,13 | STOKE (CANON). A parish in Wonford Hundred (19), called *Stoke Canonicorum* in FA i p. 377. It was granted to St. Mary's of Exeter as 6 *perticae* at *Hrocastoc* by King Athelstan (925-939), see ECDC p. 10 no. 22 = BCS no. 723 = Sawyer (1) no. 389; see also FA i p. 312, RH i p. 85a and VE ii p. 293. |
| 2,14 | TALATON. A parish in Hayridge Hundred (15), identifiable in the Tax Return for Silverton Hundred (xiii). Talaton is held from the Bishop of Exeter in FA i p. 321, see FA i p. 424, RH i p. 71a, Cal. Inq. PM vol. iii no. 599 and 2,2 note. |
| 2,15 | THE BISHOP HIMSELF HOLDS. Repeated at the beginning of 2,15-19 inclusive. |
| 2,15-17 | SIDBURY. SALCOMBE (REGIS). 'BRIGHTSTON'. The first two are parishes while 'Brightston' (*Brithricheston* in TE p. 151b) is lost in Clyst Honiton parish; all are in (East) Budleigh Hundred (14) and required by the Tax Return for that Hundred (xvi). 'Brightston' (see 1,56 and 43,2 notes and EPNS ii p. 584) probably stands for Clyst Honiton itself, earlier *Hinetune* from OE *higna* and *tūn* 'farm of a religious community'. Mrs. F. Rose Troup in DCNQ (1934) pp. 152-159 cites Harleian MS 1027 of 1319: *Bry'tt'ton id est Clyst Hineton*. In Fees p. 765 the Chapter of Exeter holds *Sidebire, Saltcumb', Bere* [most probably Treasbeare farms GR SY 0094 in Clyst Honiton, EPNS ii p. 584] and *Hynethon'* [Clyst Honiton SX 9893]; see VE ii pp. 292-293, FA i p. 365, and OJR in TDA 33 p. 529 and in TDA 35 p. 309. Sidbury (like Stoke Canon) was also a gift of King Athelstan (RH i p. 66a). |
| 2,15 | 5 HIDES .... 1 HIDE .... 2 HIDES. See Exon. Notes here. |
| 2,18 | PAIGNTON. A parish in Haytor Hundred (29); identifiable in the Tax Return for Kerswell (Haytor) Hundred (xxv). The Bishop of Exeter holds *Peinthon'* in Fees p. 769; see RH i p. 72a and FA i p. 317. Among its members, lying in Paignton and adjacent parishes, Fees p. 767 lists *Colethon'* (or *Coleton Clavill* in FA i p. 317) [Collaton St. Mary in Paignton, GR SX 8660], *Aleburne* [Yalberton in Paignton, SX 8659], *Wodeton'* (or *Wadeton* in FA i p. 317) [Waddeton in Stoke Gabriel, SX 8756], *Cumthon* (*Qumtonpole* in FA i p. 317) [Compton Pool in Marldon, SX 8665], *Stontorre* [Stantor in Marldon, SX 8863], *Loventorre*, held by John *de Arundel* [Loventor SX 8462 in Berry Pomeroy; see 17,26 note], and *Sanderig* [Sandridge in Stoke Gabriel, SX 8656]; see FA i pp. 348, 391 and OJR in TDA 40 p. 113 and in TDA 50 p. 371. |
| 2,19 | ASHBURTON. A parish in Teignbridge Hundred (23); it can be identified in the Tax Return for Teignton Hundred (xxiv). The Bishop of Exeter holds *Ayshperton* in FA i p. 378; see RH i pp. 63a, 82a. It appears to have included *Bukynton* [Bickington parish GR SX 7972] held from the Bishop of Exeter in FA i p. 390, sometimes called *Westbukyngton* to distinguish it from Bicton (51,1); see Cal. Inq. PM vol. x no. 241. Four furlongs ('ferlings') of Bickington at *Lukkecomb* ['Lurcombe' SX 798731] were held by the prior of Plympton (FA i p. 390). See the articles by Amery and Hanham.<br>10 SLAVES. The use of *Ibi*, which generally heralds a new sentence, before the slaves may imply that they were definitely not in lordship. However, it may be a scribal error. See 1,3 note on slaves. |

2,20   (CHUDLEIGH) KNIGHTON. In Hennock parish, Teignbridge Hundred (23). *Knicheton* is held of the Bishop in FA i p. 339. The holding no doubt included South Knighton (GR SX 8172); the Bishop also held the adjacent Chudleigh in Exminster Hundred (2,4-6 note).

2,21   (BISHOPS) NYMPTON. In Witheridge Hundred (7) and identifiable in that Hundred's Tax Return (x). It is *Nymid Epi* in a later hand in the margin of Exon. (folio 119b) and *Nymeton Episcopi* in FA i p. 373. In Fees p. 759 the members of this manor, besides *Nimethon'* itself, are *Uppecoth'* [Uppacott in Mariansleigh, GR SS 7521], *Buteporth'* [Port in Bishops Nympton, SS 7725], *La Chapele* (or *Alba Capella* in FA i p. 343) [Whitechapel in Bishops Nympton, SS 7527; see Cal. Inq. PM vol. iv no. 245], *Turkerig* ['Torkridge' lost in Bishops Nympton, EPNS ii p. 384], *Gerardeston'* (or *Gerelleston* with *Sepwasse* in FA i p. 343) [Grilstone' SS 7324 and Sheepwash SS 7927], *Raweston'* (*Rauleston'* in Fees p. 767) [Rawstone SS 7426] and *Kippingescoth'* [Kipscott SS 8026, see Fees p. 399 and Cal. Inq. PM vol. v no. 527, xi nos. 118, 299]. FA i pp. 343-344 adds *La Heghin* (or *Chapelheghan*, FA i p. 420) [Hayne SS 7725] and replaces 'Torkridge' held in Fees by Geoffrey *de Fayreby* with *La Fayrebie* [Veraby SS 7726] and *Kirschote* [Kerscott SS 7925], both held by William *de la Fayrebie*; see FA i pp. 363, 420 and OJR in TDA 30 pp. 401-402, TDA 33 p. 630 and TDA 40 p. 113.
14 SLAVES. In an unusual position: normally they are added after the lordship ploughs when, as here, these are given; see 1,3 note. It is interesting that in Exon. the slaves are also misplaced. The same occurs in 3,5.

2,22   BRANSCOMBE. A parish in Colyton Hundred (22); identifiable in the Colyton Tax Return (xx). Branscombe was one of the lands bequeathed to his successors in King Alfred's will (1,4 note). According to RH i p. 68b *Brankcomb'*, held by the Dean and Chapter of St. Peter's, Exeter, had been a gift of Athelstan (2,13;15-17 notes); see FA i p. 383 and OJR H7 p. 348.
1 ANIMAL. In Exon. *i. animal*. In this edition *animalia* is translated 'cattle', normally being dairy cattle, though in some instances oxen seem to be meant; see 1,3 note. 'Animal' has had to be used to translate the singular, which occurs some 27 times in Devon, but the meaning is the same as for the plural.
IT IS FOR.... In the MS ħ (a capital 'h' with the abbreviation line through it); Farley omits the abbreviation line in error.

2,23   DITTISHAM. A parish in Coleridge Hundred (30). The 1086 subtenant Baldwin, appears to be Baldwin the Sheriff since the 1 hide on which tax has not been paid according to the Tax Return for Chillington (Coleridge) Hundred (xxvii) is probably this land. In this Tax Return Oliver is given as Baldwin's tenant, though DB does not record this fact. In .FA i p. 331 *Didisham* is held by Hugh of Courtenay (descent from Baldwin, Ch. 16 note) from the Bishop of Exeter, and in FA i p. 393 is said to be held of the Courtenays' own Honour of Okehampton; see Cal. Inq. PM vol. vii no. 360. The same descent is followed by Slapton (2,24); see Cal. Inq. PM (o.s.) vol. iv no. 63 (= TDA 38 p. 328) and (n.s.) vol. iii no. 31, iv no. 428.

2,24   SLAPTON. A parish in Coleridge Hundred (30). As in the previous entry, Baldwin is probably the Sheriff: in the Tax Return for Chillington (Coleridge) Hundred (xxvii) no tax has been paid on 3 hides (the tax-paying extent of Slapton in 1086) by Robert son of Gerwy holding from Baldwin the Sheriff. In FA i p. 331 *Scalpton* is held from the Bishop of Exeter by Hugh of Courtenay and from the latter's Honour of Okehampton in FA i p. 392; see 2,23 note.
21 COTTAGERS. DB *coscet* singular, *coscez, cozets* plural (but see 3,87 note and cf. the end of this note), indeclinable (Exon. *cocetus* singular, *cotseti, coceti* plural, 2nd declension), represent Anglo-Norman versions of OE *cot-seta* singular, *cot-setan* plural, 'a cottage-dweller; cottage holder' (OE *cot, saeta*, see *English Place-name Elements* s.v. *cot-saeta*; OED s.v. *cotset*): the Anglo-Norman letter *z* represents the sound *ts* and the spelling *sc* a miscopied *st* representing metathesis of *ts*, so *coscet* = *cotset, coscez* and *cozets* = *cotsets*. The plural in *-s* represented by *cozets* (= *cotsets*) is the result of either a French adaptation or an OE change of inflexion, and is the form used in DB Wilts. Ch. 1,1-15. (JMcND)
'Cottagers' are almost entirely confined to the south-west counties in DB, Wiltshire providing about 80% of the total entries. In Devon there are 70 Cottagers recorded on ten manors, all of which, with the exception of Slapton here, were in the west of the County in Lifton (18) and (Black) Torrington (11) Hundreds. In Devon DB they are always listed after the villagers. *Cotarii* 'cottagers' (see 15,21 note) were apparently a

different class: in DB Wilts. *coscez* and *cotarii* regularly occur in the same entry. The distinction, however, is obscure and they do not occur together in Devon. The *bordarii* 'smallholders' (see 1,3 note) also had aspects in common with the *coscez*. It is interesting that in the Domesday satellite Bath A (see DB Somerset App. II) *coceti* are replaced in the corresponding Exon. and DB entries by *bordarii*. Also it may be suggestive that in Devon) smallholders are not recorded on estates which had Cottagers (5,1;4 would seem to be exceptions, but see the Details Table). See Lennard pp. 346, 353 ff. and in the Economic Journal vol. lxi (1951) p. 352 ff. and Finberg *Tavistock Abbey* pp. 61-62.

Not much is known about the status and economic position of *coscez*, though as can be seen from all the DB Devon entries they shared ploughs with the other 'villagers'. They may also have had part of the land holding that was ascribed to the *villani* as a class in Exon. For the Dorset evidence, see DB Dorset General Notes 1,8. A class of person called in OE *cotsetla* 'cottage-dweller', which seems equivalent to that of the *coscet*, has its obligations detailed in the 10th-11th century *Rectitudines Singularum Personarum* pp. 445-6. His rights varied according to local custom: in some places he had to work for his lord every Monday throughout the year or (so the Anglo-Saxon version; 'and' in the Latin) 3 days a week at harvest; in some places every day at harvest, reaping 1 acre of oats or ½ acre of other corn; he was to be allowed his sheaf by the steward; he was not to pay land-tax; he was to have 5 acres of his own, more where customary, but less would be too little because his duty-labour was frequently called for; he was to pay his hearth-penny at Holy Thursday like every free man, to relieve his lord's demesne, if required, of its obligations to sea-defences, royal deer parks and such things, according to his condition, and pay his church-dues at Martinmas.

Although the DB scribe normally uses the singular after *xxi, xxxi* etc. (see 1,3 note), the plural is used here (*xxi coscez*), the reason no doubt being that he originally wrote *xx coscez* and then corrected it to *xxi*. (It is interesting that in Exon. *xx coscetos* is similarly corrected to *xxi*; cf. notes to 3,68. 16,108. 28,10 and 32,10.)

Ch. 3   BISHOP OF COUTANCES. Geoffrey of Mowbray (from *Montbrai* in the département of Manche, France) was consecrated Bishop of Coutances in 1048 or 1049. Between then and his arrival in England in 1066 he was very active in reorganising the diocese of Coutances, finishing and endowing the new Cathedral at Coutances and promoting learning there. He was present as chief chaplain at the Battle of Hastings and played an important part in William's consecration at Westminster. He is sometimes (as in DB Glos. 6,1 and in some of the Devon and the Somerset Tax Returns in Exon.) called the Bishop of St. Lô which is close to Coutances and Montbrai and was an earlier seat of the bishopric for a time. Geoffrey was rewarded with a great number of lands in England, especially in Devon and Somerset, these lands forming his personal fief, not that of the Church of Coutances. He played a prominent part in suppressing the rebellion in the south-west in 1069, coming to the relief of Montacute Castle (Orderic Vitalis ii p. 193), and was involved in several other campaigns of suppression. He was also one of King William's chief justiciars, notably in the trial held at Penneden Heath in Kent in 1072 between Archbishop Lanfranc of Canterbury and Bishop Odo of Bayeux, and in the Ely land disputes; see also DB Worcs. App. V Worcs. H nos. 1 and 4. He joined in the rebellion against William Rufus in 1088, but was pardoned. See John Le Patourel 'Geoffrey of Mowbray, Bishop of Coutances 1049-1093' in EHR lix (1944) pp. 129-161.

On Geoffrey's death in 1093 his fief passed to his nephew, Robert of Mowbray, Earl of Northumberland, who forfeited it as the price for his rebellion in 1095 (Orderic Vitalis ii p. 223). William Rufus then granted the great majority of his Devon lands to Iudhael of Totnes (see Ch. 17 note) from whom they passed to his son Alfred. A half of Alfred's inheritance, which formed the Honour of Barnstaple, then passed to his sister who married Henry *de Tracy*; the other half went to another sister Aenor, who married Philip of Braose, and thence to her son William of Braose, but reverted in 1213 to a later Henry *de Tracy*, thus re-combining the two halves of the inheritance. The lands then passed to Henry's grand-daughter Maud, whose first husband was Nicholas son of Martin and her second was Geoffrey *de Camville*; her lands passed to William fitz Martin; see Sanders pp. 104-105, Loyd pp. 67, 104-105, and OJR in TDA 34 p. 728, 46 p. 214.

A very large number of the lands that formed this Domesday fief can be recognized in the Inq. PM of William son of William Martin (Cal. Inq. PM vol. vi no. 710) and in that of Henry *de Tracy* (Cal. Inq. PM vol. ii no. 76); see also the Inq. PM of Nicholas *Martyn* (Ch. 20 note).

THE EXON. BOOK is arranged differently from DB here and is in the following order of Hundreds:

| | | | |
|---|---|---|---|
| 3,9;86-87 | Lifton | 3,7;94;72 | Budleigh |
| 3,4;91;88,10;89;11;12 | Torrington | 3,73-79 | ?Bampton |
| | | 3,80-81;95 | Witheridge |
| 3,90 | Hartland | 3,82-84 | Tiverton |
| 3,5;13-15 | Merton | 3,97 | Teignton |
| 3,6;16-17;92;18-19 | Fremington | 3,85 | Colyton |
| | | 3,96 | Axminster |
| 3,20-22 | Tawton | 3,8 | Teignton |
| 3,23-64 | Braunton and Shirwell with South Molton | 3,98 | Plympton |
| | | 3,99 | Wonford |
| 3,65-66;93;67-68 | Wonford | 3,3;1-2 | Boroughs of Barnstaple and Exeter |
| 3,69-71 | Silverton | | |

In the Exchequer Book, the Boroughs are placed first (3,1-3), then the lands held by the Bishop himself in lordship (3,4-8) then those of his subtenants (3,9-85 all being held by Drogo).

3,1 IN EXETER 3 HOUSES .... In most other counties in DB the houses held in a borough by various holders (usually tenants-in-chief; see Warwicks. B 2, col. 238a), are described with that borough's other details (e.g. in the Wiltshire section on the Borough of Malmesbury, col. 64c), rather than at, or near, the beginning or end of the fiefs of these holders, which is the practice in Devon. For example, details of the Exeter houses also appear in 2,1. 5,15. 9,2. 16,1. 17,2 etc.
HOUSES .... PAID CUSTOMARY DUES. Probably 8d for each of the 3 (whole) houses and possibly 2d for the destroyed house; see C 1 note above.

3,2 EXEMPT. *quietae*, that is exempt from customary dues, as Exon. states; see also Exon. Notes to 9,2. In DB *quietus* can also mean 'free from tax' (as in Herefords. 19,10) or 'free from service' (as in Herefords. 1,44) or 'quit, settled, discharged' (as in Worcs. 2,74, see note, and Herefords. C 14, col. 179a, and cf. 16,72 below) or 'undisturbed' (Exon. Notes 25,3).
KEEPS THESE BACK. That is, the customary dues, *hanc* referring to *consuetud(ine)* which is generally translated in the plural in this series.

3,3 BARNSTAPLE. For its history and constituent manors, see RH i p. 63b, Cal. Inq. PM vol. viii nos. 396-397 and OJR in TDA 49 pp. 376-388 and H8 pp. 414-419. *Medeneford* [Maidenford GR SS 5833] in Fees p. 772 was probably part of this land. Iudhael of Totnes, who held the Honour of Barnstaple in the time of Henry I, granted part of the land to the Priory of St. Mary Magdalene in the town, a dependency of St. Martin des Champs in Paris; Oliver *Mon.* p. 198.
20s FROM .... KING'S BURGESSES. See 1,1.

3,4 THE BISHOP HIMSELF HOLDS. Repeated at the beginning of 3,4-8 inclusive.
ASHWATER. A parish in (Black) Torrington Hundred (11); *Esse* is held from the Honour of Barnstaple in Fees p. 772. It is *Aswalter* in FA i p. 327; see FA i p. 409 and TE p. 150b. The second element of the modern name is probably from Walter son of Ralph who held in 1166 (Black Book p. 128); see OJR H5 pp. 194, 225.

3,5 MERTON. A parish in Shebbear Hundred (4) which formerly named the Hundred (see the Appendix). The Bishop's holding can be identified in the Tax Return for that Hundred (v). In Fees p. 772 there are two Barnstaple Honour fees in *Merton'* and *Suttecumb'* [Sutcombe 3,91]; see RH i p. 93b, FA i pp. 329, 411, Cal. Inq. PM vol. iii no. 519 and OJR H10 p. 576.
3 SLAVES. Misplaced, as also in Exon. See 2,21 note.

3,6 FREMINGTON. The *caput* of Fremington Hundred (5) which it named by virtue of being a royal holding before 1066 (see the Appendix). It is identifiable in the Tax Return (iv). In Fees p. 99 Oliver *de Trascy* holds *Fremigt'* as part of his Honour of Barnstaple; see RH i p. 70a, Cal. Inq. PM vol. v no. 143, vi no. 710, viii nos. 396-397 and OJR H8 p. 506. The Church of Fremington was granted to Hartland Priory by Oliver *de Tracy*; see VE ii p. 333 and Oliver *Mon.* p. 204.
IN BARNSTAPLE .... 15d. This is written in the right margin of the MS, with a thinner pen though in the same colour ink as the rest of the entry; it is not rubricated and there are no transposition signs. See 16,65 for another instance of details concerning Barnstaple being added, and cf. 32,6 note and DB Dorset General Notes 30,4.

| | |
|---|---|
| 3,6 (cont'd.) | BURGESS WHO PAYS 15d. In the MS between the *redd'* and *xv denar'* there is an odd mark, which in the facsimile resembles an *e* (though it is unlikely that the scribe intended *redd'e xv denar'*), probably merely the dot before the *xv* was smudged or the first stroke of the *x* badly written and so done again. |
| 3,7 | CLYST (ST. MARY). A parish in (East) Budleigh Hundred (14); it can probably be identified in the Tax Return for that Hundred (xvi). In Fees pp. 763, 774, Ralph *de Sicca Villa* and the prior of St. James' hold in *Clist* and *Creulegh'* [Crealy 3,94] from Henry *de Tracy*. It is *Clistracy* in Cal. Inq. PM vol. vi no. 710. Ralph *de Sicca Villa* sold his portion (called *Clist Sechevile* in TE p. 144b) to the Bishop of Exeter by whom it was held in FA i p. 427, hence called Bishops Clist; see VE ii pp. 289-290, Cal. Inq. PM vol. xii no. 354, EPNS ii p. 586 and OJR in TDA 35 p. 289 and in VCH p. 426 note 6. |
| 3,8 | BOVEY (TRACEY). A parish in Teignbridge Hundred (23), sometimes called South Bovey to distinguish it from North Bovey (17,22). *Bovy* is held by Eva *de Tracy* in Fees p. 264. It is *Bovitracy* held from the Honour of Barnstaple in FA i p. 339, *Suthbovy* in RH i p. 82a; see RH i p. 90a, Cal. Inq. PM vol. v no. 143, vi no. 710, viii nos. 396-397. £10, LESS 30d .... £4 30d. . See C 1 note above on *minus*.
LAND OF 15 THANES. This naming of individual holdings is unusual in Exchequer DB. The material that was formed by the early stages of the DB enquiry seems regularly to have included the names of subordinate parts of the main manor, but this detail, together with others, was eliminated either before the compilation of the circuit returns or in condensing these latter to form Exchequer DB (see DB Worcs. Appendix IV). Traces of this fuller information are found in the Exon. entries for Bridestowe (16,7) and Mary Tavy (17,13); see Exon. Notes. Some of these subdivisions of Bovey are found in later documents. Thus in Fees p. 774 *Parva Bovy, Wolflegh'* and *Alenesford'* are held from the Honour of Barnstaple; see also Cal. Inq. PM vol. vi no. 710 and FA i p. 390.
DB *Adonebovi* from OE *Ofdune Bovy* or *Adoun Bovy*, meaning a Bovey holding lower down the stream, is presumably Little Bovey (EPNS ii p. 467). *Scabatore*, if correctly identified, will have been a remote outlier, now in Widecombe in the Moor parish, Haytor Hundred (EPNS ii p. 528). *Brungarstone* is identified by VCH (followed by DG) with 'Bawtor' (i.e. Bottor) in Hennock, but without evidence; see EPNS ii p. 466 note 3. *Harlei* may well be an abbreviated form of Hatherleigh (in Bovey Tracey) but is not noticed by EPNS ii p. 469.
In Exon. these lands are called booklands (*bochelandis*, ablative plural; see Exon. Notes). 'Bookland' was land taken from the common land (*folcland*) and granted by *bóc* or charter to a private owner (OED); see Maitland DBB p. 244 ff.
IN DUES. *de censu* in DB and Exon., i.e. they paid rent for their lands. See DB Dorset 16,1 note on *censores* 'tributaries'.
(THIS IS) IN ADDITION TO THE ABOVE £10. The Latin *praeter* here and in Exon. is ambiguous, with its suggestion that the thanes also paid the £10 (less 30d); it hides a longer phrase, such as 'and this £4 30d paid is in addition to/apart from the £10 (less 30d) payment (of the main manor of Bovey Tracey)'. |
| 3,9 | DROGO .... LANDS FROM THE BISHOP. Drogo is probably Drogo son of Mauger, as the Exon. for 3,9;13-14;16 states; on 'Mauger' see Exon. Notes 3,9. Mauger may have been Mauger of Carteret; see 3,70 note. Drogo was the Bishop of Coutances' chief subtenant in Devon, holding all but 19 of his manors in Ch. 3. See 3,85 note.
CORYTON. A parish in Lifton Hundred (18). In Fees p. 773 Geoffrey *de Curiton'* and Elias *de Curiford'* hold in *Curiton'* from the Honour of Barnstaple; in FA i p. 406 *Coryton* is coupled with *Coryfford* [Ford or Ford farm, GR SX 4784 or 4683, see EPNS i p. 181]; see also Fees p. 757, FA i p. 320 and OJR in TDA 46 p. 214. |
| 3,10 | HAMSWORTHY. DB *Hermodesword* (see EPNS i p. 156). It lies in Pancrasweek parish, (Black) Torrington Hundred (11). No place of this name is later found among fees of the Honour of Barnstaple, but *Hermodeswurth'* is a fee of William *Briwere* in Fees p. 396 and *Hermannesworth* is held of the Honour of Berry in Fees p. 791. It may have been an early transfer, possibly because it had been held by the daughters and heirs of William *de Braose*; see OJR H5 pp. 191, 227 and Ch. 3 note and 34,2 note on Dunsdon.
2 SLAVES. There are some 30 entries in Devon where slaves are the only inhabitants mentioned for a manor, although the details of that manor seem otherwise complete. See 17,84 note for other instances of no population at all recorded, when one would expect it to be, and cf. DB Wilts. 20,3 note. |
| 3,11 | HORTON. In Bradworthy parish, (Black) Torrington Hundred (11). Robert *de Horthon'* holds in *Horthon'* from the Honour of Barnstaple in Fees p. 772; see FA i pp. 356, 407. |

| | |
|---|---|
| 3,11 (cont'd.) | THE VILLAGERS (HAVE) ½ VIRGATE. This occurs in its usual place in Exon. after the lordship land. However, no 'villagers' other than the 2 slaves are recorded. The same occurs in 16,169, and in 16,62 where no population at all is recorded in either Exon. or DB, though Exon. similarly gives the villagers' land holding after the lordship land. Cf. notes to 3,10 and 17,84 on the lack of population recorded for some manors and Exon. Notes 23,4 for villagers recorded in Exon., but not included in DB. See also 1,3 note on slaves possibly holding land.<br>JOINED TO HORWOOD. This statement appears twice in the T.O. (see Exon. Notes), though only once in the main Exon. and in DB. Cf. 23,20 and 42,16 where some information is given twice in the main Exon. as well as twice in the T.O. Horwood is in Fremington Hundred (5), see 3,17. |
| 3,12 | HENSCOTT. In Bradford parish, (Black) Torrington Hundred (11). It is *Hengestecoth'* in Fees p. 772, *Heynstecote* in FA i p. 409, Honour of Barnstaple. Hiscott (1,40 note), which has the same etymology, is also later held of the Honour of Barnstaple.<br>THREE THANES HELD IT AS A MANOR. In the MS there is a gap between $p$ and *maner*, not shown by Farley, due to an erasure of about 4 letters, possibly *.iii.*, as the dots at the beginning and end are just visible. From the T.O. entry (see Exon. Notes here) it would seem that there were 3 manors in 1066, combined by 1086 into one. The main Exon. entry does not state in so many words that there were three manors, but implies it by saying that the Bishop now holds [Henscott] as one manor. The DB scribe may not have understood the main Exon.<br>DROGO HAS IT IN LORDSHIP. Exon. *hanc* which probably refers to the ½ virgate, i.e. he holds the whole of Henscott in lordship. Cf. 16,147 and 25,2. |
| 3,13-14 | BUCKLAND (FILLEIGH). HARTLEIGH. Buckland Filleigh is a parish in Shebbear Hundred (4) and contains Hartleigh. The former can be identified in the Tax Return for Merton (Shebbear) Hundred (v). In Fees p. 772 *Bokland'* and *Hertlegh'* are held together as one Barnstaple fee. The holder of both in FA i p. 329 is Nicholas *de Fyleleye* who names Buckland; see OJR H10 pp. 538, 576. |
| 3,15 | BARLINGTON. DB *Beldrendiland*, probably standing for OE *\*Beldredingland* 'Bealdred's land' (EPNS i p. 118) and so part of, or connected with, *Baldrintone* (3,19) 'Bealdred's farm' which had been joined to Roborough by 1086. Barlington is itself now in Roborough parish, Fremington Hundred (5), but this land is probably the *Westbaldringthon'* of Fees p. 772, held from the Honour of Barnstaple in a Shebbear Hundred group (4); it is *West Walyngton* in Shebbear Hundred in FA i p. 412; see FA i. p. 359 and 3,24-25 note. The holder in FA i p. 412 is William *de Wyrteslegh'* (from Whitsleigh in St. Giles in the Wood parish, Fremington Hundred, GR SS 5517, which is adjacent). West Barlington does not survive on modern maps, but Middle and Great Barlington do, and a 'Little Barlington' is found on the OS first edition 1-inch map (sheet 26 of 1809, reprint sheet 82 of 1969). Like Owlacombe (36,7) and Villavin (25,1), Barlington will have lain in Shebbear Hundred in 1086, though Roborough itself (3,19) was in Fremington (5); see OJR H10 p. 538 and the Appendix. |
| 3,16 | HUISH. DB *Torsewis*. It lies in Instow parish, Fremington Hundred (5), the DB form meaning 'Huish on the river Torridge'. In Fees p. 773 *Hywisse* is held by Roger *Beupel*. It is *Hywysh Beaupel* in FA i p. 375; see FA i pp. 371, 412, EPNS i p. 117 and OJR H8 pp. 496, 507. |
| 3,17 | HORWOOD. A parish in Fremington Hundred (5). The Barnstaple Honour land was at *Westhorewod'* (in Fees p. 773) or *Churchehewod* (in FA i p. 412). This place is now probably West Barton [GR SS 5027] which includes the church; see EPNS i p. 115, also FA i p. 371, OJR H8 pp. 496, 507 and 34,8 note. Horton (3,11) had been joined to this manor after 1066. It may be that the common pasture taken away from Newton Tracey (25,3) by Colswein, the Bishop of Coutances' man, had been joined to Horwood which is the Bishop's nearest manor. |
| 3,18 | WORLINGTON. It also lay in Instow parish, Fremington Hundred (5). In Fees p. 773 Simon *de Chartray* holds in *Wolvrington'* from the Honour of Barnstaple; see FA i p. 412 and OJR H8 p. 508. |
| 3,19 | ROBOROUGH. A parish in Fremington Hundred (5). It is held as *Rugheberg'* in Fees p. 773 by Alexander *de Clunny*; see FA i pp. 371, 413 and OJR H8 p. 508. Part of this land lay at *Wanteslegh'* [Wansley SS 5617] and *Emberlegh'* [Ebberly SS 5618] both in Roborough parish, Fees p. 773; see FA i p. 413.<br>BARLINGTON. See 3,15 note. *Boldringthon'*, as distinct from *Westbaldringthon'*, occurs in Fees p. 771 coupled with *Pilland'* (3,24-25 note).<br>Details of this addition are written in 1½ lines below the bottom marginal ruling and |

3,19      extending some 2 letters into the central margin; there is no rubrication. The ink is paler
(cont'd.) and the pen used thinner, which makes it hard to tell whether the scribe is the same as
          for the rest of the entry. Cf. notes to 1,45 and 3,75. The transposition signs are as in the
          translation, not the 'hands' that Farley prints. It is interesting that in Exon. details of
          this added manor are also written in the margin (see Exon. Notes). The fact that in Exon.
          the addition was written by the scribe of the next entry (= 3,20) and was thus an early
          addition, suggests that the Exchequer scribe merely missed the entry in the margin,
          rather than that the details of Barlington were written in both Exchequer and Exon. DB
          at the same, late, stage (this latter being the view of Finn in LE p. 156).
              ALFRED HELD IT FREELY. In the MS there is an oblique hair-line between *Alured*
          and *teneb'*, immediately below the interlined *lib'e*, indicating its position. Farley does
          not print it, nor the hair-line in 3,60 (see note), though it is often his practice to do so
          (e.g. in 3,52. 15,79. 17,13).
3,20      BONDLEIGH. A parish in (North) Tawton Hundred (12). In Fees p. 773 *Bonelegh'* is
          held from the Honour of Barnstaple by Robert *de Campellis* together with *Estodlegh'*
          [Stoodleigh 3,77] and *Hamptenesford* (*Little Hampteford* in Cal. Inq. PM vol. vi no.
          710), that is probably Handsford GR SS 6404 in Bondleigh rather than Hansford in
          Ashreigney; see EPNS ii p. 355, FA i p. 370 and OJR in TDA 29 p. 247.
3,21      NYMET (TRACEY). DB *Limet*, see Introductory Note 2. It lies in the modern parish of
          Bow, in (North) Tawton Hundred (12), the two names representing successive main
          settlements, Nymet Tracey around the church, Bow on the Launceston to Exeter road
          (the A3072); see EPNS ii p. 360. Oliver *de Trascy* holds *Nimet'* in Fees p. 99, a demesne
          manor of his Honour of Barnstaple; see RH i p. 75b, Cal. Inq. PM vol. v no. 143, vi no.
          710, viii nos. 396-397, FA i p. 340 and OJR in TDA 29 p. 247.
3,22      COLDRIDGE. A parish in (North) Tawton Hundred (12). In Fees p. 773 *Curig* is held
          of the Honour of Barnstaple by Ralph *de Sicca Villa*. It is *Colrygg* in FA i p. 422; see
          OJR in TDA 29 p. 247.
              ENGELBALD. DB *Ingelbald*, Exon. *Ingelbald(us)*; see Forssner pp. 70, 71.
3,23      MARTINHOE. A parish in Shirwell Hundred (2), *Mattingho* being held in Fees p. 772
          from the Honour of Barnstaple; see FA i pp. 336, 417 and OJR H8 p. 472.
3,24-25   PILLAND. PILTON. Pilland (see 3,38 note) is in (West) Pilton parish, Braunton
          Hundred (1). The DB form for Pilton, *Wiltone*, is an error. Exon. has *Piltona* (although,
          possibly due to greasy parchment, the ink did not 'take' for the middle three letters so
          that the name only reads Pi...na). It would seem likely that the Exchequer scribe misread
          the first letter as the A-S runic letter *p* (= *w*); the same mistake occurs in 3,38-39 (see
          notes) and cf. 20,10 note. The note to 16,42 gives further examples of misreadings.
              Part of the land of Pilland and Pilton was granted by Iudhael to the Priory of St. Mary
          Magdalene (in Barnstaple), a cell of the Cluniac Priory of St. Martin des Champs in Paris,
          according to a confirmation of the gift by his grandson, William *de Braose*, in 1157,
          along with half the tithe of *Taustoche* (1,40 note) and all the land called *Hole* (36,11-13
          note). A charter of Henry I (Round CDF no. 1269 p. 460; see *Regesta* ii p. 165 no. 1292
          and p. 243 no. 1667) quitclaims St. Martin des Champs and the monks of Barnstaple of
          geld, customs and dues on 1 virgate at *Pilton* and 1 *ferling* at *Cherchill* (20,4); see Oliver
          *Mon*. p. 196, VE ii p. 354 and OJR H8 pp. 421-424. The rest of *Pilland'* is a Barnstaple
          fee with *Boldringthon'* [Barlington] in Fees p. 771; see FA i p. 359 and 3,15 note.
3,26      (WEST) DOWN. A parish in Braunton Hundred (1). In Fees p. 771 Ralph *Morin* and the
          heirs of William *de Culumbariis* hold in *Dune* from the Honour of Barnstaple. The same
          holding is *Doune Columbers* in FA i p. 375, *Westdon* in FA i p. 414 and *Westdoune* and
          *Dene* [Dene in West Down, GR SS 5042] in Cal. Inq. PM vol. vi no. 710; see OJR H8
          pp. 392, 425.
3,27      HAGGINTON. East Hagginton (23,3 note) is in Berrynarbor parish and West Hagginton
          (16,70 note) in Ilfracombe, both in Braunton Hundred (1). OJR's identification with
          Kings Heanton (in Marwood, King unknown), although accepted by EPNS i p. 51, cannot
          be correct since other forms of Kings Heanton point to derivation from OE *heah* and *tūn*
          'high farm' as Heanton Punchardon (16,69), whereas the DB form points to Hagginton
          ('*Haecga's* farm', EPNS i p. 28). In spite of this, no descent of Hagginton to the Honour
          of Barnstaple has been found.
              WULFRITH. DB *Vlfert*, Exon. *Vlfert(us)*, represents OE *Wulffrith*; see PNDB pp. 418-
          419.
              2 VILLAGERS HAVE THEM THERE. That is, the 2 ploughs, as Exon. states. Cf. 1,29
          note.

| | |
|---|---|
| 3,27 (cont'd.) | AND 1 SMALLHOLDER. In the MS 7 *ū i bord'*. The 7 *ū* is a mystery: *ū* could abbreviate *vero*, but the usual abbreviation in DB for that is *ū̄* (as in C 6 and 3,2), and anyway the word would have little sense here. There is some evidence to suggest that the scribe originally wrote *cū i bord'* (cf. the formula in 3,29-30) and then partially erased the *c* and wrote 7 on top and forgot to erase the *ū*; cf. 19,42 note "And 1 slave". One might expect the Exchequer scribe to have written *cū i bord'* because Exon. states that the 2 villagers have the 2 ploughs, but the 1 smallholder appears to be separate, and in 3 other of the cases where Exon. separates the villagers with ploughs from those without, the Exchequer scribe has this formula (see 1,29. 3,29 and 14,2). However, in 14,1 and 35,19 this phrase occurs in DB, but there is no separation of villagers in Exon., and it does not occur elsewhere in DB where there is separation in Exon. (see Exon. Notes 1,9). |
| 3,28 | RALEIGH. In West Pilton parish, Braunton Hundred (1). *Ralegh'* is held with *Chaudecumb'* [Challacombe 3,33] in Fees p. 772 and is described in FA i p. 414 as *Ralegh cum parcella Metcomb'* [Metcombe 3,29]; see Cal. Inq. PM vol. xiv no. 281. |
| 3,29 | METCOMBE. In Marwood parish, Braunton Hundred (1); see 3,28 note. 2 VILLAGERS HAVE IT THERE. The *hanc* refers to the plough, as Exon. states, not the land. See 1,29 note. |
| 3,30 | (HIGH) BRAY....WHITEFIELD. Whitefield is in High Bray parish, Shirwell Hundred (2); their association in DB distinguishes this Bray from the Bray of 3,45 and this Whitefield from that of 3,34. In Fees p. 772 *Hautebray* is held by Baldwin *le Flemeng* from the Honour of Barnstaple; see FA i pp. 336, 417, Cal. Inq. PM vol. iv no. 35, xv no. 351 and OJR H8 pp. 462, 473. *Parva Bray* [Little Bray GR SS 6835 in Charles parish], held in Fees p. 772 by Robert *de Pidekewill'* (from Pickwell 3,39), may have been part of this land; see FA i p. 361 and OJR H8 pp. 463, 475. |
| 3,31 | BEARA (CHARTER). In Braunton parish and Hundred (1). In Fees p. 772 Simon *de Chartray* (whence 'Charter') holds in *Bere cum membris*. One member is given as *Puppecote* [Pippacott GR SS 5237] in Cal. Inq. PM vol. vi no. 710; see FA i pp. 360, 414 and OJR H8 pp. 393, 420. |
| 3,32 | BEFORE 1066 .... HAVE IT. The DB scribe probably intended details of this dispute as a separate section, although, since it was apparently in 1086 part of Braunton, it is not really governed by the heading above 3,9 that 'Drogo holds the undermentioned lands from the Bishop'. It does not have anything to do with Beara Charter, except perhaps the name Brictric, but it is not absolutely certain it is the same Brictric in both entries, as in Exon. he is distinguished as 'son of Camm' only for the dispute about the virgate. However, in the Exchequer MS the *B* of *Brictric* is not the ornate capital one would expect at the beginning of a new entry (cf. the *B*'s of *Braia* and *Bera* in 3,30-31, and the *V* of the *Vna hida* in the similar entry 3,71, see note), but is rubricated as for a subdivision of a manor (cf. the *H* of *Huic* in 3,26). In Exon. the details are obviously a late addition to the MS, being written at right-angles down the folio with no transposition signs; see Exon. Notes. In the Exchequer MS a slight difference in pen and ink is observable before this entry, suggesting perhaps that the scribe stopped to ponder where to include the information. (Cf. the late addition in DB, as in Exon., of the disputed manor of Werrington (1,50; see first note there), and the details of the added manor of Barlington (3,19) which are marginal in both Exon. and DB.) The parchment here is rather greasy, especially round the *Brictric*, which tends to accentuate the difference in writing. It is odd that the DB scribe should have excluded the name of the land in dispute (see next note but one), but see Introductory Note 3 for other omissions of holdings. BRICTRIC SON OF CAMM. DB *Brictric*, Exon. *[bri]stric' fili' cāmi* (see Exon. Notes here); similarly in the Exon. for the neighbouring holding 19,12 *Brestic' camesone* (not *Prestic(us)* as OEB p. 152) and in the Exon. for 17,13 his brother Brictwy son of Camm (*Bristuit camesonę*). *Camm* would be a nickname from Welsh *cam* 'crooked' (JMcND). 1 VIRGATE .... IN BRAUNTON. For Braunton, a royal manor, see 1,5. This unnamed land is identified in the corresponding Exon. entry as *Boeurda* [Boode in Braunton, wrongly said by EPNS i p. 38 to be Bugford in East Down]. WILLIAM OF VAUVILLE. See 1,15 note. THANES DO NOT KNOW HOW. The thanes were probably members of the shire court. Cf. DB Wilts. 23,7 where 'according to the evidence of the thanes of the Shire' 4 hides had wrongfully been taken away from Amesbury Church by Harold but had been returned. Cf. also DB Glos. 1,53 concerning another disputed property: 'the men of the County do not know how' Earl William and his son Roger had Dymock. |

3,33 CHALLACOMBE. A parish in Shirwell Hundred (2); see 3,28 note, FA i pp. 336, 417 and OJR H8 p. 474.
3,34 WHITEFIELD. In Challacombe parish, Shirwell Hundred (2). In Fees p. 772 Walter *Dar* holds in *Whytefeud* from the Honour of Barnstaple; see FA i p. 417 and OJR H8 p. 474. IT WAS WASTE. Whitefield lies on the very edge of Exmoor, perhaps the reason for the lack of population and resources in this manor, despite the 1086 value, but cf. Buscombe (3,35), two miles from Whitefield, which had also been waste in 1066 but for which a villager and some resources are recorded, as well as a 1086 value.
3,35 BUSCOMBE. In Challacombe parish, Shirwell Hundred (2), DB *Burietescome* corresponding to *Berwordescomb* (1330) and *Buruardescomb* (1333); see EPNS i p. 61 which does not cite the DB form; also OJR H8 p. 474. The correspondence between the place-name forms indicates that the EPNS explanation (*Beornweard's* combe) is wrong. *Burietescome* and *Buruardescomb* appear to contain respectively OE *burh-geat* 'fortified gate-house, entrance to a fortified place' and *burh-weard* 'fort-guardian, keeper of a fortified place'. Field-work, beyond the scope of this present work, is called for to establish the significance of these names.
AELFRIC. In DB Devon this personal name occurs in the form *Aluric*, with Exon. forms *Aluric(us), Alurix, Aluuritius*. However, in 17,88–89 OE *Aelfric* in DB appears to be latinized in Exon. as *Albericus* 'Aubrey' (see note).
IT WAS WASTE. Exon. *erat uastata*; *uastata* is being used here in an adjectival sense, equivalent to *uasta*: there is no implication that Buscombe, which is on the very edge of Exmoor, had been laid waste. See second note under C 3 and 3,34 note; cf. notes to 19,18. 20,2. 21,5 and 36,17.
3,36 PATCHOLE. In Kentisbury parish, Braunton Hundred (1). It is *Pachole* in FA i p. 415 held by Thomas *de Ralegh* from the Honour of Barnstaple coupled with *Trendelisho* [Trentishoe 3,48] and *Sonenasch* [Seven Ash GR SS 6044 in Kentisbury, evidently part of this holding]. *Sevenasse* on its own is coupled with *Trendeleslo* in Fees p. 771.
3,37 KILLINGTON. DB *Cheneoltone*; for the form, see EPNS i p. 66. It lies in Martinhoe parish, Shirwell Hundred (2). In Fees p. 772 *Kynewauthon'*, in FA i p. 417 *Kylweton*, is held from the Honour of Barnstaple; see OJR H8 p. 475.
6 OXEN IN A PLOUGH. There were normally reckoned to be 8 oxen to a plough-team, but there is evidence for smaller teams in the south-west; see R. Lennard in EHR lx (1945) p. 217 ff. and in EHR lxxxi (1966) p. 770 ff. and H.P.R. Finberg in EHR lxvi (1951) p. 67 ff. In Herefordshire there is evidence that, at least on the King's lordship land, a plough-team of 6 oxen was the norm; see DB Herefords. 1,50 note. The Exon. for Devon often gives the number of oxen where DB has plough(s) or a fraction of a plough, and this might be thought to be instructive in working out the number of oxen to a team. For example, in 15,29;37. 28,10. 33,2 and probably 35,23 (see Exon. note), it would seem that Exon.'s '4 oxen' equal DB's '½ plough', and in 16,82 Exon.'s '8 oxen' correspond to DB's '1 plough'. However, in 17,12. 34,32. 48,9 and 52,46 Exon. has '3 oxen' for DB's '½ plough', and in 17,28;39;66 Exon.'s 6 cattle/oxen correspond to DB's plough. Moreover, the Exchequer scribe tended to disregard odd oxen in Exon., apparently either rounding up or down to the nearest plough; see 3,44 note. The phrase *in carr(uca)* occurs several times with oxen in both DB and Exon. (and also with cattle; see 17,26 note), but does not imply that the number of oxen so detailed form a standard unit (e.g. the 6 oxen in a plough here may or may not form a team, but neither the single ox in a plough in 17,98 nor the 7 oxen in a plough in 34,35 could form a team). Cf. the phrase *ad carrucam* in the Exon. for 28,10 (see Exon. Notes). All this phrase seems to mean is that so many oxen were supplied towards a plough-team. The Exon. for 16,4, however, states that the 'villagers' "plough with 2 oxen".
3,38 PILLAND. DB *Welland*, Exon. *Pillanda*; see 3,25 and 3,39 for other examples of the Exchequer scribe's mistaking the Exon. *P* for the runic $p$ (= *w*). For the descent of the holding, see 3,24-25 note.
3,39 PICKWELL. DB *Wedicheswelle*, Exon. *Pediccheswella*; for the forms see notes to 3,24–25 and 3,38. The place lies in Georgeham parish, Braunton Hundred (1), although Pickwell appears to have been a tithing of Shirwell (2) in the Middle Ages (see, for example, LSR (1334) p. 53 and (1332) p. 25). In Fees p. 772, Robert *de Pidekewill'* holds in *Pidekewill'* and in *Gratedene* [Gratton 3,42] from the Honour of Barnstaple. In FA i pp. 335-336, Mauger *de Sancto Albino* holds in *Paddikkeswell* and in *Gracton*, while in FA i p. 416 John *Vautort* holds in *Pydekuill, Gratton, Sprecom* [Spreacombe 36,13] and *Hole* [Hole 36,11], lands said to have been held formerly by Mauger *de Sancto Albino*. Further, in FA i p. 361 these same lands appear as *Pydekewill, Gratton,*

|  |  |
|---|---|
|  | *Northole, Strodeton* [Stourton, see 36,21-23 note] and *Estwere* [unidentified]. Mauger *de Sancto Albino* held Spreacombe and Hole from the Honour of Torrington (36,11-13 note) but Pickwell and Gratton from the Honour of Barnstaple; see Cal. Inq. PM vol. iii no. 174 and OJR H8 pp. 462, 475. |
| 3,40-41 | AYLESCOTT. STOWFORD. Both lie in West Down parish, Braunton Hundred (1). In Fees p. 771 *Aylyvecoth'* is held of the Honour of Barnstaple by Mabel *de Dune*. Stowford may well be represented by the adjacent *Crakeweye* [Crackaway GR SS 5341] in Fees p. 771; see FA i p. 360. Crackaway is held by John *de Stouford* in FA i p. 414 from the Honour of Okehampton. In the same survey (FA i p. 413 of 1346) *Alescote* is coupled with other Honour of Okehampton lands (16,69 note); see OJR H8 pp. 426-427. |
| 3,42 | GRATTON. In High Bray parish, Shirwell Hundred (2); see 3,39 note. |
| 3,43 | WINSHAM. In Braunton parish and Hundred (1). The holding does not appear in the fee lists, but *Incledene* [Incledon in Braunton, GR SS 4738, see 19,12-13 note] is held from the Honour of Barnstaple by Nicholas *de Ferariis* and Robert *de Incledene* in Fees p. 771. |
| 3,44 | HELE. Probably in Ilfracombe parish, Braunton Hundred (1); see OJR H8 p. 394. 1 VILLAGER AND 1 SMALLHOLDER .... In the MS there is a space left suitable for about 7 letters between *bord'* and the side marginal ruling. It may have been left intentionally (as apparently in 20,14; see note) or, as there is a dot after *bord'*, the scribe may merely have decided to begin the resources on a new line. Cf. 3,83 note and notes to 11,1 and 25,12. 2 OXEN IN A PLOUGH. The Exchequer scribe frequently seems to have deliberately omitted odd oxen given in Exon. For example, he makes no mention of the ox in 3,88. 17,9 and 17,98, nor of the 2 oxen in 3,74;76. 16,8. 17,17 (see Exon. Notes). 17,42 and 21,18, nor of the 2 *animalia* (probably oxen) in a plough in 17,38 (cf. also the 1 *animal* (= ox) in a plough in 17,77), nor of the 3 oxen in 35,7 and 42,2 (though he records the 3 oxen in lordship in 36,17 and on several occasions he writes '½ plough' for '3 oxen'; see 3,37 note). Because of the uncertainty as to the number of oxen to a plough-team (3,37 note) it is impossible to tell sometimes how many oxen are being disregarded, e.g. in 5,1 the DB scribe may be discounting either 1 or 3 oxen and in 15,14 he may either have rounded up (at 8 oxen to a plough) or down (at 6 oxen) to the nearest plough, and in 17,61 either 2 or 3 oxen may have been ignored. However, 7 oxen recorded in Exon. for 34,35 are not mentioned in DB, which must surely be a mistake. See previous note on the possible reason for the space after the villager and smallholder in this entry. |
| 3,45 | BRAY. In South Molton parish and Hundred (6). The river names at least two holdings in the parish called 'East' and 'West' Bray in medieval documents, but more recently it seems these have become respectively 'Knights Bray' (six-inch OS map of 1891, GR SS 690260, 'Knightsbury' on 1st edition one-inch map of 1809 (sheet 26, reprint sheet 82 of 1969) and 'High Bray' (GR SS 6726, a site now abandoned, but given on the one-inch 5th edition OS map, and marked simply Bray on the 1st edition map). There is also a South Bray in Chittlehampton parish (GR SS 6624), see 1,41 note. This Bray should be distinguished from the High Bray of 3,30 and appears to be the first South Molton Hundred place to be entered in the Bishop's schedule, others (e.g. 3,56-57;61-62) being also intermixed with Braunton and Shirwell Hundred entries. This holding was certainly at *Estebray* ('East' Bray) in Fees p. 772; see FA i pp. 326, 418 and OJR H8 in TDA 36 p. 355, H3 p. 67. There was also Barnstaple Honour land at *Westbray* (Cal. Inq. PM vol. vi no. 710) held by Thomas *de Fillegh*; see 52,36 note. The holder in FA i p. 326 of *Estbraye* is Augustine *de Bathonia*; he is said to hold of Okehampton Honour in Cal. Inq. PM vol. iii no. 31. ALWARD. DB *Aluuard*, Exon. *Ailuuard(us)* for Aethelweard; PNDB pp. 188-189. Exon. also has the form *Ailuuard(us)* for DB's *Aluuard(us)* in 19,16;19. 51,3. Both DB and Exon. have the forms *Ailuuard(us), Ailuard(us)* for 3,75. 16,103. 19,25. 28,12. Cf. 1,41 note. A GARDEN. Latin *h(ortus)* is probably rendering OE *geard* 'garden, enclosure' etc. in the sense seen in *fisc-geard* 'fishery, fish pond'. Cf. DB Somerset 19,26 where a 'garden' in Langport pays 50 eels. A garden is also recorded for Ottery St. Mary (10,1), but no render is mentioned. Both Bray and Ottery St. Mary are on rivers. |
| 3,46 | NORTHCOTE. In East Down parish, Braunton Hundred (1). The identification of this and the Northcote of 3,49 has been obscured by OJR's assertion that the present holding is Incledon in Braunton (OJR H8 p. 389 and pp. 420-421; see 3,43 note). Both Northcotes were probably parts of the same vill in East Down parish (EPNS i p. 39), separately given by DB because they had different TRE holders (see 17,23-24 note). In |

3

Fees p. 771 *Northecoth'* and *Kamescoth'* [Campscott in Ilfracombe, GR SS 4944, *Camescote* in Cal. Inq. PM vol. xiii no. 18; see 3,51 note] are held from the Honour of Barnstaple; see FA i p. 415. One of these Northcotes was *Northcote Prior's* held by the prior of Pilton in Cal. Inq. PM vol. vi no. 710.

3,47 BRIDWICK. It now lies in Kentisbury parish, Braunton Hundred (1), but it was counted as a tithing of Shirwell (2) in the Middle Ages. *Brudewyk* was a fee of William *Briwere* in Fees p. 396, held of him by Hamelin *de Deaudon* and *Bridewyk'* is held of the Honour of Barnstaple in Fees p. 772; see FA i p. 336 and Cal. Inq. PM vol. ii no. 306, vii no. 297.
AELMER. The forms of this name in Devon are *Ailmar(us)*, *Ailmer*, *Elmer*, *Almaer*, *Almer*, *Almar*, *Elmar*, *Aimar* in DB and similarly in Exon. with more ending in *-us* and also *Almerd(us)*, *Elmerd(us)*. They represent either OE *Aelfmaer* or *Aethelmaer*; PNDB pp. 147-149 s.n. *Almaer*. Cf. 15,31 note.

3,48 TRENTISHOE. A parish in Braunton Hundred (1). It is *Trendeleslo* in Fees p. 771, Honour of Barnstaple; see 3,36 note.

3,49 NORTHCOTE. In East Down parish, Braunton Hundred (1); see 3,46 note.

3,50 WALLOVER. In Challacombe parish, Shirwell Hundred (2). In Fees p. 772 the Abbot of *Clive* holds in *Walleworth'* from the Honour of Barnstaple; see FA i pp. 361, 417, Mon. Ang. v p. 733 and OJR H8 p. 476.

3,51 WARCOMBE. In Ilfracombe parish, Braunton Hundred (1). The main body of the manor seems to have passed at an early date to the Honour of Okehampton, *Worcumbe* being held of it in Fees p. 784; see FA i pp. 360, 414 and OJR H8 p. 436. It is possible that Campscott (3,46 note) was part of this land.

3,52 MIDDLETON. In Parracombe parish, Shirwell Hundred (2). *Middelton'* is held of the Honour of Barnstaple in Fees p. 772; see FA i pp. 336, 416.
ANOTHER (PLOUGH). The *aliam* refers to the *caruca* in the preceding statement, but the addition of the lordship land from Exon. breaks the syntax of DB, hence the need for the bracket. Cf. 24,29 note.

3,53 STOODLEIGH. In West Buckland parish, Braunton Hundred (1), but it was counted as part of Shirwell (2) in the Middle Ages. In Fees p. 772 *Stodelegh'* is held of the Honour of Barnstaple; see FA i p. 361. The identification of DB *Stodlei* with Stoly in Shirwell (VCH p. 424 note 4) or Sloley Barton in Shirwell (OJR H8 pp. 463, 477) is impossible; see EPNS i p. 68.
IN LORDSHIP 1 PLOUGH. In the MS *In dñio e i car̄*; the dot before the *i* is larger than usual and together with a rather smudged hook at the top of the *i* makes the *i* look like an *a*; the scribe therefore clarified the number by interlining *a* (for *una*).
1 VILLAGER AND 1 PLOUGH AND 1 FURLONG. In Exon. *uill' i. ferlinū & i car̄*, but as usual it is not clear whether the *uill'* abbreviates the singular *uillanus* or the plural *uillani*, in which latter case it would be implying the slave had a share in the plough and land. Cf. 15,47 note.

3,54-55 (EAST) BUCKLAND. The Bishop apparently had three holdings here (see also 3,63). *Estbokland'* is held in Fees p. 772 from the Honour of Barnstaple; see FA i pp. 360, 414 and OJR in TDA 34 p. 731, 36 pp. 354-355, H8 pp. 395, 427. For West Buckland see 16,73.

3,54 MEADOW, 6 ACRES; WOODLAND, 6 ACRES; PASTURE, 12 ACRES. The scribe appears to have been careless when writing the resources in this entry: the acreages of both the meadow and pasture are corrected (from *iii* and *xi* respectively) and the woodland omitted and then squeezed in, mostly in the right margin (though it is hard to see where the side ruling comes here) with *siluę* interlined (though there is no gallows sign indicating the position of the *siluę*, the 7 is extra large and takes its place). All these corrections were done at an early stage in the same colour ink as the rest of the entry. The Exon. entry is neat and clear with no alterations.

3,55 THIS ENTRY is added in two lines at the foot of col. 102d below the bottom marginal ruling, extending some 4 letters into the central margin; it is not rubricated. Unlike the other additions at the bottom of columns (see 1,45 note), it is written in the same colour ink as the rest of the column, although the pen is scratchier. The transposition signs are as in the translation, not the 'hands' that Farley prints. There is no sign in the Exon. MS that this entry was a later addition, the folio being neat and by one scribe and the entries either side of it are those corresponding to 3,53 and 3,55.

3,56-57 BREMRIDGE. ALLER. Both are in South Molton parish and Hundred (6), held as *Bremelrig* and *Sudaure* [South Aller, see 42,12-13 note] by Oliver *de Tracy* in Fees p. 772; see FA i pp. 326, 418. *Cloteworth'* [Clotworthy GR SS 6828], the next entry in Fees p. 772, was no doubt part of these lands; see FA i p. 326 (*Fluteworth*), 418 and OJR H3 pp. 69, 83-84.

| | |
|---|---|
| 3,58 | PLAISTOW. In Shirwell parish and Hundred (2). It is held as *Pleystowe* in Fees p. 772 from the Honour of Barnstaple; see FA i pp. 336, 416. |
| 3,59 | VARLEY. Probably the place in Marwood parish, Braunton Hundred (1); see EPNS i p. 52. |
| 3,60 | BITTADON. In the MS there is a faint but clear hair-line between the second *E* and *D* of *BEDENDONE* (there is no gap between the *E* and *D*) to show the position of the interlined *N*; Farley does not print this line (see 3,19 last note). Exon. has *Bedendona*.
Bittadon is a parish in Braunton Hundred (1). *Bittedene* is held from the Honour of Barnstaple in Fees p. 771; see FA i p. 415. |
| 3,61 | MOLLAND. A parish near West Anstey, South Molton Hundred (6), to be distinguished from Molland in North Molton (see 36,17 note). In Fees p. 772 Robert *de Campell'* holds *Molland'* from the Honour of Barnstaple. The same place is called *Champeleston'* in FA i p. 325, *Molland Champeaux* in FA i p. 418, that is Champson in Molland, GR SS 8028; see EPNS ii p. 343 and OJR H3 pp. 69, 84. |
| 3,62 | ANSTEY. The holding lay in what is now West Anstey parish, South Molton Hundred (6). In Fees p. 772, from the Honour of Barnstaple, Roger *le Moyne* holds *Anestye*, while in FA i p. 325 William *le Moigne* holds *Westanestigh* from Ralph *de Champeus* (see 3,61 note) and the latter holds from Geoffrey *de Caumvill*. The Honour of Okehampton holds another part of Anstey (16,78) and is wrongly entered as holding this land in FA i p. 419; see OJR H3 pp. 69, 84. |
| 3,63 | (EAST) BUCKLAND. See 3,54-55 note. |
| 3,64 | ROWLEY. In Parracombe parish, Shirwell Hundred (2). *Rughelegh'* is held in Fees p. 772 from the Honour of Barnstaple; see FA i pp. 336, 417. |
| 3,65-66 | CHAGFORD. TEIGNCOMBE. Teigncombe is in Chagford parish, Wonford Hundred (19). In Fees p. 773 *Chageford'* and *Yales* [unidentified, *Heales* in Cal. Inq. PM vol. vi no. 710] are held of the Honour of Barnstaple; *Chageford* and *Teyngcomb* are similarly held in FA i p. 315; see FA i pp. 346, 387. |
| 3,67 | BRAMFORD (SPEKE). Now a parish in Wonford Hundred (19), although DB *Branfortune, Brenford* and *Branford* (see also 16,123;129. 24,2) seem to have accounted for the parishes both of Bramford Speke and Upton Pyne. In Fees p. 773 the heir of Richard *le Espek'* holds in *Branford'*, while in FA i p. 315 *Bramford Spec* is held from Hugh *de Cortenay* and he holds from Geoffrey *de Canvile*; see FA i p. 385. The four holdings at Bramford Speke, 3 hides in all, will have encompassed the 2 *mansae* at *Brentefordland* or *Brentesforlong* granted by King Edmund in 944 to Athelstan *comes* and subsequently by Athelstan to Glastonbury Abbey (ECDC nos. 29-30 p. 11 = BCS no. 799 = Sawyer (1) no. 498).
The Bishop of Coutances' holding probably included *Kouelegh'* [Cowley GR SX 9095] entered next in Fees p. 773; see FA i p. 315, Fees p. 613 and 24,2 note. |
| 3,68 | REWE. A parish in Wonford Hundred (19). Fees p. 773 records that *Rewe* is held by Robert *de Blakeford'* from the Honour of Barnstaple, together with 1 virgate of land in *Sulfertone* [Silverton, see 1,7]. In Cal. Inq. PM vol. vi no. 710 this same land appears as *Hesel* [Heazille Barton, GR SS 9500] and *Rewes*; see Fees p. 1370, FA i pp. 315, 346, 387 and RBE ii p. 558.
VALUE NOW 20s. Originally *x solid'* was written, but a second *x* was added; it is interesting that a similar correction was made in Exon. here (see Exon. Notes). Cf. notes to 2,24. 16,108. 28,10 and 32,10. |
| 3,69 | NETHER EXE. A parish in Hayridge Hundred (15); it is identifiable in the Tax Return for Silverton (Hayridge) Hundred (xiii). In Fees p. 773 Richard *de Crues* (whose family names Cruwys Morchard 3,73) holds in *Nytheresse*; see FA i pp. 322, 425, Cal. Inq. PM vol. v no. 244 and OJR in TDA 42 pp. 219, 232. |
| 3,70 | UP EXE. Now in Rewe parish (see 3,68), Wonford Hundred (19), but it was in Hayridge Hundred (15) in the Middle Ages and probably also in 1086 judging by the order of Exon. Henry *de Tracy* holds in *Uppe Esse* in Fees p. 773 from the Honour of Barnstaple; see FA i pp. 322, 368, 425, Cal. Inq. PM vol. vi no. 710, x no. 494 and OJR in TDA 42 pp. 219, 232.
IN LORDSHIP 1 PLOUGH. Possibly a mistaken item of information; see Exon. Notes here.
VILLAGERS .... WITH 1 PLOUGH. The *cū i car* is written in slightly paler ink, completely in the central margin. As there is no lordship plough recorded in Exon. (see Exon. Notes), it may be that initially the Exchequer scribe included the details of the 1 plough that Exon. records, under the lordship rather than in its correct place with the villagers; during a check of Exon. the mistake was noticed and the villagers' plough added, but for some reason the lordship plough was not deleted. |

| | |
|---|---|
| 3,70 (cont'd.) | HUMPHREY. Possibly Humphrey of Carteret (see DB Dorset 3,10 and General Notes there) who would seem to have held from Drogo in 3,80 (see note for the Tax Return evidence). This possible identification is lent support by the fact that Drogo is son of Mauger (see 3,9 note) and Mauger is probably Mauger of Carteret who holds in 15,57 and in Somerset.<br>HUMPHREY (HOLDS IT) FROM DROGO. The Exchequer scribe may have decided when copying Exon. to omit details of this lower level of subtenancy, as no doubt at 35,10 and see Exon. Notes 3,94. However, he does omit (apparently accidentally) the 1086 subtenants of the main manors of 21,1. 23,7. 24,28-29;31. 25,1. 34,16;27;47. 41,1. 47,10. 48,11 and 49,7. Except for the entries for 24,28-29;31 and 48,1 (see General Notes 24,28 and Exon. Notes 48,1), no obvious reason emerges from a study of the Exon. MS why the Exchequer scribe omitted such important details: they occur in the usual places in the Exon. entries. However, changes in tenants may have occurred in some since Exon. was compiled. |
| 3,71 | THESE DETAILS are probably intended to form a separate entry, as they do in Exon., rather than to be part of Up Exe. The *V* of *Vna* is large and rubricated like the *V* of *Vlpesse*, the first word of 3,70. Cf. 3,32 note and DB Dorset General Notes 55,15a. |
| 3,72 | (LOWER) CREEDY. DB *Cridie*. It lies in Upton Hellions parish, (West) Budleigh Hundred (14), and is probably represented by *Hassok'* [Haske GR SS 8502] in Fees pp. 762, 774; see OJR in TDA 35 pp. 282, 309. |
| 3,73-79 | A GROUP OF PLACES that all now lie on the eastern edge of Witheridge Hundred (7) apart from 3,79 which is in Tiverton Hundred (9). But in the Tax Return for Bampton Hundred (xxii), Bishop Geoffrey is allowed 1 hide 3½ furlongs (*fertinos*) of lordship land. There is no place now lying in Bampton Hundred (8) to represent them, and it is probable that this group of places (whose combined lordship is 1 hide 4 'furlongs') lay in, or was taxed in, Bampton Hundred in 1086; see the Appendix. 3,74-78 are so placed by OJR (in TDA 30 p. 454); for the sequence of the Exon. Book to be tidy, 3,73;79 should be included as well. |
| 3,73 | (CRUWYS) MORCHARD. DB *Morceth*. OJR's identification with Moor farm in Shobrooke (in TDA 30 p. 431, 35 p. 309, 36 p. 362) or with Rowlstone, a part of Morchard Bishop said to lie in Witheridge Hundred (VCH p. 426 note 9), either ignores the DB form or topography or the sequence of Hundreds in Exon. The most probable identification is with a part of Cruwys Morchard (see 3,69 note). This place now lies in Witheridge Hundred (7), but like 3,74-79 may well have been counted in Bampton Hundred in 1086. In Fees p. 773, from the Honour of Barnstaple, Robert *de Edinthon'* holds in *Northecoth'* [Northcote in Cruwys Morchard, GR SS 8613; see 19,35 note], *Coltescoth'* [Colston in Templeton, GR SS 8614, *Kolteston'* in Fees p. 760] and in *Bradelegh'* [Bradley, see 3,82 note]; see Fees p. 763. It is not unlikely that Northcote (perhaps including Colston, see 3,76 note) represents DB *Morceth*. |
| 3,74 | SPURWAY. Now in Oakford parish, Witheridge Hundred (7), but see 3,73-79 note. In Fees p. 773 *Spreweye* is held from the Honour of Barnstaple, while in FA i p. 343 it is *Estsprewey* ['East' Spurway, now Spurway Barton ] with members *Challewille* [probably now represented by Chawlmoor wood and copse, GR SS 908225] and *Falwarigge* [Valeridge GR SS 9122], held from Geoffrey *de Camvill'*; see Fees p. 759 and Cal. Inq. PM vol. x no. 241. For West Spurway see 23,14. |
| 3,75;78 | COOMBE. Probably Coombe in Templeton, now in Witheridge Hundred (7), but see 3,73-79 note. The two holdings are accounted for in Fees p. 773: (1) by *Cumb'*, one fee held by Roger *Dacastre* and John *Reyngny* (that is 3,75, the larger DB holding, found as *Cumb Acastre* and *Combe Regni* in Cal. Inq. PM vol. vi no. 710), and (2) by *Cumb' Munceus* one-sixth fee held by William *de Moncellis* (that is 3,78, the smaller holding). Both are held from the Honour of Barnstaple; see Fees p. 760 and 52,43 note. The second manor is *Cumbe Monceaus* in FA i p. 344 held from Geoffrey *de Camvill'* (see FA i pp. 362, 421); the first passes into the hands of the Knights Templars who name the parish; see RH i p. 87b and EPNS ii p. 394. |
| 3,75 | THIS ENTRY is added in 2 lines at the foot of col. 103a below the bottom marginal ruling, extending some 2 letters into the left margin; it is not rubricated. The colour of the ink is paler and the pen thinner than that of the rest of the column. Cf. the additions 1,45 and 3,19. The transposition signs are as in the translation, not the 'hands' that Farley prints.<br>ALWARD. DB and Exon. *Ailuuard(us)* for OE *Aethelweard*; see notes to 3,45 and 1,41. |
| 3,76 | CELVERTESBERIE ... COOMBE. Among fees held of the Honour of Barnstaple in Fees pp. 760, 773 is *Coltescoth'* or *Kolteston'*, now Colston in Templeton parish (3,73 |

| | |
|---|---|
| 3,76 (cont'd.) | note), which might represent the unidentified *Celvertesberie* especially if Coombe is part of the Coombe in Templeton (3,75;78 note). If, however, *Celvertesberie* simplified to 'Beer', it might be the Beer in Cruwys Morchard (GR SS 8411) in which case Coombe might be Coombe farm (SS 8511) in the same parish. More evidence is needed. <br> 3 FURLONGS AND 1 VIRGATE. The order is unusual, as furlongs ('ferlings') were subdivisions of virgates; see fourth note under 1,4. The correct order occurs in the villagers' land for 3,77 given in Exon. <br> IT IS UNOCCUPIED. Exon. *uacua* 'empty, unoccupied'. The T.O. entry (see Exon. Notes) has *uastata iacet* 'lies waste'. See second note under C 3 on *uasta, uastata*. |
| 3,77 | STOODLEIGH. A parish now lying in Witheridge Hundred (7), but see 3,73-79 note. In Fees p. 773 *Estodlegh* [East Stoodleigh, see 34,40 note] is held with Bondleigh (3,20 note) from the Honour of Barnstaple; see Fees p. 760 and FA i pp. 343, 421. |
| 3,78 | COOMBE. See 3,75,78 note. |
| 3,79 | BRADLEY. The name is now represented by Bradley (GR SS 8912), Great Bradley (SS 9013), Middle Bradley (SS 8913) and West Bradley (SS 8914), as well as by Bradleigh Down (SS 9013), all in Tiverton parish and Hundred (9). The Bishop's other Bradley (3,82) certainly lay in Tiverton Hundred, but the sequence of Exon. suggests that this land lay in Bampton (now Witheridge) Hundred (3,73-79 note) and perhaps was a part of West Bradley lying west of the river Dart, or was appurtenant to one of the Bishop's Bampton Hundred manors. |
| 3,80 | THELBRIDGE. A parish in Witheridge Hundred (7). In the Tax Return for Witheridge Hundred (x) tax is owed on 1½ virgates held by Humphrey of Carteret from Drogo which would seem to correspond to the 1½ virgates of villagers' land (the tax-paying part of the holding). Although the holder is Drogo himself in DB, this Tax Return entry must refer to Thelbridge since it is held in Fees p. 773 by Simon *de Chartray* as *Thelebrig'* and *Chatemere* [Chapner GR SS 8113]; see Fees p. 758, FA i pp. 343, 419, Black Book p. 127 and OJR in TDA 30 p. 426. Moreover, DB rarely gives details of sub-tenants, and Exon. gives them only slightly less rarely (as in 3,70, see last note). <br> IT PAID TAX FOR ½ VIRGATE OF LAND. Added later, though in the same colour ink and hand, extending into the right margin, the original dot after *M* being visible under the 7. |
| 3,81 | WORLINGTON. East Worlington parish in Witheridge Hundred (7), now united with West Worlington, see EPNS ii p. 401. In Fees p. 773 *Woluringthon'* is held from the Honour of Barnstaple. The place is *Estuuilriggton* in FA i p. 343; see Fees p. 758, and for West Worlington see 42,21 note. <br> WOODLAND, 3 ACRES. A possible reason for the omission of the woodland details in DB is that Exon. has *iii ag'nem' & iii nemcti* and the Exchequer scribe's eye travelled from one *iii nem'* to the next. Cf. notes to 1,4. 16,164 and 32,5. |
| 3,82 | BRADLEY. In Tiverton parish and Hundred (9); see 3,79 note. In Fees p. 760 (Witheridge Hundred) Robert *de Edingthon'* holds in *Norththecoth'* and *Kolteston'* (see 3,73 and 3,76 notes) and has 1 *ferling* of land in *Bradelegh'* *quod est in hundredo de Twiverton*, clearly the 1 *ferling* of this holding; see Fees p. 773 and 50,5 note. <br> IT PAYS 30d. One would normally expect *valet* instead of *reddit* here, the former being the verb used in all but three of the Value statements in Ch. 3. It is probable that the Exchequer scribe merely copied the *reddit* from the Exon. (possibly by mistake, as he changes Exon.'s *reddit* for 3,4;6;27;29 to *valet*); cf. notes to 15,53 and 24,18. It is unlikely that he meant to imply that the 30d was a payment by the smallholder (for 'farming' the manor, see 6,6 note): the wording of neither Exon. not Exchequer DB suggests this, but cf. 52,48 note. See 2,2 note on 'Value' for the apparent interchangeability of the verbs *reddit* and *valet*. |
| 3,83 | LOXBEARE. A parish in Tiverton Hundred (9). Robert *Avenel* holds *Lockesbere* in Fees p. 774 from the Honour of Barnstaple; see FA i pp. 319, 433. <br> VILLAGERS....PLOUGH. UNDERWOOD.... There is no obvious reason why the DB scribe omitted either the villagers' plough or the underwood details; neither are added in Exon. or are out of place. Although there is a small gap in the MS after *bord'* (as if left for the villagers' plough), this does not prove anything as small gaps are often left between details of population and resources etc. (as in 3,81). Cf. second note under 3,44. See second note under 1,34 on other instances of the villagers' plough(s) being omitted in DB. Underwood is also omitted for no apparent reason by the Exchequer scribe in 17,6;2. 25,12 and 47,13; cf. 1,4 note on the omissions of 'woodland'. |
| 3,84 | PEADHILL. In Tiverton parish and Hundred (9). It is *Padehill'* in Fees p. 773 held from the Honour of Barnstaple; see FA i pp. 319, 432. |

| | |
|---|---|
| 3,85 | FARWAY. A parish in Colyton Hundred (22); it should be noted that DG maps it in the wrong location. In Fees p. 773 this land (the Bishop's only holding in this Hundred) seems to be represented by *Forewod'* [Farwood Barton, GR SY 2095, in Colyton parish] held by the Abbot *de Quarera* (that is, Quarr in Ryde parish on the Isle of Wight) from the predecessors of Henry *de Tracy*; see FA i pp. 366, 428 and 21,15 note.<br>DROGO HOLDS THESE 73 LANDS. In fact there are 77 (or 75 if one excludes 3,32 and 3,71 which are not 'proper' manors; see notes). See 3,9 note on Drogo. |
| 3,86-87 | SOURTON. MILFORD. Sourton is itself a parish while Milford is in Stowford parish, both in Lifton Hundred (18). In Fees p. 773 two Honour of Barnstaple fees are held in *Surethon', Trissel* [North Russell, GR SX 5092, in Sourton parish] and *Meleford* together with *Kemmeworth'* [Kimworthy 3,89], *Niweland'* [Newland, SS 3012, no doubt part of Kimworthy] and *Thorne* [Thorne 3,88], these last three being in (Black) Torrington Hundred (11); see Fees p. 756 and FA i p. 320. In FA i p. 405 these places occur as *Sourton, Northryschel* and *Mylefford*; see OJR in TDA 46 p. 192 and H5 pp. 195, 227. |
| 3,87 | 1 COTTAGER. *i coscez* rather than the usual singular form *coscet*. The plural *coscez* is also used after *i* in 17,10 and in DB Wilts. 68,24, though in the latter an attempt was made to correct the *z* to a *t*. Exon. has the singular form here and for 17,10. Cf. 2,24 note on *xxi coscez*. |
| 3,88 | THORNE. In (Black) Torrington Hundred (11), and most likely the place in Holsworthy parish, the John *de Thorne* who holds in FA i p. 408 from the Honour of Barnstaple being probably the same man who holds land in Holsworthy in LSR (1332) p. 68. See 3,86-87 note. |
| 3,89 | THE BISHOP'S NIECE. Although Latin *neptis* can mean 'grand-daughter' as well as 'niece', the meaning here must be the latter, as Geoffrey was not married. The niece in question may have been the sister of Geoffrey's nephew and heir, Robert of Mowbray (see Ch. 3 note), though the Bishop seems to have had several brothers and a sister.<br>KIMWORTHY. In Bradworthy parish, (Black) Torrington Hundred (11). It seems to have included Newland (3,86-87 note); see Fees p. 773, FA i p. 409 and OJR H5 p. 227. |
| 3,90 | WULFRUN. DB and Exon. *Oluú*. It would seem that both scribes omitted one abbreviation sign and put the existing one in the wrong place, the correct form being *Olůū* (= *Oluerun*, OE feminine personal name *Wulfrun*). A Wulfrun held land elsewhere in Devon, but only in 1066, in common with all the *Wulf-* names.<br>WELCOMBE. A parish in Hartland Hundred (3). It is held in FA i p. 371 by Richard *de Merton* (from Merton 3,5); see Cal. Inq. PM vol. viii no. 390.<br>OSGOT. DB *Osgot*, Exon. *Ansgottus*, represent the same name in its OE and OG forms: OE *Ōsgot* = OScand *Asgautr* (the cognate OE name was *Osgeat*), PNDB p. 339, which the Normans saw as OG *Ansgaut* and wrote *Ansgot* (JMcND). In 15,77 and 16,24 the DB and Exon. forms also differ (see Exon. Notes to these). Cf. *Anger/Asgar* (1,23-24 note). |
| 3,91 | SUTCOMBE. A parish in (Black) Torrington Hundred (11). In Fees p. 772 *Suttecumb'* is held with *Merthon'* [Merton 3,5] of the Honour of Barnstaple; see FA i pp. 327, 406, Cal. Inq. PM vol. iii no. 519, viii no. 390, OJR H5 p. 226 and 3,5 note. |
| 3,92 | TAPELEY. In Westleigh parish, Fremington Hundred (5). It is held as *Tappelegh'* in Fees p. 773 from the Honour of Barnstaple, see FA i p. 413. |
| 3,93 | SOWTON. DB *Clis*. A parish in Wonford Hundred (19) formerly known as *Clist Fomison* (or *Fomyzoun*) or Clist St. Michael; see VE ii p. 309 and EPNS ii p. 445. Like Canonteign (3,97) but unlike almost all the Bishop's other Devonshire manors, this land passed to the Honour of Gloucester, thus following the same descent as the Bishop's Somerset estates. In Fees p. 779 *Clist Fomicon'* is held by Richard *Fomicun* from the Honour of Gloucester; see FA i pp. 315, 346, 386, Cal. Inq. PM vol. iii nos. 371, 532, v no. 538, ix no. 428, xvi no. 538 and OJR in TDA 44 pp. 290, 338, and in VCH p. 557. |
| 3,94 | CREALY. In Farringdon parish, (East) Budleigh Hundred (14). It is held in the fee lists with Clyst St. Mary (3,7 note).<br>2 VILLAGERS. So the MS and Farley, though part of the first *i* is not completely there and in the facsimile the number appears as ·*i*. See L 11 note. |
| 3,95 | RUSTON. DB *Rinestanedone*. It lay in the former West Worlington parish, now combined with East Worlington (3,81 note), Witheridge Hundred (7). This land passed out of the Bishop's fief, *Ringstanesdune* being held in Fees p. 761 in Witheridge Hundred of the Honour of *Gunnardeston* in Cornwall; see OJR in TDA 30 pp. 410, 427. |
| 3,96 | 'CHARLTON'. A lost place, probably in Upottery parish, Axminster Hundred (17). The DB form here is *Cheletone*, but *Cherletone* at 1,11 where it is one of the several lands said to owe dues to Axminster. It has been identified with Charton in Axmouth parish |

by Whale (in TDA 35 p. 696) and DG, but this is improbable since a place paying dues to Axminster is unlikely to have lain in Axmouth parish and Hundred. It is more likely that the place is the tithing of *Churleton* in Axminster Hundred (LSR 1334 p. 57; Reichel and Mugford (1384) p. 34). This place is stated by Pole (p. 127) to be *Charleton* coupled with *Luggeston* [Luxon GR ST 2110] and *Chanelsheghes* [Charles Hayes farm ST 2108, see EPNS ii p. 650] both in Upottery parish; see OJR in TDA 36 p. 365, in VCH p. 428 note 6 and H4 pp. 136, 155].

3,97  GEOFFREY OF TRELLY. Trelly (Exon. *de trailei*) is in the département of Manche, France; see OEB p. 116. Geoffrey is also a subtenant of the Bishop of Coutances in Bedfordshire (DB Beds. 3,4;10).

CANONTEIGN. DB *Teigne*. Now in Christow parish, Wonford Hundred (19), but it lay in Teignbridge (23) in the Middle Ages (see, for example, LSR (1334) p. 60) and the sequence of Exon. suggests that this was so also in 1086. Like Sowton (3,93) this land passed to the Honour of Gloucester, see Cal. Inq. PM vol. iii no. 371, v no. 538, ix no. 428 and xvi no. 538. It was granted *c.* 1125 by Jocelyn *de Pomeria* to the Canons of the monastery of St. Mary du Val (diocese of Bayeux in the département of Calvados); see Round CDF no. 1455 p. 536 and EPNS ii p. 431. It is *Kanone Teyng* in RH i p. 90a; see RH i p. 82a.

3,98  LANGAGE. DB *Langehewis*. It is in Plympton St. Mary parish, Plympton Hundred (26), and passed to Plympton Priory; see TE p. 153, EPNS i p. 253, Oliver *Mon*. p. 135 and OJR H6 p. 297.

3,99  ANSGER. See 1,23-24 note.

POLSLOE. In Heavitree parish, Wonford Hundred (19). It formed part of the endowment of the priory there; see RH i p. 84a and OJR in TDA 44 p. 291.

Ch. 4  GLASTONBURY CHURCH. It was said to have been founded *c.* AD 63 by St. Joseph of Arimathea and was the first Christian oratory in England. Many famous names are associated with it: St. Patrick, who retired there in 433, did much rebuilding; St. Augustine in 605 'instituted it into a more regular society' (Mon. Ang. i p. 1); but it was the Abbot Dunstan who in 942 rebuilt it after the Danish attacks and brought in Benedictine monks. King Edmund (939-946) made it large grants of land. Its position in 1086 of holding, according to DB, only one manor in Devon, 5 in Dorset, 14 in Wilts., and some 34 in Somerset, as well as single ones in Berks., Hants. and Glos., was probably due to the weakness and prodigality of Thurstan its Abbot (*c.* 1077/8-1096; see Knowles HRH p. 51) who was banished in 1083 after rioting took place in the Abbey, but was restored by William Rufus on payment of a large sum of money. Glastonbury Abbey is dedicated to St. Mary.

Although in 1086 the Church held only one manor in Devon, its property had been formerly more extensive, but in 1086 was held by other churches or by laymen. King Æthelheard of Wessex had in 729 granted 10 hides in *Torric* [i.e. on the Torridge, probably Hatherleigh and Jacobstowe which were held in 1086 by Tavistock Abbey, ECDC no. 1 p. 7; see 5,4 note]. A further 5 hides on the river *Toric* were added by King Egbert in 802 (with the enfranchisement of the first 10 hides), ECDC no. 7 p. 8. A grant in 760 by Sulca, described as *ancilla Christi* ('servant of Christ'), contained 11 hides at *Culum* and 3 at *Cumbe* [Culmstock and Culm Davy, later held by Exeter Church (2,12)], ECDC no. 6 p. 8. King Æthelwulf (839-855) granted 24 hides at *Offaculum* [Uffculme, held in 1086 by Walter of Douai (23,9)], ECDC no. 11 p. 9; he also granted land at *Occemund* [Monkokehampton; see 16,17], ECDC no. 12 p. 9. His successor, Æthelbald (855-860), gave 10 hides at *Brannocminster* [Braunton, subsequently exchanged by Edgar in 973 for 7 *mansiunculae* in Somerset; see 1,5 note], ECDC nos. 13, 40 pp. 9, 12. *Brentfordlande* [Bramford Speke; see 16,123;129] and *Lim* [Uplyme, 4,1] were grants of Athelstan *comes*, ECDC nos. 27, 31, p. 11. See Finberg *Sherborne, Glastonbury and the Expansion of Wessex* and ECDC no. 12a p. 19 (= BCS no. 472 = KCD no. 1050 = Sawyer (1) no. 303).

4,1  UPLYME. DB *Lim*. A place named from the river Lyme and lying in Axminster Hundred (17); it can be identified in the Tax Return for that Hundred (xix). The Church of Glastonbury also held 'Colway' in Lyme Regis, adjacent to Uplyme but just in Dorset (DB Dorset 8,6). Uplyme had been granted by King Athelstan in 938 to Athelstan *comes* (BCS no. 728 = ECDC no. 27 p. 11 = Sawyer (1) no. 442) and by the latter to Glastonbury; see ECDC no. 31 p. 11. While BCS no. 728 refers to the 6 hides of Uplyme, the boundary clause appears to be transposed from another charter (BCS no. 995 = Sawyer (1) no. 644) and in reality refers to Lyme Regis. On this see Fox in TDA 102

4,1 (cont'd.) and on Uplyme as a whole see Mon. Ang. i p. 50 no. XCVI; GC *passim* (especially vol. iii pp. 577-591), GF pp. xxxi, 31, 51, RH i p. 93b, TE p. 151b and FA i p. 385. In this last the Glastonbury holding is described as *Manerium de Uplym*.
IT PAID TAX FOR 6 HIDES. This was the actual size of the holding at Uplyme; see the summary of Glastonbury's land in Devon in the Exon. Notes to Ch. 4.

Ch. 5   LAND OF THE CHURCH OF TAVISTOCK. The foundation of this monastery was a project of King Edgar and Ordgar, Earl of Devon, in 961, realised by the latter's son Ordwulf; the foundation charter (ECDC p. 13 no. 43 = KCD no. 629 = Mon. Ang. ii p. 495 = Sawyer (1) no. 838; see Finberg *Tavistock Abbey* pp. 278-283) was issued in the name of Æthelred II in 974. The church was dedicated to the Virgin Mary and St. Rumon(us) and held land in Dorset, Devon and Cornwall. Among its original endowments were *Tavistok* [Tavistock 5,1], *Midelton* [Milton Abbot 5,2], *Hatherleghe* [Hatherleigh 5,4], *Berlinton* [Burrington 5,8], *Leghe* [Romansleigh 5,10] in Devon, and *Dunecheni* [Downeckney in Treneglos or Downinney in Warbstow], *Chuvelin* [unidentified] and *Lankinhorn* [Linkinhorn] in Cornwall, all given by Ordwulf. His wife Ælfwynn (who probably named Alwington 15,8) gave *Hame* [Abbotsham 5,6], *Werdgete* [Worthygate 5,7], *Orlege* [Orleigh in Buckland Brewer, GR SS 4222] and *Anri* [Annery in Monkleigh, SS 4522]. Both these last may have been part of Abbotsham (5,6). Other lands granted at the foundation were *Rame* [Rame, DB Cornwall 3,3], *Savyok* [Sheviock, DB Cornwall 3,1], *Pannastan* [Panson possibly alienated as 35,4 and originally part of Werrington, see 1,50 note], *Tornebiri* [Thornbury 5,5], *Colbrook* [?Colebrook 19,23, alienated], *Leghe* [?Leigh 5,2], *Wlsitheton* [?Woolston in West Alvington 17,47, alienated] and *Clymesland* [Stoke Climsland, Cornwall]. As stated, a number of these lands had been alienated by 1086, as also was Way in Bridestowe (16,7 note) and Werrington (see 1,50 and Exon. Notes after 5,5). Moreover, in Cornwall 3,7 the Count of Mortain is said to hold 4 of Tavistock's manors wrongfully and he appears to have 'acquired' some other of its lands there (5,1,7;16) which had been held TRE by Abbot Sihtric.

The Abbey's lands are recorded in a Bull of Exemption and Confirmation of Pope Caelestinus III, dating from 1193 (Oliver *Mon.* p. 95), as *Middelton* [Milton Abbot 5,1], *Hatherlega* [Hatherleigh 5,4], *Boryngton* [Burrington 5,8], *Lega* [Romansleigh 5,10], *Abbedesham* [Abbotsham 5,6], *Weredegat* [Worthygate 5,7], *Ordlegh* [Orleigh, see above], *Auri* [Annery, see above], *Tornebury* [Thornbury 5,5], *Rauburga* (or *Roughburgh* in VE ii p. 381) ['Roborough' near Tavistock, see Finberg in TDA 77 p. 158 and 5,1 note], one house in Exeter (5,15), *Wella* [Coffinswell 5,13], *Daggecumba* [Daccombe 5,12-13 note], *Plymstok* [Plymstock 5,14], *Raddon* [Raddon 5,9], *Hundetorre* [Houndtor 5,11] and *Odatrew* [Ottery in Lamerton 28,2, a post-1086 grant; see 5,3 note]. On the Abbey's holdings see VE ii p. 381 ff., *Regesta* ii p. 133 no. 1131, Mon. Ang. ii p. 495, Oliver *Mon*. p. 95, OJR in TDA 30 p. 291, 46 p. 220 ff., Finberg *Tavistock Abbey* and in TDA 75 and in EHR lxii (1947); also Davis MCGB p. 108.

Tavistock itself lay originally in Lifton Hundred (18), but in 1116 a new ecclesiastical Hundred, incorporating the DB manors of Leigh, Liddaton, Milton Abbot and Tavistock, was created; see the Appendix.

THIS CHAPTER has the same order in the Exon. Book, except that after 5,5 (Thornbury), there occurs an entry for Werrington (178 b 2) which in 1086 was in the King's hands, alienated from the Abbey; see below and 1,50 and 5,5 notes. The Hundredal order is:

| 5,1-3 | Lifton | 5,10 | Witheridge |
|---|---|---|---|
| 5,4-5 plus Werrington | } Torrington | 5,11 | Teignton |
| | | 5,12-13 | Kerswell |
| 5,6-7 | Merton | 5,14 | Plympton |
| 5,8 | Tawton | 5,15 | Borough of Exeter |
| 5,9 | Silverton | | |

5,1   TAVISTOCK. A parish that lay in Lifton Hundred (18) in 1086, then in Tavistock ecclesiastical Hundred (see Appendix). Prior to the foundation of the Abbey, Tavistock may already have been church land if the 8 hides at *Tauistoke* granted by King Æthelbert (860-866) to Sherborne Abbey (ECDC p. 9 no. 14) lay here rather than at Tawstock (1,40). According to RH i p. 81a it had belonged to King Æthelred and was given by him to Ordwulf his Earl, and by the latter given (with the manor of *Hurdewik* [Hurdwick GR SX 4775]) to the order of the Black Monks of St. Benedict. Both this and the manor

5,1
(cont'd.) of Milton Abbot (5,2) contained a number of separate holdings specified in feudal documents. In Tavistock parish lay *Okbere* [Ogbere SX 4474], *Hauesworth'* or *Hasworthy* ['Azores', now a field name in Kilworthy farm, GR SX 4877] and *Herdewill* or *Hurdewyk* [Hurdwick]; see Fees p. 781, TE p. 153a and FA i pp. 322, 372, 404. The manor of Tavistock stretched into the adjacent Hundred of Roborough (25) where the Abbey held *Tavyton* [Taviton SX 5074], *Northlegh* [Nutley farm SX 5075], *Codelep'* [Cudliptown in Petertavy parish, SX 5279; perhaps the *Tanylā Petri* of TE p. 153a] and *Whiteham* or *Wytehm* [now represented by a road name, Whitham Park, at SX 484736 which is a recent revival, EPNS i p. 220] and possibly 'Roborough' (Ch. 5 note); see FA i pp. 340, 402, 404 and TE p. 153a. Crebor in Tavistock was also held by the Abbot (5,4 note) and *Morwall Barton* [Morwell SX 4470] with *Morelham* [Morwellham SX 4469], both in Tavistock Hamlets parish; see VE ii p. 381.
A MILL WHICH SERVES THE COURT. *curia* regularly means the same as *aula* 'hall', that is, the lord's house. Exon. is more specific in stating that the mill served the Abbey — that is, Tavistock manor. Cf. 23,22 'a mill in lordship which renders service' (Exon. 'a mill which only serves his house'). See 1,7 note on mills.
OF THIS MANOR'S LAND .... 3 PARTS OF 1 VIRGATE. It seems likely that the '3 parts' is a scribal error in Exon. (copied by DB) for '2 parts', i.e. two-thirds of a virgate: Exon. states that the men-at-arms hold 1½ hides, and the various holdings (see Details Table) would only total this if Ralph's holding were two-thirds of a virgate. '3 parts of 1 virgate' would normally mean ¾ virgate. According to OJR in TDA 27 p. 192 note 48 the fraction of one third of a furlong ('ferling'), by which the sum of the details exceeds the total assessment, was merely disregarded.
ERMENALD. OG; see Förstemann 483 and Forssner p. 82. Probably the same man as the Ermenhald who holds six out of the seven manors belonging to Tavistock Church in DB Cornwall.
ERMENALD .... RALPH .... HUGH. For the possible identification of these subtenancies with the lands given above, see VCH pp. 429–430 and Finberg *Tavistock Abbey* pp. 13-14.
ANOTHER RALPH. Ralph of Tilly (see Details Table): Exon. *Radulfus detilio*. There are several places in France whose names derive from Latin *tilius* 'lime-tree'; see OEB p. 115.
4 PLOUGHS. In the MS *iiii car* probably corrected from *iii*, which is interesting because in Exon. 3 ploughs and 9 oxen are detailed: the Exchequer scribe may have decided that after all 9 oxen were too many to discount (see 3,44 note).

5,2 MILTON (ABBOT). A parish, first in Lifton Hundred (18), later in Tavistock Hundred. Apart from Leigh and Liddaton (see below), specifically mentioned by DB, other members of this manor (all in Milton Abbot parish unless otherwise stated) were probably (including *Middelton* itself), *Childeton'* [Chillaton parish GR SX 4381], *Wyk'* [Week in Chillaton, SX 4581], *Foghauer* or *Froggaanger* [Foghanger SX 4278], *Poghelippe* [Poflet SX 4379], *Hundcot* [Youngcott SX 4076] and *Quedre* [Quither SX 4481]; see Fees p. 781, FA i pp. 322, 372, 384, 404.
THE ABBOT HOLDS. Or possibly 'the Abbey holds', as *abb'* can abbreviate both *abbas* and *abbatia*, as well as occasionally *abbatissa* 'Abbess'. Exon. has *abbas* in full; however, it regularly has 'Abbot' for DB's 'Abbey' or 'Church' (see, for example, Exon. Notes to Chs. 4-7).
LEIGH. Now Leigh Barton in Milton Abbot parish. It is *Leghz Barton* in VE ii p. 381, *Leigh Champeaus* in FA i p. 372, *Legh'* held by Alice *de Campell'* from the Abbey in Fees p. 781; see EPNS i p. 216 and TE p. 153a.
LIDDATON. DB *Liteltone* as if from OE *litel* and *tun* 'small farm', although no place of that name is known in the locality. The Exon. form is *Lideltona*, as for 5,3 Liddaton of which this holding was no doubt a part. Although the place-name is written over an erasure in Exon. (like all of the second half of this entry) the *d* is clear enough. The Exon. form is more likely to be correct, because in several other cases where there is a discrepancy of a letter or two between the Exon. and the Exchequer place-name form, the modern name — when the place can be identified — is nearer to the Exon. than to the Exchequer form; see 16,42 note.

5,3 LIDDATON. In Brentor parish, first in Lifton Hundred (18), later (like 5,1-2) in Tavistock Hundred. Liddaton is probably derived from the river Lyd. It is *West Lidethon'* in Fees p. 781; see FA i pp. 372, 404 and OJR in TDA 46 p. 235. The later addition of Ottery (28,2 and Ch. 5 notes) gave the great rock of Brentor itself to Tavistock, and on this was reared the Church of St. Michael; see Finberg *Tavistock Abbey* p. 16.

| | |
|---|---|
| 5,3 (cont'd.) | VALUE NOW 30[s]. In the MS *solid(os)* is omitted, no doubt because of lack of space, as also in 15,11. |
| 5,4 | HATHERLEIGH. A parish in (Black) Torrington Hundred (11); it is identifiable in the Tax Return for Torrington Hundred (iii). This place is *Hatherle* in FA i p. 327; see TE p. 153a and 5,5 note. Fees p. 781 records the Abbot of Tavistock as holding various members of this manor (in Hatherleigh parish unless stated to the contrary) at *Branford'* [Broomford in Jacobstowe, GR SS 5701]; *Boleworth'* (or *Poleworthy* or *Estpoleworth[y]* in FA i pp. 357, 409) that is a part of Pulworthy SS 5104, see 16,19 note; *Langebere* [Langabeare SS 5501]; *Mannesford'* [Marshford SS 5301], *Fislegh'* [Fishleigh SS 5505] and *Hanebergh'* [Hannaborough SS 5202]. This last is held by the Abbot himself together with *Creubere* [Crebor SX 4572 in Tavistock parish]. *Carswill* [Kerswell SS 5203] was also held by the Abbot in FA i p. 409, see OJR H5 pp. 195, 217. For Jacobstowe [SS 5801], also part of this holding, see Ch. 4 note and EPNS i p. 151. |
| 5,5 | THORNBURY. A parish in (Black) Torrington Hundred (11). William *le Cornu* holds in *Thornbir'* of the Abbot of Tavistock in Fees p. 781; see FA i pp. 327, 407 and OJR H5 p. 196. |
| | FOLLOWING THIS ENTRY, Exon. includes an additional one for *Olwritona* (see Exon. Notes). This refers to Werrington (including the parishes of North Petherwin and St. Giles on the Heath) mentioned in Exchequer DB only at 1,50 (see note). It had belonged to Tavistock and was subsequently restored; see Exon. Notes. In FA i p. 327 the Abbot holds *Wolverinton* and *Hatherle* [Hatherleigh 5,4 note] in (Black) Torrington Hundred (11); see TE p. 153a. |
| 5,6 | ABBOTSHAM. DB *Hame*. A parish in Shebbear Hundred (4). It is *Abedesham* in FA i p. 329; see TE p. 153a and OJR H10 p. 577. The holding possibly included Orleigh and Annery (Ch. 5 note). |
| 5,7 | WORTHYGATE. In Parkham parish, Shebbear Hundred (4); see EPNS i p. 104. It is *Werelgete* in the foundation deed, *Werodeget* in the exemption of 1193 (Ch. 5 note); see OJR in DCNQ 10 p. 311 and H10 pp. 539, 578. |
| 5,8 | BURRINGTON. DB *Bernintone*, Exon. *Bernintona* (not *Bernurtona* as Ellis prints). It is a parish in (North) Tawton Hundred (12), and identifiable in the Tawton Hundred Tax Return (ix). The Abbot holds *Buringtune* in RH i p. 75b; see TE p. 153a and FA i pp. 340, 370. Included in the holding was *Northecoth'* [Northcote manor GR SS 6218], Fees p. 780 (see FA i p. 370) and 'Roborough' [?part of Roborough parish in Fremington Hundred, adjacent to Burrington]; see Finberg in DCNQ 23 p. 241. |
| | 4 BOORS. Latin *buri* from OE *(ge)bur*; the plural is also found as *burs* in DB (e.g. Berks. 1,31; Hants. 1,10). *Buri* are found in several counties in DB, including Worcs., Herefords., Oxfords., Bucks. and Berks., though not in any great number except on individual estates (e.g. 17 *buri* in Bampton, Oxfords. 1,6). This is the only occurrence of boors in Devon. Although in DB here they are listed separately from the villagers and smallholders and their ploughs, in Exon. they form part of the list of 'villagers' and so may have shared their ploughs (see Exon. Notes 1,26); in other DB counties, however (e.g. Herefords., Oxfords.), they do appear to have had a share in the ploughs. Boors were not exactly the same as the *geburs* of pre-Conquest documents who were of higher standing, but are equated on three occasions in DB with *coliberti* 'freedmen' (see 1,50 note). For the rights and dues of the Anglo-Saxon *(ge)bur*, see *Rectitudines* p. 446. See also DB Oxfords. 1,6 note, Maitland DBB pp. 36–37, 328–330 and Finberg *Tavistock Abbey* pp. 38, 65. |
| 5,9 | WILLIAM THE USHER. See 51,2 note. |
| | RADDON. In Thorverton parish, Hayridge Hundred (15). It is now called Raddon Court, but was formerly 'East' Raddon to distinguish it from West Raddon (15,5. 24,4). It is *Raddon* in the exemption of 1193, see Ch. 5 note. William the Usher holds another part in chief, 51,6. |
| 5,10 | ROMANSLEIGH. DB *Liege*, now the parish of Romansleigh in Witheridge Hundred (7). It is so called from the dedication of the church to St. Rumonus, the joint dedicatee of Tavistock Church; see Ch. 5 note and EPNS ii p. 391. In Fees p. 781 *Romundeylegh'* is held from the Abbot of Tavistock; see Fees p. 759, FA i pp. 344, 363, 420. The DB holding will also have included *Wodham* [Odham GR SS 7419], Fees p. 781, FA i p. 363, and *Nithercote* [?Narracott in Meshaw, SS 7619], FA i p. 363. |
| | LAND FOR 1 PLOUGH. In the MS the *i* is in dark ink and written rather close to the *ē* which is in paler ink than the *Tra* and *car̄*. There is no sign of erasure or scraping of the parchment, however. Exon. has 10 ploughs. |

| | |
|---|---|
| 5,11 | HOUNDTOR. In Manaton parish, Teignbridge Hundred (23). It is *Hundetorre* in Fees p. 781, held of the Abbot; see FA i p. 339. |
| | ABBOT SIHTRIC. See Exon. Notes to 5,8. |
| 5,12-13 | DENBURY. COFFINSWELL. Denbury is in Torbryan parish, Coffinswell is itself a parish, both lying in Haytor Hundred (29). Their combined lordship (½ hide and ½ virgate) does not fully account for the 1 hide allowed to the Abbot in Kerswell (Haytor) Hundred (Tax Return xxv). The Abbot holds *Devenebyr'* in Fees p. 769; see *Regesta* ii no. 633, TE p. 153a and FA i p. 317. Coffinswell (DB *Welles*) included *Daccumb'* [Daccombe GR SX 9068], held by the Abbot of Torre from the Abbot of Tavistock in Fees p. 781; see Fees p. 768, TE p. 153a and VE ii p. 361. Coffinswell is *Wille Coffin* in FA i p. 317 and Daccombe is *Est Daccumb* in FA i p. 322; see FA i p. 349 and W. Keble Martin in TDA 87. |
| 5,12 | ARCHBISHOP ALDRED. He was Abbot of Tavistock 1027-1042/3 (see Finberg *Tavistock Abbey* p. 4), then Bishop of Worcester 1047-1062. He held that see with Hereford 1056-1060 and with the Archbishopric of York from 1061-1062. He held York alone from 1062 until his death in 1069. He crowned William the Conqueror and Queen Matilda. |
| 5,14 | PLYMSTOCK. A parish in Plympton Hundred (26). It is held as *Plympstok'* in RH i p. 77a; see TE p. 153a, FA i p. 355 and OJR H6 pp. 261, 284. |
| | 3 PLOUGHS. Originally written *iiii*, but the first *i* has been erased to make *iii*, though it is still visible, especially in the facsimile; cf. 15,62 note. |
| 5,15 | HOUSE WHICH HE HAD IN PLEDGE FROM A BURGESS. Cf. 23,27 where Walscin/ Walter of Douai also has a house in pledge from a burgess. |
| Ch. 6 | BUCKFAST ABBEY. In Buckfastleigh parish. There is no record of its foundation or endowment and no certainty that it was originally a Celtic monastery; see Knowles MRH p. 61. It must have existed before the time of Canute (1015-1036) who gave it some of its lands; see Oliver *Mon.* p. 371 and OJR in TDA 30 p. 292. It was probably housed with Benedictine monks, but in 1136/1137 it was refounded for Cistercian monks from Savigny (Knowles MRH p. 105, J. B. Rowe in TDA 8, *Regesta* iii p. 294 no. 800, Davis MCGB p. 12 and 6,1-2 note). The Church benefited from a number of grants after 1086, including Englebourne (16,175 note), South Holne (1,34 note) and probably Wallaford (20,13 note). Its holdings at the Dissolution are given in VE ii pp. 368-370. |
| | THE EXON. ORDER of this chapter differs slightly from that of Exchequer DB. The probable Hundredal arrangement is: |

| | | | | |
|---|---|---|---|---|
| | 6,1-2 | Merton | 6,6 | ?Teignton |
| | 6,3 | Tawton | 6,7-8 | *Alleriga* |
| | 6,4 | Crediton | 6,13;9-12 | Diptford |
| | 6,5 | Exminster | | |

| | |
|---|---|
| 6,1-2 | PETROCKSTOWE. ASH. Petrockstowe is a parish in Shebbear Hundred (4) and its lordship, combined with that of Ash, accounts for the Abbot's lordship total in Merton (Shebbear) Hundred (v). The identity of Ash is uncertain. It is here assumed to be Ash in Petrockstowe, but there is at least one other 'Ash' in this Hundred, in Frithelstock parish; see EPNS i p. 92. *Petrochstona* and *Achaia* were restored to the Abbot of Savigny, mother house of Buckfast, in 1150 by a charter of Robert, Bishop of Exeter; see Round CDF p. 296 no. 816. *Patrickestowe* is held by the Abbot of Buckfast in RH i p. 94a; see RH i p. 78a and VE ii pp. 368-370. |
| 6,2 | THE CHURCH ITSELF HOLDS. Repeated at the beginning of 6,2-12 inclusive. |
| 6,3 | ZEAL MONACHORUM. DB *Limet*. A parish in (North) Tawton Hundred (12). The 1 virgate of lordship land here is not noticed in the Tax Return for Tawton Hundred (ix), although 1 virgate is not accounted for in Diptford (Stanborough) Hundred (xxvi) where the Abbey itself is situated. Outlying manors of churches are sometimes taxed with the chief manor elsewhere in the south-west counties (see, e.g., Dorset 13,6;8 note). There is no doubt as to the identity. The holding was granted by King Canute (ECDC p. 14 no. 57) and is *Sele Mo(n)aco(rum)* in RH i p. 75b; see TE pp. 146a, 153a, FA i p. 373, Oliver *Mon.* p. 374, OJR in TDA 29 p. 248, VCH p. 432 note 8, EPNS ii p. 375 and 6,4 note. |
| 6,4 | DOWN (ST. MARY). Now a parish in (North) Tawton Hundred (12), but the ½ hide lordship is counted in the Tax Return for Crediton (viii). It is *Donne* held by the Abbot of Buckfast in TE p. 144a, *Dymm'* in TE p. 153a. In VE ii pp. 368-370 *Sele* (see 6,3) and *Downe* are connected; see OJR in TDA 33 p. 582. |
| 6,5 | TRUSHAM. A parish in Exminster Hundred (24), the Abbot's 1 virgate of lordship being mentioned in that Hundred's Tax Return (xxiii); see TE p. 153a. |

6,6 ASHTON. DB *Aiserstone* recognised as Ashton parish in Exminster Hundred (24) by EPNS ii p. 487. It is also *Essestone* (44,1) and *Aysheriston* in LSR (1332) p. 57. It is unlikely to be Sherberton in Widecombe in the Moor (DG) or 'Sherwood' in Ashburton (VCH p. 433 note 1 and OJR in TDA 29 p. 228 note 8, 34 p. 292, Whale in TDA 35 p. 699). If the identification is correct, the land may have paid tax in Teignton Hundred. Although the 1½ furlongs ('ferlings') 3 acres of the DB holding are not said to be in lordship, they correspond to the 1½ furlongs ('ferlings') lordship of the Tax Return (xxiv) which are otherwise not accounted for. It may even have lain in that Hundred in 1086 since it is adjacent to the boundary of the two Hundreds.
TAX FOR 1½ FURLONGS AND 3 ACRES. This is the only occurrence in Devon of the geld-acre, which nevertheless is found often in DB Cornwall (though probably rated differently from here; see Cornwall 1,1 notes) and very occasionally in Somerset, Wiltshire and Dorset. It would seem from this entry that 3 acres formed less than ½ furlong ('ferling'), which would fit in with a 120-acre hide (7½ acres would make a 'ferling', with 16 'ferlings' to a hide), but not with a 48-acre hide (there 3 acres would form a 'ferling' and one would have expected the scribe then to have written 2½ 'ferlings' for the tax), nor with a 40-acre (where 2½ acres form a 'ferling'). See 1,4 note on the possibility of smaller hides in the south-west.
1 VILLAGER PAYS 40d. This seems to be an example of the villager 'farming' a manor, that is, holding it at a revenue or for a money rent from the tenant-in-chief; see second note under 1,5. The fact that no 'value' is given for the manor supports this view, though there are cases where it is stated that villagers pay so much and yet the manor has a present value (e.g. DB Dorset 1,23). In several entries it is expressly said that the villagers hold land at a revenue, e.g. 25,28 and 26,1 (see Exon. Notes to these) and in Middlesex 3,17 and in Kent 5,154 [where the translation should read '3 villagers now hold it at a revenue, and pay 20s. The value was always as much']. Cf. Dorset 47,7 and note. Moreover, there are some seven other cases in Devon where villagers make payments which appear to take the place of the value statement: 21,11 (see note). 28,14. 29,7;10. 34,14 (see note). 36,11 and 49,4. See also Exon. Notes 1,32 (last note). In 49,4 the payment is made to the tenant-in-chief according to Exon. In 34,11 and 36,9 it is the salt-workers' payments which appear to form the value of these manors, as also in Dorset 12,13. Lennard p. 371 states that in more than 30 entries in 11 counties in DB villagers are recorded as making payments and that nearly half these are in Devon and Kent. See Hoyt's article in *Speculum* xxx (1955).

6,7-8 '(ABBOTS) ASH'. HEATHFIELD. Heathfield is in Aveton Gifford parish, Ermington Hundred (27). The Tax Return for *Alleriga* (Ermington) Hundred (xxx) records 1½ hides of lordship for the Abbot which is not entirely accounted for by the lordship of these two holdings (1½ virgates and ½ hide). In Fees p. 771 the Abbot of Buckfast holds *Hethfeld'tone, Battekesbergh'* [Battisborough GR SX 5948, see 39,14 note], and *Esse*. In FA i p. 353 these are *Hethfeld, Battokesburgh* and *Esse Abbatis*; see TE p. 153a, RH i pp. 69a, 90b. *Esse* (which is *Esse Abbot* in 1384 (Reichel and Mugford), *Esse Abbatis* in LSR (1334) p. 64) was a tithing of Ermington Hundred and has not been located. It is unlikely to be 'Aish' in South Brent, Stanborough Hundred, if that place exists (OJR in TDA 34 p. 292), nor Ashford in Aveton Gifford (VCH), since the latter appears as *Ayshford* in 1339 (EPNS i p. 266) and is clearly a separate place from 'Abbots Ash'. It possibly lay in Holbeton parish, Ermington Hundred, since a Stephen *de Esse* holds in Battisborough in that parish in LSR (1332) p. 97. There is also an Ashridge in Modbury parish.

6,8 HEATHFIELD. HETFELD in the MS and Farley; in the facsimile the second *E* resembles an *O*, probably due to a combination of a thin middle cross-line of the *E* and the rubrication. See 1,63 note.
VALUE 40s .... 30s. There is no reason, obvious from the Exon. MS, why the Exchequer scribe omitted this important information. The whole of the value statement is also omitted in 24,12 and 45,2, although entered clearly in Exon. at the same time as the rest of the entry.

6,9 NORTON. In Churchstow parish, Stanborough Hundred (28). Its lordship needs to be included in the total of the lordship land recorded for the Abbot in Diptford (Stanborough) Hundred Tax Return (xxvi). The Abbot of Buckfast holds *Northon'* in TE p. 153a and the land also appears to be represented by *Churechestowe* [Churchstow GR SX 7145], held with *Bufestre* and *Brenth'* (6,11-13) in Fees p. 767; see TE p. 153a, VE ii pp. 368-70 and RH i p. 91b. Kingsbridge [SX 7344], a 'new borough' in RH i p. 79

|       | (*Kyngesbrigg* in VE ii p. 369), was also in this holding; see OJR in TDA 36 p. 372. |
|---|---|
| 6,10 | CHARFORD. In South Brent parish, Stanborough Hundred (28); identifiable in the Tax Return for Diptford (xxvi). It does not appear in later fee lists; see EPNS i p. 290. |
| 6,11-12 | (SOUTH) BRENT. A parish in Stanborough Hundred (28); 'South' to distinguish it from an unlocated *Overa Brenta* 'Upper Brent' (EPNS i p. 290) or, more likely, from Brentor (5,3 note) which is *Brenta* in 1238, *Northbrienta* in 1322 (EPNS i p. 213). In Fees p. 767 the Abbot holds *Brenth'*; see RH i pp. 79b, 91b. *Palston* [Palstone GR SX 7060], probably a subdivision, is mentioned in VE ii p. 370. |
| 6,13 | BUCKFAST. In Buckfastleigh parish, Stanborough Hundred (28). It is *Bufestre* in Fees p. 767 (see RH i pp. 79b, 91b) and included *Buckefastlegh cum Kylbury* in VE ii p. 368 [Buckfastleigh GR SX 7366 and Kilbury SX 749658; see 1,23 note]. |
|       | HEAD OF THE ABBEY. *caput*; the chief manor and head of the Abbey's fief. Cf. DB Dorset 12,2 where Milton Abbas is the head of (Milton) Abbey. |
|       | IT HAS NEVER PAID TAX. With the exception of three of the King's manors (1,7;11;14) and Walter of Douai's manor of Bampton (23,5) which had been held by King Edward, this manor is the only one mentioned in DB Devon as never having paid tax. |
|       | A SMITH AND 10 SLAVES WITH 2 PLOUGHS. It would appear that the slaves definitely had a share in the ploughs here; Exon. states the same with 'The Abbot has 1 smith and 10 slaves who have 2 ploughs' (not the usual formula giving the ploughs (and land) of the 'villagers' before the list of them). See 1,3 note on slaves and cf. notes to 16,6 and 28,16. A smith (*faber*) is also recorded for 19,35, but he may not have had a share in the ploughs (see Exon. Notes 19,35). See also 1,27 note on smiths. |
| Ch. 7 | HORTON ABBEY. In Dorset. It was founded as a nunnery *c.* 961 by Ordgar and his son Ordwulf (see Ch. 5 note), but was refounded *c.* 1050 as an Abbey of monks, later still becoming a Priory dependent on Sherborne; see Knowles in MRH p. 68 and in HRH p. 53, OJR in TDA 30 p. 292, Finberg in EHR lviii (1943) p. 195 and VCH Dorset ii p. 71 ff. |
| 7,1 | LITTLEHAM. A parish in (East) Budleigh Hundred (14). *Lytlanhamme*, ½ *mansa*, was granted by Edward the Confessor to Ordgar *minister* in 1042 (ECDC p. 14 no. 59 = KCD no. 1332 = Sawyer (1) no. 998). Ordgar gave it to Horton Abbey whence it came under the jurisdiction of Sherborne whose Abbot held *Littleham* in Fees p. 764; see RH i pp. 66a, 92b, TE p. 151b, Cal. Inq. PM vol. xv no. 746, FA i p. 365 and OJR in TDA 35 p. 298. |
|       | IN LORDSHIP 1 VIRGATE. As there is only one other occurrence of lordship land being given in Devon DB (2,2; see note), the Exchequer scribe may have mistakenly added the virgate in place of the lordship plough, which latter he regularly includes but omits here for no apparent reason (but cf. 1,34 note). |
| 7,2 | ABBOTSKERSWELL. A parish in Haytor Hundred (29); identifiable in the Tax Return for Kerswell (Haytor) Hundred (xxv). In Fees p. 769 the Abbot of Sherborne holds *Kareswill'*. It is *Karswill Abbatis* in FA i p. 317; see TE pp. 149b, 151b. In a grant by King Eadwig in 956 to the lady Æthelhilda (ECDC no. 35 p. 12 = BCS no. 952 = Sawyer (1) no. 601), 15½ *mansae* were given at *Iplanpen* [Ipplepen 33,1], *Doddintune* [Dainton in Ipplepen, possibly part of 33,1] and *Caerswylle*. The vill that became Abbotskerswell (as well as Kingskerswell 1,12) will probably have been included in this grant. |
|       | LAND FOR 8 PLOUGHS. There is a gap of about 4 letters' width in the MS before this statement, due to a hole in the parchment which has been very neatly filled in. Farley prints a small gap, though he leaves no gap where there is a hole in the parchment in 16,144, perhaps because it is smaller (see note). |
| 7,3-4 | SEATON. BEER. Parishes in Colyton Hundred (22), their lordship being accounted for in the Colyton Hundred Tax Return (xx). For Seaton, DB *Flueta*, see EPNS ii p. 629. One *mansa* at *Fleote* (probably covering both Seaton and Beer ½ hide each) was granted by King Æthelred II in 1005 to his minister Eadsige (ECDC p. 13 no. 48 = KCD no. 1301 = Sawyer (1) no. 910); see RH i p. 68b, TE p. 151b and OJR in TDA 30 p. 292, H7 p. 336. |
| 7,4 | 1 COW. Cows are seldom mentioned in the Exon. for Devon; as they never occur in the same list as *animalia*, it is likely that the latter term often included cows (see 1,3 note on cattle). The fact that frequently, both in Devon and in other south-west counties, only 1 cow at a time is mentioned, may indicate that it was kept to supply milk only for the lord of the manor; Round in VCH Somerset i p. 424. |
|       | FROM THIS MANOR .... COUNT OF MORTAIN. This statement was obviously added after the entry was completed, as it avoids the "Value 60s" of the main manor, which in |

| | |
|---|---|
| 7,4 (cont'd.) | itself is written on a half-line to save space. The ink colour is the same as for the rest of the entry, so it was probably an early addition. The closeness of the statement to Ch. 8 cannot be used as proof it was added later, because there is little space left between most of Chs. 7-13. In Exon. this statement also occurs at the end of the entry.<br>4 SALT-HOUSES .... TAKEN AWAY. The salt-houses were not physically removed, but the salt and the profits of the salt-houses were enjoyed by Drogo or the Count as part of one of their manors, rather than by the Abbot. As the only holding of Drogo from the Count in Colyton Hundred ('Womberford', 15,24, lost in Cotleigh parish) is not near Beer and has no reference to salt, the manor in question was probably Honiton (15,23), further away but with 2 salt-workers recorded. As Honiton itself is too far inland to have had salt-workings within its boundaries, these were probably in a detached area near Beer and Seaton on the coast or on the tidal part of the river Axe. Drogo could easily then have combined these salt-workings of his with the adjacent ones of the Abbot at Beer. See 1,23 note on salt-houses. |
| Chs. 8-13a | IN THE EXON. BOOK these chapters are grouped under the heading 'Lands of the Churches which have been given to the Saints in Alms'. Their order and presumed Hundreds are: |

|   |   |   |   |
|---|---|---|---|
| 12,1 | Merton | 9,1 | Silverton |
| 13,1. 8,1 | Tawton | 10,1 | Ottery St. Mary |
| 13a,2-3;1 | South Molton and Braunton | 10,2. 11,3;2 | Axminster |
| 11,1 | Budleigh | 9,2 | Borough of Exeter |

| | |
|---|---|
| Ch. 8 | CRANBORNE CHURCH. In Dorset. Dedicated to St. Mary (so DB Dorset Ch. 10 and Wiltshire Ch. 11), it was founded c. 980. Most of the community moved to Tewkesbury in 1102 whereupon Cranborne became a cell of the latter. See Mon. Ang. iv p. 465 and VCH Dorset ii pp. 70-71. |
| 8,1 | LOOSEBEARE. In Zeal Monachorum parish, (North) Tawton Hundred (12). The Abbot of Cranborne is allowed ½ virgate lordship in the Tax Return for Tawton Hundred (ix); see 1,64 note. |
| Ch. 9 | CHURCH OF BATTLE. DB de Labatailge (from OFr la batail(g)e, Mod.Fr la bataille 'battle'), Exon. de Proelio (from Latin proelium 'battle') and bataillię (genitive). It is sometimes styled Monasterium de Bello (Latin bellum 'war') in later documents. This Benedictine Abbey, dedicated to St. Martin, was founded in 1067 as the result of a vow made by William the Conqueror before the Battle of Hastings; it was colonised from the Abbey of Marmoutier, France (see VCH Sussex ii pp. 52-56). King William granted St. Olaf's Church in Exeter to Battle Abbey (9,2) and on the lands adjoining this church was built c. 1087 (Knowles MRH p. 65) a cell dedicated to St. Nicholas, which was dependent on Battle 'to which were removed the religious who had previously been attached to the Church of Cullompton' (Mon. Ang. iii p. 375).<br>The Church of Battle also held land at Kenbury in Exminster (1,4 note), at Sherford (1,34) and Pinhoe (1,52). In later documents it is sometimes Battle Abbey, sometimes St. Nicholas' Priory, that holds all these lands; in the Valor Ecclesiasticus (VE) of Henry VIII's reign St. Nicholas' Priory holds Brodeham [Bradham in Withycombe Raleigh, a grant of King John, 1,9 note], Bowlegh, Columpton [for both, see 9,1 note] and Sherford [1,34]. A cartulary for the Priory of St. Nicholas survives; see Davis MCGB p. 45.<br>THE HEADING IN THE MS is in red lower-case letters, not the usual capitals, as the scribe of the text did not leave sufficient room between Chs. 8-9 for the rubricator to use capitals.<br>FOR THE POSITION of this Chapter in Exon., see Chs. 8-13a note. |
| 9,1 | CULLOMPTON. It lay in Hayridge Hundred (15) and can be accounted for in the Tax Return for Silverton (Hayridge) Hundred (xiii). It is mentioned in a foundation grant (Regesta i p. 16 no. 62) which is suspect in other ways, but probably contains a true record of the church's actual holdings. Cullompton contained a number of sub-manors including Upton [ST 0306], Colbrook [ST 0006], Weaver [ST 0404] and 'Ash', and was also connected with Henland [in Kentisbeare ST 0807] and Bowley [in Cadbury SS 9004, see 21,8 note]. The Chronicon Monasterii de Bello pp. 31-33 (see Lennard p. 397) records that these estates were transferred by Battle Abbey to 'the new priory of St. Nicholas in Exeter'. Hence in Fees p. 1263 the Prior of St. Nicholas holds the church of Colinthon' and the vill of Uppeton' de veteri conquestu Willelmi Bastardi ("from the ancient conquest by William the Bastard"). In Fees p. 96 the Monks of Battle hold Bogeleg' with appurtenances and the church of Culumt' with appurtenances; see FA i p. 368, TE p. 152a, Regesta i p. 90 (no. 348a), ii p. 401 (no. 348a) and p. 385 |

9 - 10

|       | (no. 1896), iii p. 18 (no. 51), Oliver *Mon.* pp. 113-116, VE ii p. 313 and OJR in TDA 36 p. 360 and in TDA 42 pp. 220, 233. For another part of Cullompton, see 1,7 note. |
|-------|-----|
| 9,2   | CHURCH OF ST. OLAF. Also called St. Olave. St. Olaf was a half-brother of King Canute (1016-1035) and was slain in 1030; see Oliver *Mon.* pp. 113-116 and Fees p. 96. St. Nicholas' Priory was built on the lands adjoining St. Olaf's Church; see Ch. 9 note. See 2,1 note on the other churches in Exeter as recorded in DB Devon. |
|       | 7 HOUSES WHICH PAID 4s 8d. Here *redd'* abbreviates the past *reddebant* (as in Exon. in full), despite the lack of the phrase *T.R.E.*; see second note under 1,7. See also C 1 note on the customary due of 8d for a house in Exeter. |
| Ch. 10 | ST. MARY'S OF ROUEN. This is the Cathedral Church of Rouen for secular canons (Round CDF p. 1). Rouen is in the département of Seine-Maritime in France. For its complicated early history, see Mon. Ang. vi p. 1118. The Church was completed in 1063 and dedicated by Archbishop Maurilius (of Rouen); Orderic Vitalis ii pp. 373, 169, 371. This is its only holding recorded in DB. |
|       | Ellis *Introduction* i p. 481 note 6 errs in stating that this church is the Abbey of St. Mary de Prè at Rouen. |
|       | FOR THE POSITION OF THIS CHAPTER in Exon., see Chs. 8-13a note. |
| 10,1  | IN THE LEFT MARGIN beside this entry there is a O mark, apparently a checking sign contemporary with, or not much later than, DB. Similar marks appear beside other *Otri* entries (19,27;34. 23,18;21. 34,24;32;45;47;50, but see notes to 19,27;42-43 and 23,18). No further attention is drawn in these Notes to these marks. Farley only prints these O marks beside 19,27;34;42-43. See 1,65 note for similar O signs beside *Aisse*'s and 34,1 note for a similar one beside *Wiche* and cf. 16,58 note. To avoid confusion with the transposition signs of the DB scribe, these checking marks have not been entered in the margin of the translation in this edition. |
|       | OTTERY (ST. MARY). This is the sole manor in the ecclesiastical Hundred of Ottery St. Mary (21). It was granted in 1061 by Edward the Confessor to St. Mary's of Rouen as *Otregia* (KCD no. 810 = ECDC no. 69 p. 15 = Sawyer (1) no. 1033). The text of the grant, including bounds, is in TDA 71 pp. 201-220. 2 *cassati* at *Otheri* had earlier been granted (in 963) by King Eadgar to Wolfhelm *minister* (BCS no. 1104 = ECDC no. 39 p. 12 = Sawyer (1) no. 721). The 5 hides lordship of the DB holding are noted in the Tax Return (xviii); see Fees p. 763, Round CDF no. 1 p. 1 and Oliver *Mon.* p. 259 ff. |
|       | 5 PIGMEN WHO PAY 30s AND 15d. See notes to 1,26 and 1,6. |
|       | PASTURE, 8 HIDES. This entry and 23,21 are the only ones in Devon where pasture is measured in hides (but see DB Wilts. 1,11). According to VCH p. 386 this is the areal hide of 256 acres, not the geld hide, but this would make the pastureland 2,048 acres in extent, two-thirds of the extent of Ottery St. Mary. See 15,79 note on the measurement of pasture in virgates. Elsewhere in Devon, pasture is measured in leagues and furlongs and once in perches (see 16,172 note). Cf. 10,2 note. |
|       | A GARDEN. See 3,45 note. |
|       | 1 SALT-HOUSE WHICH PAYS 30d, IN SIDMOUTH. The word order of this sentence is ambiguous: it is not clear whether the salt-house pays the 30d into (the revenue of) Sidmouth, or whether the salt-house was actually in Sidmouth and the *redd' xxx denar'* interrupts the phrase *i salina in Sedemude*. The Exon. is equally ambiguous, though the use of the accusative *in terram* suggests the first meaning; however, the Exon. complicates the issue by appearing to state that the 30d was paid by both the garden and the salt-house (see Exon. Notes). However, the word order aside, it is likely that, as Ottery St. Mary is some distance from the coast, the salt-house was actually in Sidmouth. See 1,23 note on salt-houses and cf. 7,4 note. |
|       | SIDMOUTH, ST. MICHAEL'S LAND. Sidmouth was a dependency of Otterton which was held by the Church of Mont St. Michel; see 11,1 note. There was also a priory at Sidmouth which was a cell of Mont St. Michel, though this priory was often regarded as part of Otterton Priory; Mon. Ang. vi p. 1035. But see Oliver *Mon.* p. 248. |
| 10,2  | RAWRIDGE. In Upottery parish, Axminster Hundred (17); the lordship land can be identified in the Tax Return for Axminster Hundred (xix). It is held by the canons of the college of Ottery St. Mary in Cal. Inq. PM vol. xvi no. 1027; see vol. vi no. 753. These 3 hides may well be the same that were granted as 3 *mansiones* in *Upotri* by the Ealdorman Æthelmaer (in 1005) with other properties to Æthelweard, his son-in-law, in exchange for Eynsham (in Oxfordshire); see ECDC p. 13 no. 47 = KCD no. 714 = Sawyer (1) no. 911; also Round CDF p. 17 no. 63. See 1,11 for details of a customary due owing from this manor to the King's manor of Axminster. |

10,2 WOODLAND, ½ HIDE. Woodland is also, rather unusually, measured in hides in 34,51,
(cont'd.) the manor of Smallridge, which is in the same Hundred as Rawridge here, though seven
miles away. Hides are also used to measure woodland in DB Beds. 32,14 and Essex 24,1-2.
Cf. 10,1 note on pasture being measured in hides. See also 15,79 on the use of virgates to
measure both woodland and pasture and cf. 47,6 note on the *ferling* of underwood.
ROUEN PENCE. According to VCH p. 435 note 6 'Rouen pence were, at a later date,
worth half the value of English pence'; no dates or references are given, however.

Ch. 11 MONT ST. MICHEL. An Abbey for Benedictine monks situated on a rocky island,
accessible on foot at low-tide, now connected by a permanent causeway, lying just off
the coast of Normandy, near Avranches (département of Manche) in whose diocese it
lay. The Abbey was also called *in periculo maris* ('in peril of the sea'). It had several cells
in England, including St. Michael's Mount in Cornwall; see notes to 10,1 (Sidmouth) and
11,1 (Otterton).
FOR THE POSITION OF THESE HOLDINGS in Exon., see Chs. 8-13a note.

11,1 OTTERTON. In (East) Budleigh Hundred (14); it is identifiable in the Tax Return for
that Hundred (xvi) and was also known, in the Middle Ages, as *Ottery Monachorum*
(RH i p. 66b); see EPNS ii p. 593. The land was granted to the Abbey of Mont St. Michel
by the Conqueror, and a dependent priory was established here; see Fees p. 95, Davis
MCGB p. 84.
This large holding will have had a number of subordinate members. Besides
*Oteringthon'*, Fees p. 764 records *Sidemue* [Sidmouth GR SY 1287; see 10,1 note],
*Hetherland'* ['Hetherland' a lost place in Otterton according to EPNS ii p. 593,
*Hodderlond* in FA i p. 365, but there is a Hatherland in Washfield parish, (West) Budleigh
Hundred] and *Wonbogh* [Windbow SS 9116 in Washfield, (West) Budleigh Hundred,
EPNS ii p. 420]. In a Bull of 1156 (Round CDF no. 736 p. 268) Pope Adrian IV
confirmed on the Abbey *Otritone* and *Seduine* [Sidmouth], also *Cudebiria* [*Wddebir*
in Round CDF p. 279 no. 771, that is Woodbury, a later grant; see 1,33 note], *Wiscumba*
[Wiscombe in Southleigh, Colyton Hundred, GR SY 1893], *Estelleia* [unidentified],
*Erticumba* [Yarcombe 11,3] and *Bordelar* [part of East Budleigh (1,9), a later grant;
see *Regesta* ii p. 190 no. 1418]. A further charter (Round CDF no. 772 p. 279) adds
*Hapeford* [Harpford SY 0990; see 1,9 note]. On all of this, see TE p. 151b, RH i p. 66ab,
Cal. Inq. PM vol. x nos. 241-242, FA i pp. 316, 325, 365, Oliver *Mon.* p. 248 ff., DCNQ
31 pp. 1-10 and Dom. L. Guilloreau *Chartes d'Otterton*, Ligugé (Vienne) 1909. *Radway
Abbatis* [now represented by Radway Lane GR SY 0986] was no doubt also a part of
this land; see LSR (1334) p. 65 and VE ii p. 289.
COUNTESS GYTHA. See 1,29 note.
A MARKET. The only other market mentioned in Devon is at Okehampton 16,3 (in DB
that time), although there were undoubtedly other markets in the County in 1086. In
Exon. the market is interlined in paler ink, though by the same scribe as the rest of the
entry, above the first line, quite out of place, probably the reason why the Exchequer
scribe missed it.
*r* PLOUGHS. Written in the right-hand margin in pale ink, the *r* abbreviating *require*,
'enquire into the ploughs'. *r*, or *rq̃*, was usually written when the scribe lacked some
information (such as the number of villagers in DB Wilts. 2,11), but in this case there is
no sign in the MS of addition in the number of ploughs in the estimate, in lordship or
held by the villagers. Cf. DB Northants. 30,4 note. Although the gap (of 5-6 letters)
after the villagers' ploughs might suggest that space was left originally for the number,
this gap thus left would be too big for any number, and moreover the colour of ink of
the *xl* is the same as for the rest of the entry (which it would probably not be if the *xl*
were added as the result of a check). It might be that the scribe wanted to verify all the
plough numbers, as the total of villagers' and lordship ploughs exceeds the estimate by
21 — rather a lot. The fact that the *r* is in pale ink supports the view that at a later stage
someone thought the plough numbers needed checking. See l,3 note on the relationship
between the plough estimate and the actual teams recorded on manors.
PASTURE, 1½ LEAGUES.... There is no dot after *pasturę* in the MS and the rest of the
line (suitable for about 14 letters) has been left blank, perhaps intentionally (cf. the
Exon. information on the market, not in DB, which, though interlined, appears to have
been an early addition by the same scribe as the rest of the entry). See 25,12 note and
cf. notes to 3,44. 20,14 and 33,1. However, the Exchequer scribe left a similar, though
smaller, space after the resources in 11,2 (though there he puts a dot) and in several
counties spaces were normally left before the Value statement (see 15,7 note below).

| | |
|---|---|
| 11,2-3 | DENNINGTON. YARCOMBE. Dennington is in Yarcombe parish, Axminster Hundred (17). Both places can be identified from the lordship allowed in the Tax Return (xix). Yarcombe appears in various grants to Otterton or to Mont St. Michel; see Round CDF no. 734 p. 266 and 11,1 note. It included *Petrisheghis* [Peterhayes farm GR ST 2406] held later by the Bishops of Exeter from the Priors of Otterton and *Shefeheghes* [Sheafhayne ST 2509], Cal. Inq. PM vol. xvi no. 1027. See VE ii pp. 289-290 and Cal. Inq. PM vol. xii no. 354. For Dennington, see EPNS ii p. 652, Oliver *Mon*. p. 258, OJR H4 pp. 136, 167 and H7 p. 349. |
| Chs. 12 -13 | ST. STEPHEN'S OF CAEN. HOLY TRINITY OF CAEN. These two Abbeys in the département of Calvados, France, were founded by Duke William of Normandy and his wife Matilda respectively, as a penance from the Pope for marrying within the prohibited degrees of consanguinity (she was his cousin's daughter). ST. STEPHEN'S was founded in 1064, though probably not dedicated until 1077 (Orderic Vitalis ii p. 128). Lanfranc, who in 1070 became Archbishop of Canterbury, was the first Abbot. Apart from Northam in Devon, St. Stephen's held land in Dorset, Somerset, Wiltshire, Essex and Norfolk. The Nunnery of HOLY TRINITY, CAEN, was founded in 1066 and dedicated in the same year. It also held land in Dorset, Gloucestershire and Essex. See Mon. Ang. vi pp. 1070, 1072 and Ellis *Introduction* i p. 389 note 8. |
| Ch. 12 | FOR THE POSITION OF THIS HOLDING in Exon., see Chs. 8-13a note. |
| 12,1 | NORTHAM. It lies in Shebbear Hundred (4) and seems to be identifiable in the Tax Return for Merton (Shebbear) Hundred (v) (see next note but one). It was granted to St. Stephen's of Caen by Queen Matilda during her last illness with its member *Aisserugia* [probably Ashridge in Bideford, GR SS 4424]. King William's confirmation is in *Regesta* i p. 27 no. 105; see Round CDF pp. 155, 157, 162 nos. 452-453, 459, *Regesta* ii no. 1575 p. 224, Fees p. 1264, TE p. 152b, RH i pp. 63b, 78a, 93b, Cal. Inq. PM vol. xvi no. 959, FA i p. 374 and OJR H10 pp. 539, 551. BRICTRIC. Probably Brictric son of Algar, as the Exon. states that the manor was a gift of Queen (Matilda) who acquired that Brictric's lands (see 24,21 note). TAX FOR 2 HIDES AND ½ VIRGATE. The details of lordship and villagers' land total 2 hides, less ½ virgate. The Exon. MS reads *ii hidis 7 dim uirga* with an erasure after the *uirga*. It would seem that the Exon. scribe originally wrote *ii hidis dim uirga min'* ('2 hides, less ½ virgate'), then erased the *min'* and interlined the 7, then perhaps omitted to correct either of the details. The villagers' holding should probably have been corrected to 1½ hides 1½ virgates, as the Tax Return for Merton Hundred (v) states that the King had no tax from 1 hide 3½ virgates that the Abbot of St. Stephen's holds, which should refer to the villagers' holding as lordship land paid no tax. See 1,4 note on the hide and notes to 1,57. 15,10;13. 16,96 and 34,10 where alterations to the tax in Exon. resulted in the total of the lordship and villagers' land not agreeing with the tax. |
| Ch. 13 | FOR THE POSITION OF THIS HOLDING in Exon., see Chs. 8-13a note. |
| 13,1 | HOLY TRINITY CHURCH. In the MS and Farley there is the expected abbreviation sign ʼ over the last *T* of *TRINITAT*; it is not reproduced in the facsimile, probably because of its faintness and closeness to the rubricated chapter heading. See L 11 note. UMBERLEIGH. In Atherington parish, (North) Tawton Hundred (12), and probably standing for the parish. The Tax Return for Tawton Hundred (ix) records the Abbess of Caen as owing tax on 1 hide and 1 virgate, the size of the whole holding in DB (i.e. including the lordship of 1 virgate which did not pay tax). The land passed to the Honour of Gloucester; see FA i p. 340, RBE ii p. 559, Cal. Inq. PM vol. iii no. 371, viii no. 177, ix nos. 103, 218, 428, xvi no. 538, and OJR in TDA 29 p. 248. BRICTRIC. Probably Brictric son of Algar in view of the land being granted by Queen Matilda to her foundation; see 24,21 note on her acquisition of this Brictric's lands. The one holding of this church in Dorset (Ch. 21) had also been held in 1066 by a Brictric. |
| Ch. [13a] | THE RUBRICATOR of the MS gave no number to this 'chapter', no doubt because it does not appear in the Landholders' List. It has here been numbered 13a, to avoid a discrepancy in the numbering of the subsequent chapters and to indicate that it is not part of Ch. 13. FOR THE POSITION OF THESE HOLDINGS in Exon., see Chs. 8-13a note. |
| 13a,1-3 | THESE SMALL HOLDINGS were all parts of royal manors, granted in alms by the King, corresponding to Ch. 16 in DB Somerset and Ch. 24 in Dorset. |
| 13a,1 | SOUTH MOLTON. In the Tax Return for South Molton Hundred (vii), the priests of *Moltona* have 1 virgate of land in lordship, clearly this holding. |

| | |
|---|---|
| 13a,2-3 | SWIMBRIDGE. BRAUNTON. Swimbridge is a parish in South Molton Hundred (6) derived from 'Bridge' and the name of the 1086 holder Saewin (EPNS ii p. 350). It was no doubt originally part of the royal manor of South Molton (1,6). The Tax Return for Braunton and Shirwell Hundred (vi) records that the priests of *Brantona* and *Moltona* have an allowance of 1 hide and 3 furlongs ('ferlings') of lordship land. Despite the discrepancy with the actual lordship given in DB (1 virgate each), this entry appears to mean that Swimbridge was held by the priests of South Molton and, at least for tax purposes, it was regarded as lying in the adjacent Hundred of Braunton and Shirwell. |
| | The holding at Braunton probably formed the later manor of Braunton Dean, given to the Bishop of Exeter; see Oliver *Mon.* p. 134, OJR H8 p. 411 and 1,5 note. |
| 13a,2 | QUEEN M(ATILDA) GAVE .... IN ALMS. This occurs as the last statement in the Exon. entry, possibly the reason for its omission in DB. Cf. Exon. Notes 23,22 for a similar omission, though because it occurs in a sub-holding there, it was probably 'pruned out' by the Exchequer scribe. |
| 13a,3 | AFTER THIS ENTRY the scribe left a space equivalent to about a dozen lines (rather larger than is normal between chapters; cf. 7,4 note), no doubt in case more lands held in alms should be revealed, perhaps if and when more royal manors were detailed (cf. the space left at the end of the King's lands; 1,72 note), as these lands held in alms were all part of royal land. |
| Ch. 14 | EARL HUGH. Hugh of Avranches (département of Manche, France), nephew of King William; Earl of Chester from 1071/77 to 1101. His daughter Matilda married Count Robert of Mortain and his sister was the second wife of Count William of Eu. In other counties his lands form the Honour of Chester; here they pass to the Mortain Honour of Cardinan or to Herbert son of Matthew. |
| | THE ENTRIES IN THIS CHAPTER are in the same order in Exon., of which the Hundreds are: 14,1-2 South Molton and 14,3-4 Budleigh. |
| 14,1-2 | ANSTEY. There are now two adjacent parishes, East and West Anstey, both in South Molton Hundred (6). These holdings passed to the Mortain Honour of Cardinan and certainly included land in East Anstey. In Fees p. 796 the heirs of Alexander *de Crues* hold in *Anesty* from the Honour of Cardinan; Robert *de Cruues* holds *Estanestygh* from Oliver *de Dinham* and he from the heirs of Andrew *de Cardinan* in FA i p. 325. The land subsequently passes to the Honour of Bradninch; see FA i p. 418, Cal. Inq. PM vol. vii no. 462 and OJR H3 p. 91. *Westanstye* is also a Mortain fee in FA i p. 362, but this may well be an error, since the holder, William *Le Moyne*, holds West Anstey from Barnstaple and Okehampton Honours; see 3,62 and 16,78 notes. The first of these two entries (14,1) can be identified in the Tax Return for South Molton Hundred (vii). |
| | WITH 1 SMALLHOLDER. An unusual position for the smallholder after the slaves; see 1,3 note on smallholders. The slaves no doubt were recorded with the 'villagers' because of the lack of lordship ploughs (see 1,3 note on slaves). In the case of 14,2 the smallholder may have been put in this position because of the separation in Exon. of him from the villagers with ploughs (see Exon. Notes and 3,27 note above), though this does not explain 14,1. |
| 14,1 | ALNOTH. Probably Alnoth/Ednoth the Constable (*stalre*) who seems to be the same as Ednoth the Steward (*dapifer*), Earl Hugh's predecessor in Wiltshire and perhaps in other counties (see DB Berks. 7,7); see Freeman iv p. 755 ff., VCH Somerset i p. 417 ff. and DB Somerset General Notes 18,1;3-4 and 39,1. See Exon. Notes 14,3 on the forms of his name. Alnoth/Ednoth the Constable was killed in battle against Earl Harold's sons in 1067/68. |
| 14,3-4 | STOWFORD. *LANDESHERS*. Stowford is in Colaton Raleigh parish, (East) Budleigh Hundred (14); *Landeshers* (see next note) is in this Hundred but is unidentified, since in the Tax Return for Budleigh Hundred (xvi) Richard (a subtenant not mentioned in DB) owes tax on 1 hide and ½ virgate, the exact taxable size of these two lands. In Fees pp. 762, 782 Michael *de Suthcoth'* holds in *Staford'* and *Aylinewod'* ['Allen Wood' lost in Aylesbeare, EPNS ii p. 581] from Herbert son of Matthew; see FA i p. 426, Cal. Inq. PM vol. viii no. 280, x no. 241. *Huntebere* [Houndbeare farms in Aylesbeare, GR SY 0493 and 0593, see 16,136 note] is also held in Fees p. 764 by Herbert son of Matthew; see Cal. Inq. PM vol. viii no. 280, xiv no. 325. Both 'Allen Wood' and Houndbeare are some distance from Stowford and could represent the unidentified *Landeshers*, but more evidence is needed to prove the connection; see OJR in TDA 35 pp. 299, 310, 36 p. 362. |
| 14,4 | *LANDESHERS*. So MS; Farley misprints *LANDESHERG*. The final *S* is not as large as the first *S*, but it is unmistakable. In the facsimile the rubrication obscures this last letter and makes it resemble a *G*; see 1,63 note. |

Ch. 15    COUNT OF MORTAIN. Robert, half-brother of King William and younger brother of Bishop Odo of Bayeux. He held more land in England than any other follower of King William (see Freeman iv p. 762), especially in Cornwall and other south-west counties. According to the summary (in Exon. 531 a 3) of his fief in Wiltshire, Dorset, Devon and Cornwall he held 623 manors; he held a further 86 in DB Somerset Ch. 19. After Baldwin the Sheriff (Ch. 16) and Iudhael of Totnes (Ch. 17), he was the largest lay landholder in Devon. He was responsible for the 'removal' of numerous parts of manors (e.g. 1,25;50. 7,4. 34,2), illegally in many cases, and for the cessation of payment of various customary dues owed to royal manors in Somerset and Devon (see 1,11;23 in the latter). In the 'exchanges' he made of manors, he invariably got the better bargain (see 2,10 note). He also (perhaps wrongly) 'attached' lands of free TRE tenants to those of a TRE landholder whose fief, or part of whose fief, had been granted to him; see 15,31 note. After rebelling against William Rufus in 1088, he was reconciled and died in 1091.

When his fief escheated to the King, many of his tenants became tenants-in-chief, their lands forming separate baronies. Thus the Honour of Ashleigh or Ashill is formed around the lands of Bretel of St. Clair; the Honour of Montacute from lands held by Drogo and Alfred the Butler; the Honour of Cardinan and Botardel from the lands held by Richard son of Thorold/Thorulf (including the lands he held directly from the King; see Ch. 30 note); the Honour of Hatch Beauchamp from the lands of Robert son of Ivo; the Honour of Odcombe from those of Anger the Breton and Alward (with descent to *Briwere*, Chaworth, Braose and Mohun); the Honour of Trematon from Reginald of Vautortes (thence to the Earl of Cornwall; see especially Cal. Inq. PM vol. iii no. 604, xv no. 166); and the Honour of Middellaund and Launceston Castle from the lands of Erchenbald and Hamelin (with descent to the Earl of Cornwall). In addition, one or two of the Count's estates go to the Honour of Mineli and Lantyan; see OJR in TDA 38 pp. 337-351, VCH pp. 570-571 and Sanders *passim*.

Mortain (not mentioned in OEB) is in the département of Manche, France.

THE EXON. BOOK ARRANGES the Count of Mortain's Devon fief strictly in the order of Hundreds. The manner in which the Exchequer scribe rearranged the Exon. entries is interesting. First he abstracted the Count's property in Exeter (15,1) and his lordship lands (15,2-5), then he returned to the beginning of the fief in Exon. to deal with 15,6-15, of which 15,8-10 had been held by Ordwulf and 15,12-13 by Edmer Ator, two thanes whose holdings had passed to the Count. By this point the Exchequer scribe had begun dealing with lands that had been joined to Edmer's Honour (15,14-15) and so he continued abstracting them (up to 15,31), then come more lands held by Edmer himself (15,32-38) and by Ordwulf himself (15,39-46), then those added to Ordwulf's Honour (15,47-53); for each of these sections he worked through the Exon. fief afresh. He then appears to have returned to the beginning of the Exon. and dealt with the remaining entries (15,54-79) in Hundred order. The order of Hundreds in Exon. is:

| | | | |
|---|---|---|---|
| 15,6 | Torrington | 15,42 | Kerswell |
| 15,7 | ?South Tawton | 15,23 | Axminster |
| 15,8-15; 32-33; 16;47;54 | } Merton | 15,24-25 | Colyton |
| | | 15,43 | Kerswell |
| 15,39 | Fremington | 15,35 | Colyton |
| 15,55 | Exminster | 15,64-66;44;67; 36-37;45;68-72; 26-27 | } *Alleriga* |
| 15,56;40-41 | Braunton | | |
| 15,57 | Bampton | | |
| 15,58 | Cliston | 15,73;38;74 | Diptford |
| 15,59 | Wonford | 15,75-76;28; 77;49 | } *Alleriga* |
| 15,60;2;61;34; 62-63 | } Silverton | | |
| | | 15,50-51;29-30; 52 | } Plympton |
| 15,17-19;3-5; 48;21;20;22 | } Budleigh | | |
| | | 15,78-79;53;46 | Walkhampton |
| 15,31 | Witheridge | 15,1 | Borough of Exeter |

15,1    IN EXETER .... A CHURCH. According to VCH p. 446 note 2 this is St. Lawrence's Church in Fore Street. See 2,1 note on this and the other three churches in Exeter that DB Devon records.

1 ORCHARD. *uirgultum* in DB and Exon., usually in classical Latin 'a thicket' or 'shrubbery'. A ML extension of the meaning appears to be 'orchard': it is glossed in Du Cange as *viridarium, pomarium* and Charter 17 (pp. 18-19) of *Charters of the Honour of Mowbray 1107-1191* (ed. D. E. Greenway, London 1972) (= Round CDF no. 627

| | |
|---|---|
| 15,1 (cont'd.) | pp. 219-220 and see also in Orderic Vitalis v Appendix ix pp. 200-201), concerning a gift by Nigel d'Aubigny to St. Évroult *c*. 1124-1129, states that ....*duas partes tocius decime de Villaris, garbarum videlicet, lini, canabi et leguminum et ortorum et fructum omnium virgultorum ejusdem ville et omnium de quibus decima juste dari debet....* (= '....two parts of the whole tithe of Villars, namely of sheaves of corn, of flax, hemp and vegetables and of gardens and of all the fruits of the orchards of this same village, and of everything from which the tithe ought rightly to be given....'). *Virgultum* also occurs in DB Dorset 55,47 in the manor of Orchard (see General Notes there). |
| 15,2 | THE COUNT HIMSELF HOLDS. Repeated at the beginning of 15,2-5 inclusive. *STOCHELIE.* The order of the Exon. Book suggests that this land lay in Silverton (Hayridge) Hundred (15), but it has not been satisfactorily identified. It is left unlocated by OJR in VCH p. 439 note 7, but identified by him with 'Leigh and Fursden' in Cadbury parish in TDA 42 pp. 220, 233. Hoskins in DCNQ vol. 24 identifies it with Leigh Barton in Silverton. It is unlikely that *Stochelie* would shorten to 'Leigh'; the place is either lost or in a part of 'Stockleigh' (15,17-18;48) lying over the Hayridge Hundred border. |
| 15,3 | WYKE. Probably the place in Shobrooke parish (which is the next entry) in (West) Budleigh Hundred (14); this and the entries for Shobrooke and West Raddon (15,4-5) can be identified in the Tax Return for Budleigh Hundred (xvi). |
| 15,4 | SHOBROOKE. A parish in (West) Budleigh Hundred (14); see 15,3 note. *Shokebrok,* one fee pertaining to the Honour of Lantyan in Cornwall, is found in Cal. Inq. PM (o.s.) 18 Ric. II no. 31 p. 182; see Cal. Inq. PM (n.s.) vol. viii no. 280, xvi no. 875 and OJR in TDA 35 p. 300.<br>VILLAGERS....8 PLOUGHS. In the MS *iiii car* was originally written, but the first *i* was corrected to a *v* to make *viii*. Exon. has 4 villagers' ploughs and gives the plough estimate as 8, not 4 as in DB. What appears to have happened is that the DB scribe, copying from Exon., discovered he had written *iiii* for both the plough estimate and the villagers' ploughs and then corrected the second, rather than the first, *iiii*, thus making a double discrepancy between the two texts. |
| 15,5 | (WEST) RADDON. In Shobrooke parish, (West) Budleigh Hundred (14); see 15,3 note. *Raddon'* is a Mortain fee in Fees pp. 761, 791; see FA i p. 426, Cal. Inq. PM vol. ii no. 154, vi no. 710, viii nos. 396-397, x no. 461 and xvi no. 1067. 'West' distinguishes this Raddon from that in Thorverton parish, Hayridge Hundred (see 5,9 and 51,6). |
| 15,6 | STOCKLEIGH. Probably the place in Highampton parish, (Black) Torrington Hundred (11), but not positively identified from later evidence. This is the opening entry in Exon. under the Count of Mortain's fief. Since there are no Mortain lands in Lifton Hundred (18), which normally opens a fief in the order of Exon., this land will have lain in Torrington or 'South Tawton' Hundreds (see the Appendix) which are normally entered next; see OJR in TDA 36 p. 351, H5 p. 196 and 15,7 note. |
| 15,7 | GIDLEIGH. Now a parish in Wonford Hundred (19), but it lay close to South Tawton manor (1,29) and may well have been returned with it in the records on which Domesday is based. It is entered too early in the Count's fief to have been a Wonford Hundred place in 1086, but in other fiefs, places that pay dues to South Tawton are entered second (see 43,1. 45,1 and 51,2 notes and the Appendix). But no descent of this manor has so far been found to clinch the identification; see Fees p. 98, RBE ii p. 559, Cal. Inq. PM vol. i no. 740, viii no. 230, OJR in TDA 36 pp. 351, 377 and in 44 pp. 349-350.<br>LAND FOR 1 PLOUGH. .... There is a gap in the MS of about 18 letters' width, perhaps left deliberately by the scribe for some of the usual manorial details to be added if available, or perhaps merely the space left before the value, which is common in many counties in DB, e.g. Worcs. and Glos. Cf. DB Dorset General Notes 1,2 'Woodland .... wide'. See also 11,1 note above and cf. notes to 3,44;83. 20,14. 25,12. 33,1 and 40,4 on spaces left in entries. The Exon. scribe left ½ line blank at the end of the entry, but this may have been for missing details. |
| 15,8 | HAMELIN. Hamelin here and in 15,43 may be the same as the Hamelin, subtenant of the Count of Mortain in DB Cornwall Ch. 5,5 and 2,14.<br>ALWINGTON. A parish in Shebbear Hundred (4) and identifiable in the Tax Return for Merton (Shebbear) Hundred (v). In Fees p. 795 *Alwynton'* is held under the Honour of Launceston from the Barony of *Middelland;* see FA i pp. 329, 410. For Ælfwynn who probably named the place, see Ch. 5 note. |
| 15,9 | MONKLEIGH. DB *Lege.* Now a parish in Shebbear Hundred (4). This holding was granted with Frizenham (15,32) and Densham (15,31) to Montacute Priory in the reign of King Stephen by a later Alfred the Butler. In TE p. 152b the Prior of Montacute holds *Monklegh';* see Mon. Ang. v pp. 163, 166, MC nos. 1,2,4,5,6,8,9 pp. 119-125, no. 113 |

| | p. 158, no. 161 p. 181, no. 169 p. 185 and OJR H10 pp. 539, 569. |
|---|---|
| 15,10 | FRITHELSTOCK. In the MS *FREDELESTOCH*; Farley misprints *FRELELESTOCH*. It is a parish in Shebbear Hundred (4). In the Tax Return for Merton (Shebbear) Hundred (v), tax is owed on 1 hide and 1 virgate of land held by Robert from the Count of Mortain, presumably this land since it is the only one held under the Count by a Robert that could have lain in Merton Hundred. Robert son of Ivo, the 1086 holder, was a subtenant of the Count of Mortain in several of his Somerset manors and his constable (possibly of Montacute Castle; see VCH Somerset i p. 427 and Eyton *Somerset* i p. 97). He was ancestor to Robert *de Bello Campo* of Hatch Beauchamp in Somerset (see DB Somerset 19,29). The latter Robert founded a priory for Augustinian canons at Frithelstock *c.* 1220; see Fees p. 775, VE ii p. 335, Oliver *Mon.* p. 220, MRH p. 137 and OJR H10 p. 570.<br>TAX FOR 3 HIDES. The details total 2 hides 3 virgates; see 1,4 note on the hide on other cases where the total of the details does not agree with the tax. It is possible that the 'missing' virgate is the virgate mentioned in the T.O. at 506 a 9 (see after Exon. Notes 15,14) as being held in Bulkworthy by Robert son of Ivo from the Count of Mortain which 'up till now has been concealed' and which is not mentioned either in DB or in the main Exon. Robert's only holding from the Count is Frithelstock here, but though in the same Hundred (4) as Bulkworthy, it is some distance from it. It would seem either that this virgate in Bulkworthy was a detached part of Frithelstock or that both Exon. and DB have omitted a separate holding of Robert son of Ivo in Bulkworthy. Although there is a holding of 1 virgate in Bulkworthy recorded in 15,14, it is held in 1086 by Ansger the Breton.<br>It is interesting that in the Exon. MS the tax was originally written *ii hidis* with an interlined *i* with a hair-line down between the two existing minims (Ellis does not print the hair-line) to make *iii hidis*, and that there is an erasure immediately after the *hidis* which is sufficient for *& iii virg* to have been originally written. The erasure was a late one, as it is not written over, and the correction to the hides may also have been late (though not done after the Exchequer scribe had used the MS) – possibly as a result of the discovery of the concealed virgate, although, if that were the case, one would expect this to have been mentioned. Cf. notes to 1,57. 12,1. 15,13. 16,96 and 34,10 for other cases where the tax has been altered in Exon. with the result that the total of the details no longer agrees with it. |
| 15,11 | CULLEIGH. In Frithelstock parish, Shebbear Hundred (4). In Fees p. 795 *Kollelegh'* is held from the Honour of Launceston; see FA i p. 359.<br>KIPPING. See PNDB p. 221 s.n. *Cypping*.<br>VALUE NOW 12[s]. *Solid(os)* omitted through lack of space; see 5,3 note. |
| 15,12-13 | ANSGER THE BRETON. Exon. *Ansgeri(us) brito* here and in 15,13 and *Ansger(us) brito* in the T.O. entries relating to 15,14-15. He is also a subtenant of the Count of Mortain in DB Somerset and Edmer Ator was his predecessor in one manor there, as in two here. See Ch. 40 note. |
| 15,12 | BUCKLAND (BREWER). A parish in Shebbear Hundred (4). Ansger's lands descended to the Honour of Odcombe, and *Bocland'* is a Mortain fee of William *Briwere* of the Honour of Odcombe in Fees p. 796; see FA i p. 358, 411 and OJR H10 pp. 540, 571-572. Part of the land went to Dunkeswell Abbey (TE p. 152a, VE ii p. 304); the Church with chapels at Putford (15,13) and Bulkworthy (15,14) went to Torre Abbey (VE ii p. 361). Part of the land was at *Thoredoghes* [unidentified], *Todecote* [Tythecott GR SS 4117] and *Silkelond* [Silkland SS 4116], Cal. Inq. PM vol. xi no. 299.<br>EDMER ATOR. The forms of his name in Devon are *Edmer atre* in DB and *Edmarator(us), AEdmaratori(us), Edmeratori(us), Etmaratoli* (*l-r* interchange) in the main Exon. and *Elmerator(us), Almerator(us)* in the T.O. for 15,23-25. There are several occasions in DB Somerset (see General Notes 37,5 there) where the form *Almar(us), Ailmar(us)* is linked with 'Ator'. It is probable that these 'Almer' forms in Somerset and in the T.O. for Devon are scribal errors (indeed in the Exon. for Somerset 21,63 *Elmarus* has been corrected to *edmarus*): in the carolingian miniscule a badly made *ed-* might well look like *al-* (with parallel *el-, ail-*), the acceptable spelling for protothemes in *AEl-, AEthel-, AEgel-* and corresponding *El-, Ethel-, Egel-*). Certainly OEB p. 341, PNDB p. 232 and VCH for Somerset, Devon and Hertfordshire all agree that there was only one person, Edmer Ator. For a full discussion of this byname, see OEB p. 341. See also next note.<br>The Count of Mortain possessed more of Edmer Ator's land in DB Somerset, Bucks., Middlesex and Herts., and possibly also in Dorset. Edmer is described as King Edward's thane in Bucks. and Middlesex. |

15

15,12 (cont'd.) IN THE MS there is an erasure of 4 letters after *Edmer*, though Farley does not print the gap thus caused (but see 1,60 note and cf. notes to 15,74 and 50,2). Under ultra-violet light it is possible to detect an *a* as the first letter and probably an *r* as the last, suggesting that the word erased was *ator*; if so, it is not clear why it should have been erased when it is in Exon., unless the DB scribe discovered later that it was a different Edmer, not Edmer Ator, who had held Buckland Brewer. It is interesting that in 15,13 there is also an erasure after *Edmer*, apparently of 4 letters, but, unlike in 15,12, the erasure was early because *teneb'* was written over it; the scribe then interlined *atre*, presumably at some later stage though the ink colour and the hand are the same. It is perhaps suggestive that in DB Somerset 8,31 and 47,10 there is a similar erasure of 4 letters after the name *Edmer*, which in the corresponding Exon. is 'Edmer Ator'. In no other counties where Edmer Ator appears (with his byname either as *ator* or *atule* or *attile*, though the last form is unclear in the MS and probably a scribal error for *atule*) are there any signs of erasures or gaps round *Edmer*.

3 PIGMEN. This is interlined in the Exon. MS (though by the same scribe and in the same colour ink as the rest of the entry), possibly the reason for its omission in DB. Cf. 16,23 note.

GALSWORTHY .... PAID TAX FOR ½ VIRGATE. In the T.O. the ½ virgate is the extent of the added manor; the tax is not given, but no doubt was the same (see 1,4 note on the hide).

Galsworthy is in Buckland Brewer parish, see EPNS i p. 88.

15,13 (EAST) PUTFORD. A parish in Shebbear Hundred (4). *Putteford'* is a fee of William *Briwere*, Honour of Odcombe, in Fees p. 797. It is *Pottford Milf onis]* in FA i p. 358 and *Potteford Milite* in FA i p. 411; see Cal. Inq. PM vol. ii no. 306, Fees p. 400, EPNS i p. 106, OJR H10 p. 540 and 15,12 note. West Putford is in (Black) Torrington Hundred (11).

EDMER ATOR. See 15,12 note.

TAX FOR 1 HIDE. .... 1 VIRGATE. .... 2 VIRGATES. It is interesting that in the Exon. MS the *i hida* is written over a larger erasure, which may have been *iii virg*; see 1,57 note for other examples of the tax of a manor being altered and then not agreeing with the total of lordship and villagers' land.

15,14 BULKWORTHY. A parish in Shebbear Hundred (4). Like Buckland Brewer (15,12), *Bulkeworth'* was held of the Honour of Odcombe in Fees p. 797; see FA i p. 358, OJR H10 p. 573 and the second note under 15,10.

ERIC. DB and Exon. main entry *Iric*, T.O. *Irich*, represent ON *Eirikr*; see PNDB p. 299 and Fellows Jensen p. 76.

15,15 SMYTHAM. In Little Torrington parish, Shebbear Hundred (4); see EPNS i p. 111 and OJR H10 p. 574.

15,16 ALFRED THE BUTLER. Exon. *Alueredus Pincerna*. He was the Count of Mortain's butler (*Regesta* i p. xxvii) and held land from him in other counties in DB.

LITTLE TORRINGTON. DB *Liteltorelande*, now Little Torrington parish in Shebbear Hundred (4). It appears that *Toritone* and perhaps *Torilande* (see 34,9 note) can both stand for Great and Little Torrington; see also 1,31 and 16,34 notes and cf. *Beldrendiland* for Barlington (3,15) and *Birland* for Bere, i.e. Bere Ferrers (15,46). In Exon. order this entry falls in the middle of a Shebbear Hundred group and the preceding entry in DB, Smytham, lay in this parish, but conclusive evidence for the identification is lacking. OJR's identification with Woodland (VCH p. 539 note 4 and H10 pp. 541, 571) does not convince.

ALWARD RUFUS. Exon. *Eluuardus rufus* 'Alward the Red', perhaps a relation of Aelmer Rufus (15,33; see Exon. Notes), the TRE tenant of the next entry in Exon.

15,17-18 'STOCKLEIGH'. In Exon. order these two entries appear to begin a group of Budleigh Hundred places (14). The Count of Mortain held three places called 'Stockleigh' in this Hundred. Of these the third (15,48 note) is clearly Stockleigh English, but the exact identity of the first two and their relation to later Mortain holdings is not perfectly clear. In Fees p. 764 John *de Stockelegh'* holds from Walter *de Baggepuz* in *Stockelegh'* and he from Catherine *de Monte Acuto* of the Honour of *Cheselburgh'* [Chiselborough in Somerset, Sanders p. 34]. This may be the *Stokkeley Loccoumb* held by John *de Luckome* in Cal. Inq. PM vol. vi nos. 626-627. The same place is *Stokelegh' Letcomb'* of LSR 1334 p. 55 and *Stokelegh Locomb* associated with Langley [GR SS 9109] in Cadeleigh parish in FA i p. 381. If it is the 'Stockleigh' that appears (at GR SS 8808) on the 1st edition OS map (sheet 21 of 1809, reprint sheet 83 of 1969), it will have been adjacent to the other Chiselborough Honour holding at Poughill (15,19); see OJR in TDA 35 p. 296.

15,17-18
(cont'd.) The other 'Stockleigh' is probably accounted for by Fees p. 797 where Robert *de Sicca[villa]* and Gervase *de Uppecoth'* hold in *Sutton'* [Sutton in Stockleigh English, GR SS 8605] and *Uppecoth'* [Upcott in Cheriton Fitzpaine, SS 8608]. In Fees p. 400 these appear as *Luttestockeleg'* and *Hoppecote* (*Little Stokeleg*) in Cal. Inq. PM vol. ii nos. 306, 593), while Sutton is called *Sutton' Sachevill'* in LSR (1334) p. 55 and is associated with Cheriton Fitzpaine in FA i p. 381; see Fees pp. 400, 762, RH i p. 92b, FA i pp. 362, 426, OJR in TDA 35 p. 300, 36 pp. 362-363 and in VCH p. 440 notes 3-4. Since the material in the EPNS volumes is particularly sparse for these parishes, these 'Stockleighs' require further investigation.

15,18 HADEMAR. *Haimer(us)* in DB and Exon. with loss of intervocalic *ð* represents OG *Hademar, Hathumar*; see PNDB pp. 281-282 s.n. *Hademar* and § 109.

15,19 POUGHILL. A parish in (West) Budleigh Hundred (14). In Fees p. 763 *Poghill'* is held from Catherine *de Monte Acuto* from the Barony of *Cheselbergh'*; see OJR in TDA 35 p. 295 and 15,17-18 note.

2 PARTS OF 1 VIRGATE. That is, two-thirds of 1 virgate; see OED s.v. Part, sb. I, 5,(b).

15,20 BRETEL. Bretel here and elsewhere in Devon may be Bretel of St. Clair (see OEB p. 112): in the Tax Return for the Somerset Hundred of Bulstone (Exon. 526 b 1) the King did not have tax on ½ hide held by *Britellus de sancto claro*, which holding can be identified with Somerset 19,15, Swell held by Bretel from the Count of Mortain. A Bretel was also the Count's subtenant on many of his manors in Somerset and Dorset. See VCH Somerset i p. 412.

HOLBROOK. DB *Colebroch*. The DB form suggests Colebrook in Cullompton parish, Hayridge Hundred (15), and it is so identified by EPNS (ii p. 560) and DG. But the place clearly lies in Budleigh Hundred (14) in Exon. order, and in Fees pp. 763, 783 *Holebrok'* [Holbrook in Clyst Honiton parish, (East) Budleigh Hundred] is held as a Mortain fee from Walter *de Eslegh'*, that is of the Honour of Ashill (in Somerset), the anticipated descent from the 1086 holder, Bretel; see RH i p. 66b and OJR in VCH p. 441 note 2, p. 543 note 5, and in TDA 35 p. 290, 36 p. 362. The land probably included *Mora Holebrokes* [an unidentified 'Moor'], FA i p. 365; see FA i p. 427.

15,21 FARRINGDON. A parish in (East) Budleigh Hundred (14). In Fees p. 783 *Ferndon'* is a Mortain fee held from Walter *de Eslegh'* (Honour of Ashill, 15,20 note); see Fees p. 763 and FA i p. 427.

2 COTTAGERS. *Cotarii*, inhabitants of a *cote*, sometimes with land of their own (as in DB Middlesex 2,1. 3,1 etc.; see the Appendix to that county). In DB Devon they are only stated as having a share in the ploughs, though in Exon. they may be included under the general term *villani* as having land (cf. 1,3 note on slaves and Exon. Notes 1,26). Except in 17,30 (see note) and in the Exon. for 1,4 (see Exon. Notes), cottagers are either listed in Devon after the villagers and smallholders or appear on their own. There are 36 cottagers recorded, of whom only 19 appear in DB; see Exon. Notes 1,4. It is interesting that all the occurrences are in a group of four Hundreds in the south-east middle of the County. The *bordarius* ("smallholder"; see 1,3 note) seems to have been similar to the *cotarius*, though perhaps slightly further up the social scale, and the two terms were sometimes confused: in the summary of Glastonbury Abbey's lordship holding in Dorset in 527 b 4 the 72 *bordarii* corresponds to the 40 *bordarii* and 32 *cotarii* recorded in DB Dorset 8,1;3. Likewise in the Berkshire Hundreds of Blewbury, Slotisford, Wantage and Beynhurst, cottagers take the place of smallholders after villagers in the list of population; the first three of these Hundreds are adjacent, though Beynhurst is quite separate, so this phenomenon cannot be due entirely to a particular local variation. Personal preference for one term rather than the other may be the reason: it is interesting that two of the Exon. scribes dealing with the Devon material never use the terms *cotarii*, or *coceti* ("Cottagers", an allied group; see 2,24 note), but only *bordarii*, and it is more likely that the former categories were included with the latter, than that there were no 'cottagers' on so many manors; Finn LE p. 50.

15,22 ALWARD HOLDS ROCKBEARE. *de comite* 'from the Count' has been omitted, no doubt by mistake as it is in Exon. as usual; see Exon. Notes. See also Exon. Notes to 15,30;71. 16,127. 17,73-74. 34,57 and 35,25 for other cases of the Exchequer scribe omitting to state from whom a manor was held. Cf. 28,8 where the DB scribe originally omitted *de Ro(berto)* and then interlined it at the same time as another omission in the entry; similarly in 39,2 with *de Alu(redo)*.

ROCKBEARE. A parish in (East) Budleigh Hundred (14). No Mortain land appears here in later documents, but in Fees p. 763 (Budleigh Hundred) the heirs of Baldwin

15

| | |
|---|---|
| 15,22 (cont'd.) | *de Beleestane* (who names another part of Rockbeare, 16,133-134 note) hold in *La Heghland* from William *de Legh'* and he from Patrick *de Chawrces* [Chaworth], Barony of Odcombe; see Fees p. 793. Alward's holding at *Lege* [Northleigh 15,25], whence William *de Legh'* is named, descends in the same way, but *La Heghland* has not been identified: it can scarcely be Hawkerland (23,5 note), despite OJR's assertion; see OJR in TDA 35 p. 294 and in VCH p. 441 note 3. |
| 15,23-24 | DROGO. DB *Drogo*, Exon. *Dreus: Dreu(s)* is the Norman and French form of OG *Drogo* (Forssner pp. 60-61; see Reaney s.n. *Drew*). The Drogo here and in 15,25;34;62 is probably the same as the Drogo (of Montacute) who was the Count of Mortain's subtenant so frequently in Somerset and also in Dorset (DB Somerset General Notes 19,86; Dorset General Notes 26,2); see notes to 15,24;34 on the descent of these manors in the Montacute family. |
| 15,23 | HONITON. A parish in Axminster Hundred (17). Its 2 hides of lordship land are probably represented by the 2 hides noted in the Tax Return for Axminster Hundred (xix), although there the land is said to be held by the Count, not, as in DB, by Drogo under him. The land passed from the Honour of Mortain to that of Plympton. Falco *de Braute* holds *Hunetun'* in Fees p. 263; see RH i p. 74a, Cal. Inq. PM vol. viii no. 273, xiv no. 107, FA i pp. 319, 429 and OJR H4 pp. 150-151. It included *Battesthorn* [Batshorne GR SY 1599]; see Cal. Inq. PM vol. v no. 434 and x nos. 240, 384, 652. See 1,11 for details of an unpaid customary due owing from this manor to Axminster. 2 SALT-WORKERS. The salt-workings were probably near Beer and Seaton; see 7,4 note. |
| 15,24 | 'WOMBERFORD'. A lost place, that lay in Cotleigh parish, Colyton Hundred (22). The meaning 'ford over the Umborne Stream' would place it in the south of the parish; see EPNS ii p. 626. In Fees p. 782 *Wamberneford'* is held by William *Male Erbe* (with Feniton 15,34) from William *de Monte Acuto*, representing the expected descent from Drogo. According to Cal. Inq. PM vol. vi no. 238, William *de Monte Acuto* held *Fyneton* [Feniton 15,34] and *Womborneford* by *Cottele*; see RH i p. 71b, FA i pp. 330, 366, 428 and OJR H7 pp. 336, 358. |
| 15,25 | NORTHLEIGH. A parish in Colyton Hundred (22). Descent from the 1086 holder Alward is to the Mortain Honour of Odcombe (see 15,22 note). In Fees p. 793 *Legh'* is held from Patrick *de Chaworth's* portion of that Honour; it is *Northlegh* in FA i p. 330 held from the heirs of Payne *de Cadurcis*; see Fees p. 396, FA i p. 428, Cal. Inq. PM vol. v no. 527, xi nos. 118, 299 and OJR H7 pp. 336, 359. VILLAGERS .... 3 PLOUGHS. This ought not to have been included by the Exchequer scribe as he had already covered the villagers' ploughs in his statement '5 ploughs, which are there'; see the Lordship and Villagers' Table. |
| 15,26-30 | REGINALD. Without doubt Reginald here and elsewhere in this chapter, and presumably also in 1,23, is Reginald of Vautortes, a subtenant of the Count of Mortain in DB Somerset and Cornwall. He is given his byname in the Exon. for 15,44; see note below. His lands formed the Honour of Trematon (named from his holding in DB Cornwall 5,2,11), to which all his identifiable holdings in Ch. 15 descend; see Ch. 15 note. See 15,74 note on a relative, Hugh of Vautortes, also a subtenant of the Count, and 15,67 note on Godfrey, probably also 'of Vautortes'. |
| 15,26 | LUDBROOK. Now represented by Ludbrook in Ugborough parish and Higher Ludbrook and Ludbrook manor in Ermington parish, both in Ermington Hundred (27). Another part, also held by Reginald under the Count, is 15,72, the two parts being adjacent entries in Exon. In Fees p. 770 (Ermington Hundred) Stephen *de Ludebrok'* holds in *una et altera Ludebrok* ['both Ludbrooks', called 'North' and 'South' Ludbrook in FA i pp. 352, 399 and Cal. Inq. PM vol. iii no. 604], in *Baucumb'* [Bowcombe 15,75], in *Dynenton'* [Dinnaton 15,70] and in *Yedmareston'* [Edmeston, see 15,28 note] from the Honour of Trematon (descent from Reginald, Ch. 15 note); see Fees p. 796 and OJR H6 pp. 313-314. See 1,23 for details of an unpaid customary due owing to Ermington from one or other of the holdings in Ludbrook. |
| 15,27 | LUPRIDGE. Now in North Huish parish, Stanborough Hundred (28), but it lies adjacent to the boundary with Ermington Hundred (27) and was counted in the latter in the Middle Ages, as probably in 1086. In Fees p. 769 one Mortain fee in *Luperig'* (in Ermington Hundred) is held from Reginald *de Valle Torta* from the Honour of Trematon (descent from the 1086 Reginald, Ch. 15 note); see FA i pp. 351, 397, Cal. Inq. PM vol. iii no. 604, viii no. 280. In the Inq. PM of the Earl of Cornwall of fees belonging to Trematon Castle (Cal. Inq. PM vol. xv no. 168), it is associated with *Leye* [Ley GR SX 7154] and *Payneston* [Penson SX 7254]. |

15

15,28  HEWIS. An unidentified 'Huish' apparently falling in Exon. order among Ermington Hundred lands (27), although Ermington and Stanborough Hundreds are intermixed at this point in the schedule. It is tempting to identify the place with North Huish parish, now in Stanborough Hundred (28), a part of which, including Lupridge (15,27, the previous entry in Exchequer, but not in Exon., DB), lay in Ermington Hundred, but it is not found among the lands of Reginald that belonged to the Honour of Trematon. Among Reginald's lands held of that Honour in Ermington Hundred, in Fees p. 770 and p. 796 is *Edmeston* or *Yedmareston* [Edmeston GR SX 6452] with which OJR in TDA 36 p. 374 and H6 p. 313 is inclined to identify *Hewis*. There is no record of *Hewis* having become Edmeston, and although the latter is from the OE personal name *Edmer*, this land had not been held by Edmer, only added by the Count to his Honour (15,31). Moreover, Edmeston may well have been part of Reginald's holding of Modbury (15,64 note).

15,29  HARESTON. In Brixton parish, Plympton Hundred (26). Reginald held two lands here (see 15,51), separated by the order of DB, but adjacent in Exon. The larger holding (15,51) was assessed in the Hundred of East (Wivelshire) in Cornwall as *Hareston, Asseton* or *Haston*, held by Reginald *de Ferers* of the Honour of Trematon; see FA i pp. 200, 206, 212, 235. The smaller land (15,29) appears in FA i p. 334 held by William *de Collesford* as ½ fee from Bernard *de Bodbrain* and by him from the Earl of Cornwall. This is also a Trematon fee; see FA i pp. 353, 400, Cal. Inq. PM vol. iii no. 604 and OJR H6 p. 286.

15,30  REGINALD ALSO HOLDS. *de comite* 'from the Count' omitted, no doubt by mistake as it is in Exon. as usual (see Notes). See 15,22 note.
WINSTON. In Brixton parish, Plympton Hundred (26). *Wyneston* is held as a Trematon Honour fee in FA i pp. 334, 353, 401; see Cal. Inq. PM vol. viii no. 45 and OJR H6 p. 287.

15,31  DENSHAM. DB *Donevoldehame*. It lies in Woolfardisworthy parish, Witheridge Hundred (7). *Denewoldesham* was given with *Forde* [unidentified], *Leghe* [Monkleigh 15,9] and *Friseham* [Frizenham 15,32] to Montacute Priory; see 15,9 note and *Regesta* ii App. no. clx p. 348 and no. 1368, *Regesta* iii nos. 591-592. A part of Densham not included in this grant is held in Fees p. 760 from the Honour of *Tikeenbraz* in Cornwall by Roger *de Praulle*; see OJR in TDA 29 p. 257.
AETHELMER. DB *Ademar*, Exon. *Ademar(us)*, represent OE *Aethelmaer*; PNDB pp. 184-185. Cf. 3,47 note on Aelmer.
ABOVE 17 LANDS. Really 18 lands, 15,14-31 inclusive; see Exon. Notes here.
WITH EDMER ATOR'S LAND .... HANDED OVER TO HIM. BUT .... HELD .... FREELY. In other words, in spite of these lands being held freely in 1066 (*nam* is being used in an adversative sense; see also, for example, in DB Herefords. A 8, col. 179b) and the Count having no automatic right to them, they were 'added' to the lands of the important thane Edmer Ator, most of whose holding was legally transferred to the Count. (The term *deliberare*, as occurs in this phrase, is normally used of a formal transfer of property by a representative of the King; see notes to DB Glos. W 16 and Cambs. 5,22 and 13,18.) On several occasions (e.g. for 15,17-20;22; see Exon. Notes) the TRE tenants were said to have been 'men' of Edmer Ator (though still free) and this gave the Count a pretext for annexing their lands along with those of their 'master'. In many cases, however, the TRE holders had no connection with the man to whose Honour their lands were added; e.g. Alward Rufus in 15,16, Aelmer in 15,23, Wulfward in 15,24 etc. This annexation is several times said to have been done 'wrongfully' (*iniuste*); see the T.O. for 15,14-15 and DB 15,49 and 40,6-7, and see also 25,20 note and cf. notes to 23,23-24 and 24,18-19. See Exon. Notes to 15,11 and 15,47.
THANES HELD THEM FREELY. This information has already been given in DB for 15,19, and part of it (i.e. not that the TRE holders were 'thanes') in 15,26-27.

15,32  FRIZENHAM. In Little Torrington parish, Shebbear Hundred (4); see 15,16 note. It was given to Montacute Priory; see 15,9;31 notes.

15,33  WEDFIELD. Now in West Putford parish, (Black) Torrington Hundred (11), as a result of a medieval boundary change, but it lies on the Shebbear Hundred (4) side of the river Torridge and was no doubt there in 1086; see OJR H10 p. 571.

15,34  FENITON. A parish in Hayridge Hundred (15). It is held in Fees p. 782 as *Fineton'*, a Mortain fee, from William *de Monte Acuto* (descent from Drogo); see RH i p. 71a, FA i pp. 321, 367 and 15,24;62 notes.

15,35  COTLEIGH. A parish in Colyton Hundred (22), this holding being identifiable in the Tax Return for that Hundred (xx). *Cottelegh'* is held of the Barony of *Cardynan* [Cardinan] in Fees p. 795. The holder in FA i p. 330 is Oliver *de Dinham* who holds land from the Honour of Cardinan in 15,38;42 and 30,1; see FA i pp. 316, 366, Cal. Inq. PM vol. iv no. 44, Oliver *Mon*. p. 191 and OJR H7 p. 359.

15,36 CORNWOOD. A parish in Ermington Hundred (27). *Curnwod'* and *Ludeton* [Lutton GR SX 5959] are held from William *de Ferrers* of the Honour of Trematon in Fees p. 796; see Fees p. 770. In later documents there appear to be three holdings here: (1) *Crewode* or *Cornwode*; (2) *Lutton* or *Lyneton* held by Ralph *Bryt'*; and (3) another *Lodderton* or *Luddreton* held by John *de Aysschlegh'* and associated with *Littlecomb'* [possibly Combe GR SX 618611 or Watercombe SX 624613]. See FA i pp. 352, 398, TE p. 153, Cal. Inq. PM vol. ii no. 165, viii nos. 45, 648, xiii no. 99, VE ii p. 367 and Oliver *Mon*. p. 238 ff.
3 UNBROKEN MARES. Exon. *equas indomitas*. There are 155 of them recorded for 4 manors in the Exon. for Devon, of which 104 are at Brendon on Exmoor (34,14) so were probably Exmoor ponies, as these here may have been Dartmoor ponies. The remaining 48 unbroken mares, however, are on manors distant from the moors. See 1,46 note on the related group, if not the same, the *equae siluestres* 'wild mares'.

15,37 NEWTON (FERRERS). A parish in Ermington Hundred (27). In Fees p. 796 *Nyweton'* is held by William *de Ferers* from the Honour of Trematon (descent from Reginald), with *Puselynch'* [Puslinch in Newton Ferrers, GR SX 5650]; see Fees p. 770, FA i pp. 352, 399 and Cal. Inq. PM vol. viii no. 425. In the Tax Return for *Alleriga* (Ermington) Hundred (xxx) the ½ hide lordship is noted but is said to be held by the Church of St. Mary of *Niuuentona*, that is the Church of Newton Ferrers, not mentioned in DB; see OJR in TDA 30 p. 310. Among Mortain fees in Fees p. 771 is *Brunardeston'* held by John *de Alba Mara* from Geoffrey *de Crewecumbe*. This may well be Brownstone in Newton Ferrers [GR SX 5949], or possibly it is Brownstone in Modbury, although this is said to have been given at an early date to Buckfast Abbey; see Fees p. 797, FA i pp. 353, 400, Cal. Inq. PM vol. viii no. 45 and OJR H6 p. 326.

15,38 BOLBERRY. In Malborough parish, Stanborough Hundred (28). The Count had two lands here (see 15,73), entered together in Exon. The larger holding (1 hide, 15,38) held by Hugh in 1086, passes to the Beauchamps of Montacute. In Fees p. 765 (see p. 796) *Boltebir'* is held as ¼ fee by Robert *de Bello Campo* from William *de Monte Acuto*; it is *Boltebir[i] Beauchamp* in FA i p. 324, *Magna Boltebyry* in FA i p. 351 and *Mochele Boltebury* in FA i p. 396; see Cal. Inq. PM vol. viii no. 470, xi no. 35 and OJR in TDA 45 p. 184.
The smaller holding (½ hide, 15,73), held by Richard in 1086, is *Boltebir'* in Fees p. 765, held as 1/6th fee from the Honour of Cardinan. It is *Parva Boltebir[i]* in FA i p. 324, held from Oliver *de Dineham* (see 15,35 note) and by him from the Earl of Cornwall; see Fees p. 796, FA i pp. 351, 396, Cal. Inq. PM vol. vii no. 462, viii no. 280 and OJR in TDA 45 p. 184.
BUCKLAND. In Thurlestone parish, Stanborough Hundred (28); see 17,36 note.
EDEVA. DB *Eddeua* here and elsewhere in DB Devon, Exon. *Edeua, Eldeua, Eidieua*, represent OE *Eadgifu*, feminine; PNDB pp. 229-231.
LAND FOR 1½ PLOUGHS, WHICH ARE THERE. The *7 dimid'* is interlined on top of an earlier erasure which is not visible. See Exon. Notes here for the discrepancy caused by this correction. The singular verb $\bar{e}$ ('is') is equally correct after the alteration to *i caŕ 7 dimid'* as it was after the original *i caŕ*. There are numerous cases where the scribe has a singular verb after '1½', though on occasion the plural is used; see DB Dorset General Notes 26,19.

15,39 ALVERDISCOTT. A parish in Fremington Hundred (5). In Fees p. 795 Henry *de Bratton'* (from Bratton Fleming 15,40) holds from the Honour of Launceston in *Alvredescoth'* with *Aylescoth'* [Alscott in Alverdiscott, GR SS 5225], and in *Were* [?Little Weare in Weare Giffard, which should, however, have descended to Torrington Honour, see 42,5 note]; see FA i pp. 371, 413, OJR H8 pp. 497, 510 and 15,40-41 note.
OF THESE .... ORDWULF. See Exon. Notes to 3,94. 15,33 and 24,24 for other examples of the Exchequer scribe 'pruning out' details of TRE subtenancies, but cf. 15,41 note below.

15,40-41 BRATTON (FLEMING). CROYDE. The former is a parish, the latter is in Georgeham, both parishes lying in Braunton Hundred (1). In Fees p. 796 Baldwin *le Flemeng* holds in *Crideho* and also in *Bratton' cum membris*, both Mortain fees of the Honour of Launceston. In FA i p. 360 *Bratton, Cridaho* and *Alwardiscote* [Alverdiscott, see 15,39] are all held by this Baldwin; see FA i p. 415, Cal. Inq. PM vol. iii no. 413, iv no. 35 and OJR H8 pp. 396, 448.

15,40-41 (cont'd.)  In 1086 common pasture in Bratton Fleming was shared with Benton and Haxton which had belonged to the Count and were also later held by Baldwin the Fleming, but of the Honour of Bradninch; see 2,9-10 note.

15,40  THE THIRD (WAS) NOT. The exact force of Latin *minime*, unusual in DB, is notoriously difficult to judge in particular contexts: it strictly means 'very little', a meaning inappropriate here; in conversational use it has the emphatic force of 'not in the least'; in this particular context it is likely to have been preferred to *non* as giving a more satisfactory clausula.
THEY PAID TAX. The manors, as Exon. states.

15,41  ORDWULF'S SISTER .... FROM HIM. It is perhaps rather odd that the Exchequer scribe should have incorporated details of this TRE subtenant when on several occasions he seems to have deliberately omitted them; see Exon. Notes to 3,94. 15,33 and 24,24 and cf. 15,39 note.

15,42  RICHARD SON OF THORULF. *Ricard(us) fili(us) Torolui*. See Ch. 30 note on Richard son of Thorold/Thorulf.
ST. MARYCHURCH. In the MS the *cerce*, as well as the $S\bar{C}E\ MARIE$, is lined through in red for emphasis; Farley does not indicate this by the use of italics. St. Marychurch is a parish in Haytor Hundred (29). Like Woodhuish and Natsworthy (30,1-2) held by the same Richard son of Thorulf, but in chief, it passed to the Honour of Cardinan, being held in Fees p. 768 by Thomas *de Cyrencestre* as *Seintemarichurch*; see FA i pp. 316, 349, 392, Cal. Inq. PM vol. iv no. 44, vii no. 462, viii no. 397 and OJR in TDA 40 p. 122. In Fees p. 796 St. Marychurch is coupled with *Harestane* (*Horston* in FA i p. 349), that is Oar Stone, a rocky island in the sea, [GR SX 9562], off Hope's Nose; see EPNS ii p. 519 which does not, however, give these references, and Cal. Inq. PM vol. iii no. 604, xv no. 168.

15,43  HAMELIN .... VILLAGERS .... 1 HIDE. See 15,8 note on Hamelin. According to the Tax Return for Kerswell Hundred (xxv), in which Broadhempston lies, the King had no tax from 1 hide which Hamelin holds from the Count of Mortain.
BROADHEMPSTON. A parish in Haytor Hundred (29), this holding being identifiable in the Tax Return for Kerswell (Haytor) Hundred (xxv); see preceding note. In Fees p. 768 *Hemmeston*' is held by William *de Cantilupo* from the Honour of Mortain, either in chief or from the Earl of Cornwall; see Fees p. 797 and Cal. Inq. PM vol. viii no. 431. The heirs of this William hold *Hemmeston Borard* in RH i p. 72a; see FA i pp. 318, 348, EPNS ii p. 509, OJR in TDA 36 pp. 369-370, 40 p. 117, 50 p. 362 and 1,47 note.

15,44  REGINALD OF VAUTORTES. Exon. *Raginald(us) de valletorta*. Vautortes is in the département of Mayenne, France; OEB p. 117. See 15,26-30 note.
BIGBURY. A parish in Ermington Hundred (27). Descent from Reginald of Vautortes is to the Honour of Trematon (Ch. 15 note) and in Fees p. 770 William *de Bykebyr*' holds one fee in *Bykebyr*' and one in *Hugheton*' [Houghton GR SX 6546] from that Honour. Further members in Fees p. 770 are *Halewill*' [Holwell SX 6647] and *Nottedone* [Noddon SX 6547], also held by William *de Bykebyr*', and *Cumb*' held by *Juelis de Valle Torta*; see Cal. Inq. PM vol. iii no. 604, xv no. 168. This *Cumb*' is represented in FA i p. 351 by five unidentified places, all held by Michael *de Combe*: *Ieclescomb*, *Wryngoldon*, *Chochele*, *Ayneshill* and *Colewilhilt*, and appears as *Luscomb* in FA i p. 397. It could be Combe in Bigbury [SX 6748] or 'Jewelscombe', said to be a lost place in Modbury parish; see EPNS i p. 280 and OJR H6 p. 311.

15,45  HARFORD. A parish in Ermington Hundred (27). Two Mortain holdings of the Honour of Trematon (Launceston) are recognised here in Fees p. 796, Hugh *Peverel* holding in *una et altera Hereford*'; one of these is *West hertford* in Cal. Inq. PM vol. iii no. 413. See Fees p. 770, FA i pp. 352, 399 and Cal. Inq. PM vol. iii no. 604, xv no. 168.

15,46  BERE (FERRERS). DB *Birland*; for the entry see 15,16 note. It is a parish in Roborough Hundred (25). In Fees p. 796 *Ber*' and *Legh*' [Ley GR SX 4564] are held by William *de Ferers* from the Honour of Trematon; see FA i pp. 341, 354, 403 and Cal. Inq. PM vol. iii no. 604. Part of Bere was in later times assessed in the Cornish Hundred of Stratton; see FA i pp. 201, 207, 210 and OJR H3 pp. 107, 113-114.

15,47  UNDERMENTIONED SEVEN LANDS. That is, 15,47-53 inclusive. See 15,31 note on this method of acquiring lands, said to be wrongful in 15,49.

15,47-52  JOINTLY. *par*'(= *pariter*) is written in the right margin level with the first line of each of these entries; it is also added in the margin, or interlined (usually as *in paragio*), against a number of other entries in Devon DB. The ink used is more or less the same

15

15,47-52 colour throughout and is generally paler than that used for the main body of the County,
(cont'd.) suggesting they were done later, possibly as a result of checking Exon. Cf. 17,13 note. It
is interesting that in a number of cases these marginal and interlined *pariters* in DB
correspond to marginal or interlined ones in Exon.; e.g. for 15,49-50;79. 19,4;40. 35,6.
50,1. There is no indication, however, that these interlined and marginal *pariters* in Exon.
were done at a later stage: the scribe appears to be the same as for the main part of the
entry and the ink is the same colour. See 1,15 note on freely/jointly/as one manor.

15,47 HELE. Probably involving two adjacent 'Heles', one in Meeth, the other in Petrockstowe
parish, Shebbear Hundred (4). Among fees held of the Honour of Launceston (descent
from Erchenbald, the 1086 holder) in Fees p. 795 are *Hele* held by Richard *de Sechevil'*
and *Hele* held with Stockleigh (15,54) and Culleigh (15,11) by Richard *Franceis*. In FA i
p. 359 there are Mortain fees in Shebbear Hundred at *Hele Godynd* (held by Thomas
*Tyrel*, see FA i p. 411) and *Hele Pouere* and *Hele Sechevil* (both held by Robert
*de Stocheye* — from Stockey GR SS 5407, see 16,39 note — see FA i p. 411). These
three parcels of Hele probably represent: (1) Crockers Hele [GR SS 5206], formerly
*Hele Sachwill*, held by John Crokker in FA i p. 461; (2) Friars Hele [SS 5306], formerly
*Hele Pore*, held by Geoffrey *Frye* in FA i p. 461; and (3) *Hele Godyng*. The first two of
these are from Meeth parish, the last is now Hele Barton [SS 5106] in Petrockstowe.
A fourth 'Hele', Blinchs or Blanchs Hele, is found on Donn's map of 1765 at GR SS
530071 and wrongly displaces Crockers Hele, which itself displaces Giffords Hele (a fifth
'Hele') on the first edition OS map (sheet 26 of 1809, reprint sheet 82 of 1969).
These present a complex problem of identification (see also 16,42. 39,8 and 47,1 notes)
but despite EPNS's assertion that the names arose separately in different parishes, the
places are adjacent and it is more likely that the DB holdings are subdivisions of a single
'Heel' of land.
VILLAGERS .... AND 1 PLOUGH AND 3 FURLONGS. The use in DB of 7 instead of
*cum* 'with' is unusual in this phrase (but see 3,53); Exon. states that the 'villagers' have
the plough and furlongs (*ferlinos*).

15,48 STOCKLEIGH (ENGLISH). A parish in (West) Budleigh Hundred (14). It is held by
Reginald (of Vautortes; see 15,26-30 note) in 1086 and descends to the Honour of
Trematon. In Fees p. 762 Gilbert *Anglicus* holds *Stockelegh'* from a later Reginald
*de Valle Torta* of the Honour of Trematon. The place is *Stockelegh Engleys* in FA i
p. 364; see FA i p. 426, Cal. Inq. PM vol. xvi no. 1085, OJR in TDA 35 p. 282 and
15,17-18 note.

15,49 MODBURY. A parish in Ermington Hundred (27), held in 1086 in two parts by Richard
(15,49) and by Reginald (15,64) from the Count. Richard's portion passes to the Barony
of Cardinan and is held as *Parva Modbyr'* [Little Modbury GR SX 6550] in Fees p. 795;
see Fees p. 770, FA i p. 398 and Cal. Inq. PM vol. iv no. 44, viii no. 280. For Brownstone
in Modbury see 15,37 note.
WADO. DB and Exon. *Wado*, elsewhere in Devon *Wadel, Wadhel, Wadels* (rendered here
Waddell) and *Wadelo, Wadolo, Walo* (rendered here *Wadilo*) are all related and alternative
names; see PNDB pp. 407-408, especially p. 408 note 1. The basis of some instances
could be OE *Wada* (Mod.E *Wade*) and its rare derivative *Wædel*. But the range of forms
suggests rather a Norman treatment of OG *Wado*, diminutive pet-form *Wadilo, Wadil*.
*Walo* would represent a Norman treatment of *Wad(e)lo* (loss of *d* from *dl*, PNDB § 103
p. 99). (JMcND.)
THERE ALSO HE HOLDS 1 VIRGATE. See Exon. Notes here for the information that
the virgate is part of the villagers' land holding.

15,50 TORRIDGE. In Plympton St. Mary parish, Plympton Hundred (26), now swamped by a
housing development: Torridge Road and Close recall the name. Part of *Tourigg* is held
by the Prior of Plympton (FA i p. 402) and part by John *Stochay* (FA i p. 400; see
15,47 note), both of the Honour of Trematon; see FA i pp. 334, 353, Cal. Inq. PM vol.
viii no. 280 and OJR H6 p. 286.

15,51 HARESTON. In Brixton parish, Plympton Hundred (26). This is the larger half of
Reginald's holding; see 15,29 note.
SWEET. DB *Suet* probably represents OE *Swet*, though OE *Sweta* may be a possibility
because of the Exon. form *Sueta* here; PNDB p. 381.

15,52 SPRIDDLESTONE. In Brixton parish, Plympton Hundred (26). In FA i p. 334 Ralph
*[S]pridel* holds *Sprideleston* from Reginald *de Ferariis* (Honour of Trematon) and the
latter holds from the Earl of Cornwall. The DB entry probably accounted also for
*La Forsen*, similarly held in FA i p. 334 from Ralph *Spridel*, and *La Fenne* [Venn in

Brixton, GR SX 551521] in FA i p. 353; see FA i p. 401, Cal. Inq. PM vol. viii no. 45 and OJR H6 p. 288.

15,53 WEDERIGE. This place has not been identified nor any descent found. Exon. order suggests that it lay in Roborough (Walkhampton) Hundred (25) or possibly in Plympton (26). OJR's identification, following Whale, with 'Withy Hedge' in Plymstock is a mere guess (VCH p. 533 note 12 and H6 p. 262). There is a 'Wheatridge', a street name of unknown antiquity in Woodford in Plympton St. Mary parish.
IT PAYS 3s. As the Exchequer scribe has used *valet* for all the other value statements in the chapter, *reddit* here (as in 3,82 and 24,18, see notes) is probably the result of too close copying of the Exon. (which has *reddit* for DB's *valet* several times).
UP TO THIS POINT THESE ARE ADDED LANDS. This statement may refer only to the lands added to Ordwulf's fief (i.e. 15,47-53) or it may refer also to those added to Edmer Ator's holding (i.e. 15,14-31). If the latter, then it is interrupted by the lands held in 1066 by Edmer Ator and Ordwulf (15,32-46) which the Count acquired legally.

15,54 STOCKLEIGH. In Meeth parish, Shebbear Hundred (4), close to Erchenbald's other holding, at Hele (15,47). In Fees p. 795 *Stokkelegh'* is held from the Honour of Launceston; see FA i p. 359. It is *Stoklegh Dabernon* in FA i p. 411, see OJR H10 pp. 541, 570-571.
ALSI. DB forms include *Alsi, Elsi* and *Ailsi*, Exon. forms *Alsi, Alsi(us), Elsi* and *Ailsi(us)*; they represent OE *Aelfsige* or *Aethelsige*; see PNDB pp. 151-152. As with *Aluuardus* (see 1,41 note) safety indicates keeping to the base form; in previous volumes in this series the form *Alfsi* has been used.
HE COULD GO .... WOULD. This statement, although added at the end of the Exon. entry, must refer to Alsi. Cf. the similar statement in 16,10, also omitted by the Exchequer scribe (see 1,15 note on 'freely' on the omission of such phrases in DB).

15,55 MATFORD. In Exminster parish and Hundred (24). In FA i p. 346 it is a Mortain fee held by Henry *le Botour*; in FA i p. 389 it is held by John *Dynham'* of Montacute (Honour); see OJR in TDA 36 p. 368 and 47 p. 219.
ALWY TABB. Exon. *Aluuid' tabe*; from OE *Taebba*, the nickname probably referring to a tall, thin person (OEB p. 338). On the form *Aluuid(us)* for *Alwy*, see 25,2 note.

15,56 WILLIAM OF LESTRE. Exon. *Willelm(us) de lestra*; Lestre is in the département of Manche, France (OEB pp. 94-95). He is also a subtenant of the Count of Mortain in DB Somerset 19,27 and probably in Dorset 26,45;64 (in the General Notes for Somerset 19,27 and Dorset 26,64 'Eure' is a mistake for 'Manche').
TATTISCOMBE. In Trentishoe parish, Braunton Hundred (1). *Tottescomb* is held by Baldwin *de Tottescomb* of the Honour of *Bykynghull* in FA i p. 414; see FA i p. 360 and OJR H8 p. 448.

15,57 MAUGER OF CARTERET. Exon. *Mauger(us) de cartreo*. Carteret is in the département of Manche, France; see OEB p. 81. He is a frequent subtenant of the Count of Mortain in DB Somerset. Cf. 3,9 note above on Drogo (son of Mauger).
DONNINGSTONE. In Clayhanger parish, Bampton Hundred (8), named from the TRE holder Dunning. It is apparently the same place as *Duningeston'* held by the Abbot of Torre from William *Briwere* in Fees p. 396; see TE p. 153a and VE ii p. 361. Part of this holding, possibly *Alwinestone*, will have been at *Peatton* [Petton GR ST 0024 in Bampton parish], held from the Abbot of Torre in FA i p. 431. In Fees p. 797 *Peatetone* is a Mortain fee, but it is said to be uncertain whether it is held of the Honour of Plympton or of the Honour of Ashill in Somerset. Mauger's lands normally descend to Ashill Honour, but *Donnyngston'* and *Paitone* are among Plympton Honour fees in Cal. Inq. PM vol. iv (o.s.) no. 63 (= TDA 38 p. 326); see OJR in TDA 30 pp. 441, 451-452.
TAX FOR 3 VIRGATES OF LAND AND ½ FURLONG. In the MS there is an erasure by water of about 5 letters before *ferling*; part of an 7, followed by the top half of a *d*, 3 'low' letters and the top half of a second *d* with abbreviation line through the ascender, can be seen, suggesting 7 *dimid* was erased, which would then correspond to the clearly written *iii uirḡ & dim̄ & dim̄ ferdino* (3½ virgates ½ furlong) of Exon. Unfortunately the details of lordship and villagers' land do not help in discovering which was the correct tax amount (even if the details invariably agreed with the total, which they do not; see 1,4 note on the hide). It is possible that whoever checked the Exchequer MS thought that the two 7 *dimid*'s next to one another were a mistake and so erased one of them; or perhaps new information on the tax came to light which necessitated the alteration.
ALWINESTONE. Named from the TRE holder, but unidentified; see 15,57 first note.
WOODLAND, 7 ACRES. In the MS this interlineation reads 7 *vii ac̄ silue* in pale ink; under ultra-violet light it is possible to read *viii*, but the last *i* has been erased with water

|       | to make *vii* (as in Exon., where the *vii* is a correction from *iiii*); the original dot after the *viii* is still there. Farley prints *viii*, however. |
|-------|---|
| 15,58 | CLYST (ST. LAWRENCE). A parish in Cliston Hundred (20). In Fees p. 398 *Clifford* (i.e. *Clist*) *Sancti Laurencii* is a fee of William *Briwere* (Barony of Odcombe) and held of his heirs in FA i p. 333; see Cal. Inq. PM vol. v no. 527, vi no. 157, xi nos. 118 and 229 and OJR H7 pp. 364, 375. |
| 15,59 | THORNBURY. Exon. order suggests Thornbury in Drewsteington parish, Wonford Hundred (19). In Fees p. 797 Richard *Drogonis* (i.e. son of Drogo) holds in *Thornbir'* from the Prior of Montacute, Honour unknown; see OJR in TDA 36 p. 367. |
| 15,60 | ALFRED. Possibly Alfred the Breton (see Ch. 39) who has 1 virgate lordship in the Silverton Hundred Tax Return (xiii), though the main Exon. gives his lordship as 1½ virgates (see the Lordship and Villagers' Table). There may have been a change in the distribution of lordship and villagers' holding between the dates of the Tax Returns and the main Exon. returns, or one figure may be an error or a correction. This is the only holding of an Alfred in this Hundred. See 39,10 note.<br>CHITTERLEY. In Bickleigh parish, Hayridge Hundred (15). See preceding note for the possible Tax Return evidence. |
| 15,61 | BICKLEIGH. A parish in Hayridge Hundred (15). It does not appear in the fee lists; see OJR in TDA 42 p. 234. |
| 15,62 | CURSCOMBE. In Feniton parish, Hayridge Hundred (15). For the form, DB *Cochalescome*, see EPNS ii p. 563. It presumably had the same descent as Feniton (15,34), also held by Drogo from the Count.<br>INGVAR. The forms of this ODan personal name in Devon are *Ineuuar(us)* in DB and *Ineguar(us)*, *Inwarus* and *Inguar(us)* in Exon. See PNDB pp. 298-299 and §81 on the loss of the *g*.<br>1 SLAVE. In the MS *ii seru̇* was originally written, but the second *i* was erased, though it is still visible, especially in the facsimile. Cf. notes to L 11 and 5,14.<br>WITH 1½ PLOUGHS. Added later in very pale ink; as it is very squashed it might be that the scribe originally left a gap for the villagers' ploughs which did not prove large enough. However, in Exon. this information is in its usual place and written neatly like the whole entry. The rest of the line after the meadow has been erased and scraped, hence the gap, and it is possible that there were erasures under the villagers' ploughs, the *ii* of the meadow acres and, most probably, the *xl sol'* of the former value and the last *x* of the *xx solid'* present value, as they are all very pale and blurred as if written on parchment that was still damp after an erasure with water.<br>VALUE NOW 20s. The second *x* of the *xx solid'* is blurred and in pale ink, probably because written over an erasure; see preceding note. As there is a dot visible under the bottom tip of this second *x* (as well as after the *xx*), it would seem that the scribe originally wrote *xi* or *x* and then erased the last figure and corrected the value to *xx*. Because of the existence of the original dot, it is unlikely that the scribe wrote *xx* first and then tried to erase the second *x* with water to make the value 10s. In the facsimile the present value is reproduced *.x ı. solid*. |
| 15,63 | CHERITON. DB *Cherletone* from OE *ceorl* and *tūn*, EPNS ii p. 566. It lies in Payhembury parish, Hayridge Hundred (15), and was a Mortain fee in Fees p. 782, held as *Cherleton'* from Walter *de Esselegh'*, i.e. of the Honour of Ashill, Somerset, the expected descent from Bretel; see J. H. Round in TDA 38 p. 350 note 23. OJR wrongly identified it as 'Charlton' or 'Chaldon' in Cullompton or in Plymtree parishes; see VCH p. 440 note 2 and TDA 42 p. 234. Chaldon is in fact derived from OE *cealf* and *dun* 'calves' Down'; EPNS ii p. 562. Cheriton is *Brodechurleton* in FA i p. 425. |
| 15,64 | MODBURY. A parish in Ermington Hundred (27); for the other part, see 15,49. Descent from Reginald was to the Honour of Trematon, from which *Wymundeston'* [Whympston in Modbury, adjacent to Little Modbury 15,49, GR SX 6650] was held by Robert *Fort Escu* in Fees p. 770; see Fees p. 796, FA i pp. 352, 398, Cal. Inq. PM vol. iii nos. 523, 604, xi no. 459 and OJR H6 p. 313. Edmeston also lay in this parish and may have been part of this land, or it may represent *Hewis* (15,26;28 notes). In the Tax Return for *Alleriga* (Ermington) Hundred (xxx) St. Mary's of *Motberia* is said to have 1 hide in lordship, which corresponds to Reginald's lordship hide here; cf. the treatment of his lordship land in Newton Ferrers (15,37); see note). This Church was a dependency of St. Mary's of St. Pierre-sur-Dives in Normandy; see Oliver *Mon.* p. 297 and OJR in TDA 30 p. 309 note 81. |
| 15,65 | ORCHETON. In Modbury parish, Ermington Hundred (27). Like the previous entry, |

it descends to the Honour of Trematon, being held by Geoffrey *de Pridias* as *Orcherdton'* 'of the manor of *Modbyre*' in Fees p. 770; see Fees p. 796, FA i pp. 352, 397 and Cal. Inq. PM vol. iii no. 604, v no. 558.
15,66 HOLLOWCOMBE. DB *Holescome*. Exon. order suggests a place in Ermington Hundred (27); it is possibly Hollowcombe in Ermington parish for which, however, no DB reference is given in EPNS (i p. 274). On phonological grounds, it is certainly not 'Luscombe *alias* Halwell's Combe *alias* Jeclescombe *alias* Julescombe in Bigbury', VCH p. 442 note 6; see 15,44 note.
FOUR SALT-HOUSES. Presumably on the estuary of the river Erme.
PACKLOADS OF SALT. *summas salis*, accusative plural. The size of the packload is not known, but in the case of salt in DB Cheshire (S1,4 col. 268b) it contained 15 *bulliones* 'boilings'. According to OJR in VCH p. 388 the *summa* of fish or salt was 240 lbs. *Summa* is also used of corn in DB. In Exon. here the term used is probably *sagmas*, similar in meaning to *summa* (see RMLWL and Du Cange s.v. *sagma*), although the three minims after the *g* divide into *in* rather than into *m* (making *saginas*, which, however, seems only to mean 'a fishing net').
15,67 REGINALD. In the Exon. for 1,23, where details of the withheld customary due are also given, the subtenant is called Godfrey. The T.O. entry also makes Godfrey the subtenant, though this may be reflecting the name used in the main Exon. for 1,23, rather than for 15,67. Reginald was undoubtedly Reginald of Vautortes (see 15,26-30 note) and Godfrey was most likely of the same family (they both appear in the Tax Returns with the byname 'of Vautortes', but cannot be linked with this particular holding); there was probably some confusion here as to which man held Fardel from the Count.
FARDEL. In Cornwood parish, Ermington Hundred (27). *Ferthedel* is held from the Honour of Trematon in Fees p. 796; see Fees p. 771 and FA i pp. 352, 399.
ERMINGTON, THE KING'S MANOR. See 1,23.
CUSTOMARY DUES FROM PLEAS. That is, from the Hundred courts; in the T.O. for this entry and in the Exon. for 1,23 (see Exon. Notes) it is "customary dues which belong to the Hundred" and in DB 1,23 "customary dues of the Hundred".
REEVES. See 1,4 note on the reeve.
15,68-69 VENN. BROADFORD. DB *Fen, Bradeford*, both in Ugborough parish, Ermington Hundred (27), and both held by Reginald in 1086, represented by *Fenton'* and *Bradeford'* held from the Honour of Trematon in Fees p. 796; see Fees p. 770 and FA i pp. 352, 399. Broadaford owed a customary due to Ermington; see 1,23 and Exon. Notes to 1,23.
15,70 DINNATON. In Cornwood parish, Ermington Hundred (27). It is held with other of Reginald's lands of the Honour of Trematon as *Dynenton'* in Fees p. 770 (see 15,26 note). The name may be derived from Dunn who held TRE; see EPNS i p. 269. In FA i pp. 352, 399 *Langham* [Langham GR SX 6256, nearby] is coupled with *Dynyngton*; see Cal. Inq. PM vol. iii no. 604 and OJR H6 p. 314.
According to 1,23 two holdings called *Dunitone* owed a customary due to the royal manor of Ermington, although the present entry is the only other reference to the place; see 1,23 note for another possibility.
15,71 REGINALD .... HOLDS .... *de comite* 'from the Count' has been omitted, no doubt in error; it is in Exon. as usual. See 15,22 note.
PEEK. In Ugborough parish, Ermington Hundred (27). It is held as *Pek'* from the Honour of Trematon in Fees p. 796; see Fees p. 771, FA i pp. 352, 399, Cal. Inq. PM vol. iii no. 604, xv no. 149 and OJR H6 p. 319. The exact holding was Torpeek [GR SX 663562], held from John *de la Torre* in FA i p. 352.
15,72 LUDBROOK. In Ugborough and Ermington parishes, Ermington Hundred (27); see 15,26 note.
15,73 BOLBERRY. In Malborough parish, Stanborough Hundred (28); see 15,38 note.
15,74 HUGH .... VILLAGERS .... 1 HIDE. Probably Hugh of Vautortes, from whom the King had no tax on 1 hide he holds from the Count of Mortain in Diptford Hundred (Tax Return xxvi); Batson is in that Hundred and the 1 hide would be the villagers' land that was taxable. Hugh of Vautortes is a subtenant of the Count of Mortain in Somerset.
BATSON. In Salcombe parish, which it represents, Stanborough Hundred (28). In Fees p. 796 *Baddestane* is held of the Honour of Trematon; the holding included *Saltcomb* [Salcombe GR SX 7339] in FA i p. 351. See Fees p. 765, FA i pp. 324, 396, Cal. Inq. PM vol. iii no. 604, v no. 244 and OJR in TDA 45 p. 182.
VALUE NOW 15s. In the MS there is an erasure of about 4 letters after the *ual'*. Farley prints a small gap; see 1,60 note.

15 - 16

15,75  BOWCOMBE. DB *Come*. In Ugborough parish, Ermington Hundred (27). *Baucumb'* is held of the Honour of Trematon in Fees p. 770 with Ludbrook (15,26 note) and other of Reginald's lands. See Fees p. 796, FA i pp. 352, 399 and OJR H6 p. 314. The adjacent Earlscombe [GR SX 6555] seems to preserve a memory of the Earl (Count) of Mortain (EPNS i p. 287).

15,76  SHILSTON. In Modbury parish, Ermington Hundred (27). *Silvestane* is held in Fees p. 771 of the Honour of Cardinan; see FA i p. 397 and OJR H6 p. 326.

15,77  SPRIDDLESCOMBE. In Modbury parish, Ermington Hundred (27). Like Spriddlestone (15,52) it had the same 1086 holder, Reginald. In Fees p. 770 Hugh *Peverel* holds *Cumb' Spridel* from the Honour of Trematon. It is *Spridelcumb'* in Fees p. 796; see FA i pp. 352, 398, Cal. Inq. PM vol. iii no. 604 and OJR H6 p. 313.

15,78  HONICKNOWLE. In Saint Budeaux parish, Roborough Hundred (25). In Fees p. 796 *Hanecnolle* is held from the Honour of Trematon; see FA i pp. 354, 403, RH i p. 92a, Cal. Inq. PM vol. iii no. 604 and OJR H3 p. 113.
WADO. See 15,49 note on the name.

15,79  LIPSON. Now in Plymouth, Roborough Hundred (25); on the DB form, see EPNS i p. 235. *Lippeston'* is a fee of the Honour of Trematon in Fees p. 796. It is coupled with *Tongeslond* [unidentified] in FA i p. 403; see FA i pp. 340, 354 and OJR H3 p. 113.
GODWIN HELD IT FREELY (AND) JOINTLY. The marginal *par* is written in pale ink (see 15,47-52 note), whereas the interlined *libe* is in the same colour ink as the rest of the entry, suggesting that the two additions were done at different times. Cf. 17,13 note.
PASTURE, 1 VIRGATE. Pasture is also measured, rather unusually, in virgates in 21,7 and 25,24. Woodland is thus measured in 47,5. According to OJR in VCH p. 386 these are areal virgates (of 64 acres), different from the virgates used in the tax assessment. Cf. notes to 10,1-2 on the hide being used to measure pasture and woodland and 47,6 note on the *forling* of underwood.
THIS .... ALGAR'S LANDS. An odd statement because Algar nowhere else in Devon held land that passed to the Count of Mortain, whereas an Algar (perhaps a different person) is a frequent predecessor of Iudhael in Ch. 17. This statement occurs in the margin of the Exon. MS, but because Lipson is named there is no question of the scribe's adding the information beside the wrong entry.

Ch. 16  BALDWIN THE SHERIFF. Baldwin of Moeles (now Meulles in the département of Calvados, France) was the younger son of Count Gilbert of Brionne; for his elder brother Richard, see Ch. 26 note. Baldwin was delegated with other leading men-at-arms to help build a castle at Exeter after the revolt of 1068 and to remain there as part of the garrison (Orderic Vitalis ii p. 181) and the custody of the castle remained in his family. He also had his own castle at Okehampton (16,3). He was Sheriff of Devon by 1070 (*Regesta* i no. 58) and no doubt held the office until his death some time before 1096 when his son William is addressed in a charter together with Bishop Osbern and Warin the Sheriff of Cornwall (Mon. Ang. ii p. 497). His fief is the largest in Devon, but he also held land in Somerset and Dorset.
Baldwin's estates later form the Honour of Okehampton, the principal holders being the Courtenay family; see OJR in VCH p. 554 and in TDA 38 pp. 351-356. Many of the DB lands, together with later subdivisions, reappear in a series of *Inquisitiones Post Mortem* of the Courtenay family, e.g. Cal. Inq. PM vol. ii no. 71, iii no. 31, xiv no. 325. Attention should also be drawn to Cal. Inq. PM vol. iv (o.s.) no. 63, ostensibly dating from the reign of Henry VI, but the basic survey, including the names of tenants, clearly dates from the early 14th century. It is usefully divided into Hundreds and its places identified by Whale in TDA 38 pp. 318-336.
THE EXON. ORDER of this chapter, which is largely followed by the Exchequer scribe, with the presumed 1086 Hundreds is:

| | | | |
|---|---|---|---|
| 16,3-13 | Lifton | 16,106-128; 93;129;90-91; 130-132 | Wonford and Hemyock |
| 16,14-30 | Torrington | | |
| 16,31-32 | Hartland | | |
| 16,33-42 | Merton | 16,133-136 | Budleigh |
| 16,43-57 | Shebbear | 16,137 | Wonford |
| 16,58-64 | Exminster | 16,138 | Budleigh |
| 16,65-86;89; 87;94;88 | Braunton, Shirwell, Bampton, South Molton and Cliston (see Appendix) | 16,92 | Cliston |
| | | 16,139 | (unknown) |
| | | 16,140-151 | Witheridge |
| | | 16,152-157 | Teignton |
| 16,95-105 | Silverton | 16,158-159 | Tiverton |
| | | 16,160 | Teignton |

| | | | | |
|---|---|---|---|---|
| Ch. 16 | 16,161 | Halberton | 16,175-176 | Chillington |
| (cont'd.) | 16,162-163 | Kerswell | 16,2 | Barnstaple Borough |
| | 16,164-174 | Axminster, Axmouth, Colyton | 16,1 | Exeter Borough |

16,1;3 EDWARD. OSFERTH. The scribe mistakenly wrote *Edwardi* and *Offers* in capitals and the rubricator then emphasised them with a red line, which is normally reserved for personal names at the beginning of chapters, place-names and headings within chapters. DB *Offers*, Exon. *Osfers*, represents OE *Osfrith*; PNDB p. 339.

16,1 12 OTHER HOUSES .... KENN. See 16,58 and note on the 11 burgesses.
WHICH BELONGED. Exon. has *pertinuer(unt)* with an 'in 1066' phrase, but *ptiñ* in DB is more often the abbreviation for the present tense (= *pertinent* 'belong') which seems to fit in better with the phrase in 16,58 where 11 burgesses in Exeter are said to be attached (in 1086) to Kenn. According to Finn LE p. 48 the DB Commissioners were conveying the same information by the statement about the 12 houses as by that about the 11 burgesses. See second note under 1,1.

16,2 THEY PAY. The burgesses and the destroyed houses together; see Exon. Notes here. See C 1 note on other instances of 'destroyed houses' paying dues.

16,3 OKEHAMPTON. A parish in Lifton Hundred (18), *caput* of the later barony formed from Baldwin's lands. With Bratton Clovelly (16,5), it accounts for the 1½ virgates of lordship land recorded for Baldwin in the Tax Return for Lifton Hundred (i). It is represented in Fees p. 756 by *Okemeton, Alfaresdune* [Alfordon GR SX 6196], *Meledon*' [Meldon SX 5692], *La Hoke* [Hook SX 5896] and *Stokkelegh*' [Stockley SX 6095]; see Fees p. 786 and FA i pp. 320, 356, RH i p. 75a, Cal. Inq. PM vol. iii (n.s.) no. 31, vol. iv (o.s.) no. 63 and OJR in TDA 46 p. 195. The advowson of Okehampton was given to Cowick Priory (16,106 note) by Baldwin's son William; see TE p. 150b, Oliver *Mon.* p. 156 and OJR in TDA 44 p. 324, 46 p. 193.

Although DB does not describe this manor as a borough, it undoubtedly was one, though probably of recent creation and of the 'simple' kind, having only one 'owner'; see Ballard Ch. V and cf. first note under C 1 above.

16,4 CHICHACOTT. In Okehampton parish, Lifton Hundred (18); it is presumed that it descended with Okehampton and is represented by one of its members, e.g. Alfordon or Stockley (16,3 note), in later documents.
VILLAGERS ... (WHO) PLOUGH WITH 2 OXEN. An unusual variant in Exon., given as usual after the lordship plough.

16,5 BRATTON (CLOVELLY). A parish in Lifton Hundred (18); it can be identified in the Tax Return for Lifton (i), see 16,3 note. In Fees p. 785 one Okehampton Honour fee is held in *Brattone, Cumbe* [probably Northcombe GR SX 4595 and 'Southcombe', see Cal. Inq. PM vol. ii nos. 306, 593 and EPNS i p. 176] and in *Coddescot* ['Guscott', see 16,13 note, *Godescoth*' in Fees p. 756]; see FA i pp. 321, 405, Cal. Inq. PM vol. vii no. 297 and OJR in TDA 46 p. 190. The added name Clovelly is from the Claville family (who held in the 13th century), the form influenced by the place-name Clovelly (1,59); see HD p. 56 and EPNS i p. 173.
WHO HELD. In the MS *tenentʰ* (= *tenentes*, present participle, which can be used after a past verb); Farley omits the abbreviation sign in error. Both the abbreviation sign and the *dimid*' succeeding *tenentʰ* are in the same very pale ink as several of the corrections in Devon and the *dimid*' is squashed, as if added later, perhaps in correction; the scribe presumably saw at the same time that *tenent* with the preceding *erant* would make two main verbs in one phrase, which needed to be reduced to one verb or joined by an 7 (for which there would have been no room).

16,6 BOASLEY. In Bratton Clovelly parish, Lifton Hundred (18); see FA i p. 384, EPNS i p. 174 and OJR in TDA 46 p. 190.
7 SLAVES, WITH 1 PLOUGH. DB does not often state so clearly that slaves had ploughs; cf. notes to 6,13 and 28,16. Exon. records that the *villani* have the plough (and the rest of the land), but as no *villani* other than the 7 slaves are mentioned, it would seem either that they are classed as 'villagers' with land and ploughs or that for some reason the Exon. scribe omitted the true villagers and smallholders etc. (the latter being the view of Finberg *Tavistock Abbey* p. 60 note 3). Cf. Exon. Notes to 3,79. 16,145-146. 19,9. 28,16 and 35,5. See also 3,11 note on omitted 'villagers'.

16,7 BRIDESTOWE. A parish in Lifton Hundred (18); it is held of the Honour of Okehampton by Muriel *de Bollay* in Fees p. 786 as *Byrightestowe*. See Fees p. 756, FA i p. 405, TE p. 150a and Cal. Inq. PM vol. vii no. 708.

| | |
|---|---|
| 16,7 (cont'd.) | LAND OF SIX THANES. Exon. (288 b 2, see Exon. Notes) names these lands as *Carsforda* [Kersford], given as *Casforda* in T.O. 495 a 2; *Batesilla* [Battishill]; *Comba* [Combebowe]; *Etbolduswrda* [Ebsworthy], *Etboldesuuorda* in the T.O.; *Ferneurda* [Fernworthy], *Ferneuurda* in the T.O. and *Weia* [Way]; all are indexed and mapped in this volume. |
| | SAEWIN TUFT. Exon. *Sauuin' topa*. The byname may be the same as that of Haldane *Tope* and his brother Ulf *Tope sune* (DB Lincs. 7,18 and Cl.K. 10): ODan *Topi* (see OEB pp. 164, 226 and PNDB p. 386 and notes 8,9). *Topi*, however, is a rather rare and restricted ODan personal name, noted by Fellows Jensen p. 291, and appearing in DB in Lincs., Suffolk, Essex, Herts., and in Devon 16,146 (see note). The spelling *topa* here might equally well represent the rarely recorded, but surely common, word OE *toppa*, or a latinization of its more evidenced form *topp*, meaning 'a tuft, a forelock of hair' (BT; BTSuppl; OED *top* sb¹). (JMcND.) |
| 16,8 | GERMANSWEEK. A parish in Lifton Hundred (18), earlier Week Langford; see EPNS i p. 183. In Fees p. 755 Richard *de Langeford* (from Langford 16,96) holds ½ fee in *Wyk* from the Honour of Okehampton; in FA i p. 320 *Wyk Langeford* is held by the prior of Frithelstock from Roger *de Langeford*. See Fees p. 785, Cal. Inq. PM vol. viii no. 425, xiv no. 325, VE ii p. 335 and OJR in TDA 46 p. 188. |
| 16,9-10 | LEWTRENCHARD. WARSON. DB *Lewe, Wadelescote*, the latter being named from the TRE holder. Warson, which was Waddelestone until recent times (for the substitution of *-tūn* for *-cote*, see EPNS i p. 188 and cf. notes to 21,9-12 and to 42,3), is in Lewtrenchard parish, Lifton Hundred (18). In Fees p. 786 William *Trenchard* holds *Lyu* and *Wadeleston'* from the Honour of Okehampton. It is possible that *Orcherd*, the next entry in Fees [an unidentified 'Orchard', although there is one adjacent in Thrushelton parish at GR SX 4689], held by William *de Arundel*, was part of this land; see Fees p. 757, FA i pp. 320, 356, 384, 406, Cal. Inq. PM vol. xiv no. 325, OJR in TDA 46 p. 213 and 1,57 note. |
| 16,9 | ROGER OF MEULLES. DB *de Moles*, Exon. *de molis*. Meulles is in the département of Calvados, France; OEB p. 99. He appears only in Devon, not in Somerset as well (as OEB states). Other references to plain Roger in Ch. 16 may be to this man; see 16,18-20 note. |
| 16,10 | AND(?) 2 PIGMEN. The case of *porc* is not clear. It could be ablative *porcariis* (= "3 villagers with 1 smallholder and 2 pigmen with 1 plough", i.e. the plough is shared by the villagers, smallholders and pigmen); the Exon. rendering, with the pigmen after the villagers rather than in their more usual place at the end of the list of population, supports this. However, *porc͞* could abbreviate the nominative *porcarii* (= "3 villagers with 1 smallholder; 2 pigmen with 1 plough", i.e. the pigmen alone have the plough). See 1,6 note on pigmen for other examples of pigmen apparently having a share in the villagers' ploughs. |
| | HE COULD GO .... WOULD. Added at the end of the Exon. entry and referring to Waddell. Cf. 15,54 note on a similar statement in Exon., omitted in DB. |
| 16,11 | MODBERT. DB *Motbert(us), Modbert(us)*; Exon. *Motbert(us), Mobert(us)*, represent OG *Modbert*. See Förstemann 1129, PNDB p. 328 note 1 and EENS p. 55. |
| | KELLY. A parish in Lifton Hundred (18). In Fees p. 786 William *de Kelly* holds in *Kelli* and *Medwill'* [Meadwell GR SX 4081] from the Honour of Okehampton; see Fees p. 756, FA i pp. 320, 405 and OJR in TDA 46 p. 202. |
| 16,12 | RALPH OF BRUYÈRE. Exon. *Radulfus de Brueria* here and elsewhere. Bruyère is in the département of Calvados, France; see OEB p. 76. |
| | DUNTERTON. A parish in Lifton Hundred (18); it is *Dunterdune* in Fees p. 786, Okehampton Honour. See Fees p. 756, FA i pp. 320, 405, Cal. Inq. PM vol. xii no. 333 and OJR in TDA 46 p. 201. |
| 16,13 | 'GUSCOTT'. In Lifton Hundred (18) and said to be in Bratton Clovelly parish (OJR in TDA 46 p. 190 and EPNS i p. 175). It is mapped by DG in the south-east of the parish, but has not been found by the present editors on any other map. In Fees *Coddescot* (p. 785) or *Godescoth'* (p. 756) is held with 'Combe' and Bratton Clovelly; see 16,5 note and OJR in TDA 28 p. 468, 46 p. 190. |
| 16,14-30 | A GROUP OF PLACES lying in (Black) Torrington Hundred (11); the total of 2½ hides 3 furlongs ('ferlings') of lordship land (excluding 16,25 for which no detail is given) is close to the 2½ hides allowed to Baldwin in the Tax Return for Torrington Hundred (iii). |
| 16,14 | SAMPFORD (COURTENAY). A parish in (Black) Torrington Hundred (11). John *de Cortenay* holds *Sanford* in RH i p. 64b and Hugh *de Curtenay* holds *Saunford Curtenay* in FA i p. 327; see Cal. Inq. PM vol. iii no. 31, viii no. 273. Subdivisions of the Domesday |

| | |
|---|---|
| 16,14 (cont'd.) | holding, later held of the Honour of Okehampton, are given in Fees p. 784 as *Lewidecot'* [Lydcott GR SX 6297], *Cockescumb'* [Corscombe SX 6296], *Westecot'* [Westacott SS 6103], *Rokewrth'* [unidentified], all held by Richard *Cadyo*; *Herpeford* [Halford SX 6497, see EPNS i p. 165] and *Radeweye* [Reddaway SX 6295], held by Richard son of Ralph and Geoffrey *de Radeweye*; finally *Wythelgh'* [Willey SX 6495], held by Drogo *de Teynton'* FA i p. 407 adds *Doumyslond* [Dunsland 16,16]; see FA i p. 327 and OJR H5 p. 218. |
| 16,15 | BELSTONE. A parish in (Black) Torrington Hundred (11). *Belestane* in Fees p. 784 is held by the heir of Baldwin *de Belestane* of the Honour of Okehampton; see FA i p. 407 and OJR H5 p. 219. |
| 16,16 | DUNSLAND. Probably in Bradford parish, (Black) Torrington Hundred (11); there is another in Jacobstowe. *Doumyslond* (for *Dounnyslond*) is held with other Okehampton Honour places in FA i p. 407; see 16,14 note and OJR H5 p. 220. |
| 16,17 | MONKOKEHAMPTON. The DB form *Monuchemtone* (representing *Monuchaochementone* from OE *munuca* 'of the monks') implies the existence of a monastic community here before 1086, but no more is known, except that although Monkokehampton was a lay holding in 1086, it was probably the *Occemund* granted by King AEthelwulf (839-855) to Glastonbury Abbey (ECDC no. 12 p. 9 = Sawyer (1) no. 1696), and will thus have been alienated church property. In Fees p. 784 it is *Munekeokementon'*; see RH i p. 65a, FA i p. 408, Cal. Inq. PM vol. iii no. 34, EPNS i p. 153, OJR H5 p. 220 and Ch. 4 note. 2 PLOUGHS; 5 SLAVES. In the MS the 7 linking these two details is faint and shorter than usual and is not reproduced at all in the facsimile. |
| 16,18-20 | ROGER. Perhaps Roger of Meulles, who is elsewhere a subtenant of Baldwin (see 16,9 note), because of the descent of Exbourne; see next note. |
| 16,18 | EXBOURNE. A parish in (Black) Torrington Hundred (11). In Fees p. 784 John *de Molis* (possibly a descendant of Roger (of Meulles? see 16,9 note), the 1086 holder of 16,18-20) holds from the Honour of Okehampton *Lechebrok'* [Lashbrook 16,20], *Durneford* [Dornaford in Jacobstowe, GR SS 5900, and Dornaford Park in Exbourne, SX 6099], *Yekesburne* [Exbourne] and *Hyauntone* [Highampton 16,19]; see FA i pp. 327, 357, 407. An unidentified *Buston* (FA i p. 358, written *Euston* in FA i p. 407) appears to have been in this parish, a Nicholas *Buston'* being here in 1332 (LSR p. 66). It is possibly connected with Buskin [GR SS 5901]; see OJR H5 p. 221. |
| 16,19 | HIGHAMPTON. DB *Hanitone*. A parish in (Black) Torrington Hundred (11). It is *Hyauntone* in Fees p. 784 (see 16,18 note); *Hanton* in FA i p. 327; *Heghanton* in FA i p. 357, held of Okehampton Honour; see OJR H5 p. 220. In later times there were also Okehampton fees at *Buredune* [Burdon GR SS 4703] and *West Pulwrth'* [part of Pulworthy SS 5104; for 'East Pulworthy see 5,4 note] in this parish; see Fees p. 784, FA i p. 357, OJR H5 p. 225. |
| 16,20-21 | ALGAR LONG. Exon. *Algar(us) long(us)* for each entry; OEB p. 320. |
| 16,20 | LASHBROOK. Lashbrook farm and Little Lashbrook in Bradford parish (16,21), (Black) Torrington Hundred (11). It is *Lechebrok'* in Fees p. 784 (16,18 note) held from the Honour of Okehampton; see FA i pp. 327, 407 and OJR H5 p. 220. |
| 16,21 | BRADFORD. A parish in (Black) Torrington Hundred (11). In Fees p. 784 the heir of William *de Aubernun* holds in *Bradeford*; see FA i pp. 327, 357, 407 and OJR H5 p. 221. |
| 16,22 | KIGBEARE. DB *Cacheberge*, now in Okehampton parish, Lifton Hundred (18), but Exon. order clearly shows it in (Black) Torrington Hundred (11) where it is also found in medieval documents. DG identifies it with Cookbury in (Black) Torrington Hundred, but that place is *Cukebyr'* in Fees p. 788 held of Plympton Honour (see EPNS i p. 139 and 28,3 note), whereas Kigbeare is *Cakeber'* in Fees p. 784 held by Geoffrey *Coffin* of the Honour of Okehampton, with *Craffte* [Cruft GR SX 5296]; see FA i pp. 374, 409, Cal. Inq. PM vol. v no. 209, viii no. 425, xvi no. 1013, EPNS i p. 203 and OJR H5 p. 222. Part of this holding may well have been *Maddeford* [Maddaford SX 5494]; see Fees p. 784, FA i pp. 357, 405 and OJR H5 p. 225. |
| 16,23 | OTELIN. DB *Othelin*, Exon. *Otelin(us)*, represent OFr *Otelin* (Forssner p. 202) from OG *Ottelin* (Förstemann 188). INWARDLEIGH. DB *Lege*, the modern name being derived from the TRE holder *Ingvar*; see EPNS i p. 149. It is a parish in (Black) Torrington Hundred (11). In Fees p. 784 the heir of Elias *Coffin* holds from the Honour of Okehampton in *Inwardlgh'* and in *Westecot'* [Westacott GR SS 5300]; see FA i pp. 328, 408, and OJR H5 p. 222. Another Okehampton Honour holding in the same parish is *Westecomb* held by Richard |

*de Estecomb* [Westacombe and Eastacombe SX 5598, 5599], in FA i p. 408. One of these lands may represent Oak (16,24) which is otherwise not found in the fee lists.
1 PIGMAN. This is interlined in the Exon. MS (though by the same scribe and in the same colour ink as the rest of the entry), possibly the reason for its omission in DB. Cf. 15,12 note.

16,24   OAK. In Inwardleigh parish, (Black) Torrington Hundred (11); it might be represented by Westacott or Westacombe in later lists, see 16,23 note.

16,25   GORHUISH. Higher and Lower Gorhuish in Northlew parish, (Black) Torrington Hundred (11). *Gorehiwiss'* is an Honour of Okehampton holding in Fees p. 784; see FA i pp. 328, 408.

16,26   BROADWOOD (KELLY). A parish in (Black) Torrington Hundred (11). William *de Kelly* (see 16,11 Kelly, which was also held by Modbert) holds in *Brawode* from Okehampton Honour in Fees p. 784; see FA i p. 408 and OJR H5 p. 223. The next entry in Fees p. 784 records that Peter *Corbin* holds in *Corbineston'* [Corstone GR SS 6104], perhaps a part of this holding, or the second Middlecott (16,28;30 note).

16,27   HONEYCHURCH. DB *HONECHERDE*; Exon. *honechercha*, but the second *ch* is not well written, the *c* being joined to the ascender of the *h* and the hook of the *h* not reaching the line and being more curved than that of the first *h*. It is possible that on a quick glance this *ch* could be taken for a malformed *d*, which may be the reason for the DB form of the place-name (so Baring p. 316). Cf. notes to 16,44. 25,20 and 52,20, and see 16,42 note for other cases where the Exchequer scribe has misread the Exon. Honeychurch is now in Sampford Courtenay parish, but formerly a separate parish in (Black) Torrington Hundred (11). In Fees p. 784 *Hunichurch'* is held of the Honour of Okehampton; see FA i p. 409 and OJR H5 p. 223.
ALWIN BLACK. Exon. *Aluuin(us) niger*; OEB p. 292.
VALUE 30s. This is written at an angle in the right margin of the MS in the same pale ink and almost certainly by the same scribe as two other added values (34,21 and 51,14; see notes) who may be different from the scribe of the main body of Devon: these are the only occurrences in Devon of the abbreviation *sold'*, the usual form being *solid'* here. As the values are written neatly and not added in the corresponding Exon. entries, the original omission of them in DB must have been accidental, and their later inclusion perhaps due to a checking of Exon.

16,28;30 MIDDLECOTT. Probably in Broadwood Kelly parish (16,26), but the identity is open to doubt, as there was a Middlecott also in Ashwater and in Bradford, both in (Black) Torrington Hundred (11), that in Ashwater not being noticed by EPNS (see i pp. 132, 137). The fact that Middlecott in Broadwood Kelly is adjacent to Brixton (16,29) is probably significant; that both Middlecotts (16,28;30) were held by Alwold before 1066 suggests that they may be part of the same land. Another of Ranulf's estates — Whiteway 16,157 — passes to the Honour of Plympton, so 16,28 is probably the *Middlecoth'* held by Joel *Faber*, Jordan *de Fenton'* and Hugh *le Sak'* of that Honour in Fees p. 788; see FA i pp. 357, 408. The other Middlecott (16,30) does not seem to appear as such in the fee lists, but if Corstone (16,26 note) is not a part of Broadwood Kelly, it may be this second Middlecott, taking its name from the *Corbin* family who held in Fees; clinching evidence is lacking: see OJR H5 p. 224.

16,28   ALWOLD. The forms of this name in Devon are *Aluuold(us)* and *Aluuald(us)* in DB and *Aluuold(us), Aluuoud(us), Aluold(us), Aluualdus* and *Aluuardus* in Exon. and the T.O. The *Aluuardus* forms (in the T.O. for 36,23 and in the main Exon. for 36,24) are the result of AN interchange of *l-r*. All represent further OE *Aelfweald* or *Aethelweald*; see PNDB pp. 154-155. As with *Aluuardus* (see 1,41 note) safety indicates keeping to the base form; in previous volumes in this series the form 'Alfwold' has been used. See Exon. Notes 16,174.

16,29   BRIXTON. In Broadwood Kelly parish, (Black) Torrington Hundred (11). It is *Brigteneston'* in Fees p. 784, held by Ada *de Risford* (from Rushford 16,113) from Okehampton Honour; see FA i pp. 327, 408 and OJR H5 p. 225.

16,31   ASHMANSWORTHY. In Woolfardisworthy parish, Hartland Hundred (3). In Fees p. 786 *Ashmundeswrth'* is held as two half-fees, the second by three people from the Honour of Okehampton; see FA i pp. 341, 371, 410. It is *Asshemandesworthi* and *Strokesworthi* [Stroxworthy GR SS 3419] in Cal. Inq. PM vol. xiv no. 325.

16,32   YARNSCOMBE. A detached parish of Hartland Hundred (3). In Fees p. 786 there is an Okehampton fee in *Parva Ernescumb'* ['Little' Yarnscombe]; see FA i pp. 341-342 (*Litelaerneston'*), 410, 416 and Cal. Inq. PM vol. xiv no. 325, xv no. 197.

| | |
|---|---|
| 16,32 (cont'd.) | VILLAGERS .... 2½ FURLONGS. In Exon. *villani ii ferdinos & dimidiū*. VCH p. 450 translates this as 'the villeins 2 ferdings and ½ (plough)', but if this were the meaning one would expect *dimidū* (to agree with *carrucam* understood or omitted in error); in any case the placing of Latin *dimidius* after the noun (instead of immediately after the number) is very common. |
| 16,33 | PARKHAM. A parish in Shebbear Hundred (4). In Fees p. 785 the heir of Baldwin *de Belestane* (from Belstone 16,15 also held by a Richard in 1086) holds *Parkeham* from the Honour of Okehampton. See FA i pp. 329, 410 and OJR H10 p. 564. |
| 16,34 | (LITTLE) TORRINGTON. DB *Torintone*. The order of Exon. points to a place in Shebbear Hundred (as 1,31. 15,16), divided by the river Torridge from Great Torrington, which lies in Fremington Hundred, and thus indicates Little Torrington; but a consequence is that *Torintone, Toritone* and *Liteltorelande* must all be accepted as early names of Little Torrington, see EPNS i p. 111. This holding is possibly represented in Fees p. 785 by *Toniton'* (probably a misreading of *Toriton'*), held by William and Alexander *Tony* (or *Tauy* or *Touy*) from the Honour of Okehampton, the last of a group of Shebbear Hundred places; see OJR H10 pp. 536, 542, 553. |
| 16,35 | HEANTON (SATCHVILLE). In Huish parish, Shebbear Hundred (4). In Fees p. 785 John *de Sicca Villa* holds *Yauntone* of the Honour of Okehampton; it is *Heanntone Sechevill* in FA i p. 329; see FA i pp. 359, 412, Cal. Inq. PM vol. xv no. 197 and OJR H10 pp. 542, 565. |
| 16,36 | AUBREY. In DB Devon this personal name appears in the forms *Alberi, Alberic', Alebric, Alebrix*, and the Exon. forms are *Alberid(us), Alebric(us), Halebrix, Albrix, Albritius*. It appears in some instances to be a latinized form of OE *Aelfric*; see notes to 3,35 and 17,88-89. It is interesting that DB should use the form *Alebrix* (for 17,94;102-105), the -*x* ending being unusual and a peculiarity of one of the Exon. scribes and used by him for these entries, thus suggesting direct copying from the Exon. MS by the Exchequer scribe.<br>POTHERIDGE. In Merton parish, Shebbear Hundred (4). Ralph *de Estaneston'* holds one fee of the Honour of Okehampton in *Puderigh'* in Fees p. 785; see FA i p. 411 and OJR H10 p. 565.<br>WITH 2 [PLOUGHS]. In the MS *cū ii bord'* ('with 2 smallholders'), obviously a scribal error for *cū ii cař*, which is what Exon. has. |
| 16,37 | STOCKLEIGH. In Meeth parish, Shebbear Hundred (4). It is held by the heir of William *de Aubernun* as *Stockelg'* from the Honour of Okehampton in Fees p. 785; see OJR H10 pp. 542, 565. |
| 16,38 | WOOLLADON. Also in Meeth parish, Shebbear Hundred (4). Ralph *de Wulledune* holds in *Wulledune* in Fees p. 785 from the Honour of Okehampton; see FA i pp. 359, 412 and OJR H10 p. 566. |
| 16,39 | MEETH. A parish in Shebbear Hundred (4). In Fees p. 785 Roger *Giffard* holds in *La Meye* (the *y* is probably a misreading of a *p*, i.e. *La mepe* [Methe] ) from the Honour of Okehampton; the same holding is *Mete* and *Stokheye* [Stockey in Meeth, GR SS 5407] in FA i p. 329 and *Methe, Hele* and *Stokhaye* in Cal. Inq. PM vol. xiv no. 325. This *Hele* might be part of this holding at Meeth, or connected with *Helescane* (16,42). See FA i p. 412 and OJR H10 p. 566.<br>BEFORE 1066. In the MS *T.R.E.* clearly; in the facsimile the *R* comes out like a *B*. |
| 16,40 | ROBERT. Probably Robert of Beaumont (on whom, see 16,65 note): the Tax Return for Merton Hundred (v) states that the King had no tax from the ½ virgate Robert of Beaumont holds from Baldwin the Sheriff, and this is the only holding of a Robert in Merton (Shebbear) Hundred.<br>LANDCROSS. DB *Lanchers*. A parish in Shebbear Hundred (4). Philip *de Bello Monte*, no doubt a descendant of Robert (of Beaumont, see preceding note), holds *Lancarse* in Fees p. 784 from the Honour of Okehampton; see FA i pp. 329, 410 and OJR H10 p. 567.<br>AELFEVA. DB and Exon. *Alueva* represents OE *Aelfgifu*, fem.; PNDB pp. 173-174. |
| 16,41 | WOOLLEIGH. In Beaford parish, Shebbear Hundred (4), DB *Vlvelie*; see EPNS i p. 87. It does not appear in the fee lists; see OJR H10 p. 567. |
| 16,42 | HELESCANE. The DB form is not noted in EPNS and is uncertain, probably a misreading of Exon. *Helescaua* (OE *sceaga* 'a strip of rough or woodland'); cf. 28,12 DB *Beuleie*, Exon. *Benleia*, and see notes to 3,24-25;38;39. 5,2. 16,27;44. 17,18. 19,16. 25,20. 34,3 and 52,20 for other misreadings of the Exon. form by the Exchequer scribe (and cf. 28,14 note). In all those that can be identified, the modern place-name is nearer to the Exon. than to the Exchequer form, suggesting that the Exchequer scribe was |

16,42 (cont'd.)   responsible for the errors. The DB *Helescane* might be a misreading for a name *Helestane* in some earlier document, from OE *healh* and *stān*; but no later forms of a place-name in *-stone* have been found near the places called *Hele* hereabouts.

*Helescane*, like the preceding place, probably lay in Shebbear Hundred (4), the Exon. scribe changing for the next entry Chawleigh, which is first of a Tawton Hundred group (12). It has been variously identified as Hele in Meeth (DG), Hele Poure in Meeth (OJR in VCH) or Huntshaw Wood, formerly 'Henshaw' (Whale in VCH). But neither Huntshaw nor 'Henshaw' is a likely development of *Helescaua*, since the l>n interchange needs *n* or *l* or *r* in the following syllable to trigger it. It is pointed out that among Okehampton Honour fees in Fees pp. 784-785 (Shebbear Hundred) there is no fee named from Woolleigh (16,41) nor from *Helescane*, but William *le Cornu* holds ½ fee in *Hunshaue* and, in succession, Roger *Cornu* holds in *Honyschaue* in FA i p. 412. There is no need to doubt that this latter is Huntshaw, now a parish in Fremington Hundred (5), but variously in Shebbear or Fremington in the fee lists. There is also little doubt that it is the holding of William Cheever (19,5). The fact that Huntshaw appears in two Hundreds in the feudal lists led to the belief that there was a separate Huntshaw in Shebbear Hundred. Although 'Henshaw' or 'Huntbear' was rejected by OJR in TDA 29 pp. 264-266 and in TDA 36 p. 353, in H10 p. 567 he reverted to the identification 'Huntshaw *alias* Huntbere in Little Torrington' for 16,42, unfortunately using the same evidence in H8 p. 515 to identify William Cheever's holding of 19,5.

If *Helescane* later simplified to 'Hele', it is likely to be one of the Heles in Meeth or Petrockstowe parishes (see 15,47. 16,39. 39,8 and 47,1 notes), perhaps Giffords Hele.
PASTURE, 6 ACRES. The Exchequer scribe also omitted details of pasture that are given in the Exon., in 32,5 and 36,12; only for 32,5 is there a possible reason for the omission (see note).

16,43   CHAWLEIGH. A parish in (North) Tawton Hundred (12). In RH i p. 75b *Chaveleg* and *Dueltune* [Dolton 16,44] are held of the Barony of Okehampton; see FA i p. 340. In Fees p. 783 Chawleigh is probably represented by *Hardewinesl[e]gh* [Hardingsleigh GR SS 7212], *Chenneston* [Chenson SS 7009] and *Wyk* or *Wyk Chalvelegh* (FA i p. 423) [Chawleighweek SS 6813]; see Cal. Inq. PM vol. iii no. 31, viii no. 273.
SIWARD. DB *Siuuard(us)*, Exon. *Seduuard(us)*, represent OE *Sigeweard*; see PNDB pp. 357, 361.

16,44   DOLTON. DB *OVELTONE*; Exon. *Dueltona*, though the *D* is oddly shaped, narrower at the bottom than normal. Although it is unlike the *O* in *Olfus* on the same line, the Exchequer scribe seems to have read this first letter as such. See 16,27 note.
It is the parish of Dolton in (North) Tawton Hundred (12). It is held with Chawleigh (16,43) in RH i p. 75b; see FA i p. 340 and OJR in TDA 29 p. 249.
7 SLAVES. Slaves are also omitted in DB, though in Exon., in 42,16. On both occasions the word order in the Exon. may be the reason for this; see Exon. Notes here. See also Exon. Notes 34,13.

16,45   NYMET (ROWLAND). DB *Limet*. Four places in this chapter lie in the Hundred of (North) Tawton (12) and have the same basic name in DB: 16,45;48;52;55. The present holding, having the same 1086 subtenant (Walter) as Leigh and Great Beere (16,46-47), is probably the *Nimet Rollandi* held with *Legh'* and *Bere'* in Fees p. 783 from the Honour of Okehampton by Walter *de Nimet*; see FA i pp. 370, 422, Cal. Inq. PM vol. iv (o.s.) no. 63 (= TDA 38 p. 329) where the places are *Nymet Roland, Legh* and *Beare cum Rolondistone* ['Rolands *tūn*']; see also OJR in TDA 29 p. 249, 36 p. 375.
MILL .... There is no obvious reason why the Exchequer scribe omitted this important information which is in Exon.

16,46-47   LEIGH. (GREAT) BEERE. In Coldridge and North Tawton parishes respectively, (North) Tawton Hundred (12). DB *Liege* and *Bera* are identified by VCH as Rashleigh and Cherubeer (*Rasle* 1278; *Churbear* 1238, 1244; see EPNS ii p. 366). But the compounded forms of these are probably of pre-conquest origin and are likely to have been in use in 1086 rather than the simplex forms, 'Beer' and 'Leigh'. Moreover in the 13th century, there are two other places in the same Hundred, simply called *Legh'* and *Bere'*, which have the correct manorial descent: in Fees p. 783 they are coupled with Nymet Rowland; see 16,45 note and FA i pp. 370, 422.

16,48-49   BROADNYMETT. APPLEDORE. DB *Limet* (see 16,45 note) and *Apledore* lie in North Tawton and Clannaborough parishes respectively, (North) Tawton Hundred (12). They have the same 1086 holder (Ralph of Bruyère) and are held together in Fees p. 783 as *Bradenimet'* and *Apeldure* with *Niwetone* [in Zeal Monachorum, GR SS 7004] by

Ada *de Risford* (from Rushford 16,113) of the Honour of Okehampton; see FA i p. 422, Cal. Inq. PM vol. iv (o.s.) no. 63 (= TDA 38 p. 329), vol. iii (n.s.) no. 31 and OJR in TDA 29 p. 249.

16,50    HALSE. In Nymet Tracey (Bow) parish, (North) Tawton Hundred (12), held in Fees p. 783 as *Hause* by Eleanor *de Hause*; see FA i p. 423.

16,51    CLANNABOROUGH. A parish in (North) Tawton Hundred (12). It is *Cloveneburgh'* in Fees p. 783, held by Alan *de Hallesuurthe*; see FA i p. 422 and OJR in TDA 29 p. 250. BEFORE 1066; IT PAID TAX. In the MS an 7 links these two statements; Farley omits it in error.

16,52    WALSON. DB *Limet*. It lay in Clannaborough parish (16,51), (North) Tawton Hundred (12). The modern form is apparently derived from *Wado* (Exon. *Walo*; see 15,49 note on the name), the TRE holder; EPNS ii p. 365. In Fees p. 783 William *de Punchardun* holds in *Waleston'* and *La Thorne* [Thorne GR SS 7300] of the Honour of Okehampton; see FA i pp. 371, 422 and OJR in TDA 29 p. 250.

16,53-54    BRUSHFORD. A parish in (North) Tawton Hundred (12). In the Tax Return for Tawton Hundred (ix) it is stated that tax has not been paid on ½ hide held by Geoffrey from Walter of Claville. No Geoffrey holds from Walter of Claville in DB Ch. 24, so the reference is probably to these two holdings. These seem to be represented in Fees p. 783: (1) by *Brigheford* held with *Wemmewrth'* [Wembworthy 16,57] by Richard *le Espee*, and (2) by *La Heghe* [Hayne GR SS 6709] and *Pertricheswall'* [Partridge Walls SS 6708], held by John son of Roger and Iudhael *de Bosco*; see FA i p. 422 and OJR in TDA 29 p. 250.

16,53    GODFREY THE CHAMBERLAIN. Exon. *Godefrid(us) camerari(us)*; he does not occur again in DB according to OEB pp. 240-241.

16,55    BURSTON. DB *Limet*. In Zeal Monachorum parish, (North) Tawton Hundred (12). This is probably the *Burdevileston'* held in Fees p. 783 of the Honour of Okehampton by John *Burnel* and Simon *Laumpre*; see FA i pp. 373, 422, Cal. Inq. PM vol. xi no. 118 and EPNS ii p. 375.

16,56    RAINER THE STEWARD. Exon. *Rainer(us) dapifer*.
GREENSLADE. In (North) Tawton Hundred (12). Robert *de Greneslade* holds in *Greneslade* in Fees p. 783; it is probable that the next entry, *Niwelaunde* [Newland Bridge and Mill, GR SS 6500], was part of the DB manor; see FA i p. 423 and Cal. Inq. PM vol. viii no. 425, xvi no. 1013. In later times there was also an Okehampton fee in this Hundred at *Brygg* [?Bridge in North Tawton, SS 6502] close to this holding; FA i p. 423.
THE KING'S MANOR CALLED (NORTH) TAWTON. See 1,3.

16,57    RICHARD OF NÉVILLE. Exon. *Ricardus de nouilla* (not *Nouuilla* as OEB p. 102). Probably Néville in the département of Seine-Maritime, France.
WEMBWORTHY. DB *Mameorde*, Exon. *Mameorda*; the Exon. scribe appears to have written *Mameorda* for *Wameorda* and the Exchequer scribe copied his mistake (cf. notes to 34,13 and 52,10). The place is *Wemmewrth'* in Fees p. 783, held with Brushford (16,53-54 note); see FA i p. 422. It is possible that *Eggenesford* [Eggesford GR SS 6811] also in Fees p. 783, held by John *de Regni* from Okehampton Honour, is part of this holding.

16,58-64    A GROUP OF PLACES that now lie in Exminster or Teignbridge or Wonford Hundreds (24, 23, 19). Wonford and Teignbridge Hundred places are entered in distinct groups elsewhere in Ch. 16; the order of Exon. and medieval evidence makes it likely that 16,58-62;64 were all in Exminster Hundred (24) in 1086, Beetor and Shapley (16,60; 61-62;64) forming a detached portion of the Hundred. Kenn and Mamhead (16,58;63) are identifiable in the Exminster Hundred Tax Return (xxiii); see OJR in TDA 47 pp. 203-204.

16,58    LEVEL WITH THE FIRST LINE of this entry, in the left margin, is written a ४ sign, not reproduced by Farley. The colour of ink used is the same as for the entry and resembles the O checking marks beside the *Aisse*s and *Otri*s and *Wiche* (see notes to 1,65. 10,1˙and 34,1).
KENN. A parish in Exminster Hundred (24). The 3 hides of Baldwin's lordship will have formed the greater part of the 3½ hides lordship stated to be his in the Tax Return for Exminster Hundred (xxiii). In RH i p. 89b Hugh *de Curtenay* holds in *Ken*; see FA i p. 377, Cal. Inq. PM vol. ii no. 71, iii no. 31, viii no. 273 and OJR in TDA 47 p. 223.
42 VILLAGERS AND SMALLHOLDERS. That is, the combined total of the villagers and smallholders is 42, a word such as *divisi* ('divided') being understood before *inter*.

The same phrase occurs in Exon. and cf. 17,41 note. But a similar phrase of *inter* .... 7 when applied to resources means something different; see 1,4 notes on 'leagues' and 'furlongs'.

11 BURGESSES.... See 16,1 and notes. It is interesting that in Exon. this phrase is also added; see Exon. Notes here. Burgesses are regularly detailed either with the other villagers (as in 24,20) or with the resources (as in 16,3).

16,59 (GEORGE) TEIGN. In Ashton parish, Exminster Hundred (24), named from a former chapelry to St. George (EPNS ii p. 487). In Fees p. 786 Gerard *de Spineto* holds in *Teyng*; it is *Teyng Jory* in FA i p. 389; see OJR in TDA 47 p. 224.

16,60 BEETOR. DB *Begatore*, see EPNS ii p. 470. It now lies in North Bovey parish, Teignbridge Hundred (23), but it will probably have been in the same Hundred as the adjacent Shapley (16,61-62;64 note) which lay in Exminster Hundred (24) in the Middle Ages; see OJR in VCH p. 453 note 7 and in TDA 47 p. 225.

EDWULF. DB *Eddulf(us), Iadulf*, Exon. *Erdulfus, Edolf(us), Iadolf(us)*, represent OE *Eadwulf*. See 16,115 note and Exon. Notes to 19,45.

16,61- SHAPLEY. There are two places called Shapley on the edge of Dartmoor, within two
62;64 miles of each other. One is now in North Bovey parish, Teignbridge Hundred (23), the other in Chagford parish, Wonford Hundred (19). Beetor (16,60) in North Bovey parish lies between them. In DB there are five occurrences of Shapley: the present three, all of which seem to lie in an Exminster Hundred group (24); Shapley of 45,1, which probably lay in Chagford (see note), and Shapley 52,44 (see note) which according to later evidence lay in Teignbridge Hundred and so was probably the Shapley in North Bovey. The present Shapleys seem to have lain in Chagford. In Fees p. 786 Robert *de Hyliun* [from Helléan, Ch. 44 note], holds in *Shaplgh'* one fee of the Honour of Okehampton and Herbert *de Cumb'* holds in *Jurdaneston'* 1/6th fee. Unless one of these is Beetor (16,60) which is not otherwise represented in the fee lists, it is likely that 16,61-62 held by Robert, a total of 3 virgates, form the one fee in Shapley and the 1 virgate held by Godwin (16,64) is *Jurdaneston'* [Jurston in Chagford, GR SX 6984]. In FA i p. 346, in Exminster Hundred, *Schaplegh* is held by William and Hugh *le Prouz*, and *La Fenne* [Venn SX 6984] and *Jordaneston* by Robert *de Valepitte*; see FA i p. 388. Shapley, Venn and Jurston are all tithings of Exminster Hundred within Chagford parish, Wonford Hundred, in 1334 (LSR 1334 p. 59); see OJR in TDA 36 p. 368, in VCH pp. 453-454 and in TDA 47 p. 225.

16,61 ALDRED. DB and Exon. here *Aret* (on which see PNDB § 109); elsewhere in Devon DB *Adret, Eldred(us), Aldret, Aldred(us), Edred(us), Aeldret*, and in Exon. *Adret(us), Aldred(us), Aldret(us), Alred(us), Adredus*. PNDB pp. 186, 241 places these forms under the separate OE names of *Aethelred* and *Ealdred* respectively, but it would seem that by 1086 the *Aethel-* forms were becoming old-fashioned and were being superseded by *Ald-, Eld-, Ad-, Ed-*, etc. (JMcND).

Certainly there is an overlap in Exon. as compared to DB in the forms which PNDB lists as separate; e.g. in 52,27-28 DB has *Eldred* (= Aldred) and *Edred* (= Aethelred) respectively, whereas Exon. has *Adret* (= Aethelred) for both, though PNDB p. 186 explains this by stating that the DB form *Eldred* is a scribal error.

WITH 1 [SLAVE]. In the MS cū i caṙ, obviously a scribal error for *cum i servo*; in Exon. a slave is recorded after the villagers.

16,62 THE VILLAGERS (HAVE) 1 VIRGATE. No 'villagers' are recorded, however; see 3,11 and note.

16,63 MAMHEAD. A parish in Exminster Hundred (24); this holding can be identified in the Tax Return (xxiii): the 1½ virgates lordship added to the ½ hide and ½ virgate lordship of 34,10;12 account for the 1 hide of Ralph of Pomeroy's lordship in this Hundred. In Fees p. 786 Ralph Peverel holds 1 fee in *Mammehevede* of the Honour of Okehampton. It is *Mammehevede* by *Doulessh* in Cal. Inq. PM vol. vi no. 478. See FA i p. 347, Cal. Inq. PM vol. xi no. 300 and OJR in TDA 47 p. 224.

16,64 SHAPLEY. In Chagford parish, now Wonford Hundred; see 16,61-62;64 note.
16,65 ROBERT OF BEAUMONT. Exon. *de bello monte* here and elsewhere for Devon, is probably Beaumont-le-Roger in the département of Eure, France (OEB p. 71). Robert inherited the title of the Count of Meulan through his mother Adeline and, so-styled, was a tenant-in-chief in DB Warwicks., Leics. and Northants. He became Earl of Leicester in 1107. His brother Henry became Earl of Warwicks. *c*. 1089. His father, Roger of Beaumont, also held land in chief in DB Dorset and Glos. (see Dorset General Notes Ch. 28).

| | |
|---|---|
| 16,65 (cont'd.) | SHIRWELL. Shirwell parish, Shirwell Hundred (2). In Fees p. 784 Philip *de Bellomonte* holds in *Shirewill'* from the Honour of Okehampton. Richard *de Bellomonte* holds in RH i p. 78b; see FA i pp. 335, 416. There were also Okehampton Honour fees in this parish at *Shebescote* [Sepscott GR SS 5936] and *Cocklegh* [Coxleigh SS 5835] held by Robert *Beaupel* and Thomas *de Ralegh* in FA i p. 361 and at *Borygthlecote* [Brightlycott SS 5835] held with Coxleigh in FA i p. 416; see FA i p. 337 and OJR H8 pp. 464, 478–480 and 21,2 note.<br>IN BARNSTAPLE 2 HOUSES WHICH PAY 2s. Written in the left margin of the MS, surrounded on 3 sides by the same dark brown ink as the enclosed statement, but with no transposition signs to indicate its exact position in the entry. The ink is the same colour as in the main part of 16,65, though the pen appears thinner, and the addition is rubricated. Cf. another addition concerning Barnstaple in 3,6 and also 32,6 note. |
| 16,66 | ASHFORD. A parish in Braunton Hundred (1), represented by two entries in DB (16,66;85) both held by Robert from Baldwin. These correspond to *Asford* 1 fee in Fees p. 784 held by Philip *de Bellomonte* (descendent from Robert (of Beaumont, 16,65 note)) and *Westesford* ½ fee held by the heir of Richard *Beaupel* [West Ashford, adjacent but in Heanton Punchardon parish] ; see FA i pp. 359, 413 and OJR H8 p. 431. |
| 16,67–68 | LOXHORE. A parish in Shirwell Hundred (2). Descent from Robert continued in the Beaumont family, *Nitherlokysore* [Lower Loxhore] and *Overelockesore* ['Upper' Loxhore] being held from Alice *Beaumont* in FA i p. 416. *Smythepath* [Smythapark GR SS 6238] also held by Alice *Beaumont* was in this parish and probably part of this holding; see FA i p. 337, Cal. Inq. PM vol. vi no. 506, xiv no. 325 and OJR H8 p. 464. |
| 16,67 | DOLESWIF. DB and Exon. *Dolesuuif* is OE *Doles-wif*, final element OE *wif* 'woman, wife', first element the OE byname or personal name *Dol* (= OE *dol* 'foolish'; see OEB p. 344). The name indicates that Doleswif is a woman. |
| 16,68 | ALDER-GROVE also occurs in Devon at 17,9. |
| 16,69 | HEANTON (PUNCHARDON). DB *Hantone*, now a parish in Braunton Hundred (1). In Fees p. 784 William *de Punchardun* (a descendant of Robert) holds in *Hyaunton', Hakynton'* [Hagginton 16,70] and *Blakewille* [Blakewell 16,74] from the Honour of Okehampton. In FA i p. 413 these places appear as *Heannton, Blakewill* and *Westagynton* [West Hagginton] , coupled with *Alescote* [Aylescott 3,40-41 note] ; see OJR H8 p. 432. |
| 16,70–71 | ROBERT. Undoubtedly Robert of Pont-Chardon for both these entries because of the descent of the manors; see notes to 16,69 and 16,71. |
| 16,70 | HAGGINTON. West Hagginton in Ilfracombe parish, Braunton Hundred (1); see 3,27 and 16,69 notes, also OJR H8 p. 432. East Hagginton is in Berrynarbor (23,3 note). |
| 16,71 | CHARLES. DB *Carmes*, see EPNS i p. 61. It is a parish in Shirwell Hundred (2). William *de Punchardune* holds in *Charnes* in Fees p. 784; see RH i pp. 79a, 94b, FA i pp. 336, 361 and OJR H8 p. 481. |
| 16,72 | MOCKHAM. In Charles parish, Shirwell Hundred (2). It was no doubt incorporated in, and descended with, the previous entry and is not found in fee lists.<br>THIS (MANOR) SETTLED ITS TAX .... NOW .... ACCOUNTED FOR AS 2 VIRGATES. The Exchequer scribe has condensed the Exon. here (see Exon. Notes) and the result is not so clear. The position was that in 1066 Mockham and Charles paid tax together (perhaps in an attempt to conceal Mockham's size, which is never stated), the amount being 1 virgate. By 1086 the true taxable extent of the manors seems to have become clear: they were either assessed separately (at 1 virgate each presumably) or their joint tax liability was increased to 2 virgates.<br>See 3,2 note on the meanings of *quietus*, from which *adquietabat* here is ultimately derived. |
| 16,73 | (WEST) BUCKLAND. A parish in Braunton Hundred (1). In Fees p. 784 Robert *de Hokesham* holds *West Boclaunde* from the Honour of Okehampton; see FA i p. 415, OJR H8 pp. 396, 437 and 3,54-55 note. |
| 16,74 | BLAKEWELL. In Marwood parish, Braunton Hundred (1). It is held by William *de Punchardun* from the Honour of Okehampton in Fees p. 784 with Heanton Punchardon and Hagginton (16,69-70 notes); see OJR H8 p. 433.<br>BRAUNTON, THE KING'S MANOR. The cross-reference (in 1,5) proves that Braunton is intended, Blakewell lying not far from it, but both the Exchequer and Exon. versions for 16,74 have *Bractona, Bracton*, pointing rather to Bratton (Fleming), which is, however, further off and belonged to the Count of Mortain (15,40) not to the King in 1086.<br>MEN OF THE HUNDRED. These were the jurors representing each Hundred in the shire court, which, among other functions, heard pleas on disputed lands. The men of |

the Hundred are called King's men in 15,67 (see Exon. Notes). Cf. last note under 2,2 and 34,5 note.

16,75 KENTISBURY. A parish in Braunton Hundred (1); the DB holding is identifiable in the Tax Return for Braunton and Shirwell Hundred (vi). In Fees p. 784 Walter *le Lou* holds in *Kentesbir'* from the Honour of Okehampton; see FA i p. 414, Cal. Inq. PM vol. x no. 412 and OJR H8 p. 430.

16,76 ROGO. DB and Exon. *Rogo* (Forssner pp. 218-219) from OFr *Rogon* < OG *Roggo*, a short-form for OG *Rogger, Hrodger* = *Roger* (Forssner pp. 217-218). See Exon. Notes 16,158;170.

HOLCOMBE (ROGUS). A parish in Bampton Hundred (8), the added name being from the 1086 holder or a descendant. In Fees p. 786 Jordan *filius Rogonis* holds *Holecumbe* from the Honour of Okehampton; see RH i pp. 64a, 94a, FA i p. 431 and OJR in TDA 30 p. 441 note 5. Simon, a descendant, gave the Church of Holcombe to Montacute Priory *c.* 1160; see MC nos. 138, 140, 157 pp. 170, 180. This large holding of 9 hides appears to have been the *Holancumb* granted by King AEthelred II to Sherborne Abbey (KCD no. 701 = ECDC no. 45 p. 13 = Sawyer (1) no. 895) and subsequently alienated. ECDC no. 49 p. 13 (= Harmer no. 63) refers to a letter of AEthelric, Bishop of Sherborne, complaining of the loss of 33 hides and the probable loss of 9 more at *Holancombe*; see ECDC no. 50 p. 13 (= Sawyer (1) no. 1422) and ECDC no. 62 p. 14 (= Sawyer (1) no. 1474 = KCD no. 1334).

16,77 HOCKWORTHY. A parish in Bampton Hundred (8), held by Hugh *de Bynnewill'* as *Hackewrth'* from the Honour of Okehampton in Fees p. 786; see FA i p. 431. The Church was given in 1166 to Canonsleigh Priory; see Oliver *Mon.* p. 227 and OJR in TDA 30 p. 442 note 6. Hockworthy seems to have included *Trounham* [Turnham ST 0419] held by William *Barnevyle* in Cal. Inq. PM vol. iv (o.s.) no. 63 (see TDA 38 p. 332).

16,78 ANSTEY. West Anstey parish in South Molton Hundred (6). In Fees p. 784 Ralph *de Esse* (from Rose Ash 16,143) holds in *Anestye* from the Honour of Okehampton. The next entry in Fees refers to *Frodetone* and *Westecot*, also apparently in this Hundred, held by Roger *Le Moyne*. Since his family also holds West Anstey from the Honour of Barnstaple (3,62) it is possible that these two places were part of Anstey in 1086. *Frodetone* is unidentified; it cannot be Frenchstone in George Nympton, despite OJR's assertion (see EPNS ii p. 348). *Westecot* appears to have been replaced by *Monyeston* [also unidentified] in Cal. Inq. PM vol. iv (o.s.) no. 63 (= TDA 38 p. 331); but see Cal. Inq. PM vol. xiv no. 325. In FA i p. 325 the main holding is named *Westanestigh*, held by William *le Moigne* and is *Dustygh Regni* in FA i p. 418. See OJR H3 pp. 70, 85.

16,79 RINGCOMBE. In West Anstey parish, South Molton Hundred (6), and said to be joined to Anstey (16,78) in Exon. (see Exon. Notes). The DB *Ringedone* is a hill name, the modern form, if it is correctly identified, relates to the valley beneath; EPNS ii p. 337. See also 1,6 note.

16,80 FILLEIGH. A parish in Braunton Hundred (1). Nicholas *de Filelgh'* holds in *Filelgh'* in Fees p. 784 from the Honour of Okehampton; see FA i p. 415 and OJR H8 p. 430.

LOBB .... BRAUNTON .... VILLAGERS. See 1,5. The Exchequer scribe probably intentionally omitted the villagers who are given in the Exon., as unimportant in the account of Baldwin's fief because Lobb was no longer part of it. The villagers' detail should perhaps have been included in 1,5.

Lobb is in Braunton parish, Braunton Hundred (1). See EPNS i p. 33 and OJR H8 p. 397.

16,81-82 NEWTON. WHITSTONE. DB *Nevtone, Wadestan*, both lying in Chittlehampton parish, South Molton Hundred (6), and held by Ansger in 1086 like Baldwin's other holdings in this Hundred, Anstey and Ringcombe (16,78-79). *Neweton'* and *Weston'* were fees of William *Briwere* (Fees p. 401), held by Simon *de Parco*. In Fees p. 784 Vincent *de Loliwill* holds in *Niweton'* and *Weston'*; see FA i p. 325, EPNS ii p. 339.

16,83 LINCOMBE. In Ilfracombe parish, Braunton Hundred (1). In Fees p. 784 the Abbot of Dunkeswell holds in *Lincumb', Worcumb'* [Warcombe GR SS 4745, see 3,51 note] and *Middelmerwode* [Middle Marwood, see 16,87]; see Cal. Inq. PM vol. v no. 527, TE p. 152a, VE ii p. 304 and OJR H8 pp. 433, 435. *Legh'* [Lee SS 4846] was probably part of this land; see FA i p. 360.

YARD. In Ilfracombe parish. DB *Laierda* is from OE *gierd, gyrd* 'an area of land' with the French feminine definite article affixed; see EPNS i p. 48.

16,84 ILFRACOMBE. A parish in Braunton Hundred (1). In Fees p. 784 the heirs of Oliver *de Campo Ernulfi* (Champernoun) hold in *Alfrincumbe*. It is coupled with Warcombe (see 16,83 note) in FA i p. 414; see also Cal. Inq. PM vol. iv no. 312, v no. 143, vii no. 710, x no. 494 and OJR H8 p. 433.

| | |
|---|---|
| 16,85 | ROBERT. Probably Robert of Beaumont who is Baldwin's subtenant in another part of Ashford which descended, like this manor, to the Beaumonts (16,66; see note). ASHFORD. Probably West Ashford, adjacent to Ashford parish, Braunton Hundred (1); see 16,66 note. |
| 16,86 -89;94 | PLACES IN BRAUNTON AND CLISTON HUNDREDS are intermixed by Exon., the order of which is 16,86;89 (Cliston), 16,87 (Braunton), 16,94 (Cliston), 16,88 (Braunton). It appears that the DB scribe, having entered the first Cliston Hundred place (16,86) realised that two more Braunton Hundred places remained to be inserted and attempted to rectify the order. He then returned to Cliston Hundred by entering Ashclyst, but then immediately entered other lands held by churches, thus postponing the entry of another Cliston Hundred place Whimple (16,94). See 16,89-93 note. |
| 16,86 | CLYST (HYDON). A parish in Cliston Hundred (20). Richard *de Hidune* (from Clayhidon 16,111) holds *Clist* in Fees p. 786 from the Honour of Okehampton; see FA i pp. 333, 433, Cal. Inq. PM vol. x no. 384 and OJR H7 p. 377. |
| 16,87 | MARWOOD. Middle Marwood [GR SS 5338] in Marwood parish, Braunton Hundred (1). *Middelmorwude* had been a fee of William *Briwere* (Fees p. 396) and it is held with Lincombe (16,85 note) by the Abbot of Dunkeswell in Fees p. 784; see Cal. Inq. PM vol. viii no. 397, FA i p. 415 and OJR H8 p. 436. |
| 16,88 | SNYDLES. Now in Chittlehamholt parish, South Molton Hundred (6); see EPNS ii p. 338. But in LSR (1334) p. 63 *Snyddelegh'* (wrongly identified with Stoodleigh in VCH p. 457 note 4) is a part of Braunton Hundred (1) and is in a Braunton group of fees held from the Honour of Okehampton in Fees p. 784; there *Snyddelg'* is held by Nicholas *Avenel*. In FA i p. 415 it is said to be part of the manor of Meshaw in Witheridge Hundred (16,141). It was probably a detached part of Braunton Hundred in 1086; see FA i p. 360, Cal. Inq. PM vol. iv (o.s.) no. 63 (= TDA 38 p. 330), vol. iii (n.s.) no. 31, and OJR H8 p. 398 and his editor's comment (p. 398 note 1). |
| 16,89-93 | A GROUP OF PLACES scattered in Baldwin's fief in the Exon. for Devon but brought together by the DB scribe as if under a sub-heading "What the canons of St. Mary's hold", to which he adds Fursham (16,93), another church land. It appears that he decided on this grouping once he had entered 16,89 Ashclyst. He thus delays the entry of another Cliston Hundred land, Whimple, 16,94. |
| 16,89-92 | CANONS OF ST. MARY'S. Perhaps the collegiate church of St. Mary, situated within the castle of Exeter and in the patronage of St. Peter's of Plympton (see 1,17 note) to which it was given in the time of King Stephen; Mon. Ang. vi p. 1451. The patronage of St. Mary's was later given to the Abbot of Torre. See VE ii p. 361, Oliver *Mon.* p. 181 and OJR H7 p. 376. According to OJR TDA 30 p. 283 Baldwin the Sheriff had founded St. Mary's some time after the Conquest. |
| 16,89 | ASHCLYST. In Broadclyst parish, Cliston Hundred (20). It is held by the Abbot of Torre from the Honour of Okehampton in FA i pp. 367, 434. |
| 16,90 | POLTIMORE. A parish in Wonford Hundred (19). The holding was probably based on *Coteton* [Cutton GR SX 9798] according to FA i p. 315; see EPNS ii p. 444 and OJR in TDA 30 p. 283, and in 44 pp. 296, 323 and Cal. Inq. PM vol. iii no. 519, viii no. 390. WULFMER COTT. Exon. *Olmer(us) cota*; see OEB pp. 307-308. He probably named Cutton. |
| 16,91 | POLSLOE. In Heavitree parish, Wonford Hundred (19); see OJR in TDA 44 p. 324. A priory for Benedictine nuns was founded here before 1160; see Knowles MRH p. 217, TE p. 152b and VE ii p. 315. |
| 16,92 | (WEST) CLYST. Earlier *Clyst Moys*, it is now in Broad Clyst parish, Cliston Hundred (20); see EPNS ii p. 573. It seems, however, to have lain in Wonford Hundred (19) in 1086 and in the Middle Ages: DB records part added to Poltimore in that Hundred and West Clyst lies amidst Wonford Hundred places in the schedule. *Clyst Moys* is found in Wonford Hundred in feudal lists, coupled with *La Hegehen* [Moss Hayne GR SX 981948], held from the Honour of Okehampton; see FA i p. 315, LSR (1334) p. 58, OJR in TDA 26 p. 167, in 30 p. 284, in 44 pp. 295, 323 and in VCH p. 462 note 7. POLTIMORE, ODO'S MANOR. No Odo holds a manor of Poltimore in DB, but he was probably one of the unnamed canons of St. Mary's in 16,90, rather than an unmentioned subtenant of Haimeric in Poltimore (50,1). |
| 16,93 | FURSHAM. In Drewsteignton parish, Wonford Hundred (19). The 1086 subtenant, the Abbey of Mont St. Michel, is also a major holder (Ch. 11). In FA i p. 316 *Forsham* is held by the Prior of Otterton (11,1) for St. Michael's *de periculo maris* (Mont St. Michel); see RH i p. 86b. |
| 16,94 | BALDWIN'S WIFE. Emma; see 16,128. Exon. makes it clear on both occasions that |

16

| | |
|---|---|
| 16,94 (cont'd.) | Baldwin the Sheriff is meant. Emma was his second wife; his first wife, Albreda, was King William's cousin.
WHIMPLE. A parish in Cliston Hundred (20), identifiable in the Tax Return for that Hundred (xii). Hawisia *de Curten'* holds *Wimple* in Fees p. 264; see RH i p. 67a, FA i pp. 332, 382, Cal. Inq. PM vol. iii no. 31 and OJR H7 p. 371.
BEFORE 1066 ½ HIDE .... These details of Larkbeare are added after 16,95; the transposition signs are as in the translation, not the 'hands' that Farley prints. In Exon., however, the information on the ½ hide follows on from the value of the main manor with no change in scribe. It is possible that the Exchequer scribe had a break halfway through the entry and then on his return he forgot he had not finished and went on to the next Exon. entry, though he realised his mistake almost at once.
ALFRED THE BRETON .... ANOTHER MANOR .... LARKBEARE. See 39,10. |
| 16,95 | PAYHEMBURY. A parish in Hayridge Hundred (15). In Fees p. 786 Roger *Giffard* holds in *Payhaumbir'* and *Segh'lak* [Sellake 16,161] from the Honour of Okehampton; see FA i pp. 321, 368, 424, Cal. Inq. PM vol. iii no. 31 and OJR in TDA 42 pp. 221, 234-235. Part of this land was called *Cokkesputte* [Cockesputt GR ST 0801] which later went to Polsloe Priory; TE p. 152a, VE ii p. 315 and Cal. Inq. PM vol. xiv no. 325. |
| 16,96 | LANGFORD. In Cullompton parish, Hayridge Hundred (15). Richard *de Langeford* holds in *Langeford* in Fees p. 786 from the Honour of Okehampton; see FA i pp. 321, 424 and Cal. Inq. PM vol. viii no. 425, xvi no. 1013.
1 HIDE AND 3 VIRGATES. In the Exon. MS the 3 virgates were originally $\overline{dim}$ *(hida)* which would agree with the total of 1½ hides of lordship and villagers' land. It would seem that the correction to 3 virgates was the reason for this discrepancy. See 1,57 note. |
| 16,97 | WILLIAM HOLDS FROM BALDWIN. Repeated at the beginning of 16,97-103 inclusive. William may be William of Aller (*de alre*; OEB p. 36): the Tax Return for Silverton Hundred (xiii) states that the King had no tax on 1 virgate William of Aller held there. All these manors of William's are in the Hundred of Silverton (Hayridge, 15) and in three of them — 16,97;101;102 (not 16,103 which is Aller) — the villagers' holding, the tax-paying part of the total, is 1 virgate. |
| 16,97-100;102 | PONSFORD. PONSFORD. KINGSFORD. KENTISBEARE. KENTISBEARE. Ponsford is in Cullompton parish and Kingsford is in Kentisbeare parish, both in Hayridge Hundred (15). In Fees p. 786 Henry son of Henry and the heir of Hugh *de Bolley* hold in *Kentelesbere, Pauntesford', Kyngesford* and *Catteshegh'* [Catshayes in Gittisham, (East) Budleigh Hundred, GR SY 1397] from the Honour of Okehampton. In FA i p. 368 both *Kentelesbere* and *Pontesford* are held in two halves, as in DB. See HD p. 56, Fees p. 398, Cal. Inq. PM vol. ii nos. 306, 593, vii no. 297, FA i pp. 322, 425 and OJR in TDA 42 pp. 222, 236. Part of Kentisbeare was held by Christchurch Priory in Cal. Inq. PM vol. xvi no. 671 and FA i p. 322. |
| 16,99 | EDSI. DB *Ezi*, Exon. *Ezius*, represent OE *Eadsige*; PNDB p. 236. |
| 16,101 | BLACKBOROUGH. In Kentisbeare parish, Hayridge Hundred (15). Under the name of France [GR ST 0808] and Saint Hill [ST 0908], it was given to Ford Abbey from Okehampton Honour and later transferred to Dunkeswell Priory; see TE p. 152a, VE ii p. 304, Oliver *Mon.* pp. 395, 398 and OJR in TDA 36 p. 360, 42 p. 236. |
| 16,102 | KENTISBEARE. See 16,97-100;102 note. |
| 16,103 | ALLER. In Cullompton parish, Hayridge Hundred (15). Like the other part of Aller (32,3) it passed to the Peverel family, *Aur Peverel* being held in FA i p. 321 from the Honour of Okehampton; see EPNS ii p. 564. See also 16,97 note.
ALWARD. DB *Ailuuard*, Exon. *Ailuuard(us)*, for OE *Aethelweard*; see notes to 3,45 and 1,41. |
| 16,104 | '(MONK) CULM'. DB *Colun*, held in 1086 by Rogo. This place, now lost, was a tithing of Hayridge Hundred (15) in the Middle Ages (e.g. *Monkecolmp'* in LSR (1332) p. 91). It seems to have lain along the river Culm between Silverton and Bradninch; in FA i p. 382 (the *Nomina Villarum* of 1316) *Colmp Monacorum* is assessed with Upexe, Netherexe and Plymtree. Moreover, 'Combe Sackville' (52,17) is described in Cal. Inq. PM vol. viii no. 595 as *Colump Reigny* in the tithing of *Moneke Colump*. See TE p. 151b and EPNS ii p. 570. It was given to Kerswell Priory, a cell of Montacute. MC no. 11 (p. 127) records a gift of William son of Rogo of 1 virgate at *Colum*; MC no. 155 (p. 179) is a grant by William son of Rogo of lands including *Colum* and *Bernardesmore* (16,105); see MC nos. 156-157 (pp. 179-180), Oliver *Mon.* p. 312 and Mon. Ang. v p. 167. Out of this grant Rogo seems to have kept a portion called *Hele* [Hele in Bradninch, GR SY 9902] for himself, *Hele* being held by Roger *de Hele* as one fee of the Honour of |

Okehampton in Fees p. 786; see MC no. 153 (p. 178) and FA i pp. 322, 368, 425.

16,105 'BERNARDSMOOR'. In Hayridge Hundred (15). It is unidentified, but no doubt adjacent to 'Monk Culm' (16,104; see note), being similarly granted to Montacute Priory; see OJR in TDA 36 p. 360, 42 p. 237.

16,106 BALDWIN HIMSELF HOLDS. Repeated at the beginning of 16,106-109 inclusive. COWICK. In Exeter St. Thomas parish, Wonford Hundred (19), being in fact an earlier name for the parish, EPNS ii p. 437. Baldwin's holding was granted by his son William to the new priory established here, an offshoot of Bec-Héllouin. Fees p. 1386 records *Cowyke, Cristeineston* [Christow, see 16,128 note on Bridford] and *Exewyk* ' [Exwick 16,109] as held by the Abbot of Bec; see RH i p. 84a, FA i p. 314, Mon. Ang. vi p. 1068, Oliver *Mon.* p. 153, OJR in TDA 44 p. 324 and Marjorie Morgan (later Chibnall) *The English Lands of the Abbey of Bec*, London 1946.

16,107 DREWSTEIGNTON. DB *Taintone*, now a parish in Wonford Hundred (19). In Fees p. 785 the heir of Ingram *de Aubernun* (on whom see 16,21 note) hold in *Teington* from the Honour of Okehampton. It is *Teyngton Drue* in RH i pp. 84a, 85b; see FA i pp. 314, 345, 386, Cal. Inq. PM vol. iii no. 31, x no. 429 and OJR in TDA 44 p. 324.

16,108 SPREYTON. A parish in Wonford Hundred (19). In Fees p. 785 Philip *Talebot* holds *Spreiton'* from the Honour of Okehampton; see Fees p. 399, RH i p. 85b, FA i pp. 314, 345, 386, Cal. Inq. PM vol. ii no. 621, v no. 527, and OJR in TDA 44 p. 325.
14 VILLAGERS. In the MS *xiii uilli* was originally written, but corrected to *xiiii* at an early stage. In the Exon. MS the last *i* of the *xiiii* is in slightly darker ink, which might suggest a correction from *xiii*. See notes to 2,24. 3,68. 28,10 and 32,10 for instances of a correction in Exchequer DB being paralleled by one in Exon.

16,109 EXWICK. It lies in Exeter St. Thomas parish, Wonford Hundred (19), like Cowick, and was similarly granted to Cowick Priory; see 16,106 note.
EVERWACER. In the MS *Eureuuacre*, but the *c* is exuberantly written, so that it looks like an *o*, especially in the facsimile. The Devon forms of this OG name are *Eureuuacre* in DB and *Eureuuac* in Exon. See DB Somerset General Notes 27,3. According to PNDB p. 249 note 1, all the Somerset and Devon references to Everwacer are to Everwacer *minister* who in 1061 witnessed the grant of land at Ashwick, Somerset, by King Edward, to Abbot Wulfwold of Bath; KCD iv no. 811 pp. 150-151 (= Sawyer (1) no. 1034).

16,110 CLIFFORD. In Dunsford parish, Wonford Hundred (19). In Fees p. 785 Stephen *de Haccumbe* (from Haccombe 16,152) holds in *Ridmore* [Ringmore 16,112] and *Clifford* from the Honour of Okehampton. These places are *Redmor'* and *West Clifford* in RH i p. 85a; see FA i pp. 313, 345, 386. Although the place is now called Clifford Barton, an *Est Clyfford* and a *West Clyfford* occur in LSR (1332) p. 51. A Henry *de Westecomb'* [from Westacombe GR SX 7990] then lived at 'East' Clifford and a William *atte Wallen* [from Wallon SX 7790] at 'West' Clifford; thus 'West' Clifford cannot be Combe Hall in Drewsteignton (OJR in TDA 44 pp. 292, 325).

16,111 CLAYHIDON. A parish in Hemyock Hundred (16). This entry is the first of a group of Hemyock Hundred places that are intermingled with those of Wonford (16,111;121-122; 124). With Bolham Water (16,121) and Culm Pyne (16,122), this land probably accounts for the 3 hides of lordship allowed to Baldwin in the Hemyock Hundred Tax Return (xiv). In Fees p. 786 Richard *de Hidune* (see 16,86 note) holds *Hidune* from the Honour of Okehampton; see FA i pp. 367, 430, Cal. Inq. PM vol. ii no. 590 and OJR H2 p. 41.

16,112 RINGMORE. In St. Nicholas parish, Wonford Hundred (19), the parish being named from the dedication of Ringmore Church; EPNS ii p. 460. Descent of the manor is to Stephen of Haccombe, as Clifford (16,110 note).

16,113 RUSHFORD. In Chagford parish, Wonford Hundred (19). William *de Risford* holds *Risford* in Fees p. 785 from the Honour of Okehampton; see RH i p. 85b, FA i pp. 314, 345, 387 and OJR in TDA 44 p. 325.

16,114 HITTISLEIGH. A parish in Wonford Hundred (19). Philip *Talebot* holds in *Hutteneslgh'* from the Honour of Okehampton in Fees p. 785; see FA i pp. 314, 345, 387. In RH i p. 85b William *Talebot* holds from John *de Ponchardon*; see also OJR in TDA 44 p. 326.
WOODLAND. In the MS *silua* as usual; Farley misprints *siluae*.

16,115 RICHARD SON OF THORULF. Exon. *Ricard(us) fili(us) torolui*; OEB p. 201. See Ch. 30 note.
MARTIN. In Drewsteignton parish, Wonford Hundred (19). It is not apparently found in later fee lists, but the Tax Return for Wonford Hundred (xxxi) states that the King has no tax from 1 virgate of land held by Richard son of Thorold, which seems to refer to this entry. See Ch. 30 note on Richard son of Thorold/Thorulf.

| | |
|---|---|
| 16,115 (cont'd.) | EDWULF. In the MS *Iadulf*, the first letter being most likely a capital *I*, though possibly a lower-case *l*; definitely not the capital *L* that Farley prints. In the carolingian minuscule used in Domesday Book the lower-case *l* and capital *I* and *L* are fairly similar, much depending on the length of the 'foot' and the presence or absence of a hook at the top of the ascender. In Exon. the first letter of *Iadolf'* is definitely a capital *I*. Cf. 24,26 note. |
| 16,116-117 | HUGH OF RENNES. HUGH. For 16,116 Exon. has *Hugo* with *redonensis* (not *redonnensis*, as OEB p. 135) interlined in paler ink, possibly by a different scribe to the rest of the entry. The Hugh of 16,117 may also be Hugh of Rennes: although he is plain *Hugo* in DB and Exon., the scribe of the latter may have intended to interline *redonensis* there as well as in the preceding entry. Rennes is in the département of Ille-et-Vilaine, France. |
| 16,116 | MELHUISH. In Tedburn St. Mary parish, Wonford Hundred (19). In Fees p. 785 *Melehiwiss* is held of Okehampton Honour; see RH i p. 85b, FA i pp. 313, 345, 388 and OJR in TDA 44 p. 326. |
| 16,117 | TEIGNHARVEY. It lies in Stokeinteignhead parish in a detachment of Wonford Hundred (19). In Fees p. 785 Richard *de Teyng* holds in *Teing* from the Honour of Okehampton: Richard *le Baron* (see 19,41) holds the place in RH i p. 85b and Humphrey *de Beauchamp* holds *Teyng Hervy* with *Gabbewill* [Gabwell GR SX 9269] in FA i p. 346. See FA i pp. 314, 387, Cal. Inq. PM vol. ix no. 552, OJR in TDA 44 p. 326 and 48,3 note. |
| 16,118 | JOCELYN BERNWIN. Exon. *Goscelinus Beruinus*: OG *Bernwin* (OEB p. 214). On 'Jocelyn' see 16,148 note.<br>OLDRIDGE. In Whitestone parish, Wonford Hundred (19). In Fees p. 785 *Wallerig'* is divided into two portions, one held by the heirs of Richard *Cadiho*, the other by Henry *Guraunt* of the Honour of Okehampton; hence they are *Wolderigg Cadiho* and *Woldrigg Goraunt* in FA i pp. 386, 388. See FA i pp. 314, 345, RH i p. 85b and OJR in TDA 44 p. 327. |
| 16,119-120 | TEDBURN (ST. MARY). A parish in Wonford Hundred (19). Only one entry is found in Fees (p. 785) where Thomas *de Tetteburne* holds *Tetteburn* from the Honour of Okehampton. FA i p. 314, however, records two holdings: Rainer's will be *Tetteborn* held by Walter *de Honyton* from Thomas *de Tetteborn* and by him from Roger *de Langeford* (see 16,8 note); Ralph's land will be *Tetteborne* and *Coleheie* [Colley in Tedburn, GR SX 8194] held by the same Walter and the same Thomas, but from John *de Poncbardon* (on whom, see 16,52 note); see FA i p. 388, RH i p. 85b, Cal. Inq. PM vol. viii no. 425, xvi no. 1013 and OJR in TDA 44 p. 328. |
| 16,121 | BOLHAM (WATER). In Clayhidon parish, Hemyock Hundred (16). It can be identified in the Hemyock Hundred Tax Return (xiv); see 16,111 note. In Fees p. 786 the Abbot of Dunkeswell holds *Bolleham* from the Honour of Okehampton; see FA i p. 430, VE ii p. 304 and OJR H2 p. 41.<br>TAX FOR 2 HIDES. In the MS there is an erasure of six letters after this statement with a rather faint link-line written in, to indicate that the gap was not left for additional information; Farley does not print the link-line, though it is sometimes his practice to do so (e.g. in DB Herefords. 29,16 and Worcs. 15,11). The link-line is not visible in the facsimile. The erasure was probably of *7 dimid'* and was probably done when the scribe checked Exon. and decided that the *7 dimid'* there was in fact erased; see Exon. Notes.<br>LAND FOR 6 PLOUGHS. In the MS *vii car* was originally written, but the last *i* has been erased, though it is still just visible and the dot after it has not been erased. In Exon. *viii car* appears to have been corrected to *vi*, which again suggests some kind of checking of DB against Exon. The checking may have been done early, in this entry anyway, as the DB scribe did not originally write *iii* for the lordship ploughs, as the Exon. scribe did. See the three Exon. Notes for this entry. |
| 16,122 | CULM (PYNE). In Hemyock parish and Hundred (16) and identifiable in its Tax Return (xiv); see 16,111 note. It is held in Fees p. 786 by Herbert *de Pynu* as *Culum* from Okehampton Honour; see FA i pp. 339, 367, 430 and OJR H2 p. 41. |
| 16,123 | WALTER. Probably Walter the Butler (*pincerna*): the Tax Return for Wonford Hundred (xxxi) states that the King did not have tax from 1 virgate Walter the Butler holds there from Baldwin the Sheriff (which corresponds to the 1 virgate of villagers' land; see Lordship and Villagers' Table). This is the only holding of a Walter in Wonford Hundred in DB.<br>BRAMFORD (SPEKE). This is the smaller of two DB holdings (see also 16,129) called *Brenford*. It was at Rollstone in Upton Pyne parish [GR SX 904991]. Descent from the 1086 holder, Walter, was to Walter *de Nimet* (see 16,45 note) who held Rowlands Nymet (presumably the same Roland named Rollstone). It is *Rollandeston'* in Fees p. 785 held |

16,124 HOLE. In Clayhidon parish, Hemyock Hundred (16). It seems to be represented in Fees p. 786 by *Nonicote* [Newcott GR ST 1610, lying to the west; the development from *Nonicote* is strange, see EPNS ii p. 611] held by Jordan son of Rogo from the Honour of Okehampton; see FA i p. 339 and OJR H2 p. 35.
FORMERLY WASTE. *Olim uastata*; the past participle is also used in the Exon. (with the addition of *erat* 'was'), but it seems to mean no more than the adjective *uasta*. See second note under C 3 above.

16,125 BERNARD NAP(E)LESS(?). Exon. *Bernardus sine napa*, an unexplained byname according to OEB p. 390. It is probably some OE adjective in *-leas* 'lacking', but the element *napa* eludes identification — turnips, cups, boys, napkins and napes of neck might all be toyed with, but without credibility in the present state of knowledge. (JMcND)
WHITESTONE. A parish in Wonford Hundred (19). Baldwin held two manors here (see also 16,137), the larger, ½ hide, being held by Bernard Nap(e)less(?) in 1086. It appears to be *Westecot'* [West Town GR SX 8593; see EPNS ii p. 459] and *La Hacghe* (*La Heghen* in FA i p. 387), that is Hayne Barton GR SX 8693, held in Fees p. 785 by Ralph *de Alba Mara* from the Honour of Okehampton. In FA i p. 314 it is held by the heirs of Henry *Tyrel* by homage and service from Alan *filius Roualdi*; see FA i pp. 346, 387, RH i p. 85b and OJR in TDA 36 p. 375.

16,126 MAIDENCOMBE. In Stokeinteignhead parish, a detached part of Wonford Hundred (19). *Medenecumbe* is held in two portions in Fees p. 785 from the Honour of Okehampton by Warin *filius Joelis* and Peter *de la Pole*. It is found as *Medenecumb* and *Pole* in FA i p. 345. *Pole* is an unidentified 'Pool', but a Nicholas *atte Pole* and a Joel *atte Pole* are found in LSR (1332) p. 53 in Stokeinteignhead parish; see RH i p. 85b, FA i pp. 313, 386 and OJR in TDA 44 p. 329.

16,127 BERNARD HOLDS.... The scribe has omitted *de B(alduino)* 'from Baldwin', no doubt in error; it is in Exon. as usual. See 15,22 note.
ROCOMBE. In Stokeinteignhead parish lying in the detachment of Wonford Hundred (19). In Fees p. 785 the heirs of Richard *Cadyho* (on whom, see 16,118 note) hold in *Racumbe* from the Honour of Okehampton; see FA i pp. 314, 387, RH i p. 85b and OJR in TDA 44 p. 329.

16,128 BALDWIN'S WIFE. That is, Baldwin the Sheriff; see 16,94 note.
BRIDFORD. Now a parish in Wonford Hundred (19). Baldwin's land was actually at Christow [GR SX 8384] in the next parish, given by a descendant to Cowick Priory. It is *Cristenesstouwe* in FA i p. 315. See RH i p. 84a, OJR in TDA 44 p. 293 and 16,106 note.

16,129 VITALIS OF COLYTON. Exon. *Vitalis de colintona*. This is more likely to be Colyton in Devon (DB 1,13 *Culitone*, Exon. *Culitona*, compare EPNS ii p. 621 *Culinton(a)* etc.) than Collington in Herefordshire (DB *Col(l)intune*) as OEB p. 40 (where the Exon. byname is misprinted *colintuna*). See 36,13 note on the name Vitalis.
BRAMFORD (SPEKE). Now a parish in Wonford Hundred (19). This was the larger of the two DB holdings (see also 16,123) that Herbert *de Pynu* holds as 1 fee in *Braunford* from the Honour of Okehampton in Fees p. 785. In FA i p. 314 this same holding appears as *Uppeton* [Upton Pyne GR SX 9197] and *Bramford Pyn*. Pynes [SX 9196] will no doubt have been part of this holding; see RH i p. 85b, FA i pp. 344, 385, OJR in TDA 44 pp. 294, 330 and notes to 3,67 and Ch. 4.

16,130 EGGBEER. Now represented by Higher and Lower Eggbeer in Cheriton Bishop parish, Wonford Hundred (19). Descent from Modbert, the 1086 holder, is to William *de Kelly* (see 16,11 note), who in Fees p. 785 holds in *Eggebere* and *Buledune* [?Bowden in Cheriton Bishop, GR SX 7492]. In FA i p. 314 the holding is *Heggbear* and *Heilake* [Haylake SX 7892] and is described as *Heylak* and *Boledon* in FA i p. 345; see RH i p. 85b, FA i p. 386 and OJR in TDA 44 p. 330. See 52,11 note.

16,131 UPPACOTT. In Tedburn St. Mary parish, Wonford Hundred (19). In Fees p. 787 in a group of Exminster Hundred places (24), Thomas and Reginald *de Uppecot'* and the son of Geoffrey *de la Hok'* hold in *Holecumb'* [Holcombe in Dawlish, Exminster Hundred, see 2,4-6 note] and *Uppecot*; see Cal. Inq. PM vol. viii no. 425 and FA i pp. 314, 346, 347, 387. In RH i p. 85b one of the intermediate holders of *Uppecote* is John *de Kelli* (16,11 note).

(Top of page, continuation:)
by the heirs of Alexander *de Tauton* from the Honour of Okehampton for 1/6th fee. In FA i p. 314 *Roulandeston* is held from Matthew *de Wolfrynton* (Rowlands Nymet descends to William *de Wolryngton* in FA i p. 370); see FA i pp. 344, 385, OJR in TDA 36 p. 375, 44 pp. 293, 328, also the notes to 3,67 and Ch. 4.

| | |
|---|---|
| 16,132 | (GREAT) FULFORD. In Dunsford parish, Wonford Hundred (19). In Fees p. 785 the heirs of Nicholas *de Fuleford* hold in *Fuleford*. In FA i p. 314 William *de Foleford* holds from John *de Kelli* (16,11 note); see FA i pp. 345, 387 and RH i p. 85b. AETHELRIC. DB *Aric*, Exon. *Ariti(us)*, probably for *Alric* etc.; see PNDB pp. 186-187. |
| 16,133-134 | ROCKBEARE. A parish in (East) Budleigh Hundred (14). In addition to Rainer's two holdings, Gotshelm held nearly 3 hides here (16,138). Rainer's lands seem later to have formed a single manor, being held in Fees p. 787 by the heir of Baldwin *de Belestane* (see 15,22 note) as *Rakebere*, held with *Dodeton'* [Dotton 16,135]; see Fees p. 763. It is *Rokebere Baldewyn* in FA i pp. 365, 381 and in FA i p. 427 it is held from Thomas *de Langeford* (on whose family, see 16,8 note); see Cal. Inq. PM vol. viii no. 425 and OJR in TDA 35 p. 293. |
| 16,134 | 1 VILLAGER HAS IT THERE. The plough, as Exon. states. See 1,29 note. |
| 16,135 | DOTTON. DB *Otrit*. The DB form is from the river Otter and seems (by 1201) to have been supplanted by a name derived from the TRE holder, Doda (EPNS ii p. 587). It lies in Colaton Raleigh parish, (East) Budleigh Hundred (14). Descent from Rainer is the same as for his holdings at Rockbeare (16,133-134 note). It is *Doditon Abbatis* in Cal. Inq. PM vol. xiv no. 325, xvi no. 1013, from a holding of the Abbot of Dunkeswell (TE p. 152a). |
| 16,136 | AYLESBEARE. A parish in (East) Budleigh Hundred (14). John *de Curtenay* holds from the Honour of Okehampton in Fees p. 787. In FA i p. 324 it is *Aylesbear cum Popelford* [Newton Poppleford GR SY 0889]; see Fees p. 763, FA i p. 427, RH i p. 66a, Cal. Inq. PM vol. ii no. 71, iii no. 31, viii no. 273 and OJR in TDA 35 p. 293. *Huntebere* by *Ailesbere* [Great and Little Houndbeare farms in Aylesbeare, see 14,3-4 note], held of the Barony of Okehampton in the Inq. PM cited above may have been a part of this land. |
| 16,137 | WHITESTONE. It is now a parish in Wonford Hundred (19), being the smaller of Baldwin's two holdings here in 1086 (see also 16,125). The land descended in the family of Robert of Beaumont, the 1086 subtenant, Walter *de Langedene* holding *La Heith* [Heath Barton in Whitestone, GR SX 8494] in FA i p. 314 from Richard *Beaumont* from the Honour of Okehampton. In Fees p. 785 this same holding is called *Calchurch* held by Rayner *de Halleham*. The alternative names are identified by an entry in Cal. Inq. PM vol. iv (o.s.) no. 63 (= TDA 38 p. 327) *Colechurche que dicitur Sancte Marie in le Hethe*; see EPNS ii p. 459, Fees Index, RH i p. 85b, FA i p. 346, Cal. Inq. PM vol. xiv no. 325 and OJR in TDA 44 p. 331. |
| 16,138 | ROCKBEARE. A parish in (East) Budleigh Hundred (14); this is the largest of Baldwin's three holdings here (see also 16,133-134). Descent from Gotshelm is to John *Tebaut* who holds *Rakebere* in Fees p. 787 (see Fees p. 763), then to the Abbess of Canonsleigh; see FA i pp. 365, 427. It is *Rokebyar Johan* in FA i p. 381; see Cal. Inq. PM vol. viii no. 425 and OJR in TDA 35 p. 292. |
| 16,139 | PETECOTE. Identified by VCH as Pennicott in Shobrooke, largely in an attempt to account for *La Shete* of Fees pp. 762, 787 and FA i p. 426 [?Shute in Shobrooke, GR SS 8900, (West) Budleigh Hundred, see OJR in TDA 35 p. 284 and 1,9 note], and by DG, following EPNS ii p. 543, as Patcott in Tiverton parish and Hundred (9). Pennicott cannot derive from *Petecote* which is *P(e)atta's cot(e)*; while Patcott is not found in the fee lists in connection with the Honour of Okehampton and is anyway entered too early for a Tiverton Hundred place in Exon. order (see 16,158). But lying in the extreme south-west of Tiverton parish, Patcott could have been in Witheridge (7) or (West) Budleigh (14) Hundreds in 1086. The problem requires further investigation. |
| 16,140 | CHULMLEIGH. A parish in Witheridge Hundred (7) and identifiable in the Tax Return for that Hundred (x). Apart from *Chulmeleg* (RH i pp. 87b, 92a) the 5 hides will have included *Le Hospital* [Spittle GR SS 6817] and two holdings at *Hamtenesford* [Handsford in Chawleigh, SS 7210, now in (North) Tawton Hundred, called 'Little' and 'North' Handsford in Cal. Inq. PM vol. xiv no. 325], *Cadebire* [Cadbury SS 6917], *Bonevilestone* [Bunson SS 6917], *Gorelaunde* [Garland SS 7118], *Shitelesbere* [Sheepsbyre SS 7215], *Wrthi* ['Worthy' unidentified, see 16,145 note], *Baylekewrth'* [Bealy SS 7415] and *Stayne* [Stone Barton SS 7113] all given in Fees p. 783; see Fees pp. 758-759. To these can be added *Wik'* [Week SS 7316] and *Coleton'* [Colleton SS 6614] in Fees p. 761, *Benelegh* [Benley SS 7315], *Cotelonde* [Cutland SS 6817], *Panemede* [Pynamead SS 6716] and *Asselonde* [unidentified] from FA i pp. 419-421, as well as *Nywnham* by *Chilmelegh* [Newnham Barton SS 6617] in Cal. Inq. PM vol. viii no. 273. |

16,141 MESHAW. A parish in Witheridge Hundred (7). Nicholas *Avenel* holds *Mausard* in Fees p. 783; see Fees p. 759, FA i pp. 343, 420, Cal. Inq. PM vol. iv no. 367, OJR in TDA 30 pp. 401, 407 and 16,88 note.
ALFRED. DB *Aluert*, Exon. *Alueret(us)*; PNDB pp. 175-176.

16,142 YARD. In Rose Ash parish, Witheridge Hundred (7). Henry *de Yerde* holds in Fees p. 784 from the Honour of Okehampton; see Fees p. 759 and OJR in TDA 30 p. 402. It is *Yerde Beare* [?Beara in Rose Ash, GR SS 7720] in Cal. Inq. PM vol. xiv no. 325.

16,143 (ROSE) ASH. A parish in Witheridge Hundred (7). Ralph *de Esse* (see 16,78) holds in *Esse* in Fees p. 784 from the Honour of Okehampton; see Cal. Inq. PM vol. xiv no. 325 where it is *Asshe Rauf*, Fees p. 759, RH i p. 87b, FA i pp. 343, 420 and OJR in TDA 30 p. 402.

16,144 CREACOMBE. A parish in Witheridge Hundred (7); it does not appear in the fee lists; see EPNS ii p. 379.
FOURTH PART. In the MS $\bar{q}rta\ part\ e$, the gap between the *t* and *e* being caused by a hole in the parchment, not shown by Farley (but cf. 7,2 where he leaves a space; see note.
(AND) JOINTLY. In the MS $pa\bar{r}$ is written level with the first line of the Creacombe addition; Farley does not print it, perhaps because it is written quite far into the left margin which is on the inner edge of the MS.

16,145 WORTHY. It certainly lay in Witheridge Hundred (7) according to the order of the Exon. Book and it is probably the place in Rackenford parish; see EPNS ii p. 390. Unless it is the 'Worthy' included under Chulmleigh in Fees pp. 758, 783 (16,140 note), it does not appear in later feudal lists.

16,146 WILSON. DB *Welingedinge*. This cannot be Wilson in East Worlington parish (VCH and DG), whose early forms *Weveston* (1238) and *Wenede(s)ton* (1285) cited in EPNS ii p. 401 and *Wevezston* cited in 42,21 note cannot be reconciled with *Welingedinge* (see 42,21 note). Equally it cannot be Wilson in Cheriton Bishop whose early forms are *Wolgareston, Wolgerston* etc.; see EPNS ii p. 429 and 52,11 note. It may, however, be the Wilson in Witheridge parish, EPNS vol. xii (1935) addendum p. lvi. OJR's first suggestion, Woddington (in Witheridge, in TDA 30 p. 417), is phonologically impossible (see 1,32 note).
TOPI. DB *Topic*, Exon. *Topic*'; see PNDB p. 117 and §133.

16,147 CHELDON. A parish in Witheridge Hundred (7). In Fees p. 783 *Chedeledune* is held from the Honour of Okehampton. It is *Estchedeldune* ['East' Cheldon] in Fees p. 758; see also FA i pp. 343, 419. See 40,4 note on another part of Cheldon.
WHOLE OF THE LAND. See 25,2 for another example of all the land in a holding being lordship land, and cf. notes to 3,12 and 34,13. See 19,36 for a villager with all the land in lordship.

16,148 JOCELYN. The forms of this name in Devon, which represent OG *Gautselin, Gozelin, Goscelin* (Forssner p. 128), are *Gozelin(us)* in DB and *Joselin(us), Goscelinus, Gotselenus* in Exon.
RACKENFORD. A parish in Witheridge Hundred (7). In Fees p. 784 Robert *de Sydeham* holds from the Honour of Okehampton; see Fees p. 759, FA i pp. 343, 420 and OJR in TDA 30 p. 402. The land may well have included *Kanneworth* [Canworthy GR SS 8419], held by Hugh *de Courtenay* in Cal. Inq. PM vol. vii no. 344, x no. 412, xiv no. 325.

16,149 *ELTEMETONE*. It undoubtedly lay in Witheridge Hundred (7), but no satisfactory identification has been proposed; see OJR in TDA 30 p. 418.

16,150- TAPPS. WOODBURN. Both places lie in Oakford parish, Witheridge Hundred (7); for
151 Tapps, DB *Avse*, see EPNS ii p. 388. In Fees p. 784 Jordan son of Rogo (on whom, see 16,76 note) holds in *Wodeburne* and in *Westapse* [West Tapps] of the Honour of Okehampton; see Fees p. 759 and FA i pp. 343, 363. Part of Woodburn was held of Plympton Honour, see Fees p. 760, Cal. Inq. PM vol. ii no. 306. An adjacent part of Witheridge Hundred seems to have lain in Bampton Hundred (8) in 1086, but, despite OJR in TDA 30 p. 455, it should be noted that Bampton Hundred places have already been entered in Baldwin's schedule (16,76-77). Thus Tapps and Woodburn were probably in Witheridge Hundred in 1086 as later; see the Appendix and OJR in TDA 30 p. 403.

16,151 ALDRED HELD IT. In the MS *ten* was originally written (possibly due to a too close copying of Exon. which regularly has *ten* for the past tense in this formula), but was corrected to *teneb* at an early stage but without the ✝ sign being erased. A similar correction occurs in 16,165. 17,48;74. 20,4 and 36,18. Farley does not print the ✝ sign here or in 36,18 (perhaps because it is close to the abbreviation line through the *b*), though he does in 16,165 and in 20,4 (in 17,48;74 *tenƀ* the ⁷ signs may stand for the omitted *e* before the *b* and he may have left them in for that reason).

16,152 HACCOMBE. Now Haccombe with Combeinteignhead parish lying in the detached part of Wonford Hundred (19), but it was a tithing of Haytor Hundred (29) in the Middle Ages. The order of Exon. suggests that it may well have been counted in Teignton (Teignbridge) Hundred (23) in 1086; see 19,41 note. In Fees p. 786, in a group of Haytor Hundred places, Stephen *de Haccumb'* (see 16,110 note) holds in *Haccumb'* of the Honour of Okehampton; see Fees p. 768, FA i pp. 317, 349, 392 and OJR in TDA 40 p. 123.

16,153 TEIGNGRACE. DB *Taigne*, now a parish in Teignbridge Hundred (23). The alternative name *Teygnebruere* (1281) is probably derived from the 1086 subtenant, Ralph of Bruyère, or his descendants. Avicia *de la Bruwere* holds in *Teyng* in RH i pp. 82a, 90a; see EPNS ii p. 486 and OJR in TDA 29 p. 228.

16,154 LANGSTONE. In Manaton parish, Teignbridge Hundred (23); see EPNS ii p. 482. It does not appear in the fee lists.

16,155 ROGER SON OF PAYNE. Exon. *Roger(us) fili(us) Pagani* here and for 34,12; cf. 19,43 note. His byname is from Latin *paganus* 'member of a *pagus* (village or country district)', whence Mod.Fr *paysan* 'peasant, countryman' and *païen* 'pagan' (the countryfolk remained heathen long after the townspeople had become Christians).
HENNOCK. A parish in Teignbridge Hundred (23). In Fees p. 786 Richard *Treimenet'* holds from the Honour of Okehampton; see Fees p. 396, FA i p. 339 and Cal. Inq. PM vol. v no. 527, xi no. 118. In FA i p. 347 part of Hennock is held by the Abbot of Torre, and is named as *Blode in Hennock* [i.e. *Flode*, now Fludda GR SX 8479, see EPNS ii p. 471] in FA i p. 390; see Oliver *Mon.* pp. 169, 179 and TE p. 153a.

16,156 NEADON. DB *Benedone*; for the form see EPNS ii p. 482. It lies in Manaton parish, Teignbridge Hundred (23). Descent from the wife of Hervey (of Helléan, see Ch. 44 note) is to Robert *de Hyllun* who holds in *Nitheredune* in Fees p. 786; see FA i p. 348 and OJR in TDA 29 p. 229 note 11.

16,157 WHITEWAY. In Kingsteignton parish, Teignbridge Hundred (23). It seems that this land passed to the Honour of Plympton, being held in Fees p. 790 by Nicholas *Burdon* and Martin *de la Torre* in *Whyteweye* in a Teignbridge Hundred group; see Fees p. 396, FA i pp. 340, 390 and OJR in TDA 29 p. 228.

16,158 CHEVITHORNE. In Tiverton parish and Hundred (9). In Fees p. 786 William *de Chivethorn'* holds in *Chivethorne* of the Honour of Okehampton; see FA i pp. 318, 369 and Cal. Inq. PM vol. v no. 527. It is *Estchavethorne* in Cal. Inq. PM vol. xiv no. 325 (see 34,43 note). In FA i p. 433 it is held of the manor of Holcombe Rogus (16,76) which had the same 1086 holder, Rogo; see OJR H1 p. 22.

16,159 CHETTISCOMBE. In Tiverton parish and Hundred (9). In Fees p. 786 Alice *de Ros* holds in *Certecumbe* from the Honour of Okehampton; see FA i p. 318, Cal. Inq. PM vol. v no. 527, x no. 46 and OJR H1 p. 22.

16,160 MANATON. DB *Magnetone*. Despite attempts by Whale (in TDA 28 p. 422) and Finn (in TDA 89 p. 114) to connect this with Manley in Tiverton, it appears to be Manaton in Teignbridge Hundred; see EPNS ii p. 481. It will therefore be the late insertion of an omitted Teignton (Teignbridge) Hundred entry (see 16,152-157). In Fees p. 786 *Parva Maneton'* is held by the heirs of Hugh *de Langedone* (from Langdon in North Bovey); see FA i pp. 339, 390 and OJR in TDA 36 p. 358.

16,161 SELLAKE. In Halberton parish and Hundred (10). In Fees p. 786 it is held by Roger *Giffard* as *Segh'lak* coupled with Payhembury (16,95 note). There is also a separate mention of *Seghlak*, held by *Oliva de Seghlak*; see FA i pp. 368, 369, 383, 432 and OJR H2 pp. 48, 54.

16,162 SPARKWELL. In Staverton parish, Haytor Hundred (29). It appears to have been alienated from the Church of Exeter (Ch. 2 and 2,7 notes). In Fees p. 786 Henry *de Sparkewill'* holds in *Sparkewill'* from the Honour of Okehampton; see Fees p. 768, FA i pp. 318, 392 and OJR in TDA 40 p. 118.

16,163 WOLBOROUGH. A parish in Haytor Hundred (29). This land formed part of the foundation grant for Torre Abbey (Oliver *Mon.* p. 169) and in Fees p. 786 the Abbot of Torre holds *Wullebergh'* (so also Fees p. 768). RH i p. 72b mentions that in the manor of *Wolleburghe* is 'a new town (*villa nova*) held by the Abbot of Torre'; this is *Niweton* in FA i p. 318 [Newton Abbot GR SX 8671]; see FA i p. 349, TE p. 153a, VE ii p. 361, Oliver *Mon.* pp. 169, 172, OJR in TDA 40 p. 124 and 1,10 note.

A further Okehampton Honour holding in this Hundred, not named in DB and either omitted, included under another manor or a post-DB acquisition, was *Blakedune* [Blackaton in Widecombe in the Moor, GR SX 6977], held by John son of Richard in Fees p. 786; see Fees p. 768, FA i pp. 348, 392, Cal. Inq. PM vol. xiv no. 325 and OJR in TDA 40 p. 120. In Fees p. 768 the intermediate holder is Hugh *de Bollay*, suggesting descent from Ralph of Pomeroy: Ralph holds 16,7, Bridestowe, which later passes to Muriel *de Bollay* (16,7 note).

16,164 MUSBURY. Now a parish in Axminster Hundred (17). In the Middle Ages 5 of its hides lay in Axmouth Hundred, 2 in Axminster (OJR H4 pp. 138, 151, 179). In 1086 its 4 lordship hides seem to have been divided equally, 2 hides lordship together with the 1 lordship hide of Thorncombe (16,165) accounting for the 3 hides allowed to Baldwin in the Axminster Hundred Tax Return (xix), while another 2 hides lordship together with ½ hide each of the lordship of Stedcombe and Combpyne (16,169;171) accounting for his 3 hides of lordship in Axmouth Hundred (xxi). Hawise *de Curten'* holds *Musbiri* in Axminster Hundred in Fees p. 264; see FA i pp. 319, 328 (where it is divided between the two Hundreds) and Cal. Inq. PM vol. iii no. 31. It included *Broclonde* [Bruckland, for another part see 34,53 note] and *Esse* [Chapel Ashe GR ST 2795], Cal. Inq. PM vol. ii no. 71.

WOODLAND. The Exchequer scribe may have omitted the woodland details because in Exon. they come before the mill, rather than after it (as in the entries for 16,163;166). See Exon. Notes here. Cf. notes to 1,4. 3,81 and 32,5.

16,165 THORNCOMBE. A detached part of Axminster Hundred (17), its lordship being accounted for in that Hundred's Tax Return (see 16,164 note). Adeliza, daughter of Baldwin, granted it to Ford Abbey (established at Forde, GR ST 3604, within this parish); see VE ii p. 299, Oliver *Mon.* p. 338 ff. and OJR H4 pp. 151-154. Thorncombe was finally transferred to Dorset in 1844.

EDWARD HELD IT. In the MS *ten* was originally written, but corrected to *tenet* but without the *t* sign being erased. Farley prints the *t* sign, but see 16,151 note.

16,166 'FORD'. Lost in Musbury parish, Axminster Hundred (17); see EPNS ii p. 646. In Fees p. 785 Henry *de la Forde* holds in *La Forde*; see FA i pp. 319, 366, 429 and OJR H4 pp. 138, 154. It is *Forde* near Trill in Cal. Inq. PM vol. xiv no. 325.

16,167 *ALREFORD*. Identified by DG with Aller in Upottery, by OJR in VCH p. 466 note 1 with 'Allerford' in Axminster parish or Rosamondford in (East) Budleigh Hundred, by OJR H4 p. 154 with 'Ford' (see 16,166 note) and by EPNS ii p. 634 with the site of Newenham Abbey in Axminster (see 1,11 note). Clinching evidence is lacking.

IFING. DB *Juin*, Exon. *Juin'*; see PNDB p. 300.

16,168 SMALLICOMBE. It now lies in Northleigh parish, Colyton Hundred (22), but it is regularly coupled with Trill (in Axminster parish) in feudal documents and seems to have been a detached part of Axminster Hundred (17) in the Middle Ages. In Fees p. 785 John *de Tril* holds in *Smalecumb'* and in *Tril* [Trill in Axminster, GR SY 2995]; see FA i pp. 319, 366, 429 and OJR in TDA 36 p. 365, H4 p. 154 and H7 p. 351.

16,169 STEDCOMBE. DB *Stotecome*, in Axmouth parish, formerly Axmouth Hundred (17). In Fees p. 785 Roger *le Ver* and Stephen *de Uffewille* (from Offwell 16,172) hold in *Suttecumbe* (in error for *Stuttecumbe*) from the Honour of Okehampton; see FA i pp. 328, 430, EPNS ii p. 636 and OJR H4 pp. 175, 180.

THE VILLAGERS (HAVE) 2 VIRGATES. No villagers are detailed, however, only slaves. See 3,11 note and 1,3 note on slaves on the possibility that they held land.

16,170 COLWELL. In Offwell parish, Colyton Hundred (22). In Fees p. 785 William *de Colewill'* holds in *Colewill'* from the Honour of Okehampton; see FA i pp. 330, 428, Cal. Inq. PM vol. xi no. 309, xii no. 333, 51,10 note and OJR H7 p. 353.

16,171 COMBPYNE. A parish, now in Axminster Hundred, formerly in Axmouth (17), where it can be identified in the Tax Return (xxi). In Fees p. 785 Robert *de Shete* holds in *Cumb'* from the Honour of Okehampton; in FA i p. 328 (Axmouth Hundred) the holder is Thomas *de Pin*, the manor being called *Comb Coffyn* in FA i p. 429, Cal. Inq. PM vol. xi no. 300; see OJR H4 p. 180.

16,172 OFFWELL. A parish in Colyton Hundred (22). Roger *le Ver* and Stephen *de Uffewill'* (on whom, see 16,169 note) hold in *Uffewill'* in Fees p. 785; see FA i pp. 330, 428 and OJR H7 p. 352.

PERCHES. DB *pertica* or *perca*, a measure of length, usually reckoned at 5½ yards, though a 20-foot perch was in use for measuring woodland until last century; see Zupko s.v. *perch*. In Devon both woodland and underwood are measured in perches, as here and in 17,10;16 and 33,2, but 1 perch of meadow is also recorded in 24,9.

FORMERLY 12d; VALUE NOW 13s. This is a large increase in value. It is possible, however, that 12d may be a scribal error for 12s, or 13s an error for 13d. See 48,1 note and cf. Dorset General Notes 56,12.

16,173-174 MORIN. Probably Morin of Caen; see next note and cf. 51,14 note.
WILMINGTON. 'BEER'. In Offwell parish, Colyton Hundred (22). The Tax Return for Colyton (xx) records Morin of Caen not paying tax on ½ hide of land, probably parts of one or other of these two holdings. Wilmington does not appear in the fee lists; see OJR H7 p. 338.
DB *Collebere* survived as Culbear meadow (1708 Parish Account Book) and as Culley Bear, a field on the 1843 tithe map. It is now represented only by Beer Copse (6-inch OS map of 1890), see EPNS ii p. 629, Lysons ii pp. 142, 374 and OJR H7 p. 353.

16,175 W..... In the MS a space suitable for about 5 letters is left after *W*, presumably for the scribe to complete the name when he could discover it. There is no *r* for *require* 'enquire' (see 11,1 note) in the margin. Exon. merely has .*W*. with no space left; the scribe may have thought he had already written the name in full earlier in the entry (details of the 1086 holder generally occur after the plough estimate in Exon.); no other *W*.s hold Baldwin's land on this folio. Tenants of Baldwin elsewhere in Ch. 16 whose names begin with *W* are William (9 times), Walter (6 times) and William son of Wimund (once). The later descent of the manor does not help in ascertaining which *W*. was intended. Cf. Exon. Notes 16,131.
ENGLEBOURNE. Englebourne Abbots in Harberton parish, Coleridge Hundred (30). In Fees p. 786 the heir of William *de Bykebir*' holds in *Engelburne*; it was granted to the Abbot of Buckfast in 1244. See FA i pp. 350, 394, VE ii pp. 368-370 and OJR in TDA 43 p. 211.

16,176 PRAWLE. West Prawle in East Portlemouth, Coleridge Hundred (30), not East Prawle in Chivelstone, EPNS i p. 319. In Fees p. 786 Roger *de Praulle* holds in *Praulle* from the Honour of Okehampton; it is *West Praull* in FA i p. 349; see FA i pp. 332, 394, OJR in TDA 43 p. 211 and 52,53 note.

Ch. 17 IUDHAEL OF TOTNES. DB *Judhel*, Exon. *Juhellus*, represents Breton Iudhael, Judhael, which according to Dauzat (s.n. *Juhel*) is an alternative of the Breton name *Iudicael, Judicael*; Reaney (s.nn. *Jekyl, Joel*) disagrees.
Totnes was the chief seat of his fief in Devon and *caput* of the later Barony. He is also styled Iudhael of Barnstaple from his holding of that Barony and as such witnessed a charter of Henry I in 1123 (*Regesta* ii no. 1391). He is sometimes called Iudhael son of Alfred; see the charters on Totnes and Barnstaple in Mon. Ang. iv p. 630 and v p. 198. After Baldwin the Sheriff (Ch. 16) he was the largest landholder in Devon; he also held a manor in Cornwall (Ch. 6). He was dead by 1130 (in Pipe Roll 31 Hen. I p. 153 his son Alfred appears as paying a relief on his father's lands).
Iudhael was expelled from Totnes in 1087 and the barony granted by William II to Roger I *de Nonant*, although Iudhael himself was granted the Barony of Barnstaple (lands formerly held by the Bishop of Coutances, see Sanders p. 104 and Ch. 3 note) some time between 1095 and 1100. The Barony of Totnes descended in the *de Nonant* family and in 1206, during the possession of Henry *de Nonant*, it was divided. One part, the Honour of Totton or Totnes, was granted to William *de Braose*, then descended to *de Cantelou* (Cantilupe), then to Millicent who was married first to *de Montalt* then to *de la Zouche*. The other part, usually called the Honour of Hurberton [now Harberton, a post-1086 subdivision of Chillington 1,34; see note there and OJR in TDA 43 p. 205], was retained by Henry *de Nonant* then acquired by Roger *de Vautortes* and descended in his family. It was divided in 1305 between Peter Corbet and Henry *de Pomeroy*, then reunited with the Totnes portion of the Barony shortly after 1315. See OJR in VCH pp. 558-560 and Sanders pp. 89-90. Many of the lands of this barony appear in *Inquisitiones Post Mortem*; see especially Cal. Inq. PM vol. i no. 63 (Reginald *de Valle Torta*), ii no. 17 (George *de Cantilupo*), ii no. 165 (Walter *de Bathonia*), iv no. 296 (Henry *de la Pomeray*) and xii no. 119 (John *de Bello Campo*).
THE EXON. ORDER OF THIS CHAPTER (apart from the placing of the Boroughs (17,1-2) at the end) is identical to that of Exchequer DB. The Hundredal arrangement seems to be:

| 17,3-14 | Lifton | 17,23-31 | Kerswell |
| 17,15-20 | Torrington | 17,32-47 | Diptford |
| 17,21 | Wonford | 17,48-58 | Chillington |
| 17,22 | Teignton | 17,59-68 | *Alleriga* |

| | | | |
|---|---|---|---|
| | 17,69-82 Walkhampton | 17,1 | Borough of Totnes |
| | 17,83-107 Plympton | 17,2 | Borough of Exeter |

It will be noted that the great majority of Iudhael's manors lay in the southernmost Hundreds of the County.

17,1    IUDHAEL .... TOTNES. He has both the King's two-thirds of the total revenues of Totnes and the third penny that had belonged to Earl Leofwin; see 1,55 and note.
TOTNES. Head of the later barony. In Fees p. 98 Henry *filius Comitis* holds the Castle and Borough of *Toton'* along with *Cornewrth'* [Cornworthy 17,48] and *Lodiswill'* [Loddiswill 17,32]. The Church of St. Mary at Totnes, with the Chapel of St. Peter, was given by Iudhael to the Church of St. Sergius and St. Bacchus at Angers, *Regesta* ii p. 50 no. 735a; see OJR in TDA 30 p. 309. For 'Little' Totnes see Cal. Inq. PM vol. i no. 650, vi no. 710 and xi no. 597.
BURGESSES .... 15 OUTSIDE THE BOROUGH WHO WORK THE LAND. Cf. DB Shrops. 3h,1 (col. 253a) where 2 burgesses (presumably in Shrewsbury) work on the land and pay 3s, and Worcs. 19,12 (the manor of Wychbold) '13 burgesses in Droitwich who reap for 2 days in August and March'. See 1,1 note above on the phrase 'burgesses .... outside the Borough'.
BOROUGH ... 40d in TAX. That is, ¼ silver mark, which corresponds to 2½ hides (see C 4 note above). In Exon. the past tense is used, as if the 40d payment no longer took place.
TOTNES, BARNSTAPLE AND LYDFORD, BETWEEN THEM, THEY PAY.... This sentence is ungrammatical. In Exon. *Barnestablam, Totenais* and *Lidefordam* are clearly in the accusative dependent on *inter*, but the meaning obviously cannot be that 'if an expedition travels by land or sea between Barnstaple, Totnes and Lydford, they pay....'. The Exon. scribe should have written either *Barnestabla, Totenais & Lideforda inter se reddunt*.... or *inter Barnestablam .... tantum redditur seruitii....* ('among/between Barnstaple, Totnes and Lydford, as much service is paid (as Exeter pays)'). The Exchequer scribe perpetuated the confused construction of the Exon. (Cf. 20,13 note.)
In C 6 Barnstaple, Lydford and Totnes are stated to provide as much service as Exeter does, but the phrasing there (and in the corresponding Exon.) is ambiguous and could be taken to mean that these Boroughs (individually) paid as much as Exeter (this meaning cannot be read into the statement in 17,1). However, grammar aside, the truth seems to have been that when an expedition took place, Barnstaple, Totnes and Lydford collectively paid as much as Exeter, that is they provided 1 man-at-arms (see C 5 note). No payment of any sort is mentioned under the entry relating to Barnstaple (1,1), but Lydford in 1,2 is said to pay as much service as Barnstaple or Totnes when an expedition goes out (see note). It may be relevant that Totnes' tax payment of 40d recorded in the previous sentence in 17,1 is half Exeter's tax of ½ silver mark (i.e. 6s 8d) recorded in C 4.
BARNSTAPLE. In the MS *Barnestaple*; Farley misprints *Rarnestaple*.

17,3    THRUSHELTON. A parish in Lifton Hundred (18). In Fees p. 776 Guy *de Brettevil'* holds in *Thrysselthon'* of the Honour of Totnes (Hurberton); see Fees p. 757, FA i pp. 320, 406 and OJR in TDA 46 pp. 209-210.

17,4    RADDON. In Marystow parish, Lifton Hundred (18). In Fees p. 795 John *de Raddune* holds in *Raddune* and *Aureford* [Allerford GR SX 4285] from the Cantilupe Honour of Totnes; see Fees p. 757, FA i pp. 320, 355, 405-406 and OJR in TDA 46 p. 211.

17,5    BROADWOODWIDGER. DB *Bradewode*. Now a parish in Lifton Hundred (18). In Fees p. 775 Richard *de Veteri Ponte* (whence *Bradewode Vypund*, French *vieux pont* 'old bridge'; see EPNS i p. 179) holds in *Brawod', Bradelegh* [Bradaford 17,11, *Bradeford* in Fees p. 756], *Middelcoth'* [Middelcott in Virginstow, GR SX 3893, part of Bradaford 17,11] and *La More* [Moor 17,10] from the Honour of Totnes (Hurberton). In FA i p. 321 *Brawode* is held from the Honour of Hurberton by the heirs of *Wiger*; see FA i pp. 355, 405, Cal. Inq. PM vol. ii no. 265 and OJR in TDA 46 pp. 207-209. According to the T.O. (496 a 3) a place called *Bradeoda* (probably Broadwoodwidger) owes a customary due in *Listona* (Lifton, 1,25); see last note under Exon. Notes to 1,25.

17,6    NORTON. In Broadwoodwidger parish, Lifton Hundred (18). In Fees p. 776 Richard *Baucan* holds *Northon'* from the Honour of Totnes (Hurberton); see Fees p. 757, FA i pp. 321, 405, Cal. Inq. PM vol. viii no. 45 and OJR in TDA 46 p. 206.

17,7    DOWNICARY. DB *Kari*. In Broadwoodwidger parish, Lifton Hundred (18). In Fees p. 794 William *Pipard* holds in *Cary* from the Cantilupe Honour of Totnes; see Fees pp. 775, 1425, Cal. Inq. PM vol. i no. 650, FA i pp. 321, 403 and OJR in TDA 46 p. 187.

17

| | |
|---|---|
| 17,8 | SYDENHAM. In Marystow parish, Lifton Hundred (18). This 'Little' Sydenham (1 virgate) is to be distinguished from Sydenham Damerel (½ hide) in the same Hundred (17,14). In Fees p. 776 Maurice *de Sideham* holds in *Parva Sideham* from the Honour of Totnes (Hurberton) of Reginald of Vautortes; see Fees pp. 757 and 795 (the latter referring to a part held by the Prior of Plympton from William *de Cantilupe's* Totnes Honour), also FA i pp. 321, 355, 405 and OJR in TDA 46 pp. 204–205. |
| 17,9 | ASHLEIGH. In Lifton parish and Hundred (18). Nicholas *de Eslegh'* holds in *Eslegh'* from the Honour of Totnes in Fees p. 795; see Fees p. 756, FA i pp. 321, 405 and OJR in TDA 46 p. 203. |
| | 1½ VIRGATES. In the MS *7 dimid'* written in the left margin, rather squashed and in paler ink, with transposition signs to indicate its correct place in the entry. It is not added in Exon. |
| 17,10 | NIGEL HOLDS FROM IUDHAEL. Repeated at the beginning of 17,10-14 inclusive. MOOR. In Broadwoodwidger parish, Lifton Hundred (18), and held with it in Fees p. 776 as *La More* by Richard *de Veteri Ponte* (see 17,5 note) of the Honour of Totnes (Hurberton). It is *More Veteris Pontis* in Cal. Inq. iv no. 296 (EPNS i p. 180) and *More Malherbe* in FA i p. 405. Another part of *More* is held from the Cantilupe Honour of Totnes in Fees p. 795 by the Knights Hospitalers of *Bokelaunde* [Buckland in Somerset]. It is *More Fyz Estevene* in FA i p. 355; and *More Malherbe* and *Wydyamore* [Withymore, see 17,36 note] held by the Prior of the Hospital of St. John in Cal. Inq. PM vol. vi no. 486; see OJR in TDA 46 p. 209. |
| 17,11 | BRADAFORD. Bradaford and Middlecott in Virginstow parish, Lifton Hundred (18); see 17,5 note and FA i p. 406. |
| 17,12 | TILLISLOW. In Virginstow parish, Lifton Hundred (18). *Tullesle* and *Bikecote* [Beckett GR SX 4196, part of Tillislow, but in Broadwoodwidger parish] are held of the Cantilupe Honour of Totnes in Fees p. 795; see Fees p. 755 and FA i p. 320. *Toleslo* and *Bykcote* are held with *Thorne* [North Thorne and Thorndon in Broadwoodwidger parish, both SX 4095] in FA i p. 405; see Cal. Inq. PM vol. vi no. 486 and OJR in TDA 46 p. 188. SAEWIN .... THESE LANDS. That is 17,11-12. Cf. Exon. Notes here. |
| 17,13 | (MARY) TAVY. DB *Tavi*. Now distinguished from Peter Tavy (39,21) by the dedication of the Church. It is a parish in Lifton Hundred (18). In Fees p. 776 John *de Alba Mara* holds one part of *Tavy* from the Honour of Totnes (Hurberton) and another in Fees p. 794 from the Cantilupe Honour of Totnes; see Fees p. 756. *Tavy* is coupled with *Wagheffenne* [Warne, see below] in FA i p. 406; see 17,14 note and OJR in TDA 46 p. 197. It is *Tavy St. Mary* in Cal. Inq. PM vol. xii no. 119 (of John *de Bello Campo*); see Cal. Inq. PM vol. ii no. 789, vi no. 486 and viii no. 230. BRICTWY SON OF CAMM. See 3,32 note. LANDS OF THREE THANES. Exon. 317 b 3 and T.O. 495 a 5 name these as *Wagesfella* [Warne, see EPNS i p. 201], *Berna* [Burntown] and *Wereingeurda* or *Weringheorda* [Wringworthy]. THEY HELD THEM AS THREE MANORS AND COULD GO.... In the MS *ꝑ iii man*ʰ was interlined at the same time as the rest of the entry, its position indicated by the hairline. However, the *7 poterant ire quo voleb'* was done later, in smaller writing and in paler ink, possibly as a result of checking over the Exon. MS, where this information comes after a more detailed account of the added lands (see Exon. Notes). It is interesting that in 23,6 and 34,10 similar information is interlined in paler ink (and cf. 40,5 note), suggesting — together with the evidence of the marginal and interlined *par(iter)s* (see 15,47-52 note) and the *lib(er)es* (e.g. 15,79 and cf. 24,28-29 and 25,20) — that the Exchequer scribe decided late on that details of how a manor was held in 1066 were important. |
| 17,14 | SYDENHAM (DAMEREL). The 'Greater' Sydenham (17,8 note), a parish in Lifton Hundred (18). Descent is to John *de Alba Mara* (as 17,13) who holds *Sideham* and *Waghefen* [Warne, 17,13 note] in Fees p. 776 from the Honour of Totnes (Hurberton); see Fees p. 756, FA i pp. 321, 406, Cal. Inq. PM vol. viii no. 230 and OJR in TDA 46 p. 198. |
| 17,15 | CLAWTON. A parish in (Black) Torrington Hundred (11). In Fees p. 775 the constituents of Reginald *de Valletorta's* manor of *Clauton'* (Honour of Totnes-Hurberton) are given as *Kymethorne* [Kempthorne GR SX 3497 in Clawton parish], *Fernhille* [Fernhill SX 3398 in Clawton], *More* [?Moor in Pyworthy, 17,18 note], *Kiletre* [Killatree SS 3203 in Pyworthy], *Blakedone* [Blagdon SX 3696 in Tetcott], *Tynacre* [Tinacre SS 3600 in Clawton], *Frenecoth'* [?Kennicott in Clawton, SX 3598], |

17,15 (cont'd.) *Winescoth'* [Winscott SS 3301 in Pyworthy], *Loveworth* [Leworth SS 3201 in Clawton] and *Byestedone* [Eastdown SX 3499 in Clawton]. In addition, in FA i p. 357 *Clauton* is coupled with *Cratesworth[y]* ['Crossworthy', EPNS i p. 138].
    Between them these lands above will have accounted for the bulk of Iudhael's three lordship manors (17,15-17) in this Hundred and this large unit of land interspersed with the manors of no other lord may have been mistaken as a separate Hundred of 'Clawton' by the compilers of the Hundred Returns (see Appendix); see also FA i pp. 327, 406, 409, Cal. Inq. PM vol. ii no. 165, VE ii p. 335 and OJR H5 pp. 199, 229, 230.
    LESS 1 FURLONG. *uno ferling minus*, interlined in pale ink, probably later.

17,16 PYWORTHY. A parish in (Black) Torrington Hundred (11), probably represented in part by Killatree and Winscott in Fees p. 775 (17,15 note) and possibly by 'Moor' (17,18 note). The Prior of Totnes holds *Pyworth'* in TE p. 150b; see Cal. Inq. PM vol. v no. 213, viii no. 280 and OJR H5 p. 231.

17,17 TETCOTT. A parish in (Black) Torrington Hundred (11). In Fees p. 794, from the Honour of Totnes, William *Pipard* holds *Tetticot'* from the manor of Clawton; see RBE ii p. 558, FA i pp. 358, 409, Cal. Inq. PM vol. i no. 650, ix no. 137, xiv no. 151, xv no. 807, OJR H5 p. 231 and 17,15 note.
    2 VILLAGERS HAVE IT THERE. The plough; see Exon. Notes and cf. 1,29 note.

17,18 AIULF. DB and Exon. *Aiulf(us)* represent OE *Aethelwulf*.
    LIDEMORE. The Exon. form *Liclemora*, which is more likely to be correct than the DB form *Lidemore* (see 16,42 note), suggests 'Little Moor' and it is tempting to identify this place with the 'Moor' given as a member of Clawton in Fees p. 775 (17,15 note). But all the other lands forming that complex manor in Fees are parts of Iudhael's lordship manors (17,15-17) in 1086, whereas *Lidemore* is held by a subtenant Aiulf. Moreover, the identity of 'Moor' is uncertain for there is also a Moortown in Tetscott (SX 3396), presumably the same place, where John *atte More* lived in the parish in LSR (1332) p. 68; see OJR H5 p. 230.

17,19 BRADFORD. Seemingly in Pyworthy parish in (Black) Torrington Hundred (11), though it is little evidenced in later documents; it went to the canons of St. Stephen's at Launceston; see OJR H5 p. 231.
    AELEVA. DB and Exon. *Aileua* represent OE *Aethelgifu*, feminine; PNDB p. 183.

17,20 HENFORD. In Ashwater parish, (Black) Torrington Hundred (11). In Fees p. 794 John *de Hyndeford* holds in *Hyndeford* of the Honour of Totnes; see FA i pp. 358, 409 and OJR H5 p. 231.
    BRODER. DB *Brodre*, Exon. *brorus*; see PNDB p. 218 s.n. ON *Brothir*. Probably the same as the Broder who held land in the adjacent Cornish Hundred of Stratton.

17,21 BRIDFORD. A parish in Wonford Hundred (19); identifiable in the Tax Return for that Hundred (xxxi). It is held from the Honour of Hurberton by the heirs of Roger *de Waletort* in FA i p. 316; see RH i p. 84a, Cal. Inq. PM vol. iii no. 523 and OJR in TDA 44 p. 339.

17,22 THORGILS. This ON personal name (PNDB p. 393) occurs in Devon in the forms *Turgisus, Turgis* and *Torgis* (DB) and *Turgisus, Turgin(us)* and *Torgic(us)* (Exon.). The name-forms are Norman variants, with loss of final *s*, *l* before *s*, and dissimilation of *r-l* to *r-n*.
    (NORTH) BOVEY. A parish in Teignbridge Hundred (23) and identifiable in the Tax Return (xxiv) for that Hundred. William *Pipard* holds in *Nortbuvy* from the Cantilupe Honour of Totnes in Fees p. 795; see RH i pp. 82a,b and 90a,b, FA i p. 389, Cal. Inq. PM vol. i no. 650, xi no. 597, xv no. 807, xvi no. 151, OJR in TDA 29 p. 229 and notes to 3,8 and 17,49.

17,23-24 COMBE (FISHACRE). DB *Cumbe* lay in Haytor Hundred (29), although the individual identities are not entirely clear. The first is held by Ralph of Pomeroy in 1086, the second by an undifferentiated Ralph (see next note), and one holding is certainly Combe Fishacre in Ipplepen parish, held as *Cumb'* by Roger *de Punchardun* from the Cantilupe Honour of Totnes in Fees pp. 767, 795. It is *Come Fishacre*, held from Millicent *de Monte Alto*, in FA i pp. 317, 392. OJR, tentatively in TDA 36 p. 370, then firmly in VCH p. 469 no. 10 and TDA 40 p. 116, followed by EPNS and DG, identified the second 'Combe' with Longcombe in Berry Pomeroy, but evidence is lacking. These could simply be parts of the same village separately listed by DB, as often, since they had different TRE holders.

17,24 RALPH. Although one would expect the scribe to have written 'Ralph also (*idem*) holds' for this entry if he intended the same Ralph as in 17,23, Ralph here is probably

Ralph of Pomeroy because of his other holding in *Cumbe* (17,23) — if in fact both refer to Combe Fishacre (see 17,23-24 note). Exon. very rarely uses *idem* (see Exon. Notes 15,21) and has plain *Radulf(us)* here, though the entry is among a group of holdings of Ralph of Pomeroy (= DB 17,23;25-28) and it is interesting that *de pomario* is interlined above plain *R[adulfus]* in the next entry (= 17,25).

17,25   RALPH OF POMEROY ALSO HOLDS FROM IUDHAEL. Repeated at the beginning of 17,25-28 inclusive, though without Ralph's byname (which occurs in the Exon. for each entry).
LITTLEHEMPSTON. DB *Hamestone*. A parish in Haytor Hundred (29); for Broadhempston, see 15,43. In Fees p. 795 Guy *de Brianne* and Jacob *de Vado* hold in *Hemmeston'* from the Cantilupe Honour of Totnes; it is *Hemeston' Chatard* in Fees p. 767; see FA i pp. 349, 391 and OJR in TDA 36 p. 369, 40 p. 115.

17,26   LOVENTOR. In Berry Pomeroy parish, Haytor Hundred (29). In Fees p. 795 John *de Arundel'* (John *de Luvenetor'* in Fees p. 768) holds in *Luventor* from the Cantilupe Honour of Totnes; see FA i p. 318 and OJR in TDA 40 p. 121.
2 CATTLE IN A PLOUGH. Exon. *ii animalia in carr̃*; these are almost certainly oxen, as also in 17,28;38-39;53;77. See 1,3 note on cattle and 3,37 note on the phrase *in carr(uca)* which occurs with the cattle in all the above entries except 17,53 (see Exon. Notes there).

17,27   (SHIPHAY) COLLATON. In Cockington parish, Haytor Hundred (29). Iudhael had three manors called *Coletone* in 1086 (17,27;31;35). The first two fall in a group of Kerswell (Haytor) Hundred places in the order of Exon. and the last in a Diptford (Stanborough) Hundred group. The first of the two Haytor places, held by Ralph of Pomeroy, was Shiphay Collaton, purchased by William *Briwere* from the Pomeroy family and given to Torre Abbey; see FA i p. 349, TE p. 153a, VE ii p. 361, Oliver *Mon.* pp. 174, 176, OJR in VCH p. 470 note 3, in TDA 36 p. 370, 40 p. 126 note 1, and Watkin p. 797.
The second *Coletone* in Haytor Hundred (17,31) lay in Brixham parish and was held by Warin in 1086 and by Martin *de Fisacre* from the Honour of Totnes (Hurberton) in Fees pp. 769, 776, then by Matthew son of John of the Barony of *Almeton* (Yealmpton, see 1,18) in FA i p. 317 and as *Coleton Fysacre* from the Honour of Stoke in Hamme in FA i p. 391; see Cal. Inq. PM vol. viii no. 280, xvi no. 875 and OJR in TDA 36 p. 370, 40 p. 126.
A third Haytor Hundred *Coletone* was part of Paignton (2,18) in 1086. See 1,34 note for Collaton in Halwell parish, Coleridge Hundred (30).

17,28   LUPTON. DB *Lochetone*; for the form see EPNS ii p. 508. It lies in Brixham parish, Haytor Hundred (29). Roger *de Penilles* holds in *Lughetone* from the Cantilupe Honour of Totnes in Fees p. 795; see Fees p. 767, FA i pp. 316, 391 and OJR in TDA 40 p. 112.

17,29   BRIXHAM. A parish in Haytor Hundred (29); its lordship is identifiable in the Tax Return for Kerswell (Haytor) Hundred (xxv). In Fees p. 769 Reginald *de Valletorta* holds the manor of *Brixham* from the Honour of Totnes (Hurberton); see RH i pp. 72a, 89a, Cal. Inq. PM vol. iii no. 523, vi no. 318, ix no. 109, xi no. 35, xii no. 163, FA i p. 378 and OJR in TDA 40 p. 128. A further part of this land was at *Hoo* [Hoodown GR SX 8852] ; see FA i p. 348 and Cal. Inq. PM vol. ii no. 165.

17,30   CHURSTON (FERRERS). A parish in Haytor Hundred (29) and identifiable in the Kerswell (Haytor) Hundred Tax Return (xxv). William *Buzun* holds in *Churcheton'* in Fees p. 776 from the Honour of Totnes (Hurberton). The holder in FA i p. 348 is Hugh *de Fereris*; see Fees p. 767, FA i p. 391 and OJR in TDA 40 p. 112.
3 COTTAGERS. They are listed in an unusual place before, rather than after, the villagers and smallholders; see 15,21 note. It is possible that the Exchequer scribe intended them to be more closely linked with the slaves and the lordship, though it is more likely that they are merely misplaced (as the smallholders appear to be in 17,56; see note): in Exon. they occur in their usual place between the smallholders and slaves. The Exon. addition of the lordship land dictates their listing in this edition at the beginning of the villagers' paragraph.

17,31   COLETON. In Brixham parish, Haytor Hundred (29); see 17,27 note.

17,32   LODDISWELL. A parish in Stanborough Hundred (28). The lordship land, together with that of Thurlestone (17,33), accounts for Iudhael's hidage in the Tax Return for Diptford (Stanborough) Hundred (xxvi). In Fees p. 98 *Lodisswill* with Totnes (17,1) and Cornworthy (17,48) is held by Henry *filius Comitis* formerly by Reginald *de Brause*. Eva *de Breusa* holds in Fees p. 1371 and William *de Cantilupo* in Fees p. 766; see Fees

p. 264, RH i pp. 79b, 91b, TE p. 151a, Cal. Inq. PM vol. x nos. 240, 384, 652, FA i p. 323 and OJR in TDA 45 p. 194. It is possible that *Hach'* [Hatch in Loddiswell, GR SX 7146] held by John *de Arundel* in Fees p. 777 (Honour of Hurberton) was part of this land; see Fees p. 766, FA i pp. 323, 396 and OJR in TDA 45 p. 191.

17,33 THURLESTONE. A parish in Stanborough Hundred (28), identifiable in the Tax Return for Diptford (Stanborough) Hundred (xxvi); see 17,32 note. William *Buzun* holds *Thurlestane* in Fees p. 777 from the Honour of Totnes (Hurberton); see Fees p. 766, RH i pp. 79b, 91b, FA i p. 323, OJR in TDA 45 p. 187 and 17,41 note. Two other holdings from the Honour of Totnes, Buckland and possibly North Upton (17,36 note), lay in this parish.
A THANE HELD .... FROM JOHN. See Exon. Notes to 3,94. 15,33 and 24,24, and 15,39 note above, for other examples of the Exchequer scribe 'pruning out' details of TRE subtenancies.

17,34 BAGTON. In West Alvington parish, Stanborough Hundred (28). It is held from the Cantilupe Honour of Totnes in Fees p. 795 as *Baggetone* by Ralph *de Beaumis*; see Fees p. 766, FA i pp. 323, 396 and OJR in TDA 45 p. 188.

17,35 COLLATON. In Malborough parish, Stanborough Hundred (28), the name being derived from the TRE holder, Cola. In Fees p. 777 Roger *de Praulle* holds *Colethon'* of the Honour of Totnes (Hurberton). It is *Coleton Pral* in Cal. Inq. PM vol. xii no. 119; see Fees p. 765, FA i pp. 323, 396, OJR in TDA 45 p. 183 and 17,27 note.

17,36 (SOUTH) HUISH. A parish in Stanborough Hundred (28); for North Huish see 17,46 and note. Both South Huish and Galmpton (17,37) have the same 1086 holder (Ralph) and the same later holders. In Fees p. 795 Gilbert son of Stephen holds 1 fee from the Cantilupe Honour of Totnes in *Gaumeton* [Galmpton] and 1 fee in *Hiwiss* and *Boclaunde* [Buckland, now in Thurlestone, GR SX 6743]; see Fees p. 766, FA i pp. 323, 396 and OJR in TDA 45 p. 186. This Buckland may have been an outlying portion of Huish in 1086 or a later sub-infeudation of Iudhael's lordship manor of Thurlestone (17,33) or the Buckland (in Thurlestone) added to the Count of Mortain's Bolberry (15,38). Adjacent also was *Uppetone* held by *Ada Bernard* and the heirs of Ralph *de Uppetone* from the Cantilupe Honour of Totnes in Fees p. 795; see FA i pp. 323, 397. This is either North Upton in Thurlestone [SX 6844] or Upton in South Milton [SX 7043]; see OJR in TDA 45 p. 189. A further holding was at *Wydyamore* [Withymore in South Huish SX 7040], associated with Moor (17,10) and *Bokland Cammel* [Buckland, see above] in Cal. Inq. PM vol. vi no. 486.

17,37 GALMPTON. DB *Walementone*, see EPNS i p. 304. It lies in South Huish parish, Stanborough Hundred (28); see 17,36 note.
MEADOW, 2 ACRES. There is no obvious reason why the Exchequer scribe omitted this information from Exon. He also omits meadow details in 32,5. 36,12 and 47,3, though there may be a reason for their omission in 32,5 (see note).
VALUE NOW 50s. In the MS *xl sol'* was originally written, but the *x* was scratched out to make *l sol'*, though it is still visible. The figure was never *xxx sol'* as in Exon.

17,38 (WEST) PORTLEMOUTH. In Malborough parish, Stanborough Hundred (28). East Portlemouth is in Coleridge Hundred (30) and is wrongly identified by EPNS i p. 328 with the DB place (see 52,53 note). In Fees p. 777 Guy *de Brettevill'* holds in *Porlemue* from the Honour of Totnes (Hurberton); see Fees p. 766, FA i pp. 323, 396 and OJR in TDA 45 p. 191.

17,39 ILTON. Likewise in Malborough parish, Stanborough Hundred (28). It is held by Gerard *de Spineto* as *Ydelthon'* of the Honour of Totnes (Hurberton) in Fees p. 777; see Fees p. 766, FA i pp. 323, 396 and OJR in TDA 45 p. 192.

17,40 ALSTON. DB *Alwinestone*, named from the TRE holder. This is Alston in Malborough parish, Stanborough Hundred (28). In Fees p. 776, from the Honour of Totnes (Hurberton), John *de Rak'* holds in *Surlegh'* [Sorley 17,42], *Rak'* [Rake GR SX 7247 adjacent to Sorley] and *Alwyneston'*. In FA i p. 323 this holding at Alston is described as *Alwyneston'* and *La Herd* or *Virga* in FA i p. 351, *La Eyrd* in FA i p. 396, that is Yarde in Malborough, SX 7140; see OJR in TDA 45 p. 181.

17,41 SOAR. Or Sewer, in Malborough parish, Stanborough Hundred (28). In Fees p. 777 Robert *Buzun* holds *Sure* from the Honour of Totnes (Hurberton). In FA i p. 396 *Soure* is coupled with *Thorleston'* (17,33); see Fees p. 765, FA i p. 323 and OJR in TDA 45 p. 183.
240 SHEEP AND GOATS. Exon. *ccxl inter oues & capras*; that is, the sheep and goats together numbered 240; see 16,58 note.

17,41 NINE MANORS .... LAID WASTE BY IRISHMEN. That is, 17,33-41, all in
(cont'd.) Stanborough Hundred in the extreme south of the County. They were probably laid
 waste when two of Earl Harold's sons, who had taken refuge in Ireland, staged a series
 of raids on the south-west in 1069 and following years; Loyn p. 105. See Exon. Notes
 here. See the article by Alexander in TDA 55.
17,42 SORLEY. In Churchstow parish, Stanborough Hundred (28). Descent is with Alston,
 another of Fulk's lands, of which Rake was probably a sub-manor (17,40 note). It seems
 that this was the *Swurdleage*, 3 *perticae* granted by King Edgar to *Æthel...e minister* in
 962 (ECDC p. 12 no. 38 = Sawyer (1) no. 704).
17,43 POULSTON. Now in Halwell parish, Coleridge Hundred (30), but it lies adjacent to the
 Stanborough Hundred boundary and was counted in the latter Hundred in the Middle
 Ages. The order of Exon. points to the same. In Fees p. 776 Alan *Bughedon'* holds in
 *Pollekeston'* from the Honour of Totnes (Hurberton); see Fees p. 765, FA i pp. 323,
 395 and OJR in TDA 45 p. 182.
17,44 CURTISKNOWLE. In Diptford parish, Stanborough Hundred (28). In Fees p. 795 John
 *de Alba Mara* holds *Curtescnolle* from the Cantilupe Honour of Totnes; a descendant is
 called William *Albemarle de Northiwis* (from North Huish 17,46) in FA i p. 323; see
 Fees p. 766, FA i p. 395 and OJR in TDA 45 p. 188.
17,45 BROADLEY. In North Huish parish (see 17,46), Stanborough Hundred (28). In Fees
 p. 795 William and Adam *de Bradelg'* hold in *Bradelg'* from the Cantilupe Honour of
 Totnes; see Fees p. 766, FA i pp. 324, 395 and OJR in TDA 45 p. 189.
17,46 (NORTH) HUISH. A parish in Stanborough Hundred (28). While the link with Galmpton
 established the 'Huish' of 17,36 as South Huish, this present entry is *Hiwiss'* held by
 John *de Alba Mara* from the Cantilupe Honour of Totnes in Fees p. 795. It is *Northywys*
 held by another John *Daumarle* in FA i p. 395. See Fees p. 765, FA i pp. 323-324, Cal.
 Inq. PM vol. viii no. 230, OJR in TDA 45 p. 181 and 17,44 note.
17,47 WOOLSTON. In the MS *Vlsistone* is in lower-case letters for some reason, instead of
 the capitals usual for the names of manors. Cf. 17,98 note. It is in West Alvington
 parish, Stanborough Hundred (28), and is held by Richard *Crespin* of the Honour of
 Totnes (Hurberton) in Fees p. 777 as *Wolsingthon'*; see Fees p. 766, FA i pp. 323, 396,
 Cal. Inq. PM vol. v no. 462, OJR in TDA 45 p. 188 and Ch. 5 note.
17,48 CORNWORTHY. A parish in Coleridge Hundred (30). In Fees p. 795 Henry *de
 Tiddewrth'* holds in *Cornnewrth'* from the Cantilupe Honour of Totnes. In FA i p. 393
 this holding seems to be represented by ¼ fee held by the Prioress of Cornworthy in
 *Allelegh* [Allaleigh GR SX 8153] and *Tortysfenne* [unidentified] and ½ fee held in
 *Tyddeworth[y]* [Tideford SX 8254] by William *Tyddeworth[y]* of the Honour of
 Torrington (an error for Totton or Totnes); see VE ii p. 335, OJR in TDA 43 pp. 195,
 214 and 17,1 note.
 HELD IT. In the MS *ten* corrected to *tenb*; see 16,151 note.
17,49 CHARLETON. This large holding presumably represents Charleton parish in Coleridge
 Hundred (30); see EPNS i p. 319, OJR in TDA 43 p. 215 and Cal. Inq. PM vol. xi no.
 597 of Margery wife of William *Pippard* who also held North Bovey (17,22). See also
 Cal. Inq. PM vol. i no. 650, ii nos. 165, 470, iv no. 31, xiv no. 151 and xv no. 807.
 11 SLAVES. In the MS the *xi* is written over an erasure, but there is not enough room
 for the figure to have been *xii* as in Exon. It is interesting that there is a correction in
 Exon. too, a *v* having been originally written before the *xii* but then erased with water.
17,50 LEIGH. DB *Lege*, now East and West Leigh in Harberton parish, Coleridge Hundred
 (30), so VCH p. 472 note 8. Although there is no evidence to support the exact
 identification, it seems more likely than Dorsley where there were also Totnes Honour
 holdings. In Fees p. 795 John *de Regni de Sumerset* holds 1/6th fee in *Thurislgh'* from
 the Cantilupe Honour of Totnes and in Fees p. 777 Robert *le Bastard* and Durand son
 of Richard each hold 1/6th fee there of the Honour of Totnes (Hurberton); see FA i
 pp. 331, 394, OJR in TDA 43 pp. 195, 216 and EPNS i p. 325. But Dorsley (which is
 probably part of Harberton, 1,34 note), being derived from *Dur* or *Duri* (an Anglo-
 Scandinavian personal name) should have appeared in compounded form in DB, not
 simply as *Lege*. The present 'Leigh' is possibly the *Leygh Duraunt* of Cal. Inq. PM
 vol. vii no. 494.
 PASTURE, 10 ACRES. The second of these two identical phrases is underlined for
 deletion in pale ink in the MS, though this underlining is not reproduced in the
 facsimile despite its being the same colour as the 7s (which often appear in paler ink).
 To complete the correction the scribe should have interlined the 1 acre of woodland
 which is written clearly in Exon.

17,51   POOL. South Pool parish in Coleridge Hundred (30). In Fees p. 795 William *de la Pumeray* holds *Pole* from the Cantilupe Honour of Totnes. It is *Suthpole* in FA i p. 332; see FA i p. 392, TE p. 151a, Cal. Inq. PM vol. iii no. 401, xi nos. 35, 309, xii no. 333 and OJR in TDA 36 p. 371, 43 pp. 195, 216.
17,52   COMBE. Presumably Combe in South Pool parish (17,51), Coleridge Hundred (30); see OJR in TDA 43 p. 195.
        ALRIC. DB and Exon. *Alrist* which is a scribal error; see PNDB p. 151. See the Introduction to the Exon. Notes for other examples of scribal errors in both DB and Exon., suggesting direct copying of the one from the other.
17,53   (SOUTH) ALLINGTON. In Chivelstone parish, Coleridge Hundred (30). There has been some confusion with East Allington (EPNS i p. 313) which was in Stanborough Hundred (28) in 1086 and sometimes later; see 30,3 note and the Appendix. In Fees p. 777 Gilbert *Crespin* (who also holds Stancombe (17,54), likewise held by Thorgils in 1086) has *Aylington'* from the Honour of Totnes (Hurberton). It is *Alyngton Crispyn* in Cal. Inq. PM vol. xii no. 119. Also in Fees p. 777, Richard *Crespin* and William *de la Pomeray* hold in *Burgh'* [Borough in Chivelstone, GR SX 7937]. In FA i p. 331 *Stancumb'* [Stancombe 17,54], *Alinton* and *Burge* are held together by John of Cirencester; see FA i pp. 393-394 and OJR in TDA 43 p. 217.
17,54   STANCOMBE. In Sherford parish, Coleridge Hundred (30). Gilbert *Crespin* holds *Stonecumb'* in Fees p. 777 from the Honour of Totnes (Hurberton); see FA i pp. 331, 393 and OJR in TDA 43 p. 195.
17,55   MALSTON. Also in Sherford parish, Coleridge Hundred (30). Aubrey *de Pynu* holds in *Mallestone* from the Cantilupe Honour of Totnes in Fees p. 795; see FA i pp. 332, 393, Cal. Inq. PM vol. xvi no. 875 and OJR in TDA 43 p. 217.
17,56   FORD. In Chivelstone parish, Coleridge Hundred (30); see OJR in TDA 43 p. 217 and 17,57 note.
        1 SMALLHOLDER. Listed in an unusual position before, rather than after, the villagers, as also in 21,9. 36,7. 42,16. 52,3 and 52,38. It almost seems from the Latin that the smallholder here is linked with the lordship plough (the necessary addition of the lordship land from Exon. somewhat obscures this), but it is possible that the *ii uitti* should have been written *ii uittis* (i.e. "In lordship 1 plough, with 1 smallholder and 2 villagers with 2 ploughs") which is more normal. In Exon. the smallholder appears after the villager, the lordship and villagers' ploughs (and land) being detailed in the previous sentence as usual. See 1,3 note on the smallholder.
17,57   CHIVELSTONE. A parish in Coleridge Hundred (30). In Fees p. 795 William *de Bykelg'* holds in *Cheveleston'* from the Cantilupe Honour of Totnes. *Chevylston* and *Forde* [Ford 17,56] are coupled in FA i pp. 349, 392; see Cal. Inq. PM vol. vi no. 486 and OJR in TDA 43 p. 217.
17,58   FOLLATON. In Totnes parish, Coleridge Hundred (30). It was bestowed by Iudhael on the Priory Church of St. Mary of Totnes, a cell of the church of SS Sergius and Bacchus at Angers; see VE ii p. 367, Oliver *Mon*. p. 238, OJR in TDA 30 p. 285, 43 p. 218 and 17,1 note.
17,59   WORTHELE. In Ermington parish and Hundred (27). This and the next manor, Leigh, both held by Iudhael in lordship in 1086, can be identified from the 1 hide of lordship given for Iudhael in the Tax Return for *Alleriga* (Ermington) Hundred (xxx). In Fees p. 776 Herbert son of Matthew and Hugh *de Foresta* hold *Worthyel* of the Honour of Totnes (Hurberton); see Fees p. 770, TE p. 153, Cal. Inq. PM vol. viii no. 280, xvi no. 875, FA i p. 398 and OJR H6 p. 317.
17,60   LEIGH. In Modbury parish, Ermington Hundred (27). It can be identified in the Tax Return for *Alleriga* (Ermington) Hundred (xxx); see 17,59 note. Guy *de Brettevil'* (for whom see 17,3) holds *Legh'* in Fees p. 776 from the Honour of Totnes (Hurberton); see Fees p. 770. It is *Legh' Brytevyll* in FA i p. 398; see EPNS i p. 280 and OJR H6 p. 318.
17,61-62 BUTTERFORD. Now in North Huish parish, Stanborough Hundred (28), but in the Middle Ages it was counted as part of Ermington Hundred (27), where it lies in Exon. order. In Fees p. 776 William *de la Pomeray* (who later holds part of South Allington (17,53) which was also held by Thorgils in 1086) holds in *Buterford'*; see Fees p. 769, FA i pp. 351, 397, Cal. Inq. PM vol. xii no. 333 and OJR H6 p. 308.
17,63   RALPH HOLDS FROM IUDHAEL. Repeated at the beginning of 17,63-67 inclusive.
        STADBURY. In Aveton Giffard parish, Ermington Hundred (27). Ralph *de Stodbiri* holds in *Stodbir'* in Fees p. 795 from the Cantilupe Honour of Totnes; see Fees p. 771, FA i pp. 352, 400, Cal. Inq. PM vol. i no. 740, vi no. 486, viii no. 230 and OJR H6 p. 325.

| | |
|---|---|
| 17,64 | RINGMORE. A parish in Ermington Hundred (27). It is held in Fees p. 795 as *Redmore* from the Cantilupe Honour of Totnes by Gilbert son of Stephen (on whom see 17,36 note); see also Fees p. 770, Cal. Inq. PM vol. vi no. 486 and 17,65 note. |
| 17,65 | OKENBURY. In Ringmore parish, Ermington Hundred (27). In FA i p. 397 *Ridmore* [Ringmore 17,64], *Wokenobeare* [Okenbury], *Merewild* [Marwell in Ringmore, GR SX 6547] and *Fuggeslangeston* [Langston or South Langston in Kingston, GR SX 6448, see EPNS i p. 279] are held from the Honour of Totnes. They are *Wokkenebiri, Langeston* and *Marlewille* in Cal. Inq. PM vol. vi no. 486. |
| 17,66 | BLACHFORD. In Cornwood parish, Ermington Hundred (27). In Fees p. 795 Richard *Bauceyn* holds in *Uvereblachesuurthe* ('Over' Blachford) from the Cantilupe Honour of Totnes; see Fees p. 771, FA i pp. 353, 399, Cal. Inq. PM vol. vi no. 486, OJR H6 p. 325 and 29,5 note. |
| 17,67 | LAMBSIDE. In Holbeton parish, Ermington Hundred (27). It is held as *Lamsede* with *Alnetheston'* [Alston GR SX 5848] in Fees p. 795 by Gilbert *Crespin* of the Cantilupe Honour of Totnes; see Fees p. 770, FA i pp. 352, 398, TE p. 153 and OJR H6 p. 315. MEADOW, 3 ACRES. In the MS *ii ac pti* was originally written, but a final *i* was added in slightly paler ink which is smaller and does not reach down as far as the other *ii*. As Exon. has '2 acres' with no sign of correction, this may suggest that the Exchequer MS was corrected from other sources as well as against Exon. |
| 17,68 | MEMBLAND. In Holbeton parish, Ermington Hundred (27). In Fees p. 795 Walter *de Mimilaunde* holds in *Mimilaunde* from the Cantilupe Honour of Totnes. The next Fees entry, *Calsintone* [Caulston GR SX 5647] held by the heirs of Henry *le Deneys*, is probably part of this land; see Fees p. 770, FA i pp. 352, 399 and OJR H6 pp. 315-316. |
| 17,69 | EGGBUCKLAND. DB *Bocheland*, the name of the TRE holder Heca being prefixed. It is a parish in Roborough Hundred (25) and can be identified in the Tax Return for Walkhampton (Roborough) Hundred (xxix). Like Compton Gifford (17,78) and Hooe (17,106) it passed as a result of purchase by William *Briwere* to the Honour of Plympton. In Fees p. 789 the heir of Isabella *Giffard* holds 2 fees in *Eckebocland'*, *Compton'* and *Ho'*; see Fees p. 401, RH i p. 92a, HD p. 56, FA i pp. 354, 403, Cal. Inq. PM vol. i no. 112, ii nos. 306, 593, v no. 527, vii no. 347 and OJR H3 pp. 123-124. It is possible that Leigham, associated in later lists with Manadon, was part of this land (17,75 note). |
| 17,70-71 | MUTLEY. Now in Plymouth, Roborough Hundred (25); see EPNS i p. 235. |
| 17,70 | 2 VILLAGERS HAVE IT THERE. The plough, as Exon. states. See 1,29 note. |
| 17,71 | VIRGATE. Farley prints a capital *V* for *Virg'*, but in the MS the *v* is not large but the normal size used when the scribe writes *v̄*. |
| 17,72 | ODO ALSO HOLDS. Repeated at the beginning of 17,72-77 inclusive. LEURICESTONE. Formally, neither Leigham in Eggbuckland (OJR in TDA 36 p. 372 and H3 pp. 125-126, see 17,75 note) nor Laira (Whale in TDA 28 p. 426 and DG) can be derived from the DB form; see EPNS i pp. 20, 228. The place certainly lay in Roborough Hundred (25) according to the order of Exon., but the matter needs further research. |
| 17,73-74 | THE SCRIBE HAS OMITTED *de Ju*. 'from Iu(dhael)' in error; it is in Exon. as usual. See 15,22 note. |
| 17,73 | WESTON (PEVERELL). A parish in Roborough Hundred (25), now absorbed by Plymouth, the name being represented by the separate Weston Mill (GR SX 4557) and Peverell (SX 4756). In Fees p. 776 Hugh *Peverel* holds in *Weston'* from the Honour of Totnes (Hurberton); see FA i pp. 341, 403 and OJR H3 p. 126. |
| 17,74 | BURRINGTON. Burrington and Burraton (EPNS i p. 246) in Weston Peverel parish, Roborough Hundred (25). It does not appear in the fee lists; see OJR H3 p. 126. HELD IT. In the MS *ten* corrected to *tenb*; see 16,151 note. |
| 17,75 | MANADON. Similarly in Weston Peverell parish, Roborough Hundred (25). In Fees p. 776 William *Buzun* holds in *Legham* [Leigham in Eggbuckland, GR SX 5158, see 17,69;72 notes] and *Manedone* from the Honour of Totnes (Hurberton); see FA i p. 404 and OJR H3 p. 125. Leigham (*Legham Bozon* in FA i p. 403) later forms a part of the Honour of Trematon. |
| 17,76 | WHITLEIGH. In St. Budeaux parish, Roborough Hundred (25). In Fees p. 776 Peter *de Alnedeston'* (from Alston 17,67 note) holds in *Whytelegh'* from the Honour of Totnes (Hurberton). It appears as *Thorn* [unidentified] and *Wytele* in FA i p. 354 and as *Thorne* and *Estwytelegh* (though held from the Honour of Trematon) in FA i p. 404; see FA i p. 341, OJR H3 p. 126 and 28,15-16 note. |

17,77 COLERIDGE. In Eggbuckland parish, Roborough Hundred (25). In Fees p. 776 Augustine *de Courig* holds in *Courig* from the Honour of Totnes (Hurberton); see FA i pp. 341, 354, 403 and OJR H3 p. 127.
1 ANIMAL IN A PLOUGH. Here the Exon. *animal* must be an ox; cf. '1 ox in a plough' in 17,98. See notes to 1,3 on cattle and 2,22 on 'animal', also 17,26 note.
WASTE. DB *uastata est*, Exon. *erat uastata*; see second note under C 3 and cf. notes to 3,35 and 16,124.

17,78 COMPTON (GIFFORD). Compton or Compton Gifford (EPNS i p. 227), a parish in Roborough Hundred (25); see OJR H3 pp. 123-124 and 17,69 note.
VALUE .... 30s. So the MS; Farley misprints *xiii solid'*.

17,79-82 MEAVY. A parish in Roborough Hundred (25). It is difficult to relate these four DB holdings exactly to later evidence. Fees p. 776 records four holdings: (1) *Mewy*, ½ fee held by Richard *de Mewy*; see FA i p. 402. (2) *Godemewy* [Goodameavy GR SX 5364], ½ fee held by Walter *Pomeray* which must have descended from Thorgils (see 17,53;61-62 notes); it is *Godmeuwaie Pomeray* in Cal. Inq. PM vol. xii no. 119; see vol. xii no. 333 and FA i pp. 354, 403. (3) A fortieth fee held by Richard *de Mewy*, called *Hughemewy* [Hoo Meavy SX 5365] in FA i pp. 354, 404 where it is held by Richard *Giffard*. (4) *Gropeton* [Gratton SX 5267] also held by Richard *de Mewy*, then by John *de Asshlegh* in FA i pp. 355, 404; see TE p. 153. All these are held from the Honour of Totnes (Hurberton). From the Cantilupe Honour of Totnes is held *Hugemewy* [Hoo Meavy, see above] by William *Giffard* and Richard *de Mewy* in Fees p. 795.

A portion of Goodameavy is called *Cadeworth[i]* [Cadover SX 5564] and is held by the Prior of Plympton; see FA i pp. 341, 403. A further land appears to be *Brittenesworth[y]* [Brisworthy SX 5565] held by Richard *de Mewy* (Honour of Hurberton) in FA i pp. 355, 403; see OJR H3 pp. 127-129.

Part of Meavy (see also 29,9) appears to have been the *Maewi* granted as ½ *mansa* by King Canute to *AEtheric minister* in 1031 (ECDC no. 58 p. 14 = KCD no. 744 = Sawyer (1) no. 963).

17,83 SHERFORD. East and West Sherford in Brixton parish, Plympton Hundred (26). Parts of *Shireford'* or *Sireford'* are held both from the Canitlupe Honour of Totnes and the Honour of Hurberton by the Prior of Plympton in Fees pp. 776, 794; see FA i p. 401 and OJR H6 p. 289.
MOOR. DB and Exon. *mora*. Sherford is about 3 miles south of the present edge of Dartmoor, so the 'moor' here may have been a detached part of the manor. The only other reference to moorland in Devon is in 1,41.

17,84 WILLIAM ALSO HOLDS FROM IUDHAEL. Repeated at the beginning of 17,84-89 inclusive. After this statement in 17,84 in the MS is erased *ten*, though still visible. Farley does not print the gap thus caused, but see 1,60 note.
CHITTLEBURN. In Brixton parish, Plympton Hundred (26). Like Sherford (17,83), it is in later times held in two parts: *Chycheberg'* held by Richard *de Cynnock'* from the Honour of Totnes (Hurberton) and *Chicheburgh'* held by John *de Regni* from the Cantilupe Honour of Totnes; see FA i pp. 335, 354, 401 and OJR H6 p. 290.

It is odd that no population was recorded for this manor, although most of the manorial details are given, including resources. It was similarly omitted for 19,22. 23,25. 34,37;54. 35,23. 42,19 and 47,2. It is possible that Chittleburn was worked by some of the villagers from nearby manors, such as Sherford or Wollaton or Brixton (17,83;85-87); cf. notes to 19,22. 23,25. 34,37 and 42,20. In eleven other entries (e.g. 14,3-4. 17,18) no population is recorded but neither are any resources, though the plough estimates and sometimes the actual ploughs on the land are nonetheless given. See 3,10 note on the occurrence of only slaves in some thirty manors, and cf. 3,11 note. There seems to be no obvious reason for the omission of the villagers from these manors.

17,85 WOLLATON. In Brixton parish, Plympton Hundred (26). It is coupled with Brixton in later documents; see 17,86-87 note.

17,86-87 BRIXTON. A parish in Plympton Hundred (26). A second place with the same modern name, Brixton Barton in Shaugh parish (17,91) is found in this Hundred, but the names have a different origin. The first, DB *Brisestone*, is perhaps from the Celtic personal name *Brioc* (EPNS i p. 249), the second, DB *Brictricestone*, is from the OE personal name *Beorhtric* (EPNS i p. 258). These differences in spelling are preserved in medieval documents, the two present holdings (17,86-87) being represented (1) by *Brighton'* held in Fees p. 794 by John *de Regni* of the Cantilupe Honour of Totnes, and (2) by *Brigston'* held in Fees p. 776 by Gilbert *Anglicus* of the Honour of Totnes (Hurberton).

The first, later known as *Brixton Regny*, passes to Robert *de Blakeford*, being coupled with *Gorlowfenne* [Gorlofen GR SX 5652] in FA i p. 334 and *Wolvyngton* [Wollaton 17,85; for the form see EPNS i p. 251] in FA i p. 402; see FA i p. 353. The second (17,87) is held in FA i p. 334 by Roger *le Engleys*; see FA i pp. 353, 401 and, on both the holdings, OJR H6 pp. 291-292.

17,88-89 AELFRIC. DB *Aluric*, Exon. *Alebric'*, in both entries. It would appear from this equation (and see also DB Cornwall Exon. Notes 5,3,6) that OE *Aelfric* (see 3,35 note) has been latinized *Albericus* (usually OG *Alberic*, OFr *Aubri*, whence English *Aubrey*, cf. OEB pp. 169-170); see PNDB p. 180 and Forssner p. 19 s.n. *Albericus*. It is interesting that DB Somerset 1,27 has *Aluric paruus*, whereas in the corresponding Exon. 113 a 2 the scribe originally wrote *Albric' paruus*, but corrected the first name to *Aluuric'*. It is quite likely that the various Aelfrics and Aubreys who in 1066 held manors in the large group of Plympton Hundred (26) places (17,83-107) were one and the same man. The 1066 tenant of 17,84, *Alric*, may also be the same person; see 1,11 note. For example, in 17,83-85;87 'Aubrey', 'Alric' and 'Aelfric' held in 1066 manors very close together which all passed in 1086 to a certain William.

17,88 DOWN (THOMAS). In Wembury parish, Plympton Hundred (26). Thomas *Joelis* holds in *Dune* in Fees p. 776 of the Honour of Totton (Hurberton); see FA i pp. 335, 401 and OJR H6 p. 292.

17,89 STADDISCOMBE. In Plymstock parish, Plympton Hundred (26). It is held by Guy *le Breth'* as *Stottecumb'* in Fees p. 776 from the Honour of Totnes (Hurberton); see FA i pp. 335, 353, 401 and OJR H6 p. 292.

17,90 STADDON. In Plymstock parish, Plympton Hundred (26). It is later divided between the Honour of Totnes and Hurberton, 1/3rd fee being held of the latter and 1/6th fee of the former by Guy *le Bret* and Henry *de Waleford* in *Waleford* ['Walford' 17,93] and *Stoddune* in Fees pp. 776, 794; see FA i pp. 335, 401 and OJR H6 p. 292.

17,91 BRIXTON. DB *Brictricestone*, now Brixton Barton in Shaugh parish, Plympton Hundred (26); see 17,86-87 note. It is *Brigtrichest'* held by Henry *de Brigtricheston'* in Fees p. 794 of the Cantilupe Honour of Totnes; see FA i pp. 335, 402, Cal. Inq. PM vol. vi no. 486 and OJR H6 p. 294.

17,92 'BACCAMOOR'. In Plympton St. Mary parish, Plympton Hundred (26), an unfruitful and depopulated place, represented on six-inch maps by Baccamoor Waste. In Fees p. 794 Ralph *de Stadbir'* holds in *Backemore* and *Hunelaunde* [Holland 17,94] from the Cantilupe Honour of Totnes; see FA i pp. 334, 402, Cal. Inq. PM vol. vi no. 486 and OJR H6 p. 294.
?HELOISE. DB *Elous*, Exon. *Ealous*, not explained by PNDB p. 247. In this form and *Alous* 25,7 (Exon. *Aloiss*) the *-us* probably represents an integral part of the name, not a Latin *-us* inflexion. The Exon. *Aloiss* indicates that the *-ous* form also represents *-ouis* or *-oüis*, for which we should seek personal names in the OFr (<OG) feminine theme *-wis*, with *o(u)* for *w* (PNDB §55 p. 76) and elision (or mere scribal omission?) of *i*. This might offer an alternative model to OE *-gyth* for ME fem. personal names in *-usa*, *-use* (cf. Reaney s.n. *Aldous*). *Elous* might well represent OFr *Heloise*, OG *Helewis* (Forssner p. 145), *Heilwid(is)* (Förstemann 729). Cf. *Helewis* in DB Norfolk 10,81. DB *Alous* in 25,7 (Exon. *Aloiss*) represents ME *Halewise*, OFr *Alweis* (Forssner p. 24), OG *Adalwid(is)* (Förstemann 180). The Exon. spelling *Eal-* may be an attempt to reflect some persistence of the diphthong of OG *Heil-*; or an anticipation of the diphthong in *-ewis*; or a spelling analogous with personal name forms in *El-*, *Eal-* from *Eald-* (PNDB § 102.2(c) and p. 240). (JMcND.)
ANOTHER 'BACCAMOOR'. Another holding in 'Baccamoor', rather than another village called 'Baccamoor'; see Exon. Notes here and to 14,2. *Alia* has a similar meaning in 17,105 and also elsewhere in DB (e.g. with Seaborough in Somerset 3,1; Franche and Ribbesford in Worcs. 1,2). Cf. 1,23 note on *altera Dunitone*.
SIGERIC. DB and main Exon. entry *Seric(us)*, T.O. *Siric(us)*, represent OE *Sigeric*.
VALUE 20s. *Valent*, plural, meaning the value of both the manors of 'Baccamoor'. Cf. 17,105.

17,93 'WALFORD'. A lost place in Plympton St. Mary parish, Plympton Hundred (26); see EPNS i p. 254. It is *Waleford* in Fees pp. 776, 794 held with Staddon (17,90 note). OJR identified it wrongly with Collaford, see editor's note in OJR H6 p. 286.

17,94 HOLLAND. In Plympton St. Mary parish, Plympton Hundred (26). In later documents it is coupled with 'Baccamoor' (17,92 note).

17,95-96 LANGDON. In Wembury parish, Plympton Hundred (26). In Fees p. 794 *Langedune* is

|         | held by William *Pipard* from the Cantilupe Honour of Totnes; see FA i pp. 335, 401, RBE ii p. 558 and Cal. Inq. PM vol. i no. 650, iii no. 598, iv no. 31, xi no. 597, xiv no. 151, xv no. 807. |
|---|---|
| 17,97 | COLDSTONE. In Shaugh parish, Plympton Hundred (26); it is not found in later fee lists. |
| 17,98 | THORGILS ALSO HOLDS FROM IUDHAEL. Repeated at the beginning of 17,98-101 inclusive. |
|         | FERNHILL. In the MS only the last two *E*s of *Fernehelle* are in capitals, the rest being in lower-case for some reason (cf. 17,47 note); Farley misprints two capital *L*s as well. It is in Shaugh parish, Plympton Hundred (26). In Fees p. 775 it is held of the Honour of Totnes (Hurberton) as *Fernhille* by Nicholas *de Fernhille*; see FA i p. 401, Cal. Inq. PM vol. xii no. 333 and OJR H6 p. 296. |
| 17,99 | PETHILL. In Shaugh parish, Plympton Hundred (26); it does not appear in later lists of fees. |
| 17,100 -101 | SHAUGH (PRIOR). A parish, sometimes simply Shaugh, in Plympton Hundred (26). In Fees p. 776 the Prior of Plympton holds *Saghe* from the Honour of Totnes (Hurberton); see TE p. 153, FA i pp. 333, 400, OJR H6 p. 296 and 21,20 note. |
| 17,102 | TORRIDGE. In Plympton St. Mary parish, Plympton Hundred (26); see 15,50 note. This, the smaller of the two holdings, was 'Little' Torridge. It is held as *Parva Thorz* with *Lughetorr'* [Loughtor 17,103] by William *Le Abbe* from the Cantilupe Honour of Totnes in Fees p. 794; see FA i pp. 333, 402 and OJR H6 p. 294. |
| 17,103 | LOUGHTOR. In Plympton St. Mary parish, Plympton Hundred (26), like the preceding entry, and held with it in later times (see 17,102 note). |
| 17,104 | ELFORDLEIGH. DB *Lege*. In Plympton Hundred (26), but the identity is not firmly established, although, since 17,102-3;5 are all in Plympton St. Mary parish, Elfordleigh in the same is not unlikely; see EPNS i p. 253. OJR (H6 pp. 265, 294) suggests Higher and Lower Leigh in Shaugh parish. |
| 17,105 | WOODFORD. In Plympton St. Mary parish, Plympton Hundred (26). In Fees p. 794 Muriel *de Bolley* holds in *Wodeford* from the Cantilupe Honour of Totnes; see FA i pp. 333, 400, Cal. Inq. PM vol. vii no. 708, viii no. 230. The 1086 holder Ralph appears to be Ralph of Pomeroy, since Matilda *de Pomeray* before 1155 gave one third of Woodford to Plympton Priory; see OJR H6 p. 295. |
|         | ANOTHER WOODFORD. Another holding in Woodford; see 17,92 note. |
| 17,106 | HOOE. In Plymstock parish, Plympton Hundred (26). Like Compton Gifford and Eggbuckland (17,78;69) with which it is associated in Fees p. 789, it passed to the Honour of Plympton. The holding seems to have encompassed both *Westhoe* (FA i pp. 335, 401) and *Estho* (FA i p. 353); see FA i p. 354, Cal. Inq. PM vol. vii no. 297 and OJR H6 p. 285. |
| 17,107 | HALWELL. In Brixton parish, Plympton Hundred (26). In Fees p. 776, from the Honour of Totnes (Hurberton), William *de Haleghewelle* holds in *Haleghewell'*; see FA i pp. 334, 401 and OJR H6 p. 293. |
| Ch. 18 | WILLIAM OF MOHUN. DB *de Moion*, Exon. *de Moione*. Although he came from Moyon in the département of Manche, France, he is rendered William of Mohun in this series in deference to the more popular 13th century spelling of the English form of his surname. He was Sheriff of Somerset from *c.* 1068 and he 'farmed' various royal manors there (see DB Somerset General Notes 1,14). Dunster in Somerset was the seat of his barony and his lands later formed the Honour of Dunster. |
| 18,1 | CLAYHANGER. In Bampton Hundred (8); EPNS ii p. 533. It does not appear in later fee lists. William appears to have held a part of Bampton (23,5 note) unlawfully with this land. |
| Ch. 19 | WILLIAM CHEEVER. DB *Chieure, Cheure, capra* (not *de Chieure, de Chievre*, as OEB p. 360 states), Exon. *capra*: OFr *chievre* (Mod.Fr *chèvre*) from Latin *capra* 'a she-goat'. This is William's only holding in DB. |
|         | Although neither DB nor Exon. states in so many words that William's brother was Ralph of Pomeroy (Ch. 34), the T.O. (at 496 b 2) records that William Cheever and his brother added William's manor in Instaple (= DB 19,3) to the manor of Bradworthy (= 34,6, held by Ralph of Pomeroy); see Exon. Notes 19,3. And the Tax Return for Fremington Hundred (iv) states that Ralph of Pomeroy has ½ hide lordship and his brother William has ½ hide: these can be identified as 34,8 and, probably, 19,5-6. Moreover, their lands are held in virtually the same Hundreds (see the next note and the second note under Ch. 34) and follow the same Hundredal order. Many villages were divided between the two men, such as West Putford (19,4 and 34,7), Awliscombe |

Ch. 19    (19,25-26;32 and 34,23;26), Weston (19,27 and 34,24), Rapshays (19,34 and 34,32)
(cont'd.) and Ivedon (19,42-43 and 34,45;47) and, according to Exon., Yowlestone was held
jointly by William Cheever and Ralph of Pomeroy (see Exon. Notes 19,33). Even the
services of one villager were divided between the two men; see 19,43 note. Likewise, the
lands of both men had previously been held by a number of the same tenants: for
example, Alward son of Toki who appears only as a TRE tenant in Chs. 19 and 34 (see
19,16 note); Viking — most of the occurrences of this name, which is unusual in DB, are
in Devon and again only in the fiefs of William and Ralph; Saemer, who had held the
manor of Ivedon which was in 1086 divided between the two men (19,43 and 34,45);
Aelmer, three of whose manors passed to Ralph's and William's sister Beatrix (19,40;46
and 34,43); see also the division of Ivedon and Weston between Warin and Rozelin
(19,42 and 34,24 notes). Other TRE tenants of lands that passed to both William and
Ralph include Brictmer, Edric, Edmer, Godric, Ulf, Alric, Wulfnoth, Aelfric, Edwin and
Burgred, but theirs are common names and may not apply to the same man every time.
However, one must not assume that because DB records a William holding in 1086 from
Ralph or a Ralph holding from William, that the brother is meant, because, for example,
Exon. identifies DB's plain William (the subtenant of 34,27-28) as 'of Poitou', and in
19,43 the subtenant Ralph is called 'son of Payne' in the Exon.
    It is possible that the fiefs of the brothers had been returned together (and then
divided into two by the compilers of Exon.); cf. the fiefs of Walter of Claville and
Gotshelm (also apparently brothers), Chs. 24-25, which still form one section in Exon.
as they probably had done in the 'original returns'.
    William's estates fell to the crown in the reign of Henry I and were granted by Henry
to his own illegitimate son, William I *de Tracey*, forming (with Ch. 31 lands) the Honour
of Braneys or Bradninch (from Bradninch 19,31); see VCH pp. 560-563 and Sanders
p. 20. Most of these lands are found later in the *Inquisitiones Post Mortem* of the Honour
of Braneys or of the Earls of Cornwall; see, for example, Cal. Inq. PM vol. iii no. 604,
xv no. 166.
THE ORDER OF THIS CHAPTER, with the exception of Exeter (19,1, placed by Exon.
as the final entry), is the same in both Exon. and Exchequer DB. It should be noted that
the Exon. MS is misfoliated between the entries relating to DB 19,8 and 19,27 (see Exon.
Notes to 19,8. 19,20 and 19,27) and this disguises the correspondence between Exon.
and DB. The Hundredal order, which seems to show a number of dislocations or later
entries (see 19,21-43 note), is:

|  |  |  |  |
|---|---|---|---|
| 19,2-4 | Torrington | 19,33-34 | Budleigh |
| 19,5-6 | Fremington | 19,35 | Witheridge |
| 19,7-10 | Exminster | 19,36 | Hemyock |
| 19,11-14 | Braunton | 19,37 | Witheridge |
| 19,15-18 | Shirwell | 19,38 | Wonford |
| 19,19 | South Molton | 19,39-40 | Witheridge |
| 19,20 | Cliston | 19,41 | ?Teignton |
| 19,21-24 | Silverton | 19,42-43 | Tiverton |
| 19,25-27 | Hemyock | 19,44-45 | Axminster |
| 19,28-30 | Wonford | 19,46 | Colyton |
| 19,31 | Silverton | 19,1 | Borough of Exeter |
| 19,32 | Hemyock |  |  |

19,2    VIRWORTHY. DB *Fereurde*. It is Virworthy in Pancrasweek parish, (Black) Torrington
Hundred (11), like 24,32 (see note). William's three holdings in this Hundred (19,2-4)
seem to be represented in Fees p. 792 by *Alfardesworth'* [Alfardisworthy in Bradworthy,
GR SS 2911, close to Virworthy], *Sessecoth'* [Sessacott SS 3516 in West Putford, 19,4],
*Scotteworth'* ['Scotworthy' in West Putford, 19,4, represented by John *de Scotteworth'*
in LSR (1332) p. 70] and *Hethestapele* [Instaple 19,3], all held by Robert *Tyrel* from
the Honour of Bradninch; see FA i pp. 356, 409 and OJR H5 p. 235.

19,3    INSTAPLE. In Bradworthy parish, (Black) Torrington Hundred (11); see 19,2 note. The
T.O. records it as added to Bradworthy, 34,6 (see Exon. Notes here), but neither
Exchequer nor the main Exon. DB mentions this in either place.

19,4    (WEST) PUTFORD. In the MS and Farley *POTEFORDE*; in the facsimile the first *E*
resembles an *S* because of the rubrication; see 1,63 note. It is a parish in (Black)
Torrington Hundred (11), probably represented by Sessacott and 'Scotworthy' in Fees;
see 19,2 note. William's brother Ralph holds another part, 34,7.
TWO THANES HELD. In the MS there is an erasure of about 5 letters between *taini*

|   |   |
|---|---|
|  | and *teneb'*; Farley does not print the gap caused, the *teneb'* being printed next to the *taini* with the result that there is a sizeable gap left after *teneb'*, which is not there at all in the MS. See 1,60 note on Farley's varied treatment of MS erasures. |
| 19,5-6 | ALWARD. Probably Alward son of Toki; see last note under Exon. Notes 19,35. |
| 19,5 | HUNTSHAW. Now a parish in Fremington Hundred (5): this entry must account for part of William's lordship total in the Tax Return for Fremington Hundred (iv); see 19,6 note. In a series of Inq. PM of the *Welyngton* family (Cal. Inq. PM vol. viii no. 177, ix nos. 103, 218, xv nos. 154, 866, 875), Huntshaw is held of the Honour of Bradninch, or of the Duchy of Cornwall (which included Bradninch Honour); in the feudal lists, however, it appears to be held of the Honour of Okehampton (see 16,42 note), and to lie either in Shebbear or in Fremington Hundred. In Fees p. 785, in a Shebbear Hundred group, *Hunshaue* is held by William *le Cornu* of the Honour of Okehampton; Roger *Cornu* holds in FA i p. 412 in Shebbear Hundred; John *de Wylyngton* holds in FA i p. 358 (in Shebbear) and in FA i p. 375 (in Fremington); see Cal. Inq. PM vol. iv (o.s.) no. 63 (= TDA 38 p. 330) and OJR H8 p. 515. |
| 19,6 | EASTLEIGH. In Westleigh parish, Fremington Hundred (5): William's ½ virgate lordship here combines with his 1 virgate in Huntshaw (19,5) to form most of the ½ hide of lordship land recorded for him in the Tax Return for Fremington Hundred (iv); see also last note under 19,6. In Fees p. 792 Geoffrey *de Legh'* holds in *Estlegh'* of the Honour of Bradninch; see FA i pp. 371, 412, Cal. Inq. PM vol. xvi no. 106 and OJR H8 p. 516. TAX FOR ½ HIDE. After the *p* in the MS a *.i.* is erased and its final dot made into a comma-type omission mark immediately below the interlined *dimid'*, both of which are in paler ink. Farley does not show the omission mark nor the gap caused by the erasure (see 1,60 note). ½ VIRGATE .... CONCEALED. The existence of the ½ virgate was not revealed to the authorities. Cf. the previously concealed virgate in Bulkworthy which is only recorded in the T.O. (see Exon. Notes 15,14). See also DB Dorset 27,10 and in the Exon. Notes 55,16 there where tax has been concealed on land with the result that the King had no tax from it; also Bucks. 18,3. KING HAS NO TAX. The Tax Return for Fremington Hundred (iv) states that the King had (*habuit*) no tax from ½ virgate that Ansketel holds from William Cheever. The main Exon. entry and the T.O. entry also have *habuit* in full in this phrase, so it is quite possible that *hab̃* here abbreviates the past *habuit* rather than the present *habet* and that the scribe only wrote *hab̃* (which usually = *habet*) because of lack of space on the line. Moreover, once the ½ virgate had been 'discovered' by the DB Commissioners, the reason for the King's not having the tax (implied by the *ita quod* construction) would disappear. |
| 19,7 | SHILLINGFORD. A parish in Exminster Hundred (24); this and the following two entries probably account for the lordship of 1 hide, 3 virgates and 1 furlong (*fertinum*) allowed William in the Tax Return for Exminster (xxiii). The estate was later known as North Shillingford or Shillingford Abbot, being held by the Abbey of Torre, granted to it by William *Briwere* and purchased by him from William *de Tracey*, William Cheever's successor; see Oliver *Mon.* pp. 169, 173, TE p. 153a, VE ii p. 361, Cal. Inq. PM vol. vi no. 710, x no. 390, EPNS ii p. 503, OJR in TDA 47 p. 229 and 49,1 note. |
| 19,8 | EXMINSTER. A parish in Exminster Hundred (24); see 19,7 note. The holding was actually at *Tuz Seinzton'* [Higher and Lower Towsington GR SX 9387], held of Bradninch Honour in Fees p. 792 by Lucas *de Tuz Seinz* and Lucas *de Barevil'*; see Cal. Inq. PM vol. vi no. 506 and FA i pp. 346, 389. |
| 19,9 | MATFORD. In Exminster parish and Hundred (24); see 19,7 note. It is *Matteford'* held of the Honour of Bradninch in Fees p. 793; see FA i pp. 346, 389 and OJR in TDA 47 p. 230. |
| 19,10 | HACCOMBE. Now the parish of Haccombe with Combeinteignhead in a detached portion of Wonford Hundred (19). The order of Exon. strongly points to a place lying in Exminster Hundred (24) like the preceding entries. The next hundred group is then begun (19,11) with William's lordship manor of Woolacombe. The land probably lay at *Nithereton'* [Netherton GR SX 8971], held by John *le Barun* (on whom see 19,41 note) and Walter *le Tut* from the Honour of Bradninch in Fees p. 792. It is *Nitherton* and *Nytherecote* [an unidentified 'Nethercote'] in Exminster Hundred in FA i p. 346; see FA i p. 388 and OJR in TDA 47 p. 231. Netherton is now in Haccombe parish in the same detachment of Wonford Hundred. 1 SALT-HOUSE; 1 FISHERY. No doubt on the estuary of the river Teign. |
| 19,11 | WOOLACOMBE. In Mortehoe parish, Braunton Hundred (1), although Woolacombe |

| | |
|---|---|
| 19,11 (cont'd.) | itself was a tithing of Shirwell Hundred (2) in the Middle Ages. In Fees p. 792 Oliver *de Tracy* holds in *Wollecumb'* from the Honour of Bradninch; see FA i pp. 336, 416 and OJR H8 p. 486. |
| | VALUE .... £13.... In the MS the *xiii lib'* was originally *iii lib'*. It is interesting that in Exon. the scribe seems to have written *xiii*, then erased the *x*, only to add another *x* in front of it close up against the *ann̄* (the result being *ualet p̄ ann̄x iii lib'*): the Exchequer scribe no doubt only saw the *iii* at first glance because of the gap before it and the unusual closeness of the *x* to *p̄ ann̄*. |
| 19,12-13 | (NORTH) BUCKLAND. BUCKLAND. The first lies in Georgeham parish, the second in Braunton, both in Braunton Hundred (1). They are close together and may originally have been parts of the same 'Bookland'. The larger (19,12), 1 hide, is the ¼ fee (formerly a ½ fee) held by the heirs of Ralph *de Bray* in *Bockland'* from the Honour of Bradninch in Fees p. 792; this is *Bokelond Deneham* in FA i p. 415; see FA i p. 360, Cal. Inq. PM vol. iii no. 604 and EPNS i p. 43. The smaller (19,13), 1 virgate, is presumably the 1 fee (¼ fee in FA) of Fees p. 792 held by Geoffrey *Challo* in *Incledone* [Incledon in Braunton, SS 4738; see 3,43 note] and in *Bocland'*, later 'Little' Buckland in Braunton; see Cal. Inq. PM vol. iii no. 604, vi no. 506, xiv no. 325, FA i pp. 359, 464, EPNS i p. 32 and OJR H8 pp. 446-447. |
| 19,14 | ASH. Apparently in Braunton parish and Hundred (1), later *Asshroges* or *Asshe Rogus* (EPNS i p. 32). In Fees p. 792 Baldwin *le Flemeng* holds in *Esse, Hakeston'* [Haxton 2,9] and *Duntingthon'* [Benton 2,10] of the Honour of Bradninch; see FA i pp. 437, 439 and OJR H8 pp. 447-448. |
| | ALWARD. Probably Alward son of Toki; see last note under Exon. Notes 19,35. |
| 19,15 | COUNTISBURY. A parish in Shirwell Hundred (2). It was granted with Lynton (19,16) *c*. 1200 to the Abbot of Ford by Henry *de Tracy*; see VE ii p. 299, Oliver *Mon*. p. 347 and OJR H8 pp. 486-487. *Cunteshyr'* is held by the Abbot in RH i pp. 79a, 94b. |
| 19,16 | LYNTON AND ILKERTON. Ilkerton is *Crintone* in DB, *Incrintona* in Exon.; the latter is the more correct form, which in its turn may represent a Norman French modification of a form **Ilcrintona*. The Exchequer scribe obviously thought that the Exon. scribe had mistakenly made one word out of two (*in crintona*) and so omitted the *in* as it was not needed in this phrase. Lynton is a parish in Shirwell Hundred (2) and Ilkerton lies within it. Lynton itself was given with Countisbury (19,15, see note) to Ford Abbey, but other portions of the DB holding are accounted for in the fee lists: in Fees p. 792 three men (one of them Mauger *de Speranger*, named from North and South Sparhanger GR SS 7146, and another *Marioth' de Radespree*, named from Radsbury SS 7145) hold *Hilcrinton'* [Ilkerton] from the Honour of Bradninch. It is East and West Ilkerton in FA i p. 417. Other subdivisions are *Welanger* [Woolhanger SS 6945] and *Furshille* [Furzehill SS 7244]. In FA i p. 337 *Welhanger* is coupled with *Thorneworth'* [Thornworthy SS 7145] and in FA i p. 417 *Forshull* is coupled with *Stock* [South Stock SS 7145 and Stock Castle SS 7146]; see FA i p. 361, OJR H8 p. 487 and 20,2 note. |
| | ALWARD SON OF TOKI. The forms of this byname are *Tochisone* in DB 19,35, and in Exon. *tocheson(e?)* here and for 19,19;39, *toquisone* for 19,35 and *tochesona* for 34,14 and in the T.O. *filius Tochi* for 19,35. See OEB p. 164 s.n. *Tokes sune* and p. 200 s.n. *filius Tochi*. Alward is *Ailuuard(us)* in the Exon. for this entry and for 19,19; the name probably represents *Aethelweard* (see 3,45 note and cf. 1,41 note). Many, if not all, of the references to plain 'Alward' in Chs. 19 and 34 are probably to the son of Toki; see last note under Exon. Notes 19,35 and Ch. 19 note. |
| 19,17 | LYN. In Lynton parish, Shirwell Hundred (2). In Fees p. 791 *Lyn* is held of the Honour of Bradninch; it is *Estlyn* and *Westlyn*, coupled with *Sperhangre* [Sparhanger, see 19,16 note], in FA i p. 417; see FA i p. 361, RH i p. 79a and OJR H8 p. 488. |
| 19,18 | 'BADGWORTHY'. In Brendon parish, Shirwell Hundred (2). The change of name — DB *Bicheordin, Bygworthy* (1379), *Baggeworth* (12th century) — makes the identification less than secure; see EPNS i p. 59. In Fees p. 792 Hamelin *de Deudone* holds in *Bykeworth'* and *La Fenne* [unidentified] from the Honour of Bradninch; see Fees p. 396, HD p. 57, Cal. Inq. PM vol. ii no. 306, v no. 527, vii no. 297, FA i pp. 337, 361, 417, OJR H8 p. 489 and 19,19 note. The last settlement here, Badgworthy Cottage, is now abandoned; see 34,14 note on 'Lank Combe'. |
| | IT WAS WASTE. Exon. *erat uastata*; see second note under C 3 and cf. notes to 3,35. 20,2. 21,5 and 36,17. 'Badgworthy' is on the edge of Exmoor, so there is no implication that it had been 'laid waste'. |

# 19

19,19     RADWORTHY. North and South Radworthy in North Molton parish, now South Molton Hundred (6); to be distinguished from 'Radworthy' in Challacombe (21,1 note). In Fees p. 792 *Radeworth'* is held from the Honour of Bradninch by Roger *de Rem*; Maurice *de Rotomago* holds in Fees p. 396 from William *Briwere*; in the same list of Fees *Radewurh* is connected with *Bykewurth* and *La Fenne* (see 19,18 note). This Radworthy does not appear in subsequent feudal lists, but the Fees p. 792 entry cannot be 'Radworthy' in Challacombe in Shirwell Hundred (despite EPNS i p. 60), since it is an isolated entry there between places in Haytor and Exminster Hundred, Shirwell places having been entered earlier; see Cal. Inq. PM vol. iii no. 604 (*Suthradeworth*), v no. 527 and OJR H9 p. 525.

19,20     WHIMPLE. A parish in Cliston Hundred (20). The Honour of Bradninch holding was at *Cobbewimple* in Fees p. 792, now Cobden in Whimple (EPNS ii p. 579), *Cobbeton* in FA i p. 332; see FA i pp. 367, 433 and OJR H7 p. 379.

19,21-43     THE BASIC SEQUENCE is of places in Silverton Hundred (19,21-24), Hemyock (19,25-27), Wonford (19,28-30), Budleigh (19,33-34), Witheridge (19,35;37;39-40), Teignton (19,41), Tiverton (19,42-43), which agrees well enough with the normal sequence within a fief (see the Appendix). It is complicated, however, by a number of late entries for Hundreds previously entered: 19,31-32;36;38.

19,21     PIRZWELL. In Kentisbeare parish, Hayridge Hundred (15). In Fees p. 792 Thomas *de Orweye* holds in *Pisewill'* of the Honour of Bradninch, and in FA i p. 321 he holds in *Orweye* [Orway, see 38,1-2 note] and *Piseweyll*; see FA i p. 424 and OJR in TDA 42 p. 240.

19,22     HEWISE. The holding, apparently in Hayridge Hundred (15) from the order of the Exon. Book, has not been identified. It can scarcely be Orway's Hayes (OJR in TDA 36 p. 361, 42 p. 240) or Hays Park (DG), since *Hewise* 'Huish' (from OE *hiwisc* 'household, hide') will not yield 'Hayes' (which is from OE *gehaeg* or *hege*, meaning 'enclosure'). Orway and Pirzwell are both held later of the Honour of Bradninch (19,21 note); if Orway is not part of Pirzwell, it might be that Orway at a later stage came to stand for *Hewise*, but firm evidence is lacking.
ON THE LACK OF POPULATION see 17,84 note. It is possible that this manor was worked by some of the villagers in the nearby holding at Orway (38,2).

19,23     COLEBROOK. In Cullompton parish, Hayridge Hundred (15). It was given to Ford Abbey by Henry *de Tracy*; see Oliver *Mon*. p. 347, OJR in TDA 42 p. 241 and Ch. 5 note.

19,24-25     ALWARD. Probably Alward son of Toki; see last note under Exon. Notes 19,35. For 19,25 the DB form is *Ailuuard* and the Exon. is *Ailuard(us)* for OE *Aethelweard*; see notes to 3,45 and 1,41.

19,24     CADELEIGH. A parish in Hayridge Hundred (15). It is perhaps the *Parva Kidel* held by William *Briwere* in Fees p. 398, coupled with *Furesden* [Fursdon GR SS 9204 in Cadbury], called *Little Cadelegh* in Cal. Inq. PM vol. iii no. 604, but it does not otherwise appear in the fee lists; see OJR in TDA 42 p. 241 and 51,5 note.

19,25     RALPH. Probably William's brother, Ralph of Pomeroy, who holds another part of Awliscombe himself in 34,23: in Fees pp. 791-792 Roger *Giffard* holds both parts.
AWLISCOMBE. DB *Aulescome*, similarly for 19,26 and 25,14. In Hemyock Hundred (16). Other 1086 forms, to be added to EPNS ii p. 608, are *Orescome* (19,36. 34,23; 26), *Holescome* (19,43), *Holescumbe* (34,45) and *Horescome* (19,32). There were six holdings here in 1086 (19,25-26;32. 25,14. 34,23;26) and a number of lands added to Awliscombe (19,36;43. 34,45); the later position is also complex, with a number of lands called 'Awliscombe' in 1086 being represented by more particular names in the locality. The present holding appears, like 19,9 and 19,33 (also held by a Ralph in 1086), to have passed to the *Spek* and *Tremenet* families. In Fees p. 792 Roger *Giffard'* holds *Aulescumb'* from the Honour of Bradninch; in FA i p. 338 Matthew *Gyffard* holds from the heirs of Richard *Tremenet* and they from William *Spek*; a later holder is Reginald *de Ashborn*, FA i pp. 367, 430. See Fees p. 398 (*Aulescumbe Tremettes*), Cal. Inq. PM vol. v no. 527, ix no. 288 and OJR H2 p. 44.

19,26     AWLISCOMBE. A parish in Hemyock Hundred (16); see 19,25 note. This second Awliscombe, held by Hamo in 1086, together with the third Awliscombe (of 19,32), are probably accounted for by (1) *Godeford'* [Godford GR ST 1302 in Awliscombe] held in Fees p. 792 of the Honour of Bradninch by Reginald *de Albo Monasterio* as 1/8th fee, later by Richard, then by Reginald *de Clifford* (see FA i pp. 338, 367, 430 and OJR H2 p. 44); and (2) another part of Awliscombe (*Ouliscomb*) held by the Abbot of Dunkeswell of the Honour of Bradninch as ¼ fee (FA i pp. 367, 430). That Reginald

19

*de Clifford* also holds Combeinteignhead (19,28) held in 1086 by William, suggests that 19,32, the smaller DB holding, is Godford and this is borne out by the comparative size of the fees.

19,27 LEVEL WITH THE FIRST LINE of this entry in the left margin of the MS is written O, probably a checking mark similar to the Os beside other *Otris* (see 10,1 note). The O sign appears to have been written first and then the X added with a thinner, scratchier pen. Although there is no other mark exactly like this one in Devon, two other entries for *Otri* have both an O and a X sign (see notes to 19,43 and 23,18) and cf. 19,42 note. Farley prints this mark, the one at 19,42 and part of the one at 19,43, although with the exception of the O at 19,34 he has not printed these checking marks. See the end of 10,1 note for the treatment of these marks in this edition.
WESTON. DB *Otri*, now Waringstone or Weston in Awliscombe parish, Hemyock Hundred (16), named from the 1086 holder; see EPNS ii p. 609. In Fees p. 792 the heirs of Geoffrey son of William hold in *Otery*, this same appearing as *Weringeston* in FA i pp. 338, 430; see Cal. Inq. PM vol. iii no. 604, vii no. 141 and viii no. 238. A subinfeudation is *La Hokederis* or *Hokerigg* [Hookedrise in Dunkeswell, ST 1207]. On Weston see OJR H2 pp. 42, 44 and 34,24 note. Weston went to Dunkeswell Abbey; see TE p. 152a and VE ii p. 304.
VALUE 12s. Written in paler ink completely in the central margin between the two columns; the 'gallows' sign is ⌐, not as Farley prints it. In Exon. it is *x* with *ii* interlined, but otherwise a clear, neat entry.

19,28- THESE PLACES lie in Wonford Hundred (19) with a total lordship of 1½ hides, 2½
30;38 virgates and ½ furlong ('ferling') which represents William's lordship land of 1½ hides 2½ furlongs recorded in the Tax Return for Wonford Hundred (xxxi).

19,28 WILLIAM HIMSELF HOLDS. Repeated at the beginning of 19,28-32 inclusive.
COMBEINTEIGNHEAD. DB *Cumbe*. Now the parish of Haccombe with Combeinteignhead (from 'Ten Hides') in the detached part of Wonford Hundred (19) lying south of the Teign estuary. In FA i p. 316 Reginald *de Clyfford* (on whom see 19,26 note) holds in *Comb in Tynhyde* from the Earl of Cornwall; see FA i p. 387 and OJR in TDA 44 p. 341.

19,29 ROCOMBE. In Stokeinteignhead parish, in the detached part of Wonford Hundred (19). Although the holding does not appear in later fee lists, whereas *Haurig* [Horridge GR SX 7674 in that part of Ilsington parish that lay in Wonford Hundred], held of the Honour of Bradninch in Fees p. 792 (see FA i pp. 316, 346, 387), does so and lacks a DB counterpart, there is no other reason to connect the two; see OJR in TDA 36 p. 376 and in 44 p. 341.

19,30 TEDBURN (ST. MARY). A parish in Wonford Hundred (19). It is *Tetteburne* held by Ralph *de Alba Mara* of the Honour of Bradninch in Fees p. 792, particularised as *Fairewode* [Great Fairwood GR SX 8194] held by John *Daumarle* of the same Honour in FA i p. 316; see FA i pp. 346, 388 and OJR in TDA 44 p. 342.

19,31 BRADNINCH. A parish in Hayridge Hundred (15), *caput* of the later Barony; see Fees p. 1368, FA i p. 321, Cal. Inq. PM vol. iii no. 604, EPNS ii p. 555 and OJR in TDA 42 p. 242.

19,32 AWLISCOMBE. DB *Horescome*; see 19,25 note. This place is probably another part of Awliscombe, a parish in Hemyock Hundred (16), since Wonford, Hayridge and Hemyock Hundred entries are mingled at this point in the schedule (see 19,21-43 note). It will probably have been at Godford (19,26 note). OJR in TDA 36 p. 361 and in TDA 42 p. 225 identifies Owlacombe in Bradninch, but see EPNS ii p. 562 (Cullompton parish).

19,33 RALPH .... RALPH. Perhaps two different people; see Exon. Notes here.
YOWLESTONE. DB *Ædelstan*, Exon. *Aeldestan* (see Exon. Notes). It is now in Puddington parish, Witheridge Hundred (7), but was a part of (West) Budleigh Hundred (14) in the Middle Ages. In Fees p. 793 Henry *de Yaldestane*, who also has Coombe (19,39 note) similarly held by Ralph in 1086, is tenant of *Yaldestane* from the Honour of Bradninch; see Fees p. 763 and FA i pp. 362, 365, 419, 427. OJR confuses the place with 'Yardlestone' in Tiverton; the latter is in fact Yearldstone and has a different derivation (EPNS ii p. 546); see OJR in TDA 35 p. 292.
HALF OF THIS LAND FROM WILLIAM. The *de W*. is written into the right margin, perhaps a little later, though the colour of the ink is the same as for the rest of the entry. It may have been added in an attempt to clarify the confused details of this entry; see Exon. Notes.

19,34 RAPSHAYS. DB *Otri*. In Gittisham parish, (East) Budleigh Hundred (14). Although the

| | |
|---|---|
| 19,34 (cont'd.) | order of the Exon. Book is not clear at this point, it is probable that this place lay in Budleigh Hundred and is the *Rappinghegh'* held by the Abbot of Dunkeswell in Fees p. 793 from the Honour of Bradninch; see Fees p. 762, FA i p. 426, VE ii p. 304, EPNS ii p. 589, OJR in TDA 35 p. 311 and notes to 25,15 and 34,32.<br>BRICTRIC HELD IT IN 1066. In the Exon. MS part of this phrase occurs on the inner edges which were damaged by water or damp (see Exon. Notes 19,28-46). It is just possible that if this damage were done at a very early stage, this might be the reason for the omission of this detail in DB (cf. 19,37 note). However, there is no other real indication that the Exchequer scribe had difficulty in reading material on these folios which is now illegible due to this damage. Moreover, he omitted from the Exon. details of several other 1066 tenants for some reason, see Exon. Notes 2,7 and cf. Exon. Notes 3,94. 15,33 and 40,6.<br>WOODLAND, 1 ACRE. In the MS the woodland is unusually abbreviated *sit* because it was written over an erasure, apparently of *p̃ti* 'meadow'; in the facsimile the *i* of *sit* resembles a capital *E* because of the erased *t* of *p̃ti*. |
| 19,35 | (CRUWYS) MORCHARD. A parish in Witheridge Hundred (7). It is *Morceth'* held in Fees p. 793 from the heirs of Alexander *de Crues* from Bradninch Honour; see Fees p. 758, FA i pp. 342, 419, RH i pp. 87b, 92a and OJR in TDA 30 p. 418. It is possible that *Northecote* [Northcote GR SS 8613 in Cruwys Morchard; see 3,73 note], FA i p. 342, was part of this holding.<br>ALWARD SON OF TOKI. He was probably William's immediate predecessor (as also in several other manors; see last note under Exon. Notes 19,35), as both the main Exon. and T.O. entries state (see Exon. Notes here), rather than the victim of Aelmer's rapacity. The *Aluuardo* here would thus be a scribal error for *Aluuardus*. It is possible, however, that the Exchequer scribe was correcting the Exon., having received new information. The final phrase in the entry, that William holds this with Alward's land, would support the view that Aelmer had held the manor immediately before William, because only then would it have meaning: William was not automatically given Cruwys Morchard with Alward's other lands, but he added it to them because it had once been held by Alward. Cf. the phrases after 15,31 and before 15,47 referring to manors held in 1066 by people other than Edmer Ator and Ordwulf, but added to these men's lands by the Count of Mortain (see 15,31 note). However, Exon. and the T.O. also have the phrase 'William holds it with the Honour of Alward', which would not be necessary if, as they both state, Alward took the manor from Aelmer (unless, of course, Aelmer had claimed the land and this phrase was stating William's counter-claim to it).<br>See 19,16 note on the form of Alward's name.<br>A SMITH. See 6,13 note. |
| 19,36 | MACKHAM. This place is left unidentified by DG and assimilated to Woodscombe in Cruwys Morchard by OJR (in TDA 30 p. 428 and in VCH p. 505 note 9) on the grounds of sequence (it lies between two Witheridge Hundred places). But it will be noted that entries for a number of Hundreds are here intermixed (see 19,21-43 note). The fact that this land has been added to *Orescome* [Awliscombe, see 19,25 note] strongly suggests a place in Hemyock Hundred (16); Hamo will presumably have added it to his particular holding at Awliscombe (19,26). It further suggests that the land rightly belonged to another manor or another holder. *Madescame* does not descend to the Honour of Bradninch, but in Cal. Inq. PM vol. ii no. 590 (of Richard *de Hydon*), following an entry for *Hem[yo]c* [Hemyock 1,8] held by Richard, is one for *Meddesamele alias Madddescamele* and *Maddeford*. These places are Mackham and Madford [the latter at ST 1411] in Hemyock parish; see EPNS ii pp. 616, 618. They are not adjacent to Awliscombe, but it is possible that Hamo, having seized them, claimed them as a detached part of Awliscombe, his only manor in this Hundred. The later descent of Mackham suggests that the alienation was temporary; see 1,8 note.<br>1 VILLAGER .... LORDSHIP. It is very unusual for a villager − not the tenant − to hold land in lordship. See Exon. Notes 3,91 for other examples of odd tenure of lordship land. |
| 19,37 | OAKFORD .... MILDON. Oakford is a parish, Mildon lying within it, in Witheridge Hundred (7). In Fees p. 761 Herbert son of Matthew holds *Hakeford'* from Reginald *de Mohun'* and in Fees p. 792 Roger *de Middeldon'* holds *Middeldone*, both from the Honour of Bradninch; see Fees p. 759, Cal. Inq. PM vol. v nos. 213, 527, FA i pp. 344, 421 and OJR in TDA 30 p. 419. The DB form *Alforde* (Exon. *Alforda*) is an error for *Acforde*, see EPNS ii p. 387. |

| | |
|---|---|
| 19,37 (cont'd.) | IT PAID TAX FOR 1 HIDE. Interlined in paler ink, probably later. Although in Exon. part of the tax statement has been damaged by damp (see Exon. Notes 19,28-46), it is very unlikely that the MS was hard to read when the Exchequer scribe used it (and for this reason the omitted tax was not discovered until later), because he had apparently no difficulties with deciphering other information which is now illegible; cf. 19,34 note. |
| 19,38 | WHIPTON. In Heavitree parish, Wonford Hundred (19), apparently a late entry, out of order. William *de Tracy*, a successor to William Cheever, granted the bulk of the manor to Polsloe Priory; a portion not given to the Priory was at *Ryngeswille* [Ringwell in Heavitree, GR SX 955924], held of the Honour of Bradninch in FA i p. 316, see FA i pp. 346, 387 and OJR in TDA 44 p. 342. |
| 19,39 | PUDDINGTON. A parish in Witheridge Hundred (7). In Fees p. 793 Ralph *de Sicca [Villa]* holds from the Honour of Bradninch in *Putiton*; see Fees p. 758, Cal. Inq. PM vol. ii no. 6, v no. 148 and FA i pp. 342, 419. A portion of this holding may have been at *Cumb* [Coombe in Puddington, GR SS 8411] held with *Petinton* in FA i p. 342, probably the *Comb'* connected with *Olleston* or *Oldeston* [Yowlestone 19,33] in FA i pp. 362, 419. The Templars, then the Hospitalers, are said to hold a *Come* from the Honour of Bradninch in FA i p. 421, but this may be Coombe in Templeton (3,75;78 note). |
| 19,40 | BEATRIX, WILLIAM'S SISTER. She also holds from William in 19,46 and probably from her other brother Ralph (of Pomeroy) in 34,43 (all three manors were held by an Aelmer in 1066). Ralph of Pomeroy also has his sister Beatrix as subtenant in DB Somerset 30,1. BRADFORD. In Witheridge parish and Hundred (7); the particular manor was Bradford Tracy [GR SS 8116] which William *de Tracy* holds as *Bradeford'* in Fees p. 792; see Fees p. 759, FA i p. 342 and OJR in TDA 30 p. 419. TOREDONE. The identification of this place, added to Bradford, with Thorne in Rackenford, GR SS 8417 (*Thorne* in LSR (1332) p. 30), or Downe in Witheridge, SS 8316, is not established. AELFRIC COLLING. Exon. *Aluric(us) colim*, T.O. *Aluric(us) Colin*; see OEB pp. 141-142. |
| 19,41 | BUCKLAND. Buckland Barton in Haccombe with Combeinteignhead parish, now in the outlying part of Wonford Hundred (19), but in 1086 it may well have lain, like part of Haccombe (16,152 note) in Teignton (Teignbridge) Hundred (23), being similarly a detached part of Haytor (29) later in the Middle Ages. In Fees p. 792 John *le Barun* holds in *Bocland'* from the Honour of Bradninch; see Fees p. 768, FA i pp. 317, 349, 392 (all in Haytor Hundred) and OJR in TDA 40 p. 123. Robert's holding of Netherton (19,10 note) will have been adjacent, but apparently in a different Hundred. |
| 19,42 | LEVEL WITH THE FIRST LINE of this entry in the left margin of the MS is written a ♂ sign, unlike any other in Devon; it is not as Farley prints it which would make it identical to the signs beside 19,27 (see note), although both manors were held in 1086 by Warin. From a study of the MS it would appear that this mark was done in two stages, the *o* first and the ⚔ added in a thinner pen, which suggests that the *o* part is the same checking mark as those done against other *Otri*s (see 10,1 note); the other part, however, does not resemble the crosses of 19,27;43 and 23,18. IVEDON. DB *Otri*. In the Tax Return for Tiverton Hundred (xi) Warin and Rozelin are said to have failed to pay tax on 1 hide 3½ virgates they hold from Ralph of Pomeroy. Rozelin is Ralph's tenant in 34,47, but Warin is a tenant not of Ralph but of Ralph's brother, William Cheever, in several Ch. 19 holdings. They do not hold jointly, but both hold a place or places called *Otri*. Although the lordship size of the holdings is not given in Exon., the Tax Return clearly points to land in Chs. 19 and 34 lying in Tiverton Hundred. It must have been at Ivedon, which lies on the river Otter and in Awliscombe parish, but was a detached part of Tiverton Hundred (9) in the Middle Ages. The present holding is probably the ¾ fee at *Yvedon'* held by Robert *de Stanton'*, Richard *de Bembyr* [i.e. *Membyr*, see 19,44 note] and William *de Tracy* of the Honour of Bradninch in Fees p. 792; see FA i pp. 369, 432 and OJR in TDA 36 p. 358 and H1 p. 28. This is the expected place in Exon. order for a Tiverton Hundred place (see the Appendix). AND 1 SLAVE. In the MS *cū i seruo* was originally written, then with a thinner pen an *7* was squashed in, half-covering the *c* of *cū*, obviously intended to replace it, as a *cū* had already been written before the villager. Farley misprints *7 cū i seruo*. Cf. 3,27 note. |
| 19,43 | LEVEL WITH THE LAST LINE of 19,42 in the central margin of the MS is written an *o* sign, printed by Farley. It seems likely that this sign, together with the ✕ written with |

| | |
|---|---|
| 19,43 (cont'd.) | a thinner pen at an angle 2½ lines below and not printed by Farley, refers to the *Otri* of 19,43 and that they are placed like this, rather than level with the first line (as apparently for 19,27 and 23,18), because of the presence in the central margin of the added value of 19,27 in the opposite column (which of course means they were written after the correction to the text). See notes to 10,1. 19,27 and 23,18. |
| | RALPH SON OF PAYNE. Exon. *Radulf(us) pagani filius*; see 16,155 note. He only holds half of Ivedon from William, the rest presumably being held by William himself; see Exon. Notes here and to 34,27 and cf. Exon. Notes to 19,33 and 23,22. |
| | IVEDON. DB *Otri*. Following as it does the *Otri* of 19,42 this might be expected to be a portion of the same place, a detached part of Tiverton Hundred. Saemer also held an *Otri* TRE, similarly added to Awliscombe, but held by Ralph of Pomeroy in 1086 (34,45; see note). The ½ villager (see note below) makes it certain that 19,43 and 34,45 were parts of the same place; see OJR in TDA 36 pp. 358-359. |
| | ½ VILLAGER. *Dimidius uillanus*. See 34,45, Ivedon, for the other 'half' of this villager. In other words, in the part of Ivedon held TRE by Saemer and added to Awliscombe, the services of one villager were divided between William Cheever and his brother, Ralph of Pomeroy. Thirty-eight half-villagers (*villani dimidii*) occur in DB Glos. (see W 1 note there) and in DB Shrops. 2,2, in which latter they are contrasted with 'whole' (*integri*) villagers. It is more likely, however, that these last-mentioned half-villagers were men who held half the normal holding of the average villager in the area, rather than that two lords shared their services. |
| | HAS IT THERE. The *hanc* refers to the ½ plough, as Exon. states. See 1,29 note. |
| | ADDED TO AWLISCOMBE. Presumably the addition was to Awliscombe (19,25) also held by a Ralph. The entry in the T.O. (502 b 7) reverses the process adding *Holescoma* to *Otria*. This may be an error although a similar reversal occurs in the T.O. for 34,45 and for 39,16 (see Exon. Notes to these). |
| 19,44 | MEMBURY. A parish in Axminster Hundred (17) and required by its Tax Return (xix). When Robert *de Chandos* founded Goldcliff Priory in Monmouthshire (in 1113, see Mon. Ang. vi p. 1021, *Regesta* iii p. 143 no. 373), his wife Isabella gave West Membury to St. Mary of Bec-Héllouin, the mother house of Goldcliff. *Membyry* is held by the prior of Goldcliff in FA i p. 384; see TE p. 152a and Fees p. 97. The other part of Membury, East Membury, was held by Roger *de Rem* and Richard *de Membyr*' as *Est Membyr*' of the Honour of Bradninch in Fees p. 792; see FA i pp. 320, 366, 429 and OJR H4 p. 158. It went to Newenham Abbey, Oliver *Mon.* p. 357. |
| | See 1,11 for details of a customary due unpaid by Membury. |
| | ALDHILD. DB *Eldille*, Exon. *Eldillus*; see PNDB p. 241 s.n. *Ealdhild*. |
| 19,45 | AXMINSTER. Axminster parish, Axminster Hundred (17). Stephen *de Haccumb*' holds in *Axeministre* of the Honour of Bradninch in Fees p. 792; see FA i p. 429 and OJR H4 p. 159. |
| 19,46 | SOUTHLEIGH. A parish in Colyton Hundred (22). John *de Legh*' holds in *Suthlegh*' in Fees p. 792; see FA i pp. 330, 428, Cal. Inq. PM vol. xv no. 967, xvi no. 673 and OJR H7 p. 357. According to the Tax Return for Colyton Hundred (xx) the King had no tax from 1 hide held there by Beatrix, sister of William Cheever; probably the villagers' hide of Southleigh, as her only other holdings in Devon, 19,40 and 34,43, are in the Hundreds of Witheridge (7) and Tiverton (9) respectively. |
| Ch. 20 | WILLIAM OF FALAISE. He was married to the daughter of Serlo of Burcy (DB Som. 27,3). William's daughter Emma married William *de Curcy*. Falaise (DB *de Faleise*, Exon. *de Falesia, de faleisa*) is in the département of Calvados, France. |
| | William's lands later form the Honour of Dartington, which was joined to the Honour of Blagdon (Somerset) formed around the fief of his father-in-law, Serlo of Burcy. Many lands are held in the 12th and 13th centuries by the Martin family, see VCH p. 565, Sanders p. 15. A part of the DB fief is found in Cal. Inq. PM vol. vi no. 710 (of William son of Martyn) and in Cal. Inq. ad Quod Damnum no. 193 (no. 4) = Cal. Inq. PM (o.s.) vol. ii I Edward III no. 40 p. 10 (of Nicholas *Martyn*). |
| | THE EXON. ORDER OF THIS CHAPTER is followed by Exchequer DB. The lands fall into Hundred groups as follows: |

| | | | |
|---|---|---|---|
| | 20,1-4 Braunton and Shirwell | 20,10 | Kerswell |
| | 20,5-9 Witheridge | 20,11-17 | Diptford |

| | |
|---|---|
| 20,1-4 | THESE PLACES lay in Braunton or Shirwell Hundreds (1-2), and 20,1;3-4 with a total lordship of 1 hide 1 virgate are no doubt accounted for by the same amount in the Tax Return for Braunton and Shirwell Hundred (vi) allowed to William of Falaise. It is |

20

possible that Twitchen, also held by Brictwold before 1066, subsequently added to Arlington, should rightly be in this group of William's lands; see 38,1 note.

20,1 COMBE (MARTIN). A parish in Braunton Hundred (1). It is held as *Comb' Martin* by Nicholas son of Martin in RH i pp. 66a, 95a and from the Honour of Blagdon in FA i p. 415. See Cal. Inq. PM vol. vi no. 710, viii nos. 396-397 and OJR H8 pp. 399, 440.

20,2 FURZE. DB *Ferse* from OE *fyrs* 'furze'. This holding seems to have left no trace in the fee lists, but is identified with Furze in West Buckland, Braunton Hundred (1), by OJR H8 p. 398 and by EPNS i p. 35. Foss *alias* Fairlinch (VCH p. 489 note 6) is phonologically unlikely and Furzehill in Lynton (DG) is held of Bradninch Honour and so is probably part of William Cheever's Lynton (19,16, see note).
IT IS WASTE. Despite the use of the past participle and verb (*est uastata; Exon. est penitus uastata*), the meaning is that Furze, as its name suggests, was wasteland. See second note under C 3 and cf. notes to 3,35. 19,18. 21,5 and 36,17.

20,3 PARRACOMBE. A parish in Shirwell Hundred (2), held as *Parrecumb* by William son of Martin in FA i p. 335; see Cal. Inq. PM vol. iii no. 174.
NOW 40s. In the MS *xl solid*'; Farley misprints a capital *L* in *xl*.

20,4 CHURCHILL. In East Down parish, Braunton Hundred (1). It is held as *Churchehille* among Dartington Honour fees in Fees p. 782; see FA i p. 414 and 3,24-25 note.
HELD IT. In the MS *ten̄* corrected to *teneƀ*, but without the ⁊ sign being removed; see 16,151 note.

20,5 'BEARE' from OE *bearu* 'grove, wood'. If this place lay in Witheridge Hundred (7) like those following, there is a Beara in Kings Nympton [GR SS 6919] and one in Romansleigh [SS 7219]. OJR in VCH p. 489 note 9 identifies it as Bar *alias* Beare in East Worlington. But Middle, East and West Bar of the first edition OS one-inch map (sheet 26 of 1809, reprint sheet 82 of 1969) appear as Burrow on recent maps and are not derived from OE *bearu*; see EPNS ii p. 402. Nor is it Mouseberry, which is not Mouse *bearu*, but Mouse *burh*. This place is most likely a lost 'Beare' in Worlington (20,7 note), with which it merged soon after 1086. In the Inq. PM of Nicholas *Martyn* (cited in Ch. 20 note above) it appears as the manor of *Beare* and *Wolrington* held from Dartington Honour; see OJR in TDA 30 p. 419, 34 p. 295.

20,6 WASHFORD (PYNE). A parish in Witheridge Hundred (7); this holding does not appear in the fee lists.
IT PAID TAX. In the MS *geldb*' at the end of the line; in the facsimile for no apparent reason the curve of the *b* is not reproduced.

20,7 HUGH OF DOL. Exon. *Hugo de dol*. Dol (or Dol-de-Bretagne) is in the département of Ille-et-Vilaine, France; OEB p. 86.
WORLINGTON. Now a single parish in Witheridge Hundred (7), formerly East and West Worlington; see 3,81 note. For the Dartington Honour holding, see 20,5 note.
2 VILLAGERS HAVE IT THERE. The *hanc* refers to the plough, as Exon. states. See 1,29 note.

20,8-9 BRADFORD. DENSHAM. To be identified respectively with Bradford in Witheridge parish and Hundred (EPNS ii p. 398), rather than with an unidentified 'Bradford in Cruwys Morchard' (VCH p. 490 note 2), and with Densham in Woolfardisworthy parish. Both lands were granted to the Prioress of Polsloe who in Fees pp. 760-761 holds *Bradeford*' and *Munecheneland*' in alms. The latter is derived from OE *mynecena-land* 'nuns' estate' and is now Minchingdown from OE *mynecena-tūn* 'nuns' farm' [GR SS 8210 in Woolfardisworthy] adjacent to Densham, which it probably represents; see EPNS ii p. 400 and TE p. 152b.

20,8 1 VILLAGER HAS IT THERE. The *hanc* probably refers to the plough; see 1,29 note. Exon. here is ambiguous; see Exon. Notes.

20,10 COCKINGTON. A parish in Haytor Hundred (29); it can be identified in the Tax Return for Kerswell (Haytor) Hundred (xxv). As *Cokinthon*' it is held from Nicholas son of Martin of the Honour of Dartington in Fees p. 768; see Fees p. 781, FA i pp. 317, 348, 392 and notes to 20,15 and 51,12.
OF THIS LAND ALRIC HELD. *ten̄* in DB and Exon. must abbreviate *tenebat* rather than the present *tenet*, because in Exon. Alric is described as *idem* (that is, the same man as the TRE holder of the main manor), and William holds it with Cockington.
'DEWDON'. An outlying part of Cockington lying in Widecombe in the Moor parish, which is itself isolated from the bulk of Haytor Hundred (see Appendix). The name survived until at least 1737 (EPNS ii p. 527) but is said to have been merged with Blackslade farm, itself now an abandoned site (see 34,46 note); see Fees p. 400, Cal. Inq. PM vol. ii no. 672 and the article by Lineham (1962).
It is probable that *Deptone* (Exon. *Depdona*) came from an original *Dewdone*

(OE *dēaw-dune* 'dewy upland') spelt with a runic 'wynn' (*p*) for the *w* and that this was misread as a minuscule *p*, the reverse of the process observed in the case of DB *Wiltone* (Exon. *Piltona*) for 3,25 (see 3,24-25 note); see also notes to 3,38 and 3,39.

20,11-17 A GROUP OF MANORS in Stanborough Hundred (28). In the Tax Return for Diptford (Stanborough) Hundred (xxvi) William of Falaise is allotted 3 hides 1 virgate of lordship land − 1 virgate less than the total lordship of these manors (see 20,17 note). A successor, William son of Martin, holds several manors in this Hundred whose exact relation to the DB holdings has yet to be determined. They lay in the adjacent parishes of Dean Prior, South Brent, Rattery and Dartington and are here mentioned under the modern parishes in which they lie; see OJR in TDA 45 pp. 172-178.

20,11 HOLNE. A parish in Stanborough Hundred (28). *Northamme* ['North' Holne] is held by Nicholas son of Martin of the Honour of Dartington in Fees p. 766; see Fees p. 265, Cal. Inq. PM vol. vi no. 710, viii nos. 396-397 and FA i p. 323. 'South' Holne was part of Harberton, then held by Buckfast Abbey (1,34 note).

20,12 STOKE. In Holne parish, Stanborough Hundred (28), EPNS i p. 302.

20,13 DEAN (PRIOR). A parish in Stanborough Hundred (28). In Fees p. 764 *Uveredene* ['Upper' Dean] and *Nitheredene* ['Lower' Dean, see EPNS i p. 298] are both held from Nicholas son of Martin of the Barony of Dartington, the latter by the Prior of Plympton whose holding named the parish; see Fees p. 781, RH i pp. 79b, 91b, FA i pp. 323, 394, TE p. 153 and VE ii p. 375.

*Walleworth'* [Wallaford in Buckfastleigh, GR SX 7265] of Fees p. 765, held from the Dartington Barony in FA i pp. 324, 395, is adjacent to this holding and may have been part of it. Another part was held by Buckfast Abbey in FA i p. 395 (see Ch. 6 note).

AS MUCH LAND AS PAYS 10s. *tantum terrae unde reddit x solidos*. The scribe obviously intended the subject of *reddit* to be the land, but he has confused two Latin constructions: *tantum ... quantum* ('as much as') and *aliquantum terrae unde reddit* ('some land from which he (the Englishman) pays'). The Exon. scribe made the same grammatical error and it would seem likely that the Exchequer scribe copied it directly. Cf. penultimate note under 17,1 and 23,22 note.

20,14 RATTERY. A parish in Stanborough Hundred (28). It is held in alms by the Abbot of *Cameis* [i.e. of St. Dogmael's in Pembrokeshire, now Dyfed], a gift of the predecessors of Nicholas son of Martin in Fees p. 766; see RH i pp. 79b, 91b.

*Morlegh* [Marley GR SX 7261] was a holding of Nicholas son of Martin in this parish, as was *Whittekesdon'* [White Oxen manor SX 7261] also held by the Abbot of St. Dogmael's in Fees p. 782; see FA i pp. 324, 395. Part of White Oxen lay in Dean Prior parish.

8 VILLAGERS AND 7 SMALLHOLDERS .... There is no dot after *bord'* and the remaining two-thirds of this line is blank in the MS, perhaps left by the scribe for some of the details of resources given in Exon., although he had already included them under the main manor (see Exon. Notes here). Cf. 3,44 note.

20,15 DARTINGTON. A further parish in Stanborough Hundred (28). It was *caput* of William son of Martin's Honour and is held in Fees p. 98 as *Dertint'* with various unnamed members, a grant said to originate from the Conquest (*de conquestu*); see Fees pp. 264, 765, RH i pp. 79b, 91b, FA i pp. 323, 350, 395 and Cal. Inq. PM vol. ii no. 440, vi no. 710, x no. 494. The Church was conferred on SS. Sergius and Bacchus at Angers; see *Regesta* ii p. 50 no. 735a.

Land at *Hode* [Hood manor GR SX 7763, part of which may have lain in Rattery parish] was probably part of this holding; see Fees p. 765 and FA i pp. 324, 395. *Fenthon'* [Venton SX 7560] in FA i p. 350 was another part: a John *de Fenthon'* holds in the manor of *Derthingthon'* in Fees p. 765. In FA i p. 324 *Lokinton'*, said to be in Haytor Hundred (29), is associated with Hood and with Wallaford and Marley (20,13-14 notes). This is unlikely to be Lupton in Brixham (OJR in TDA 45 p. 177); it is more probably an error for *Cokinton'* [Cockington 20,10] as in Fees p. 781.

2 FISHERMEN .... SALMON. In Exon. this detail is interlined after the pigmen (though by the same scribe and in the same colour ink), possibly the reason for its omission in DB. These are the only fishermen mentioned in Devon, though no doubt more existed. See 1,4 note on the fisheries recorded.

Next to this entry in Exon. is a marginal note in a 16th century (or possibly later) hand *Salmones in Darte fluvis* (an error for either *fluvio*, sing., or *fluviis*, pl.) "salmon on the Dart river(s)".

BEFORE 1066 A THANE .... The *T.R.E.* could well belong to the previous statement (= "It paid tax for as much before 1066. A thane held it"), although in Exon. the phrase

belongs to the statement about the thane. Cf. Dorset General Notes 55,23 for a similar ambiguity with *T.R.E.*
LUSCOMBE. William appears to have held two 'Luscombes': one in Rattery parish, the other in Harberton (20,17 note), both in Stanborough Hundred (28) in 1086. The former, adjacent to Dartington, is probably the subject of the present entry, held in Fees p. 765 from the Honour of Dartington as *Loscumb'* by Jordan *Barnage* and as *Loscumb Baruge* by the Abbey of *St. Doumelle* [St. Dogmael's, see 20,14 note] in FA i p. 324; see Fees p. 781, FA i p. 396 and EPNS i p. 310.

20,16 HARBOURNEFORD. In South Brent parish, Stanborough Hundred (28), held as *Hurberneford'* from the Barony of Dartington in Fees pp. 765, 781; see FA i pp. 324, 395. It is *Northhurberneford* ['North' Harbourneford] in FA i p. 350.

20,17 ENGLEBOURNE. Now in Harberton parish, Coleridge Hundred (30). No lordship is, however, allowed William of Falaise in the Tax Return for Chillington (Coleridge) Hundred (xxvii), whereas there is a shortfall of 3 'ferlings' in that for Diptford (Stanborough), unless this land is included, although its inclusion makes a 1-virgate excess; see 20,11-17 note. It may well have counted as a detachment of Stanborough Hundred in 1086. It does not appear in the feudal lists but may well be represented by a second series (see 20,15) of entries for *Luscomb'* [Luscombe in Harberton, GR SX 7957] in Fees p. 765, FA i pp. 324, 396 and by *Herneford* [Hernaford in Harberton, SX 7855, EPNS i p. 326]; see FA i pp. 324, 395 and Cal. Inq. PM vol. xiii no. 99. In FA i p. 350 Hernaford is coupled with *La Wode* held by the Abbot of St. Dogmael's, possibly the same place as *Boys* (from Latin *boscus*, Fr. *bois* 'wood') that is Woodcourt SX 7755; see EPNS i p. 327, Fees pp. 765, 781.

Ch. 21 WILLIAM OF POILLEY. Poilley (DB *de Poilgi, de Poillgi*, Exon. *de Poilleio* with *Poillei* interlined in the section heading, also *de Poileio*, and *Poillelo* in the T.O.) is in the département of Manche, France. See OEB p. 107.

William's lands later form part of the large Honour of Plympton, being granted to Richard I *de Redvers* (died 1107), whose son Baldwin was created Earl of Devon in 1141; see Sanders p. 137 and 1,17 note. Other DB fiefs in Devon which contributed all their manors, or a large number, to this Honour are Chs. 28,29,32,35,37,39,43,44, 46,47,48 and 49. Many of the DB lands belonging to the Honour of Plympton can be found in the great Inq. PM of Hugh *de Courtenay* (Cal. Inq. PM vol. iv (o.s.) no. 63 = TDA 38 pp. 321-326; see Ch. 16 note) and in Cal. Inq. PM (n.s.) vol. i no. 564, xiv no. 325.

In a grant of 1093 to the Abbey of St. Martin at Sées (Round CDF no. 661 p. 235), William *de Polleio* grants tithes from a number of manors which can be closely compared with DB: *Bochelande* [Buckland Monachorum 21,20], *Calcantone* [perhaps Walkhampton, see 21,1 note], *Guichelia* [?Bickleigh 21,19, although the *gu* might be an OFr substitute for OE *w*, and the *ch* for *th*, and so represent an unidentified 'Whitleigh'], *Botteford* [Battisford 21,17], *Cadeberia* [Cadbury 21,7], *Boeleia* [Bowley 21,8], *Blacaleia* [Blagrove 21,9], *Pedeleiga* [Pedley 21,10], *Stoch* [Stoke Rivers 21,3], *Sirigvilla* [Shirwell 21,2] and from "the three manors of Ralph son of Jocelyn (*Goiscelin*), and *Sandfort* the manor of *Ascelin* and the other manor held by him of William *de Polleio*, and the two manors of Herbert 'the seneschal' ", and from *Orfadesora* [Woolfardisworthy 21,12]. A man called Ralph holds Pedley (but this has already been mentioned above) and three other manors: Dart 21,6, Dart Raffe 21,13 and Worth 21,14, which are presumably the three intended by the grant. *Sandfort* is Sampford Spiney (21,21), held in DB by a Robert (TRE by Brictmer). A Robert also holds Goosewell (21,18), and it is probable that these are the two manors of *Ascelin*. Only one manor (Farwood 21,15) is held in DB by a Herbert. The only other manors not accounted for are 21,4;11 (21,5 is waste) and of these 21,11 *Assecote*, being joined with Pedley to Blagrove, was probably counted with them in the above, which leaves 21,4, Beaworthy: it is possible that after 1086 Herbert became William's subtenant here.

Another grant (Round CDF no. 662 p. 235) records that William also gave (in 1096) to St. Martin's the tithe of *Leuga* [probably 21,16 Challonsleigh] and also a manor called *Baraberga* [Harrowbeer, GR SX 5168; EPNS i p. 225], a member of Buckland Monachorum.

THE EXON. BOOK has the same order as DB, the Hundred groupings being:

| 21,1-3 | Shirwell | 21,14 | Budleigh |
| 21,4-5 | Torrington | 21,15 | Colyton |
| 21,6-8 | Silverton | 21,16-18 | Plympton |
| 21,9-13 | Witheridge | 21,19-21 | Walkhampton |

| | |
|---|---|
| 21,1-3 | A GROUP OF PLACES probably all lying in Shirwell Hundred (2). In the Tax Return for Braunton and Shirwell Hundred (vi) William of Poilley is allowed ½ hide of lordship land, which can be accounted for by 21,2-3, leaving the ½ virgate of 'Radworthy' (if it is in this Hundred) as an excess. |
| 21,1 | 'RADWORTHY'. Perhaps in Challacombe parish, Shirwell Hundred (2), to be distinguished from Radworthy (19,19) in North Molton parish, now in South Molton Hundred. But it does not appear in fee lists and its identity, though not improbable, is not certain. OJR bases his identification on the fact that *Calcantone* of William's grant (Ch. 21 note) is Challacombe (TDA 36 p. 355 and H8 p. 489). But *Calcantone* is unlike early forms of Challacombe (EPNS i p. 60) and its position in the grant (which seems to be grouped by Hundreds) suggests a corrupt form of Walkhampton (*Walkamtone* etc., EPNS i p. 243) adjacent to Buckland Monachorum (see 1,19 and 21,20 notes). The site of 'Radworthy' is now abandoned, the name surviving in Radworthy Common. |
| 21,2 | WILLIAM HIMSELF HOLDS. Repeated at the beginning of 21,2-5 inclusive. SHIRWELL. A parish in Shirwell Hundred (2) of which it is *caput*. A portion of *Schirewell* is held in Fees p. 787 by Philip *de Bello Monte* from the Honour of Plympton; see Cal. Inq. PM vol. i no. 564 and FA i p. 335. The same man holds another part under Hugh of Courtenay; 16,65 note. THEY ARE (INCLUDED) IN THE ABOVE VALUE. Exon. *sunt in predicto pretio*; the use of *sunt*, plural, implies that the ploughs are included in the 40s value of the main manor, but the meaning was more likely to have been that the value of the 1 virgate subtenancy was included in the 40s. See Exon. Notes 1,66 where ½ virgate of Irishcombe attached to Lapford is accounted for in the value of Lapford; cf. DB Somerset Exon. Notes 9,3. See also Exon. Notes 16,58 where *isti sunt in supradicto pretio* refers to the 4s 5d of the burgesses' payment forming part of the manor's value. |
| 21,3 | STOKE (RIVERS). A parish in Shirwell Hundred (2). *Stokes* is held in Fees p. 787 from the Honour of Plympton by Ralph *de Welinton'* and is *Stoke Ryvers* in FA i p. 336; see FA i pp. 361, 417, Cal. Inq. PM vol. ix no. 103, x no. 238, xv nos. 154, 866 and OJR H8 p. 490. The additional name is said by EPNS (i p. 69) to be from the Redvers family, Earls of Devon and holders of Plympton Honour, but see OEB p. 110. |
| 21,4-5 | BEAWORTHY. MELBURY. They lie in (Black) Torrington Hundred (11), Melbury being in Beaworthy parish. The places are held together from the Honour of Plympton in Fees p. 788 as *Beghworthy* and *Mellebir'*; see FA i pp. 328, 357, 408 and OJR H5 p. 214. It is probable that Beaworthy can be identified in the Tax Return for Torrington Hundred (iii). |
| 21,5 | WHOLE OF IT IS WASTE. *Vastata est tota*; despite the past participle and verb (similarly in Exon.) the meaning is that Melbury is wasteland: it lies 5 miles from Dartmoor, but there are still patches of uncultivated land there, reflected in such local names as Stoney and Bogtown. See second note under C 3 on *uasta/uastata* and cf. notes to 3,35. 19,18. 20,2 and 36,17. |
| 21,6-8 | PLACES IN HAYRIDGE HUNDRED (15). In the Tax Return (xiii) for Silverton (Hayridge) Hundred ½ hide of lordship is allowed to William and probably represents the 1 virgate of Cadbury combined with the 1 virgate of Bowley (21,7-8). |
| 21,6 | RALPH. Probably Ralph son of Jocelyn; see Ch. 21 note. DART. Places of this name (see also 21,13. 36,24. 42,20) lie on the Dart or Little Dart rivers. The first is a tributary of the Exe, the latter of the Taw. Both rivers rise in Witheridge Hundred; the Dart first divides Witheridge Hundred from Tiverton Hundred, then Tiverton from Hayridge. The Little Dart for much of its length divides Witheridge from North Tawton Hundred. In Ch. 21 a Dart in Witheridge Hundred appears among other Witheridge places at 21,13. It is likely therefore that this Dart, appearing earlier in the schedule, is in another Hundred, probably Hayridge, like the places 21,7-8. Since the Dart only briefly touches this Hundred, in Cadeleigh parish, Dart Cottages have been mapped as the likely location. For OJR's identification with Welltown *alias* Welesbere (TDA 42 pp. 225, 243), see Ch. 44 note. |
| 21,7 | CADBURY. A parish in Hayridge Hundred (15). It is held by Joanna *Brywere* and Baldwin *de Wayford'* from the Honour of Plympton in Fees p. 794; see FA i pp. 322, 368, 425, Cal. Inq. PM vol. xvi no. 1085 and OJR in TDA 42 p. 243. |
| 21,8 | BOWLEY. Apparently in Cadbury parish, Hayridge Hundred (15); see 21,6-8 and 9,1 notes. |
| 21,9-12 | BLAGROVE. PEDLEY. *ASSECOTE*. WOOLFARDISWORTHY. Blagrove and Pedley |

are in the parish of East Worlington (see 3,81 note); Woolfardisworthy is itself a parish
(all three places being in Witheridge Hundred), while *Assecote* is unidentified but likely
to be adjacent to the others. It is possibly a miscopying of *Affecote* in one of the
documents preceding Exon., and it might now be represented by Affeton Barton
[GR SS 7513] in East Worlington, 'Aeffa's Farm' (EPNS ii p. 402) with substitution
of *-tūn* for *-cote* as in Warson (DB *Wadelescote*, 16,10) and Alminstone (DB
*Almerescote*, 42,3).
 In Fees p. 787 *Alfeton* is held with North Tawton (1,3) by Iudhael *de Valletorta*
from the Honour of Plympton: the same man also holds 21,13 Dart Raffe and 21,14
Worth. This place is *Affeton* in FA i p. 422, but in both Fees and FA is regarded as a
part of North Tawton. The remaining places are held by John *le Despenser* from the
Honour of Plympton in Fees p. 787 as *Wolfaresworth', Piddelegh'* and *Blakegrave*; see
Fees p. 758, FA i pp. 362, 419 and OJR in TDA 30 p. 420.

21,11 HILDWINE. DB *Elduin(us)*, Exon. *Holduin(us)*. The spellings are probably an early
 evidence for the evolution of an eME form *Holdwine* < OE *Hildwine*, an AN treatment
 of *Hild-* producing *(H)ild-* > *(H)eld-* > *Hold-* (PNDB pp. 119, 50, 78 and § § 138, 12, 61).
 Cf. the discussion by O. von Feilitzen *Namn och Bygd* 33 (1945), p. 83 s.n. *Holdburh*,
 feminine, ME, for which he suggests OE *hold* 'gracious, friendly', cites *Holduine* 12th
 century (Liber Vitae Hyde Abbey p. 66, Searle p. 300) as the only other example, and
 refers to Forssner p. 154 s.nn. *Holdabrand*, *Holdegrim*, *Holdiard* for instances of *Hold-*
 representing OG *Hild-* (*Hildebrand*, *Hildegrim*, *Hildegard*), whence a possibility that
 names in *Hold-* developed from forms from OG or OE names in *Hild-* with AN
 *-ol<el<il* in pretonic position. (JMcND.)
 1 VILLAGER; HE PAYS 30d. It is unlikely that the *redd' xxx denar* in DB refers to
 the manor's value, as Exon. clearly states that the villager pays 30d. See 6,6 note on
 villagers 'farming' a manor and cf. 28,14 where the villager's payment, also of 30d,
 forms the manor's value. See also 34,14 note and cf. 52,48 note.
 THESE TWO LANDS....12s 6d. This statement is written two letters into the central
 margin in the MS; Farley does not show this. As it is not written below the bottom
 ruling, it is unlikely to have been a later addition. The villager's payment of 30d (see
 note above) seems to be added with the 10s present value of Pedley (21,10) to make
 the 12s 6d.
21,12 WITH 1 SLAVE. In the MS the *seru* is written on top of an erasure and is very blurred
 and in paler ink; the *i* before it is in darker ink.
21,13-14 RALPH. Probably Ralph son of Jocelyn; see Ch. 21 note.
21,13 DART (RAFFE). In Witheridge parish and Hundred (7) and held in Fees p. 787 from
 the Honour of Plympton as *Derth'* by Ralph *de Derth'*. It is called *Derte Rau* in FA i
 p. 364, *Deterauf* in FA i p. 421 either from the later Ralph or from the 1086 holder; see
 Fees p. 760, where the intermediate holder is Iudhael *de Valletorta*, and 21,9-12 note.
 See also 21,6 note.
21,14 WORTH. In Washfield parish, (West) Budleigh Hundred (14). It is *La Worth'* in Fees
 p. 762 held from Iudhael *de Valletorta* of the Honour of Plympton; see Fees p. 790,
 FA i pp. 364, 427, OJR in TDA 35 p. 284 and 21,9-12 note.
21,15 HERBERT. Probably Herbert 'the Seneschal'; see Ch. 21 note.
 FARWOOD. In Colyton parish, Colyton Hundred (22). There seem to have been two
 manors here, both later held by the Abbey of *Queraria* [Quarr, Isle of Wight], one from
 the fees of Henry *de Tracy* (see 3,85 note on Farway), the other from the Earls of
 Devon, Honour of Plympton; see RH i pp. 68b, 94b, TE p. 152a, FA i pp. 366, 428,
 OJR in TDA 36 p. 364 and H7 pp. 339, 351. In Cal. Inq. PM vol. iv (o.s.) no. 63 (= TDA
 38 p. 325) *Forewode* is coupled with *La Hille* ['Hill' unidentified]; the latter is *La Hille
 abbatis de Quarera* in Fees p. 788, associated with Sutton (51,10). For the grant to
 Quarr, see Mon. Ang. v pp. 318-319 nos. viii, ix.
21,16 CHALLONSLEIGH. In Plympton St. Mary parish, Plympton Hundred (26). *Legh'* is
 held by Ralph *de Chalun* from the Honour of Plympton in Fees p. 789. It is *Leghe
 Chaluns* in FA i p. 334; see FA i pp. 353, 400 and OJR H6 p. 283.
21,17 BATTISFORD. In Plympton St. Mary parish, Plympton Hundred (26); see Cal. Inq. PM
 vol. i no. 50 (Baldwin of Redvers) and EPNS i p. 252. It cannot be 'Butless in Brixton'
 (OJR H6 p. 283); see EPNS i p. 250.
21,18 ROBERT. In view of the later descent of Goosewell (see next note), this Robert must
 be Robert Bastard, tenant-in-chief of Ch. 29.
 GOOSEWELL. In Plymstock parish, Plympton Hundred (26). *Gosewill'* is held by

|       |       |
|-------|-------|
|       | Nicholas *le Bastard* from the Honour of Plympton in Fees p. 789; see FA i pp. 335, 353 and OJR H6 p. 283. |
| 21,19 | BICKLEIGH. In Roborough Hundred (25); it can be deduced in the Tax Return for Walkhampton (Roborough) Hundred (xxix) and is possibly the *Guichelia* of William's grant (Ch. 21 note); see Cal. Inq. PM vol. ii no. 573 and 21,20–21 notes. |
| 21,20 | BUCKLAND (MONACHORUM). A parish in Roborough Hundred (25) and identifiable in the Tax Return for Walkhampton (Roborough) Hundred (xxix). An Abbey was founded here in 1278 and endowed with various lands including *Boclond* and *Bikelegh* [Bickleigh 21,19] from the Honour of Plympton by Amice, mother of Isabella Countess of Devon. It is *Byckleght cum Shaght* [Shaugh Prior, 17,100–101] in VE ii p. 378; see Cal. Inq. PM vol. i no. 564, FA i p. 341, Oliver *Mon.* p. 383, OJR H3 pp. 103, 117–118 and 1,19 note. |
| 21,21 | SAMPFORD (SPINEY). A parish in Roborough Hundred (25). In Fees p. 789 Gerard *de Spineto* holds *Sanford'* from the Honour of Plympton; it is *Sandford Spynee* in FA i p. 354; see Fees p. 398, FA i pp. 340, 402. Touching the eastern edge of the parish is Sheepstor [GR SS 5567] also held from the Honour of Plympton as *Sytelestorre* in the next entry in Fees (p. 789) or as *Sychestorr* in FA i p. 402; see FA i p. 354. This was either a part of this holding or of Bickleigh (21,19) of which Sheepstor was a chapelry. In VE ii p. 378 the Abbey of Buckland Monachorum (21,20 note) holds *Heyle* [Hele in Bickleigh, SX 5262], *Shittistor'* and *Rynmore* [Ringmoor in Sheepstor, SX 5566]. |
| Ch. 22 | WILLIAM OF EU. William, Count of Eu (but see *Anglo-Saxon Chronicle*, ed. D. Whitelock etc., p. 173 note 7 and Eyton *Dorset* p. 120 note 7), was the second son of Count Robert of Eu. More than half his fief lay in Wiltshire and Dorset. His first wife, Beatrice, was the sister and heir of Roger II of Bully (son of Roger I of Bully, see Ch. 27 note) and his second wife was the sister of Earl Hugh of Chester; Sanders pp. 119–120. He rebelled against William Rufus in 1088 and in 1094 and was charged with treason in 1096, was blinded and castrated and probably died soon after; Orderic Vitalis iii p. 411. He was executed in 1096 according to Eyton *Dorset* p. 76. On his death his fief was re-allotted. Both his Devonshire manors pass to the Earldom of Hereford. |

Eu (DB *de Ow*, Exon. *de Hou* and *de Ou*) is in the département of Seine-Maritime, France (OEB p. 105).

EXON. ORDER. This fief, enumerated separately in Exchequer DB, is grouped in Exon. with a number of others to which the Exchequer scribe also gave separate chapters (see Exon. Notes Ch. 22), under the general title 'Lands of the French Men-at-Arms in Devonshire'. The Exon. order and probable Hundred groupings of these chapters are:

| 43,1. 45,1 | ?South Tawton | 46,1-2 | Tiverton |
|---|---|---|---|
| 45,2 | Torrington | 40,4 | Witheridge |
| 45,3 | Hartland | 26,1 | Budleigh |
| 40,2 | Fremington | 43,5. 32,6-7 | Teignton |
| 40,1 | Tawton | 32,8 | Tiverton |
| 40,3 | Shebbear | 32,9 | Witheridge |
| 22,1. 32,1 | Exminster | 27,1. 40,5-6 } | Halberton |
| 31,1-3 | Braunton | 41,1-2. 51,14 } | |
| 43,2 | Cliston | 32,10 | Kerswell |
| 31,4 | Braunton | 40,7 | Tawton |
| 43,3-4 | Wonford | 33,1-2 | Kerswell |
| 32,2-3 | Silverton | 43,6 | Borough of Exeter |
| 32,4-5. 22,2 and *Sotrebroc* } (see below) | Wonford | | |

This order, while generally corresponding to the expected sequence, has a few dislocations and late entries (e.g. for Tawton Hundred 40,7), perhaps caused when the 'Lands of the French Men-at-Arms' were drawn from a mass of material arranged by Hundreds. Moreover, at a later stage, in the process of abstracting individual fiefs from Exon. to form separate chapters, the scribe appears to have missed a single manor held by Flohere (*Sotrebroc*), lying at 459 a 3 between 22,2 Whitestone held by William of Eu and 46,1 (West) Manley held by Gerard (translated in Exon. Notes Ch. 22). This manor was in Wonford Hundred (19) in an area now absorbed by Exeter. The lost Exeter street-name 'Shutbrook Street' (named from a stream called the *Schutebroke*, EPNS i p. 23) may have preserved the name. In later times this holding was called from the 1086 holder or his descendants 'Floyers Hayes'. It was held under the Barony of Okehampton and appears at GR SX 917918 in Donn's map of the City included in his Map of Devon (1765); it is also pictured in G. Braun *Civitates Orbis Terrarum* (1572-1618) in Tome 3, Book 6 (*Theatri praecipuarum totius mundi urbium Liber Sextus* (1618) no. 1) and lay between Haven Road and Alphington Street near Williams Avenue. See Cal. Inq. PM (n.s.) vol. xiv no. 325, (o.s.) vol. iv no. 63 (= TDA 38 p. 327) where it is *Floyerslond iuxta Exham*, OJR in TDA 44 p. 298, Mrs. Rose-Troup in DCNQ (1936) p. 168 and J. K. Floyer *Annals of the Family of Floyer* in TDA 30 pp. 505-524.

22,1 POWDERHAM. A parish in Exminster Hundred (24). It is held as *Pouderham* in FA i p. 347 from the Earl of Hereford; see Cal. Inq. PM vol. ix no. 65 and OJR in TDA 47 p. 236.

½ VIRGATE .... WHICH LAY IN EXMINSTER. See 1,4.

22,2 WHITESTONE. A parish in Wonford Hundred (19). In the order of Exon. it lies in a group of Wonford places and is held in FA i p. 317 as *Westeton* by John *de Pouderham* (see 22,1) from the Earl of Hereford; see Cal. Inq. PM vol. ix no. 65 and OJR in TDA 44 p. 334.

TOLI. DB *Toli*, Exon. *Tolus*, represent ODan *Toli*, latinized *Tolus, -i*, which must have developed from an anglicized derivative *Tol*. See DB Dorset General Notes 34,2 on other forms of his name. He held many of William of Eu's lands before 1066, e.g. in Dorset, Wilts., Hants., in which last county he is called Toli the Dane.

6 VILLAGERS HAVE IT THERE. Grammatically the *hanc* refers to the *terra* (or possibly the *una virgata*), but in Exon. (see Exon. Notes) the villagers have 2 ploughs on the land; the Exon. phrase *in ea* "on it" (referring to the *terra* that Ranulf holds) may have confused the Exchequer scribe. See 1,29 note on the phrase.

Ch. 23 WALTER OF DOUAI. He is sometimes referred to by his name 'Walter' (OG *Walt(h)er*, Forssner p. 243), as in the Exchequer and some Exon. entries here and in DB Surrey, Kent, Essex, Suffolk and in some entries in DB Somerset (see Somerset General Notes L 24), and sometimes, as in DB Dorset and Wiltshire and in some entries in Somerset and in some in the Exon. for Devon, by 'Walscin', the nickname variant of it (not discussed by PNDB, OEB or Ellis *Introduction*; Searle is misleading). This *Walscin* appears to be the Norman French version of an OG *Walzin* (*sc* etc. for *z*; see Zachrissen pp. 37-38, PNDB pp. 110-111, Forssner p. 39 and compare his spelling for *Azelin*) which would be a double-diminutive pet-form of *Walter* (an -*in* suffix derivative — see Forssner pp. 278-279 — of the recorded -*z* suffix form *Walz(e)*, see Bach 1,i para. 97,1; 100,2); JMcND.

In the Exon. for Devon his first name takes the form *Valscini* (genitive) in the chapter heading, *Walteri(us)* in the entry corresponding to 23,1, but for the rest of the time, including the T.O. entries, the form is *Walscin(us)* or *Walcin(us)*. In the entry for 23,3 the Exon. scribe originally wrote *Walter*̃ but interlined *soiñ* (presumably for *sciñ*; the first letter is not a capital as Ellis prints) above the last 4 letters to correct to *Walsciñ*; an early change in the same colour ink, as two lines below the form *Walscino* (ablative) is used and repeated as the end of the entry. Whale in TDA 37 p. 274 takes the interlined *soiñ* as a byname of Walter, but this is very unlikely.

After 23,1 in the Exchequer DB *Walterius* is abbreviated to W., as is usually the case. In this translation the W. has been expanded into the form used by the Exon. scribe, in keeping with the method adopted for the Somerset volume in this series.

Douai (DB *de Douuai, de Dowai*; Exon. *de duaco*, T.O. *duacensis*) is in the département of Nord, France; OEB p. 87.

Walter had apparently also another byname: Walter of Flanders in the Tax Return for Uffculme Hundred (xv); see 23,9 note. He was married to the Edeva who was the 1066 tenant of 23,9 (see note there).

The descent of Walter's manors is not entirely clear. Most seem to have formed the Honour of Bampton and to have passed on his death *c*. 1107 to his son Robert who rebelled in 1136, thence to Robert's daughter Juliana who was first married to Fulk Paynel (Sanders p. 5). The lands remained in the Paynel family and were held in 1242-43 (Fees p. 793) by Herbert son of Matthew. Other lands passed to the Honour of Marshwood (in Dorset) which had been granted by Henry I to Geoffrey I de Mandeville (see Sanders p. 64 and Cal. Inq. PM vol. ii no. 154). Some estates passed to other Honours, others are not found in the fee lists; see OJR in TDA 43 p. 220 and VCH pp. 563-565 and H. M. Peskett in DCNQ 32 p. 183.

THE EXON. BOOK has the same order as DB, the places apparently falling in the following Hundreds:

|        |         |             |        |                   |
|--------|---------|-------------|--------|-------------------|
| 23,1-4 | Braunton    | 23,15   | Teignton          |
| 23,5-9 | Bampton     | 23,16   | Kerswell          |
| 23,10-11 | South Molton | 23,17-21 | Axminster   |
| 23,12  | Wonford     | 23,22-26 | Chillington     |
| 23,13-14 | Witheridge | 23,27  | Borough of Exeter |

23,1 HOLLACOMBE. Presumably the place in Kentisbury parish, Braunton Hundred (1); see OJR H8 p. 398 note 2, although a number of other Hundreds normally precede Braunton in Exon. order (see the Appendix). Both 23,1 Hollacombe, 34,11 Holcombe and 36,9 Hollowcombe are DB *Holecome*, from OE *holh* and *cumb* 'hollow valley' and all apparently refer to different places, though in each case the identity is not completely certain. It is perhaps interesting that all three Exchequer entries contain details that are not in Exon. (a plough estimate here and the amount of tax paid for 34,11 and 36,9), as if additional information relating to a single village had come to light after the compilation of Exon., but it is possible that the DB scribe 'deduced' this extra information (see Exon. Notes to these entries).

23,2 BERRYNARBOR. DB *Hurtesberie*, 'Heort's *burh*' which simplified to 'Berry' before gaining the name of the 13th century holder *Nerebert* as a suffix; see EPNS i p. 27. It is a parish in Braunton Hundred (1) and can be deduced from the Tax Return for Braunton and Shirwell Hundred (vi). In Fees p. 400 *Bery*, held by Philip *de Nerbert*, is a fee of William *Briwere*, while in Fees p. 793 *Byri* is held of the Honour of Bampton; see FA i p. 414, Cal. Inq. PM vol. v no. 527, xv no. 628, *Regesta* ii p. 77 no. 866 and OJR H8 p. 438. In the first list of Hundreds bound up with Exon. DB (see the Appendix) *Hertesberia* constitutes a separate Hundred.

23,3 HAGGINTON. East Hagginton in Berrynarbor parish, Braunton Hundred (1). Hagginton had the same late 12th/early 13th century family holding it as Berrynarbor (William *Nerbert*). He exchanged it and it is subsequently held of the Honour of Dartington; see OJR H8 pp. 398, 439. In Fees p. 782 *Hakinton'* is held of the Barony of Dartington. It is *Yesthagynton* [East Hagginton] in FA i p. 414, *Westagynton* in FA i p. 360, the latter probably in error, as West Hagginton is in Ilfracombe (see 3,27 and 16,70 notes).

23,4 ?STOODLEIGH. It is not improbable that it is the place in West Buckland parish, Braunton Hundred (1), although it has not been positively identified: Exon. order suggests a place either in Braunton or Bampton Hundreds and the fact that there is a change of scribe after this entry inclines to the former. If in West Buckland, Stoodleigh will have been shared with the Bishop of Coutances (3,53 note), but it might have lain in the Stoodleigh that is now in Witheridge Hundred, but which probably lay in Bampton (8) in 1086; see 3,77 note. OJR in VCH p. 486 note 1 suggests 'Stoodleigh' in Berrynarbor (which is not to be found). Slew (OJR in TDA 36 p. 367) or Sloley (OJR H8 p. 399) have a different etymology. Reichel's editor (H8 p. 399) accepts the place in West Buckland.

23,5 BAMPTON. A parish, *caput* of Bampton Hundred (8). This large holding had been obtained by Walter in exchange for Ermington and Blackawton (1,23-24 notes), having previously been the royal manor that named the Hundred (see the Appendix). The manor was the head of the later barony of Bampton and had connections with Walter's Somerset manors of Huntspill and Horsey. Fees p. 793 lists its members as *Deuval* [Duvale GR SS 9420], *Hele* [?Hele in Clayhanger, ST 0222], *Doddescumb'* [Doddiscombe SS 9823], *Hakeworth'* [Hockworthy 23,7], *Havekareland* [?Hawkerland in Colaton Raleigh, (East) Budleigh Hundred, SY 0588, EPNS ii p. 587; see Cal. Inq. PM vol. v no. 527] and *Legh* [Lea Barton in Hockworthy, EPNS ii p. 534, part of 23,7]. In FA pp. 430-431 *Baunton* and *Of Colmp* [Uffculme 23,9] are coupled with the manor of *Honspill* in Somerset [Huntspill, DB Somerset 24,28;34]; there also *Duvale* is connected with *Exebrigg* [?Exbridge in Morebath, SS 9320], *Dodiscomb* is said to be held from the Honour of Torrington (see OJR in TDA 30 p. 439) and *Hele* and *Legh Poulet* are held from the manor of *Horsi* in Somerset [Horsey, DB Somerset 24,25]. See FA i p. 369, RH i pp. 65a, 94a, Cal. Inq. PM vol. i no. 139, iv no. 89, v no. 530, xii no. 220, xv no. 733. Hawkerland subsequently went to Dunkeswell Abbey, VE ii p. 304, TE p. 152a.

LAND FOR 4 PLOUGHS. This Exon. addition means 4 carucates of land (see 1,2 note): Bampton had not been hidated. See Exon. Notes here.

PIGMEN WHO PAY 106½ PIGS. They probably paid 106 one year and 107 the next. Cf. DB Herefords. 1,6 where freedmen paid 2½ sheep with lambs.

RADEMAR. A Rademar, probably the same man, is a frequent subtenant of Walter of

23,5       Douai in DB Somerset Ch. 24. According to Eyton *Somerset* i p. 62 he is Rademar the
(cont'd.)  Clerk, Walter's brother: in Somerset 24,35 a Raimer (*Raimar*) the Clerk is described in
           Exon. as Walter's brother. Although *Raimar* usually represents OG *Ragimar* (Forssner
           p. 207, Förstemann 1235) and *Rademar* usually represents OG *Radmer* (Forssner p. 206,
           Förstemann 1216), it is possible that *Rad(e)mar* and *Rag(e)mer* may have become
           confused: *Rademar/Radmer* could have lost its *d*, producing a French variant *Ramer*
           (cf. *Rodbert/Robert, Leodmaer/Lemar*, see PNDB § 103 p. 98). JMcND.
           GERARD. According to Eyton *Somerset* i p. 62 the Gerard who held Bratton Seymour
           (Somerset 24,15) was Walter's steward (*dapifer*) and was also his subtenant in Devon.
           There is no mention in either DB or Exon. of Gerard as *dapifer*.
           WILLIAM OF MOHUN .... ½ FURLONG. He holds Clayhanger (18,1), adjacent to
           Bampton.
           DESPITE WALSCIN. *super Walscinum* in both DB and Exon.; *super* 'over, against' is
           difficult to render in this sense. The primary notion contained in the Latin word is that
           of a battle or contest, fair or unfair, in which William 'wins' and Walscin 'loses'. *Super*
           may, however, be a translation of OE *ofer* 'despite, in spite of, contrary to'. The reality
           was probably that the land was taken, or encroached upon, against Walscin's wish or
           even without his knowledge. Cf. DB Dorset 55,23, Cambs. 3,5 and Notts. 20,7.
23,6       DIPFORD. In Bampton parish and Hundred (8). It was held from the Queen, and
           Walter's citation of the King suggests uncertainty about its tenure; see last note under
           this entry. It may be for this reason that it did not descend with the rest of Walter's
           lands. It passes in fact to the Honour of Torrington (see Ch. 36 note), being held as
           *Depeford'* in Fees p. 775; see FA i p. 431 and OJR in TDA 30 p. 440.
           IT PAID TAX FOR ½ HIDE. Written in very pale ink in the left margin of the MS,
           surrounded on 3 sides by the same pale ink, but with no transposition signs. The
           distinctive ink colour is the same as that used in the additional entries on col. 117c
           (48,12 and 49,7) and in several other interlineations and corrections.
           2 ASSES. *ii asinos*, very rarely recorded in Exon.: apart from these two, there were
           three in Somerset and only one in Dorset (DGSW pp. 206, 123).
           TWO THANES....TWO MANORS. This sentence is squeezed in at the end of the line in
           the same very pale ink as the marginal tax assessment; the scribe appears to be the same
           as for the rest of the entry. See 17,13 note.
           HE CALLS UPON THE KING (TO WARRANT) IT. *inde regem aduocat*. He calls upon
           the King to vouch that he holds the land lawfully; he could no longer call upon the
           Queen as she was dead. The Exon. scribe puts it more fully and clearly with his use of
           *advocatus* in apposition to the King (see Exon. Notes). An *advocatus* in this sense would
           be someone, by no means always the King, though with his authority (e.g. the Bishop of
           Bayeux in DB Surrey 1,5), who could 'guarantee' that the land was held lawfully and
           could protect the holder against claimants to it. Cf. DB Somerset 22,19 and Dorset 54,8.
23,7       HOCKWORTHY. A parish in Bampton Hundred (8), 'Hocca's farm', EPNS ii p. 534.
           *Hakeworth'* is held with other Bampton Honour places in Fees p. 793, including probably
           Lea Barton (23,5 note). The exact holding may have been at Hockford Waters [GR ST
           0220], the 'Waters' preserving Walter's name as in Bridgwater, Somerset; see FA i
           pp. 369, 431 and OJR in TDA 30 p. 443 note 9.
23,8       GERARD. See 23,5 note.
           KERSWELL. DB *Cressewalde* from OE *caerse wielle* 'cress spring', EPNS ii p. 535. It
           lies in Holcombe Rogus parish, Bampton Hundred (8).
23,9       W(ALSCIN) HOLDS UFFCULME. The Tax Return for Uffculme Hundred (xv) states
           that Walter of Flanders (*flandrensis*) has 5 hides of lordship land there, which corresponds
           to this holding. Douai is in Flanders.
           UFFCULME. Now in Bampton Hundred (8). Uffculme had its own Tax Return (see
           above note) and continued as a separate Hundred in later times (see the Appendix). In
           FA i pp. 430-431 it is coupled with Bampton (23,5 note) and its members are given as
           *Stenhal* and *Yundecote* [Stenhill GR ST 0610 and Yondercott ST 0712]; Stenhill is held
           as *Stenenhalle* in Fees p. 782 from the Honour of Worle [Somerset DB 24,1 held by
           Walter of Douai in 1086].
           Uffculme had belonged to Glastonbury Abbey (see Ch. 4 note), being granted by King
           AEthelwulf (839-855) as 24 hides at *Uffaculum* (ECDC no. 11 p. 9 = Sawyer (1) no.
           1697; see ECDC p. 15 no. 66). GC p. 126 no. 172 records its lease to Edeva (the 1066
           holder), widow of Hemming, who married Walter of Douai. DB does not mention the
           Glastonbury tenure, the implication being that the land was confirmed on Walter by the

| | |
|---|---|
| 23,9 (cont'd.) | Conqueror. It passed to Walter's son Robert and was restored to Glastonbury Abbey by King Stephen in 1136 (GC i p. 126 no. 172), an act which led to a prolonged revolt by Robert and other nobles; see Hoskins and Finberg DS pp. 59-77. It did not long remain in Glastonbury's possession, but reverted to Walter's heirs; see Cal. Inq. PM vol. i no. 139, iv no. 89, v no. 530, xii no. 220 and xv no. 733. |
| | 2 PIGMEN .... PIGS. It is interesting that this statement is interlined in Exon., above the second line containing the livestock, but at the same time as the rest of the entry; this is probably the reason for its misplacement in Exchequer DB. Cf. 42,6 note. |
| 23,10-11 | KNOWSTONE. A parish in South Molton Hundred (6). In Fees p. 793 the heir of Richard *Beupel* holds in *Cnuston'* of the Honour of Marshwood; in FA i pp. 325, 418 *Knouston Beaupel* is held by John *de Maundevill'* from the same Honour. This manor is now represented by Beaples Barton, Hill and Moor in this parish. If the second DB entry represents a separate manor, it may have been the Knowstone that passed to William *de Botreaux* and was given by him to the Canons of Hartland in 1160 (Oliver *Mon.* p. 207, VE ii p. 333; see OJR H3 pp. 71, 89-90). But the descent of the other Knowstones (52,41;51) is also obscure. |
| 23,12 | GERARD. See 23,5 note. |
| | DUNSFORD. A parish in Wonford Hundred (19) divided in 1086 between two lords (see also 52,47). The two portions had the same middle lords in the Middle Ages, which makes the descent difficult to trace with certainty, although the larger land (23,12) was held of the Honour of Marshwood, the smaller of Okehampton Honour. In Fees p. 793 Robert *de Blakeford'* holds *Dunesford'* from the Honour of Marshwood. In FA i p. 316 it is held by the Bishop of Exeter from John *de Blakeford* then by William *de Servyngton* who in FA i p. 346 holds in *Parva Sotthon* [Sowton, 52,47 note], *Donesford* and *Spreweye* in Witheridge Hundred [Spurway 23,14]. Finally William *de Servyngton* holds *Parva Dunsford* from the Honour of Marshwood in FA i p. 387. If the Honour is correctly recorded in this last, the place-name must be an error (probably for *Parva Sotthon* and *Dunsford*), since the Marshwood holding is the larger. This misled OJR into reversing the identifications in the later descent of these holdings; see RBE ii p. 558, Fees pp. 612, 1370, RH i p. 84a, Cal. Inq. PM vol. i no. 799, ii nos. 154, 239 and OJR in TDA 44 p. 332. |
| 23,13 | LITTLE RACKENFORD. DB *Litelracheneford*, in Rackenford parish, Witheridge Hundred (7); DB unusually distinguishes this place from Rackenford (16,148). The other lands held by Ludo from Walter in 1086 (23,17-20;22) are later held of the Honour of Marshwood by the Mohun family of Dunster in Somerset; cf. 25,23 note. No such holding appears in the fee lists although the Mohuns hold the adjacent Nutcott (46,2) from the Honour of Plympton; see OJR in TDA 30 p. 418, 36 p. 357. In Fees p. 761 Little Rackenford appears as *Parva Rakeneford'* held by Robert of *Sideham* (from Sydeham 24,7), but held of the Honour of Gloucester. *Little Rakerneford* and *Sidham* are associated in Cal. Inq. PM vol. vii no. 344. |
| 23,14 | SPURWAY. In Oakford parish, Witheridge Hundred (7). In Fees p. 793 Ivo *de Servinton'* holds in *Spreweye*. The place is *Westsprewey* held from John *de Mandevill'* of *Coker* [Coker in Somerset] in FA i p. 343; see Fees p. 759, Cal. Inq. PM vol. ii no. 154. For East Spurway, see 3,74. |
| 23,15 | ANSGER .... ASGAR. Although the forms *Ansger* and *Asgar* represent the same name (see 1,23-24 note), it is unlikely that the same man held *Sutreworde* both in 1066 and 1086, as the formula one would expect in such a case would be 'Ansger holds .... He also held ....'. |
| | SUTREWORDE. DG's identification of this place with Southbrook in North Bovey parish, Teignbridge Hundred (23), is over-hasty since EPNS ii p. 469 reports early forms as *Sudbroc, Suthbroke*. Nonetheless, this entry is in the right place in the schedule for a Teignbridge Hundred place and it might be the place later called *Leuestelegh'* [Lustleigh GR SX 7881], otherwise unrepresented in DB, and which is held in that Hundred in Fees p. 793 by the heirs of John *de Mandevill'* from the Honour of Marshwood; see Cal. Inq. PM vol. ii nos. 154, 236, FA i pp. 339, 389, VE ii p. 335, OJR in TDA 29 p. 236. But the connection has yet to be proved. For another view see J. V. Somers Cocks in DCNQ (1965-67). |
| | 5 BEEKEEPERS. *v mellitarios*, accusative, instead of the usual nominative; probably the result of direct copying from Exon. where the beekeepers (like the rest of the population) are the object of 'Ansger has'; cf. 1,27 note on 'smiths'. Nine beekeepers are also recorded in DB Wilts. 1,16 and a 'keeper of 12 beehives' in DB Herefords. 1,47. |

23

23,15     SESTERS OF HONEY. The sester is a measure, sometimes of liquid, as here, sometimes
(cont'd.) dry (e.g. it is used of salt in DB Glos. 1,47-48 and of wheat, malt and oats in Wilts. 24p).
It was of uncertain and probably variable size (see DB Glos. G 1 and 19,2 notes). It was
reckoned at 32 oz. for honey; see Zupko p. 155. Sometimes the sester payment was
commuted: in Wilts. 24p Edward of Salisbury had, among other commodities as his
annual payment as Sheriff, '16 sesters of honey, or instead of honey, 16s'. Cf. Warwicks.
B 5 (col. 238a) where the Borough of Warwick pays '6 sesters of honey, that is a sester
at 15 pence'.

23,16     GOODRINGTON. In Paignton parish, Haytor Hundred (29). In Fees p. 767 *Goderington',
Ledwycheton'* [now Boohay in Brixham, GR SX 8952, EPNS ii p. 507], and *Bruneston'*
[Brownstone in Brixham, SX 9050] are held as one fee of Geoffrey *de Mandevil'* of the
Honour of Marshwood; see Fees p. 793, Cal. Inq. PM vol. ii no. 154 and FA i pp. 317,
348, 391.

ASGAR. DB *Asgar*, Exon. *Ansgar(us)*; see 1,23-24 note.

23,17     LUDO HOLDS FROM W(ALSCIN). Repeated at the beginning of 23,17-20 inclusive.
He is called Walscin's man-at-arms in the T.O.; see Exon. Notes 23,20.

HETFELLE. It would not be unreasonable to suppose, from Exon. order, that this place
lay in Axminster Hundred along with 23,18-20. Moreover, there is a Heathfield in
Honiton parish (at GR SY 1599) and DG identifies *Hetfelle* with this place. But there are
at least eleven other 'Heathfields' in Devon and convincing evidence for this identification
is lacking. A holding of Ludo in 1086 normally passes to the Mohun family (23,13 note)
and they hold *Holedich* or *Holedych* [Holditch in Thorncombe, GR ST 3402] otherwise
unaccounted for in DB. But there is at present no evidence to connect *Hetfelle* with
Holditch; see Fees pp. 612, 793, 1263, 1423, FA i p. 319, HD *passim*, Cal. Inq. PM vol.
ii nos. 154, 306, 539, vi no. 602, vii no. 297 and OJR H4 pp. 139, 159.

23,18-19 (MOHUNS) OTTERY. LUPPITT. The former lies in Luppitt parish, Axminster Hundred
(17). Ludo's *Otri* will have passed to the Mohuns, has the same 1066 and 1086 holders as
Luppitt and occurs as *Oterymoun* with *Loveput* in FA i p. 429, held from John *Mohun*
of Dunster. Earlier this place appears as *Otery* held by Reginald *de Mohun* from Geoffrey
*de Mandevil* of the Honour of Marshwood and is also known as *Ottery Flemeng*; see FA
i pp. 319, 366, HD p. 56, Cal. Inq. PM vol. ii nos. 154, 306, 436, 593, iii no. 415, vi no.
478, vii no. 297, xi no. 300, xii no. 436, OJR H4 pp. 139, 160 and 23,21 note.

23,18     LEVEL WITH THE FIRST LINE of this entry in the left margin of the MS is an *O* sign
and in the right margin a † sign, neither shown by Farley. The cross is in a thinner pen
and possibly in paler ink than the *O*, though it is hard to be certain as the *O* is written on
the darker parchment at the inner edge of the folio. See notes to 10,1. 19,27 and 19,43.

23,20     GREENWAY. Also in Luppitt parish, Axminster Hundred (17), and with the same
manorial descent as Luppitt; see OJR H4 p. 163 and 23,18-19 note.

SHAPCOMBE ... BROADHEMBURY. See 42,16 although the details do not tally,
perhaps because they originated from two different returns.

23,21     COMBE RALEIGH. DB *Otri*. A parish in Axminster Hundred (17). This second 'Ottery'
held by Walter in 1086 (the first is 23,18) is found in Fees p. 793 as *Cumb'* held by
Matthew *de Banton* (from Bampton 23,5) of the Honour of Marshwood, later as *Otercomb*
held by John *Ralegh* from the Mohun Honour of Dunster (FA i p. 429). This is *Combe
Banton* in FA i p. 319, *Combe Mathei de Bampton* in HD p. 57 and Cal. Inq. PM vol. ii
nos. 306, 593, *Cumb Coffyn* held by the heirs of Matthew *de Baunton* in Cal. Inq. PM
vol. ii no. 154. It is now Combe Raleigh (EPNS ii p. 638), although FA i p. 489 says of
the same land *Otercombe alias dicta Uppeotery* [Uppottery] ; see OJR H4 pp. 140, 163
and in DCNQ 21 p. 201. 'Combe Bampton' went to Newenham Abbey, Oliver *Mon*. p. 357.

23,22     STOKE (FLEMING). A parish in Coleridge Hundred (30). In Fees p. 793 *Stokes* is held
by Reginald *de Mohun* of the Honour of Marshwood. It is *Stok Flemeng* in FA i p. 331.
This manor or Townstall (23,26) also contained lands at Kinsgwear, Norton, Clifton,
Dartmouth and 'Hardness'. In Cal. Inq. PM vol. xiv no. 325 Hugh *de Courteney* holds
*Norton* [Norton GR SX 8551] by *Stokeflemmyng*, *Clyfton* [Clifton SX 8850],
*Dertemuth* [Dartmouth SX 8751] and *Hardenesse* ['Hardness', see EPNS i p. 321].
Kingswear [SX 8851] had also been part of this land before going to Torre Abbey
(EPNS ii p. 515, VE ii p. 361). On the whole manor see FA i pp. 350, 391-392, HD p. 56,
Cal. Inq. PM vol. ii nos. 306, 436, 593, iii no. 415, vi no. 478, vii no. 297, xi no. 300,
xii no. 436, xiii no. 18, xvi no. 959, and OJR in TDA 36 p. 371, 43 pp. 197, 221-222.

A MILL IN LORDSHIP WHICH RENDERS SERVICE. *molinum in dominio seruiens*.
The Exon. (see Exon. Notes here) makes it clear that this is a mill that only serves the lord

| | |
|---|---|
| 23,22 (cont'd.) | (of the manor). However, *seruiens* is an awkward addition to the set phrase *in dominio* (= 'a mill in lordship, serving'), whereas the Latin should read *molinum domui/domino seruiens* (= 'a mill serving the house/lord'), the verb *seruio* taking its object in the dative case. See 1,7 note on mills and cf. notes to 17,1 and 20,13 on other examples of bad construction of the Latin in DB.<br>RALPH .... ½ HIDE. Probably at *Northton* [Norton SX 8551], a Marshwood fee in Fees p. 793, FA i pp. 331, 393, later joined to Townstall (23,26) which Ralph also held; see OJR in TDA 43 p. 222. |
| 23,23-24 | ADDED TO ASGAR'S LANDS. The implication is that the addition was illegal, that Walter should not have annexed these lands, held freely in 1066, to those of Ansger/Asgar whose holding he had (legally) acquired. Cf. 15,31 note. |
| 23,23;25 | COLERIDGE. In Stockenham parish, Coleridge Hundred (30); see OJR in TDA 43 p. 197. |
| 23,23 | BICCA. DB *Biche*, Exon. *Bichus*; see PNDB p. 202. |
| 23,24 | ?WOODCOMBE. DB *Wodicome*. The order of Exon. places it clearly in Chillington (Coleridge) Hundred (30); it may well be the place in Chivelstone parish, although neither this place nor the entries for Coleridge (23,23;25) are found in fee lists. It is unlikely to be Widdicombe in Stockenham parish (OJR in TDA 43 p. 197, EPNS i p. 333) which is derived from *withig* 'withy'. Moreover, the Fees reference (p. 780) cited by EPNS actually relates to Withycombe Raleigh (24,3). The DB form points rather to Woodcombe (EPNS i p. 320).<br>ALRIC HOLDS .... FROM. In the MS *teneb'* ('held') written originally, but corrected to *teñ de* (the *d* covering the original *b*) without the second *e* of *teneb'* being erased. |
| 23,25 | ON THE LACK OF POPULATION recorded for this manor, see 17,84 note. It is possible that the land was worked by some of the 3 smallholders recorded for the other manor in Coleridge (23,23). |
| 23,26 | TOWNSTALL. In Dartmouth parish, Coleridge Hundred (30). After 1086 this manor was combined with Norton (23,22 note), but was later separated again and granted to Torre Abbey before 1346 when the Abbey is found holding *Tounstalle* (FA i p. 393). See VE ii p. 361, TE p. 153a, Oliver *Mon*. p. 169 and OJR in TDA 43 p. 222. |
| 23,27 | HOUSE IN PLEDGE FROM A BURGESS. Cf. 5,15 and note.<br>CUSTOMARY DUES. That is, 8d; see Exon. Notes and C 1 note. |
| Chs. 24 -25 | THE LANDS OF WALTER OF CLAVILLE AND OF GOTSHELM are entered together in the Exon. Book (see Exon. Notes Chs. 24-25) in the following order of Hundreds: |

| | | | | |
|---|---|---|---|---|
| | 24,32 | Torrington | 24,5-7 | Witheridge |
| | 24,22. 25,1-2 | Merton | 24,8-10. | } Tiverton |
| | 25,3-4 | Fremington | 25,16-19 | |
| | 25,5-10. | } Tawton | 25,20-22. | } Halberton |
| | 24,23-25 | | 24,11-16 | |
| | 24,26 | Fremington | 24,17. 25,23 | Colyton |
| | 24,27-29. 25,11 | Tawton | 25,24-25. 24,18-19 | Coleridge |
| | 24,30-31. 25,12 | Bampton | 24,20. 25,26 | *Alleriga* |
| | 25,13 | Silverton | 24,21 | Diptford |
| | 25,14. 24,1 | Hemyock | 25,27 | (unknown) |
| | 24,2 | Wonford | 25,28 | Cliston |
| | 25,15. 24,3-4 | Budleigh | | |

| | |
|---|---|
| Ch. 24 | WALTER OF CLAVILLE. DB *de Clauile*; Exon. entries for 24,1;3 *de clauilla* (elsewhere in the section he is called plain Walter). Walter may have come from one of several places in France called Claville or Clasville: Claville near Évreux in the département of Eure or Claville-Motteville near Yvetot in the département of Seine-Maritime or Clasville near Cany Barville also in Seine-Maritime (see Dauzat s.n. *Clasville*). OEB p. 82 seems to confuse both the départements and the villages; see also Loyd p. 29. Walter also held land in chief in Dorset; see DB Dorset General Notes 41,1 and cf. notes to 16,5 and 24,8 here. See Ch. 25 note on Walter's brother Gotshelm.<br>Walter's lands later form a part of the Honour of Gloucester, other contributors being Gotshelm (Ch. 25), Ansger (Ch. 40), Aiulf (Ch. 41), Morin [of Caen] (51,14 note), Colwin (52,4-6 notes), Godric (52,20-21 notes) and Godwin (52,9-19 note), in addition to the lands of Queen Matilda (1,57-72). The Honour of Gloucester lands reappear in a number of Inq. PM; see in particular that of Henry *de Wylyngton* (Cal. Inq. PM vol. ix no. 218). |
| 24,1 | BYWOOD. In Dunkeswell parish, Hemyock Hundred (16); it can be identified in the Tax Return for that Hundred (xiv). *Biuuode* is held in FA i p. 338 by the Abbot of |

|  |  |
|---|---|
|  | Dunkeswell from John *de Clavill* and by him from the Honour of Gloucester; see FA i pp. 367, 430, TE p. 151b, Oliver *Mon.* p. 396, OJR H2 p. 43 and 24,16 note. |
| 24,2 | BRAMFORD (SPEKE). A parish in Wonford Hundred (19); see 3,67 and 16,123 notes. This particular ½ hide holding appears to be represented in Fees p. 779 by *Steveneston'* [Stevenstone Barton in Upton Pyne, GR SX 9199], *Couelegh'* [Cowley in Upton Pyne, SX 9096] and *Yendecoth'* [Yendacott in Shobrooke, SS 8900, see 24,4 note] held by Agnes *de Esford'* from the Honour of Gloucester; see FA i pp. 346, 387 and OJR in TDA 44 p. 296. |
|  | PAID TAX. In the MS the *g* of *geldb'* covers an *r*: the scribe probably began to write *redd'* for *reddit gildum*, as in Exon., but realised his mistake. |
| 24,3 | WITHYCOMBE (RALEIGH). A parish in (East) Budleigh Hundred (14). In Fees p. 780 William *de Clavill'* holds *Wydecumb'* from the Honour of Gloucester; see Fees p. 763, RH i pp. 66b, 92b, FA i pp. 364, 427 and OJR in TDA 35 p. 288. A mill here was given to Canonsleigh Priory by a later Walter *de Claville*; see Canonsleigh Cartulary no. 12 p. 2. |
| 24,4 | WALTER THE STEWARD. Exon. here and for 24,13 *dapifer*. (WEST) RADDON. In Shobrooke parish, (West) Budleigh Hundred (14); 'West' to distinguish it from 'East' Raddon in Thorverton parish, Hayridge Hundred (5,9. 51,6). It is probably represented in Fees p. 779 by Yendacott (in Shobrooke parish); see 24,2 note. OJR in TDA 30 p. 421 and TDA 36 p. 357, without evidence, identified the place with 'Fremanscot *alias* Westyeo' in Witheridge; see 24,6 note. |
| 24,5 | WASHFORD (PYNE). A parish in Witheridge Hundred (7); this holding can be identified in the Tax Return for that Hundred (x). In Fees p. 778 Herbert *de Pinu* holds in *Wasford* and in *Sideham* [Sydeham 24,7] ; see Fees p. 758, FA i p. 419 and OJR in TDA 30 p. 398. |
| 24,6 | DRAYFORD. In Witheridge parish and Hundred (7) and identifiable in the Tax Return for that Hundred (x). In Fees p. 778 *Drayford'* is held by John *le Despenser* from the Honour of Gloucester; see Fees p. 758, FA i p. 419 and OJR in TDA 30 p. 421. It may well be that the next entry in Fees p. 778 was part of this holding, that is *Fremanescoth'* ['Freemancott' lost in Witheridge, EPNS ii p. 398]. In FA i p. 342 *Drayford* is coupled with *Hille juxta Specthcote* [an unidentified 'Hill' near Speccot in Merton parish, Shebbear Hundred]. It is not clear to which holding of Walter this should be referred, unless it is the 1 virgate belonging to Iddesleigh 24,22. |
| 24,7 | SYDEHAM. In Rackenford parish, Witheridge Hundred (7); see OJR in TDA 30 p. 421, and notes to 23,13 and 24,5. |
| 24,8-16 | THESE PLACES lie in Tiverton and Halberton Hundreds (9-10). It is difficult to reconcile their lordship with the Tax Returns, and the order of Exon. with the later contents of these Hundreds, which are often counted as a joint Hundred and where a number of boundary adjustments have been made. In Exon. the places fall in the order 24,8-10. 25,16-22. 24,11-16. It seems likely that, as he did with the other Hundreds in Chs. 24-25, the scribe first entered Walter's lands in Tiverton Hundred, then Gotshelm's lands in Tiverton followed by those in Halberton Hundred, then Walter's lands in Halberton, 25,20 being the first place in Halberton Hundred. See Exon. Note Chs. 24-25. |
| 24,8 | (CRAZE) LOWMAN .... 'KIDWELL'. Craze Lowman is earlier 'Claville's Lowman' from the family that held in 1086 and later under the Honour of Gloucester, 'Craze' being a corruption of Claville via the dissimilated form *Craville (see EPNS ii p. 542). It lies in Tiverton parish and Hundred (9). 'Kidwell', now only represented by Kidwell Lane, is in Uplowman parish, Halberton Hundred (10). It was probably, like Uplowman itself, in Tiverton Hundred in 1086 as in the Middle Ages (see LSR (1332) p. 36). In Fees p. 780 *Lomene* and *Cadewill'* are held by William *de Clavill'* from the Honour of Gloucester; see FA i pp. 318, 433, Cal. Inq. PM vol. ix nos. 326, 428 and OJR H1 pp. 2, 24. |
| 24,9-10 | MURLEY. COOMBE. Both lie in Uplowman parish, now Halberton Hundred (10), but they were part of Tiverton Hundred (9) in the Middle Ages and probably in 1086. In Fees p. 780 John *Lancelevee* and Robert *Avenel* hold in *Cumb'* and *Morlegh'* from the Honour of Gloucester; see FA i p. 318 (Tiverton Hundred), FA i p. 432 and OJR H1 p. 25. |
| 24,9 | WALTER THE WILD. Exon. *Walteri(us) saluagi(us)* with *siluestris* interlined above by the same scribe and in the same colour ink, apparently as a gloss, as *saluagi(us)* is not underlined for deletion. *siluestris* is the word used in 24,10;31. The two words do not mean exactly the same, *saluagius* deriving from OFr *salvage* (Mod.Fr *sauvage*), LLat. *salvaticus, silvaticus* 'wild, untamed' from *silva* 'wood' (OEB p. 355), while *siluestris* is 'of, from, belonging to, a wood' (OEB p. 136). Cf. Edric the Wild (*saluage*) in DB Herefords. 9,3 (see note). PERCH. See 16,172 note. |

24,11-12 BOEHILL. In Sampford Peverell parish, Halberton Hundred (10). In Fees p. 780 *Behille* is held by William *de Clavil'* of the Honour of Gloucester together with Appledore and Burlescombe; see Cal. Inq. PM vol. viii no. 363 and notes to 24,14 and 24,30. The tithe of the rents of *Buelle* was given to Canonsleigh Priory; see Oliver *Mon.* p. 228 and OJR H2 p. 58. The DB division into two manors survived, reference to 'the two Boehills' being found in later documents.
    Boehill and Ayshford (24,13) totalling 2 hides 1 virgate and 1½ furlongs ('ferlings') in 1086 appear to be the 2½ *mansae* and 25 *segetes* granted in 958 by King Eadwig to Eadheah at *AEscforda* and *Byohylle*; see ECDC no. 36 p. 12 = BCS no. 1027 = Sawyer (1) no. 653.

24,11     4 SMALLHOLDERS HAVE IT THERE. Although in phrases such as this the *hanc* would normally refer to the plough (see 1,29 note), it may here refer to the land. Cf. 25,28 note. As Exon. records neither plough-team nor land holding for the smallholders (see Exon. Notes) it is possible that the Exchequer scribe had access to information from another source.

24,12     IT PAYS 10s A YEAR. See 6,8 note.

24,13     AYSHFORD. It lies in that part of Burlescombe parish that has always been in Halberton Hundred (10). *Esford'* is held in Fees p. 780 by Agnes *de Esford'* from the Honour of Gloucester; see FA i pp. 338, 369, 432, OJR H2 p. 58 and 24,11-12 note.

24,14     WALTER HIMSELF HOLDS. Repeated at the beginning of 24,14-18 inclusive.
    APPLEDORE. DB *Suraple*. It lies, like the preceding entry, in that part of Burlescombe parish that was always in Halberton Hundred (10). In Fees p. 780 *Sureapeldor'* is held with Burlescombe and Boehill (see notes to 24,11-12 and 24,30) by William *de Clavil'* from the Honour of Gloucester; see FA i pp. 338, 432, Oliver *Mon.* p. 224 ff., Canonsleigh Cartulary no. 12 p. 2 and OJR H2 p. 58.
    WULFWY. *Vluui*, possibly a mistake for *Vluiet*; see Exon. Notes.

24,15     CANONSLEIGH. DB *Leige*. It lay in that part of Burlescombe parish that was in Halberton Hundred (10) and it can be accounted for in the Tax Return for Halberton (xvii). The second Walter of Claville gave 'all the land at Leigh' *c.* 1170 to the priory for Augustinian Canons he established there; henceforth Leigh was called Canonsleigh. It was later a nunnery (Knowles MRH pp. 132, 227); see Cal. Inq. PM vol. xvi no. 538, Oliver *Mon.* p. 228, Canonsleigh Cartulary *passim*, Davis MCGB p. 19, OJR H2 p. 59 and 41,2 note.

24,16     LEONARD. DB *Lannor*. It lies in Halberton parish and Hundred (10). In Fees p. 780 the Abbot of Dunkeswell holds *Lynor* from the Honour of Gloucester. It had been granted to the Abbey with Bywood (24,1) in 1206; see FA pp. 338, 432, Cal. Inq. PM vol. viii no. 363, VE ii p. 304, Oliver *Mon.* p. 396 and OJR H2 p. 60.

24,17     BERE. It appears to have lain, like the next entry in Exon. (Farway 25,23), in Colyton Hundred (22), since Walter of Claville is allowed 1 virgate of lordship in that Hundred's Tax Return (xx). There was Claville land at Netherton [GR SX 1895] in Farway parish, given by the second Walter of Claville to Canonsleigh (see Oliver *Mon.* p. 228, Canonsleigh Cartulary no. 12 p. 2, OJR in TDA 36 p. 366 and H7 pp. 338, 354 and 24,15 note). Both VCH and DG identify *Bere* as Netherton, but there is no evidence to connect the two.
    WORDROU. DB and Exon. *Wordrou*; see PNDB p. 417, where Feilitzen suggests this may be based on the OBret personal name *Woret*. The second element *-rou* may represent an unidentified byname; hence the name may be *Woret 'Rou'*. (JMcND)

24,18-19 BRICTRIC'S LANDS .... BRICTRIC. Most probably Brictric son of Algar, on whom see 24,21 note. According to the T.O. entry (see Exon. Notes) this addition of Buckland Tout Saints to those held, apparently legally, by Walter as being part of Brictric's fief, was wrongful; the DB hints at this by stating that it was free before 1086. Walter's brother Gotshelm also seems to have indulged in this method of acquiring lands; see 25,20 note and cf. 15,31 note.

24,18     BUCKLAND (TOUT SAINTS). A parish in Coleridge Hundred (30); it takes its second name from the 13th century holder of Gotshelm's manor here (see 25,25 note). This particular land was at *Wodemaneston'* held in Fees p. 780 by Thomas *de Wodemaneston'* from the Honour of Gloucester; see FA i p. 393. Formerly 'Woodmanstone', named from Woodman the 1066 holder, the place is now Bearscombe [GR SX 7544]; see EPNS i p. 318 and OJR in TDA 43 p. 224.
    IT PAYS 10s. *Reddit* here may perhaps be the result of a too close copying of Exon., as *valet* is used elsewhere in Ch. 24; see notes to 3,82 and 15,53.

24,19     POOL. North Pool in South Pool parish, Coleridge Hundred (30). William *de Bykelegh'* holds in *Northpole* and in *Colemore* [Colmer, see 24,20 note] in Fees p. 780 from the Honour of Gloucester; see FA i pp. 332, 393, Cal. Inq. PM vol. viii no. 273, xiv no. 325 and OJR in TDA 43 p. 225.

24,20 LUPRIDGE. Now in North Huish parish, Stanborough Hundred (28), but it appears to have lain in Ermington (27) in the Middle Ages and was probably in *Alleriga* (Ermington) in 1086 (see 15,27 note). This particular holding seems to have been at *Colemore* [Colmer GR SX 7053], held in Fees p. 780 from the Honour of Gloucester with North Pool (24,19). Colmer appears to have been named from Cola, the TRE holder; see FA i p. 400, EPNS i p. 303 and OJR H6 p. 327.

WITH 1 BURGESS. Totnes is the nearest borough to Lupridge and so it is likely that the burgess was there (Walter had no property in Exeter). However, Finberg (*Tavistock Abbey* p. 75) thinks that *cū i burg(en)si* here is a slip for *cū i bord(ario)* 'with 1 smallholder'.

IT WAS WASTE. Exon. *erat uastata*; the past participle *uastata* probably means the same as the adjective *uasta*; see second note under C 3.

24,21-22 IN THE MS there is a gap of a line between these entries (not shown by Farley), and *Walterius* is written in capitals and is rubricated, treatment usually reserved for the first entry in a chapter or, as in Ch. 51, for a change in holder in a chapter devoted to several holders. This later confused the scribe when he came to write the Landholders' List; see L 25 note above. There is no evidence, however, that the Walter of 24,22-32 is a different man from Walter of Claville. Individual manors throughout Ch. 24 descend to the Claville family. The reason for this gap and the capitals may lie in the fact that after 24,21 the scribe moved from the end to the beginning of the section in Exon. dealing with the fiefs of Walter and Gotshelm, perhaps because he had originally mislaid the booklet containing the first part of the Exon. section (see Exon. Note Chs. 24-25). Cf. 24,32 note below.

24,21 LEIGH. In Churchstow parish, Stanborough Hundred (28); it can be identified in the Tax Return for Diptford (Stanborough) Hundred (xxvi). In Fees p. 780 Geoffrey *de Insula* holds in *Legh'* from the Honour of Gloucester; see Fees p. 765, FA i pp. 350, 395, Cal. Inq. PM vol. iii no. 413. It is sometimes known as All Hallowsleigh or Leigh All Saints; see EPNS i p. 296 and OJR in TDA 36 p. 372, 45 p. 179.

BRICTRIC SON OF ALGAR. A great English thane who had held much land in the west. Although Brictric is only given his full name here and in DB Glos. and Worcs., many of the references to plain Brictric in Somerset, Cornwall, Dorset, Wilts. and Herefords., as well as in Devon, are undoubtedly to the son of Algar (see, for example, 13,1 note). In DB Cornwall 1,19 a Brictric was also the predecessor of land held by Walter of Claville.

Many of Brictric's lands passed to Queen Matilda before going to the King on her death in 1083 (see 1,57 note). A romantic tale told by the Continuator of Wace and others (Freeman iv App. Note 0) alleges that Matilda had seized his lands because in youth he had spurned her hand. See 27,1 and notes.

W(ALTER) HOLDS THESE. In Exon. the *has* probably refers to the two 1066 manors of Leigh which Walter has combined, though according to Whale in TDA 37 p. 272 it refers to the preceding manor Lupridge and the present one Leigh. Cf. third note under 34,54.

24,22 1 VIRGATE .... IDDESLEIGH. The King's manor is 1,63 in Shebbear Hundred (4). Iddesleigh itself also passed to the Honour of Gloucester and this virgate may well be one of the members named in the fee lists (1,63 note); see 24,6 note.

AELFEVA THIEF. DB *Aleuesdef*; Exon. *Aleuesclef* with a slight gap between *Aleues* and *clef* (the *cl* being a scribal error for *d*). The first part, *Aleues*, represents OE *Aelfgifu*, fem. (PNDB p. 173; see 16,40 note), the *-s* being an inorganic composition suffix (see PNDB §112). The second part is a byname from OE *theof* 'thief'; OEB p. 375. Cf. 25,1 note. See 1,63 note. (JMcND)

24,23;25 THE RUBRICATED TRANSPOSITION SIGNS in the left margin beside these entries are probably intended to indicate that the virgate in Dowland 24,25 is part of the main manor there in 24,23, rather than a separate manor of Dowland. In Exon. the order of the entries is as in DB, but the scribe there makes it clear that the virgate is a sub-holding of the main manor of Dowland.

DOWLAND. A parish in (North) Tawton Hundred (12). In Fees p. 778 Henry *de Nuny* and his wife Matilda hold in *Dugheland'* from the Honour of Gloucester; see FA i pp. 370, 422 and OJR in TDA 29 p. 251. The church and ½ furlong ('ferling') were given to

Canonsleigh (24,15 note) by the second Walter of Claville, see Oliver *Mon.* p. 224 ff. and Canonsleigh Cartulary no. 12 p. 2.

24,23 ALWARD MART. Exon. *Auuard' merta*; see PNDB §64 on the loss of the *l* in *Auuard'* and see OEB p. 323 on Mart being 'a short, stumpy person'. See also 24,28 note on his naming one of the 'Nymets'.

24,24 LOOSEDON. In Winkleigh parish, (North) Tawton Hundred (12). Another part was held by Gotshelm (25,6) in 1086 and it is possible that the two lands were combined under the same later lord, or that one of the 'Loosedons' descended with Winkleigh (1,64) which also went to the Honour of Gloucester. In Fees p. 778 Roger *Cole* holds ½ fee and 1/8th fee in *Lullardeston'* from the Honour of Gloucester; see FA i p. 423 and OJR in TDA 29 p. 251.
BRICTRIC. Most probably Brictric son of Algar, on whom see 24,21 note.

24,25 IN DOWLAND 1 VIRGATE OF LAND. See notes to 24,23 and 24,23;25. According to the T.O. entry this land was added to Loosedon after 1066; see Exon. Notes to 24,24 and 24,25. It may be that Walter 'acquired' the main manor of Dowland (24,23) by the well-known expedient of having part of it attached to a manor which had fallen to him with other of the 1066 holder's lands (in this case Brictric's manor of Loosedon); cf. 15,31 note. However, it is just possible that Brictric did in fact hold the main manor of Dowland in 1066, because Alward Mart, the TRE tenant given there (though said to have been free), held Loosedon from Brictric according to Exon.
1 VIRGATE .... IT PAID TAX FOR AS MUCH. Elsewhere in Devon when the hidage of a holding is given, the tax is not mentioned (e.g. in 24,22), as it is generally thought to be the same in Devon; see 1,4 note on the hide. See also 34,32 note and Exon. Notes 34,11.
TWO THANES. One of them may have been Alward Mart who had held the main manor of Dowland in 1066 and was a thane (see 52,30).

24,26 INSTOW. In the MS the first letter resembles a capital *I*, rather than the *L* Farley prints (cf. the *I* of *IWESLEI*, 24,22). See third note under 16,115 and fourth note under 34,14. It is called *Iohannestou* from the dedication of the church to St. John the Baptist; see EPNS i p. 117. Though it certainly lay in Fremington Hundred (5), it is entered in the order of Exon. among Tawton places (see Chs. 24–25 note), having perhaps been missed when the Fremington Hundred lands of Gotshelm (25,3-4) were being entered earlier. In Fees p. 779 John *de Sancto Johanne* holds *Jonestowe* from the Honour of Gloucester; see FA i pp. 371, 413 and OJR H8 p. 514. See 42,6 last note.
A PRIEST. This is the only occurrence in Devon of a priest being listed with the 'villagers' rather than as holding a separate piece of land.

24,27 CHETELESCOTE. Identified by OJR as Gillscott in Coldridge parish, (North) Tawton Hundred (12); see TDA 29 p. 251, 36 p. 356 and VCH p. 496 note 10. But although *Chetelescote* is clearly named from Ketel the TRE holder, Gillscott has a different origin; see EPNS i p. 85, ii p. 365.

24,28 WALTER HOLDS. Repeated at the beginning of 24,28-31 inclusive. This formula implies that Walter of Claville held these four manors himself, but Exon. states that he had subtenants, also called Walter, for 24,28-29;31 (called Walter the Wild for 24,31). This subtenant Walter may be the Walter 'the man of Walter of Claville' whom the Tax Return for Tawton Hundred (ix) states collected the King's tax on 1 hide (*accepit Gildum regis*) but 12d remained from this 1 hide which the King had not had. Unless the Exchequer scribe had received contrary information, it is likely that he was confused by the subtenants here in Exon. having the same name as the tenant-in-chief. Cf. notes to 34,14. 47,2 and 48,8.
WOLFIN. DB *Nymet*, named like 25,8-9 from the river 'Nymet' now the Yeo (see Introductory Note 2). This particular holding lay in Down St. Mary parish, (North) Tawton Hundred (12). The TRE holder, Alward Mart, seems to have given his name to the place which is called *Merdesnymeth'* in Fees p. 778 held with *Bradeford'* [Bradiford GR SS 7306 in the same parish] of the Honour of Gloucester by Walter *le Lou*. Walter's byname is derived from Latin *lupus* 'wolf', OFr *le lou, le leu*, and he named this place *Wolvysnymet* (in 1359, see EPNS ii p. 368). It is *Wellek Nymet* in FA i p. 370 held with *Bradeford*. *Wolvesnymet* is held by Richard Wolf in Cal. Inq. PM vol. xiii no. 153; see Cal. Inq. PM vol. x no. 412 and OJR in TDA 36 pp. 356-357.

24,29 SHOBROOKE. Now in Morchard Bishop parish, Crediton Hundred (13), but like Wolfin (24,28) and Morchard Bishop itself (1,68) it appears to have been in (North) Tawton Hundred (12) in 1086; see EPNS ii p. 409 and OJR in TDA 29 p. 252.
VILLAGERS .... HAVE THESE (PLOUGHS) THERE. *Has habent ibi....*, a regular

formula, the *has* referring to the *ii carucas* in the preceding sentence. However, the addition of the lordship land from Exon. breaks the syntax of DB, hence the need for the bracketed ploughs. Cf. 'another (plough)' in 3,52.

24,30   BURLESCOMBE. Much of the parish is in Halberton Hundred (10), but Burlescombe itself is a tithing of Bampton Hundred (see the Appendix). This holding can be accounted for in the Tax Return for Bampton (xxii), where Walter is allowed 3 virgates less ½ furlong *(fertinum)* of lordship; this seems to be made up of the 2 virgates 1 furlong *(ferdinum)* lordship of Burlescombe together with the unspecified lordship of *Ciclet* (24,31). In Fees p. 780 William *de Clavil'* holds in *Bordlescumb', Sureapeldor'* [Appledore 24,14] and in *Behille* [Boehill 24,11-12]; see RH i pp. 64a, 94a, FA i p. 431, Cal. Inq. PM vol. iii no. 371, v no. 538, ix nos. 326, 428, xvi no. 538 and OJR in TDA 30 pp. 439, 444.

The Church of *Burwoldescumbe* with ½ virgate at *Byestebrok* [Eastbrook GR ST 0817]; EPNS ii p. 548] and 1 virgate in *Rukeknolle* [Rocknell ST 0516] was granted to Canonsleigh (see 24,15 note) by the second Walter of Claville; see Oliver *Mon*. p. 224 ff., Canonsleigh Cartulary no. 12 p. 2.

24,31   CICLET. Unidentified, but apparently in Bampton Hundred (8) in 1086 from the evidence of the Tax Return (see 24,30 note) and Exon. order.

24,32   THERE IS A GAP of 1 line before this entry in the MS and the *W* of *Walter'* is large and ornate, like the *W* of *Walterius* in 24,1 and 24,22 and other *W*s at the beginning of chapters. The scribe probably thought it important to draw attention to the joint tenure of Walter and Gotshelm in 24,32, linking, as it were, the fiefs of the two men. It is noteworthy that he adds the phrase *de rege* 'from the King', treatment usually reserved for the first entry or two in a chapter (cf. 25,28 note). The fact that after writing 24,31 the scribe had to turn back several folios in Exon. to where this entry is described, may have been a contributory factor in causing the gap, as seems to have been the case for the space between 24,21 and 24,22 (see note).

VIRWORTHY. DB *Fereordin*; see 19,2 note. It lies in Pancrasweek parish, (Black) Torrington Hundred (11), and appears in the fee lists associated with Stevenstone (40,2 note). It is wrongly identified by OJR H5 p. 201 as 'Farworthy an outlier of Sutcombe'.

Ch. 25   GOTSHELM. DB *Goscelmus*, Exon. *Goscelm(us), Gotselm(us), Goscem(us), Goselm(us)*, represent OFr *Goscelm*, OG *Gozhelm*. He was the brother of Walter of Claville (see Ch. 24) according to Finn in LE p. 79 and in MDeD p. 118; this would explain the intertwining of their manors in Exon. (see Exon. Note Chs. 24-25). As in the fiefs of William Cheever and his brother Ralph of Pomeroy (Chs. 19, 34; see Ch. 19 note), several manors in both Ch. 24 and Ch. 25 had been held by the same person before 1066; e.g. Brictric (son of Algar, see notes to 24,18-19 and to 25,20), Aelfeva (who may be the Aelfeva Thief of 24,22 and see 25,1 note), Alward (who was perhaps Alward Mart, Walter's subtenant in three manors), Wulfgeat (who had held the adjacent holdings of Appledore and Burlescombe in 24,14;30 and Fenacre in 25,12) and Alnoth (though this is a common name in DB and more than one person may be involved). Moreover, both Walter and Gotshelm hold part of Buckland Tout Saints (24,18 and 25,25) and Lupridge (24,20 and 25,26) and they hold Virworthy (24,32) together.
See 25,28 note on Gotshelm of Exeter.

Gotshelm's lands descend to the Honour of Gloucester; see Ch. 24 note.
FOR THE EXON. ORDER of this chapter, see Chs. 24-25 note.

25,1   VILLAVIN. DB *Fedaven*. Now in Roborough parish, Fremington Hundred (5), but it seems, like the nearby Barlington (3,15 note) and Owlacombe (36,7 note), to have been in Shebbear Hundred (4) in the Middle Ages. In Fees p. 779, in a group of Shebbear Hundred places, *Feldefen* is held of the Honour of Gloucester; see FA i pp. 359, 411, Cal. Inq. PM vol. vi no. 710 and OJR H10 pp. 544, 563.

EDLUFU THIEF. DB and Exon. *Edlouedief* represents OE *Eadlufu*, feminine, with byname OE *theof* 'thief'. See PNDB p. 245 and OEB p. 375. The Exon. entry immediately succeeds the one for DB 24,22 where the TRE tenant is Aelfeva Thief (see note); it may be that the two women were related (their holdings are only 5 miles apart and had passed to the brothers Walter and Gotshelm) with names in *Ead-l-* and with the same byname.

WALTER OF BURGUNDY. Exon. *Walter(us) borgundiensis* here, *Walter(us) borgoin* for 25,3-4; see OEB pp. 133, 127.

25,2   HUISH. A parish in Shebbear Hundred (4). The holding is probably represented by

| | |
|---|---|
| 25,2 (cont'd.) | *Lovelleston* [Lovistone GR SS 5410] held by Robert *Pollard'* of the Honour of Gloucester in Fees p. 779; see FA i pp. 359, 412, Cal. Inq. PM vol. ix no. 218 and OJR H10 pp. 544, 563.<br>ALWY. DB *Aluui* throughout Devon, Exon. *Aluius, Alueius, Aluuid(us)*, represent OE *Aelfwig* or *Aethelwig*; see PNDB pp. 157-158. The form *Aluuid(us)* has *-d* by phonetic substitution for *-t*, a graphic substitution for *-c*, a phonetic substitution for *-g*, in an original personal name *Alwig* (→ *Aluui*); see PNDB § 133. As with *Aluuardus* (see 1,41 note) safety indicates keeping to the base form; in previous volumes in this series the form *Alfwy* has been used. See 38,1 note.<br>IN LORDSHIP, AND THE WHOLE LAND. See 16,147 for another example of all the land in a manor being in lordship, and cf. notes to 3,12. 19,36 and 34,13. |
| 25,3 | NEWTON (TRACEY). A parish in Fremington Hundred (5). In Fees p. 779 Henry *de Tracy* holds in *Nywethon'* from the Honour of Gloucester; see FA i p. 371 and OJR H8 p. 513. It is possible that the neighbouring Gloucester Honour fee at *Heyscote* in FA i p. 413 [Hiscott GR SS 5426 in Tawstock parish, see EPNS i p. 121] was part of this holding; see 40,2 note. See also 42,6 last note.<br>COLSWEIN .... COMMON PASTURE. The nearest holding of the Bishop of Coutances is Horwood (3,17).<br>HAS TAKEN AWAY. *Aufert*, present, both in Exon. and in DB, meaning 'is taking away', instead of the more usual perfect *abstulit* 'has taken away' (e.g. in 16,92). The present tense was probably influenced by the scribe's thought that Colswein was at that moment in illegal possession of the common pasture. |
| 25,4 | DODSCOTT. In St. Giles in the Wood parish, Fremington Hundred (5), named from the 1066 holder Doda. In Fees p. 779 *Duddecoth'* is held from the Honour of Gloucester by Simon *de Bosco* and in FA i p. 371 by the heirs of Henry *de Tracy*; see OJR H8 p. 513. Another portion of Dodscott was held of the Honour of Torrington, see 42,6 note. |
| 25,5 | RIDDLECOMBE. In Ashreigney parish, (North) Tawton Hundred (12). In Fees p. 778 Richard *de Lumene* (on whom see 25,16 note) holds in *Ridelcumb'* and *Northecot'* [Northcott GR SS 5914]; see FA i p. 423, Cal. Inq. PM vol. vi no. 540, viii no. 176, ix no. 103, x no. 238 and OJR in TDA 29 p. 252. |
| 25,6 | LOOSEDON. In Winkleigh parish, (North) Tawton Hundred (12); see 24,24 note. |
| 25,7 | BRUSHFORD. A parish in (North) Tawton Hundred (12). It is coupled in feudal documents with Woodbeare (25,13) and Ash Thomas (25,20) and included 'Titterton' (1,64 first note); see OJR in TDA 29 p. 252 and 25,13 note.<br>?HALEWISE. DB *Alous*, Exon. *Aloiss*; see 17,92 note under ?Heloise. |
| 25,8-9 | HAMPSON. (NICHOLS) NYMET. DB *Nimet*; see 24,28 note and Introductory Note 2. These two places lie in Nymet Tracey (*alias* Bow) parish and in North Tawton parish respectively, both in (North) Tawton Hundred (12). Hermer's holding, the smaller, appears to have been at Hampson, named after him (EPNS ii p. 360). In FA i p. 370 the heirs of Walter *de Wasshborn* (from Washbourne 25,24, also held in 1086 by Hermer) hold in *Hermaneston* and *Assh*. These places occur as *Choldasshe* [unidentified] and *Hermeston* in FA i p. 422; see Cal. Inq. PM vol. ix no. 218.<br>The larger 'Nymet' will probably have been *Nymet Nicole* held by William *Lampre* in FA i p. 370; see FA i p. 422 and Cal. Inq. PM vol. ix no. 218. The same family held Fenacre (25,12) which was also a tenancy of Osmund in 1086. Simon *Lamperie* and John *Burnellus* also hold in *Notteston'* [Natson GR SS 7100 in Bow] in Fees p. 778, but this is probably the holding of Godwin in 1086 (see 52,9 note). On the identity of these 'Nymets' see OJR in TDA 29 pp. 252-253 and Barbara Carbonel in TDA 60 p. 301. |
| 25,8 | ½ FURLONG. In the MS a not very well written *ferling* is interlined in paler ink and with a thicker pen with the *f* (not a hair-line as Farley prints) extending down after the *dim̃* to show its position. |
| 25,10 | NEWTON. Presumably the place in Zeal Monachorum parish, (North) Tawton Hundred (12). Simon *Lamprey* (on whom see 25,8-9 note) sold some land here to the Abbot of Buckfast in 1225; see J. Brooking Rowe in TDA 8 p. 820, OJR in TDA 29 p. 253 and 47,4 note. |
| 25,11 | GOODCOTT. DB *Godevecote*, named from the TRE holder. It lies in Ashreigney parish, (North) Tawton Hundred (12); see EPNS ii p. 355 and OJR in TDA 30 p. 449. The indexer of Fees wrongly identifies it with the *Godwynescoth* of Fees p. 778; see OJR in TDA 30 p. 449 and 52,9 note. |
| 25,12 | FENACRE. It lies in Burlescombe tithing of Bampton Hundred (8), most of Burlescombe parish being in Halberton Hundred (10). In Fees p. 780 Simon *Lamperee* |

25

| | |
|---|---|
| 25,12 (cont'd.) | (on whom see 25,8-9 note) holds in *Fenacre* of the Honour of Gloucester; see FA i p. 431 and OJR in TDA 30 pp. 439, 445. |
| | PASTURE, 5 ACRES. .... In the MS the rest of the line is left blank (space for some 12 letters) after *pasture*, which has no dot after it. Exon. includes underwood among the resources (in its usual place before the meadow and pasture) and there is no obvious reason why the Exchequer scribe should have omitted it, unless perhaps he wanted to check it. See 11,1 note and cf. notes to 3,44 and 20,14. |
| 25,13 | WOODBEARE. In Plymtree parish, Hayridge Hundred (15). In Fees p. 779 William *de Wodebere* holds in *Wodebere, Esse* [Ash Thomas 25,20] and in *Brigeford'* [Brushford 25,7] from the Honour of Gloucester. In FA i p. 368 Juliana *de Wodebur[y]* holds in "*Wodebur[y], Tare* [unidentified] and *Esse* in Halberton Hundred, *Toyterton* in (North) Tawton Hundred ['Titterton' GR SS 6605 in Coldridge, EPNS ii p. 365; no doubt part of Brushford 25,7] and *Britteford* in the Hundred of Winkleigh [Brushford 25,7]"; see FA i pp. 322, 425, Cal. Inq. PM vol. ix no. 218 and OJR in TDA 42 p. 240. |
| 25,14 | GOTSHELM HIMSELF HOLDS. Repeated at the beginning of 25,14-18 inclusive. |
| | AWLISCOMBE. A parish in Hemyock Hundred (16); see 19,25-26 notes. This particular holding seems to have been at *Marlecumb'* [Marlcombe GR ST 1103], held by William *de Colehegh'* from the Honour of Gloucester in Fees p. 780. It passed to Dunkeswell Abbey being known then as *Colehey* [Colhays ST 1299], FA i p. 338. Another part was *Wolveston* [Wolverstone in Awliscombe, ST 1204], Cal. Inq. PM vol. ix no. 218. See FA i pp. 367, 430, OJR in TDA 36 p. 362 and H2 pp. 36, 43 and 25,16;21 notes. |
| 25,15 | GITTISHAM. A parish in (East) Budleigh Hundred (14). In Fees p. 762 (Budleigh Hundred) Richard *de Lumene* holds in *Giddesham* from Ralph *de Wylingthon'* and he from the Honour of Gloucester; see RH i pp. 66b, 92b, FA i p. 426, Cal. Inq. PM vol. vii no. 26 and OJR in TDA 35 p. 285. It is possible that a part of this holding was at Rapshays, *Rapelyngheyes* in Cal. Inq. PM vol. ix no. 218 (of Henry *de Wylyngton*); see 19,31 and 34,32 notes. |
| 25,16-22 | PLACES IN Tiverton and Halberton Hundreds (9-10); see 24,8-16 note. |
| 25,16 | UPLOWMAN. DB *Lonmine*, a settlement named from the river Lowman. Although DB seems to distinguish this 'Lowman' held by Gotshelm himself in 1086 from *Oplomie* [Uplowman 25,19] held by Aelmer the priest, the present land appears to have been part of Uplowman. In Fees p. 780 Richard *de Lomene* holds in *Lumene* and *Whytenech'* [Whitnage 25,22] from the Honour of Gloucester. This same land is *Lumene Ricardi* in FA i p. 318 in Tiverton Hundred, but *Uplomene, Beden* [unidentified], *Manelegh* [East Manley 25,21] and *Marlcomb* [Marlcombe, 25,14 note] in FA i p. 370, and *Uplomene, Wytenishe* and *Manalegh* in FA i p. 433. It will be noted that *Lonmine*, Manley, Marlcombe and Whitnage are all held by Gotshelm himself in 1086, and have the same manorial descent. Since 'Lowman' is later replaced by Uplowman in this group, it is likely that DB *Lonmine* is in fact Uplowman; this is more likely than that DB *Oplomie* (25,19) held by Aelmer in 1086 came to descend with lands held by Gotshelm in chief. The forms given by EPNS (ii p. 552) fluctuate between *Lomene, Lumene* and *Uplomene*. Uplowman is generally counted as a parish in Halberton Hundred (10), but was a medieval tithing in Tiverton Hundred (9). OJR in VCH p. 499 note 3 identified Chieflowman but that appears to have been a part of the royal manor of Halberton (1,70 note); see OJR H1 p. 27. |
| 25,17 | COOMBE. Presumably the Coombe in Uplowman parish, locally in Halberton Hundred (10) but a tithing of Tiverton (9); see OJR H1 p. 25 and 24,9-10 note. |
| 25,18 | LOTELANDE. An unidentified place, presumably in Tiverton Hundred (9) according to Exon. order; see OJR H1 p. 8. |
| 25,19 | UPLOWMAN. DB *Oplomie*. See 25,16 note. If the identification there proposed is correct, this holding does not appear in later fee lists; see OJR H1 p. 25. |
| 25,20 | ASH (THOMAS). DB *DISA*; in Exon. probably *Aisa*, though the first letter is oddly shaped: Ǫ, neither like the ᴆ of *Aiseforda* in 395 a 3 (DB 24,13) nor like a *D* which is invariably less round and has no central cross-line. The Exon. scribe seems to have begun with a capital *O* and then added the hooks at the top and bottom and the line in the middle, intending it as a capital *A*. The Exchequer scribe, however, read it as a *D*, as did Ralph Barnes. Cf. notes to 16,27. 16,44 and 52,20 and Exon. Notes to 19,33. |
| | Ash Thomas is in Halberton parish and Hundred (10). It is held with Woodbeare (25,13) in Fees p. 779 and later; see 25,13 note and OJR H2 p. 58. |
| | THIS LAND .... ADDED TO BRICTRIC'S LANDS. Probably Brictric son of Algar. See 15,31 note on this method of obtaining lands by attaching them to a fief which |

|   |   |
|---|---|
| | has been legally transferred. In the T.O. for 25,25 (see Exon. Notes) the land there is said to have been added 'wrongfully' (*iniuste*) to Brictric's lands and note the statement here that the TRE holder was 'free', as also in the similar statement in 25,25 and cf. 25,27. Gotshelm's brother also acquired lands in this way; see 24,18–19 note. |
| 25,21 | (EAST) MANLEY. In the MS and Farley *MAENELEGE*; in the facsimile the first *E* resembles a *G* because of the rubrication. See 1,63 note. East Manley is in Halberton parish and Hundred (10); for West Manley, see 46,1. In Fees p. 780 William *de Manelegh'* holds in *Manelegh'*. It is similarly *Manelegh* coupled with *Colehaye* [Colhays, see 25,14 note] in FA i p. 338 and is associated with Uplowman and Marlcombe in FA i p. 370; see OJR in TDA 36 p. 362, H2 p. 57 and 25,16 note. |
| | AND ½ VIRGATE OF LAND. Interlined in rather paler ink than the rest of the entry. It is not marked for erasure as VCH p. 499 note 7 states; the abbreviation sign over the *T* of *T̃ra* (which Farley omits) has become part of the *i* of *dim̄*, and this and the top stroke of the *T* and the abbreviation line over the *e* in the same phrase may have misled Reichel. It may have been added when a check was made of Exon. where it is perfectly clear. |
| 25,22 | WHITNAGE. In Uplowman parish, Halberton Hundred (10). It was a tithing of that Hundred in the Middle Ages, while most of the parish was in Tiverton Hundred (9); see LSR (1332) p. 40, FA i p. 383 and the Appendix. For the descent see OJR H2 p. 58 and 25,16 note. |
| 25,23 | FARWAY. A parish in Colyton Hundred (22), held by Ludo in 1086. In Fees p. 779 Reginald *de Mohun* (cf. 23,13 note) holds in *Fareweye* from the Honour of Gloucester; see FA i pp. 330, 366, 428, Cal. Inq. PM vol. ii no. 306, xv no. 967, xvi no. 673 and OJR H7 p. 353. |
| 25,24 | WASHBOURNE. In Halwell parish, Coleridge Hundred (30); see 1,34 note and OJR in TDA 43 p. 219. |
| 25,25 | BUCKLAND (TOUT SAINTS). A parish in Coleridge Hundred (30). In Fees p. 780 William *de Tuz Seynts* holds in *Bocland'*. The same man holds Lupridge (25,26); see FA i pp. 332, 393, OJR in TDA 43 p. 224 and 24,18 note. |
| 25,26 | LUPRIDGE. Now in North Huish parish, Stanborough Hundred (28), but it probably lay in *Alleriga* (Ermington) Hundred (27) in 1086 as it did later in the Middle Ages; see 15,27 and 24,20 notes. In Fees p. 780 William *de Tuz Seynts* (who holds Buckland Tout Saints 25,25) holds in *Loperig'*; see Fees p. 769, FA i pp. 351, 397 and OJR H6 p. 309. |
| | SNOTTA. DB *Snode*, Exon. *Estnota*; see PNDB p. 368. |
| | WOODLAND, AS MUCH. In the MS *siluę* appears to have been added: it is compressed and written at an angle and is blurred and in slightly paler ink, as if it were written over an erasure. It is perhaps interesting that in Exon. it is not woodland, but underwood (*nemusculus*), which in DB is normally *silua minuta* and for which there would have been even less room. Cf. Exon. Notes 1,27. |
| 25,27 | VLESTANECOTE. Standing for OE *Wulfstānescote* 'Wulfstan's *cote*'. Unless this is a late entry of land whose Hundred has been included earlier, this place, named from the TRE holder, ought to lie in Roborough or Plympton Hundreds (25-26). Evidence is lacking however; DG's Woolston Green in Staverton (Haytor) Hundred, is out of sequence and has no evidence to connect it with Gotshelm or the Honour of Gloucester. OJR in TDA 36 p. 362 and H2 p. 36 identifies Wolverstone in Awliscombe, the *Ulverston* of FA i p. 338. But Wolverstone is not derived from the personal name *Wulfstan* but from *Wulf* (EPNS ii p. 609) – although this may be a short-form for *Wulfstan* – and it appears to have been part of Marlcombe or of Colhays (25,14 note). The problem needs further study. |
| 25,28 | GOTSHELM OF EXETER. It is possible that he is a different person to the Gotshelm of the rest of Ch. 25. The inclusion of the phrase *de rege* 'from the King' may indicate this: it is normally reserved for the first entry or so in a chapter, though there are exceptions (cf. 24,32). In Exon. his holding is separate from those of Walter of Claville and his brother Gotshelm; however, as the entry is the only one on the folio, details of it may have been late coming in and hence were separated from the rest. See Exon. Notes. In the DB MS there is a slightly larger gap between this entry and 25,27 than is normal between entries, but not as large as between 24,21 and 24,22 and between 24,31 and 24,32 (see notes). See next note for the possibility that Gotshelm was one of the canons of Exeter. |
| | HERSTANHAIA. Perhaps representing the OE personal name *Heorstan* and *(ge)hāeg*, or from *hierra Stanhaia* 'Higher Stanhay', though this would imply the existence of a *nidera* |

| | |
|---|---|
| 25,28 (cont'd.) | *Stanhaia* 'Lower Stanhay' and no places of this or similar name have been found in the expected locality. The land seems to have lain in Cliston Hundred. The Tax Return for Cliston Hundred (xii) states that *Gotselin(us)* the Canon had ½ hide of lordship land there. *Gotselinus* usually represents OG *Gautselin* 'Jocelyn' (see 16,148 first note), but it is likely that *Gotselinus* is a scribal error for *Goscelmus*: the same scribe as wrote this Tax Return also wrote parts of the Exon. section corresponding to DB Chs. 24–25 where he used the form *Gotselm(us)* for 'Gotshelm' (see Ch. 25 note), so a mere mistake in the joining up of the minims (i.e. *m* became *in*) would account for the apparent change in name. (It is less likely that both the main Exon. and DB made a mistake in the man's name.) There is no obvious holding in DB of a Gotshelm (or of a Jocelyn) in this Hundred and of the unidentified places held by either the only candidate in terms of size is this entry; unfortunately Exon. does not clinch the matter by giving the lordship land here. Gotshelm might thus be one of the canons of Exeter Cathedral.<br>Identifications such as 'Cliston Hayes' (Pole p. 172, followed by OJR in VCH p. 501 note 7 and H7 p. 383) and Blue Hayes (DG) appear to be conjectures. Since this entry in Exon. might appear to represent a different fief or be the land of Gotshelm in a different county, it has been thought (by Whale in TDA 37 pp. 249–250) that the place might be in Dorset, there being a *Herstanesheia*, now Hursey in Burstock parish, Whitchurch Canonicorum Hundred (see A. Fägersten *The Place-Names of Dorset*, Uppsala 1933, reprinted East Ardsley 1978, p. 284). But Dorset lands in the surviving portion of Exon. form a single block and are not intermingled with those of Devon, Cornwall and Somerset.<br>6 VILLAGERS HAVE THEM THERE. The *has* probably refers to the 3 ploughs, as it usually does; see 1,29 note. However, Exon. states that the villager had the 1½ hides as well as the 3 ploughs, so it is possible that here the *has* refers to the 1½ hides in the tax statement. Cf. 24,11 note and DB Dorset General Notes 3,14 and 13,7.<br>IT PAYS 20s. See 2,2 note on 'Value' for DB's *reddit* perhaps indicating that a manor was being 'farmed' (in this case by the villagers; see Exon. Notes here). |
| Ch. 26 | RICHARD SON OF COUNT GILBERT. The elder son of Count Gilbert of Brionne (département Eure, France) and brother of Baldwin the Sheriff (Ch. 16); Orderic Vitalis ii p. 122. He also held land in DB Kent, Wilts., Cambs., Beds. etc. and his wife Rohais held in DB Herts. and Hunts. He was also called Richard of Tonbridge (Kent Ch. 11).<br>FOR THE EXON. ORDER of this chapter, see Ch. 22 note. |
| 26,1 | LYMPSTONE. A parish in (East) Budleigh Hundred (14). In later times it was a serjeanty, held in Fees p. 764 as *Leveneston'* by Reginald *de Albamara* from Muriel *de Bollay*; see RH i p. 66b, FA i p. 325, Cal. Inq. PM vol. vi no. 271, vii no. 672 and OJR in TDA 35 p. 299. Part of the manor lay at *Southedon* [Sowden GR SX 9983], Cal. Inq. PM vol. vi no. 753.<br>VALUE NOW, IT PAYS. In the MS *redd* 'pays' is interlined above *uat* with the *r* extending down before *uat* to act as an omission sign (Farley prints a separate hair-line, as he does on several occasions, e.g. 25,8); *uat* is not underlined for deletion. The colour of the ink is the same, so it does not appear to be a later correction. There are two possible explanations for the double verb. Firstly, the DB scribe may have re-read the Exon. entry which has the villagers etc. paying (*reddunt*) William £8 in revenue, and half-heartedly 'corrected' his version, omitting to delete the superfluous *uat*. This would imply a difference in meaning between *reddit* and *valet* which their use elsewhere in DB and Exon. does not seem to support; see 2,2 note. Secondly, the Exchequer scribe may have interlined the *redd* in the wrong place: in 26,1 instead of in the similar value statement in 28,1 which lacks a verb, although there is plenty of room for one. |
| Ch. 27 | ROGER OF BULLY. DB *de Busli*, Exon. *de Busleio*, is perhaps Bully-en-Brai in the département of Seine-Maritime, France; see OEB p. 78. His main holdings, which were considerable, were in the north.<br>FOR THE EXON. ORDER of this chapter, see Ch. 22 note. |
| 27,1 | SAMPFORD (PEVERELL). Now a parish in Halberton Hundred (10), but in 1086 it seems to have been divided between Tiverton and Halberton Hundreds (9–10) since in the Tax Return for Halberton (xvii) ½ hide lordship (only part of the 1½ hides ½ furlong (*fertinum*) lordship of this holding) is recorded for Roger of Bully, while the Tax Return for Tiverton (xi) states that the King had no tax on the 1 hide held by Roger (this would be part of the villagers' 2 hides less ½ furlong (*fertinum*), which was taxable).<br>Roger's land passed to the Peverel family, Hugh *Peverel* holding *Sanford, Haur* [Aller 32,3] and *Carswill* [Kerswell 32,2] in Fees p. 96; see Fees p. 782, RH i p. 71b, FA i p. 338, MC no. 9 p. 126, Cal. Inq. PM vol. iii no. 599, viii nos. 49, 363, ix no. 663, |

27 − 28

27,1 (cont'd.) OJR H2 p. 52 and 1,23 note. Sampford Peverell itself (so called to distinguish it from Sampford Arundel just over the border in Somerset) went to Kerswell Priory, a cell of Montacute, Oliver *Mon.* p. 312.
BRICTRIC. No doubt Brictric son of Algar (on whom see 24,21 note); see DB Glos. 1,37, Clifford Chambers, which had belonged to him and which Queen Matilda, his successor, also gave to Roger of Bully.
QUEEN MATILDA GAVE IT TO ROGER WITH HIS WIFE. Her name was Muriel: she and her husband were co-founders of the Benedictine Priory of Blythe (Notts.) in 1088; for the charter see British Library Harleian MS 3759 f. 106a (Mon. Ang. iv p. 623 no. 1). Muriel may have been the daughter of Eudo *Dapifer* ('the Steward') whose wife (also called Muriel) was King William's half-sister; Ellis DTY p. 143. See note above on Matilda's other gift to Roger.

Ch. 28 ROBERT OF AUMALE. DB *de Albemarle*, Exon. *de Albamarla, de Albamarula* (not plain *Alba Marula* as OEB p. 126 states). Aumale is in the département of Seine-Maritime, France; OEB pp. 66-67. The majority of Robert's lands form part of the large Honour of Plympton; see Ch. 21 note.
THE EXON. ORDER of this chapter, with the probable Hundreds, is:

| | | | |
|---|---|---|---|
| 28,2 | Lifton | 28,11 | *Alleriga* |
| 28,1;3-5 | Torrington | 28,12-14 | Diptford |
| 28,6 | Fremington | 28,15-16 | Walkhampton |
| 28,7-9 | Braunton | 28,17 | Borough of Barnstaple |
| 28,10 | Witheridge | | |

28,1 MILTON (DAMEREL). A parish in (Black) Torrington Hundred (11); the added name is from the 1086 holder or his descendants. The land can be identified in the Tax Return for Torrington Hundred (iii). In FA i p. 327 John *de Albemarle* holds *Middelton* from Isabella, Countess *Albemarlie* (of Devon), from the Honour of Plympton; see FA i p. 374, Cal. Inq. PM vol. x no. 240 and OJR H5 p. 215.
½ LEAGUE WIDE. In the MS *lata* with a line over the first *a*, not shown by Farley, left from an original, erased, word (probably *lg*).
[VALUE]. See 26,1 note.

28,2 OTTERY. In Lamerton parish, Lifton Hundred (18). DB *Odetrev* ('Odda's tree', EPNS i p. 186) is to be distinguished from the many places called 'Ottery' (DB *Otri* etc.) from the river Otter. The two Ottery manors (see Exon. Notes) together with Collacombe and Willestrew can be identified in the Tax Return for Lifton Hundred (i), accounting for the ½ virgate lordship of Robert of Aumale there. Ottery is held in Fees p. 757 by the Abbot of Tavistock (see Ch. 5 and 5,3 notes) as *Oddetrewe*, a gift of the predecessors of Ralph *de Alba Mara* (Honour of Plympton); see OJR in TDA 46 p. 219. The customary dues of *Oddetriwe* had already been granted to Tavistock by Queen Matilda, see *Regesta* ii p. 29 no. 632.
COLLACOMBE AND WILLESTREW. Held in Fees p. 789 from the Honour of Plympton as *Collecumb'* and *Willestre'*; see FA i pp. 320, 355, 405 and Cal. Inq. PM vol. xiv no. 325.
THREE THANES. Oslac and Burgred and either a second Oslac or a second Burgred; see second note under Exon. Notes to this entry.
FOUR MANORS. That is, Collacombe, Willestrew and the two manors in Ottery which had been held by Burgred and Oslac; see the first two Exon. Notes to this entry.

28,3 (COOKBURY) WICK. DB *Wiche*. Lying in Cookbury parish, (Black) Torrington Hundred (11), the manor consisted of a number of members, given in Fees p. 788 as *Cukebyr'* [Cookbury GR SS 4005], *Stapeldon'* [Stapledon SS 3804], *Fagelefenne* [Vaglefield SS 3606], *Uppecoth'* [Upcott SS 3804] and *Halesdone* [Halsdon Barton SS 3805], all in Cookbury parish and all held by William *Avenel* from the Honour of Plympton; see FA i pp. 356, 407, OJR H5 pp. 204, 215 and 16,22 note.

28,4 THUBOROUGH. In Sutcombe parish, (Black) Torrington Hundred (11). From the Honour of Plympton in Fees p. 787, Ralph *de Alba Mara* holds in *Thefebergh'* and *Kystemeldon'* [Kismeldon in West Putford, GR SS 3416, EPNS i p. 161]; see FA i pp. 356, 407. Kismeldon is not adjacent to Thuborough and may either have been a detached part or a portion of another Honour of Plympton land, such as West Putford (35,9). See OJR H5 p. 215.

28,5 GIDCOTT. In Milton Damerel parish, (Black) Torrington Hundred (11). DB *Gildescote*, Exon. *Gildescota*, is probably an error by the Exon. scribe for *Giddescote*, i.e. Gydda's *cote*, EPNS i p. 153. It is held in Fees p. 788 of the Honour of Plympton as *Giddecoth'*; see FA i pp. 356, 407, Cal. Inq. PM vol. xvi no. 113 and OJR H5 p. 216.

28,6    WESTLEIGH. DB *Weslege*, a parish in Fremington Hundred (5); it can be identified in the Tax Return for Fremington Hundred (iv). Ralph *de Alba Mara* holds in *Westlegh'* in Fees p. 788 from the Honour of Plympton; see FA i pp. 371, 412 and OJR H8 p. 517.
28,7    GOODLEIGH. A parish in Braunton Hundred (1). In Fees p. 787 *Godelegh* is held from the Honour of Plympton by Roger *Giffard*, the Prioress of *Cantingthon'* [Cannington in Somerset] and the heir of William *Daubernun*; see Fees p. 400, FA i p. 415, HD p. 56, Cal. Inq. PM vol. ii nos. 306, 593, v no. 527, vii no. 297, xi no. 118 and OJR H8 p. 450.
28,8    MARWOOD. A parish in Braunton Hundred (1). The land was at Church Marwood, held as *Churimerwod* in Fees p. 787 from the Honour of Plympton by Henry *de Tracy* and the Prior of Pilton; see Fees p. 790, 414 and OJR H8 pp. 401, 452.
        TAX FOR 1 VIRGATE .... ½ VIRGATE .... ½ HIDE. It is possible that the '½ hide' of villagers' land in Exon. is a mistake for '½ virgate', although it is clearly written and the entry is neat. However, there are other examples of the lordship and villagers' land holding exceeding the taxed land; see 1,4 note on the hide.
28,9    WHITEFIELD. In Marwood parish, Braunton Hundred (1). It is held from the Honour of Plympton as *Whytefeld'* in Fees p. 787; see FA i p. 414 and OJR H8 p. 453.
28,10-11 BICKHAM. FLETE. They lie respectively in Oakford parish, Witheridge Hundred (7), and in Holbeton parish, Ermington Hundred (27), Flete being probably identifiable in the Tax Return for *Alleriga* (Ermington) Hundred (xxx). The places are coupled in Fees p. 770 (Ermington Hundred) where John *de Alba Mara* holds from Ralph of the same byname of the Honour of Plympton in *Flethe et in Bikecumb' et in Wardeslegh' quae sunt in Hundredo de Wyrig*; see Fees p. 789 and FA i pp. 352, 398. *Wardeslegh'* is thus clearly in Witheridge Hundred and is not likely to be Warleigh in Tamerton Foliot, Roborough Hundred (25), despite EPNS i p. 242. It might be a misspelling of *Warbeslegh'* i.e. Waspley (52,43) in Stoodleigh parish (EPNS ii p. 394 s.n. *Warbrightsleigh*). Flete is *Fluto Daumarll* in FA i p. 352; see EPNS i p. 276, Cal. Inq. PM vol. ii no. 789, viii no. 230, xiv no. 925 and OJR in TDA 30 p. 421 and H6 p. 314.
28,10   ROBERT OF 'HEREFORD'. Exon. *de Herrefort*; OEB p. 44 has 'of Hereford'. However, it is more likely that he is Robert of Harford (15,45), of which the DB form is *Hereford*, Exon. *Hereforda*. Cf. EPNS i p. 275. The spelling in the surname shows an early ME doubling of *r* after the short vowel, and unvoicing of the final *d*.
        TAX FOR 4 VIRGATES. In the MS *iii v* clearly corrected to *iiii* by the addition of a final *i* (under which can be seen the original dot after the *iii*), the reason for the scribe's not writing '1 hide'. It is very interesting that in Exon. *iii uirgis* has also been corrected to *iiii uirgis*. Cf. notes to 2,24. 3,68. 16,108 and 32,10. See also 31,1 note.
28,11   BRICTWOLD. In the MS *Brictualdes* with a badly formed *u* interlined at an angle over the *e*; the *e* has a deletion dot under it, which Farley fails to print. In Exon. the form is *Bristualdus*.
28,12   BEENLEIGH. DB *Beuleie*, Exon. *Benleia*; the Exchequer scribe merely misread the *n* as a *u*. As with the other examples quoted in 16,42 note, the Exon. form is correct, but could, at a distance or in poor light, be misread as the Exchequer scribe did.
        The place lies in Diptford parish, Stanborough Hundred (28), and is held from Ralph *de Alba Mara* of the Honour of Plympton as *Benlegh'* in Fees p. 766; see Fees p. 790. In FA i p. 324 it is coupled with *Lenercombe* (probably for *Levercombe* that is Larcombe in Diptford, GR SX 7457, EPNS i p. 301) and can thus be distinguished from Beenleigh in Harberton parish, Coleridge Hundred (30); see EPNS i p. 325, FA i pp. 350, 395, OJR in VCH p. 516 note 9 and in TDA 45 p. 190.
        ALWARD. DB and Exon. *Ailuuard(us)* for OE *Aethelweard*; see notes to 3,45 and 1,41.
        FOR ½ HIDE. Squeezed into the right margin of the MS, outside the side ruling; an early addition because it is in the same colour ink as the rest of the entry, though the pen looks thinner and the script is smaller.
28,13   WOODLEIGH. A parish in Stanborough Hundred (28). It is held as *Wodelegh'* by Ralph *de Alba Mara* of the Honour of Plympton in Fees p. 765; see Fees p. 790, FA i pp. 323, 351, 396 and OJR in TDA 45 p. 179.
        AELFRIC PIKE. Exon. *Alurix pic*; see OEB pp. 326-327.
        WOODLAND, 100 ACRES. Apparently added, half in the right margin of the MS, in the same smaller script with thinner pen as the tax in 28,12 and the plough estimate in 28,14 (see notes).
        A FISHERY. In Exon. the word *piscatoriã* spans two lines at the top of 421b, possibly the reason for its omission by the Exchequer scribe.
28,14   'HALSTOW'. DB *Haletrev*, Exon. *Haletrou*. In view of the preceding entry, it seems

| | |
|---|---|
| 28,14 (cont'd.) | natural to connect this place with the lost *Halestowe, Halstowe* in Woodleigh parish, the DB form being either a faulty transcription (cf. 28,12 note) or the representation of an earlier name, with OE *treow* 'tree', later replaced by OE *stow* 'place of resort or assembly; religious establishment'; see EPNS i p. 313 and OJR in TDA 45 p. 201.<br>1 VILLAGER WHO PAYS 30d. As only the past value of the manor is given, it would seem that the villager's payment here formed the present value. See 6,6 note on villagers 'farming' land.<br>LAND FOR 1 PLOUGH. Added outside the side ruling of the right margin of the MS; like the tax in 28,12 and the woodland in 28,13 it is written in the same colour ink as the rest of the entry, but with a slightly thinner pen. |
| 28,15-16 | STOKE. WIDEY. WHITLEIGH. These three places lie in Roborough Hundred (25). Stoke, now in Devonport, was formerly the parish of Stoke Damerel (EPNS i p. 240); Widey is in Eggbuckland parish and Whitleigh is in St. Budeaux. In Fees p. 789 Ralph *de Alba Mara* holds of the Honour of Plympton *Stokes, Whytelegh'* and *Wythy*; see FA i pp. 340-341, 354, 403, Cal. Inq. PM vol. xiv no. 325, OJR H3 pp. 103, 120 and 17,76 note. |
| 28,16 | WADILO. See 15,49 note on Wado.<br>IN LORDSHIP .... 3 SLAVES, WITH 1 VILLAGER HAVE ½ PLOUGH. Unless *hñt* (*habent*) is a mistake for *hñte* (*habente*, ablative after *cum*, 'having', referring only to the villager), then it would seem that, despite the two main verbs (*est* and *habent*) in the sentence, the slaves in this manor had a share in the ploughs. The Exon. may also be stating this; see Exon. Notes here and cf. those for 28,5. See 1,3 note on slaves generally. Cf. DB Wilts. 67,39 and note.<br>WOODLAND .... 4 FURLONGS. In the MS the first *i* of the *iiii* is blurred and appears to have been attacked with water; as Exon. has *iii* it is possible that (when a check was made against it) the DB scribe tried — not very successfully — to erase the first *i* to make *iii*. Farley prints *iiii*. |
| 28,17 | THEY PAY 4d. It is probable that the site of the 'destroyed' houses had some value. It is just possible, however, that *uastatas* here is being used more in the sense of *uasta* 'unoccupied'. See second note under C 3 and C 1 note on the rate of payment of customary dues for houses generally. |
| Ch. 29 | ROBERT BASTARD. DB *Bastard, Bastardus*, no Exon. surviving, from OFr *bastard* 'bastard'; OEB p. 373. He only held land in chief in Devon, but he seems to have been a tenant of William of Poilley; see 21,18 note. His estates continue in his family and form part of the Honour of Plympton (see Ch. 21 note).<br>THIS FIEF IS ABSENT from the Exon. Book, but its Hundred order in the Exchequer version appears to be regular: |

|  |  |  |  |
|---|---|---|---|
| 29,1 | Witheridge | 29,4-5 | *Alleriga* |
| 29,2-3 | Diptford | 29,6-10 | Walkhampton and Plympton |

| | |
|---|---|
| 29,1 | BACKSTONE. In Rackenford parish, Witheridge Hundred (7). *Baggestane* is a fee of Nicholas *le Bastard'*, Honour of Plympton, in Fees p. 759 in Witheridge Hundred; see Fees p. 787, FA i p. 343 and OJR in TDA 30 pp. 403, 421. |
| 29,2 | HAZARD. Now in Harberton parish, Coleridge Hundred (30), but it lay in Stanborough Hundred (28) in the Middle Ages. Nicholas *le Bastard'* holds in *Herewaldeshore* from the Honour of Plympton in Fees p. 765; see Fees p. 790, FA i pp. 350, 395 and OJR in TDA 45 p. 178.<br>1 VIRGATE OF LAND. In the MS *uirg⁺* is interlined above *v'* in the same colour ink and almost certainly by the same scribe, though the letters are smaller. See 29,8. 34,2;4 and 47,8 for other corrections of *v'* to *virg⁺*; *v⁺* is a standard abbreviation for *uirga(ta)* and the DB scribe uses it regularly in Devon without attempts at correction. |
| 29,3 | COMBE (ROYAL). In Churchstow parish, Stanborough Hundred (28). The additional name is derived not from a royal holding, but from William *Royel* who is stated to have held it in FA i p. 396. In Fees p. 766 *Cumb'* in Stanborough Hundred is held from Nicholas *Bastard'* who holds from the Honour of Plympton; it is *Cumb Ruel* in FA i p. 351, *Comb Regis* in FA i p. 396; see Fees p. 790, FA i p. 324 and OJR in TDA 45 p. 190. In Cal. Inq. PM vol. xii no. 143 it is described as *Combe Royel* within the manor of *Dodebrok* [Dodbrooke 52,53]. |
| 29,4 | DUNSTONE. With Blachford (29,5) this entry can be identified in the Tax Return for *Alleriga* (Ermington) Hundred (xxx). It is now part of Yealmpton parish, Plympton Hundred (26), and is not to be confused with Dunstone in Stockenham in Coleridge Hundred (30) with which it is identified by OJR in TDA 43 p. 199, DG and EPNS i p. 332. See LSR (1332) p. 97, (1334) p. 64 and 52,42 note. |

29,5 ROBERT HIMSELF HOLDS. Repeated at the beginning of 29,5-9 inclusive.
BLACHFORD. In Cornwood parish, Ermington Hundred (27); see 29,4 note. It is held as *Nythereblachesworth*' ['Nether' or 'Lower' Blachford] in Fees p. 771 in Ermington Hundred by Walter *Tremeneth'* from Nicholas *le Bastard'* of the Honour of Plympton; see Fees p. 789, FA i pp. 353, 399, OJR in TDA 36 p. 374 and H6 p. 325. 'Over' Blachford was held from Iudhael (17,66), but the separate settlement names have not survived.

29,6 EFFORD. In Eggbuckland parish, Roborough Hundred (25). It can be identified in the Tax Return for Walkhampton (Roborough) Hundred (xxix). In Fees p. 789 Nicholas *le Bastard'* holds in *Eppeford* from the Honour of Plympton; see FA i pp. 340, 403 and OJR H3 p. 120.

29,7 STONEHOUSE. In the MS and Farley *STANEHUS*; in the facsimile the *E* resembles a *B*, probably due to the rubrication; see 1,63 note. Stonehouse is in St. Andrew's parish, Plymouth, Roborough Hundred (25). It followed the same descent as Efford (29,6), being held with it in FA i p. 493; see Cal. Inq. PM vol. v no. 461, Oliver *Mon*. p. 130 and OJR H3 p. 121.
1 VILLAGER WHO PAYS 5s. See 6,6 note on villagers 'farming' land.

29,8 BICKFORD. In Plympton St. Mary parish, Plympton Hundred (26). It is identifiable in the Tax Return for Plympton Hundred (xxviii). In Fees p. 788 Ralph *de Bykeford'* holds an unnamed place, clearly this land, from the Honour of Plympton; William *de Bikeford* holds *Bikeford* from Baldwin *le Bastard* in FA i p. 334. See OJR H6 p. 284. For another part of Bickford, see 52,28.
1 VIRGATE. In the MS *v*ᵗ corrected immediately to *virg*ᵗ (see 29,2 note), but without the first ᵗ sign being erased; Farley omits this superfluous sign, as he often does (e.g. in 16,151. 34,2. 36,18. 47,8).

29,9 MEAVY. DB *Metwi*. A parish in Roborough Hundred (25). A number of DB places, later differentiated, share this same basic river name; see 17,79-82 note. This holding is to be identified with *Lovyeton'* [Lovaton in Meavy, GR SX 5466], held in Fees p. 789 by Ralph *de Cilterne* from the Honour of Plympton. It is held by Richard *de Meuwy* as *Loviaton* from Baldwin *le Bastard* in FA i p. 341 and is *Loveton Bastard* in FA i p. 354; see FA i p. 403 and OJR H3 pp. 104, 121.

29,10 LAND OF ST. PETER'S OF PLYMPTON. Unnamed, but lying in Plympton Hundred; see 1,17 notes.
THEY PAY 5s. That is, the villagers; presumably another example of villagers holding land for a money-rent (see 6,6 note).

Ch. 30 LAND OF RICHARD SON OF THOROLD. *Terra Ricardi filii Turoldi*. *Turoldi* is the genitive of *Turoldus* which represents ON *Thoraldr* (PNDB p. 390). However, in 30,1 and in the Landholders' List (col. 100a) the form is *Torulf* which represents ON *Thorolfr*, ODan *Thorulf* (PNDB p. 396), and in the T.O. for 30,4 the form is *filius Turulfi* (see Exon. Notes). What may have happened is that in the Exon. heading (corresponding to DB Ch. 30) for this section, (which has not survived), Richard's father was written *turol* which can represent either Thorold or Thorulf, and that the Exchequer scribe expanded it to *Turoldi* instead of to *Turolfi*. [In 30,1 the Exchequer scribe either expanded it correctly or *Torulf* was how the name was written in the Exon.] However, as the rubricated chapter headings in DB were done after the main text had been written, it is very odd that the rubricator did not take the form of the name given in 30,1 or in the Landholders' List (i.e. Thorulf); it seems unlikely that he would have returned to the Exon. MS merely for the heading. Thus it would seem that the form *Turoldi* is a mere scribal error for *Turolfi*. It is just possible, though, that the rubricator was correcting the name from Thorulf to Thorold as the result of some information received after the main text had been written. It is interesting that in the Tax Return for Kerswell Hundred (xxv) a Richard son of Thorold (*filius turoldi*) holds 1 hide in lordship which seems to refer to the holdings of Richard son of Thorulf in 30,1-2; likewise in the Tax Return for Diptford Hundred (xxvi) a Richard *filius turoldi* holds 1 hide in lordship which seems to refer to the holding in 30,3. The Exon. for 15,42 and 16,115 give DB's plain Richard the byname of *filius Torolui* 'son of Thorulf' (see OEB p. 201 s.n. *Torulf*). And the descent of the 15,42 holding is the same as for 30,1-2 (see second note under 15,42). But again, the Tax Return for Wonford Hundred (xxxi) states that the King has no tax from 1 virgate held by Richard son of Thorold (*filius turaldi*), which seems to refer to 16,115 (see note). Meanwhile, the Exon. for Cornwall 5,3,1 states that a Richard son of Thorulf (*filius Turolfi*) was a subtenant of the Count of Mortain, and for 2,5 that a Richard *filius*

| | |
|---|---|
| Ch. 30 (cont'd.) | *turol* was a subtenant of the Bishop of Exeter: this latter was translated 'son of Thorold' in DB Cornwall, but the *turol* could equally well represent 'Thorulf' (a study of the Exon. MS here has revealed the interesting fact that a 'tall' letter was erased after the *turol*, possibly a *d* or an *f*). There are no more occurrences of either Richard son of Thorold or Richard son of Thorulf in DB (OEB p. 202 mistakenly includes under Richard son of Thorold references to Glos. and Worcs. which in fact belong to Gilbert son of Thorold).<br>Later manorial history does not help with the problem of Richard's father's name. The holdings of Richard son of Thorulf in this chapter, together with his holding at St. Marychurch under the Count of Mortain (15,42, see note) and probably that at Martin under Baldwin the Sheriff (16,115; see OJR in TDA 44 p. 331) pass to the Honour of Cardinan (see Ch. 15 note). Meanwhile it is possible that the names Thorold and Thorulf might have fallen together in a common form *Thorol, Thorul* in the colloquial vernacular.<br>THIS CHAPTER has no corresponding entries in the surviving portion of the Exon. Book. Its Hundred order is:<br>30,1-2   Kerswell                           30,4      Borough of Exeter<br>30,3      Diptford |
| 30,1-2 | WOODHUISH. NATSWORTHY. Woodhuish is in Brixham parish, Natsworthy in Widecombe in the Moor, both in Haytor Hundred (29). Both are required to make up the Tax Return for Kerswell (Haytor) Hundred (xxv); see first note under Ch. 30. In Fees p. 796, held from the Honour of Cardinan, are *Wodhywisse, Reftercumb'* [Raddicombe in Brixham adjacent to Woodhuish, GR SX 9053; see EPNS ii p. 508] and *Nottesworth'*; see Fees pp. 767, 768, FA i pp. 316, 348, 391-392, Cal. Inq. PM vol. iii no. 401, iv no. 44, vi no. 710, vii no. 462, xii no. 333 and OJR in TDA 40 p. 111. |
| 30,3 | (EAST) ALLINGTON. A parish in Stanborough Hundred (28), although it was sometimes counted in Coleridge Hundred (30). This holding is required by the Tax Return for Diptford (Stanborough) Hundred (xxvi); see first note under Ch. 30. It is held as *Allyngthon'* in Fees p. 766 from the Barony of Cardinan, then as *Alinton'* in FA i p. 324 from the Earl of Cornwall; see Cal. Inq. PM vol. iv no. 44, vii no. 462, OJR in TDA 45 p. 194 and 17,53 note. |
| Ch. 31 | RALPH OF LIMESY. Ralph held much land in Somerset, Notts., Essex, Herts., Norfolk, Suffolk, Glos., Warwicks. and Northants. Three of his four manors in Devon pass to the Honour of Bradninch (see Ch. 19 note).<br>Limésy is in the département of Seine-Maritime, France.<br>FOR THE EXON. ORDER of this chapter, see Ch. 22 note. |
| 31,1-4 | THESE MANORS will between them more than account for the 1 hide ½ virgate lordship allowed to Ralph in the Tax Return for Braunton and Shirwell Hundred (vi). |
| 31,1-2 | (EAST) DOWN. BRADWELL. Both places lie in Braunton Hundred (1), the first being a parish, the second lying in West Down parish. In Fees p. 794 *Bradewill'* and *Dune* are fees of the Honour of *Odingeseles* (or *Doddynghele* in FA i p. 414), held respectively by Ralph *de Pinu* and Henry *de Dune*. Philip *de Doune* holds in *Estdoune* in FA i p. 360 (see FA i p. 414), while *Bradewill* is held in FA i p. 415 by William *Pyn* from the Honour of Bradninch (see Cal. Inq. PM vol. v no. 411 and OJR H8 pp. 402, 454). |
| 31,1 | 5 VIRGATES. It is interesting that Exon. also has '5 virgates', instead of 1 hide 1 virgate, for the tax. Cf. '4 virgates' in both Exon. and DB for 28,10 (see note). |
| 31,3-4 | ROADWAY. MORTEHOE. In Braunton Hundred (1), Roadway lying in Mortehoe parish. Roadway passes to the Honour of Bradninch, being held as *Radeweye* and *Settesbergh'* [Shaftsboro GR SS 4845] in Fees p. 792; see FA i p. 360. *Burgh'* [Borough SS 4844], the next entry in Fees, may well have been part of this holding. DB *Radehide* 'Red Hide' is presumably a corrupt form; EPNS i p. 53.<br>*Morteho* (Fees p. 771, FA i p. 415) passes to the Honour of Barnstaple; see Cal. Inq. PM vol. iv no. 710 and OJR H8 pp. 428, 449, 454. |
| 31,3 | VALUE 31*d*(?). In the MS a *i*, written in much darker ink and at an angle and extending down below the level of the *xxx*, appears to have been added to the *xxx*. Because of the slope of the *i* the original dot after *xxx* is still in the correct place for *xxxi*. There is a very pale ink blot over the last *x* and the *i*, but this looks as if it were there before the *i* was added. Exon. has *xxx* clearly. Farley prints *xxx*: he may have thought that the added *i* was part of the ink blot (perhaps the reason why the *i* is not reproduced in the facsimile — it was covered up at the same time as the blot). |
| Ch. 32 | RALPH PAGNELL. DB *Pagenel*, Exon. *paganus* for 32,1;3;6;8;10, *paganell(us)* for 32,2;5, but plain *Radulfus* for 32,4, *Idem Radulfus* for 32,7 and *Radulfus predictus* for |

| | |
|---|---|
| Ch. 32 (cont'd.) | 32,9. Although *paganellus* is a diminutive of *paganus*, which is usually translated 'Payne' in this series (see 16,155 note on Payne), both the Exon. byname forms refer to the same person (see OEB p. 223 and cf. DB Glos. 44,2 note). Ralph Pagnell's lands lay mainly in Lincs., but he also held in Yorkshire, Devon, Somerset, Glos. and Northants. With the exception of his manor at Edginswell (32,10), all Ralph's Devon lands lay within 15 miles of Exeter, although in seven Hundreds. Ralph was Sheriff of Yorkshire in 1088 and an enthusiastic supporter of William Rufus. See last note under 32,1 on his predecessor Merleswein.<br>Many of Ralph Pagnell's estates pass subsequently to the Honour of Plympton; see Ch. 21 note.<br>FOR THE EXON. ORDER of this chapter, see Ch. 22 note. |
| 32,1 | DUNCHIDEOCK. A parish in Exminster Hundred (24), perhaps identifiable in the Tax Return for that Hundred (xxiii). It is probably the *Donnsidiock* held by Plympton Priory in TE p. 153; see OJR in TDA 47 p. 213.<br>MERLESWEIN. He had been an important man in the reign of King Edward and was Sheriff of Lincs. at some stage during King William's reign (see *Regesta* i no. 8 of 1067), until he joined the Danes in 1069 in their attack on York (ASC 'D' s.a. 1068 [1069]). All Ralph Pagnell's lands in Devon, Somerset and Yorks. and almost all his others in Glos. and Lincs. had been held in 1066 by Merleswein (see the statement at the end of 32,10 here and the similar one at the end of Ralph's fief in DB Somerset Ch. 31). |
| 32,2 | KERSWELL. In Broadhembury parish, Hayridge Hundred (15). The land passes to the Peverel family, Hugh *Peverel* holding *Carswill* with *Haure* [Aller 32,3] and *Sanford* [Sampford Peverell 27,1] in Fees p. 96. Kerswell was granted to Montacute Priory by Matilda *Peverel* and became a cell of it; see MC nos. 141-142, 150 pp. 171-172, 177, Oliver *Mon.* p. 313 and OJR in TDA 42 pp. 226, 244.<br>GUNTER. DB *Gonther*, Exon. *Gonher(us)*; see PNDB p. 276 note 4. |
| 32,3 | RALPH HIMSELF HOLDS. Repeated at the beginning of 32,3-7 inclusive.<br>ALLER. In Cullompton parish, Hayridge Hundred (15), positively identifiable in the Tax Return for Silverton (Hayridge) Hundred (xiii). The descent is similar to Kerswell (32,2, see note), *Aure* being held with *Sanford'* [Sampford Peverell 27,1] in Fees p. 782; see Fees p. 96, RH i p. 70b, Cal. Inq. PM vol. viii no. 363, OJR in TDA 42 p. 245 and 16,103 note. It also went to Montacute Priory. Places called *Wytehethfeld* [Whiteheathfield Barton GR ST 0103] and *Frieland* [unidentified] lay within this manor; MC no. 148 p. 176, Cal. Inq. PM vol. ii no. 590. Bolealler [GR ST 0204] might have been part of this land, but (despite OJR in VCH p. 519 note 8) is not derived from 'Peverel's Aller'; see EPNS ii p. 562. |
| 32,4 | THROWLEIGH. A parish in Wonford Hundred (19). *Throulegh'* is held from the Honour of Plympton in Fees p. 788 by Fulk *de Ferers*; see RH i p. 85a, Cal. Inq. PM vol. i no. 564, FA i pp. 313, 345, 386 and OJR in TDA 44 p. 317. It is probably the land mentioned in a notification of King Canute to Burhwold, Bishop of St. German's, concerning an exchange of *Thrulea* for lands in Cornwall (ECDC p. 14 no. 53 = KCD no. 728 = Sawyer (1) no. 951). |
| 32,5 | CHAGFORD. A parish in Wonford Hundred (19); see OJR in TDA 44 pp. 298, 318.<br>WOODLAND .... MEADOW .... PASTURE. Details of these occupy exactly one line in Exon. and it would seem likely that in copying from there the Exchequer scribe skipped the line by mistake, his eye travelling from the 7 before the woodland to the 7 immediately below before the value. Cf. notes on the omission of woodland in 1,4. 3,81 and 16,164 and of meadow in 17,37 and of pasture in 16,42. |
| 32,6-7 | ILSINGTON. INGSDON. In Teignbridge Hundred (23), Ingsdon lying in Ilsington parish. Both are identifiable in the Tax Return for Teignton (Teignbridge) Hundred (xxiv). In Fees p. 790 the Earl of Devon holds *Aylekesdon'* [Ingsdon, EPNS ii p. 476] and Philip *de Bello Monte* holds *Ilstinthon'* from the Honour of Plympton; see RH i pp. 82a, 90a, TE p. 150a, FA i pp. 339, 347, 390, Cal. Inq. PM vol. i no. 564, iii no. 532, vii no. 462 and 43,5 note.<br>In later times there is a Plympton Honour one-third fee at *Holrig* [Horridge in Ilsington, GR SX 7674] in Teignbridge Hundred, held in Fees p. 790 by the heirs of David *de Holrig*, then (in FA i pp. 347, 390) by the Abbot of Torre; see Oliver *Mon.* p. 175 and TE p. 153a. It is not clear to which DB holding this belongs; it could have been a part of Ilsington 32,6 which is in Teignbridge Hundred, whereas other adjacent Plympton Honour places (Sigford (35,23) and Bagtor (48,7)) are in Wonford Hundred, as is another part of Horridge (19,29 note); see OJR in TDA 29 p. 240. |

| | |
|---|---|
| 32,6 | IN EXETER....10s. This statement is compressed and in paler ink. It is interesting that in Exon. the statement is interlined (though by the same scribe and at the same time as the rest of the entry), suggesting that the Exchequer scribe originally missed the interlineation and added it later. In Exon. there is a ; omission mark after the *xxii uill'* (not printed by Ellis) corresponding to one before the interlineation (cf. Exon. Notes 1,40), though usually in Exon. details of houses appear either in a separate section or, as in 2,4, with the resources. 10s as a payment for 1 house is far higher than normal, 8d being the usual customary due for a house in Exeter (see C 1 note above). Although there is no mention of this being a customary due, it is likely that it was, and possible that *sol'* is an error for *den'*, bringing the payment more into line with the others. However, see DB Herefords. 1,44 where a house in Worcs. paid 1 silver mark (13s 4d), whereas the normal rate there seems to have been 7½d (C 3). See VCH p. 397 for a different view of the 10s payment. |
| 32,8-9 | GERARD. Perhaps Gerard the tenant-in-chief of Ch. 46; see Ch. 46 note. |
| 32,8 | TIVERTON. In Tiverton Hundred (9). The only evidence for OJR's more precise identification with Little Tiverton *alias* West Exe (in TDA 29 p. 495, in VCH p. 520 note 12 and H1 pp. 9, 18) is that Robert *de Bykelege* who also held 'Little Washfield' (32,9) was holder in the 13th century; see Whale in TDA 33 p. 398. Tiverton itself went to the Honour of Plympton and this small manor was probably numbered among its several members; see 1,35 note. |
| 32,9 | '(LITTLE) WASHFIELD'. DB *Wasfelte*. Washfield parish is a triangular outlier of (West) Budleigh Hundred (14), closed on two sides by Tiverton Hundred (9) and on its northern edge by Witheridge (7). The main Washfield holding is land of Ralph of Pomeroy (34,39), but a part of Washfield, *Parva Wassefeld'* [an unlocated 'Little Washfield', presumably this holding], lay in Witheridge Hundred and appears to be the land held in socage in Fees p. 761 by Robert *de Bykelegh'* from the heirs of William *Brywerre* of the Honour of Plympton; see OJR in TDA 30 p. 408, 35 p. 313, 36 pp. 357-358, in VCH p. 521 note 1 and Whale in TDA 33 pp. 397-398. |
| 32,10 | EDGINSWELL. In Cockington parish, Haytor Hundred (29). *Welles* is held by Richard *Folioth'* from the Honour of Plympton in Fees p. 768; see Fees p. 790. Fulk *de Ferariis* (on whom see 32,4 note) holds *Wille Eggelf* in FA i p. 317; it is *Eggereswill* in FA i p. 349; see EPNS ii p. 511. |
| | TAX FOR 2 HIDES. In the MS *i hida* originally written, but corrected to *ii hid'* (the original dot can be seen under the added *i*); there are signs in the Exon. MS that there the hidage was originally *i* and corrected to *ii*. Cf. notes to 2,24. 3,68. 16,108 and 28,10. |
| Ch. 33 | RALPH DE FEUGERES. DB *de Felgheres, de Felgeres*, Exon. *de felgeriis* (but plain *Radulfus* for 33,2), may be surnamed from Feugères, département of Manche, France, as mentioned in OEB p. 88, a suggestion taken up by the late General Editor and followed in some volumes of the present series. A fuller reading of OEB pp. 88-89 would indicate the stronger likelihood of derivation from Fougères (département of Ille-et-Vilaine, France), the name adopted in the Norfolk volumes of the present series. The problem is that the old spellings would represent either place-name, but Tengvik's philological arguments for Fougères (OEB pp. 88-89, where the reference to Mawer should be p. 90), are strong. (JMcND.) The fact that part of Ipplepen went to the Canons of Fougères (33,1-2 note) may possibly support the derivation from Fougères; see 33,1-2 note. |
| | FOR THE EXON. ORDER of this chapter, see Ch. 22 note. |
| 33,1-2 | IPPLEPEN. GALMPTON. Ipplepen parish and Galmpton (in Churston Ferrers parish) are both in Haytor Hundred (29) and both can be identified in the Tax Return for Kerswell (Haytor) Hundred (xxv). After Ralph of Feugères (also known as Ralph *de Meulent* [of Meulan] ), the land continued with his heirs then was successively granted to Henry, son of Earl Reginald, to Nicholas *de Lestre* and to Amaric *de St. Armand*. Ralph *de Sancto Armando* holds *Ipelepenne* and *Gaumeton'* from the King in Fees p. 782; see Fees pp. 97, 612, 768, 1262, 1372, RH i pp. 72a, 89a, FA i pp. 317-318, 348, 391, Cal. Inq. PM vol. ii nos. 306, 436, 593, iii no. 415, vi no. 478, xi no. 300, xii no. 436, xv no. 581, OJR in TDA 40 p. 116, 50 p. 360 and 7,2 note. Part of Ipplepen went to the Canons of Fougères, Oliver *Mon.* p. 300. |
| | GODA. Probably Countess Goda who had held one of the two manors comprising Ralph's fiefs both in DB Bucks. and in Surrey. She was the sister of King Edward (DB Glos. 24,1) and the wife first of Count Drogo of Mantes and then the first wife of Count Eustace of Boulogne; she died *c.* 1056. |
| 33,1 | PASTURE, 10 ACRES. In the MS the remaining three-quarters of the line is blank |

33 - 34

after *pasture*, which surprisingly has no dot after it. The value of this manor is given at the end of 33,2 together with that manor's value. It is interesting that in Exon. the joint value of these manors is also given at the end of the entry for Galmpton, though in slightly different wording. Cf. 40,4 note on a similar gap left and also 11,1 note.

33,2   14 VILLAGERS. In the MS and Farley *xiiii uitti*; in the facsimile the *xii* at the beginning of the number are poorly reproduced and the figure resembles *xxiii*.

Ch. 34   RALPH OF POMEROY. DB *de Pomerei*, Exon. *de Pomaria, Pomeria*; see OEB p. 107 and Loyd pp. 78-79. Ralph also held land in chief in Somerset (DB Ch. 30). He was brother of William Cheever; see Ch. 19 note. See also 19,40 note on his sister Beatrix.

Several entries in Devon suggest that Ralph was a rapacious man: he had seized Ash (34,5) and the case went to court, he 'took possession of' Aunk and *Heppastebe* (34,34), he had appropriated Panson before exchanging it for three manors (34,54 note) and, like many of the noblemen, he withheld customary dues on houses in Exeter (34,58). It is interesting that his manor of Dunsdon (34,2) had lost a virgate to that other great land-thief, the Count of Mortain.

Ralph's estates later form the Honour of Berry, named from Berry Pomeroy (34,48); see VCH p. 561 and Sanders p. 106. Many of these lands are found in the Inq. PM of Henry *de la Pomeray*, Cal. Inq. PM vol. iv no. 296.

THE EXON. ORDER of this chapter is followed almost exactly by DB; the sequence of Hundreds is very similar to that of Ch. 19 (see note), the latter part of the order similarly being disrupted by late entries for Hundreds already included. The order is:

| 34,3;1 | Lifton | 34,44 | Teignton |
| 34,2;4-7 | Torrington | 34,45 | Tiverton |
| 34,8-9 | Fremington | 34,46 | Kerswell |
| 34,10-13 | Exminster | 34,47 | Tiverton |
| 34,14-17 | Shirwell | 34,48-49 | Kerswell |
| 34,18 | Cliston | 34,50-53 | Axminster |
| 34,19-22 | Silverton | 34,54 | Colyton |
| 34,23-26 | Hemyock | 34,55 | Chillington |
| 34,27-29 | Wonford | 34,56 | Wonford |
| 34,30-39 | Budleigh | 34,57 | Axminster |
| 34,40-42 | Witheridge | 34,58 | Borough of Exeter |
| 34,43 | Tiverton | | |

34,1   IN THE LEFT MARGIN of the MS beside this entry is written an *O* mark, not printed by Farley. It resembles other contemporary, checking signs in Devon (see notes to 1,65 and 10,1), but is the only one found beside a *Wiche* here.

SOUTHWEEK. DB *Wiche*. It lies in Germansweek parish, Lifton Hundred (18). In Fees p. 791 the heirs of Henry *le Deneys* hold in *Sudthwik*' from the Honour of Berry; see Fees pp. 399, 756, HD p. 56, FA i pp. 321, 355, Cal. Inq. PM vol. ii nos. 306, 593, v no. 527, vii no. 297, OJR in TDA 46 p. 189 and 16,8 note.

ALWARD. Alward here and in 34,8 is probably the son of Toki, who is Ralph's predecessor in 34,14 and Ralph's brother's predecessor several times in Ch. 19; see last note under Exon. Notes 19,35 and Ch. 19 note.

FORMERLY .... 50s. In the MS the *O* of *Olim* is oddly shaped: the scribe appears to have written *I* first (perhaps the first letter of *Ipse* for a new entry?).

34,2   DUNSDON. In Pancrasweek parish, (Black) Torrington Hundred (11). This holding seems to have included a number of places that lay in the later parish and which are named in Fees p. 791: *Pankardeswik*' (or *Wyke pranhard* in FA i p. 328) that is Pancrasweek GR SS 2905, see 34,6 note, *Decnesbere* [Dexbeer SS 2909], *Huttesdon*' [Hudson, also SS 2909] and *Heremannesworth*' [Hamsworthy SS 3108]. This last was probably held by the Bishop of Coutances in 1086 (3,10 note); see Fees pp. 396, 399, FA i pp. 328, 357, 407, Cal. Inq. PM vol. ii no. 306, v no. 527, xi nos. 118, 299 and OJR H5 pp. 232-233.

34,2;4   TAKEN AWAY 1 VIRGATE. ½ VIRGATE. In both cases $v^t$ has been changed to *virg* and *virga\** respectively (see 29,2 note). In the first the original *t* over the *v* has not been erased, but Farley does not print it (as also in 29,8; see note). There is no sign of the 1 virgate of 34,2 in the Count of Mortain's lands either in Devon or in Cornwall.

*virga instead of the usual Exchequer form *virgata* is no doubt the result of copying Exon. too closely; cf. 1,22 second note.

34,3   LYDFORD. DB *TIDEFORD*; Exon. *lidefort*. The *l* in the Exon. has a smudge running from the top towards the left, outside the side marginal ruling, which probably misled the Exchequer scribe into thinking it was a *T* (though without the right-hand part of the cross-bar). See 16,42 note for a list of other misreadings of Exon. by the Exchequer scribe.

|  |  |
|---|---|
|  | Lydford is a parish in Lifton Hundred (18); see 1,2 note for the Borough of Lydford. See OJR in TDA 36 p. 350. |
| 34,4 | *ALWINECLANCAVELE*. It clearly lay in a group of (Black) Torrington Hundred places (11), but is so far unidentified. There is no reason to agree with OJR's East Youlstone in Bradworthy (TDA 28 p. 465 note 5, 36 p. 351, H5 p. 235) even though one of the members of Bradworthy (34,6 note) may account for it. |
| 34,5 | ASH. In Bradworthy parish, (Black) Torrington Hundred (11). It is *Esse* in Fees p. 791 held of the Honour of Berry; see Fees p. 400 (52,31 note) and 34,6 note.<br>LEDMER. DB *Leimar*, Exon. *Letmarus*, represent OE *Leodmaer*; PNDB p. 310.<br>FRENCH AND ENGLISH TESTIFY. According to the ICC (see DB Cambs. Appendix) there were 4 French and 4 English jurors for each Hundred in the shire court. Cf. last note under 2,2 and 16,74 note. |
| 34,6 | BRADWORTHY. A parish in (Black) Torrington Hundred (11). The various members of this large manor, which seems to have included Ash (34,5) and West Putford (34,7), are given in Fees p. 791 (Honour of Berry) as: *Worthy* [Worden GR SS 3013, see EPNS i p. 135], *Putteford* [West Putford 34,7], *Atteworth* [Atworthy SS 3117], *Stane*, or *Stoneford* in FA i p. 358, [Stowford SS 2913], *Esse* [Ash 34,5], *Dune* [probably West Down SS 2914; OJR's *Berridon* (H5 p. 234) is not derived from the Honour of Berry but from OE *bearu*], *Lewenescoth'* [Lymscott SS 2912], *Brighteneswych'*, or *Brictenestworth[y]* in FA i p. 388, [Brexworthy SS 2813; see EPNS i p. 133], *Dunneworth'* [Dimworthy SS 3115] and *Braworth'* [Bradworthy]. All these lie in Bradworthy parish except for West Putford; see Fees p. 396, FA i pp. 326, 356, 358, 407, 409, Cal. Inq. PM vol. ii nos. 306, 593, v no. 527, OJR H5 pp. 232-234 and 19,3 note. A mill at *Bradeworthi* and the chapel of *Pankardeswike'* [Pancrasweek, see 34,2] were given to Torre Abbey; see Oliver *Mon*. p. 169, VE ii p. 361. See Exon. Notes 19,3 for the statement in the T.O. that Ralph and his brother added Instaple (19,3) to Bradworthy. |
| 34,7 | (WEST) PUTFORD. A parish in (Black) Torrington Hundred (11); East Putford lies in Shebbear Hundred (4). See 19,4 and 34,6 notes. This holding appears as *Puteford Henrici* in Fees p. 398. |
| 34,8 | HORWOOD. A parish in Fremington Hundred (5). The Honour of Berry lands lay at *Esthorewod'* [?East Barton GR SS 5127, EPNS i p. 115] and *Pinhorwod'* [Penhorwood SS 5028] held by Jocelyn *de Lancell'* in Fees p. 791 and at *Lovenescote* [Lovacott SS 5227 in Fremington] in FA i p. 371; see Fees p. 400, FA i pp. 412-413, Cal. Inq. PM vol. v no. 527, OJR H8 p. 511 and 3,17 note.<br>ALWARD. See 34,1 note. |
| 34,9 | (?GREAT) TORRINGTON. DB *Torilande*. There are two adjacent places called Torrington (see 1,31. 15,16 and 16,34 notes): Great Torrington lies in Fremington Hundred (5), Little Torrington in Shebbear Hundred (4). Little Torrington in 15,16 is separately specified in DB as *Liteltorelande*, but DB *Toritone* also seems to account for Little Torrington (1,31) as well as for Great Torrington (40,2. 42,5-6). *Torilande* here (with substitution of *-lande* for *-tūn*, see 15,16 note) may, in the same way, be assumed to stand for Great or Little Torrington. Since Shebbear Hundred places are consistently entered before those for Fremington in Exon. order (see the Appendix), so this land, partly unidentified but following Horwood, a Fremington Hundred place, will probably have lain in the latter Hundred; see OJR in VCH p. 480 note 3, in TDA 36 p. 351 and H10 p. 579. But land just over the river in Shebbear Hundred was held of the Honour of Berry, called *Magdalene* in FA i p. 358, that is 'Magdalene Hospital' (GR SS 487186) in Taddiport, Little Torrington. |
| 34,10 | ASHCOMBE. A parish in Exminster Hundred (24). The ½ hide of lordship land here together with the ½ virgate of lordship in Peamore (34,12) plus the 1½ virgates lordship of Ralph's subtenancy at 16,63 probably account for his allowance of 1 hide in the Tax Return for Exminster Hundred (xxiii). In Fees p. 1308 *Assecomb'* is held by Nicholas *de Kirkham* of Henry *de Pomeray*. The place appears as *Alleston* held by Baldwin *de Countevill'* in FA i p. 346, *Alychyston alias dicta Ayshcombe* in FA i pp. 389, 487; see OJR in TDA 47 p. 226.<br>AELFRIC PIG. Exon. *Aluric' piga*; see OEB p. 364.<br>TAX FOR 2 HIDES. The details total only 1 hide, but it is interesting that in Exon. the tax was originally written *i hid'*, but a second *i* was interlined in slightly darker ink to make *ii* — perhaps the Exon. scribe meant to change the lordship and/or villagers' land holding too. (There are numerous corrections in this Exon. entry, including the villagers' |

| | |
|---|---|
| 34,10 (cont'd.) | ploughs.) See 1,4 note on the hide and 1,57 note on other cases of the tax figure being altered and then disagreeing with the sum of the details. JOINTLY AS THREE MANORS. Interlined in very pale ink and with a thicker pen than the rest of the entry; see 17,13 note. |
| 34,11 | HOLCOMBE. It lies between two Exminster Hundred places in Exon. order and is presumably a part of Holcombe, in Dawlish parish, Exminster Hundred (24), that was not held by the Church of Exeter, despite OJR in TDA 47 p. 227; see Fees p. 398 and notes to 2,4-6 and to 23,1. 4 SALT-WORKERS WHO PAY.... Their payment seems to form the manor's value; see 6,6 note and cf. 36,9, Hollowcombe, where the salt-workers' payment also appears to take the place of the value statement. |
| 34,12 | PEAMORE. In Exminster parish and Hundred (24); see 34,10 note. It passed to the Honour of Lancaster; see FA i pp. 346, 389, Cal. Inq. PM vol. v no. 527 and OJR in TDA 47 p. 228. |
| 34,13 | MOWLISH. DB and Exon. *Bolewis*. Despite the form, taken by DG as pointing to Bowlish in Whitestone parish, Wonford Hundred (19), the order of entries requires a place in Exminster Hundred (24). The Exon. scribe no doubt wrote *B* for *M* (cf. 19,42 second note) and the Exchequer scribe copied his mistake (cf. notes to 16,57 and 52,10), since later evidence points to Mowlish in Kenton parish. *Molehywisse* is held from the Honour of Berry in Fees p. 791; see FA i p. 347 and OJR in TDA 36 p. 368, 47 p. 228. THE WHOLE OF THIS (MANOR). Exon. *hanc totam*, possibly to be translated 'the whole of this (virgate)', as *virga* is also feminine. Of the preceding two *hancs* in the Exon. entry, the first refers to either *virga* or *terra* understood and the second to the manor. See notes to 16,147 and 25,2 for cases where the whole of a manor's land was in lordship and cf. notes to 3,12 and 19,36. |
| 34,14 | RALPH HIMSELF HOLDS. Repeated at the beginning of 34,14-23 inclusive. However, according to the Exon. he has a subtenant, Helgot, for 34,16 (see Exon. Notes there), probably the same man as Ralph's subtenant in 34,26. See notes to 24,28. 47,2 and 48,8. BRENDON. A parish in Shirwell Hundred (2). It passed to Robert *de Beaupeyl*; see RH i pp. 79a, 94b and OJR H8 p. 482. ALWARD SON OF TOKI. See 34,1 note and 19,16 note on the form of his name. 'LANK COMBE'. DB *lacombe* (Farley misprints a capital *L*; cf. second note under 16,115 and 24,26 note), Exon. *Lancoma*. The DB form appears either to have a nunnation mark omitted or is a mistaken attempt to resolve the place-name into *Combe* with the French feminine definite article 'la' (this would suggest that the use of the lower-case *l* was intentional); see EPNS i p. 59. The place, if correctly identified, lies in Brendon parish, Shirwell Hundred (2); the site is now abandoned, like 'Badgworthy' (19,18) which is nearby. 1 VILLAGER WHO PAYS 3s. It is interesting that in the T.O. entry (see Exon. Notes) the value of 'Lank Combe' is given as 3s. This may be because the villager's payment dated from a different time to that at which the T.O. were written or it may indicate that the villager's payment formed the manor's value as on several other occasions; see 6,6 note on villagers holding land for a money-rent. In the T.O. for 21,11 the value of 21,10-11 is given as 12s 6d, but this value seems to include the 30d payment of the villager in 21,11, as it does in DB (see 21,11 note). |
| 34,15 | CHERITON. In Brendon parish, Shirwell Hundred (2); see OJR H8 p. 482. |
| 34,16 | (CAFFYNS) HEANTON. In Lynton parish, Shirwell Hundred (2). Hugh *Coffin* holds *Yanton'* in Fees p. 791 of the Honour of Berry. It is *Heanton Coffyn* in Cal. Inq. PM vol. xv no. 197 and is called *Hanton Coffyn* held with *La Worth, Kynetete* and *la Brunthuchene* [all unidentified] from the heirs of Henry *de la Pomeray* in FA i p. 336; see Fees p. 396, FA i pp. 361, 417 and OJR H8 p. 483. |
| 34,17 | STANDONE. Apparently in Braunton or Shirwell Hundreds (1-2), it has not been satisfactorily identified. DG's 'Eastanton' drawn from TWW in VCH p. 481 note 1 seems to be a mere extrapolation of the DB form; see OJR H8 p. 465. |
| 34,18 | AUNK. DB *Hanc*. It lies in Clyst Hydon parish, Cliston Hundred (20), and is identifiable in the Tax Return for that Hundred (xii). On the descent, see FA i pp. 333, 367, 433 and OJR H7 p. 378. |
| 34,19 | SHELDON. A parish in Hayridge Hundred (15). *Seldene* was a gift of the Pomeroys to Gloucester Abbey; see History of St. Peter's, Gloucester, i pp. 88, 113, 123, ii pp. 125-126 and *Regesta* ii p. 113 no. 1041. It seems later to have been in the hands of Dunkeswell Abbey, TE p. 152a, VE ii p. 304. |

34,20 BLACKBOROUGH. In Kentisbeare parish, Hayridge Hundred (15). In Fees p. 791 the heir of Hugh *de Bollay* holds in *Blakebergh'* from the Honour of Berry. In Cal. Inq. PM vol. vii no. 708 (of John *de Cobeham*), *Blakeburgh* is held of John *de Bello Campo* as of his manor of *Bokerel* [Buckerell, see 34,23 note]. See FA i p. 345, Cal. Inq. PM vol. xvi nos. 670-671 and OJR in TDA 42 p. 237. Allhallows farm [GR ST 0910; EPNS ii p. 564] marks the site of the manor. Cf. 51,7 note.

34,21-22 TALE. In Payhembury parish, Hayridge Hundred (15). Geoffrey *de la Pomeray*, a descendant of Ralph, gave land here to Ford Abbey; see Oliver *Mon.* p. 346, VE ii p. 299 and OJR in TDA 42 p. 238.

34,21 VALUE 20s. Added later in very pale ink; see 16,27 note.

34,22 BURGRED. In the MS *Borgaret* but a diphthong squiggle was added to the *a*, probably later though the colour of the ink is the same, making it *Borgaeret*. Farley misprints *Borgaret*. The form in Exon. is *Borgaret(us)*.

34,23 AWLISCOMBE. DB *Orescome*. A parish in Hemyock Hundred (16); for the form, see 19,25 note. A Ralph holds another portion of Awliscombe under William Cheever in 19,25 (see first note there). Both parts seem to have passed to Roger *Giffard* who holds this *Aulescumb'* from the Honour of Berry in Fees p. 791; see FA i p. 338. It was subsequently given to the Abbot of Dunkeswell, FA i pp. 367, 430; see OJR H2 p. 42. Part of Pomeroy's holding at Awliscombe must have included *Bokerel* [Buckerell ST 1200] now an adjacent parish; see Fees pp. 400 (52,31 note), 1308, 1443, Cal. Inq. PM vol. ix no. 288 and 34,20 note.

½ MILL. The other manor which shared the use of this mill with Awliscombe is not mentioned in DB. VCH p. 400 states that it is Feniton (15,34), but there is no record there of ½ mill and, though adjacent to Buckerell (accounted for in DB under Awliscombe, see above note), Feniton is in a different Hundred. See 1,7 note on mills.

34,24 WESTON. DB *Otri*, held by Rozelin. The modern place-name is from Warin, the 1086 holder of the *Otri* of 19,27; it is Warinstone or Weston in Awliscombe parish, Hemyock Hundred (16). Warin and Rozelin also share Ivedon (19,42. 34,47). In Fees p. 791 the Abbey of Dunkeswell holds in *Otery*; this same land is called *Weryngyston* in FA i p. 430; see OJR H2 p. 42.

Another Pomeroy estate in this Hundred, possibly a subordinate part of Weston, was at *Trilbehegh'* [unidentified, unlikely to be Trebblehayes in Membury, GR ST 2606] held in Fees p. 791 by William and Alexander, later given to the Prior of Taunton; see FA i p. 430 and OJR H2 p. 42.

34,25 DUNKESWELL. A parish in Hemyock Hundred (16). It passed to William *Briwere* and was given by him in 1201 as part of the foundation of Dunkeswell Abbey; see Cal. Inq. PM vol. xi nos. 118, 299, Oliver *Mon.* p. 395 and OJR H2 p. 42. It included *Bourehays* [Bowerhayes GR ST 1408] in VE ii p. 304, *Burhei* and *Steintewode* [Stentwood ST 1309] in TE p. 151b.

34,26 HELGOT. DB *Helgot*, Exon. *Hegotus*; see PNDB §61 for the vocalised *l* before the *g*.
AWLISCOMBE. A parish in Hemyock Hundred (16); see 34,23 note.

34,27-28 WILLIAM OF POITOU. Poitou (Exon. *pitauensis*, *pictauensis*) is in the central west of France; OEB pp. 134-135. He also held some land in Kent (DB Kent M 15, col. 1d).
OGWELL. East and West Ogwell in a detached part of Wonford Hundred (19). In Fees p. 791 Robert *le Peytevin* (from Poitou) holds *Cridie* [Lower Creedy 34,35], *Denescumb'* [Dunscombe 34,33] and *Westwogewill'* and *Estwogewill'* from the Honour of Berry. See FA i pp. 316, 345, 388 and OJR in TDA 36 p. 375, 44 p. 340.

34,27 MEADOW, 1 ACRE; .... In the MS there is a plain gap of about 16 letters' width after the meadow details. There is a faint *7* visible after the *pti*, but no other sign of erasure. Exon. attributes 12 acres of underwood, as well as the meadow and pasture, to William's holding (see Details Table). The different treatment of the tenancy of this entry (see Exon. Notes) may be the reason for the space left.

VALUE NOW 30s. In the MS *xx solid'* was originally written, perhaps as a result of the scribe copying the value only of William's holding in Exon. (see Details Table), then corrected to *xxx*, the final *x* being added in paler ink and at an angle to fit in.

34,29 ROGER. Probably Roger Blunt; the Tax Return for Wonford Hundred (xxxi), in which Huxham lies, states that Roger *flavus* (see OEB p. 313) has ½ hide in lordship there. This is the only holding of a Roger in this Hundred in DB.

HUXHAM. A parish in Wonford Hundred (19); see above note. The place is *Hokesham* held from the Honour of Berry in Fees p. 791; see Fees p. 396, FA i pp. 316, 387, Cal. Inq. PM vol. i no. 352, v no. 527 and OJR in TDA 44 p. 340.

34

34,30 CLYST (ST. GEORGE). DB *Chisewic*, now a parish in (East) Budleigh Hundred (14). In Fees p. 764 *Clistwyk* is held of the Honour of Bradninch (descent from William Cheever, see Ch. 19 note; an error for Berry) from Geoffrey *de la Pomeraye*. It is *Clist* held of Henry *de la Pomeraye* of his manor of *Bukerel* (34,23 note) in Cal. Inq. PM vol. iv no. 312 and *Clystwik Sči Georgii* in 1327 (EPNS ii p. 585); see FA i p. 365 and OJR in TDA 35 p. 299. The lordship land of this manor with that of 34,31;39 probably accounts for Ralph's allowance of 1 hide in the Budleigh Hundred Tax Return (xvi).
One *mansa* at *Clystwicon* was given by King Edgar to Æthelnoth *c*. 961, see ECDC p. 12 no. 37 = BCS no. 1103 = Sawyer (1) no. 669.

34,31 STOCKLEIGH (POMEROY). A parish in (West) Budleigh Hundred (14); see 34,30 note. In Fees p. 764 the heirs of Henry *de la Pomeraye* hold in *Stokkelegh'* from the Honour of Berry; see Fees p. 1314, FA i p. 325, Cal. Inq. PM vol. xii no. 163, RH i p. 66a, OJR in TDA 28 pp. 362-390, 35 p. 295 and 15,17-18 note.

34,32 RAPSHAYS. In Gittisham parish, (East) Budleigh Hundred (14); see 19,34 and 25,15 notes. In Fees p. 791 Roger *le Poer* holds in *Rappinghegh'* of the Honour of Berry; see Fees p. 762, FA i pp. 364, 426 and OJR in TDA 35 p. 286. Ralph's holding here is probably remembered in Pomeroy at GR SY 1398.
BEFORE 1066. .... In the MS there is a gap of about 11 letters' width after *T.R.E.* The parchment appears to be very slightly scraped, but nothing is visible. It is possible that the scribe originally wrote the tax liability, though there is scarcely room for it and in any case it would not have been necessary as the hidage had already been given (but see 24,25 and note and also Dorset 27,6 where 3 hides attached to Clifton Maybank are stated to have paid tax for 3 hides, and see also Dorset Exon. Notes 55,15). Exon. does not state the tax paid. Cf. 34,37 note and Exon. Notes 34,11.

34,33;35 WILLIAM. Perhaps William of Poitou because the descent of these manors to Robert of Poitou is the same as that for 34,27-28 (see second note there), which are held by William of Poitou in 1086.

34,33 DUNSCOMBE. In Cheriton Fitzpaine parish, (West) Budleigh Hundred (14). It is held with the Ogwells (34,27-28 note) in Fees p. 791; see FA i pp. 364, 426 and OJR in TDA 35 p. 281.

34,34 HEPPASTEBE. In the order of Exon. it lies among places in East or West Budleigh Hundred (14), but has not been identified. Among Berry Honour fees in this Hundred are *Hille* [?Hill farm in Farringdon, GR SY 0090] and *Eston'* or *Exton'* [Exton in Woodbury, SX 9886] in Fees pp. 763, 791. These two lands do not seem to be accounted for by another DB holding, but the connection with *Heppastebe* has not been established; see FA i pp. 365, 427 and OJR in TDA 35 p. 291.
AUNK. See 34,18.

34,35 (LOWER) CREEDY. In Upton Hellions parish, (West) Budleigh Hundred (14). Robert *le Peytevin* holds *Cridie* in Fees p. 791; see Cal. Inq. PM vol. ii no. 265, FA i p. 426, OJR in TDA 35 p. 281 and 34,27-28 note. North Creedy lies in Sandford parish, Crediton Hundred (13).

34,36 YEADBURY. Now in Cruwys Morchard parish, Witheridge Hundred (7), but it was a tithing of Budleigh Hundred (14) in the Middle Ages. The order of the Exon. Book suggests that it also lay there in 1086. In Fees pp. 762, 791 Robert *de Horthon'* holds in *Addebyr'* from the Honour of Berry; see RH i pp. 66b, 92b, FA i p. 426 and OJR in TDA 35 p. 283.

34,37 (LOWER) CREEDY. Presumably this 1 furlong (*ferling*), having a different TRE holder from *Cridie* (34,35), but the same 1086 tenant, was later combined with it. It would seem that as no population was recorded for this holding, the land here was worked by some of the smallholders and slaves at the larger manor in Lower Creedy; see 17,84 note and cf. 23,25 note. See OJR in TDA 36 p. 362, 54 p. 173.
BEFORE 1066. .... In the MS there is a gap of about 11 letters' width after *T.R.E.*, possibly due to an erasure of at least 6 letters; an 7 and part of a *d* and a *b* can be seen, suggesting 7 *geldb'* may have been originally written. Cf. 34,32 note.

34,38 STRETE (RALEGH). Now in Whimple parish in Cliston Hundred (20), but it was in (East) Budleigh (14) in the Middle Ages and seems to have been so included by the order of Exon. In Fees p. 792 Henry *de Ralegh'* holds in *Strethe* from the Honour of Berry; see Fees p. 763, FA i p. 427 and OJR in TDA 35 p. 293.

34,39 WASHFIELD. A parish in (West) Budleigh Hundred (14); see 32,9 note. This holding is identifiable in the Tax Return for Budleigh Hundred (xvi); see 34,30 note. In an unfinished entry in Fees p. 762 William *Le Abbe* holds in *Wassefeld'* from Muriel *de Bollay*. Although

           the Honour is not stated and it is from the Honour of Totnes (see Ch. 17 note) that
           Walter *Abbot* holds in FA i p. 427, these entries appear to refer to this holding; see
           FA i p. 365 and OJR in TDA 35 p. 284.
34,40-41   THESE PLACES now lie in Witheridge Hundred (7) but they are placed by OJR (in
           TDA 30 p. 455) in Bampton Hundred (8). While it is true that Bampton Hundred
           seems to have been larger in 1086 than later and to have included a number of places
           that were afterwards in Witheridge Hundred, if these two particular lands lay in Bampton
           in 1086, they should have been entered at an earlier point in the schedule; see the
           Appendix and 16,150-151 note.
34,40      STOODLEIGH. West Stoodleigh in Stoodleigh parish, Witheridge Hundred (7). In Fees
           p. 791 Robert *de Campellis* holds in *Weststodlegh'* from the Honour of Berry; see Fees
           pp. 398, 760, FA i pp. 344, 421, OJR in TDA 30 pp. 404, 421 and 3,77 note.
34,41      HIGHLEIGH. DB *Henlei*. Apparently Highleigh in Oakford parish, Witheridge Hundred
           (7), for which EPNS ii p. 388 only quotes the form *Heghelegh* (1325). It was given by
           Henry *de la Pomeray* to the Priory of St. Mary at Pilton and is called *Hellegh'* in TE
           p. 152b, *Seyntemarilegh'* in Fees p. 761; see Oliver *Mon.* p. 247 and OJR in TDA 30
           p. 422.
34,42      ADWORTHY. In Witheridge parish and Hundred (7). It is held as *Oddeworth'* of the
           Honour of Berry in Fees p. 761. OJR in TDA 30 p. 422 and VCH p. 483 note 7 identifies
           Woodford in Thelbridge, but see EPNS ii p. 398.
           SAERIC. DB *Seric*, Exon. *Seric(us)*, could represent OE *Sigeric*, rather than OE *Saeric*;
           see PNDB p. 352 s.n. *Sae-* and p. 354 s.n. *Saeric*.
34,43      [HOLDS]. In the MS *ten*' omitted in error.
           CHEVITHORNE .... UPLOWMAN. Chevithorne is in Tiverton parish and Hundred (9);
           Uplowman is now counted in Halberton Hundred (10), but was a tithing of Tiverton
           Hundred in the Middle Ages; see 25,16 note and, for example, LSR (1332) p. 36. In
           Fees p. 791 Alice *de Ros* holds in *Chyfethorn'* from the Honour of Berry. It is
           *Westchyvethorne* (see 16,158) in FA i pp. 370, 433, having passed into the King's hands
           by 1303 and being granted to Edmund of Woodstock, Earl of Kent; see Fees p. 396,
           Cal. Inq. PM vol. iv (o.s.) no. 63 (= TDA 38 p. 326) and OJR H1 p. 23.
34,44      GAPPAH. In Kingsteignton parish, Teignbridge Hundred (23). In Fees p. 791 the land
           seems to have had three parts: (1) *Gatepath'* held by William *de Beldemerse*, called
           *Gatepath* and *Bealdemerse* [Bellamarsh GR SX 8577] in FA i p. 339; (2) another
           *Gatepath'* held by the heirs of Hugh *de Bollay*; and (3) *Babbecumb'* [Babcombe SX
           8677] held by John *de Babbecumb'*; see Cal. Inq. PM vol. ii nos. 306, 593, vii no. 297,
           HD p. 56, FA i pp. 347, 390 and OJR in TDA 29 pp. 239, 241, 36 p. 368.
34,45      IVEDON. DB *Otrie*. Now in Awliscombe parish, Hemyock Hundred (16), but this entry
           appears to be a delayed part of Tiverton Hundred (9), Teignton and Tiverton Hundred
           places being intermixed at this point in the schedule as in 16,152-160; see 34,43 note.
           Ivedon was a detached part of Tiverton Hundred in the Middle Ages and this particular
           holding, whose TRE tenant was Saemar, was split after the Conquest between William
           Cheever (who holds the other part and ½ villager, 19,43 note) and Ralph of Pomeroy.
           Both of these parts of Ivedon are recorded as being added to Awliscombe. The 19,43
           holding was probably added to 19,25; in the present case Ivedon was probably added to
           the Awliscombe of 34,23 also held by Ralph himself, whereas the Awliscombe of 34,26
           has Helgot as subtenant. It is interesting that in the T.O. entries for 19,43 and 34,45
           Awliscombe is stated to have been added to Ivedon, the reverse of what the main Exon.
           and Exchequer DB entries state; see Exon. Notes. Cf. Exon. Notes 39,16.
           ½ VILLAGER. In the MS *uitto* corrected from *uitti* (nominative plural); the scribe also
           appears to have written a *c* as the first letter and corrected it to a *v*. For the other half
           of the villager, see 19,43 and note.
34,46      DUNSTONE .... 'BLACKSLADE'. Both lie in Widecombe in the Moor, a detached part
           of Haytor Hundred (29). On the DB form of 'Blackslade' see EPNS ii p. 526. If this
           holding is later represented by *Widecumb'* [Widecombe in the Moor], held by Richard
           son of Ralph in Fees p. 768 (see Fees p. 790, FA i pp. 318, 349, 392), then the
           overlordship early passed to the Honour of Plympton; see OJR in TDA 40 p. 124.
           'Blackslade farm' (GR SX 736754) is now represented only by 'Blackslade Down';
           see H. French and C. D. Lineham in TDA 95 especially p. 175.
           PASTURE, 30 ACRES. The scribe originally wrote *xxx ac p̄ti* 'meadow, 30 acres', then
           corrected the *p̄ti* to *p̄stē*; the *p̄stē* is squashed in and the first abbreviation sign is very
           faint (it is not reproduced in the facsimile). The whole word is written in such pale ink

34

(like some of the other corrections and additions) that one could almost think it had been erased, especially as *pti* is still visible underneath, but in the same dark ink as the rest of the entry. However, the compression of the *p̃tẽ* and the obvious need for a correction to the *p̃ti* (to avoid two sets of details for meadow; cf. 17,50) contradict this notion. The Exon. entry is neat and clear.

34,47  IVEDON. Now in Awliscombe parish, Hemyock Hundred (16), but long a tithing of Tiverton Hundred (9); see 19,42-43 and 34,45 notes. This holding can be identified in the Tax Return for Tiverton Hundred (xi): Rozelin, Ralph's tenant here (in Exon.), has failed to pay tax on land held with Warin (the tenant of another part of Ivedon under Ralph's brother William Cheever, 19,42). This holding does not appear in later lists, but it may have been coupled with the Ivedon held of Bradninch Honour; see OJR in TDA 36 p. 358, 362 and H1 p. 28.

34,48  RALPH HIMSELF HOLDS. Repeated at the beginning of 34,48-51 inclusive.
BERRY (POMEROY). A parish in Haytor Hundred (29); identifiable in the Tax Return for Kerswell (Haytor) Hundred (xxv). It is *caput* of the later Honour of Berry. In Fees p. 769 the heirs of Henry *de la Pomeraye* hold *Beri*; see RH i p. 72a, Fees p. 1307, Cal. Inq. PM vol. xii no. 163, FA i pp. 318, 349 and OJR in TDA 40 p. 129, 50 p. 565.

Tithes and various renders from *Bercium* and *Otrevum* [Berry and one of Ralph's 'Otter' holdings, 34,24;32;45;47;50] were granted *c*. 1125 by Jocelyn *de Pomeria* to the Abbey of St. Mary du Val in the Diocese of Bayeux; see Round CDF p. 536 no. 1455.

34,49  AFTON. In Berry Pomeroy parish, Haytor Hundred (29); see Fees p. 1311.
34,50  UPOTTERY. DB *Otri*. A parish in Axminster Hundred (17), this holding being identifiable in the Axminster Hundred Tax Return (xix). For the descent see OJR H4 p. 155. It included *Fayrook* [Fair Oak GR ST 1808] in Cal. Inq. PM vol. xvi no. 1027; see vol. vi no. 753.

34,51  SMALLRIDGE. In Axminster parish and Hundred (17). In Fees p. 791 *Wymundus de Ralegh'* holds in *Smalerig'* from the Honour of Berry; see HD p. 56, Cal. Inq. PM vol. ii nos. 306, 593, vii no. 297, FA i pp. 320, 366, 429 and OJR H4 p. 157. Both Smallridge and Weycroft (34,52) went to Newenham Abbey (see 1,11 note); see Oliver *Mon*. p. 357 ff.

See 1,11 for details of a customary due owing from this manor.

34,52  ROGER. Possibly Roger of Courseulles. The Tax Return for Axminster Hundred (xix) states that the King had no tax from ½ hide which Robert holds from Roger of Courseulles: this is the only holding of a Roger in this Hundred in DB (Roger of Courseulles is not a tenant-in-chief in Devon). Lower layers of subtenancy are often omitted in Exon. and DB (see 3,70 note), though it is possible that a change had taken place in the subtenancy of Weycroft between the compilation of the Tax Returns and of Exon.
WEYCROFT. Also in Axminster parish and Hundred (17). Henry *Gobaud'* holds in *Wicrofte* in Fees p. 791 from the Honour of Berry; see FA i pp. 320, 366, 429, OJR H4 p. 157 and 34,51 note.

34,53  BRUCKLAND. In Axmouth parish, formerly in Axmouth Hundred, but now in Axminster (17). In Fees p. 791 John *de Tryl* holds from the Honour of Berry in *Brocland'* and in *Borcumb'* ['Radish', 34,54 note]; see FA i pp. 328, 430, OJR H4 p. 181 and 16,164 note.
AETHELHARD THE MONK. DB and Exon. *Ailard(us)* with Exon. *monac(us)*. This OE personal name is also represented in DB by *Aelard* (Sussex 11,8) and, with AN interchange of *l-r*, by *Airard* (Dorset 49,7). See PNDB p. 184.

34,54  'RADISH'. In Southleigh parish, Colyton Hundred (22); it is identifiable in the Colyton Hundred Tax Return (xx) and is now represented only by 'Radish Plantation'. In Fees p. 791 it appears to be *Borcumb'* [Borcombe lying adjacent, also in Southleigh parish, GR SY 1991], held by John *de Tryl* with Bruckland (34,53); see FA i pp. 331, 428 and OJR in TDA 36 p. 366 and H7 p. 356.
ON THE LACK OF POPULATION recorded for this manor, see 17,84 note.
THESE THREE MANORS. That is, Bruckland and the two TRE manors of 'Radish'.
GIVEN TO RALPH IN EXCHANGE FOR ONE MANOR OF 1 VIRGATE. The manor was Panson, 'given' to Roald Dubbed, 35,4. The T.O. entry there (see Exon. Notes 35,4), by stating that Ralph had appropriated Panson, suggests a reason why he was keen to exchange it. Apart from ridding himself of a manor to which he was not legally entitled, Ralph gained lands of larger extent though worth only a fifth of the value of Panson in 1086.

34,55 KEYNEDON. In Sherford parish, Coleridge Hundred (30). In Fees p. 792 Roger *de Praulle* holds in *Kynedon'* and in *Ernecumb'* [said to be 'Yarnscombe' in Stockenham, EPNS i p. 333] from the Honour of Berry; see FA i pp. 332, 350, 393, Cal. Inq. PM vol. xvi no. 875 and OJR in TDA 43 p. 196.
POOL. Presumably part of North Pool in South Pool parish, adjacent to Keynedon in Coleridge Hundred (30).

34,56 HEAVITREE. A parish in Wonford Hundred (19), now incorporated in Exeter. In Fees p. 791 William *de Kelly* holds in *Hevetre* from the Honour of Berry; see FA i pp. 316, 387, Cal. Inq. PM vol. v no. 527 and OJR in TDA 44 p. 341.
2 CARUCATES. See 1,2 note.
2 PLOUGHS. In the MS and Farley clearly *ii carucẹ*; in the facsimile only the bottom half of the first *i* is reproduced for some reason.

34,57 ROGER HAS .... The scribe has omitted *de Ra.* 'from Ra(lph)', probably in error; it is in Exon. as usual. See 15,22 note.
A MILL WHICH PAYS 30d. *moliñ redđ xxx den'*. It is possible that the Exchequer scribe omitted an *7* between *moliñ* and *redđ* or some form of punctuation after *moliñ* or a capital *R* for *redđ*, to make the reading 'A mill. It (the manor) pays 30d'. The main Exon. is almost as ambiguous as to what the *valet per annum xxx den'* refers, but the T.O. entry clearly makes the ½ virgate worth 30d; see Exon. Notes. However, one would have expected the Exchequer scribe to have used *valet* here if he meant it for the ½ virgate, *redđ* in Devon being used almost entirely in the Value statements of royal manors (see 1,32 note and cf. notes to 3,82. 15,53 and 24,18), though in Devon the two words probably meant the same (see 2,2 note on Value). Cf. 52,48 note.
AELFRIC HELD IT JOINTLY. The marginal *par'* obviously belongs here with the TRE holder, despite its being written level with the first line of the entry. Without exception, these marginal *par'*s (see 15,47-52 note) refer to the TRE tenants, who are normally written on the first line. Presumably the scribe adding these *par'*s did not read the entries or he would have noticed that here the details of the 1066 holder were misplaced (as they are in Exon.).
ADDED TO WEYCROFT. That is to 34,52.

34,58 6 HOUSES .... 3s 4d. As the rate of payment of customary dues is given as 8d a house in almost every other instance in Devon (see C 1 note), it is possible that *vi domos* here is a scribal error for *v domos* (i.e. 5 × 8d = 40d or 3s 4d). In the MS the *i* of the *vi* is in darker ink, but this may be incidental (the scribe may have merely dipped his pen into the ink again), as the distance between the figure and *domos* does not suggest an addition to the figure. There is no sign of correction in the Exon. MS.

Ch. 35 ROALD DUBBED. DB *Adobed*, Exon. *Adobatus*, represent OFr *adobed* or *adubé*, the past participle of the verb *aduber/adouber/adubber* 'to equip a knight, to array'. Cf. Mod.E *adub* 'to invest with the insignia of knighthood, to dub'; OEB p. 373.
The majority of Roald's holdings later form part of the great Honour of Plympton (Ch. 21 note), many being held by the Giffard family. On the descent of Roald's lands, see the articles by the Earl of Halsbury cited in the Bibliography.
THE MANORS FALL in the following Hundred groupings, the order being the same in DB as in Exon., except that the Exon. entries corresponding to 35,26-31 have not survived:

| 35,1 | Lifton | 35,24 | Budleigh |
| 35,2-9 | Torrington | 35,25 | Witheridge |
| 35,10-19 | Merton | 35,26 | *Alleriga* |
| 35,20 | Braunton | 35,27-28 | Plympton |
| 35,21 | Wonford | 35,29-30 | Walkhampton |
| 35,22 | South Molton | 35,31 | Borough of Exeter |
| 35,23 | Wonford | | |

35,1 LAMERTON. A parish in Lifton Hundred (18). Walter *Giffard* holds *Lamerthon'* from the Honour of Plympton in Fees p. 789; see Fees p. 756, FA i pp. 321, 355, 405, Cal. Inq. PM vol. xv no. 597 and OJR in TDA 46 p. 199.

35,2 BRIDGERULE. DB *Brige* with Roald's name affixed. It is a parish in (Black) Torrington Hundred (11), positively identifiable in the Tax Return for Torrington (iii). In Fees p. 787 Ralph *de Dune* holds in *Bruge Ruardi* of the Honour of Plympton; see FA i pp. 327, 406 and OJR H5 p. 213.

35,3 WALTER OF OMONVILLE. Exon. *de Osmundi uilla*; see OEB p. 104.
WONFORD. In Thornbury parish, (Black) Torrington Hundred (11). In Fees p. 788

|  |  |
|---|---|
|  | *Wanford* is held by Alexander *de Heremanesdon'* (from Hemerdon, 35,28); see FA i p. 357 and OJR H5 p. 212. |
| 35,4 | ALFRED THE BRETON. DB *Alured*, Exon. *Aluid(us) brito*. The personal name is OBret *Alfrit*, *Alfred*, not OE *AElfred*, although of course the English would identify it with their name. The *Aluid(us)* form represents OBret *Alfrid* with loss of *r*. See PNDB p. 176 and note 3. On *brito*, see OEB p. 133. |
|  | PANSON. In St. Giles in the Heath parish, (Black) Torrington Hundred (11). Panson had been given to Tavistock Abbey before the Conquest (Ch. 5 note) and was also held by it in later times. This entry may refer to a temporary alienation or to another part; see OJR H5 p. 213. |
|  | BRUCKLAND AND 'RADISH'. See 34,53-54, exchanged with Ralph of Pomeroy for Panson. |
| 35,5 | TAMERLANDE. Named from the river Tamar, this holding of Roald clearly lies in (Black) Torrington Hundred (11) and must have been adjacent to Peeke (35,6) since the T.O. entry (496 a 4) records that it has been added to Peeke. Neither *Tamerlande* nor Peeke appears in fee lists, but one of them must be represented by the *Leghyngecoth'* of Fees p. 787, held from the Honour of Plympton. It appears as *Loghingecote* [Luffincott GR SX 3394, the parish in which Peeke lay] in FA i p. 327; see FA i pp. 358, 409. The other could well be the *Northcote* by *Loghincote* [Northcott SX 3492] of Cal. Inq. PM vol. xiv no. 325; see Cal. Inq. PM vol. iv (o.s.) no. 63 (= TDA 38 p. 324) and OJR H5 p. 213. |
|  | 1 VILLAGER; 1 PLOUGH.... In DB it is not clear whether *i car* is in the ablative after *cum* (i.e. 'In lordship .... with 1 slave and 1 villager and 1 plough....'). However, Exon. makes it clear that the villager (or 'villagers', see Exon. Notes) has the plough and furlongs ('ferlings'). |
| 35,6 | PEEKE. East and West Peeke in Luffincott parish, (Black) Torrington Hundred (11); see 35,5 note. |
|  | JOINTLY. In the MS *par* was originally interlined, but corrected at an early stage to *in paragio* but without the ⁺ abbreviation sign being erased (Farley does not print it); all of the interlineation is in pale ink. |
|  | LAND. .... In the MS there is a plain gap of about 11 letters' width, probably left for the plough estimate (which is also absent in Exon.; see Exon. Notes); or possibly because there was a query about the lordship land given in Exon. (though Exchequer DB only includes the lordship land for two entries in Devon; see 2,2 note). |
| 35,7-8 | ROGER OF FLANDERS. Exon. *Roger(us) flandrensis*; OEB pp. 133-134. |
| 35,7 | KIMBER. East and West Kimber in Northlew parish, (Black) Torrington Hundred (11). In Fees p. 788 the heir of Robert *le Brok'* and the priest (*persona*) *de Lyu* hold in *Kemppebere* from the Honour of Plympton; see FA i pp. 357, 409 and OJR H5 p. 212. Grendon [Greendown GR SX 4899 in Northlew] has the same later holders as Kimber (FA i p. 408) and was probably part of it. |
| 35,8 | RUTLEIGH. DB *Radeclive*. Great Rutleigh, now in Northlew parish, (Black) Torrington Hundred (11); see EPNS i p. 155. Robert *le Brok'* (on whom see 35,7 note) holds *Radeclive* from the Honour of Plympton in Fees p. 788; see FA i pp. 357, 408 and OJR H5 p. 213. |
| 35,9 | (WEST) PUTFORD. A parish in (Black) Torrington Hundred (11). It is held by Walter *de Morthon'* as *Churiputteford'* ['Church' Putford] in Fees p. 787 from the Honour of Plympton, is *Westpoteford* in FA i p. 327 and *Churche Poteford* in FA i p. 407 and Cal. Inq. PM vol. xiv no. 325, probably now Julian and Chollaton GR SS 3614, 3714; see EPNS i p. 161, OJR H5 p. 214 and 28,4 note. |
| 35,10 | WEARE (GIFFARD). A parish in Shebbear Hundred (4), named from the fish-weir or fishery there. In Fees p. 788 Walter *Giffard* holds 1 fee in *Were*, *Holnam* [Hollam 35,12] and *Polam* [Pulham 35,22]; this last is said to be in North Molton Hundred in FA i p. 358. See FA i pp. 329, 411, Cal. Inq. PM vol. xiv no. 325 and OJR H10 pp. 545, 555. |
|  | ORDWULF. Farley misprints *Ordulf* in capitals; it is in lower-case as usual in the MS (but cf. 16,1;3 note). |
|  | ½ FISHERY. There is no record in DB Devon of which other manor shared this fishery on the river Torridge. |
|  | COUNT OF MORTAIN HOLDS ½ VIRGATE. He may hold it as part of his manor of Culleigh (15,11) which is a couple of miles away on the other side of the river Torridge and is also held by Erchenbald from the Count in 1086. |
|  | ERCHENBALD HOLDS FROM HIM. The Exchequer scribe probably deliberately omitted this detail of a subtenancy of a sub-holding; cf. 3,70 note and Exon. Notes 3,94. |
| 35,11 | HUXHILL. In Weare Giffard parish, Shebbear Hundred (4); see OJR H10 p. 555. |

35,12   HOLLAM. In Little Torrington parish, Shebbear Hundred (4); in later lists it is associated with Weare Giffard and Pulham (35,10 note).
35,13   (PETERS) MARLAND. A parish in Shebbear Hundred (4), 'Peters' from the dedication of the church. In Fees p. 788 Roger *le Mareschal* holds in *Petermerland* from the Honour of Plympton; see FA i pp. 359, 412 and OJR H10 p. 556. For Little Marland see 36,6.
35,14   ROALD HIMSELF HOLDS. Repeated at the beginning of 35,14-18 inclusive.
35,14;18   TWIGBEARE. In Peters Marland parish, Shebbear Hundred (4). In Fees p. 788 William *del Chenne* holds in *Twykkebere* from the Honour of Plympton; see FA i pp. 329, 359, 411 and OJR H10 p. 557.
35,15   WINSCOTT. Also in Peters Marland parish, Shebbear Hundred (4). In FA i p. 359 Philip *de Cruce* holds in *Twykkebere* [Twigbeare 35,14;18] and in *Wynescote* and *Wyneslegh* [unidentified]; see OJR H10 p. 557.
35,16   WINSWELL. In the MS *WIFLESWILLE*; in Farley the second *I* appears only as a dot. It is now represented by Willeswell moor and Winswell, the latter influenced by Winscott (35,15). Both are in Peters Marland parish, Shebbear Hundred (4); see EPNS i p. 98 and OJR H10 p. 557.
IT PAID TAX. In the MS *7 geldb'* is written twice in the same colour ink, at the end of the first line and at the beginning of the second, with no attempt at erasure of the error or application of deletion dots.
35,17   LOVACOTT. In Shebbear parish and Hundred (4), it is named from the TRE holder; see OJR H10 pp. 546, 557.
35,18   TWIGBEARE. See 35,14;18 note.
35,19   HANKFORD. In Bulkworthy parish, Shebbear Hundred (4); see OJR H10 p. 557.
1 VILLAGER HAS IT THERE, WITH 1 SMALLHOLDER. The *hanc* probably refers to the plough; see 1,29 note. Exon. states that the villager and the smallholder had the plough, so there seems to be no reason for the Exchequer wording "with 1 smallholder"; cf. notes to 3,27 and 14,1-2.
35,20   LOBB. In Braunton parish and Hundred (1). Philip *de Lobbe* holds in *Lobbe* in Fees p. 787 of the Honour of Plympton. It is *Lob Phelip* in FA i p. 375; see FA i pp. 359, 414 and OJR H8 p. 450.
1 SALT-HOUSE. The Exchequer scribe probably missed this in the Exon. because it was unusually sandwiched between the smallholders and the slaves and written in the right margin (though by the same scribe as the rest of the entry, so not added after Exon. had been used at Winchester).
35,21   CROKERNWELL. In Cheriton Bishop parish, Wonford Hundred (19); see OJR in TDA 44 p. 321.
35,22   PULHAM .... PRAUNSLEY. Both lie in Twitchen parish, now South Molton Hundred (6), but Pulham was in North Molton Hundred in the Middle Ages; see the Appendix, 35,10 note and OJR H9 p. 522.
THIS (LAND) .... 3s. A very confused sentence, as also in the main Exon. entry, which suggests direct copying of it by the Exchequer scribe. The *q̄* would seem to abbreviate *quae* referring to the *illa* which in turn refers to an understood *terra* or perhaps *mansio*. However, the subject of the common phrase *poterat ire ad quemlibet dominum* is almost invariably in Devon the TRE holder, and the phrase often seems included to suggest that a manor was wrongfully taken over (as, for example, in 40,7 and see 1,15 note on 'freely'). The T.O. entry, itself corrected (see Exon. Notes here), explains that Praunsley was added to Pulham, using the normal formulae for cases where two or more manors held freely in 1066 (often by thanes) had been combined by a 1086 holder; the surrounding T.O. entries are all of this sort. The Exon. scribe, followed by the DB scribe, for some reason omitted the vital information of Praunsley being added.
35,23   SIGFORD. Now in Ilsington parish, Teignbridge Hundred (23), but in the Middle Ages it was a detached part of Wonford Hundred (19); the order of Exon., interrupted though it is by Pulham (35,22), suggests a place in Wonford Hundred. In Fees p. 788, in a Wonford Hundred group, Joel *de Bukethon'* holds in *Sygeford'* from the Honour of Plympton; see RH i p. 85a, FA i pp. 313, 345, Cal. Inq. PM vol. x no. 241, OJR in TDA 44 p. 321 and 32,6-7 note.
ON THE LACK OF POPULATION recorded for this manor, see 17,84 note.
35,24   POUGHILL. A parish in (West) Budleigh Hundred (14). The church was given by Roald to St. Nicholas' Priory; Oliver *Mon.* p. 119, TE p. 152a. The holding may have been at, or included, *Braderig* [Broadridge GR SS 8508], held with Langley (1,9 note) in Fees p. 761 of the Honour of Plympton; see OJR in TDA 35 pp. 280, 312.

| | |
|---|---|
| 35,25 | WALTER HOLDS.... The scribe has omitted *de Ru.* 'from Roald', no doubt by mistake as it is in Exon. See 15,22 note.<br>DOCKWORTHY. Now in Chawleigh parish, (North) Tawton Hundred (12), but it lies geographically on the Witheridge Hundred (7) side of the Little Dart river and was in that Hundred in the Middle Ages, as also apparently in 1086, this point in the schedule being too late for a North Tawton Hundred place. In Fees p. 787 *Dockeworth'* is held from the Honour of Plympton; see Fees p. 759 and OJR in TDA 30 p. 422.<br>AELFLED. DB *Alflet*, Exon. *Alfleta*, represent either OE *Aelflaed* or *Aethelflaed*, feminine; PNDB p. 144.<br>PASTURE, 1 FURLONG LONG .... *una q̈x pasturae lg̃*.... (*q̈x* = *quarentena*); one would normally expect either *in longitudine* with this phrase (as in 16,78) or the nominative *pastura* preceding the measurement (as in 35,29). Perhaps the Exchequer scribe was copying the Exon. too closely, as in 1,57 (see note), but this cannot be checked as the pasture details are on the missing Exon. folios; see Exon. Notes here. |
| 35,26 | AVETON (GIFFORD). A parish in Ermington Hundred (27), this holding probably being identifiable in the Tax Return for *Alleriga* Hundred (xxx: Roald is recorded as having 1 hide of lordship there, but, as there is no Exon. surviving for this entry, this cannot be checked, though it is likely, being his only holding in this Hundred). In Fees p. 789 Walter *Giffard* holds in *Aveton'* and in FA i p. 351 the Prior of Plympton holds a part of *Aveton Giffard* called *Tottewill* [Titwell GR SX 6849] and *Cumb* [Combe and Challons Combe SX 6748]; see TE pp. 149, 153, RH i p. 69b, Fees p. 769, FA i p. 397, Cal. Inq. PM vol. ii no. 205, viii no. 230, xiv no. 325 and OJR H6 p. 309. |
| 35,27 | TRAIN. DB *Alfelmestone*, apparently 'AElfhelm's *tūn*'. It is identified by OJR (in VCH and H6 p. 282), by EPNS (i p. 254) and by DG as Yealmpstone in Plympton St. Mary parish, Plympton Hundred (26). In Fees p. 788 William *Le Abbe* holds in *Alfamescoth'* from the Honour of Plympton; it is *Alfemeston* in FA i p. 334, held from Robert *de Dynham* who holds from the Countess *Albemarlie*, see FA i pp. 353, 402. The manor is described as *Alphameston juxta Wenbury* [Wembury GR SX 5148] in 1318 and is thus unlikely to have been Yealmpstone which is some distance from Wembury. Moreover, in LSR (1332) p. 12 the tenants of *Alfameston'* are John *atte Treawen*, Thomas *de Nytheretreawen*, John *de Sprirewille* and Elias *atte Forde*. These places are all in Wembury parish, being now Train, 'Nether Train', Spirewell and Ford. The manor is described as *Alphemeston* otherwise *Treawyn* in 1561-1562. Its modern representative is thus Train in Wembury, now Train, Train Wood, Train Brake and Higher Train; see OJR's editor in H6 p. 282, F. B. Prideaux 'Alfelmestone Manor' in DCNQ 14 para. 271 pp. 300-304, EPNS i p. 261 and R. C. Rowland 'Traine Farm, Wembury, Devonshire' in JEPN 10 (1977-1978) p. 40. Train is from OE *trēowum* 'at the trees'. |
| 35,28 | HEMERDON. Also in Plympton St. Mary parish, Plympton Hundred (26). In Fees p. 788 Alexander *de Heremannesdon'* holds in *Heremannedon'* from the Honour of Plympton; see FA i pp. 334, 400 and OJR H6 p. 283. |
| 35,29 | WHITCHURCH. A parish in Roborough Hundred (25). Since the corresponding Exon. entry is missing, there is no record of the proportion of this 1 hide holding that was lordship land, but the Tax Return for Walkhampton (Roborough) Hundred (xxix) allows Roald 1 virgate of lordship which must apply to this holding, his only one in this Hundred. Walter *Giffard* holds in *Whytechurch'* from the Honour of Plympton in Fees p. 789; see FA i pp. 340, 354, 402, Cal. Inq. PM vol. xv no. 597 and OJR H3 p. 119. |
| 35,30 | MONKSWELL. DB *Macheswelle*. In Sampford Spiney parish, Roborough Hundred (25), long unidentified, but see the editor in OJR H6 p. 328. The place was *Mankeswill(e)* in 1340; see EPNS i p. 238. |
| 35,31 | 1 HOUSE .... CUSTOMARY DUES. That is, 8d; see the T.O. entry in the Exon. Notes here and C 1 note above. |
| Ch. 36 | THEOBALD SON OF BERNER. He is the Theobald who is the father-in-law of Odo son of Gamelin (Ch. 42) who is described in the T.O. entry relating to 42,4 as having (joined) an appropriated furlong (*ferdinum*) of land to Odo's manor of Huish. It is interesting that both Theobald and Odo have in common a number of predecessors in their manors, e.g. a Vitalis, a Norman, an Aelmer, a Leofgar, a Brictric, an Edmer, a Saewin, an Alwold (although most of these are common names and could refer to more than one person); cf. the 'shared' 1066 tenants in the fiefs of other related tenants-in-chief (see notes to Ch. 19 and Ch. 25). They may also have shared the holding of 'Dart' (36,24 and 42,20).<br>Both Theobald's and Odo's lands later form the Honour of (Great) Torrington; see Sanders p. 48 and Ch. 50 note. Many of these lands are found in the Inq. PM of Richard *de Merton* (Cal. Inq. PM vol. xiii no. 268). |

Ch. 36       IN THE EXON. BOOK these places fall in the same order as in the Exchequer volume.
(cont'd.)    Their Hundred groupings are:
             36,1-4     Hartland                        36,18      Hemyock
             36,5-7     Merton                          36,19-20   Budleigh
             36,8-9     Fremington                      36,21-25   Witheridge
             36,10-16   Braunton and Shirwell           36,26-27   Colyton
             36,17      South Molton
36,1         YARNSCOMBE. A detached parish of Hartland Hundred (3); it can be identified in the
             Tax Return for that Hundred (ii: the King has not had his tax from ½ virgate 1 furlong
             (fertinum) held by Theobald there, which corresponds to the 3 furlongs (ferlinos) of
             villagers' land that paid tax in this entry). It is held as *Muchelaerneston* ['Much'
             Yarnscombe, contrasting with 'Little' Yarnscombe 16,32] in FA i p. 342 from John
             *de Umfravill'* who is elsewhere a tenant of the Honour of Torrington (36,26 note);
             see RH i p. 89b, Cal. Inq. PM vol. iii no. 599, viii no. 363, ix no. 663.
36,2         BUCKS (CROSS). In Woolfardisworthy parish, Hartland Hundred (3). In Cal. Inq. PM
             vol. vi no. 710 (of William son of William son of Martyn) John *de Morton* holds as one
             fee *Ailmer[sdon]* [Alminstone 42,3], *Buckish* and *Lane* [Lane Mill and Lane Barton,
             GR SS 3420, part of Alminstone in 1086]. DB *Bochewis* is found on Greenwood's map
             of 1827 in the forms West Buckish in Hartland Hundred (3) and East Buckish just in
             Shebbear Hundred (4); the boundary between these two Hundreds seems to have been
             altered in the Middle Ages; see 42,4 note. The name is now represented by Bucks Mills
             and Bucks Cross; EPNS i p. 81.
36,3-4       (SOUTH) HOLE. MILFORD. Both lie in Hartland parish and Hundred (3). In Fees
             p. 775 Reginald *Beupel*, Roger *Giffard'* and the Prior of *Frythelarestok'* [Frithelstock,
             see 15,10 note] hold from the Honour of Torrington in *Melleford'*, *Hole* and *Herdeswik*
             [Hardisworthy GR SS 2220 near South Hole]. These places are *Hele Beaupel* and
             *Herdesworth[i]* in FA i p. 342 and *Hole, Herdesworthe, Millford* and *Mannesleghe*
             [Mansley SS 2221] in Cal. Inq. PM vol. vi no. 710; see FA i p. 410, Cal. Inq. PM vol. v
             no. 527, xi no. 118, xvi no. 258. These places form a unit in the south-west of the
             parish; North Hole is at its northern end.
36,5         SPECCOTT. In Merton parish, Shebbear Hundred (4). *Spekcoth'* is held from Torrington
             Honour in Fees p. 775; see FA i p. 411, Cal. Inq. PM vol. vi no. 710 and OJR H10 p. 574.
36,6         (LITTLE) MARLAND. In Petrockstowe parish, Shebbear Hundred (4). The basic name
             is also found in Peters Marland parish (35,13). It is *Merlond Pye* in FA i p. 359; see Cal.
             Inq. PM vol. vi no. 710, EPNS i p. 106 and OJR H10 p. 575.
36,7         OWLACOMBE. Now in Roborough parish, Fremington Hundred (5), but it lay in
             Shebbear Hundred (4) in the Middle Ages. In Fees p. 775 *Ullecumb'* [Owlacombe],
             *Blythemesham* [Blinsham in Beaford, GR SS 5116, perhaps carved out of Beaford 1,51]
             and *Wollecumb'* [Woolacombe, 36,15, in Shirwell Hundred (2)] are held by Robert
             *filius Pagani* and his wife Nesta from the Honour of Torrington; see Cal. Inq. PM vol. vi
             no. 710, FA i pp. 359, 412 and OJR H10 p. 575.
             3 PLOUGHS THERE. The villagers' 2 ploughs (see Lordship and Villagers' Table) seem
             rather too many for the people recorded. It is possible that the teams were shared with
             the adjacent manor of Barlington (3,15) which has 3 villagers and 2 smallholders and no
             recorded ploughs; though, as this Barlington seems to have been part of, or connected
             with, that added to Roborough (3,19), despite the difference in TRE holder, the lack of
             teams there may have been supplied by Roborough itself.
36,8-9       BICKLETON. HOLLOWCOMBE. Bickleton is in Instow parish and Hollowcombe in
             Fremington, both in Fremington Hundred (5). *Bykanthon'* is held in Fees p. 774 from
             the Honour of Torrington; see FA i p. 371, Cal. Inq. PM vol. iii no. 519, OJR H8 p. 513,
             and, for the DB form of Bickleton, EPNS i p. 117. On Hollowcombe, see OJR H8
             pp. 499, 513 and 23,1 note.
36,9         THEOBALD HIMSELF HOLDS. Repeated at the beginning of 36,9-14 inclusive.
             3 SALT-WORKERS [WHO] PAY.... See 6,6 note on villagers 'farming' manors and
             cf. 34,11 note. As there are two main verbs in this sentence, *sunt* and *reddunt*, it seems
             likely that the scribe mistakenly omitted a *qui* before *reddunt*; Exon. has one there.
36,10        SAUNTON. In Braunton parish and Hundred (1). It is *Santon'* held in Fees p. 774 from
             the Honour of Torrington; see FA i p. 414, Cal. Inq. PM vol. iii no. 519, viii no. 390 and
             OJR H8 p. 413.
36,11-13     HOLE. GEORGEHAM. SPREACOMBE. These places are respectively North and South
             Hole in Georgeham parish, a detachment of Shirwell Hundred (2) in the Middle Ages;

36,11-13 Georgeham parish, Braunton Hundred (1); and Spreacombe in Mortehoe parish, which
(cont'd.) with Woolacombe (36,15) in the same parish was also a detachment of Shirwell Hundred
in the Middle Ages, although Mortehoe itself was and is in Braunton Hundred. In Fees
p. 774, in two consecutive entries, *Hamme* is held by Robert *de Edinthon'* from the
Honour of Torrington and with *Sprecumb'* and *Hole* and *Thaungelegh* [Thongsleigh in
Budleigh Hundred (14), see 36,20 note] from the same Honour. In FA i p. 360 Mauger
*de Sancto Albino* holds in *Hamme* in Braunton (Hundred), in *Spreycomb* and *Southole*
in Shirwell and *Twangeslegh* [Thongsleigh, see above] in Budleigh. In the same schedule
(FA i p. 361) he holds *Pydekewill* [Pickwell], *Gratton* [Gratton], *Northole, Strodeton*
[see Stourton 36,21-23 note] and *Estwere* [unidentified], the first two being held by
the Bishop of Coutances in 1086; see 3,39 note. Georgeham is so called from the
dedication of the church; EPNS i p. 43. On these holdings see Cal. Inq. PM vol. xiii
no. 268 and OJR H8 pp. 444, 485.

36,11   2 VILLAGERS .... PAY 5s. See 6,6 note on villagers 'farming' land.

36,13   VITALIS. In Devon the forms of this Latin name ('vital, full of life, lively') (whence
OFr *Vit(t)el*, ME *Vidal*) are *Vitalis* in DB and *Vitalis, Fitellus, Vithel&, Vital(us)* in
Exon. See PNDB pp. 405-406.

36,14   OSSABOROUGH. Now in Mortehoe parish, Braunton Hundred (1). It does not appear
in the fee lists but may well have been a detached part of Shirwell Hundred (2) in the
Middle Ages; see EPNS i p. 53 and OJR H8 p. 389.

36,15   WOOLACOMBE. Now in Mortehoe parish, Braunton Hundred (1), but it was a
detachment of Shirwell Hundred (2) in the Middle Ages. It is accounted for in Fees
p. 775 with Owlacombe (36,7 note), is *Wollecombe* 'in the Hundred of Shirwell' in
FA i p. 359 and *Overewelecumb* [now Over Woolacombe Barton ᶜ R SS 4643] in
FA i p. 336; see FA i p. 416 and OJR H8 pp. 467, 485.
BRICTITH. DB and Exon. *Brisidus* represents OE *Beorhtgyth*, feminine; PNDB p. 194.

36,16   MARWOOD. A parish in Braunton Hundred (1). In Fees p. 774 this holding is
particularised as *Westecoth'* [Westcott Barton GR SS 5338] held by Eustace *de
Merewod'* of the Honour of Torrington. In FA i p. 360 the same land is *Westecote* and
*Patford* [Patsford SS 5339]; see FA i p. 414, Cal. Inq. PM vol. iv (o.s.) no. 63 (= TDA 38
p. 330) and OJR H8 p. 401.

36,17   MOLLAND. Now in North Molton parish, South Molton Hundred (6), distinct from
the Molland (1,41. 3,61) that was a separate Hundred and is now a parish in South
Molton Hundred. For the 'Hundred' of North Molton, see the Appendix. In Fees p. 775
Ralph *Sarazenus* holds in *Molland'* from the Honour of Torrington. A Thomas *Sarazin*
is an assessor in the later North Molton Hundred in LSR (1332) p. 109; see OJR H9
p. 522.
WHOLE .... IS WASTE. Exon. *est tota uastata*; Molland is close to the south-west edge
of Exmoor. See second note under C 3 and cf. notes to 3,35. 19,18. 20,2 and 21,5.

36,18   CULM (DAVY). DB *Cumbe*. It lies in Hemyock parish and Hundred (16). It is called
Culm 'Davy' and sometimes *Cumbe Wydeworth* (FA i p. 367) from David *de Wydworth'*
[from Widworthy 36,26] who held *Cumb'* in Fees p. 775 from the Honour of
Torrington. It is *Combe Davi* in FA i p. 339; see FA i p. 430 and OJR H2 p. 45. The
modern form has been influenced by the nearby river Culm. See 2,12 note.
COLBRAN HELD. In the MS *ten'* originally written, then corrected to *teneb'* but
without the ᵇ sign being erased. Farley does not print the ᵇ sign; see 16,151 note.
OLIVER HOLDS GORWELL .... ½ VIRGATE. According to the Tax Return for
Hemyock Hundred (xiv) the King had no tax from ½ virgate that Oliver held from
Theobald son of Berner; this is Oliver's only holding of the right size in this Hundred.

36,19   CHERITON (FITZPAINE). A parish in (West) Budleigh Hundred (14) and identifiable
in the Budleigh Hundred Tax Return (xvi). In Fees p. 775 Thomas *de Santon* (from
Saunton 36,10) holds in *Churiton'*; see Fees p. 762, FA i p. 426, Cal. Inq. PM vol. iii
no. 519 and OJR in TDA 35 p. 283. In Fees p. 761 Baldwin *de Raddun'* (who also held
West Raddon 15,5) holds *La Furse* [Furze GR SS 8800 in Shobrooke] from the Honour
of Torrington. It may have been part of this land; see Fees p. 775, FA i p. 426 and OJR
in TDA 35 p. 281.

36,20   JAGELIN. In the MS *Jagelin*; Farley prints *Iagelin*, but the first letter has a pronounced
'tail', and no 'foot' like an *I*. In Exon. it is *Iagelin(us)*.
COOMBE. Probably in Cheriton Fitzpaine parish, Budleigh Hundred (14). It does not,
however, appear under this name in the fee lists, but it may well be represented by the
*Thaungelegh'* of Fees p. 774, coupled with Georgeham, Spreacombe and Hole (36,11-13

note). This place is Thongsleigh [GR SS 9011] in that part of Cruwys Morchard parish that lay in Budleigh Hundred. There is a further entry for *Twangeslegh'* in Fees p. 775; see FA i p. 426. If this is so, the *Cumbe* of DB could have been, or included, Coombeland (GR SS 9010 in Cruwys Morchard parish) which lies between Coombe and Thongsleigh and refers to a different valley, though one rising to the same ridge. OJR in TDA 35 p. 283 counts Thongsleigh as a part of Cheriton Fitzpaine (36,19).

36,21-23 WASHFORD (PYNE). Now the parish of Washford Pyne in Witheridge Hundred (7). The DB name seems to have covered a number of separate places. One was probably *Stordethon'* in Fees pp. 760, 774 or *Stordeton* in FA i p. 421 [Stourton in Thelbridge, GR SS 8012, see 3,39 and 36,11-13 notes] held from the Honour of Torrington. Other parts are represented by *Wasford', Westecoth'* [Westcott SS 8011] and *Dertth'* ['Dart' 36,24] held by the Prior of Barnstaple and Robert *de Horthon'* in Fees pp. 760, 774; and by *Wafford* held by Herbert *de Pin, Strethe* [Stretch SS 8113; see EPNS i p. 396], *Derte, Uppecote* [Upcott SS 8212] and *Westcote* in FA i p. 344; and by *Wasseford, Strath, Westecote* and *Derte* in FA i p. 421. Cal. Inq. PM vol. iii no. 519 includes *Dupeford* [Deptford SS 8412 in Cruwys Morchard] with several of these places. On these manors see Cal. Inq. PM vol. xiii no. 268 and OJR in TDA 30 p. 405, 36 p. 317.

36,22 FOUR THANES. In the MS *Duo taini* originally written, but with the first 3 letters altered to *Qua* followed by a comma to indicate the *ttuor* interlined.

36,23 ALWOLD. DB *Aluuold(us)*, Exon. main entry *Aluualdus*, but in the T.O. *Aluuard(us)*. The T.O. form probably represents AN dissimulation of *l-r* (PNDB p. 155 and §60), rather than a discrepant name *Alward* (OE *Aelfweard* or *Aethelweard*, see 1,41 note). See also 36,24 note.

THESE THREE MANORS. That is, the three manors of Washford Pyne (36,21-23).

36,24 'DART'. There are three holdings (21,13. 36,24. 42,20) in Witheridge Hundred (7) named from the Little Dart river; see 21,6 note. The first of these can be positively identified with Dart Raffe; see note. Theobald's holding falling after the three entries for Washford Pyne is probably the *Derte* associated with it (and so perhaps adjacent to it) in feudal documents (36,21-23 note), in particular called *Estderte* in Cal. Inq. PM vol. xiii no. 268. Identified by VCH p. 509 note 6 with Queen Dart (followed by EPNS ii p. 399 — Queen unknown) and said by the Indexer of Fees to be in Thelbridge, it awaits positive identification and location. The places associated with it lie in a compact area south of the Little Dart river in Thelbridge and Washford Pyne parishes; see OJR in TDA 30 pp. 404, 422 and Oliver *Mon.* p. 202.

ALWOLD .... ALWOLD ALSO. DB *Aluuald(us)*, Exon. *Aluualdus* for the 1066 holder and *predictus Aluuardus* for the 1086 tenant; see 36,23 note on *l-r* interchange in *Aluualdus* and *Aluuardus*.

36,25 RIFTON. DB *Restone* from OE *(ge)rēfantūn* 'reeve's farm'; EPNS ii p. 393. It lies in Stoodleigh parish, Witheridge Hundred (7), but might have lain in Bampton Hundred (8) in 1086 (see the Appendix). *Refthon'* is held from the Honour of Torrington (Fees pp. 760, 774) but seems to have passed to the Honour of Berry (on which, see Ch. 34 note); see FA i pp. 363, 421 and OJR in TDA 30 p. 423.

36,26 WIDWORTHY .... WILMINGTON. Widworthy is a parish in Colyton Hundred (22); Wilmington is now in Widworthy, but was formerly in Offwell parish, in the same Hundred. One of these manors must account for the arrears of tax on 1 virgate held by Oliver from Theobald recorded in the Tax Return for Colyton Hundred (xx). In Fees p. 775 *Wideworth'* is held of John *de Humframvill* of the Honour of Torrington; see FA i pp. 330, 428 and OJR H7 pp. 339, 354-355.

36,27 WHICH PAYS 8d. Or perhaps 'which paid 8d', as *reddt* can abbreviate the past *reddebat* as well as *reddit* (see 1,7;37 notes). Exon. has *reddebat*, as has also the T.O. entry with the additional information that Theobald was withholding the due. However, the Exchequer scribe may have had access to the information that he was in fact now paying his dues. Cf. 39,22 note.

Ch. 37 THURSTAN SON OF ROLF. *filius Rolf* in DB, *filius Rofi* in Exon.; the Exon. form is not mentioned in OEB p. 196, though it also occurs in the heading for his Somerset lands (382 b 1). Thurstan may have been the standard bearer at Hastings (see Ellis DTG pp. 186-187) who was rewarded with land in Glos., Somerset, Herefordshire, Berkshire, Dorset, etc.

37,1 CHURCHSTANTON. A parish in Hemyock Hundred (16), transferred to Somerset in 1896. In Fees p. 794 John *de Tuddeham* holds in *Stanton'* a ½ fee of the Honour of *Kerlihun* [Caerleon] of Nicholas *de Molis*. It was also known as *Churystanton* or

37,1        *Staunton Todeham*, see FA i pp. 338, 366, 430, Cal. Inq. PM vol. viii no. 69 and OJR H2
(cont'd.)   p. 43.
            GERO. DB *Geron*, Exon. *Gereon*, represent OG *Gero*, a personal name of uncertain
            origin (Forssner p. 108). The form *Geron* was mistakenly used in the 'Elsewhere' section
            of the Somerset volume in this series.
Ch. 38      ALFRED OF 'SPAIN'. The forms *de Ispania* in the Landholders' List (col. 100a), in this
            chapter heading and 38,1 and in the T.O., and *Ispaniensis* in the main Exon. section
            heading, are a kind of word-play. Alfred came from Épaignes in the département of Eure,
            France (OEB pp. 92, 134 and see Loyd pp. 51–52) and he held land also in Dorset,
            Somerset, Wiltshire, Gloucestershire and Herefordshire. Alfred's lands pass to the Honour
            of Stowey (in Somerset), then to the Chandos and Columbières families.
            THE EXON. ORDER of this chapter is the same as in DB and the places will have lain
            in Shirwell and Silverton (Hayridge) Hundreds respectively in 1086.
38,1–2      ARLINGTON. ORWAY. Arlington is a parish in Shirwell Hundred (2) and Orway lies in
            Kentisbeare parish, Hayridge Hundred (15). They are held in Fees p. 782 as *Auvrington'*
            by William *de Ralegh'* and *Orweye* by Thomas *de Orweye*, both from Philip *de Culumbers*.
            Thomas *de Orweye* holds another part of Orway of the Honour of Bradninch (19,21
            note); see FA i pp. 322, 336, Cal. Inq. PM vol. xiv no. 281 and OJR in TDA 42 p. 238
            and H8 pp. 465, 484.
            ALWY. DB *Aluui*, Exon. *Ailuuid(us), Ailuuius*, for OE *Aethelwig*; see PNDB pp. 189–
            190. Cf. 25,2 note. This Alwy is undoubtedly the same as Alfred's predecessor *Aluui*
            in his lands in Somerset, Dorset and Wiltshire, who on several occasions in the Exon.
            for Somerset is called Al(f)wy son of Banna and who may also have been Al(f)wy the
            King's reeve; see Somerset Exon. Notes to 35,24 and Somerset General Notes 35,1.
38,1        TWITCHEN. DB *Tuichel*, Exon. *Tuchel*, accepted by EPNS i p. 57. It lies in Arlington
            parish, Shirwell Hundred (2), and was probably alienated from William of Falaise's fief
            (20,1–4 note).
Ch. 39      ALFRED THE BRETON. See 35,4 note on his name. His manors pass to the Honour
            of Plympton (Ch. 21 note).
            THIS FIEF IS ABSENT from the Exon. Book, but its Hundred order is what would be
            expected in Exon:

| | | | |
|---|---|---|---|
| 39,1–2 | Lifton | 39,11 | Kerswell |
| 39,3 | (uncertain) | 39,12–13 | Chillington |
| 39,4–7 | Torrington | 39,14–17 | *Alleriga* and Diptford |
| 39,8 | Merton | 39,18–21 | Walkhampton |
| 39,9 | Braunton | 39,22 | Borough of Exeter |
| 39,10 | Cliston | | |

39,1        WILLSWORTHY. Now in Peter Tavy parish, Roborough Hundred (25), but it formerly
            lay in Lifton (18) and can be identified in the Tax Return for the latter Hundred (i).
            In Fees pp. 756, 789 *Wyvelesworth', Stondon'* [Standon GR SX 5481] and *Burydon'*
            [Beardon SX 5184] are held from Geoffrey *de Mandevil'* of the Honour of Plympton
            in a Lifton Hundred group; see FA i pp. 320, 355, 406, Cal. Inq. PM vol. i no. 154,
            xiv no. 325 and OJR in TDA 46 p. 196.
39,2        WIHENOC. *Wihuenech* here, *Wihuenec* in 39,7, are poor spellings of the Breton personal
            name *Wihenoc*, seen also in DB Glos. 32,9 (see note) and Norfolk 21,1. He was the
            founder of Monmouth Priory; when he became a monk his Devonshire lands largely
            passed to William *le Poer* son of his brother Baderon; see OJR in TDA 46 p. 215.
            SPRYTOWN. In Stowford parish, Lifton Hundred (18). It is *Spree* held of the Honour
            of Plympton by John *de Sicca Villa* from William *le Poure* and by William ultimately
            from Geoffrey *de Mandevil'* in Lifton Hundred in Fees p. 757; see Fees p. 789, FA i
            pp. 321, 356, 406, Cal. Inq. PM vol. ii no. 154, OJR in TDA 46 p. 215 and 39,8 note.
39,3        FERDING. 'A ferding/ferling/furlong of land'. The place-name has disappeared, if it
            really was one, and the Hundred is uncertain. There is no evidence to connect it with
            Willsworthy (39,1) as OJR in TDA 36 p. 351 and in VCH p. 535 note 2 states.
39,4        INGLEIGH. In Broadwood Kelly parish, (Black) Torrington Hundred (11). DB *Genelie*
            is also represented by Yenne Park and Copse [GR SS 619068] to the east of Ingleigh,
            EPNS i p. 137. In Fees p. 788 *Jonelegh'* is held by Matthew *de Bello Monte* from the
            Honour of Plympton; see FA i p. 408, Cal. Inq. PM vol. i no. 564, iii no. 309 and
            OJR H5 p. 216.
39,5        EXBOURNE. A parish in (Black) Torrington Hundred (11). It is *Yekkesburne* in Fees
            p. 789, held by Alan *de Buddekeshyde* (from Budshead 39,18) from the Honour of

|       |  |
|-------|--|
| | Plympton. The land included *Cokeswell* [Coxwell GR SS 6003]; see Cal. Inq. PM vol. xiv no. 325, OJR in VCH p. 535 note 4, H5 pp. 205, 216 and next note. |
| 39,6 | CURWORTHY .... THREE MANORS. DB *Corneurde*. It lies in Inwardleigh parish, (Black) Torrington Hundred (11). The other two manors are named in the T.O. (see Exon. Notes here) as *Corneorda* [a second holding in Curworthy] and *Witefelda* [Widefield GR SX 5596]. In Fees p. 789 *Whitefeud'* and *Cureworth'* are coupled with Exbourne (39,5) held by Alan *de Buddekeshyde* (from Budshead 39,18) from the Honour of Plympton. In FA i p. 328 in (Black) Torrington Hundred, Roger *de Cokeswell* (from Coxwell, see 39,5 note) holds *Widefeld* from the Countess *de Albemarle*; see FA i p. 374, OJR in VCH p. 537 note 13 and H5 pp. 206, 216. |
| 39,7 | ASHBURY. A parish in (Black) Torrington Hundred (11). It is represented by *Aysbyri* or *Aysbery* and *Scobbechestre* [Scobchester GR SX 5196 in Ashbury] in Fees p. 788, FA i pp. 328, 408–409, held of the Honour of Plympton; see Cal. Inq. PM vol. ii no. 154, OJR H5 pp. 206, 216 and 39,8 note. |
| 39,8 | HELE. Earlier identifications with 'Luttocks Hele' in Cullompton (39,9 note) or Hele in Bradninch have been replaced by the certainty that it is Hele *Poer* (see first note under 39,2) in Meeth parish in Shebbear Hundred (4). In Cal. Inq. PM vol. xiv no. 325 (of Hugh *de Courteney*) *Hele Poure, Spry* (39,2) and *Asshebury* (39,7), all held by Wihenoc in 1086, are held together of the Honour of Plympton. This *Hele* is held in Fees p. 788 from the Honour of Plympton by Roger *Giffard*, William *Lampree* and Thomas *de Aureford'* and is now Giffords Hele in Meeth; see Cal. Inq. PM vol. ii no. 154, EPNS i p. 99, OJR in TDA 42 p. 233, 46 p. 221, H10 pp. 548, 558 and notes to 15,47. 16,42 and 47,1. |
| 39,9 | ?ROADWAY. DB *Radewei* 'red road', possibly the place in Mortehoe parish, Braunton Hundred (1); see 31,3-4 note. The earlier identification of this place with Rudway in Rewe was affected by that of Hele (39,8), once thought to be 'Luttocks Hele' in Cullompton, Hayridge Hundred (15); see OJR in TDA 28 p. 477, 29 p. 265, 36 p. 361, 42 pp. 227, 248 and EPNS ii p. 445. Rewe is in Wonford Hundred (19), but Rudway, like Up Exe (3,70), could well have been in Hayridge. But Hayridge Hundred places are consistently entered after those for Cliston (20), so Rudway would be expected after Larkbeare (39,10). If, however, Alfred held land in Braunton or Shirwell Hundreds (1-2), it would have been entered here, so this place could be Roadway in Mortehoe, which has the same derivation as Rudway (EPNS i p. 53). |
| 39,10 | LARKBEARE. Part now lies in Talaton parish, Hayridge Hundred (15), part in Whimple parish, Cliston Hundred (20). Alfred the Breton is allowed 1 virgate of lordship land in the Tax Return for Silverton (Hayridge) Hundred (xiii) and ½ hide lordship in that for Cliston (xii). There is no corresponding Exon. entry for this manor to supply the lordship detail that Exchequer DB omits, but it is likely that the Cliston Tax Return entry stands for the present land (½ hide plus the added ½ hide being sufficient to allow ½ hide lordship), as there is no other holding in this Hundred of either Alfred the Breton or a plain Alfred; meanwhile, the lordship in the Silverton Tax Return may well be the 1½ virgates an unspecified Alfred held at Chitterley under the Count of Mortain (15,60). For the descent of Larkbeare in the Pipard family, see FA i pp. 367, 434, Cal. Inq. PM vol. i no. 650, ix no. 137 and OJR H7 pp. 366, 383.<br>WHIMPLE, BALDWIN'S MANOR. See 16,94 for Baldwin the Sheriff's manor of Whimple and further details of this ½ hide. |
| 39,11 | BATTLEFORD. In Ipplepen parish, Haytor Hundred (29). *Bakeleford'* or *Bakeford'* is held from the Honour of Plympton in Haytor Hundred (29) in Fees pp. 767, 790; see FA i pp. 317, 348, 391. The holder in FA i p. 317 is Peter *de Fishacre* who also holds Grimpstone (39,12) in FA i p. 332, Grimpstonleigh (39,13 note) and Moreleigh (39,16) in FA i p. 324; see OJR in TDA 40 p. 115. |
| 39,12 | GRIMPSTONE. In Blackawton parish, Coleridge Hundred (30). It is *Grimeston'* held from the Honour of Plympton by William *de Morlegh'* (from Moreleigh 39,16) in Fees p. 790; see FA i pp. 332, 350, 394, OJR in TDA 43 p. 226 and 39,11 note.<br>IN LORDSHIP, HOWEVER, 1 PLOUGH. The *tamen* was included to indicate that the lordship plough, when added to the villagers' ploughs, exceeded the plough estimate; see fourth note under 1,3 and cf. notes to 49,1 and 40,4. |
| 39,13 | GRIMPSTONLEIGH. DB *Lege*. Now in Woodleigh parish, Stanborough Hundred (28), but, as its modern name suggests, it was long associated with Grimpstone (39,12), being coupled with it in LSR (1334) p. 64 as *Grymeston' cum Legh*; see LSR (1332) p. 95. Both in Domesday and in the Middle Ages it seems to have been a detachment of |

39 - 40

Coleridge Hundred (30). *Legh Artour* and *Grymeston* are adjacent entries in Cal. Inq. PM vol. xiv (n.s.) no. 325 and vol. iv (o.s.) no. 63 (= TDA 38 p. 322); see OJR in VCH p. 535 note 12 and in TDA 43 pp. 199, 226.

39,14 BATTISBOROUGH. In Holbeton parish, Ermington Hundred (27). Together with 39,17 (Ugborough), this holding probably accounts for the 2 hides lordship recorded for Alfred in the Tax Return for *Alleriga* Hundred (xxx). The land passed to the Abbot of Buckfast and is held as *Battekesbergh'* in Fees p. 771 with 'Abbots Ash' and Heathfield (6,7-8); see TE p. 153a, RH i p. 90b, FA i p. 353 and OJR H6 p. 327.

CREACOMBE. In Newton Ferrers parish, Ermington Hundred (27); see EPNS i p. 283.

39,15 (SOUTH) MILTON. A parish in Stanborough Hundred (28). The 2 hides of the tax assessment will no doubt have included the 1 hide of Alfred's lordship allowed in the Tax Return for Diptford (Stanborough) Hundred (xxvi), there being no other holdings in DB of an Alfred in this Hundred. This holding appears as *Middelton* in FA i p. 324 in Stanborough Hundred (28) and probably included *Nyweton* [Osborne Newton in Churchstow, GR SX 6945] and *Horswyll* [Horswell SX 6942]; see FA i pp. 351, 396. It represents the unnamed lands of Fees pp. 766, 790 held by Baldwin *de Wayford* and Ralph *Le Abbe*; see OJR in TDA 45 p. 185.

LAND FOR 12 PLOUGHS. In the MS and Farley *xii car⁷*; in the facsimile the first *i* is blurred (probably because it is written over an erasure) making it resemble an *x*. There are several erasures and corrections in this entry.

39,16 MORELEIGH. A parish in Stanborough Hundred (28). It is held from the Honour of Plympton in Fees pp. 765, 790 as *Morlegh'* and included *Starig'* [Storridge GR SX 738532]; see FA i pp. 324, 351, 396, OJR in TDA 45 p. 180 and 39,11-12 notes.

ADDED TO .... GRIMPSTONLEIGH. See Exon. Notes here.

39,17 ALFRED HIMSELF HOLDS. Repeated at the beginning of 39,17-21 inclusive.

UGBOROUGH. A parish in Ermington Hundred (27); see 39,14 note. In Fees pp. 771, 789 Alice *de Mohun* holds *Uggebergh'* from the Honour of Plympton; see FA i p. 399, Cal. Inq. PM vol. ii nos. 306, 436, vii no. 297, RH i p. 69b, TE p. 149b and OJR H6 p. 324. One *ferling* in *Uggeburgh'* was given to Torre Abbey; Oliver *Mon.* p. 169.

39,18 BUDSHEAD. In St. Budeaux parish, Roborough Hundred (25). The DB form *Bucheside* indicates a hide of land belonging to the Celtic saint, St. Budoc, who named the parish (EPNS i pp. 236-237). *Buddekeshid'* is held in Fees p. 789 from the Honour of Plympton; see Cal. Inq. PM vol. i no. 564, FA i pp. 341, 403, OJR H3 pp. 104, 123 and 39,5 note.

39,19-20 TAMERTON (FOLIOT). BLAXTON. They are in Roborough Hundred (25), the former being a parish in which the latter lies. In Fees p. 789 *Tamerton'* and *Blakestane* are held of the Honour of Plympton by Robert *Folioth'*; see FA i p. 403 (*Tamerton Folyet*), FA i p. 340, Cal. Inq. PM vol. i no. 564, iii no. 231, iv no. 295, xiv no. 325 and OJR H3 pp. 121-122. According to TE p. 153, part of this land was held by Plympton Priory in *Tamton* and *Martinescube* (*Martynstowe* in VE ii p. 376), that is Maristow GR SX 4764 (EPNS i p. 242).

39,21 (PETER) TAVY. A parish in Roborough Hundred (25). It is *Tawy* held by Robert *Folioth'* from the Honour of Plympton in Fees p. 789, *Peterstavy* in FA i p. 340, *Tavifolys* in FA i p. 402; see OJR H3 p. 122. For Mary Tavy, see 17,13.

39,22 WHICH PAYS 8d. Or perhaps 'which paid 8d', as *redd* can abbreviate the past *reddebat* as well as the present *reddit* (see 1,7;37 notes). The T.O. entry has *reddidti* with the additional information that Alfred was withholding the due. However, the Exchequer scribe may have been told that he was now paying his due. Cf. 36,27 note.

Ch. [40] AT THIS POINT IN THE MS the rubricator appears to have checked the numbering in the Landholders' List and, seeing that Ansger was numbered XLI there, decided to make the numbers tally once again (see L 25 note above) by giving him the same number in the text. This led to there being no Ch. 40 in the text, so the present editors have thought it best to renumber Chs. 41-53 inclusive as Chs. 40-52, to avoid misleading the reader into thinking that there were 53 chapters in Devon, instead of 52. However, this does mean that the chapter numbers no longer tally with those of the Landholders' List.

ANSGER. He is called Ansger of Montacute in 40,1 and Ansger of Senarpont (département of Somme, France) in the T.O. entries for 40,4-7 and in the Tax Return for Tawton Hundred (ix); see Exon. Notes to 40,1-2. He is apparently the same man as Ansger the Breton (see 15,12-13 note on him); VCH Somerset i p. 412. His holdings later form part of the Honour of Gloucester (Ch. 24 note).

FOR THE EXON. ORDER of this chapter, see Ch. 22 note.

# 40

40,1      STAFFORD. In Dolton parish, (North) Tawton Hundred (12). Stafford will account for the 1 furlong (*fertinum*) of lordship land allowed to Ansger (of Senarpont, see Ch. 40 note) in the Tawton Hundred Tax Return (ix).

40,2      ANSGER HIMSELF HOLDS. Repeated at the beginning of 40,2-7 inclusive.
(GREAT) TORRINGTON. A parish in Fremington Hundred (5). This holding does not occur under its own name in the feodaries, but there are a number of Honour of Gloucester holdings that could account for it and for the 3 virgates held by the three Frenchmen — Gotshelm, Walter and Ansger — in Great Torrington (see 42,6 note). In Fees p. 779 Richard *de Whyteslegh'* holds in *Whytefeld* [unidentified], called *Wyteslegh* in FA i pp. 371, 413 [Whitsleigh in St. Giles in the Wood parish, GR SS 5517]. In FA i p. 413 the heir of William *de Wyteslegh'* holds an unidentified *Als* (apparently the same as *Assh* held by Simon *de Wybbery* in FA i p. 371). Another Gloucester Honour fee is *Steveneston'* [Stevenstone GR SS 5219] in Fees p. 779. In FA i p. 371 *Steveneston* is associated with *Viraworth[y]* [Virworthy 24,32]; see FA i p. 413. Hiscott, a further Gloucester fee, may be part of Newton Tracey (25,3 note). On all this, see OJR H8 pp. 513-514.

40,3      BRIMBLECOMBE. It now lies in Iddesleigh parish, Shebbear Hundred (4), EPNS i p. 94, but is close to the boundary of (North) Tawton Hundred (12) where Stafford (40,1, the previous entry in Exon.) lies. Part of Iddesleigh (1,63) also lay in (North) Tawton Hundred in 1086. In later times the Honour of Gloucester holds Iddesleigh manor and it is probable that Brimblecombe is included in one of its members enumerated in Fees p. 779 (see 1,63 note). It is not well evidenced in later documents, but a William *de Bremylcomb'* is found in Iddesleigh parish, Shebbear Hundred, in 1332 (LSR p. 19).
ALCHERE. DB here and for 47,7 *Alcher*; Exon. *Algher(us)* and *Alger(us)* respectively. See PNDB p. 242 s.n. OE *Ealhhere*.

40,4      CHELDON. A parish in Witheridge Hundred (7). *Chedeldun'* is held from the Honour of Gloucester in Fees p. 778 by William *Calleweye*; see Fees p. 758, FA i p. 419 and notes to 16,147 and 40,7.
IN LORDSHIP, HOWEVER, 1 PLOUGH. The scribe usually writes *tamen* only when, as in 40,6, the ploughs actually on the land exceed the estimate (and by no means always then; see fourth note under 1,3). Here, however, because for some reason he omitted the villagers' 2 ploughs, the *tamen* makes no sense; no doubt he intended to add them when he wrote the *tamen*, as he did in the similar 39,12 and 49,1. Although in the Exon. there is an erasure under most of the sentence on the lordship and villagers' land and ploughs and the villagers' ploughs themselves are corrected from *i* to *ii*, the Exchequer scribe must have seen the entry in its corrected state because of his use of *tamen*; it is possible he had a break after he wrote the word.
PASTURE, 10 ACRES. In the MS the remaining two-thirds of this line is blank after *pasturę* which surprisingly has no dot after it. As in 33,1 (see note) the value of the manor comes later. Cf. 11,1 note on other spaces left in entries.
THESE TWO LANDS PAY 50s. The main manor of Cheldon must pay 25s, as the value of the added land is given as 25s in the T.O. entry (see Exon. Notes).
TO THIS MANOR HAVE BEEN ADDED.... The added land is also called Cheldon, *Chadeledona* in the main Exon. entry, *Chaldeldona* in the T.O.; see Exon. Notes. It is possible that it was subtracted from Chulmleigh (16,140) which is adjacent and was held by a Brictmer TRE.

40,5-6    MUXBERE. SUTTON. Both lie in Halberton parish and Hundred (10). In Fees p. 780 *Mukelebere* and *Sweteton'* are held from the Earl of Gloucester; see FA i pp. 338, 369, 432 and OJR H2 p. 61. Sutton is 'Sweta's *tūn*' (EPNS ii p. 550) assimilated to Sutton ('south *tūn*); see 41,1 note.
BRICTRIC. Probably Brictric son of Algar (on whom see 24,21 note); cf. next note but one.

40,5      ANSGER....AS ONE MANOR. This is written at a slant in the MS, the *p* being ½ line higher than the preceding *xxx solid'*, so that it resembles a capital, but with the *Ansger* somewhat below the line. It was probably added, though it is in the same colour ink as the rest of the entry. It occurs at the end of the Exon. entry and the Exchequer scribe could have briefly missed it. Cf. notes to 17,13. 23,6 and 34,10.

40,6-7    WRONGFULLY ADDED TO BRICTRIC'S LANDS. That is, Ansger legally acquired some of Brictric's lands (only 40,5 in Devon), but neither Sutton nor Dolton was among them. See 15,31 note and cf. notes to 24,18-19 and to 25,20.

40,7   DOLTON. A parish in (North) Tawton Hundred (12); it is not clear why the entry is out of sequence in Exon. order (see Ch. 22 note). The land actually lay at Iddlecott [GR SS 5712] held as *Aderichescote* in Fees p. 98, *Yedescoth'* in Fees p. 778, where it is held with Cheldon (40,4) by William *Calleweye* from the Honour of Gloucester; see Fees p. 758 and FA i p. 419 and also p. 422 where the former holder is named as Philip *de Stafford* (named from 40,1 Stafford). The name 'Edric's *cote*' is derived from the 1066 holder; EPNS ii p. 367.

Ch. 41   AIULF. Probably Aiulf the Sheriff; VCH p. 521 note 5. He had succeeded Hugh son of Grip as Sheriff of Dorset by 1082/84 (*Regesta* i no. 204; Round CDF no. 1206 p. 435) and was Sheriff of Somerset by 1091 (*Regesta* i no. 315) holding both offices in the reign of Henry I and perhaps until 1120. He is called Aiulf the Chamberlain in DB Dorset Ch. 49 heading (Aiulf the Sheriff in the Landholders' List there), and was the brother of Humphrey the Chamberlain (VCH Somerset i p. 416). He was probably also at court a deputy to Robert Malet, the King's great Chamberlain; Morris in EHR xxxiii (1918) p. 151 note 48. He held land in Wiltshire as well. On the form *Aiulf*, see 17,18 note.
    Aiulf's lands descend to the Honour of Gloucester (see Ch. 24 note).
    FOR THE EXON. ORDER of this chapter, see Ch. 22 note.

41,1   SUTTON. In Halberton parish, Halberton Hundred (10). In Exon. this *Suetetona* comes directly after the entry for *Suetatona* (40,6); see OJR H2 pp. 51, 61.
    FLOHERE. See OEB p. 155 and Forssner p. 284. Another holding of his in Devon, not recorded by DB, appears in Exon. 459 a 3; see Exon. Notes Ch. 22.
    No obvious reason emerges from a study of the Exon. MS why the Exchequer scribe omitted Flohere and the lordship and villagers' ploughs from this entry. These details occupy the last line on folio 461a and the first ¾ of a line on the reverse, but the writing is neat and by the scribe of the rest of the entry, and the DB scribe obviously saw and copied the remainder of this manor's details.

41,2   WESTLEIGH. DB *Lege*. It is in that part of Burlescombe parish that lay in Halberton Hundred (10); see 24,30 note and the Appendix. In Exon. order it falls in a group of Halberton Hundred places. OJR in VCH p. 521 note 7 identifies it as "Leigh Boty *alias* Besley in Holcombe Rogus, Halberton Hundred", but this is confused. Holcombe Rogus (16,76) is in Bampton Hundred (8), and Besley (wrongly mapped by DG in the north of the parish), earlier *Beasselegh* (EPNS ii p. 535), is not connected with 'Leigh Boty'. But *Legh'* is held in a Halberton Hundred group by Ralph *Buty* in Fees p. 780 from the Honour of Gloucester. In FA i p. 338 *Botislegh* is shared between John *de Asford* and the Abbess of *Legh* [Canonsleigh] via several middle lords from the Earl of Gloucester. In FA i p. 383 it is associated with Sampford Peverell and Ayshford (27,1. 24,13); see FA i pp. 369, 432. Despite the absence of a mention in EPNS ii p. 547, there is little doubt that 'Leigh Boty' is the manor later known as Westleigh. This *Lege* was held in two parts in DB, the other holder being Walter of Claville (24,15 and note) whose portion was *c*. 1170 granted to 'Leigh' Abbey which was first for canons (whence it was called Canonsleigh) then for canonesses. Half of Aiulf's manor of Westleigh was later granted to Canonsleigh; see LSR (1332) p. 40, (1334) p. 56 and OJR H2 pp. 51, 59.

Ch. 42   ODO SON OF GAMELIN. He also held a manor in DB Somerset Ch. 38. According to the T.O. entry for 42,4 (see Exon. Notes there), his father-in-law was called Theobald, that is Theobald son of Berner (see Ch. 36 note). Odo's son William was a Constable; see G. H. White p. 151 of 'The Household of the Norman Kings' in TRHS 4th series vol. xxx (1948) and Round FE p. 487. Odo's Devonshire lands later form part of the Honour of Torrington; see Ch. 36 note.
    THE ORDER OF ENTRIES in the Exon. Book with their probable Hundredal groupings is:

|       |                        |         |            |
|-------|------------------------|---------|------------|
| 42,2  | Lifton                 | 42,14   | Bampton    |
| 42,1;3| Hartland               | 42,15   | Braunton   |
| 42,4  | Shebbear               | 42,16-18| Silverton  |
| 42,5-6| Fremington             | 42,19-21| Witheridge |
| 42,7  | Tawton                 | 42,22   | Budleigh   |
| 42,8-9| Braunton and Shirwell  | 42,23   | Tiverton   |
| 42,10-13| South Molton         | 42,24   | Halberton  |

42,1   DELLEY. In Yarnscombe parish, Hartland Hundred (3). The first element of the name, the OE personal name *Dealla*, is also present in Delworthy [GR SS 5423]; see EPNS i p. 82. The ½ virgate of lordship land here, together with the 1 furlong (*ferlinum*) lordship in 42,3, probably account for most of the 1 virgate lordship recorded for Odo in the Tax Return for Hartland Hundred (ii).

42,1 (cont'd.)   BRICTRIC HELD IT BEFORE 1066. In the MS *Brictric teneb' T. T.R.E.* The first *T* comes at the end of the first line in the central margin. The scribe, realising he had overrun the line limit, wrote *T.R.E.* on the next line, but failed to delete the first *T*.

42,2   RALPH VITALIS. Exon. *Radulfus uitalis* here and in 42,4; OEB p. 226.
STOWFORD. A parish in Lifton Hundred (18). In Fees p. 775 William *de Hywisse* (perhaps from Huish 42,4) holds *Staford'* from the Honour of Torrington; see Fees p. 757, FA i pp. 321, 355, 405, Cal. Inq. PM vol. iii no. 413 and OJR in TDA 46 p. 211.

42,3   COLWIN. Probably Colwin the reeve who according to the Tax Return for Hartland Hundred (ii) held ½ virgate in lordship; the remaining 1 furlong ('ferling') of this ½ virgate was probably his lordship of Woolfardisworthy (52,4).
ALMINSTONE. DB *Almerescote*, 'AElfmaēr's *cote*' with a later substitution of *-tūn* for *-cote*; cf. 16,9-10 note and 21,9-12 note. It lies in Woolfardisworthy parish, Hartland Hundred (3), and can be identified in that Hundred's Tax Return (ii); see above note and 42,1 note. In Fees p. 775 *Almereston* 'with members' is held from the Honour of Torrington; see FA i p. 342. One of the members will probably have been Lane and another, Walland; see 36,2 and 42,4 notes.

42,4   HUISH. A parish in Shebbear Hundred (4). This holding can be identified in the Tax Return for Merton (Shebbear) Hundred (v). In Fees p. 775 William *de Hywis* holds in *Hywis, Wyddene* [Whiddon 42,8] and *La Walle* from the Honour of Torrington; see FA i pp. 359, 411, Cal. Inq. PM vol. iii nos. 413, 519 and OJR H10 pp. 543, 574. The entry in FA i p. 359 makes it clear that *La Wallen* is in Shebbear Hundred; it is thus not in Shirwell Hundred and it is certainly not Woolley in Shirwell (OJR H10 p. 574) which is formally impossible. It may well be Walland in Woolfardisworthy (GR SS 3522) and have formed a part of Alminstone (42,3) in 1086. The Shebbear/Hartland Hundred boundary seems to have been redrawn in this area in the Middle Ages; see 36,2 note. It is less likely to be Waldons [GR SS 5706] in Iddesleigh parish in Shebbear Hundred; see EPNS i p. 94.

42,5   LITTLE WEARE. Now part of Weare Giffard parish, in that portion of Shebbear Hundred (4) that lies on the east, or Fremington Hundred side, of the river Torridge. DB makes it plain that it lay in (Great) Torrington (42,6) and thus in Fremington Hundred (5); see OJR·H10 p. 544 and 15,39 note.

42,6   (GREAT) TORRINGTON. In Fremington Hundred (5); *caput* of the later Barony. It is positively identifiable in the Tax Return for Fremington Hundred (iv); see also next note. This large holding probably extended into the modern parish of St. Giles in the Wood and included a part of Dodscott [GR SS 5419], named from Doda the TRE holder of another portion (25,4). *Doddelescoth'* is held in Fees p. 774 from the Honour of Torrington; see FA i pp. 371, 413, Cal. Inq. PM vol. iii no. 519, iv no. 428 and OJR H8 pp. 498, 512.
VILLAGERS .... 2 HIDES. The Tax Return for Fremington Hundred (iv) states that the King had no tax from 1 hide which the villagers of Odo son of Gamelin hold. This is the only villagers' holding of sufficient size in this Hundred in Ch. 42.
25 PIGMEN .... 110 PIGS. In Exon. this statement is also misplaced, after, instead of before, the resources. Cf. 23,9 and note.
THREE FRENCHMEN. Exon. names them as Gotshelm, Walter and Ansger. If they are the Gotshelm, his brother Walter of Claville and Ansger of Montacute/Senarpont who are tenants-in-chief of Chs. 25, 24, 40, then they held land at Newton Tracey (25,3), Dodscott (25,4), Instow (24,26) and Great Torrington (40,2) in this Hundred. Their subtenancies in Odo's Torrington may well have passed to the Honour of Gloucester; see OJR H8 p. 514 and 40,2 note.

42,7   BUCKLAND. In Dolton parish, (North) Tawton Hundred (12). In Fees p. 774 *Bokland'* is held of the Honour of Torrington and in FA i p. 370 *Boclond* is associated with Halgheston [Halsdon GR SS 5512, also in Dolton] and *La Wode* ['Wood' unidentified, but there is a William *at Wode* in Dolton parish in LSR (1332) p. 76; adjacent in Merton parish, Shebbear Hundred, is Great Wood, GR SS 5414]; see FA i p. 422 and OJR in TDA 29 p. 253.

42,8   WHIDDON. In Marwood parish, Braunton Hundred (1). In FA i p. 359 Richard *de Hywysh* holds *Wydedon* "in the Hundred of Braunton", with *Hywysh* [Huish 42,4] and *La Wallen* (42,4 note).

42,9   SHIRWELL. A parish in Shirwell Hundred (2). This particular holding seems to have been named *Fytelecoth'* [unidentified] after the TRE holder. It is *"Fytelcote* in the tithing of *Shirewell"* in Cal. Inq. PM vol. xiv no. 281 and so is unlikely to be Fiddlecott

42,9      in Chawleigh parish, (North) Tawton Hundred: EPNS ii p. 364. It is held in Fees p. 774 by
(cont'd.) the heir of Richard *Beupel'* from the Honour of Torrington and is *Vyttelecote* in FA i
          p. 417; see FA i p. 361 and OJR H8 p. 466.
          VITALIS HELD. The TRE tenant Vitalis here and in 42,13 is probably the same man as
          the 1066 holder of Odo's manor of Luccombe in DB Somerset 38,1, who also held it in
          1086 (see PNDB p. 405 note 8); Odo's subtenant Vitalis in 42,24 may also be the same
          person.
42,10     (GEORGE) NYMPTON. A parish in South Molton Hundred (6), its lordship being
          identifiable in the Tax Return for that Hundred (vii); see Cal. Inq. PM vol. ii no. 76,
          iv no. 428, v no. 143, vi no. 710, viii nos. 396-397, xvi no. 1067 and OJR H3 pp. 71, 88.
42,11     HONITON. In South Molton parish and Hundred (6); see EPNS ii p. 347 and OJR H3
          p. 88.
42,12-13  ALLER. HACCHE. In South Molton parish and Hundred (6). In Fees p. 774 *Aure* and
          *Hach'* are held from the Honour of Torrington by Hawisia *de Aure* and William *de
          Wolvrinton'* (from Worlington 42,21) respectively. Alwy was Odo's subtenant at Hacche
          in 1086 and it will be noted that he also held Worlington which likewise descended to
          William *de Wolvrington'*. From FA i p. 326 it is apparent that the first is *Northalle* [North
          Aller GR SS 6928] held by John *de Aur*; see FA i p. 418, Cal. Inq. PM vol. i no. 740,
          vi no. 710, and OJR H3 pp. 71, 88-89. For South Aller, see 3,56-57 note.
42,13     VITALIS. See 42,9 note.
42,14     STALLENGE (THORNE). In Hockworthy parish, Bampton Hundred (8). It is positively
          identifiable in the Bampton Hundred Tax Return (xxii); see FA i p. 381.
          HIS MANOR OF HUNTSHAM. That is 42,23. It is less than 2 miles away, just inside
          Tiverton Hundred (9). There was an outlying part of Huntsham parish adjacent to this
          holding; see OJR in TDA 30 p. 446 note 14.
42,15     BRAYLEY. In East Buckland parish, Braunton Hundred (1). In Fees p. 774 *Braylegh'* is
          held by Philip *Pulayn* from the Honour of Torrington; see FA i p. 414 and OJR H8 p. 443.
42,16     BROADHEMBURY. A parish in Hayridge Hundred (15) and identifiable in the Silverton
          (Hayridge) Hundred Tax Return (xiii). Fees p. 1263 records how *Brodehambur'* had
          been held by William *de Thorinton'* of the Barony of Torrington and was given to
          William *Bruere* (Briwere) who in turn gave it to the Abbot of Dunkeswell; see RH i
          pp. 70b, 95a, Cal. Inq. PM vol. xi nos. 118, 299, TE p. 152a, VE ii p. 304 and OJR in
          TDA 42 pp. 223, 238.
          1 HIDE IN. Farley prints a capital *I* for *In*, but in the MS it is *in* with a long 'tail'
          extending down after *adiaceb'* to show the position of the interlineation.
          SHAPCOMBE .... WITH WALTER'S LAND. In the MS and Farley *COBECUME*; in the
          facsimile the first *E* resembles a *B* because of the rubrication. See 1,63 note. 'Walter's
          land' is Walter of Douai's manor of Greenway (23,20), although the details to not agree,
          perhaps because they originated from two different returns. Like Broadhembury,
          Shapcombe went to Dunkeswell Abbey, VE ii p. 304.
42,17     PLYMTREE. A parish in Hayridge Hundred (15); it is identifiable in the Tax Return for
          Silverton (Hayridge) Hundred (xiii). In 1095 Plymtree was given to St. Peter's, Gloucester,
          by Odo (History of St. Peter's, Gloucester, i p. 74; see *Regesta* ii p. 410) and was thence
          acquired by Nicholas the Bowman *alias* Nicholas de la Pole (see Ch. 48 note) in exchange
          for Ailstone in Warwickshire (DB Warwicks. 40,1; see VCH Warwicks. i p. 280). There-
          after it is counted among Plympton Honour lands. It is *Plimtre* in Fees p. 264; see FA i
          pp. 322, 368, 425, Cal. Inq. PM vol. xii no. 333 and OJR in TDA 42 p. 239.
42,18     HILLERSDON. In Cullompton parish, Hayridge Hundred (15). *Hilderesdon'* is held of
          the Honour of Torrington in Fees p. 775, as are both *Esthillerysdon* and *Westhillerysdon*
          in FA i p. 425; see OJR in DCNQ 6 (pt. i) p. 22.
42,19     ESSEBEARE. In Witheridge parish and Hundred (7), presumably the *Beare* held with
          *Rowedon* [Rowden in Witheridge, GR SS 8016] and *Grenedon* [Grendon in Witheridge,
          SS 8017] by the Prior of Barnstaple from Thomas *de Merton* (one of the co-heirs of the
          Barony of Torrington) in FA i p. 344; see Cal. Inq. PM vol. xiii no. 268 and OJR in TDA
          30 p. 429.
          ON THE LACK OF POPULATION recorded for this manor, see 17,84 note. It is possible
          that Essebeare was worked by some of the villagers on the nearby manor of 'Dart'
          (42,20).
42,20     'DART'. Exon. order places this in a Witheridge Hundred group (7); see 21,6 note. In
          Fees pp. 760, 774 *Derth'* is held of the Honour of Torrington by Henry *de Dune*. The
          same holding is *Derte Tracy* in FA i p. 344 held by Thomas *de Merton*. Like the 'Dart'

of 36,24 held of the same Honour and similarly named from the Little Dart river (see note), this 'Dart' has not been positively located; there was an *Overederta* ['Upper Dart' in Witheridge] in 1332 (LSR p. 29) and a Queen Dart (EPNS ii p. 399), the latter poorly represented in the records.

42,21   WORLINGTON.  East and West Worlington were adjacent parishes in Witheridge Hundred (7), now combined into the single parish of East Worlington. In Fees pp. 758, 774 William *de Wolvrington'* holds *Wolvringthon'* and *Wevezston'* [Wilson GR SS 7814 in East Worlington, EPNS ii p. 401; see 16,146 note]. This same holding is *Westwolryngton* in FA i p. 419; see Cal. Inq. PM vol. x no. 241.

Worlington descends from Alwy to William *de Wolvrington'* as does Hacche (42,13; see 42,12-13 note). In Fees p. 775 William also holds *Baddekesworth'* from the Honour of Torrington; see FA i p. 433. This place lay in Tivertón Hundred (9) and from the names of the tenants in LSR (1332) p. 37 — Walter *de Netelworthi* (from Nettleford GR SS 8018) and Walter *Dichyet* (from Ditchett SS 8119) — this place is unquestionably Batsworthy [GR SS 8219], now in Creacombe parish, Witheridge Hundred (7), but a detached part of Tiverton Hundred (like Nutcott, 46,2) in the Middle Ages. It is possibly one of the lands added to Worlington; see editor's note in OJR H1 p. 24.

42,22   CHILTON.  In Cheriton Fitzpaine parish, (West) Budleigh Hundred (14). Since the place does not appear in the fee lists, the identity is not certain. It cannot, however, be Kyllon Barton in Holcombe Rogus, Bampton Hundred (OJR in TDA 30 p. 446) which is philologically impossible; moreover, Bampton Hundred places have already been entered in the schedule. If this is Chilton (so EPNS ii p. 414) it may have been combined with Thomas *de Santon*'s fee in *Churiton'* held of the same Honour (see 36,19 note).

The final sentence of the fief of Hervey of Helléan's wife (after 44,2 Hackworthy) reads 'Hervey's wife holds these lands in exchange for Chilton'. No other Chilton is mentioned in DB and the identification of the 44,2 Chilton with this Chilton is lent some support by the fact that in 1066 Aelmer held both 44,1 Ashton and 42,22 Chilton, suggesting that they may once have been part of the same fief; see 44,2 note.

42,23   HUNTSHAM.  A parish in Tiverton Hundred (9); it is positively identifiable in the Tax Return for that Hundred (xi) where Odo son of Gamelin is recorded as having 1 virgate of lordship and where tax is owed on 2 furlongs (*fertinis*) held from Odo son of Gamelin by Alfgeat (*Aluiet'* in the MS; Ellis misprints *Aliuet'*), a subtenant who is not mentioned in connection with Huntsham in DB but who is the 1086 holder of Buckland (42,7) in another Hundred. In Fees p. 775 Thomas *de Santon* (from Saunton 36,10) holds *Honesham* from the Honour of Torrington; see FA i pp. 318, 432, TE p. 144a and OJR H1 p. 24.

42,24   VITALIS HOLDS.  Perhaps the same man as the 1086 subtenant of Odo's manor of Luccombe in DB Somerset 38,1; see also 42,9 note above.

WILLAND.  A parish in Halberton Hundred (10). It was given to Taunton Priory (hence called *Wildelonde Prior* in FA i p. 383) by William son of Odo, Mon. Ang. vi p. 166 no. II; see FA i pp. 338, 432 and OJR H2 p. 54.

Ch. 43   OSBERN OF SACEY.  See Exon. Notes here on the form of his first name. Sacey (in Devon DB *Salceid*, Exon. *Salciet, Salceio, Salceit, Salcet*) is in the département of Manche, France, but see OEB p. 112 for other places possibly the origin of the byname. This is Osbern's only fief in DB; OEB errs when referring to him in the Exon. sections relating to Somerset. A Ralph of Sacey, probably a relative, is recorded in DB Herefords. 1,61.

Most of Osbern's manors in Devon later form part of the Honour of Plympton (see Ch. 21 note).

FOR THE EXON. ORDER of this chapter, see Ch. 22 note.

43,1   PARFORD.  For the form, DB *Patford*, see EPNS ii p. 432. It lies in Drewsteignton parish, Wonford Hundred (19). Being the first entry in the 'Lands of the French Men-at-Arms' in Exon. (Ch. 22 note), it and ?Shapley (45,1) are unexpectedly early for a Wonford Hundred group in the schedule of lands, so it is possible that, although Parford lay in Wonford Hundred (Tax Return xxxi), it was returned with South Tawton (1,29), to which it paid a customary due, and thus like ?Shapley, Gidleigh (15,7) and Taw Green (51,2) it came into the scribes' hands on a separate list; see the Appendix. Shilstone (43,3), which is geographically close, occurs in the correct place for a Wonford Hundred group in the schedule; see OJR in TDA 36 p. 377, 44 p. 350. Parford does not appear in the fee lists; the EPNS citation of Fees p. 769 refers in fact to Combe Pafford (2,7-8 note).

1 OX OR 30d.  A common customary due; see 51,2 and DB Cornwall 1,15.

| 43,1 | (SOUTH) TAWTON. See 1,29 note.
| 43,2 | OSBERN HIMSELF HOLDS. Repeated at the beginning of 43,2-5 inclusive.
CLYST (GERRED). DB *Clist*. It lies in Broad Clyst parish, Cliston Hundred (20), and can be positively identified in the Tax Return (xii) for that Hundred. In Fees p. 789 William *de Clist* holds *Clist* and *Brighteneston'* from the Honour of Plympton. In FA i p. 333 *Clist Giraud* is held from Simon of Montacute who holds from Walter *le Deneys* who holds from John *de Maundevil'* of the Honour of Plympton; see FA i p. 434, Cal. Inq. PM vol. ii no. 154, vi no. 238, xiv no. 325 and OJR in VCH p. 553 and H7 pp. 366, 379-380.
 *Brighteneston'* ('Beorhtwine's farm') is a tithing of Cliston Hundred (see, for example, LSR (1334) p. 56) and is not the same place as another lost 'Brightston' ('at Beorhtric's stone', EPNS ii p. 584; 2,15-17 note) which is in, or the same as, Clyst Honiton parish, Budleigh Hundred (14); see also 1,56 note.
| 43,3 | SHILSTONE. DB *Selvestan*; see EPNS ii p. 433. It can be identified in the Tax Return for Wonford Hundred (xxxi) and now lies in Drewsteignton parish in that Hundred (19); see 43,1 note. In Fees p. 788 *Silvestane* is held of the Honour of Plympton; see Fees p. 1371, FA i p. 345, Cal. Inq. PM vol. i no. 564 and OJR in TDA 44 p. 317. In FA i p. 312 *Schilston* is held with *Toppysham* and *Rohorn* (1,44 note) and in FA i p. 388 *Shilston* is held with *Lamford* (43,4). See 1,26 note.
| 43,4 | LAMBERT. DB *Lanford*; for the form see EPNS ii p. 428. It lies in Cheriton Bishop parish, Wonford Hundred (19). In Fees p. 788 *Parva Lampford* is held by the Prior of Plympton from the Honour of Plympton; see TE p. 153, FA i p. 345, OJR in TDA 44 p. 218 and 52,11 note.
| 43,5 | INGSDON. In Ilsington parish, Teignbridge Hundred (23). It can be positively identified in the Tax Return for Teignton Hundred (xxiv) and with 32,6-7 forms a Teignton Hundred group in the order of Exon. The Ingsdon of 32,7 also passes to the Honour of Plympton; see Cal. Inq. PM vol. i no. 564 and OJR in TDA 29 p. 229.
 125 WETHERS. *Berbices*: male sheep kept for mutton. There is only one other occurrence of them in the Exon. for Devon (30 in 52,26); probably more manors had them, but they were not recorded there.
| Ch. 44 | (WIFE OF) HERVEY OF HELLÉAN. The Landholders' List (col. 100a) and the entries in this chapter indicate that it is the fief of Hervey of Helléan's wife (or, rather, widow), the word *uxoris* being omitted after *Terra* in this chapter heading. Cf. DB Dorset Ch. 55 heading (*Terra Uxoris Hugonis Filii Grip*). She may have been called Emma: the Tax Return for Exminster Hundred (xxiii) states that Emma a widow has 1 hide 1 virgate lordship there, and this seems to represent the whole of her holding at Ashton, 44,1; see also below and the Exon. Notes here for the evidence of the Colyton Hundred Tax Return (xx). (The wife of Baldwin the Sheriff was also called Emma, but she was not a widow and her holdings at 16,94;128 are in different Hundreds.) She only holds lands in Devon: OEB p. 91 mistakenly includes under Hervey of Helléan references to Norfolk which in fact belong to Tihel of Helléan — *alias* Tihel the Breton — who also held in Essex, perhaps some relative. Helléan is in the département of Morbihan, France.
 The wife of Hervey's lands pass to the Honour of Plympton (Ch. 21 note). Her fief, which is not in the surviving portion of Exon., included Ashton in Exminster Hundred (24) and Hackworthy in Wonford (19), but seems to have been more extensive in 1086 than is recorded in Exchequer DB. These other lands may have been accidentally omitted in the compilation of Exon. (hence their omission in Exchequer DB) or the details arrived too late for inclusion. The Tax Return for Budleigh Hundred (xvi) allows the wife of Hervey ½ hide and ½ virgate lordship. Later evidence suggests that this land lay at Clyst St. Mary [GR SX 9790] and Lower Creedy [SS 8402], both in Budleigh Hundred (14), since in Fees p. 763 the heirs of Gilbert *le Blund* hold in *Clist Sancte Marie* from Robert *de Helihun'* who holds from the Honour of Plympton; see FA i pp. 364, 427. *Crye* is held in Fees p. 790 by William *de Helihun'* from Robert *de Helihun'* from the Honour of Plympton and occurs as *Crydihelyhun* in Fees p. 762; see FA i pp. 364, 426. *Assherton* [Ashton 44,1], *Clyst St. Mary*, *Hakeworthi* [Hackworthy 44,2] and *Cridie Hilion* are coupled together in Cal. Inq. PM vol. xiv no. 325; see Cal. Inq. PM vol. i no. 564. 'Creedy Hellions' was one of the medieval manors in Lower Creedy (3,72. 34,35;37 were others) and has given its name to the parish Upton Hellions; see EPNS ii p. 419.
 A further omitted land was Whitley, mentioned in the T.O. (see Exon. Notes here). Whitley must be the ½ hide and ½ virgate lordship recorded for *ima vidua* ('?Emma, a widow') in the Tax Return for Colyton Hundred (xx), see Exon. Notes here. In Fees p. 788 Robert *de Helyhun'* holds in *Whytelegh'*; it is *Whitelegh* by *Fareweye*, coupled

| | |
|---|---|
| Ch. 44 (cont'd.) | with *Wydecomb* (48,12 note), in Cal. Inq. PM vol. xiv no. 325, and the holder in FA i p. 428 (in Colyton Hundred) is Hugh *Proutz*; see 44,1-2 notes, FA i p. 366 and OJR H7 p. 350.<br>    Another land is mentioned in the T.O. (see Exon. Notes) where ½ furlong (*ferdinus*) of *Esseorda* ['ash-tree enclosure', OE *aesc, worth*, unidentified, but probably in Hayridge Hundred (15)] has been added to the King's manor of Silverton (1,7). It is possible that other lands were involved in this fief. For example, in Fees p. 789, from the Honour of Plympton, Peter *de Hakeworthi* (from Hackworthy 44,2) holds land called *Welebere* [Welsbere in Poughill, GR SS 8408, (West) Budleigh Hundred (14); see EPNS ii p. 416] ; see FA i pp. 345, 368, 382 and 21,6 note. This may be the same as the land called *Fenne* by *Poghull* [Venn Channing in Poughill] in Cal. Inq. PM vol. xiv no. 325. |
| 44,1 | ASHTON. DB *Essestone* 'Æschere's *tūn*'; see EPNS ii p. 487 and 6,6 note. It is a parish in Exminster Hundred (24). William *le Prouz* holds *Aysseriston* in Exminster Hundred in FA i p. 346; see OJR in TDA 47 p. 216 and Ch. 44 note.<br>THESE THREE LANDS. That is, the main manor of Ashton held by Aelmer and the two added manors of the two thanes. |
| 44,2 | HACKWORTHY. In Tedburn St. Mary parish, Wonford Hundred (19). In Fees p. 788 *Hakeworth'* is held from the Honour of Plympton and is held from Richard *le Prouz* in FA i p. 313; see RH i p. 85a and OJR in TDA 44 p. 321.<br>CHILTON. The only place of this name mentioned elsewhere in DB is Chilton in Cheriton Fitzpaine parish, (West) Budleigh Hundred (14), in the fief of Odo son of Gamelin (42,22). This land would have touched the eastern edge of Hervey's holding at Lower Creedy (Ch. 44 note), but the exchange, if it is for 44,1-2, will have been rather unequal, as Odo's Chilton is rated at only ½ virgate as against the almost 2 hides of 44,1-2 which are also worth four times as much; see 42,22 note. Chilton is DB *Cillitone*, probably 'Cilla's farm' (EPNS ii p. 414); it is therefore not possible to identify it with the Chilton in Thorverton (1,7 note) which is *Childetun* in Fees p. 96, *Chilleton* in FA i p. 425, probably from OE *cild* and *tūn* ('child's farm'). |
| Ch. 45 | GERALD THE CHAPLAIN. He appears in Exon. under the heading of French Men-at-Arms; see Exon. Notes here. This seems to be his only holding in DB.<br>FOR THE EXON. ORDER of this chapter, see Ch. 22 note. |
| 45,1 | ?SHAPLEY. This may well be part of the Shapley that now lies in Chagford parish, Wonford Hundred (19), other portions being 16,61-62;64. If so, its treatment in Exon. is different from that of the other parts. It is second in the list of 'Lands of the French Men-at-Arms' (see Ch. 22 note) which suggests that, together with the first entry (43,1 Parford), it came into the scribes' hands with a return originating in South Tawton (1,29); see the Appendix. The other parts of Shapley were in Exminster Hundred (24) in 1086, later in Wonford (19); see OJR in TDA 36 p. 377 and 44 p. 350.<br>(SOUTH) TAWTON. See 1,29 note. |
| 45,2 | (ABBOTS) BICKINGTON. DB *Bichetone*, a parish in (Black) Torrington Hundred (11). It was granted by Geoffrey, son of Oliver *de Dynham* (who later held Hartland 1,30), to the Canons of Stoke St. Nectan (i.e. Hartland Abbey) some time before 1189, Oliver *Mon.* p. 207; see OJR H5 pp. 204, 210 and 45,3 note.<br>2 PARTS OF 1 VIRGATE. That is, two-thirds of a virgate; see 15,19 note.<br>IT PAYS 20s .... AS MUCH. See 6,8 note. |
| 45,3 | STOKE. DB *Nistenestoch*, known from the 13th century as 'Stoke St. Nectan' doubtless after the Irish saint. It lies in Hartland parish and Hundred (3). Held in 1086 by the Canons of Hartland Abbey (see Exon. Notes), it remained with the Church; see Oliver *Mon.* p. 204, EPNS i p. 75 and OJR in TDA 26 p. 416, 30 p. 288. |
| Ch. 46 | GERARD. Both his lands lay in Tiverton Hundred (9) and passed to the Honour of Plympton. In view of the location and descent of these lands, Tiverton and '(Little) Washfield' (32,8-9) may also have been held by this Gerard but under Ralph Pagnell.<br>FOR THE EXON. ORDER of this chapter, see Ch. 22 note. |
| 46,1-2 | ALSTAN TILLEY. DB *Alestan*, Exon. *Alestantilia* and *Alestilla* respectively. Tilley means 'tiller, cultivator'. This instance of the byname antedates Reaney's 13th century record s.n. *Tilley* (ii), OE *tilia* 'one who tills' (OE *tilian* 'to till, to cultivate'). It is not explained in PNDB pp. 152-153; nor contained in OEB, where cf. *Til* p. 356 (Redin p. 55 s.n. *Tila*) from OE *til* 'good', forbidden here by the *-ia* form. *Alestilla* would be a mistake for *Alest'tilia*. (JMcND) |
| 46,1 | (WEST) MANLEY. It lies in Tiverton parish and Hundred (9); the Exon. order (Ch. 22 note) strongly points to a place in Tiverton Hundred rather than to one in Halberton |

46,2  Hundred (East Manley, 25,21 note). It does not appear in the fee lists under its own name, but the Honour of Plympton holds Tiverton (1,35) and a number of sub-manors. Of these Pool Anthony [GR SS 9712] is adjacent to West Manley and like Nutcott (46,2) had been held in the early 13th century by William *Briwere*. It is *Pole* in Fees p. 399, *La Pole* in Fees p. 789, FA i pp. 319, 370, *Pole Antony* in FA i p. 433; see OJR in TDA 36 p. 364 and H1 p. 17.

46,2  NUTCOTT. DB *Nochecote*. This place, which has proved difficult to identify (and whose name is not well explained in EPNS ii p. 390, JMcND), lies now in Rackenford parish, Witheridge Hundred (7), but was a tithing of Tiverton Hundred (9) in the Middle Ages. It was among the estates of William *Briwere* in the early 13th century, passing at the division of the lands to Alice *de Mohun*. In Fees p. 789 it is held as *Nochecote* by Robert *Mauduth'* of the Honour of Plympton; in FA i p. 319 it is *Nouchecote* held by the heirs of John *de Mohun* from the Countess *Albemarlie*; the same place is *Neutecote* in HD p. 56, *Noggecote* and *Nuggecote* in FA i pp. 370, 433, *Nuchecote* in Cal. Inq. PM vol. ii no. 306 and *Nettecote* in Cal. Inq. PM vol. vii no. 297. All these forms point to Nutcott in Rackenford parish despite the shortage of examples cited in EPNS loc. cit. The form *Neatecote* given there is either a development of *Nettecote* (above) or belongs under another place. Nutcott appears as *Nuthecote* (LSR (1334) p. 55) and *Nuchecote* (Reichel and Mugford p. 21) where it is a tithing of Tiverton Hundred (9); it probably lay in that Hundred in 1086. These early forms make it unlikely to be Neddycott in Uplowman (for which EPNS ii p. 553 gives only *Nythecott alias Newcott*) or Northcote in Tiverton (OJR H1 pp. 2, 9, 18); see Reichel's editor in H1 p. 18 note 11 and 23,13 note above. Another medieval detachment of Tiverton Hundred, Batsworthy (42,21 note), lay in the same area.

Ch. 47  GODBOLD. Godbold the Bowman; see Exon. Notes Chs. 47-50. He is probably the same as the Godbold who holds one manor in Somerset Ch. 43. Most of his lands here later form part of the Honour of Plympton (see Ch. 21 note).
IN EXON. the entries of this chapter are grouped under the heading "Land of Nicholas the Bowman in Devonshire" together with those for Chs. 48-50 and the first entry of Ch. 51; see Exon. Notes Chs. 47-50. The Hundredal arrangement is:

| | | | |
|---|---|---|---|
| 47,1 | Merton | 50,1. 47,11-12. 49,4. | Wonford |
| 48,1 | Fremington | 48,3-7. 49,7 | |
| 47,2-4 | Tawton | 47,13. 50,2-4 | Witheridge |
| 47,5-6. 49,1 | Exminster | 49,5. 51,1 | Budleigh |
| 47,7 | Braunton | 48,8-10. 47,14 | Teignton |
| 47,8 | South Molton | 50,5. 49,6 | Tiverton |
| 49,2-3 | Cliston | 48,11 | Kerswell |
| 47,9-10. 48,2 | Silverton | 48,12 | Colyton |
| | | 47,15 | Borough of Exeter |

47,1  HELE. In Petrockstowe parish, Shebbear Hundred (4), one of two 'Heles' that passed to the Honour of Plympton (39,8 note). It can be identified in the Tax Return for Merton Hundred (v). In Fees p. 788 John *Goding* holds in Hele of the Honour of Plympton. It is *Hele Godyng* in FA i p. 359; see FA i p. 411, Cal. Inq. PM vol. xiv no. 325, EPNS i p. 105, OJR H10 p. 558 and the notes to 15,47 and 16,42.

47,2-4  HOOK. BRUSHFORD. NEWTON. Hook is in Ashreigney parish, Brushford is its own parish and Newton is in Zeal Monachorum parish, all in (North) Tawton Hundred (12). In Fees p. 787 the heir of Miles *Corbyn* holds in *Brigeford', Hoke, Nyweton'* and *Foldehegh'* [Foldhay GR SS 7004 in Zeal Monachorum, part of Newton in 1086] of the Honour of Plympton. In FA i p. 422 an entry for *Mileston* (named from Miles *Corbyn*), that is Millsome GR SS 6605, has apparently replaced Brushford; see FA i p. 370, Cal. Inq. PM vol. xiv no. 325 and OJR in TDA 29 pp. 253, 263.

47,2  GODBOLD HIMSELF HOLDS. Repeated at the beginning of 47,2-12 inclusive. However, according to Exon., Godbold has a subtenant at 47,10; see notes to 24,28. 34,14 and 48,8. Cf. 23,7 where DB has Walter (of Douai) holding Hockworthy 'himself' and Exon. gives him a subtenant, and similarly for 49,7. In none of these cases are the details of the subtenant added in Exon.
ON THE LACK OF POPULATION recorded for this manor, see 17,84 note.

47,5  DODDISCOMBSLEIGH. DB *Leuge*. It is a parish in Exminster Hundred (24), this and the next entry being identifiable in the Tax Return for Exminster Hundred (xxiii). The 13th century forms of the name, *Leghe Gobol* or *Guobol*, *Gobaldeslegh*, go back to the 1086 holder or his successors; EPNS ii p. 494. In FA i p. 346 John *de Dodescomb* and

Hugh *Gubbewolt* hold in *Legh* and *Lowedoum* [Lowton 47,14] from the Honour of Plympton. The same place is *Legh Doddyscomb* in Cal. Inq. PM vol. iv (o.s.) no. 63 (= TDA 38 p. 322); see Cal. Inq. PM vol. i (n.s.) no. 564, FA i p. 388 and OJR in TDA 47 p. 213.

47,6 LOWLEY. In Doddiscombsleigh parish, Exminster Hundred (24); it does not appear in later fee lists, but may have followed the same descent as Doddiscombsleigh (47,5 note).
UNDERWOOD, 1 FURLONG. The use of *ferling* (DB; *ferd(inum)*, accusative, in Exon.) as a measure of underwood (or of any other 'resource') is extremely rare. It is almost invariably used in Devon, together with the hide and virgate, in the tax statement and in measuring the lordship and villagers' land holding; see 1,4 note 'lordship .... 1 furlong'. It is possible that the Exon. scribe wrote *ferd'* by mistake for *quadrag(enariam)* 'furlong' (see 1,4 note '12 furlongs') and the Exchequer scribe followed suit, but it is odd that one furlong ('ferling') is needed to add up with the 1 furlong and ½ virgate of lordship and villagers' land (see Lordship and Villagers' Table) to make up the 1 virgate tax payment. It is also interesting that both hide and virgate are occasionally in Devon used to measure resources; see notes to 10,1. 10,2 and 15,79.

47,7 MULLACOTT. In Ilfracombe parish, Braunton Hundred (1), and positively identifiable in the Tax Return for Braunton and Shirwell Hundred (vi). In Fees p. 787 Robert *de Mullecoth'* holds *Mullecoth'* from the Honour of Plympton. It is *Mollecote Corbyn* in Cal. Inq. PM vol. xiv no. 325; see FA i p. 360 and OJR H8 p. 453.
REST OF THE LAND IS LYING WASTE (AND IS USED) FOR PASTURE. Exon. *et alia terra iacet uastata ad pasturam*, written at the end of the entry immediately after the smallholder, but with no change in scribe or ink colour. It is an unusual phrase; the *alia terra* would seem to refer to the remainder of the furlong ('ferling') which the smallholder was presumably not cultivating. It cannot refer to the rest of the ½ hide, as that has already been fully described (see Lordship and Villagers' Table). Meanwhile, the T.O. entry (see Exon. Notes here) omits reference to the smallholder (as one would expect, but see Exon. Notes 1,11 'Deneworthy' ... said manor) and states that 1 furlong (*ferdinus*) added to Mullacott is completely waste (*penitus uastata est*). (Cf. Exon. Notes 34,37 where the phrase *alia terra est ita uastata* seems to refer to all the manor apart from 1 acre of meadow.)

47,8 SATTERLEIGH. Now a joint parish with Warkleigh in South Molton Hundred (6); it is positively identifiable in the Tax Return for the same Hundred (vii). It appears to have descended with Warkleigh (1,41 second note); see OJR H3 p. 94.
1 VIRGATE. In the MS *v*⁺ altered to *virg*⁺. The first ⁺ sign is not erased, though it is not entirely there; Farley does not print it. See notes to 29,2 and 29,8.

47,9 BURN. In Silverton parish, Hayridge Hundred (15). In Fees p. 789 Nicholas *de Burne* holds in *Burne* from the Honour of Plympton; it is *Borne* by *Silferton* in Cal. Inq. PM vol. xiv no. 325 and *Borne* and *Dowrygge* [?Dorweeke in Silverton, GR SS 9506] in Cal. Inq. PM vol. iv (o.s.) no. 63 (= TDA 38 p. 326); see FA i p. 368 and OJR in TDA 42 p. 245.

47,10 YARD. Probably in Silverton parish, Hayridge Hundred (15). It may be the *Yurdon* [Yard Down] held with Greenslinch (48,2) of the Honour of Plympton in FA i pp. 368, 425; see Cal. Inq. PM vol. xiv no. 325 and OJR in TDA 42 p. 245.
2 VILLAGERS HAVE IT THERE. The *hanc* refers to the ½ plough, as Exon. makes clear. Cf. 1,29 note.

47,11-12 CLIFFORD. HALSTOW. Both lie in Dunsford parish, Wonford Hundred (19), and both are positively identifiable in the Tax Return for Wonford Hundred (xxxi). In FA i p. 312 *Clyfford* and *Halftouwe* are held from the heirs of Ralph *de Dodescomb'* (see 47,5) by Geoffrey *de Radeweye*. Clifford is *Clyfforde Corbeyn* in Cal. Inq. PM vol. xiv (n.s.) no. 325 and vol. iv (o.s.) no. 63 (= TDA 38 p. 321); see RH i p. 85a, FA i pp. 346, 388 and OJR in TDA 44 pp. 299, 321.

47,13 JAGELIN. DB *Lachelin(us)*, Exon. MS *lachelin(us)* (Ellis misprints *Iachelin'*, which is in fact the more correct form). See Forssner p. 170: a diminutive of Breton, Cornish, Welsh *Iago, Jago*. Reaney s.n. *Jacklin* overlooks a possibility (JMcND). The initial *L*, though very clear in the Exchequer DB MS, is due to the original misreading by the Exon. scribe of *I* as *l*.
(WEST) WHITNOLE. In Stoodleigh parish, Witheridge Hundred (7); it is included in Bampton Hundred (8) by OJR in TDA 30 p. 454 (see the Appendix). In Fees p. 760 Roger *Dacastre* holds in *Warebrigthelegh'* [Waspley, 52,43 note), *Blackesworth'* [Blatchworthy GR SS 8817, probably part of West Whitnole] and *Whytecnolle* from

|        | Geoffrey *de Mandevil'* who holds from Ralph *de Doddescumb'* (see 47,5) of the Honour of Plympton; see Fees p. 787, FA i pp. 343, 421 and OJR in TDA 30 pp. 404, 424. |
|--------|---|
| 47,14  | LOWTON. In Moretonhampstead parish, Teignbridge Hundred (23); see EPNS ii p. 484. It can hardly be Lowton in Bridford (DG) which is in the wrong Hundred (Wonford, 19), nor is it Liverton in Ilsington (OJR in TDA 29 p. 229) which has a different derivation. It has the same medieval holders as Doddiscombsleigh (47,5): in FA i p. 390 Cecilia *de Dodiscom[b]* holds in *Lughedon* in Teignbridge Hundred from the Honour of Plympton. It is *Lowedon Peverel* in FA i p. 348. In Fees p. 790 and FA i p. 346 it is included in Exminster Hundred (24) probably because *Lowedoum* and *Legh'* [Doddiscombsleigh 47,5, in Exminster Hundred] are associated. But there was a detached portion of Exminster Hundred adjacent at Shapley; see 16,61-62;64 note and the Appendix. On the descent of the manor, see OJR in TDA 47 p. 213. |
| Ch. 48 | NICHOLAS THE BOWMAN. *Balistarius* in DB, *archibalistarius* and *arbalestari(us)* in Exon. (see Exon. Notes here). The Latin word *ballista* covered all missile-throwing weapons, from cross-bow to large artillery piece. The English word 'gun' was used of such weapons before the introduction of gun-powder. In earlier volumes in this series (as in Warwickshire, where Nicholas also appears as tenant-in-chief; see below) the translation 'Gunner' was used, but it has been decided that the modern reader might think it implied the use of firearms, hence the change to 'Bowman'. According to Ellis DTY pp. 245-246 the *balistarius* was "the captain or officer in charge of the stone-and-missile-discharging engines used in sieges . . . it was probably the *balistarii* who planned and superintended the works of military engineering as well". |
|        | Nicholas also had the byname 'de la Pole': some time between 1095 and 1100 Abbot Serlo of St. Peter's, Gloucester, exchanged the manor of Ailstone belonging in 1086 to Nicholas the 'Gunner' (DB Warwicks. 40,1) with Plymtree (42,17 above; see note) and in the History of St. Peter's, Gloucester, i p. 74 and ii pp. 125-126 the holder of Ailstone is given as Nicholas de la Pole. See VCH Warwickshire i p. 280. Most of Nicholas' Devon manors are later held of the Honour of Plympton (see Ch. 21 note). |
|        | FOR THE EXON. ORDER of this chapter, see Ch. 47 note. |
| 48,1   | WEBBERY. In Alverdiscott parish, Fremington Hundred (5); the land seems to be identifiable in the Tax Return for Fremington (iv). It appears to have passed to the Honour of Launceston (Ch. 15 note), being held of it by Baldwin *le Flemeng* as *Wybbebeyre Nicholai Pulain* in Fees p. 795; see FA i pp. 371, 413 and OJR H8 p. 510. |
|        | FORMERLY 12d; VALUE NOW 15s. This is a large increase in value; it is possible that the Exon. scribe (whom the Exchequer scribe then copied) made a mistake in either the *den'* or the *sot* and the reading should be either 'Formerly 12s; value now 15s' or 'Formerly 12d; value now 15d'. See 16,172 note for a probable error of the same sort and cf. Exon. Notes 15,22. (Elsewhere in Devon the largest increase in value seems to be of the manor of Alminstone (42,3) where it is almost sevenfold, less than half the increase here.) |
|        | ROGER GOAD. Exon. *Reger(us) aculeus* here, *Roger(us) aculeus* for 48,6, the first *e* in *Reger(us)* obviously being a scribal error for *o*. See OEB pp. 372-373 on this byname. |
| 48,2   | GREENSLINCH. In Silverton parish, Hayridge Hundred (15); it is positively identifiable in the Tax Return for Silverton Hundred (xiii). In Fees p. 789 Nicholas *de Greneslingh'* holds in *Greneslinch'* from the Honour of Plympton and in FA i p. 368 William *Thorlock* holds *Grenelinch, Northwill* [unidentified] and *Yurdon* [Yard Down, see 47,10 note]; see FA i pp. 322, 425 and OJR in TDA 42 p. 245. |
|        | NICHOLAS HAS THIS MANOR BY EXCHANGE. Exon. *pro escanbiis* literally "in place of exchanges", i.e. more than one land was exchanged with Greenslinch. According to Round in VCH Essex i p. 386 a method often adopted to conceal a defective title to a piece of land was to state that it had been 'exchanged'. It would seem particularly likely that some legal fiction was being practised when, as here, there is no mention in Exon. or DB of which manors formed the other half of the exchange (presumably because they did not exist). In the Exon. MS 1½ lines have been left blank at the end of this entry (not shown by Ellis), possibly for the later inclusion of details of the lands exchanged (if they could be found). Cf. notes to 48,12. 51,3 and 51,10 and see also 2,10 and notes on the Count of Mortain's 'exchanges'. |
| 48,3   | STOKEINTEIGNHEAD. A parish in the detached part of Wonford Hundred (19) that lies south of the Teign estuary. In Fees p. 788 the heir of Roger Fitzpayne holds *Stokes* with two manors called *Gabewill'* [Higher and Lower Gabwell in the parish, GR SX 9169, 9269]. *Stoke in Tynhyde* is held with Staplehill (48,9) in FA i p. 313. It is |

*Stok cum Nytheregabewill* in FA i p. 345, *Stoke in Tynehide* "with both *Gabewilles*" in Cal. Inq. PM vol. xiv no. 325; see FA i p. 386, RH i p. 84a, Fees p. 1370, Cal. Inq. PM vol. ii no. 403, v no. 607 and 16,117 note. The modern place-name is influenced by the proximity of the parish to the river Teign, but in fact it refers to 'ten hides', presumably the original extent of the Wonford Hundred detachment.

48,4  ROCOMBE. In Stokeinteignhead parish in the detached part of Wonford Hundred (19); see 48,3 note. In Fees p. 788 Reginald *de Albo Monasterio* holds in *Racumb'* from the Honour of Plympton; it is *Rocombe Blaumoster* (OFr *blanc moutier* 'white monastery', a translation of the Latin) in FA i pp. 345, 388, and OJR in TDA 44 p. 320. Charlecombe (48,10 note) may have been part of this holding.

48,5  OGWELL. East Ogwell. A parish in the 'Teignhead' section of Wonford Hundred (19). In Fees p. 788 Humphrey *de Dune* holds in *Estwogewill'* from the Honour of Plympton; in FA i p. 345 the holder of *Estwogwyll* and *Malleston* [Malston 17,55] is Thomas *Peytevyn*. Ogwell is said to be held from *Stoke in Tynhid* (48,3) in FA i p. 386; see FA i p. 313 and OJR in TDA 44 p. 319.

48,6  HOLBEAM. In Ogwell parish, Wonford Hundred (19). William *de Holebem* holds *Holebem* in Fees p. 788 from the Honour of Plympton; see RH i p. 85a, FA i pp. 313, 345 and OJR in TDA 44 p. 319. In FA i p. 386 it is held from the manor of Stokeinteignhead (48,3).

48,7  BAGTOR. In Ilsington parish, now Teignbridge Hundred (23), but it lay in that part of the parish that was a detachment of Wonford Hundred (19) in the Middle Ages; Bagtor seems to have been in Wonford Hundred in 1086 according to the order of Exon. In Fees p. 788 William *de Baggetorre* holds in *Baggetorre* of the Honour of Plympton in a Wonford Hundred group; in FA i p. 345 it is connected with *Aure* in Haytor Hundred [Aller 48,11]; see FA i pp. 313, 388, RH i p. 85a, OJR in TDA 44 p. 319 and 32,6-7 note.

48,8  NICHOLAS HIMSELF HOLDS. Repeated at the beginning of 48,8-12 inclusive. However, Exon. gives him a subtenant for 48,11. See notes to 24,28. 34,14 and 47,2. IDEFORD. DB *Ludeford*, though the first letter may be an *I* as the 'foot' is very short (it is certainly not a *Y* as in DG and EPNS ii p. 474); the initial letter of the Exon. form is not *L* (as Ellis prints) but probably *I* or possibly *l*; see 16,115 note on 'Edwulf' on the similarity of *L*, *I* and *l*, and cf. 24,26 note and the fourth note under 34,14. Ideford is a parish in Teignbridge Hundred (23) and positively identifiable (with Staplehill 48,9) in the Teignton Hundred Tax Return (xxiv). In Fees p. 790 Aubrey *de Boterellis* holds in *Ioweford* from the Honour of Plympton. It is *Hiddeford* in FA i p. 339, *Yuddeford* in RH p. 82a, *Jorford* in Fees p. 264, *Yudesford* in FA i p. 390; see Cal. Inq. PM vol. x nos. 240, 384, 652 and OJR in TDA 29 p. 229.
[ACRES]. In the MS *ac* either omitted in error or implied after the 'acres' of meadow. Exon. has 'acres'. Cf. 48,12 note.

48,9  STAPLEHILL. In Ilsington parish, Teignbridge Hundred (23); it is positively identifiable (with Ideford 48,8) in the Tax Return for Teignton Hundred (xxiv). It seems in the Middle Ages to have been absorbed by the outlying portion of Wonford Hundred (19) that formed part of Ilsington parish; thus in Fees p. 788 among a group of Wonford places Roger *de Stapelhille* holds in *Stapelhille* from the Honour of Plympton; see FA i pp. 313, 345, 386 (all Wonford Hundred) and OJR in TDA 44 pp. 300, 319.

48,10  BUCKLAND (IN THE MOOR). It is now a parish in the moorland detachment of Haytor Hundred (29). Exon. order (see Ch. 47 note) suggests that it was in Teignton (Teignbridge) Hundred (23) in 1086. In Fees p. 790 in a group of Haytor Hundred places, Roger *de Bokland'* holds from the Honour of Plympton in *Bocland'* and in *Cherlecumb'*. This latter place is *Cherleton'* in Fees p. 768, *Therlecumbe* in FA i p. 318 and is probably Charlecombe in Stokeinteignhead parish, Wonford Hundred, GR SX 9070, possibly part of Rocombe 48,4 or a dependency of Buckland in the Moor. It is called *Churleton* and *Bukelond in la More* in Cal. Inq. PM vol. xiv no. 325; see FA i pp. 318, 348, 392 and OJR in TDA 40 p. 120.

48,11  ALLER. In Abbotskerswell parish, Haytor Hundred (29). In Fees p. 790 William *de Baggetorre* (see 48,7) holds in *Aure* from the Honour of Plympton. It is *Alre juxta Carswill* in Cal. Inq. PM vol. iv (o.s.) no. 63 (= TDA 38 p. 322); see FA i pp. 318, 345, 349, Fees p. 768 and OJR in TDA 40 p. 125.

48,12  THIS ENTRY IS WRITTEN in the left margin of the MS in very pale ink and with a thicker pen, suggesting a later addition; it is not rubricated and has no transposition signs to show its correct position. In Exon., however, it occurs after the entry

48,12 corresponding to 48,11 and there is no sign of its being added later there, the scribe
(cont'd.) being the same as for the preceding entry.
?NORTHLEIGH. DB *Lege*. It seems to have lain in Colyton Hundred (22), since Nicholas is allowed 1 virgate of lordship land in that Hundred's Tax Return (xx). There are at least two 'Leighs' in the Hundred, Northleigh and Southleigh, both with Domesday representatives. This land may have been at *Wydecumb* [Widcombe Barton farm in Farway parish, GR SY 1894, adjacent to Northleigh], which in FA i p. 330 is an Honour of Plympton holding by Hugh *le Pruz* and Richard *le Despensar* from Baldwin *de Specote*; see Ch. 44 note. The descent of this holding needs further investigation; OJR H7 pp. 340, 350, without supporting evidence, identifies 'Bramleigh in Farway'.
1 SMALLHOLDER. There is no reason for the omission in DB of the smallholder detailed in Exon. See also Exon. Notes 19,20.
[ACRES] .... [ACRES]. The words *acrae* were no doubt omitted by the Exchequer scribe before the pasture and meadow through lack of space; they are in Exon. as usual (but see Exon. Notes for the discrepancy in the meadow's measurement). However, it is possible that he thought the *ac̄* given before the woodland would cover for the other measurements; cf. 48,8 note and Exon. Notes to 1,3 and 16,75.
(PART) OF NICHOLAS' (LANDS ACQUIRED BY) EXCHANGE. Exon. *de escanbiis nicholai*. See 48,2 note and cf. notes to 51,3 and 51,10. The Exon. scribe hopefully left the rest of the line after *nicholai* blank, with no dot after it, in case details of the exchanged manor(s) were forthcoming.

Ch. 49 FULCHERE. He is called Fulchere the Bowman in the main Exon. and T.O. entries referring to 49,7; see Exon. Notes here. Most of his lands in this chapter are later held of the Honour of Plympton (see Ch. 21 note).
FOR THE EXON. ORDER of this chapter, see Ch. 47 note.

49,1 SHILLINGFORD. A parish in Exminster Hundred (24), this holding being positively identifiable in the Tax Return for that Hundred (xxiii). In Fees p. 790 Richard son of Ralph holds in *Sillingeford*' from the Honour of Plympton. William *Briwere* held *Sullingford*' and *Ferendon*' [Farringdon 49,5] in Fees p. 399 and was possibly an earlier holder of this land; he also held another part of Shillingford (19,7 note). On the descent of the manor see FA i pp. 346, 389, Cal. Inq. PM vol. i no. 129, v no. 527, xi no. 118, and OJR in TDA 47 p. 214.
2 PLOUGHS THERE, HOWEVER. The scribe wrote the *tamen* because the 2 lordship ploughs, when added to the 3½ villagers' ploughs, exceed the plough estimate; see the fourth note under 1,3 and cf. notes to 39,12 and 40,4.

49,2 COLUMBJOHN. DB *Colum*. Named from the river Culm, it lies in Broad Clyst parish, Cliston Hundred (20). It can be identified in the Tax Return for that Hundred (xii); see Exon. Notes Ch. 49. John *de Culum* holds *Culum* from William *Briwere* in Fees p. 396; the same man holds *Colm* of the Honour of Plympton in Fees p. 789. See FA i pp. 333, 367, 433, Cal. Inq. PM vol. v no. 527, xi nos. 118, 299, xiv no. 325, and OJR H7 p. 381.

49,3 'EVELEIGH'. This holding can be identified in the Tax Return for Cliston Hundred (xii; see Exon. Notes Ch. 49) and is said to have lain in Broad Clyst parish, EPNS ii p. 574. There is an 'Eveleigh' in the adjacent parish of Sowton, Wonford Hundred (19), marked on the first edition OS 1-inch map (sheet 22 of 1809, reprint sheet 91 of 1970) at SS 986927 where Dymonds farm now is. *Yevelegh* is held with *Colome Johan* (49,2) in Cal. Inq. PM vol. xi no. 299, xiv no. 325; see OJR H7 p. 381. An approximate location for 'Eveleigh' in Broad Clyst parish is given by the fact that Comberoy farm [GR ST 0100] is an *alias* of 'East Eveleigh', EPNS ii p. 576.

49,4 ?CULM (VALE). The order of Exon. points to a place in Wonford Hundred (19), the place-name points to the river Culm. It might be Culm Vale in Stoke Canon parish. Successors to Fulchere held Whiteheathfield in Cullompton parish, Hayridge Hundred (15), but there is no proof that this land represents DB *Colun*; see OJR in TDA 36 pp. 359–360 and 42 p. 226.
1 VILLAGER .... 10s. He pays Fulchere 10s (see Exon. Notes here) and see 6,6 note on villagers 'farming' land.

49,5 FARRINGDON. A parish in (East) Budleigh Hundred (14), identifiable in the Tax Return for Budleigh Hundred (xvi). In Fees p. 790 Richard son of Ralph holds in *Ferndon* from the Honour of Plympton. Fees p. 763 makes it clear that Richard holds from the heirs of William *de la Bruere*; see Cal. Inq. PM vol. i p. 129, v no. 527, Fees p. 399 and 49,1 note.
The next entry in Fees p. 790 (see Fees p. 763, FA i p. 427), *La Ford'*, may be part of

this land as it has the same holders; see Cal. Inq. PM vol. xiv no. 325. It is perhaps Rosamondford [GR SY 0291] in Aylesbeare parish, adjacent to Farringdon.
Part of Farringdon was given to Exeter Church and it is possible that *Storsan* and *Whythen* [Within Furze and Within SY 0290] held by the Dean and Chapter of Exeter in Cal. Inq. PM vol. xi no. 118 were part of this gift; see OJR in TDA 35 pp. 290-291.

49,6      LEIGH. In Loxbeare parish, Tiverton Hundred (9). In Fees p. 759 Robert *de Legh'* holds *Legh'* from the Honour of Plympton. It is *Legh' Roberd* in Cal. Inq. PM vol. v no. 527 and had been a fee of William *Briwere*, Fees p. 396; see FA i pp. 319, 433, OJR in TDA 35 p. 313 and H1 p. 19.

49,7      THIS ENTRY IS WRITTEN in the same very pale ink as 48,12 some 12 letters into the left margin of the MS below the bottom marginal ruling of col. 117c; it is not rubricated. It seems likely that the scribe simply failed initially to abstract this entry from the Exon. section dealing with Godbold, Nicholas the Bowman, Fulchere and Haimeric (see Exon. Note Chs. 47-50), rather than that details of the holding came in late (there is no sign of this in Exon.). Cf. his failure to abstract Flohere's manor of *Sotrebroc* from the Exon. section on French men-at-arms (see Exon. Notes Ch. 22).
HUISH. DB *Chiwartiwis*, probably for OE *Cyneweard-hiwisc* 'the Cyneweard estate' (JMcND). Apparently Great Huish and East Huish in Tedburn St. Mary parish, Wonford Hundred (19), although EPNS ii p. 452 does not give the DB reference. In Fees p. 788 Richard *Tremeneth'* holds in *Hywisse* from the Honour of Plympton; see FA i pp. 313, 345, 388, RH i p. 85a, HD p. 56, Cal. Inq. PM vol. ii nos. 306, 593, vii no. 297, and OJR in TDA 44 p. 320.

Ch. 50      HAIMERIC. Haimeric of Arques (Exon. *de arcis, de archa*; see Exon. Notes here). Arques is in the département of Pas-de-Calais, France. One of his manors in Devon passes to the Honour of Plympton (Ch. 21 note), others to Torrington (Ch. 36 note).
FOR THE EXON. ORDER of this chapter, see Ch. 47 note.

50,1      POLTIMORE. A parish in Wonford Hundred (19). The Tax Return for Wonford Hundred (xxxi) states that Haimeric has 1½ hides, 2½ furlongs (*fertinos*) in lordship there, which agrees with the lordship given in Exon. In Fees p. 788 Bartholomew *de Pultimor* holds in *Pultimor* from the Honour pf Plympton; see RH i p. 85b, Cal. Inq. PM vol. xiii no. 268, FA i pp. 313, 386 and OJR in TDA 44 pp. 299, 320. It is associated with *Hille* in Witheridge Hundred [Hill 50,3] in FA i p. 345.

50,2      HAIMERIC HIMSELF HOLDS. Repeated at the beginning of 50,2-5 inclusive.

50,2-3    RUCKHAM. HILL. Both lie in Cruwys Morchard parish, Witheridge Hundred (7); see EPNS ii p. 380 and EPNS vol. xiv (1937) p. lii. In Fees p. 760 John *le Despenser* holds in *Hille* and in *Throucumb'*, together with 1 furlong (*ferlingo*) in *Bradelegh'* [Bradley 50,5] "which is in the Hundred of Tiverton", from Roger *Dacastre* who holds ultimately from the Honour of Torrington; see Fees p. 774 and FA i pp. 344, 364, 421, OJR in TDA 30 pp. 406, 424 and 50,1 note.

50,2      WITH 1 .... SLAVE. In the MS there is a gap of about 9 letters' width between *cū i* and *seruo*, due to an erasure. Under ultra-violet light an 7 is visible with a gap for a number immediately before the *seruo* and part of a *d* can be seen before the 7. It is possible that the scribe originally wrote *cū i bord'* 7 *i seruo*. Farley shows the gap caused by the erasure, though he does not always do so; see 1,60 note.

50,4      COOMBE. Exon. order (see Ch. 47 note) suggests that it lay in Witheridge Hundred (7), but it does not appear in feudal lists; if it lay in Cruwys Morchard parish (where it is mapped in this edition), it would form a unit with Ruckham and Hill (50,2-3). There is another Coombe close by [GR SS 8411] and a Woodscombe [SS 8312] both in Puddington parish. There are also two places named Coombe in Witheridge parish.

50,5      BRADLEY. 'East' Bradley in Tiverton parish and Hundred (9). It can be identified in the Tax Return for Tiverton Hundred (xi); see Exon. Notes Ch. 50. In Fees pp. 760, 744 it is held with Hill and Ruckham (50,2-3 note) as *Bradelegh'* or *Estbradelegh'* [probably the village now known as Great Bradley] of the Honour of Torrington; see FA i pp. 319, 370, 433 and OJR H1 p. 9.

Ch. 51      KING'S SERVANTS. Only the holders of 51,1-13 can really be described as 'servants', i.e. people who held land by serjeanty, the rest of the chapter being filled with holders who did not fit in under any of the other chapter headings of Exchequer DB; see Exon. Notes to 51,14 and 51,15-16.
IN EXON. the bulk of this chapter is under the heading 'Lands of the King's Servants in Devonshire', in the following Hundredal order:
    51,2    Wonford                              51,3-4    Tawton

|         |           |          |          |          |
|---------|-----------|----------|----------|----------|
| 51,5-7  | Silverton |          | 51,12;9  | Kerswell |
| 51,11   | Witheridge|          | 51,10;13 | Colyton  |
| 51,8    | Tiverton  |          |          |          |

The first entry in the chapter is included in Exon. under 'Land of Nicholas the Bowman' (Ch. 47 note); 51,14 is among 'Lands of the French Men-at-Arms in Devonshire' (Ch. 22 note) and 51,15-16 are in 'Lands of English Thanes in Devonshire' (Ch. 52 note).

51,1 WILLIAM THE PORTER. DB *portō* for *port(it)o(r)* (although when the scribe added the † which is in paler ink, he should have added a final *r*); Exon. *portitor* and in the Tax Return for Budleigh Hundred (xvi), in which Bicton lies, he is William *portarius* with ½ hide 1 virgate lordship. On the byname OEB p. 129 is irrelevant, p. 265 pertinent. William seems to have held Bicton by service of guarding the gate of Exeter Castle (Round KS p. 14), and probably also Exeter jail as his successors did (see the quote from Fees p. 96 in the next note), hence his byname describes his occupation rather than that of a predecessor; cf. 1,64 note on 'Norman Parker' and DB Dorset General Notes 57,17 on 'Osmund the Baker'. See also Exon. Notes here.
BICTON. A parish in (East) Budleigh Hundred (14). This entry can be identified in the Tax Return for Budleigh (xvi); see note above. It later forms a serjeanty involving the gate of Exeter Castle and the jail: in Fees p. 96 John *Janitor* (from Latin *ianua* 'door') holds *Bukint' cum pertinenciis de domino rege per sergenteriam custodiendi januam castri Exonie et gaiolam prisonum* ("Bicton with dependencies from his lord, the King, by a serjeanty of guarding the gate of Exeter Castle and the prisoners' jail") by gift of King Henry I to his predecessors for the same service. The holder in RBE ii p. 452 is Roger *Portarius* (from Latin *porta* 'gate'); in RH i pp. 66b, 92b the holder is Reginald *le Arbelestr'*, in Fees pp. 764, 1368, 1424 Ralph *Balistarius* and in FÂ i p. 325 Geoffrey *Arblaster*. The place is called *Estbuketon* in Cal. Inq. PM vol. x no. 241 to distinguish it from Dickington (?,19 note); see Fees p. 342, Cal. Inq. PM vol. vi no. 6, ix no. 38, OJR in TDA 35 p. 298 and 1,9 note.

51,2 WILLIAM THE USHER. DB *hostiarius*, Exon. *hostiarius* and perhaps *hestiarius*, Latin for 'usher, door-keeper'; OEB p. 255. He also holds land in DB Notts. Ch. 29 and his son Robert holds in DB Leics. 43,9 ff. William's Devonshire manors are later held by William *Briwere* (Fees pp. 396-401), then by the Mohuns (of Dunster in Somerset) either in chief from the Honour of Dunster or from the Honour of Plympton (see Ch. 21 note). Many reappear in the Inq. PMs of the Mohuns; see, for example, Cal. Inq. PM vol. vii no. 297.
TAW (GREEN). DB *Tauelande*. The DB place was named from the river Taw and, if correctly identified, it lay in South Tawton parish, now in Wonford Hundred (19), but its position at the head of 'Lands of the King's Servants in Devonshire' in Exon. (475 a 1) suggests that it may have been contained in a return originating from South Tawton royal manor in 1086; see notes to 1,29. 15,7. 43,1 and 45,1. The holding probably included the adjacent Cocktree [GR SX 6698], held as *Coketrewe* by Roger *Burnel* in 1303 (FA i p. 356), a member of the same family which held Crooke Burnell (51,3); see Cal. Inq. PM vol. ii nos. 306, 593, vii no. 297, and OJR in TDA 27 p. 198 note 55 and 44 pp. 345, 351.
1 OX OR 30d. See 43,1 note.
(SOUTH) TAWTON, THE KING'S MANOR. See 1,29 note.

51,3-4 WILLIAM. Almost certainly William the Usher; the Exon. scribe no doubt did not feel it necessary to repeat his byname after the first entry on folio 475a (though it is repeated on folios 475b-476b, but these entries show signs of being added at different times). Also all of this section in Exon., with the exception of the last entry on Ansger the King's servant (= DB 51,13), is on William the Usher. Moreover, 51,3 descends to the same family of *Burnel* as 51,2 and 51,5 (see note to latter on William there being William the Usher).

51,3 CROOKE (BURNELL). In (North) Tawton parish and Hundred (12). In Fees p. 787 Robert *Burnel* holds in *Cruk'* from the Honour of Plympton; see Fees p. 400, HD p. 56, Cal. Inq. PM vol. ii nos. 306, 593, vii no. 297, FA i pp. 370, 422 and OJR in TDA 29 p. 253.
ALWARD. DB *Aluuard*, Exon. *Ailuuard(us)*; see 3,45 note and cf. 1,41 note.
IN EXCHANGE FOR (SOME OF) WILLIAM'S LANDS. *de excambio terrarum Willelmi*. William told the DB Commissioners that he acquired Taw Green and Crooke Burnell by exchanging them for some other of the manors originally granted to him. The fact that he did not apparently name the manors suggests that they may not have existed; see notes to 48,2. 48,12 and 51,10.

| | |
|---|---|
| 51,4 | 1 VIRGATE. This entry has not been identified or even located in a Hundred; see OJR in TDA 36 p. 357 and VCH p. 526 note 10 for speculation. It is not part of the previous entry in the DB MS since the *R* of *Radulf'* is rubricated in a similar fashion to the initial letters of other sections. Moreover, 1 virgate is not needed in 51,3 to make the lordship and villagers' land add up to the amount of taxed land. This latter is not definitive proof, but the equation of taxed land = the total of lordship and villagers' land works out for the majority of entries (see 1,4 note on the hide). This land also forms a separate entry in Exon. Cf. notes to 3,32 and 3,71.<br>1 FEMALE SLAVE. This is the only occurrence of *ancilla* in Devon, though female slaves were commonly specified in other DB counties, such as Gloucestershire. Their almost complete absence from Devon does not mean that they did not exist, merely that, like much of the female population, they were not counted, or that they were included among the *serui* as a class. |
| 51,5 | WILLIAM. William the Usher; the Tax Return for Silverton Hundred (xiii) states that he had ½ hide lordship there, which seems to correspond to his 1 virgate lordship in this entry and his 1 virgate in Raddon, 51,6, where Exon. supplies his byname.<br>CADELEIGH. A parish in Hayridge Hundred (15), identifiable in the Tax Return for Silverton Hundred (xiii); see note above. *Cakelee* is held by John *Burnell* (see 51,3-4 note) in HD p. 56 from the Mohuns; see RH i pp. 70b, 95a, Cal. Inq. PM vol. ii nos. 306, 436, vii no. 297, viii no. 273, FA i pp. 321, 367, 424 and OJR in TDA 42 p. 246. For 'Little' Cadeleigh see 19,24 note. |
| 51,6 | RADDON. In Thorverton parish, Hayridge Hundred (15), and identifiable in the Tax Return for Silverton (xiii); see first note under 51,5. It is held in FA i p. 368 by the heir of Augustine *de Bathonia* as *Estroddon* ['East' Raddon; for West Raddon see 15,5 and 24,4] and from the Honour of Plympton in FA i p. 425; see Cal. Inq. PM vol. ii no. 165, OJR in TDA 42 p. 246 and 5,9 note. |
| 51,7 | RALPH BOTIN, Exon. *Radulf(us) Botin(us)*. The byname is parallel with *Bodin* (Forssner p. 50), but a distinct name, although rare. This is an OG or OFr formation with the diminutive suffix *-in(us)*, derived from the OG personal name stem *Boto*, alternative to OG *Bod-* (Förstemann 219-323, see also Bach § 203, para. 2). (JMcND)<br>BLACKBOROUGH. In Kentisbeare parish, Hayridge Hundred (15). There were two manors here in 1086, the other being Allhallows farm (see 34,20 note). This manor was *Blakeburu' Boydin* in Fees p. 398, held by William *Briwere*, and *Blakebergh'* held in Fees p. 794 by Ralph *Buty* (presumably a descendant of the 1086 holder Ralph Botin) from the Honour of Plympton; see FA i pp. 368, 425 and OJR in TDA 42 p. 247. An eighth part of the manor lay in *Ashforde* [unidentified], Cal. Inq. PM vol. iv (o.s.) no. 63 (= TDA 38 p. 326).<br>LEOFWIN SOCK. Exon. *Leuuin(us) socca*; see OEB p. 371.<br>9 VILLAGERS AND 2 SLAVES (HAVE) ½ HIDE AND ½ VIRGATE. Exon. merely states that the *uill(ani)* have the ½ hide and ½ virgate; see the last paragraph in 1,3 note on slaves on the question of slaves having land, and cf. Exon. Notes to 3,57. 16,145-146. 17,58 and 19,9. |
| 51,8 | BOLHAM. In Tiverton parish and Hundred (9) and positively identifiable in that Hundred's Tax Return (xi). It passed to the Honour of Dunster and was held in FA i p. 319 by Hugh *Ralegh* as *Bolleham* from the heirs of John *de Moun*; see HD p. 39 and OJR H1 p. 29. |
| 51,9 | ILSHAM. In St. Marychurch parish, Haytor Hundred (29); either this holding or Tormoham (51,12) accounts for the lordship of ½ (hide?) just *dim̃* in the Exon. MS, though *hida* is probably implied from the previous lordship statements) that is allowed to William the Usher in the Tax Return for Kerswell (Haytor) Hundred (xxv). Ilsham seems to have been regarded as a part of Tormoham in later times and to have had the same descent, being held with it by Torre Abbey; see TE p. 153a, Oliver *Mon.* pp. 170, 173 and OJR in TDA 40 p. 127, 50 p. 372. |
| 51,10 | SUTTON. In Widworthy parish, Colyton Hundred (22). In Fees p. 788 (Honour of Plympton) Robert *de Bulkeworth'* holds in *Sutthon'* together with *La Hille abbatis de Quarera* [an unidentified 'Hill', see 21,15 note]. *Moricius de Lucy* holds *Sutton* in FA i p. 366; it is *Sutton Lucy* coupled with *Colewill* [Colwell 16,170] in Cal. Inq. PM vol. xii no. 333. See also FA i pp. 330, 366, 428 and OJR H7 pp. 340, 350.<br>THE ABOVE MANORS .... EXCHANGE. This refers to 51,4-10 (see Exon. Notes), though of course the same was true of 51,2-3 (see the statement at the end of 51,3). The idea that William may have stated that these manors were exchanges to cover the |

fact that he had acquired some at least of them illegally (see 48,2 note) may be strengthened by the fact that a priest had held Raddon (51,6) in 1066 (so VCH p. 381), though William was a subtenant of Tavistock Abbey's holding at Raddon (5,9). The Exon. scribe may have left 1¾ lines blank at the end of 476 b 1 (= 51,10), for the later inclusion of the manor(s) exchanged. Cf. notes to 48,12 and 51,3.

51,11 MARIANSLEIGH. DB *Lege*. A parish in Witheridge Hundred (7) and positively identifiable in its Tax Return (x). It is so called from the dedication of the church, now to St. Mary, perhaps formerly to St. Marina; EPNS ii p. 382. In Fees p. 761 William *de Mohun* holds *Marinelegh'* from Reginald *de Mohun* who holds from the Honour of Plympton; see HD p. 56, Cal. Inq. PM vol. ii no. 306, vii no. 297, and OJR in TDA 30 pp. 408, 424.

51,12 TORMOHAM. DB *Torre*. It is a parish in Haytor Hundred (29), containing both Torre and Torquay; the second element is a corruption of *Mohun*, see EPNS ii p. 523. In Fees p. 769 William *de Mohun* holds *Torre Brywere* (named from William *Briwere* to whom these manors descend, see 51,2 note) from Alice *de Mohun* of the Honour of Plympton; see HD p. 39, FA i p. 318 and Cal. Inq. PM vol. i no. 564, ii no. 306. Part of the manor was granted by William *Briwere* in 1196 for the foundation of the Abbey of Torre; see Cal. Inq. PM vol. vii no. 297, Oliver *Mon*. p. 172 and OJR in TDA 40 p. 127, 50 p. 372. It is *Torre Mohun cum capella de Cokyngton* ("... with the chapel of Cockington", see 20,10) in VE ii p. 361.

51,13 ANSGER, THE KING'S SERVANT. Perhaps either Ansger (the) Cook (*coquus*) or Ansger Fower (*fouuer, focarius*, 'the hearth-keeper'), both of whom appear in the chapter devoted to the King's servants in DB Somerset (46,16 and 46,12-15 respectively), although none of their holdings descends to the Honour of Berry (see next note). Ansger Cook also held in 1086 land in DB Wilts. 66,3 (as one of the King's Servants) and in Essex Ch. 75 (as a tenant-in-chief).
GATCOMBE. In Colyton parish and Hundred (22). The land passed to the Honour of Berry, Robert *de Helihun* holding *Gatecumb'* in Fees p. 791; see FA i pp. 330, 365, 428 and OJR H7 p. 355.

51,14 MORIN. DB *Morin(us)*, Exon. *maurin(us)*; see Reaney s.n. *Morin*. He is probably Morin of Caen (*de Cadomo*; OEB p. 79) who has 1 virgate in lordship in Halberton Hundred (Tax Return xvii). See 16,173-174 note and Exon. Notes here.
LEONARD. In Exon. this entry lies among the 'Lands of the French Men-at-Arms in Devonshire' at the end of a group of Halberton Hundred places (10); see Ch. 22 note. It lies in Halberton parish and Hundred and is identifiable in that Hundred's Tax Return (xvii); see above note. It is probably represented by *Moriston'* [Moorstone Barton GR ST 0109] in Fees p. 780 held by Geoffrey *Gambun* from the part of the Honour of Gloucester held by Earl Richard. *Moriston'* is probably derived from Morin, the 1086 holder, EPNS ii p. 549. See FA i pp. 338, 349, 432 and OJR H2 pp. 51, 60.
[VALUE] .... 15s. This last line is written in paler ink and probably by a different scribe to the rest of the entry. See 16,27 note.

51,15-16 THESE TWO ENTRIES are among the 'Lands of English Thanes in Devonshire' (Ch. 52 note) in the Exon. Book.
PRIESTS OF BODMIN. Of St. Petroc's, Bodmin. See DB Cornwall 4,3-22 for this priory's holdings in that county, most of them with the Count of Mortain as subtenant; see also Cornwall Exon. Notes 4,3. See Mon. Ang. ii pp. 459-460 for St. Petroc's chequered history.

51,15 HOLLACOMBE. A parish in (Black) Torrington Hundred (11). In the Tax Return for Torrington Hundred (iii) the clergy of *Holecoma* have failed to pay tax on 1 virgate, that is on the whole of their holding here (including their ½ virgate lordship land detailed in Exon., which does not pay tax). These clergy were dependent on St. Petroc's of Bodmin (see note above) which continued to hold the land: in Fees p. 1264 the Prior *de Bonne* [Bodmin] holds *Slecumbe* [an error for Hollacombe] 'by gift of some ancient King'. The King may well have been Athelstan who was a great benefactor of the priory (Mon. Ang. ii pp. 459-460). See FA i p. 327 and OJR H5 pp. 205, 211.

51,16 NEWTON (ST. PETROCK). A parish in Shebbear Hundred (4). In the Tax Return for Merton (Shebbear) Hundred (v) the priests of *Niuuetona* have failed to pay tax on 1 hide of land, that is on the whole of their holding here (including, apparently, the non-taxable lordship land; cf. 51,15 note). These priests, like their brethren at Hollacombe (51,15 note), were subject to St. Petroc's of Bodmin. In RH i p. 93b the Prior of Bodmin holds *Niweton*; see TE p. 146b and OJR H10 p. 552. The land was granted to the priory by

# 51 - 52

51,16 (cont'd.) King Eadred between 946 and 955; see ECDC p. 10 no. 25 (= BCS no. 725 = Sawyer (1) no. 388) and ECDC p. 12 no. 32, Oliver *Mon*. p. 411 and 1,39 note.
WHICH PAYS TAX. Although *geld* can abbreviate the past *geldabat* as well as the present *geldat* (see 1,7 note) and although *geldabat* is the usual word in the tax payment formula, Exon. has *reddit gildum* in full, probably because of the lack of TRE holder for the manor which means that the tax statement immediately succeeds the statement that the priests of Bodmin have a manor called Newton (St. Petrock) — and this is in the present tense. Cf. 2,2 note on 'pays tax'.

Ch. 52  LANDS OF THE KING'S THANES. See 1,32 note on thanes. In Exon. the entries for this chapter (with 51,15-16) fall under the heading 'Lands of English Thanes in Devonshire'. The order of Hundreds is:

| | | | |
|---|---|---|---|
| 52,26;29; 1-3. 51,15 | } Torrington | 52,50 | Wonford |
| | | 52,41;51 | South Molton |
| 52,4;31 | Hartland | 52,20 | Witheridge |
| 52,5-8;32-33. 51,16 | } Merton | 52,35;18 | Budleigh |
| | | 52,43 | Witheridge |
| 52,30;9 | Tawton | 52,21 | Tiverton |
| 52,34 | Crediton | 52,44 | Teignton |
| 52,36 | South Molton | 52,27 | ?Exminster |
| 52,37 | ?Wonford | 52,46 | Teignton |
| 52,38 | Cliston | 52,52 | Kerswell |
| 52,10 | South Molton | 52,28 | Plympton |
| 52,11-15 | Wonford | 52,24;19;25 | Axminster and Axmouth |
| 52,16 | Teignton | 52,53 | Chillington |
| 52,40 | South Molton | 52,42 | *Alleriga* |
| 52,17;22 | Silverton | 52,45 | Diptford |
| 52,23 | Budleigh | 52,47 | Wonford |
| 52,39 | Silverton | 52,48-49 | Exminster |

These last three entries (52,47;48-49) in the right column appear to be late entries, out of sequence.
Exchequer DB arranges the chapter not by Hundreds but by 1086 holders, thus:

| | | | |
|---|---|---|---|
| 52,1-8 | Colwin | 52,38-39 | Edwin |
| 52,9-19 | Godwin | 52,40 | Ulf |
| 52,20-21 | Godric | 52,41-42 | Algar |
| 52,22-25 | Odo | 52,43-45 | Alric |
| 52,26-28 | Aldred | 52,46 | Leofric |
| 52,29-30 | Alward (Mart) | 52,47-49 | Saewulf |
| 52,31-33 | Ansgot | 52,50 | Aelfeva |
| 52,34-35 | Dunn   *r* | 52,51 | Alfhild |
| 52,36 | Alnoth | 52,52-53 | Godiva |
| 52,37 | Alwin | | |

52,1  COLWIN. Colwin here and in 52,2-8 is perhaps Colwin the reeve who, according to the Tax Return for Hartland Hundred (ii), seems to have held 52,4; see 42,3 note. See C 2 note above on Colwin the reeve.
CHILSWORTHY. In Holsworthy parish, (Black) Torrington Hundred (11). Like Culsworthy (52,3), Chilsworthy (*Cheleswrth'* or *Chulaworth*) belonged to Robert *de Sancto Dionisio*, then to William *de Arderne* also known as William *le Sauser* because he had been a *salsarius* (an officer of the King's saucery), before it escheated to the King; see Cal. Inq. PM vol. i no. 815, Fees pp. 265, 613, 1369, 1426, RH i p. 64b and OJR H5 pp. 204, 211.
OSEVA. DB *Odeua*, Exon. *Oseua*, represent OE *Osgifu*. In PNDB p. 334 the DB form is supposed erroneous and it is identified with a quite different name, OG feminine *Odgiva*, at Forssner p. 196. The spellings can only be reconciled with each other as representatives of OE *Osgifu* if we suppose a most intricate and hypothetical manipulation of phonetics (JMcND). Clerical error seems more likely. For the other cases where the Exchequer scribe seems to have miscopied Exon., see Exon. Notes 24,14.

52,2  COLWIN ALSO HOLDS. Repeated at the beginning of 52,2-8 inclusive.
BREXWORTHY. DB *Bristelesworde*. It lies in Bradworthy parish, (Black) Torrington Hundred (11); see EPNS i p. 133, OJR in TDA 36 p. 351, H5 pp. 191, 204, 211 and 34,6 note.
3 SLAVES, WITH 1 VILLAGER. In the MS both *serui* and *uitto* are written over erasures; as the order in Exon. is the normal one ('1 villager and 3 slaves'), it is possible that the Exchequer scribe originally wrote *iii uitti cū i seruo* by mistake.

| | |
|---|---|
| 52,3 | CULSWORTHY. In Abbots Bickington parish, (Black) Torrington Hundred (11); see EPNS i p. 125. In Fees p. 1426 *Colteswurth'* had belonged to Robert *de Sancto Dionisio* (see 52,1 note), then to Maurice *de Culteswurth'*, then to Ralph *de Sicca Villa* before being held by Gervase *de Horton'*; see Fees p. 1369. In Fees p. 797 Maurice *de Coltesuurth'* is said to hold from an unknown Honour; subsequently the land appears under the Honour of Okehampton; see FA i pp. 357, 408 and OJR H5 p. 205. |
| 52,4 | WOOLFARDISWORTHY. DB *Olvereword*. It is a parish in Hartland Hundred (3) and this holding is identifiable in the Tax Return for that Hundred (ii); see 52,1 note under Colwin. In Fees p. 780 William *de Hamptenesford'* holds in *Wolfarysworth'* from the Honour of Gloucester. It is *Est Wolfordisworth[y]* in FA i p. 371 and it is held with *Dynnesber'* [Dunsbeare 52,5] in Cal. Inq. PM vol. iii no. 371 and xvi no. 538; see FA i pp. 342, 410, Cal. Inq. PM vol. ix no. 428 and OJR in TDA 26 p. 417. Its church went to Hartland Abbey, see Oliver *Mon*. p. 204 and VE ii p. 333. |
| 52,5-6 | DUNSBEARE. ALLISLAND. In Merton and Petrockstowe parishes respectively, Shebbear Hundred (4). In Fees p. 779 William *de Hampteneford'* (see 52,4 note) holds in *Haleyslond', Dynesbere* and *Childedon'* [Chelsdon GR SS 4810 in Petrockstowe] from the Honour of Gloucester. In FA i p. 411 William *de Hauttysford* holds in *Allyslond, Wynesbear* [i.e. *Dynesbear*] and *Chillesdon*, formerly held by Richard *de Hauttysford* and David *de Servyngton*. This latter may be the man who named *Dainesheaunton* or *Davysheanton*, otherwise West Heanton in Buckland Filleigh parish (EPNS i p. 91); this suggests that West Heanton (52,8), also held by Colwin, had the same descent. If Chelsdon is not a part of Allisland, which is adjacent, it might stand for West Heanton which is also close by but in the next parish; see FA i p. 359, Cal. Inq. PM vol. v no. 538, ix no. 428 and OJR H10 pp. 547, 563. |
| 52,7 | *HAME*. It clearly lay in Shebbear Hundred (4) and was probably close to Colwin's other holdings (52,5-6;8) in that Hundred, but it has not been positively identified, since identifications with Embury or Galmington, both in Buckland Filleigh parish, are unsupported by evidence; see EPNS i p. 91, OJR in VCH p. 529 note 3 and H10 pp. 547, 563. |
| 52,8 | (WEST) HEANTON. In Buckland Filleigh parish, Shebbear Hundred (4). It is not found in the fee lists unless it is represented by Chelsdon, see 52,5-6 note and OJR H10 pp. 547, 563. |
| 52,9-19 | GODWIN. His lands are later held of the Honour of Gloucester, the holders in the late 13th century being the Umfravilles. |
| 52,9 | GODWIN HOLDS. Repeated at the beginning of 52,9-12 inclusive. These Godwins and those in 52,13-18 may be Godwin of Chittlehampton; see notes to 52,17 and 52,19. He is called plain Godwin, however, in the Tax Return for Wonford Hundred (xxxi) which refers to 52,11-15 (see 52,11 note on Cheriton Bishop), and in that for Teignton (xxiv) which refers to 52,16 and in that for Budleigh (xvi) which refers to 52,18. But the Tax Returns do not always give a man his full name: e.g. in the Return for Torrington Hundred (iii) plain Roald's ½ virgate of lordship is clearly the ½ virgate lordship detailed for Roald Dubbed in 35,2. NATSON. DB *Limete*. The sequence of entries in the Exon. Book points to a place in (North) Tawton Hundred (12), one of several designated from an earlier name of the river Yeo (see Introductory Note 2). This 'Nymet' should be looked for among one of the fees of the Honour of Gloucester in (North) Tawton Hundred; see 52,9-19 note. It is tempting to identify it with *Godwynescoth'* held of that Honour in Fees p. 778 by Baldwin *Lovel* and Robert *Pollard* and possibly called after the 1086 holder of 'Nymet'. But the place has not been located (it is wrongly identified with Goodcot in Ashreigney (DB *Godevecote* 25,11) by the indexer of Fees). A clear identification is Natson in Bow parish, held in Fees p. 778 by John *Burnellus* and Simon *Lamperie* as *Notteston'* from the Honour of Gloucester (see 25,8-9 note). See 52,11 note, FA i pp. 346, 371, 423 and OJR in TDA 29 p. 253. |
| 52,10 | CHITTLEHAMPTON. The Exon. form is *Curemetona* (not *Citremetona* as Ellis prints, although this was probably its correct form and the Exon. scribe misread his original); by writing *Curemtone* the Exchequer scribe perpetuated the Exon. mistake, as in 16,57 and 34,13. Chittlehampton is a parish in South Molton Hundred (6). In Fees p. 778 Herbert son of Matthew holds *Chedelhampton'* from the Honour of Gloucester; Cal. Inq. PM vol. ix no. 428 makes it clear that *Chitelhamholte* [Chittlehamholt GR SS 6421, a separate parish since 1885] was the woodland belonging to the manor; see RH i pp. 80b, 93a, FA i pp. 326, 418, Cal. Inq. PM vol. iii no. 371, iv no. 434, v no. 538, x no. 88, xiv no. 209, xvi no. 1067, EPNS ii p. 337 and OJR H3 p. 79. |

| | |
|---|---|
| 52,10 (cont'd.) | 5 CARUCATES. It is unusual to have carucates used when land has been hidated; see 1,2 note and cf. 1,3;5. |
| 52,11 | CHERITON (BISHOP). Now a parish in Wonford Hundred (19). This holding is identifiable in the Tax Return for that Hundred (xxxi): Godwin's 3½ virgates of lordship there correspond to the sum of his lordship in 52,11-15.<br>This holding appears to be represented in Fees p. 779 (Honour of Gloucester) by: (1) *Churiton'* and *Wolgareston'* [Wolfgar farm or Wilson, GR SX 7595; see EPNS ii p. 429] held by John *de Melewis*, Simon *Lamperee* (on whom see 52,9 note) and Hugh *de Loges*; (2) *Tryfebel* [Treable farm SX 7192] held by Eleanor *de Hause*; and (3) *Alricheston'* [Easton Barton SX 7293; see EPNS ii p. 428] held by the heirs of William *le Barun*. All these are held from John *de Umfravile* in FA i p. 315 with the addition of *La Mille* ['Mill farm' SX 7694 on the 1st edition OS 1-inch map, sheet no. 26 of 1809, reprint sheet no. 82 of 1969] and *Stoddon* [Staddon SX 7594]. In FA i pp. 345-346 *Nithereparkyng* [Partridge SX 7393] is said to be part of Treable, *Aereston* [Easton] is coupled with *Somerton* [unidentified] 'in Shebbear Hundred' and *Churiton* is associated with *Notteston* [Natson, see 52,9] 'in the Hundred of (North) Tawton'; see FA i pp. 387-388 and OJR in TDA 36 p. 376, 44 pp. 334-335.<br>Cheriton was a lay holding in 1086, later called 'Cheriton Bishop' from a holding of the Bishop of Exeter which he acquired in the late 13th century; see EPNS ii p. 427. Much earlier, Cheriton seems to have been part of a grant by Edward the Martyr to AElfsige in 976 of 1 *pertica* at *Hyples eald land*; this appears in DB divided into six portions: Eggbeer (16,130), Lambert (43,4), Cheriton Bishop and Lambert, Medland and Coombe (52,11-13;15); see ECDC pp. 20-31 and no. 42 p. 13. |
| 52,12 | LAMBERT. DB *Lanford*; see EPNS ii p. 428. It is in Cheriton Bishop parish, Wonford Hundred (19); see 52,11 note. In FA i p. 315 Baldwin *de Specote* holds *Lamford* from John *de Umfravile* who holds from the Honour of Gloucester; see FA i pp. 345, 386 and OJR in TDA 44 p. 336. |
| 52,13 | GODWIN ALSO HOLDS. Repeated at the beginning of 52,13-18 inclusive; see 52,9 note.<br>MEDLAND. Like 52,11-12 it lay in Cheriton Bishop parish, Wonford Hundred (see 52,11 note). *Middellond* is held in FA i p. 315 from the Earl of Gloucester and was given to the Abbot of Tewkesbury (Gloucestershire) by Robert son of Hamon, Mon. Ang. ii p. 65; see FA i p. 356 and OJR in TDA 44 p. 337. |
| 52,14 | OGWELL. A parish in the 'Ten Hide' or 'Teignhead' section of Wonford Hundred (19); see the Appendix. William *de Boyvil'* and Anastasia his wife hold in *Wogewill'* from the Honour of Gloucester in Fees p. 779; it is *Westwoggewill* [West Ogwell] held from John *de Umfravile* in FA i p. 315; see FA i p. 387 and OJR in TDA 44 p. 335. |
| 52,15 | COOMBE. In Drewsteignton parish, Wonford Hundred (19); see 52,11 note. In FA i p. 315 it seems to be represented by *Burgh'* [Burrough farm, just to the east of Coombe, GR SX 7491], held from John *de Umfravile*; see OJR in TDA 36 p. 376, 44 p. 337. |
| 52,16 | WRAY. In Moretonhampstead parish, Teignbridge Hundred (23). It can be identified in the Tax Return for Teignton Hundred (xxiv); see 52,9 note on Godwin. *Wrey* is held from John *de Humfravill* (Honour of Gloucester) in FA i p. 339. |
| 52,17 | 'COMBE (SACKVILLE)'. DB *Colun*, named from the river Culm. The manor corresponds to what is now Silverton park in Silverton parish, Hayridge Hundred (15), the remains of a manor house being marked as an antiquity on OS maps; see EPNS ii p. 570. In the Tax Return for Silverton (Hayridge) Hundred (xiii) Godwin of *Cillemetona* (from Chittlehampton 52,10) has 1 virgate of lordship which probably refers to this land, the only holding of a Godwin in this Hundred in DB; see notes to 52,19 and 52,9. In Fees p. 779 *Colm Reyngny* is held by Robert *de Sicca Villa* from the Honour of Gloucester, while in FA i p. 322 *Culm Reng[n]y* is held from John *de Humfravill*; see FA i pp. 368, 425, Cal. Inq. PM vol. viii no. 595 and OJR in TDA 42 pp. 227, 247. |
| 52,18 | HOLBROOK. In Clyst Honiton parish, (East) Budleigh Hundred (14). It can be positively accounted for in the Tax Return for Budleigh Hundred (xvi); see 52,9 note on Godwin. In Fees p. 763 Henry *de Holebrok'* holds in *Holebrok'* from Gilbert *de Unfranvil'* who holds from the Honour of Gloucester; see Fees p. 780, FA i pp. 365, 427 and OJR in TDA 35 p. 290. |
| 52,19 | GODWIN. Probably Godwin of Chittlehampton (*de cicemetona*; OEB p. 39), whom the Tax Return for Axmouth Hundred (xxi) states has ½ hide lordship there: this is the only holding of a Godwin in this Hundred in DB. See notes to 52,17 and 52,9.<br>'DOWN (UMFRAVILLE)'. DB *Dune*. 'Down' is the name of a hill lying between Axmouth and Lyme Regis from which Rousdon (52,25) and Dowlands (in Axmouth |

parish, not in DB) are also named. The present holding lay in Axmouth Hundred in 1086; see note above. 'Down Umfraville' cannot now be precisely located, but was probably adjacent to Rousdon, the two places being called *Estdon* and *Westdon* and associated with Musbury and Combpyne in FA i p. 384 (the *Nomina Villarum* of 1316). In FA i p. 328 John *de Humfravill* holds *Done* from the Earl of Gloucester; Gilbert *de Umfrevil* holds *Doune Sancti Leonardi* in FA i p. 366, the additional name deriving from a chapel there dedicated to St. Leonard which was given with 16 acres of land to Montebourg Abbey by Gilbert *de Hunfrancvilla* (Round CDF p. 318 no. 893). See also FA i p. 429, LSR (1334) p. 57 (where *Doune Umframvill* is associated with *Comb Pyn*), Pole p. 126 and OJR H4 pp. 176, 182. Reichel's identification (loc. cit.) with Charton in Axmouth is unfounded.

52,20   BULWORTHY. DB *Boleborde*, Exon. *Bolehorda*; the Exchequer scribe no doubt mistook the *h* for a *b* (it is rather 'hooked' and the ink may have been as pale in 1086 as it is today); see 16,42 note on other misreadings of Exon. by the DB scribe.

The place lies in Rackenford parish, Witheridge Hundred (7), and has the same later descent as Calverleigh (52,21) that is to the Honour of Gloucester: in Fees p. 779 *Boleworth'* and *Coldethorn* [unidentified] are held from that Honour 'from the part of Earl Richard'; *Boleworthi* is held by Ralph *de Calwodelegh'* in FA i p. 342; see Cal. Inq. PM vol. v no. 538, ix no. 428, xvi no. 538, and OJR in TDA 30 pp. 424, 430, 36 p. 357.

52,21   GODRIC. No doubt Godric of Calverleigh (*de calodeleia*; OEB p. 39), who in the Tax Return for Tiverton Hundred (xi) holds ½ virgate lordship (see Lordship and Villagers' Table).

CALVERLEIGH. DB *Calodelie*. A parish, now united with Loxbeare, in Tiverton Hundred (9), It is clearly identifiable in the Tax Return for that Hundred (xi); see the note above. Ralph *de Kalewodel[egh]* holds in *Kalewodel[egh]* from the Earl of Gloucester in FA i p. 316; see FA i pp. 342, 370, 433, Cal. Inq. PM vol. iii no. 371 and OJR H1 p. 27.

52,22-25 ODO. The Exchequer scribe, by removing these four entries of Odo from the large Exon. section (see Ch. 52 note) and putting them together, implies that the same man holds these four manors. In the Tax Returns are references both to Odo son of Edric and to Odo the Englishman, which probably refer to these holdings, the former to 52,22-23;25 and the latter to 52,24; see notes on these manors below. There is no reason why Odo son of Edric could not also have had the byname 'the Englishman'. (Odo, as an Englishman, would really have been called *Odda*; at some stage this OE personal name probably became confused with ContGerm *Odo*; JMcND.)
In later times Odo's estates are held of the Honour of Plympton (see Ch. 21 note).

52,22   PAYHEMBURY. A parish in Hayridge Hundred (15). The 3 virgates of this holding must account for the major part of the 3 virgates 1 furlong (*fertinum*) lordship of Odo son of Edric in the Tax Return for Silverton (Hayridge) Hundred (xiii); see 52,23 note for the likely remainder. The land seems to have lain at *Hugeton* [Uggaton has GR ST 0903 in Payhembury] held with Wyke Green and Rousdon (52,24-25) by Ralph *de Dune* in Cal. Inq. PM vol. i no. 141. It was given by Thomas *de Doune* together with Coddiford (52,23) to Dunkeswell Abbey, Oliver *Mon.* p. 396; see VE ii p. 304, TE p. 152a and OJR in TDA 42 pp. 227, 248, H4 p. 184.

52,23   CODDIFORD. The sequence of the Exon. Book suggests that this place lay in Silverton (Hayridge) Hundred (15); its lordship may well be accounted for in the Tax Return for Silverton (Hayridge) Hundred (xiii); see 52,22 note. Moreover, *Codeford* was closely connected with Uggaton in Payhembury (52,22) and given with it to Dunkeswell Abbey: a charter of King John, printed in Oliver *Mon.* p. 396, confirms the grant by Thomas *de Cumba Duna* of *totam terram quam habuit in Uggatona cum toto tenemento suo in Codeford* ("all the land he had in Uggaton with his whole holding in Coddiford"). There appears, however, to be no place of this or similar name either in Payhembury or in Hayridge Hundred; Coddiford in Cheriton Fitzpaine in (West) Budleigh Hundred (EPNS ii p. 414) may well be the correct identification. If this is so, Coddiford will apparently have been an outlying part of Hayridge Hundred because it was a sub-manor of Uggaton, just as Smallicombe (16,168, see note), by virtue of its association with Trill, was a detachment of Axminster Hundred (17); see OJR in TDA 42 p. 248.

52,24   WYKE (GREEN). In Axminster parish and Hundred (17). It seems likely that this is the land implied by the Tax Return for Axminster Hundred (xix) in which Odo the Englishman has ½ virgate lordship land; see 52,22-25 note on Odo. In Fees p. 788 Ralph *de Dune* (from Rousdon 52,25, another of Odo's lands) holds in *Wyk'* from the Honour of Plympton; see FA i pp. 319, 366, 429, Cal. Inq. PM vol. i no. 141, OJR H4 pp. 141, 149 and 52,22 note.

52,25 ROUSDON. DB *Done*, which is also found as the basic element in Down Ralph (the site of Allhallows School), originally an alternative name for Rousdon. It is one of two places called 'Down' in this chapter, both lying in Axmouth Hundred (which was absorbed into Axminster Hundred (17); see Appendix); see 52,19 note. This particular holding seems to be represented by the 3 furlongs (*fertinos*) of lordship land allowed to Odo son of Edric in the Tax Return for Axmouth Hundred (xxi). Odo's 'Down' passed to the Honour of Plympton, *Dune* being held by Ralph *de Dune* (whence Rousdon and Down Ralph) in Fees p. 788. In FA i p. 328 another Ralph *de Done* holds *Rawesdon*; see Cal. Inq. PM vol. i no. 141, FA i pp. 366, 429. The chapel of Rousdon was dedicated to St. Pancras and was given *c.* 1155 by Alfred *de Douna* to the Abbey of Montebourg, Round CDF pp. 319-320 nos. 898-900; see Hoskins *Devon* p. 375 and OJR H4 pp. 176, 182.

52,26-28 ALDRED. DB *Eldred, Edred*; Exon. *Aldretus, Adret*; see 16,61 note on Aldred/Aethelred. He may have been Aethelred/Aldred the Forester; see 52,27 note. Round (in VCH Somerset i p. 417 and Hampshire i p. 427) maintains that the Aldred here is the same man as the Aldred of DB Somerset 45,16-17 (who also held TRE), the Aldred of DB Wilts. 67,34-38* (who held two of the five manors TRE), and the Aldred brother of Odo of DB Hants. 69,45. 6,16 and 53,2 (who held two out of the three TRE; his wife had held the third); this Odo is called Odo of Winchester in the Landholders' List to Sussex, in which county he shares a chapter with Aldred (his brother).
*The three Tax Returns for the Wiltshire Hundred of Blackgrove (Exon. 3 a 6, 9 b 1 and 16 a 4) state that Aldred brother of Odo has 8 hides lordship, which probably refer to Aldred's holding in Wilts. 67,38.

52,26 ?WEEK. This land is the first entry in the Exon. section entitled 'Lands of English Thanes in Devonshire'. The following five places lay in (Black) Torrington Hundred (11) and it is not unlikely that this holding also lay there. It may have been at Week in Thornbury parish, known as Lashbrook Week on the OS first edition 6-inch map, North Week on the first edition 1-inch map (sheet 26 of 1809, reprint sheet 82 of 1969); see OJR in TDA 36 p. 352 and H5 pp. 191, 204, 211.

.... BEFORE 1066. In the MS a plain gap of about 15 letters has been left for the 1066 holder's name and *teneb'*. There is nothing in the margin such as *r* (= *require* 'ask'; see 11,1 note) to remind the scribe to fill it in. In Exon. there is no sign of the TRE holder, nor any space left for one to be added. Aldred may have held this manor TRE, as well as 52,27-28.

52,27 MANATON. A parish in Teignbridge Hundred (23). In the order of Exon. this entry lies between two (52,44;46) relating to places that lay in Teignton (Teignbridge) Hundred in 1086, the first probably, the second certainly; moreover, another part of Manaton (16,160) probably lay in Teignbridge Hundred where the place consistently belongs in later documents. In the Tax Return for Exminster Hundred (xxiii) however, *Aderet* (= Aethelred/Aldred) *foristarius* ('the Forester') has ½ virgate of lordship land which is most likely to refer to this holding. It may be that this land was regarded as an outlying part of some manor in the main body of Exminster Hundred (see OJR in TDA 47 p. 217) or as forming an outlying portion of the Hundred with Beetor and the Shapleys in Chagford (16,61-62;64 note). The only other possible explanation of the Tax Return entry is that it refers to the land at Shapley (16,61) of which, according to DB, an Aldred was the TRE holder and Robert the 1086 holder, but at the time the Returns were compiled Aldred might also have held Shapley for he held both Manaton and Bickford (52,28) before and after 1066.

This land passed to William *Briwere* (Fees p. 399), then to the Honour of Berry, Gervase *de Horthon'* holding *Manethon'* in Fees p. 791; see FA i pp. 339, 390 and OJR in TDA 29 pp. 238, 241, 47 pp. 208, 217-218.

52,28 BICKFORD. In Plympton St. Mary parish, Plympton Hundred (26); see also 29,8. This holding does not appear in the fee lists; see OJR H6 pp. 267, 284.

52,29 ALWARD. Probably Alward Mart, as he holds 52,30 and appears as a TRE tenant in Ch. 24 as he does here.
COLSCOTT. DB *Colsovenescote*. If the identification with Colscott in West Putford parish, (Black) Torrington Hundred (11), is correct, the DB form has been drastically reduced; see EPNS i p. 160 and OJR H5 pp. 204, 211.

52,30 ½ VIRGATE OF LAND.... In the MS there is a plain gap of about 15 letters' width after the land holding, probably for the name of the village in which the ½ virgate lay.

| | |
|---|---|
| 52,30 (cont'd.) | There is nothing in the margin and Exon. adds nothing to the entry. The ½ virgate may have lain in Shebbear Hundred (4), the handwriting in Exon. being the same as for the previous entry (= 51,16). But there is ½ virgate 'missing' from Ashreigney (1,65), held by Queen Matilda till 1083. This second identification is given further support by the fact that Alward Mart was a subtenant of Brictric (son of Algar) in 1086 (see Exon. Notes 24,24) and Brictric's lands passed to Queen Matilda (see 1,57 note).<br>IN ALMS. In the MS and Farley clearly *in elemosina*; in the facsimile only half of the *n* of *in* is reproduced for some reason. |
| 52,31 | MEDDON. In Hartland parish and Hundred (3) and clearly identifiable in its Tax Return (ii). It appears to have passed to William *Briwere*, being held of him in Fees p. 400 as *Meddon'* with *Aurescumb'* and *Esse* [Awliscombe 34,23;26 and Ash 34,5] by Jordan *Speciarius*. It then went to the Honour of Berry, Jordan *de Esse* holding in *Mededon* and in *Dupeford'* [Deptford in Hartland, GR SS 2618] in Fees p. 791; see FA i pp. 342, 410 and Cal. Inq. PM vol. ii no. 306, v no. 527. |
| 52,32 | VARLEYS. In Petrockstowe parish, Shebbear Hundred (4); see OJR in TDA 36 p. 354 and H10 p. 580. |
| 52,33 | SEDBOROUGH. In Parkham parish, Shebbear Hundred (4); see OJR H10 p. 568.<br>PARKHAM, BALDWIN THE SHERIFF'S MANOR. See 16,33. |
| 52,34 | NEWTON (ST. CYRES). DB *Niwetone*, the added name being from the dedication of the church to St. Ciricius. The place lies and lay in Crediton Hundred (13) and can be identified in the Tax Return for that Hundred (viii). Crediton was an ecclesiastical Hundred and this land had been alienated from the Church of Exeter: Dunn's claim to hold and to have held from the King is stated here; the Bishop's claim is stated in 2,2 (see notes there). |
| 52,35 | NUTWELL. In Woodbury parish, (East) Budleigh Hundred (14), and identifiable in that Hundred's Tax Return (xvi). Together with Harpford (part of Budleigh in 1086, see 1,9 note), Nutwell was confirmed by Henry I on Oliver *de Dinant* [from Dinan in the département of Ille-et-Vilaine]. Harpford had been granted to Oliver's predecessors by William I (Fees p. 96); Oliver gave both places to a priory established near Dinan that was a daughter house of Marmoutier (Tours). In Fees p. 96 the monks of Dinan hold *Herpeford* and in Fees p. 764 the Prior of *Dynam* holds *Harepeford'* and *Nutewill'* from Geoffrey *de Dinam*; see RH i p. 92b, FA i pp. 325, 365, Cal. Inq. PM vol. iii no. 532, iv no. 44, and OJR in TDA 35 p. 297. |
| 52,36 | ALNOTH. No doubt the Alnoth of Bray (*de braio*; OEB p. 38), from whom the King had no tax on ½ virgate he held in the Tax Return for South Molton Hundred (vii). This ½ virgate would have been part of the villagers' land holding (not given in the main Exon.), as the lordship land (½ virgate; see Lordship and Villagers' Table) does not pay tax.<br>BRAY. One of several 'Brays' in South Molton parish and Hundred (6); see 3,45 note. This land can be identified in the Tax Return for South Molton Hundred (vii); see note above. It seems most likely to have been 'West' Bray held in Fees p. 794 by Robert *de Cantelo*, Richard son of John and Walter *de Ralegh'* as *Westbray*, a fee of John *de Nevil'*, that is of the Honour of Stoke Courcy [Stogursey, Somerset]. It thus seems to have followed the same descent as Blackpool 1,41 (see note); see FA i pp. 326, 362, 376, 418 and OJR H3 pp. 72, 92. |
| 52,37 | MIDDLECOTT. It may well have lain in Chagford parish, Wonford Hundred (19); see OJR in TDA 36 p. 376. No clue to its 1086 Hundred is, however, given by the order of Exon., although it is entered too late to have been a member or a dependency of South Tawton; see OJR in TDA 44 pp. 300, 346, 352 and the Appendix. |
| 52,38 | EDWIN. Probably Edwin of Butterleigh; see 52,39 note on the Tax Return evidence and next note on a likely descendant with the same family name.<br>BUTTERLEIGH. A parish in Cliston Hundred (20). It can be positively identified in the Tax Return for that Hundred (xii). A Brian *de Boterlegh'* gave the church of this manor to St. Nicholas' Priory, Exeter, between 1161 and 1184 (Oliver *Mon.* p. 114); in 1258 the holder was Joel *de Grenelinche* (Fees p. 1263) and in 1285 (FA i p. 333) Thomas *Poleyn* holds from the Honour of Plympton. See FA i pp. 367, 434 and OJR H7 pp. 366, 383. |
| 52,39 | EDWIN. Probably Edwin of Butterleigh (*de buterleio*; OEB p. 38 and see 52,38) who has 2 furlongs (*fertinos*) of lordship in Silverton Hundred Tax Return (xiii). The only other Edwin in DB, holding in 1086, is in 52,38 and his lordship land is already identified in the Tax Returns (see note), though it is likely, as he held Butterleigh, that he is the same man as this Edwin. |

| | |
|---|---|
| 52,39 (cont'd.) | CLYST (WILLIAM). In Plymtree parish, Hayridge Hundred (15); the added name is from OE *aēwielm* 'source' (of the river Clist); compare Toller Whelme in Dorset. It seems to be identifiable in the Tax Return for Silverton (Hayridge) Hundred (xiii); see note above. Robert *Ryvel* holds in *Clist Ewelme* in Fees p. 782 from Nicholas *de Mereyeth*'; see OJR in TDA 42 pp. 227, 248. |
| 52,40 | WADHAM. In Knowstone parish, South Molton Hundred (6); it can probably be identified in the Tax Return for that Hundred (vii). See OJR H3 pp. 72, 91. |
| 52,41 | KNOWSTONE. A parish in South Molton Hundred (6); see 23,10-11 note. This holding does not appear in later fee lists. OJR (H3 pp. 73, 90) offers no evidence for his identification with Shapcot; cf. 52,51 note. |
| 52,42 | DUNSTONE. Now in Yealmpton parish, Plympton Hundred (26), but in the Tax Returns it was clearly included in *Alleriga* (Ermington) Hundred (xxx) where Algar has 1 virgate of lordship land. Dunstone is close to the Ermington Hundred border; see OJR in TDA 35 p. 709 and H6 p. 328, also 29,4 note above. |
| 52,43 | WASPLEY. Earlier Warbrightsleigh, DB *Wasberlege*; EPNS ii p. 394. It lies in Stoodleigh parish, Witheridge Hundred (7), and appears to be a late entry for Witheridge (see 52,20) rather than a part of Bampton Hundred (8) as suggested by OJR in TDA 30 p. 454; see the Appendix. In Fees p. 612 Roger *de Acastr'* holds *Warbritteslegh'* and a half of *Cumbe* [Coombe, 3,75;78 note] formerly belonging to Henry *de Tylly*, by gift of Robert *de Mandevill'*. In Fees p. 760 Roger *Dacastre* holds in *Warebrigthelegh'*, *Blackesworth'* [Blatchworthy, see 47,13 note] and in *Whytecnolle* [West Whitnole, see 47,13 note] from Geoffrey *de Mandevil'* who holds from Ralph *de Doddescumb'* of the Honour of Plympton; see Fees p. 787, FA i pp. 343, 421, Cal. Inq. PM vol. ii no. 154 and OJR in TDA 30 pp. 404, 425. |
| 52,44 | SHAPLEY. The five places called 'Shapley' in DB now lie in two parishes, Chagford and North Bovey, and in different Hundreds (Wonford and Teignbridge respectively); see notes to 16,61-62;64 and to 45,1. Like the following entry for Skerraton, also held by Aelfric, this land later formed a serjeanty, that of supplying two arrows for the King when he hunted on Dartmoor. In Fees p. 98 David *de Scyredun'* holds 1 virgate in *Scyredun'* [Skerraton 52,45] and *Sappeleg'*, said to have been held by his predecessors since the Conquest. Shapley has the same descent as Skerraton, but in later documents the name is displaced by the adjacent Hookney [GR SX 7182] and Kendon [SX 7181], both in North Bovey parish: in RH i p. 81b in Teignbridge Hundred the manors of *Kingdon*, *Sekiredon* and *Hokneton* are held together by Roger *Mirabel*, then by Walter *de Skiredon'*, then by John *de Bovyle*; see RH i p. 90a and Cal. Inq. PM vol. i no. 165. Two 'ferlings' of Kendon went to Buckfast Abbey; RH i p. 79a. <br> All this points to an identification with the Shapley that lies in North Bovey parish, Teignbridge Hundred, where it is placed in Fees p. 264. This is the anticipated place in Exon. order for a Teignton (Teignbridge) Hundred holding (see Appendix) and 52,46 (the next entry but one in Exon.) was in this Hundred, but 52,27 (the next entry), although later in Teignbridge Hundred, may be identifiable in the Tax Return for Exminster Hundred in which the other Shapleys lay (16,61-62;64 and 45,1, see notes). All the Exminster Hundred entries (see also 52,48-49) are out of order in this section of Exon.: in other fiefs, Exminster Hundred places are entered after those for (North) Tawton and Crediton Hundreds; see OJR in TDA 36 p. 368. |
| 52,45 | SKERRATON. In Dean Prior parish, Stanborough Hundred (28). Like Shapley (52,44), also held by Aelfric in 1086, this land later formed a serjeanty, in this case of providing three arrows for the King's hunt in Dartmoor Forest. David *de Scyredun'* held in 1212 (see 52,44 note), then Robert *de Scyredon'*, then Roger *Mirabel* who forfeited it for murder. It was given by Henry III to Walter *le Deveneys*, then passed to John *de Boyville* and to his son William who died in 1320; see Fees pp. 98, 264, 1188, 1250, 1371, 1425, RBE ii p. 560, RH i pp. 79a, 91b, Cal. Inq. PM vol. i no. 165, vi no. 230, xii no. 211, and OJR in TDA 45 p. 200. |
| 52,46 | TWINYEO. DB *Betunie* from OE *betwēon* and *ēa* 'between the rivers', the farm lying at the confluence of the Bovey and Teign rivers in Kingsteignton parish, Teignbridge Hundred (23); see EPNS ii p. 479 and 52,44 note. In Fees p. 790 Richard son of Ralph holds in *Twyneya* from the Honour of Plympton; see FA i pp. 347, 390, Cal. Inq. PM vol. i no. 564, xiv no. 325, DCNQ 10 pp. 114-115, 165 and OJR in TDA 29 p. 239. |
| 52,47 | DUNSFORD. A parish in Wonford Hundred (19). In the Middle Ages it had the same middle lords as Dunsford (23,12) but while the latter (like many Ch. 23 lands) was held of the Honour of Marshwood, the former seems to have been held of Okehampton |

52 - E

Honour, even though Saewulf's land at Mowlish (52,49) passes to Marshwood. Dunsford is sometimes replaced by Sowton [GR SX 8388] in later lists. In Fees p. 785 John *de Nevile* holds *Dunesford*, while in FA i p. 314 William *de Servyngton* holds *Suttheton* [Sowton] from John *de Mandevile* who holds from Hugh *de Courtenay*. The Abbess of Leigh (Canonsleigh) holds *Donysford* from Okehampton Honour in FA i p. 345, the prioress of Canonsleigh in FA i p. 385; see RH i p. 85b, OJR in TDA 44 pp. 300, 323, 332 and 23,12 note.

52,48 MAMHEAD. A parish in Exminster Hundred (24); both this and the following entry probably account for the 1 virgate of lordship allowed to Saewulf in the Tax Return for Exminster Hundred (xxiii). It passed to the Honour of Plympton and was known as 'Ashford', see EPNS ii p. 501. William *de Molehywis* (see 52,49) and Ralph *Bonvallet* hold in *Esseford'* in Fees p. 790. It is *Ay[s]hford Peverel* in FA i p. 389, *Assheford* by *Mammeshed* in Cal. Inq. PM vol. xiv no. 325; see FA i p. 347, Cal. Inq. PM vol. v no. 527, OJR in TDA 47 pp. 206, 215 and 52,44 note.
1 VILLAGER. IT PAYS 45d. Or perhaps "1 villager; he pays 45d", in other words he held Mamhead for a money-rent (see 6,6 note on villagers 'farming' manors). The Latin of the Exon. is equally ambiguous: *In ea (mansione) est i uillanus et reddit per annum xlv denarios*. Cf. 3,82 and note (though the Latin of the Exchequer DB, by omitting the 7 before the *Redd* there, is less ambiguous, and also notes to 1,32 and 21,11 (but there the Exon. is clear). Cf. also 34,57 second note.

52,49 MOWLISH. In Kenton parish, Exminster Hundred (24); see 52,48 note. It passed to the Honour of Marshwood, being held as *Molehiwis* by Robert *de Molehiwis* in Fees p. 793; see FA i p. 389, Cal. Inq. PM vol. ii no. 154 and OJR in TDA 47 pp. 207, 229.

52,50-53 IN THE MS there is a space of 1 line before these four holdings, possibly indicating that these three women were to be regarded as separate from the rest of the 'King's Thanes'. However, women were often classed as 'thanes' in DB; see, for example, Somerset Exon. Notes to 5,65. 19,72 and 37,8. Moreover, in several counties in DB women appear in the chapter devoted to King's thanes and their holdings are not 'tacked on' at the end of these chapters; see Wilts. 67,25;48;80;83;87-88;90, Dorset 56,23, Glos. 78,7-8, Hants. 69,34, Staffs. 17,20 etc. The space left and *Alueva* in 52,50 being written in capitals and lined through in red, rather resemble the treatment in Ch. 51 when there is a new tenant, especially 51,12-15.

52,50 ST. JAMES CHURCH. In Heavitree parish, Wonford Hundred (19); see EPNS ii p. 441. It was held as the *villam de Sancto Jacobo* by the Prior of St. James in alms from the Barony of Plympton in FA i p. 312; see RH i p. 85a, Oliver *Mon*. p. 193, DCNQ 1 p. 41 and OJR in TDA 44 pp. 301, 317.

52,51 ALFHILD. DB *Alfhilla*, Exon. *Alfilla*, represent OE *Aelfhild*, feminine; see PNDB p. 175.
KNOWSTONE. A parish in South Molton Hundred (6); see 23,10-11 note. OJR (H3 pp. 73, 90) identifies Harpson in Knowstone on the grounds that that name is derived from Alfhild the 1086 holder. But Harpson is 'Herbert's *tūn*; EPNS ii p. 340.

52,52-53 GODIVA. It is just possible that Godiva had other land in Devon, not recorded by Exon. or Exchequer DB. The Tax Return for Teignton Hundred (xxiv) states that Godiva wife of Brictric has ½ hide lordship there. But these are her only holdings recorded in Devon DB and they are dealt with in the Tax Returns for Kerswell (xxv) and Chillington (xxvii) Hundreds respectively, under the name of plain Godiva, with her lordship there agreeing with that given by the main Exon. entries.

52,52 TORBRYAN. DB *Torre*. A parish in Haytor Hundred (29), accountable in the Tax Return for Kerswell (Haytor) Hundred (xxv); see 52,52-53 note. It passed to the Honour of Okehampton, being held by Guy *de Brionne* as 1 fee in *Torre* and *Weston'* [?Weston in Staverton, GR SX 7564] in Fees p. 768; see Fees p. 786, FA i pp. 317, 348, 391, Cal. Inq. PM vol. xvi no. 959 and OJR in TDA 40 p. 117, 50 p. 374.

52,53 DODBROOKE. Now combined with Kingsbridge parish, Stanborough Hundred (28), but it was formerly in Coleridge Hundred (30). It is identifiable in the Tax Return for Chillington (Coleridge) Hundred (xxvii); see 52,52-53 note. This holding passed to the Honour of Okehampton; in Fees p. 786 Richard son of Alan holds in *Doddebrok'* and *Porlemue* [?East Portlemouth, perhaps part of Prawle 16,176] and in *Lamsede* [unidentified]; see FA i pp. 332, 393, Cal. Inq. PM vol. vi no. 180 and OJR in TDA 43 pp. 199, 225.

PLACES ELSEWHERE
DB sometimes includes details of a holding that lay in one county in 1086 in the folios of another. There are no such cases in Devon. All the lands listed here lay outside the

# E - EC, ED

|  |  |
|---|---|
|  | County in 1086; for their dates of transfer, see Introductory Note 4 on the county boundary. For the full text, translation and notes, see the relevant county volume in this series. |
| EC 1-2 | BOROUGH. TACKBEAR. Held by Alfred and Bernard the priest respectively under the Count of Mortain. These two holdings, which lie west of the Tamar, were only brought into the County in the 19th century with the transfer from Cornwall of a part of West Bridgerule parish. |
| ED | SOME UNNAMED LANDS included by Dorset DB under other manors were also later transferred to Devonshire. Hawkchurch and Dalwood parishes were transferred in 1896 and 1832 respectively. A portion of Hawkchurch was probably included in the 22 hides of Cerne Abbas (Dorset General Notes 11,1), and Philleyholme in Hawkchurch [GR ST 3500], if correctly identified, was an outlier of Frampton, held by Caen Abbey (Dorset General Notes 17,1). Dalwood [GR ST 2400] was an outlying part of the royal manor of Fordington (Dorset General Notes 1,4). |
| ED 1 | [LAND OF THE MONKS OF SHERBORNE]. The compiler of DB was uncertain how to treat the lands of the former see of Sherborne. In attempting to distinguish the lands of the Bishop (who had transferred his seat to Salisbury) and of the monks, he half-heartedly inserted a chapter number III in the left-hand margin of col. 77a, but no heading. This figure really only governs 3,1 which belongs to the monks (but the entry includes the value for the Bishop's holding 2,6). 3,2-9 could just be said to belong to the new chapter since, although they are held by the Bishop, they are for the monks' supplies. But the subsequent entries (3,10-18) belong only to the Bishop. CHARDSTOCK. The 12 hides will have included Wambrook [GR ST 2907] which an 1896 boundary change placed in Somerset. |
| ED 2 | STOCKLAND. A detached part of Whitchurch (Canonicorum) Hundred, Dorset, until its transfer to Devon in 1832. |

Exon. Introduction

## EXON. EXTRA INFORMATION AND DISCREPANCIES WITH DB

### INTRODUCTION

### Scope of these Notes
The Notes below incorporate material supplied by the Exon. Domesday returns and the T.O. for Devon, which is not in DB and which it has not proved possible to include either in small type in the translation or in the Lordship and Villagers' Table or in the Details Table following these Notes. Also mentioned in the Notes below are any differences between the texts, other than simply of phrasing, and information given in DB that is not in Exon. Information given in DB or the corresponding Exon. main entry, that is omitted in the T.O., is not generally mentioned.

The Tax Returns are occasionally cited in these Notes (e.g. for Ch. 44), though reference to them is more often made in the General Notes; see the fifth introductory paragraph at the head of the General Notes for the grounds on which their evidence is used in the Notes.

The summary of the one land of Glastonbury Abbey in Devon is given under Ch. 4 note below, and reference is made in General Notes Ch. 15 to the summary of the Count of Mortain's fief.

Scribal errors in the Exon. MS, of which there are a great many, are given only when they occur in a quotation. Ralph Barnes' errors of transcription (see below) are pointed out as far as possible.

### Relationship between Exon. and Exchequer DB
The relationship between the Exon. main returns and Exchequer DB has been the subject of much discussion. According to Eyton *Somerset* i pp. 4-5, OJR in VCH pp. 377, 378 ff. and Salzmann in VCH Cornwall ii, part viii, pp. 45-46 etc., Exon. was completely unconnected with DB, though Eyton did suggest that the same 'Commissioners' Notes' that preceded Exon. were later sent to Winchester to be used in the production of Exchequer DB; at the same time OJR and Salzmann believed that the Dorset and Wiltshire sections in Exon. were taken from Exchequer DB, but that for Devon, Cornwall and Somerset, DB and Exon. were 'independent compilations'. Meanwhile, Vinogradoff (p. 228) maintained that Exon. was a later document "written for the use of the Abbey of Tavistock or, at any rate, by scribes prejudiced in its favour"! Round (in VCH Somerset i 'Introduction to the Somerset Domesday' pp. 383-432) professed himself uncertain as to the character, origin and object of the Exon. Domesday. However, Baring in his article in EHR for 1912 (see Bibliography) came to the conclusion that DB was derived from Exon. More recently, the idea has been put forward that a fair copy was made of the Exon. we now possess, and it was sent to Winchester and was used in the compilation of DB and afterwards destroyed, having served its purpose ('our' Exon. MS meanwhile remained at Exeter); see Finn LE pp. 28, 52-54 and his articles 'The Immediate Sources of Exchequer Domesday' and MDeD p. 114 ff., also Galbraith pp. 31-32 and Ch. VIII.

The present editors, however, are convinced that the Exchequer DB scribe had in front of him the Exon. MS in its present form, no doubt with the portions of Devon, Dorset and Wiltshire that have not survived. The evidence for this is various.

One of the first aspects of the five south-western counties that strikes the reader of Domesday Book, is the lack of Hundred headings. Although the policy throughout DB was to include them, it would seem that for some reason they were omitted in Exon. (perhaps because not thought necessary, on which see Galbraith pp. 114-115) and by the time that volume reached Winchester it was too late to discover in which Hundreds the thousands of places lay and so the Exchequer scribe was forced to follow his copy in not including them. Secondly, within a fief the order of entries in Exchequer DB frequently, especially in Devon, Somerset and Dorset, follows almost the exact order of those in Exon. (see, for example, the General Notes on Exon. order towards the beginning of Chs. 2, 5, 6, 16-17, 19-21, 23, 28-30, 34-36, 39, 42).

But it is when one comes to study the manuscripts of Exon. and Exchequer DB closely that the immediate dependence of the latter on the former becomes unmistakable. Firstly, numerous items of information, misplaced in Exon., are often similarly misplaced in Exchequer DB (for example, the salt-workers in 15,23, the fishery in 1,60, the slaves in 2,21 and 3,5, the pigmen in 23,9 and 42,6,

# Exon. Introduction

the details of Maker in 1,22; see the Exon. Notes to the first, the General Notes to the rest). Compare also the details of Barlington (DB 3,19) which were written in the margin of the Exon. MS (though at an early stage) and missed by the Exchequer scribe and then added later at the foot of the column, and the case of the marginal *par(iter)*s (General Notes 15,47–52) which are also often marginal or interlined in Exon. If a copy had been made of Exon., all or a great majority of these items would have been entered in their correct places. (Although the Exchequer scribe was capable of adding information in the wrong place, there are too many such misplacements of the same items in both MSS to be coincidental.) It might be thought that late information was added to both DB and Exon. at the same time, but in the vast majority of cases in Exon. the ink colour and the scribe of the misplacements and additions are the same as for the main part of the entry, which would be unlikely if they were done much later, considering the number of scribes employed in writing Exon. (Although there is overwhelming evidence that the Exon. MS was checked, this was done early on and the majority of the corrections were seen and incorporated by the Exchequer scribe.)

Secondly, errors in personal and place-names and figures, bad grammar and confused constructions in Exon. are perpetuated in DB (e.g. see General Notes to 17,52. 16,57. 34,13. 52,10. 5,1 (third note). 20,13. 35,22 and the penultimate note under 17,1); again, one would have expected the scribe of the fair copy to have corrected at least a major proportion of these errors, this after all being the main purpose of a 'fair copy'.

Thirdly, peculiarities in terms and formulae that appear in Exon. regularly find their way into Exchequer DB, such as the 5 virgates, in place of 1 hide 1 virgate, in 31,1 (and cf. 4 virgates for 1 hide in 28,10), the rare -*x* ending in the personal name *Alebrix* (see General Notes 16,36), the unusual phrase *cum omnibus ibi pertinentibus* in 1,7; see also General Notes 1,6 (second note).

Fourthly, although the DB scribe largely adjusted the words and formulae of Exon. to accord with the standardized Exchequer forms (see below), there are several occasions where these are preserved (apparently by accident) in DB, such as the use of *mansiones* instead of *maneria* (see General Notes 1,22, second note). In numerous instances the Exchequer scribe has followed his copy too closely and this has led to errors; for example, the smiths in 1,27 and the beekeepers in 23,15 are in the accusative case as they are in Exon., not in the nominative as they should be in the DB formula (and cf. General Notes 1,57), *qui* has been mistakenly retained in a phrase which has been partially altered (see General Notes 2,1) — see also General Notes 16,151 and cf. General Notes 3,82 and 24,2. The fact that on several occasions a figure correction in DB is paralleled by one in Exon. (see the end of General Notes 2,24 on 'Cottagers') might be due to the Exchequer scribe's correcting the Exon. MS at the same time as, or soon after, he corrected the DB MS; but see General Notes 19,11 on the value.

It would be hard to explain away the countless discrepancies between Exon. and DB by saying that there would have been few, if any, discrepancies between DB and the 'fair copy' of Exon., because this would mean that the compiler and/or scribe involved in this fair copy had either received a mass of information, presumably correcting the original Exon. MS, or had himself introduced the mistakes (which the Exchequer scribe then copied). Incorporating corrections to the original Exon. would have taken an immense time, and time was very short: in fact it is far from clear whether there would have been time to make a copy at all of such a vast document. There is much evidence that 'our' Exon. MS was corrected and this must have been a separate earlier exercise to that envisaged by the upholders of the 'fair copy' view because the corrected material is reproduced in the Exchequer MS, and because, if only one set of corrections had been done, then the figure and other errors in the original Exon. (which form the discrepancies with DB) would have been altered at the same time as the ones we see in the MS today — and if this had been the case, then there would be far fewer discrepancies.

Moreover, a study of the Exon. MS explains a great many of these discrepancies: in several cases interlineations or marginal additions in Exon. (though done at the same time as the main body of the entry, judging by the colour of the ink and with no change in scribe) led to omissions by the Exchequer scribe (e.g. of the subtenant in 48,1, the pigmen in 15,12 and 16,23, the market — which is also misplaced — in 11,1) or to delayed inclusion (e.g. of the house in Exeter in 32,6) or to incorrect figures (e.g. the DB scribe missed the interlined 7 *v* of the value in 17,4 and the *i*

# Exon. Introduction

in the woodland acres in 21,13, see Exon. Notes to these). Again, the Exchequer scribe has obviously in some cases misread an Exon. correction, such as in the number of pigs in 20,15 and in the value in 42,6 (see Exon. Notes to these), and in several cases a portion of an erasure in Exon. seems to have been read as part of the correction, such as in the number of pigs in 23,15 and in the former value in 5,4 and the present value in 21,13 (see Exon. Notes there), and cf. Exon. Notes to 16,121 and 17,85. Bad writing in Exon. may well have caused several of the discrepancies with DB (see, for example, Exon. Notes 7,1 and General Notes 16,27;44 and 25,20), and the greasy parchment of the Exon. MS caused parts of the number of villagers in 7,4 and of slaves in 31,1 and of the value of the mill in 15,23 not to be clearly visible and the Exchequer scribe omitted these parts. The fact that in several instances part of a number or measurement overruns a line in Exon. and the DB scribe only copied the first part (see Exon. Notes to 3,86. 17,69 and 34,25), is further proof that the existing Exon. MS was used by the Exchequer scribe: the composition of individual lines would be totally different in a copy. In 23,5 the Exchequer scribe misunderstood $carr$ in the Exon. MS because he missed the interlined $\bar{tra}$ (see fourth note under Exon. Notes there and cf. 52,10 note), and also in this entry an interlineation may have caused the omission of some of the villagers (see penultimate note under Exon. Notes 23,5). For explanations of other discrepancies between DB and Exon. see General Notes to 15,4 and Exon. Notes to 19,16 and 28,12 (place-names), also to 1,50. 2,6 and 5,4 (figure discrepancies), to 15,38 (ploughs) and to 16,30;87. 17,71 and 48,1 (on lordship and villagers' ploughs).

The omission in DB of items of information that are clearly written in the Exon. MS and are of a type that the Exchequer scribe normally includes, such as the lordship ploughs in a dozen manors, is harder to explain.* Sometimes, however, one can see why the Exchequer scribe failed to include an item – perhaps it was misplaced (like the salt-house for 35,20) or interlined (like the fishermen for 20,15 or the subtenant for 48,1), though in each case by the same scribe who wrote the rest of the entry, or a whole line was obviously accidentally omitted (see General Notes 32,5) or the phrasing of Exon. misled him (see Exon. Notes 23,4 and 49,3 on the omitted villagers); see also Exon. Notes to 1,4 (first note). 3,84 and 16,44 and General Notes 1,4 on 'woodland'.

Of course, not all the differences between the two texts can be explained away by looking at the MSS. There is some evidence that the Exchequer scribe had access to other sources of information (such as, perhaps, Tax Returns or Hundred lists, local data or to the results of lawsuits; cf. Exon. Notes 24,17 and 34,11), or had recourse to simple deductions (as probably for 3,51 and 23,1, see Exon. Notes to these), which would explain the few instances of information in DB which is not in Exon. (see Exon. Notes 3,51). Moreover, information to correct the Exon. may have come to light after it was compiled: this might be the case with changes in tenants (e.g., see Exon. Notes 24,14, and in some of the cases where DB has the tenant-in-chief holding a manor 'himself' and Exon. gives a subtenant, the manor may have reverted to the tenant-in-chief, for which see Exon. Notes to 23,7. 34,16. 47,10 etc.) or in numbers of population or present values or acreage (see, for example, General Notes 17,67). Finally, simple error on the part of the Exchequer scribe no doubt played a large part in the discrepancies (e.g., see Exon. Notes 5,4 and 15,70); certainly the Exchequer scribe's carelessness can be proved in a number of cases (for example, see his misreading of several place-names, a list of which is given in General Notes 16,42).

According to Finn LE pp. 52-54 this fair copy of Exon. contained some extra information, but perhaps did not include later additions to the surviving Exon. MS, and the foliation was different. However, it seems odd that if such a copy were made, so few new details were added to it, in other words that it was so like its original, as can be seen from Exchequer DB. One would have expected, at least, that the obvious absences of certain items of information usually included would have been rectified, such as the full name of Baldwin's subtenant $W$ for 16,175 (and cf. General Notes 52,26;30) and the plough estimate in 35,6. The Hundred heads could also have been inserted in a fair copy. Finn's point about the later additions was intended to explain many of the

---

* At the first occurrence of each category of omissions, a note in made in the General Notes (or in the Exon. Notes if the omitted phrase is not added from Exon. in small type in the translation) of other omissions of it and possible reasons for this, i.e. for the omission of woodland in some DB entries, see General Notes 1,4, or of villagers see Exon. Notes 23,4.

# Exon. Introduction

discrepancies between Exon. and DB — the corrections in our Exon. which cause the discrepancies were done *after* the copy had been made — but a study of the Exon. MS shows that, though undoubtedly some corrections were done at a later stage (though not necessarily after the MS had been used to produce DB), the great majority are 'immediate' corrections. In any case, it would be very odd if these so-called 'later' additions to the original Exon. MS were not transferred to the copy for inclusion in the official Exchequer DB: there would be little point spending time neatly correcting a MS which had already been superseded. The omissions in Exchequer DB of material that appears in our Exon. might be due to the accidental omission of such items in the copy — or to errors made by the Exchequer clerks; Finn MDeD p. 115. As to the foliation in the copy being different, this might explain the original omission in DB of Dorset 36,4–11 (see Dorset General Notes on these), but the method and order of the Exchequer scribe's excerpting of Walter's lands from the composite section in Exon. can only be explained by the 'booklet' arrangement of the present Exon. MS at this point (see Exon. Notes Chs. 24–25); Finn attempts to avoid this objection by stating that in this case the booklets were the same. For Finn's view of the phrases *hoc* (or *haec* or *hic*) *scripsit Ricardus* and *usque huc* (not *hoc*, as Finn MDeD p. 115) *scripsit R.* in the margins of the Exon. MS being the work of the scribe making this fair copy, see Exon. Notes 17,5.

According to Galbraith pp. 105-107 (though Finn LE p. 54 disagrees) some attempt was made in the fair copy of Exon. to organise the King's lands and those of his thanes and servants in an order closer to that adopted for the other counties in DB (see General Notes to Ch. 1, and Exon. Notes to Ch. 22, Chs. 24–25, Chs. 47–50, Ch. 52). These rearrangements, however, were neither too extensive nor too complicated to have been done entirely by the compiler of DB at the time of writing. Indeed, several aspects of the rearrangement in DB of the composite Exon. sections can only be explained by assuming that the Exchequer scribe had in front of him the extant Exon. MS. If, for example, the large Exon. section of French Men-at-Arms (see General and Exon. Notes to Ch. 22) had been re-organised into individual chapters in the copy (as in DB), the reason for the Exchequer scribe's omission of Flohere's manor of *Sotrebroc* in his repeated scanning of this section during excerpting the holdings of tenants-in-chief, would disappear. Finally, the Exon. MS is a document so regular and neat as a whole (in fact many folios are less corrected than those of Exchequer DB for Devon) that it would not really need to be recopied to improve its legibility.

For specific examples of the dependence of the Dorset DB on the Exon. MS see the Introduction to the Exon. Notes for that county.

## The *Terrae Occupatae* for Devon

Devon has 193 entries in the *Terrae Occupatae*, filling folios 495a–506b inclusive of the *Liber Exoniensis*. They are arranged, it would seem, partially by Hundred (the first eight are in Lifton Hundred, and on 496a–497a with one exception come 11 in Chillington/Coleridge Hundred) and partially by subject (e.g. 11 consecutive entries on 505b–506a contain details of withheld customary dues from houses in Exeter and, with one break, 9 at 505a,b deal with lands added to the Honours of Edmer Ator and Ordwulf). These are condensed entries, containing for the most part information already recorded in the main Exon.; it is just possible that, despite several cases of information not to be found in the main Exon. returns (see Exon. Notes to 1,25 (last note) and Ch. 44), these T.O. entries were taken from those returns. However, it is more probable that while our Exon. MS (itself a condensation) was at Winchester being used in the compilation of Exchequer DB, some of the earlier material relating to the Inquiry remained at Exeter for the hearing of claims and the sorting out of illegal tenure and occupation; this material, either fuller in itself or amplified or corrected at the hearings, may have produced the T.O. (This would perhaps explain the omission from the T.O. of some abstractions or additions one would expect to find therein, such as the dispute over Werrington (in Exon. Notes after 5,5) and see Exon. Notes 3,32 and General Notes 2,2 on Newton St. Cyres; other instances of 'omissions' in the T.O. seem to have been accidental, see Exon. Notes 20,1.) For Finn's views on the origin of the T.O., see LE p. 57 ff. As with the main Exon. returns, a number of scribes were employed in the production of the T.O. and the entries show no signs of being written continuously at a single time.

As the name implies, these *Terrae Occupatae* are lands, either whole manors or parts of manors, which had been 'seized' or 'appropriated', though sometimes only in the weakened sense of

# Exon. Introduction

'disputed' or containing some illegality in tenure; they are of the same genre as the *Clamores* ('Claims') and 'Declarations' recorded at the end of Yorkshire, Lincolnshire and Huntingdonshire and are related to the *Inuasiones* ('Annexations') at the end of Norfolk, Suffolk and Essex. The entries of the T.O. fall into several categories. The largest group, comprising some 98 entries, has two subdivisions which sometimes overlap: there are those entries which concern manors which DB merely states had been held by two or more thanes, but for which the T.O. formula is basically "*A* (1086 holder) has a manor called *B* which a thane held freely/jointly in 1066; *e* hides which 1 or 2 (or more) thane(s) held freely/jointly in 1066 (*or* "the lands of 1 or 2 (or more) thane(s) which they held . . . They (lands) paid tax for . . . *or* "another manor which . . . It paid tax for . . .") have been added to it. *C* holds from *A*. Value (of the added lands) £*y*; when (*A*) acquired them £2". In these T.O. entries the TRE holders are often called 'thanes' and they regularly held 'freely' or 'jointly' (see General Notes 1,15 on these terms; the main Exon. and DB entries also sometimes designate the manner of tenure thus in this type) and in several entries (see Exon. Notes 17,14. 19,4 etc.) the added manors are said not to have belonged in 1066 to the manor to which they were added, hence the idea that they had been wrongly combined. This type of T.O. entry is given next to the manor's name in the Exon. Notes; see, for example, notes to 3,12;40. 20,7. 28,2. 35,9. 36,2. 39,6;15. 47,14. 49,7. 50,1 etc. The second subdivision of this largest group comprises entries which state either that a whole manor has been added to another manor or that parts of manors have been added. Where it is the case of a whole manor being added, neither the main Exon. nor Exchequer DB always records this fact for some reason (see Exon. Notes 16,9 for these cases). In this subdivision are details of two additions not recorded either in the main Exon. or in DB (see Exon. Notes to 1,66 and Ch. 44).

A second category of T.O. entry, containing some 14 entries, deals with removals of land from manors (e.g., see Exon. Notes to 1,10. 3,92. 7,4 etc.), including one only recorded there (see Exon. Notes Ch. 44). A third group of 36 entries concerns manors that had been added to the Honour/ lands of a particular thane; again reference to such entries appears in the Exon. Notes next to the manor's name (see, for example, notes to 15,16;17-19;20-22). The 1066 holders are regularly said to have held 'jointly' or 'freely' or to be able to 'go to whichever lord they would with their land' and the land held is often said to have been added 'wrongfully' or to have 'not belonged' to the lands (generally of some important Anglo-Saxon thane such as Edmer Ator, Ordwulf or Brictric) which had been (legally) transferred to the 1086 holder (see Exon. Notes to 15,14;15. 40,1;3 etc.). See General Notes 15,31 on this method of acquiring lands.

Details in some 30 entries of withheld customary dues, whether owed to a royal manor (e.g. see Exon. Notes 1,11;23) or from houses in Exeter (e.g. see Exon. Notes 3,2. 9,2. 5,15), form a fourth group. Among them are details of two withheld dues not recorded either in the main Exon. or in DB (see Exon. Notes 1,25 and 15,14); see also last note under 1,41. There are a few miscellaneous entries such as those on the appropriation of the whole or part of a manor (see Exon. Notes 34,5. 35,4. 42,4. 1,70) and those where some illegality of tenure is implied (see Exon. Notes 5,9. 24,28-29) and there is the entry at 500 a 4, not mentioned in the main Exon. nor in DB, about the unclaimed furlong (*ferdinus*) in Molton Hundred (see last note under Exon. Notes). See also those entries referred to in the next paragraph.

Occasionally it is not clear why an entry was made in the T.O. For example, the entry at 506 a 11 merely states that "The Bishop of Coutances has a manor called (Lower) Creedy which Goda held jointly in 1066. Value 5s", unless in this case the scribe meant to include the fact that Lower Creedy belonged to Cruwys Morchard (which the main Exon. and DB both state, 3,72-73). See also the entries relating to DB 1,11 (Exon. Notes "½ hide . . . 20s") and 2,2 (first Exon. note) and to 2,15. 13a,2 and 42,10 (Exon. Notes).

Finally, the case of the T.O. entry referring to the ½ virgate added to Eastleigh (DB 19,6), falls in two of the above categories because it was both added and had not paid tax (because concealed).

Reference is always made in the notes below to the existence of a T.O. entry and in many cases the whole of the entry is given in translation, otherwise only discrepancies or additions are recorded there.

# Exon. Introduction

## Exon. and Exchequer Formulae

Without altering the sense of the Exon., the Exchequer scribe changed many of the words and formulae in Exon. and condensed not only the material but the elaborate phraseology. For example, for Exon.'s *nemus, nemusculum* and *pascua* he used *silua, silua minuta* and *pastura*, for Exon.'s *mansio* he substituted *manerium*, for *quadragenaria, quarentena*. He changed the lengthy *ea die qua rex Eduuardus fuit vivus et mortuus* ("on the day on which King Edward was alive and dead", i.e. 5th January 1066) to the standard phrase (which is also to be found in Exon.; see Exon. Notes 5,6) *T.R.E. (tempore regis Eduuardi* "in King Edward's time", translated "before 1066" in this edition). The Exon. phrase for the plough estimate "(*z* hides) which *y* ploughs can plough" was likewise altered to "Land for *y* ploughs", and Exon.'s *reddidit gildum* was shortened to *geldabat*. For the Exchequer scribe's alteration of Exon.'s *reddit* to *valet* in many entries (and occasionally vice versa), see Exon. Notes 1,32 ('Value £6') and General Notes 2,2 on Value. See the specimen of Exon. and DB at the beginning of this edition for other changes made by the Exchequer scribe.

Exon. often omits nouns (as DB less often), as in "the King has 3 ploughs in lordship and the villagers 4" where "4 ploughs" are intended: where DB gives the expected noun no attention is generally drawn here to the Exon. omission. Exon. regularly abbreviates personal names to the initial letter (e.g. *B.* for *Balduinus*), generally when the name has already occurred in full in the entry. In these Notes the name thus abbreviated is always written, e.g. "B(aldwin)", except in the cases of *rex E.* and *rex W.* (e.g. in the phrase *quod tenuit rex E.*) which are so common that there is no doubt about the full version of the names. The Exon. for Devon rarely states, as DB usually does, that the 1086 holder held his manor "from the King" and references to these 'omissions' are not therefore made in the Notes below, but see Exon. Notes 51,14 for the occasions when the phrase *de rege* is used in Exon. for Devon.

In the statement "the villagers have *y* hides ... *z* ploughs" Exon. regularly uses the term *villani* in the general sense of the inhabitants of a *villa*, covering smallholders, Cottagers (*coscez*), cottagers (*cotarii*) – and possibly also other classes of population such as pigmen, salt-workers, etc. – as well as villagers in the strict sense. See Exon. Notes 1,26. Often no villagers are mentioned in the holding, just smallholders and slaves (e.g. for 16,50; 90; 100) and occasionally just slaves (see General Notes 16,6, also 1,3 on slaves). However, on several occasions in Exon. (though not for Devon) where there are only smallholders and slaves on a manor, the term *bordarii* takes the place of *villani* in the statement of their land and ploughs; see Exon. Notes 3,63.

## Ellis' Text of Exon. and the VCH Translation

Ellis' edition of Exon. is not as accurate as Farley's one of the Exchequer DB. Apart from larger errors and omissions, there are numerous occasions when either the transcriber Ralph Barnes (or Ellis or his printer) leaves gaps where there are none in the MS and vice versa (e.g., see Exon. Notes 40,6), omits underlining (indicating deletion) or puts it in wrongly (e.g., see Exon. Notes 16,74. 23,12. 25,27. 34,6. 1,52), positions interlineations incorrectly, includes parts or all of erased words and figures (see the three notes under Exon. Notes 16,121), omits transposition signs, etc. There is also inconsistency in the use of dots for material that can no longer be read because the MS is faded or damaged, as distinct from their use for erasures. It must be said, however, that many entries in the MS are untidy with much erasure, overwriting and correction; also, some of the letters are malformed and misled the Exchequer scribe as well as Mr. Barnes (e.g., see Exon. Notes 25,20 and cf. the last note under Exon. Notes 24,22). The scope of this edition prohibits mentioning all but the more important mistakes of Mr. Barnes and checking the transcription of all the place-names, though it is worth noting here that 7 out of the 8 textual notes on the table of Hundred names in the Tax Returns and Hundred Lists (near the beginning of the Appendix below) concern errors of transcription. Ellis' text has misled a number of people, especially in the case of the place-names. The present editors hope in the near future to produce a full list of corrections to his text.

The main Exon. returns and the T.O. are translated in the Victoria County History for Devon vol. i by O. J. Reichel; where the Exon. folios have not survived (i.e. those corresponding to DB Chs. 29, 30, 39, 44 and a few entries at the ends of Ch. 28 and Ch. 35), it is the Exchequer DB text that is translated. The VCH translation is not entirely satisfactory. Although Reichel seems to have looked at the Exon. MS for the first few entries and possibly for the damaged folios 403a–405b, he appears to have used only Ellis' text for the rest and thus reproduced all Barnes' errors in transcription. He occasionally gives Exchequer variants, though his method is inconsistent: at times figure discrepancies are given in brackets, at others it looks as if only the major differences are included (as for 19,35). Moreover, Reichel does not have a standard policy when dealing with the damaged folios, sometimes giving the Exchequer reading in brackets for what is under the gall, but sometimes merely printing dots instead of reproducing the DB, and sometimes making guesses as to the correct reading without mentioning this fact; see Exon. Notes to 19,38;39;41. (Ellis' treatment here is inconsistent also, see Exon. Notes 19,32.) Again, Reichel varies in his translation of terms and phrases; for example, in the first T.O. entry (495 a 1) he translates *pariter* as 'independently', then three entries later he uses the more usual translation 'in parage' (pp. 536–537). He also occasionally omits material, such as on p. 433 the pasture and meadow with their measurements at 183 b 2 (= DB 6,12). Finally, he sometimes writes the Exon. folio reference in the wrong place in the translation.

In the Notes below quotations are from, and references to, the Exon. folios given beside the translation, unless otherwise stated. In these quotations the abbreviated forms of the Latin are extended only where there is no reasonable doubt; elsewhere either the exact form of the abbreviation is reproduced when this seems important (e.g., see the second note under 1,11) or an apostrophe is used in place of the abbreviation sign (e.g., see last note under 1,11). References to notes are to the Exon. Notes, unless otherwise stated. References to DB, DB scribe and DB MS are to the Exchequer Domesday Book, scribe and MS, as distinct from the Exon. DB, scribe(s) and MS.

| | |
|---|---|
| C | DETAILS OF THE CITY OF EXETER appear in Exon. as the last entry under the heading of "The King's lordship belonging to the throne in Devonshire"; see 1,1–24 note. The rest of folio 88 is blank after it. |
| C 3 | SINCE THE KING HAS COME TO ENGLAND. "since King William has had England". The whole of this detail of the Exeter houses appears later in the Exon. entry, immediately before the part about the burgesses (DB C 7). |
| C 4 | ½ SILVER MARK FOR THE USE OF THE MEN-AT-ARMS. "½ silver mark for the soldiers (*dimidia marca argenti ad solidarios*)"; Ellis omits *marca*. |
| C 5–6 | WHENEVER AN EXPEDITION .... AS THIS CITY. These entries, apparently separate in the Exchequer DB, are part of the same sentence in Exon., an & joining the two statements, thus implying that the service of Barnstaple, Lydford and Totnes equalled that of Exeter when (and perhaps only when) an expedition took place. |
| C 7 | BURGESSES OF THE CITY. "The above-mentioned burgesses", though in fact none has been previously mentioned. |
| | LAND FOR 12 PLOUGHS. So Exon. MS; Ellis misprints *xii carrucatū* for *xii carrucarū*. |
| Ch. 1 | FOR THE DIFFERENT GROUPINGS of the King's lands in Exon. and in the Exchequer DB, see General Notes Ch. 1 and also notes above to C and below to 1,1–24. 1,25-56 and 1,57-72. |
| 1,1–24 | THESE MANORS, as well as the details of Exeter (see note to C above), are entered in Exon. under the heading of "The King's lordship belonging to the throne (*regnum*) in Devonshire", folios 83a to 88a inclusive. |
| 1,1 | BARNSTAPLE. KING EDWARD HAD IT IN LORDSHIP. "Barnstaple, which King Edward held in 1066"; *in dominio* omitted, probably because the Exon. scribe believed it to be covered by the heading (see preceding note). |
| | 40 BURGESSES.... In 1086: "The King has 40 burgesses....". Similarly for 1,2. |
| 1,1–2 | SINCE THE KING HAS COME TO ENGLAND. "since King William has had England" in both entries. |
| 1,2 | LYDFORD. KING EDWARD HELD IT IN LORDSHIP. "Lydford, which King Edward held in 1066"; *in dominio* omitted, see 1,1 note. |
| | 2 CARUCATES OF LAND OUTSIDE THE BOROUGH. "Land for 2 ploughs outside the city"; see the General Notes here. |
| | 40 HOUSES DESTROYED .... ENGLAND. This sentence occurs before the statement of the burgesses' tenure of 2 carucates. See the General Notes here. Exon. uses the past participle *uastatae* for "destroyed" (DB *uastae*), but no difference appears intended; see General Notes C 3 (second note). |

# Exon. 1

1,3     THE KING HOLDS (NORTH) TAWTON. "The King has 1 manor called (North) Tawton"; in virtually every entry in Exon. the formula is "*A* holds a manor called *B*". Attention is not therefore drawn again in these Notes to this designation of the place-name as a manor.
IN LORDSHIP.... "The King has .... in lordship"; Exon. almost always states that it is the 1086 holder who has the land and ploughs in lordship; attention is not drawn to this again in these Notes.
MEADOW, 40 ACRES. "40 of meadow". As the word *agros* has already occurred with the woodland and underwood, the scribe no doubt felt there was no need for it a third time. This omission of *agros* occurs fairly regularly in Exon. (and see General Notes 48,8;12) and no further attention is drawn to it in these Notes unless there is doubt as to what was omitted (see 16,75 note).

1,4     18 VILLAGERS AND 7 SMALLHOLDERS. ".... and 12 cottagers (*quotarios*)", added after the slaves on a new line; this and perhaps the unusual spelling* may account for the omission of the cottagers by the Exchequer scribe. However, there is no apparent reason for the omission of the 5 cottagers in Brixham (17,29), especially as the DB scribe includes the cottagers for three other manors on the same Exon. folio (17,30;32-33). Likewise, some 46 cottagers in Somerset and 15 in Dorset appear in Exon. but not in DB. See General Notes 15,21 on cottagers.
*The same scribe has *quoliberti* for *coliberti* in 98 a 3 (= 1,50) and seems to be the same as the writer of *quosceti* for *cosceti* and *quocetum* for *cocetum* in 121 a 2 and 121 b 1 (= 3,86-87).
OF THIS MANOR'S LAND .... 1066. Also in the T.O. at 498 a 8.
BELONGED THERE. "lay (*iacebat* in the MS; Ellis misprints *acebat*) in the said manor". In 498 a 8 "belonged to the King's lordship manor called Exminster".
VALUE 5s A YEAR. Only in 498 a 8.
ECCHA ... HOLD IT. Also in the T.O. at 498 b 1.
ECCHA THE REEVE. "Eccha the King's reeve" in 498 b 1.
1 FURLONG OF LAND. ".... which is (part) of the King's lordship manor called Exminster" in 498 b 1.
VALUE 2s A YEAR. Only in 498 b 1.

1,5     IN LORDSHIP 1 PLOUGH .... 1 CARUCATE. "The King has there 1 carucate of land and 1 plough"; *in dominio* omitted, as on several other occasions in Exon. when it is in DB (1,6;44;61. 2,14-15. 28,5. 43,3. 51,10) and on some 35 occasions in Exon. when no lordship detail is given in DB. Lack of space prohibits further mention in these Notes of this omission of *in dominio*; attention is, however, drawn to instances in Exon. where it is implied, but is *not* in DB.
WHEN BALDWIN .... AS MUCH. *quando Balduinus uicecomes recepit hanc qui tenet eam ad firmam de rege reddebat tantundem*. This has been translated on the assumption that, bearing in mind the order of the Latin, *qui* is resumptive (= "and he") and refers to Baldwin, but it might possibly be translated "when Baldwin the Sheriff acquired it, he who holds it at a revenue from the King paid as much"; in other words, the Sheriff had charge of Braunton but it was 'farmed' by someone else (so Lennard p. 148 note 1), rather than that Baldwin 'farmed' the manor himself. However, it seems more probable from the point of view of Latin grammar, that the subject of the two verbs *reddit* (in the 1086 value statement preceding this) and *reddebat* is the same (i.e. the manor), rather than that *ille* ("he") is understood as antecedent of the *qui*-clause and is the subject of the second verb. Moreover, the entry corresponding to 1,36 states that Baldwin acquired (Bradstone) at a revenue (i.e. 'farmed' it): *quando .... recepit eam ad firmam reddebat....* . See General Notes here.
1 VIRGATE .... TAKEN AWAY .... ADDED 1 VIRGATE.... So also in the T.O. at 498 b 6, the details of the virgate taken away being added in the margin of the Exon. MS.
1 VIRGATE OF LAND HAS BEEN TAKEN AWAY. ".... which lay there in 1066"; so also in 498 b 6.
IN KING'S REVENUE. "to the revenue in the King's manor (*ad firmam in manerio regis*)"; so also in 498 b 6. See the General Notes here.

1,6     12 PIGMEN. Added after the villagers, smallholders and slaves, as generally; they may have held the 20 ploughs as well as the other 'villagers' as DB 1,9 implies (but see Exon. Note to it). See 1,26 note.
½ VIRGATE....5s. Also in full in the T.O. at 499 b 3.

1,9     16 VILLAGERS, 20 SMALLHOLDERS .... 12 PLOUGHS. "The King has there 16 villagers and they have 12 ploughs. He has there 20 smallholders, 10 pigmen and 4 slaves". See the Exon. Notes to DB Somerset 5,21 and perhaps Dorset 55,25 for other examples

Exon. 1

of Exon.'s separating the villagers — or in some cases the smallholders — who hold the ploughs from other categories of population who apparently do not. See also notes below to 2,3. 3,27. 14,2. 15,16. 23,4. 24,16;31. 36,21. 49,3. This formula is not the work of one or even two particular scribes (in Devon in any case), so must have reflected an actual situation.

1,10  KINGSTEIGNTON. Details of this manor begin as the third entry on folio 84a, with 84b beginning after 3 lines with *& xii carr̄*. Ellis misprints folio 85 as beginning in the middle of the manor of (East) Budleigh (DB 1,9); whereas in fact folio 85a begins with the manor of Kingskerswell (DB 1,12), the marginal entries (see third note under 1,11) all appearing on 84b.
IT PAID TAX FOR.... "It paid for....": *redd(id)it p(ro)*; the scribe no doubt omitted *gildum* "tax" in error.

1,11  LAND FOR 40 PLOUGHS. *per xl carrucas potest arari terra* "the land can be ploughed by means of/using 40 ploughs", instead of the usual Exon. formula "y ploughs can plough it".
UNDERWOOD. In the Exon. MS *nemor* with '*cti* interlined to correct to *nemusculi*; Ellis fails to reproduce the underlining (see the section on Ellis' text in the Introduction to these notes) and misprints '*ati* as the interlineation.
TO THIS MANOR....THIS MONEY. This paragraph is condensed in DB from 5 entries in Exon. which are neatly added in the left margin of the MS probably by the same scribe as the main entry. They read:
84 b 5: "The Count of Mortain has a manor called Honiton, which before 1066 paid 30d a year to this manor of the King's, Axminster, but since the Count has had it, it has not paid".
84 b 6: "Ralph of Pomeroy has a manor called Smallridge which before 1066 paid 30d a year to the said manor, but Ralph has kept them (30d) back during the last 12 years (*retinuit eos radulfus xii anni sunt transacti*)". This last phrase occurs several times in this section and seems to lack a conjunction such as *dum* "while" before *retinuit*, since otherwise the two main verbs are unconnected.
84 b 7: "William Cheever has a manor called Membury, which likewise before 1066 paid 30d (*xxx den* in the MS; Ellis misprints *xxx. de.i*) a year to this manor of the King's, but William has kept them back during the last 12 years (*xii anni sunt transacti*)".
84 b 8: "The Bishop of Coutances has a manor called 'Charlton', which before 1066 paid 15d a year to the above manor of the King's, but since the Bishop has had it, it has not paid".
84 b 9: "The Canons of St. Mary's of Rouen have a manor called Rawridge, which before 1066 paid 30d a year to the above manor of the King's, but they have kept back this customary due during the past 18 years (*xviii anni sunt praeteriti*)".
The *Terrae Occupatae* entries run thus:
503 b 1: "The Count of Mortain has a manor called Honiton, which in 1066 paid 30d a year in customary dues to the King's manor called Axminster, but since the Count has obtained this land they (30d) have not been paid into the King's revenue (*ad firmam regis*). Drogo holds it from the Count" (this last phrase is interlined, though by the same scribe).
503 b 6: "Ralph of Pomeroy has a manor called Smallridge, which before 1066 paid 30d a year in customary dues into the revenue of Axminster, the King's manor, but since Ralph has had the land the King has had no customary dues".
503 b 7: "William Cheever has a manor called Membury, which before 1066 paid 30d in customary dues to Axminster, the King's manor, but for 12 years William has kept back this customary due".
503 b 8: "The Bishop of Coutances has a manor called 'Charlton', which before 1066 paid 30d (not 15d, as the main Exon. entry and as DB) in customary dues to Axminster, the King's manor, but since the Bishop has had this land, he has not paid this customary due".
503 b 9: "The Canons of Rouen have a manor called Rawridge, which before 1066 paid 30d in customary dues to the King's manor called Axminster, but for a long time now the Canons have kept back this customary due".
'DENEWORTHY' .... SAID MANOR. Also, in full, in the T.O. at 503 a 2; it is very unusual for the T.O. to give details of population, but see fifth note below and notes to 1,32 and 1,70 for other examples. See also Finn LE p. 75.
'DENEWORTHY'. "another manor called 'Deneworthy' "; so also in 503 a 2.

# Exon. 1

| | |
|---|---|
| 1,11 (cont'd.) | UNDERCLEAVE .... 5s. Abbreviated details of this added manor also appear in the T.O. at 503 a 3.<br>UNDERCLEAVE IS ATTACHED ALSO TO THIS MANOR. "In Axminster itself is another manor called Undercleave". Similarly in 503 a 3.<br>EDWARD SON OF EDRIC HOLDS IT. "Edward son of the same Edric holds it from King William". So also in 503 a 3.<br>½ HIDE .... 20s. Also in the T.O. at 503 a 4, again in full with the smallholders unusually included (cf. fifth note above). It is not clear why this should be recorded in the T.O. as there is no implication that the ½ hide should not have belonged to the church, although it is possible that, as Axminster church had formerly belonged to St. Peter's, York (Finn LE p. 72 note 1), the change in ownership had not been authenticated. Cf. notes to 2,2;15. 13a,2 and 42,10 and the Introduction to the Exon. Notes for other entries in the T.O. which have no hint of illegality in them.<br>2 PLOUGHS THERE. "2 ploughs can plough it (the ½ hide), which are there". So also in 503 a 4. No detail of the ploughs is given, but this is not unusual in a sub-holding of a manor. See also 17,18 note.<br>VALUE 20s. In 503 a 4 *ualent ... xx sol'*: the plural would seem to refer to the smallholders, though this must be a mistake. The main Exon. entry has *ual' ... xx sol'*. |
| 1,12 | MANOR'S CHURCH. "village's church". |
| 1,13 | IN (THE LANDS OF) .... 5s. "This said manor has a church where (i.e. in whose lands) ½ virgate lies. Value 5s". |
| 1,15 | FARLEIGH .... KING'S REVENUE. Abbreviated details of this added manor appear also in the T.O. at 504 a 3.<br>A THANE HELD IT FREELY BEFORE 1066. "which a thane held jointly in 1066; he could go to whomever he would". But in 504 a 3 just "which a thane held jointly in 1066".<br>IT PAYS 10s BY WEIGHT IN KING'S REVENUE. "It pays 10s a year by weight in the above revenue", referring to the revenue of Diptford. In 504 a 3 "it pays 10s a year by weight in revenue to the said manor (of Diptford)". |
| 1,17 | BESIDES THIS LAND. "Apart from these 2½ hides (*exceptis his ii hidis & dim'*)".<br>CANONS OF THIS MANOR. "Canons of St. Peter's of Plympton". The Tax Return for Plympton Hundred (xxviii) also designates them thus ("St. Peter's of Plympton (have) 2 hides (lordship)"; although a wavy line has been drawn under this statement, it is not likely to be a deletion line as it is in 'greyer' ink and is probably not contemporary).<br>12 VILLAGERS HAVE 4 PLOUGHS. "The canons have there 12 villagers who have 4 ploughs". |
| 1,18 | CLERGY. "priests (*sacerdotes*)". |
| 1,22 | THIE ENTRY appears in Exon. as part of the details of (Kings) Tamerton, the scribe originally having written "From this manor (i.e. Kings Tamerton) has been taken away...." and then erased the *hac* "this" and interlined *Wachetona*, Walkhampton. Abbreviated details of this entry also occur in the T.O. at 505 a 2.<br>IT PAID .... IN KING'S REVENUE. "This manor paid .... to Walkhampton in 1066"; in 505 a 2 "to Walkhampton".<br>IN THE LORDSHIP OF KING EDWARD.... This information is added under each manor in the form of "which King Edward held in 1066", with the exception of North Tawton (1,3), in the Exon. entry for which the only reference to King Edward is in the payment of tax "in King Edward's time"; the omission is probably because this manor is the first to be written under the heading (see 1,1 note) which covers the lordship part of it. |
| 1,23 | TO THIS MANOR .... DUES OF THE HUNDRED. As with 1,11 this paragraph is condensed from 5 entries neatly written, probably by the same scribe as the main entry, in the left margin of the Exon. MS. They read:<br>85 b 2: "The Count of Mortain has a manor called Fardel, which Godfrey holds from him and which before 1066 paid 30d in customary dues to Ermington, the King's manor, and the other customary dues which [belong] to the Hundred. But since King William has come to the throne (*regn̄*) the said customary dues have been taken away from the King's manor".<br>85 b 3: "Reginald has a manor from the Count of Mortain called Dinnaton, which before 1066 paid 30d in customary dues to Ermington, the King's manor, and the other customary dues belonging to the Hundred, but they have been taken away from there since King William has obtained the land". |

Exon. 1

| | |
|---|---|
| 1,23 (cont'd.) | **85 b 4**: "Reginald holds a manor from the Count of Mortain called Dinnaton, which before 1066 paid 30d in customary dues to Ermington, the King's manor, and the other customary dues of the Hundred. But since King William has obtained the throne (*regnū*) the customary dues and pence have been taken away from there". |
| | **85 b 5**: "And from Broadaford, the Count's manor, which Reginald holds from the Count, the customary dues and 30d have been taken away from the said manor of the King's". |
| | **85 b 6**: "And from Ludbrook, which Reginald holds from the Count, 30d and the customary dues of the Hundred have been taken away from the said manor of the King's". |
| | After this follows the name *Raginal* ('Reginald') preceded by a gallows sign: the scribe may have intended to add further details of withheld customary dues later when available, or he may have begun in error and forgotten to erase it. |
| | The *Terrae Occupatae* entries, 504 a 7-8 and 504 b 1-3, are virtually identical to the main Exon. entries quoted above (except for "since King William has held England" for the main entry's "since King William has come to the throne" in the Fardel entry), so are not given here. |
| 1,24 | THESE TWO MANORS .... BAMPTON. That is, Ermington and Blackawton. Exon. has this statement at the end of the Blackawton entry, but also states at the end of the main Ermington entry (85 b 1) that that manor is in exchange for Bampton. |
| 1,25-56 | THESE MANORS are separated in Exon. from the ancient demesne (lordship) lands (1,1-24) by the King's lordship land in Somerset, and are entered under the heading of "The King's lordship in Devonshire", folios 93a-98a inclusive. With the exception of the manor of Broadclyst held TRE by Ordwulf (1,56), they deal entirely with the lands held by the family of Godwin in 1066 (which were extensive in the west and were almost all held by the King in 1086). They are arranged by Hundred, not by holder as in DB, hence the lack of correspondence in consecutive numbering (see General Notes Ch. 1). Cf. the similar arrangement in the Exon. sections for Somerset Ch. 1 (see Somerset Exon. Notes 1,11-25), although there Queen Edith is given a section of her own (see Somerset Exon. Notes 1,26-31). This large section in Exon. also contains a short list of payments from 'farmers' of various of King William's lands; see after 1,55 note. |
| 1,25 | QUEEN EDITH HELD .... KING HOLDS. In each of the entries relating to 1,25-28 inclusive Exon. states "The King has .... which Queen Edith held in 1066", with the exception of the entry for 1,27 where 'Edith' is omitted, no doubt in error or because understood. |
| | TWO LANDS .... 60s. Full details of these two manors appear also in the T.O. at 495 b 3, where Lifton is described as the King's lordship manor. |
| | LANDINNER. In the Exon. MS *Lamliner*; Ellis misprints *Laniliner*. In the T.O. the form is *Lanliner*. |
| | THE COUNT HAS .... 60s. These details only appear in 495 b 3, written at the same time as the other details there. The fact that there is a gap of 1½ lines in the main Exon. entry after the preceding statement, with no full-stop after *ten&*, suggests either that the scribe needed to check these details, or that he realised details were unnecessary because already in Cornwall. |
| | ALSO IN THE T.O., though the information appears neither in the main Exon. nor in DB, is the following entry: |
| | **496 a 3**: "Iudhael and Alfred hold 1 hide of land in *bradeoda*, which as a customary due paid 7s 6d a year in customary dues to the King's lordship manor called Lifton. Since these two have held it, the King has not had his customary dues". |
| | *Bradeoda* is probably Broadwoodwidger, 17,5, held by Nigel from Iudhael, which paid tax for ½ hide, less 1½ furlongs ('ferlings'). But there is no record of a second holding in Broadwoodwidger by an Alfred which would account for the remaining ½ hide and 1½ furlongs of the hide. See notes to 1,66. 2,2. 15,14 and the last entry in these Notes for other instances of whole entries in the T.O. which appear neither in the main Exon. nor in DB. See also Ch. 44 note. |
| 1,26 | PIGMEN....SALT-WORKERS. As the land and ploughs of the *uillani* as a class are given before the detailed list of villagers, smallholders, cottagers, slaves, pigmen, salt-workers etc., it is not clear whether the pigmen and salt-workers here had a share in them (see General Notes 1,6). This uncertainty occurs almost every time pigmen (and other classes of population other than villagers, smallholders and cottagers — but see 1,9 note) are given in DB, as in the next entry, or are added from Exon., as in 1,39;67, and attention |

# Exon. 1

is not drawn to it again in these notes, because of lack of space, except on occasion when the phrasing of DB appears to exclude the pigmen etc. from those having a share in the ploughs (e.g. in 1,64). Cf. 2,2 note where Exon has "the villagers and men-at-arms" instead of just "villagers", and see also 19,35 note on 'a smith'.

SMITHS. DB *ferrarios*. In the Exon. MS *ferrạnos*, the dot under the *a* indicating deletion with the interlined *ũ* to replace it (not to add to it, as VCH p. 408 *ferruarii*). Ellis prints *ferrũrios*, but the *ri* are definitely an *n*, though probably a scribal error for *ri*. The Latin for 'smith, farrier' is *farrarius* and for 'an ironworker' *ferruarius* (RMLWL). Although neither *ferrũnos* nor *ferrũrios* (acc. pl.) are recognised forms, it is possible that *ferrun(n?)os* is a latinization of OFr *un ferron* 'an iron-worker; an iron-dealer', itself ultimately derived from Latin *ferrum* 'iron'. Ferron is also a personal name; see DB Northants. 6a,27 and note. Du Cange has only *ferrarius (equorum): Qui equos calceat* ("who shoes horses"), with no entry for *ferruarius*. The correction seems to have been done at the same time as the rest of the entry.

WOODLAND. *nemusculum*, the usual word for DB's *silua minuta* "underwood". There are some 11 occurrences in Devon, as in Somerset and Dorset, of DB putting "woodland" for Exon.'s "underwood", and 3 examples of the reverse (see 16,37 note).

1,29 GYTHA .... FOLLOWING MANORS. In each of the entries corresponding to 1,29-35 inclusive Exon. states "which Gytha held in 1066".

WOODLAND 2 LEAGUES LONG AND 2 WIDE. "woodland, 2 leagues in length and 2 furlongs in width". DB implies the width is 2 leagues too. The discrepancy is probably due to careless omission of *quarentinas* by the DB scribe, although it is possible that he had received information to correct the Exon. statement.

ASH .... KING WILLIAM'S TIME. Abbreviated details of this added manor also appear in the T.O. at 498 a 3.

WULFRIC HELD IT BEFORE 1066 AS A MANOR. "Wulfric held it jointly in 1066". So also in 498 a 3.

6 VILLAGERS WITH 1 SLAVE HAVE THEM THERE. "The King has 6 villagers and they have 3 ploughs; the King has 1 slave".

1,30 BEFORE BALDWIN('S TIME) IT PAID £23. "When B(aldwin) the Sheriff acquired it, it paid £23 by weight". As the DB scribe regularly has "Value was", "Value formerly" for this Exon. phrase, there are probably three dates of payment here: now, when Baldwin acquired it, and before he did. The same occurs for 1,33. Cf. DB Dorset 55,33. In some counties in DB (e.g. Bedfordshire) the value at three dates was regularly given for manors.

1,32 VALUE £6. In the Exon. MS the scribe wrote *uat*, then another scribe interlined *reddit* above it in much darker ink and with a thinner pen. It is possible that this interlineation was done after the Exchequer scribe had used Exon. and is the reason for the use of *valet* (instead of *reddit*) in DB (see General Notes here). In three other cases which occur consecutively in the Exon. for DB Ch. 1 (= DB 1,27;41-42) a different scribe has interlined *reddit* above an original *uat*, though *uat* is not underlined for deletion in any of these entries; the Exchequer scribe either saw these interlineations or he deliberately changed the *ual(et)*s to *reddit*. Exon. has *valet* also for 1,35;56;66, the other instances in Ch. 1 of DB having *valet*; perhaps in all four cases the Exchequer scribe was merely guilty of following his copy too closely (see the section on the relationship between DB and Exon. in the Introduction to these Notes, and cf. General Notes 3,82. 15,53. 24,18.

TO THIS MANOR .... 5s. Also in the T.O. at 500 b 5 in slightly abbreviated form.

WHICH THEY HELD FREELY. "which they held jointly". In 500 b 5 "thanes who could go with their lands to whichever lord they would in 1066".

3 VILLAGERS. IT PAYS 5s. "On these ('ferlings') 3 villagers still live who pay 5s a year to the said manor". In 500 b 5 "On this thaneland (*teglanda*) are 3 villagers who pay 5s to the said manor". This appears to be an example of villagers holding land at a revenue ('farming' it); see General Notes 6,6. See also 1,11 note ('Deneworthy' .... said manor) for other examples of the rare inclusion in the T.O. of villagers. Thaneland (of which this is the only mention in Devon Exon. or DB) was usually part of the lordship land (see DB Somerset 8,16) of either a lay or an ecclesiastical landholder, set aside to maintain a thane, armed and mounted. In return for the land the thane would provide certain services, often military. This thaneland, especially if it was part of the church's land, was usually inalienable: the holder was not free to transfer his allegiance to another lord nor to sell the land (see DB Dorset 49,10;17 and Exon. Notes there to 11,2;13, but cf. Dorset 1,31). Thaneland was not automatically hereditable, though it could sometimes be granted for a period of 'three lives' (a common length of lease). The holder of

Exon. 1

thaneland was not necessarily a thane: in Dorset 1,31 he is a priest and see Dorset Exon.
Notes 11,13 where the holder is a French man-at-arms. However, from several entries,
this one included, it would seem that thaneland was often simply land once held by
a thane.

1,33 BEFORE BALDWIN('S TIME) £18. "When B(aldwin) acquired it, £18". See 1,30 note.
THE CHURCH OF (MONT) ST. MICHEL .... 1 HIDE .... 20s. "The Abbot of Mont St.
Michel has there the church and land which a priest held in 1066; that is, ½ hide, 1
virgate and ½ furlong (*ferlinum*). Value 20s a year with common pasture".

1,34 WHEN BALDWIN ACQUIRED IT, AS MUCH. Originally "£18", but *xviii lib*' is
underlined for deletion and *tantūd*' is interlined in correction.
SHERFORD .... £3. Abbreviated details of this removed manor also appear in the T.O.
at 503 b 10.
VALUE WAS.... "when the Abbot acquired it". So also in 503 b 10.

1,35 THIS ENTRY is given twice in the main Exon. returns, once (in 98 a 2) under the
heading of the King's lordship in Devonshire (see 1,25-56 note) and once (in 110 b 2),
misplaced and surrounded on 3 sides by brackets in dark ink (not printed by Ellis) under
the heading of Queen Matilda's land in Devonshire (see 1,57-72 note). The entries are
virtually identical and are by different scribes; the entry at 110 b 2 has several corrections
and interlineations.

1,36 EARL HAROLD .... LANDS. Earl Harold is given as the TRE holder in each of the
entries relating to 1,36-49 inclusive, with the exception of 1,41-42;45 where the title
'Earl' (*comes*) is omitted, no doubt in error or because understood.

1,37 (WEST) PUTFORD. "The manor of (West) Putford"; see 34,7. In the T.O. at 497 a 4:
"Ralph (of Pomeroy) has a manor called (West) Putford which paid 30d a year in
customary dues to the King's lordship manor of (Black) Torrington. Since Ralph has
held this land the King has not had his customary due from it".

1,38 WOODLAND, 1 ACRE. "woodland, 1 furlong". DB similarly has acres for Exon.'s
furlongs in 23,12, though in that entry there is a possible reason for the discrepancy
(see note). Cf. 17,79 note.

1,39 500 SHEEP. In the Exon. MS *Ď oues*; the number is badly written. '500' is normally
written *D, Đ, d* etc., but this is unlike this scribe's usual *Ds* or *ds*, looking more like a
capital *O* with an extension at the top left. However, the scribe probably intended '500',
which is a common number for sheep (cf. in 1,40).

1,40 IN EXETER 5 HOUSES. This is interlined in the Exon. MS above the pigmen and with
an omission sign (;) after the *lx uillanos* which precede the pigmen (there is only a faint
mark before the interlineation, but cf. General Notes 32,6).
FROM THIS MANOR LANGLEY .... (HIGH) BICKINGTON. In Exon. these details
are added by the same scribe in 4 lines at the foot of folio 94b below the last ruling,
*c*. 13 letters into the left margin, with a cross beside them but with no corresponding
one after the Tawstock entry at the top of the folio. Both Langley and (High) Bickington
are described as manors, as also in the T.O. entry at 499 a 6 where abbreviated details of
the removal are also to be found.
THIS LAND .... (HIGH) BICKINGTON. "Now it has been wrongfully added to the
King's manor called (High) Bickington which is (part) of Brictric's lands (*bristricii*;
Ellis misprints *bristicii*)" .... 499 a 6. The last phrase is interlined.

1,41 BLACKPOOL .... 20s. Abbreviated details of this added manor also appear in the T.O.
at 499 a 5.
ALWARD HELD IT. DB and Exon. MS *Eluuardus*; Ellis misprints *Eduuardus*. In
499 a 5 "which a thane held jointly".
VALUE 20s WEIGHED AND ASSAYED. "Value 20s a year" .... 499 a 5.
NIMETE .... 15s. Mostly written in the right margin of the Exon. MS, the value being
squashed in, probably later. Details of this added land also appear in the T.O. at
499 b 4.
WRONGFULLY JOINED. Not in 499 b 4.
½ VIRGATE .... 1066. Only in 499 b 4; Ellis misprints *sr̃s* for the MS's *fr̃s* (= *fratres*
'brothers'). VCH p. 541 translates 'sisters' reading *sr̃s* for *sorores*. In the Exon. MS the
word is written thus ﬀ̃ and the reading of the first letter as *f* or *s* hinges on whether or
not it has a cross-line; in this case the *r* joins this letter, adding to the difficulty. However,
this scribe writes an *r* as *ꝛ*, so the bar to the left of it must be the cross-line of an *f*.
TO THE MANOR .... ENGLAND. These details are added in darker ink at the bottom
of folio 95a (after the entry for Broadclyst, DB 1,56) with no transposition signs. The

# Exon. 1

scribe is the same as for the Molland entry earlier on the folio. These details also occur in the T.O. at 499 b 9, where the information about the King no longer having the due is given in a slightly different form and the third penny is attached to Molland "from the time of King Edward".

1,46 WOODLAND, 40 ACRES. *xl agros* only; *nemoris* omitted, but probably correctly supplied by the DB scribe, this being the usual place in Exon. for the woodland details (see General Notes 1,53). It is unlikely that the Exon. scribe meant '40 + 16 acres of woodland' (i.e. two stretches of woodland, one of 40 acres and one of 16 acres), though cf. General Notes 1,35 where this may be the meaning. Other examples of Exon. omitting the noun but giving the measurement, and the Exchequer scribe adding it, are 6,12. 16,133. 19,44. 21,19. 36,19. 42,15 and see also DB Dorset Exon. Notes 36,3 and Somerset Exon. Notes 22,8 and 47,16. This entry in Exon. is a neat one. Cf. notes to 1,53. 22,1. 28,2 and 32,6 below.
TO THIS MANOR .... 4s. Also in full in the T.O. at 502 a 3.
WHICH A THANE HELD FREELY BEFORE 1066. "which a thane held jointly in 1066; he could go to whichever lord he would". In 502 a 3 "which a thane held jointly in 1066".

1,49 PASTURE, 1 LEAGUE IN LENGTH AND WIDTH. "pasture, 1 league in each direction (*ab omni parte*)".
TO THIS MANOR .... REVENUE. Also in full in the T.O. at 502 a 4.
½ VIRGATE OF LAND. "A manor of ½ virgate"; so also in 502 a 4.
WHICH A THANE HELD FREELY BEFORE 1066. "which a thane held in 1066; he could go with his land to whichever lord he would". In 502 a 4 "which a thane held jointly in 1066".
IN KING'S REVENUE. "into the King's revenue (*ad firmam regis*)".

1,50 16 VILLAGERS. "116 villagers"; *c & xvi uill'*; the splitting of the number, very frequent in Exon., is probably the reason for the discrepancy. This entry, the last under the King's lands in Devon, is written by 2 (possibly 3) different scribes in a browner ink than 98 a 1-2 (though the ink changes during the entry) and is very messy with several erasures (perhaps the result of its disputed ownership; see General Notes here). Cf. 17,51 note for another Exon. entry written by 2, or 3, scribes.
REST OF THE LAND. *aliam terram*, a very common phrase in the parts of Exon. relating to Cornwall, but see also in the translation here for 3,86. 15,14;19. 28,2, and 16,6 note and 42,2 in the Lordship and Villagers' Table.
25 CATTLE. *xx 7 v animal'* is written over an erasure. After the *v* are 2 faint minim strokes which may be part of the erasure, or *xx 7 vii animal'* may be intended: no new dot is written after the *v* as after the *xx*.
FORMERLY. "before 1066 (*tempore regis Eduuardi*)".
GYTHA HELD IT. "which Earl Harold's mother held", who was of course Gytha.
THE COUNT OF MORTAIN .... 1066. Details of this ½ hide occur among the *Terrae Occupatae* for Cornwall:
    508 a 5: "The King has a manor called Werrington, from which ½ hide has been taken away which belonged there in 1066. The Count of Mortain holds it now. Value 40s; value when the Count acquired it £4".
Werrington is on the county boundary. There is no record of the abstraction in the *Terrae Occupatae* for Devon. See General Notes here. Cf. 1,25 where details of the two Cornish manors are in the T.O. for Devon, but not for Cornwall.

1,51 EARL LEOFWIN HELD .... BELOW. In each of the entries corresponding to 1,51-55 inclusive Exon. states "which Earl Leofwin held in 1066".

1,52 10 CATTLE. In the Exon. MS *xi* underlined for deletion and *x* interlined in correction; Ellis misprints $x^{\cdot}_{i}\cdot$

BATTLE ABBEY. "The Abbot of Battle".

1,53 PASTURE, 12 FURLONGS AND 12 ACRES. *xii quadrā̆ & xii ağ pascuę*. It is not entirely clear whether the 12 furlongs are a measurement of the pasture; *nemusculi* "underwood" could perhaps have been omitted after the *xii quadrā̆* (as also perhaps at 28,2; see note). This entry, however, is a neat one with no gaps or erasures. See General Notes here and cf. 22,1 note below.

1,55 TO THIS MANOR .... IUDHAEL. "From this manor the King gave 20s to Iudhael which the Borough of Totnes paid to this manor in revenue (*reddebat .... huic mansioni ad firmam*)".
AFTER THIS ENTRY IN EXON. there appears a gallows sign followed by 3 blank lines,

Exon. 1

1,55 (cont'd.)  possibly an entry neatly erased, the space perhaps being left for details of another manor. Then the following items of information, preceded in each case by a gallows sign and occupying 2½ lines at the bottom of folio 97b:
 **97 b 2**: "Baldwin pays the King in revenue (*ad firmam*) £375 a year from the lands of the Earls".
 It is not clear how the sum £375 was reached. If one adds up the payments made by the manors held in 1066 by Countess Gytha (1,29-35;50), by Earl Harold (1,36-49) and by Earl Leofwin (1,51-55) the total is £393 (or £398 1s if the payments and values of the added manors are included). OJR in VCH p. 389 states that if the £18 payment of Kings Nympton (1,49) were discounted, the total would be £375, but there is no reason why that manor's payment should be disregarded rather than the £18 payments from 1,35 or 1,37 or 1,39 (or indeed several smaller payments totalling £18). Whale in TDA 32 p. 529 arrives at a total of £375 by adding together the present values of 1,29-49;51-55 (discounting the added lands, but deducting the 20s value of the church at Woodbury, 1,33, though including the £3 value of the similar 'removed' land of Sherford, 1,34 — which he later states he has excluded); there seems no reason for this treatment or his exclusion of 1,50 in his reckoning.
 It is more likely that the discrepancy is a scribal error or that this statement originated from a different source to the returns for these comital manors.
 **97 b 3**: "Jocelyn (*Gotselenus*; see General Notes 16,148) pays the King £108 a year for the lands of Queen Edith".
 Queen Edith's lands (1,25-28) pay £108, but 93 a 2 states that it was Colwin (not Jocelyn) who held Lifton (1,25) at a revenue (see General Notes C 2); however, as this statement is an interlineation, apparently by a different scribe to the rest of the entry, it could have been missed by the scribe of this entry, or added after these totals had been written.
 **97 b 4**: "Reginald pays* to the King's revenue £24 a year for Ordwulf's land".
 * *reddi*, possibly abbreviating *reddidi* "I have paid", referring to Reginald (of Vautortes) — see VCH p. 377 — but more likely being a scribal error for *reddit*.
 Ordwulf's land appears to be Broadclyst, 1,56, whose value was £24, but there is no mention there of a Reginald holding it 'in charge for the King' (so VCH *ibidem*). Reginald (of Vautortes) was Ordwulf's successor in much of the latter's land that passed to the Count of Mortain; e.g. 15,44 and see General Notes 15,26-30.
 1½ blank lines, possibly erased neatly, follow this.

1,57-72  THESE MANORS (and also 1,35; see note to it) are dealt with in Exon. under the heading of "Land of Queen Matilda in Devonshire", folios 108a-111a inclusive, although 1,72 does not appear to have anything to do with either Queen Matilda or her predecessor Brictric.

1,57  BRICTRIC HELD. "held in 1066" for each entry. Queen Matilda, though she heads the section, is only mentioned again in this first entry in Exon. and for 1,66;68.
 IT PAYS £9 AT FACE VALUE. "Gotshelm has this manor at a revenue (*ad firmam*) and pays from it £9 a year at face value".

1,58  IT PAYS 70s AT FACE VALUE. "Gotshelm has this manor at a revenue and pays from it 70s a year at face value".

1,59  IT PAYS £12 .... £6. "This manor pays £12 at face value. Gotshelm has this manor at a revenue and when he acquired it himself, it paid £6".

1,63  ALWARE PET HELD IT .... FROM HIM. "Alware Pet held it in 1066; she could not be separated from Brictric with this land".
 2½ VIRGATES .... TAWTON HUNDRED. This detail appears to be an addition in Exon., the last 3 words being written in the right margin. The Exchequer scribe may only have seen the last 3 words when checking Exon. and then added them to DB in the same size script as he used for Hundred headings; see General Notes here.

1,64  60 VILLAGERS WITH .... 10 PIGMEN. Listed as usual in Exon.: "The King has 60 villagers, 16 slaves and 10 pigmen", the ploughs and land of the *uillani* as a class being given separately; see 1,26 note.

1,66  LAPFORD. In the T.O. at 497 b 5: "The King has a manor called Lapford, to which 4 manors have been added which 4 thanes held jointly in 1066 and which did not belong to the said manor before 1066. Walter of Claville holds them in the revenue of Lapford. They pay (MS *reddi*; Ellis misprints *reddit*) 20s a year in this revenue". There is no cross-reference to these lands under Walter of Claville's fief, probably because he 'farmed' Lapford rather than held it. See notes to 1,25 (last note). 2,2. 15,14. Ch. 44 and the last

| | |
|---|---|
| 1,66 (cont'd.) | entry in these Notes for other instances of whole entries in the T.O. where information does not appear either in the main Exon. or in DB. |
| | IRISHCOMBE....THERE. "To this manor is attached ½ virgate which is accounted for in the above value (*in supradicto pretio cumputatur*; cf. General Notes 21,2); it is called Irishcombe". No record of this ½ virgate appears in the T.O. unless as part of the lands of the "4 thanes" in the above note. |
| 1,67 | 2 PIGMEN; THEY PAY.... *ii porcaŗ & reddī*; despite the & for the more usual *qui* (as for 2,2;4 etc.) it is doubtless the pigmen's annual payment of pigs that is recorded. In the Exon. for 3,14. 16,43 and 19,17 & is similarly used for *qui* and all these four entries are by the same scribe. It is interesting that in a similar phrase for the manor of Dolton (16,44), another entry by this scribe, *& reddi* has been corrected by him to *ą reddī*. |
| | LANGLEY. Described as a manor. See 1,40 note for the entry. |
| 1,70 | OF THIS MANOR'S LAND .... HALBERTON. In the T.O. at 502 b 5: "From the King's manor called Halberton Gotshelm appropriated (*occupavit*) 1 virgate of villagers' land; he has on it 1 plough, 1 smallholder and 1 slave and paid 10s to the revenue of (*firmę\* de*) Halberton". See 1,11 note ('Deneworthy' .... said manor) for other examples of the very rare inclusion in the T.O. of details of inhabitants. |
| | \* *Firmę*, dative, instead of the more usual *ad firmam*. |
| | OF THIS MANOR'S LAND. "Of these 5 hides". |
| | IT PAYS 10s TO HALBERTON. "It paid 10s to the revenue of (*firmę de*) Halberton when G(otshelm) received it". No mention is made of the present (1086) payment. |
| 1,71 | IUDHAEL HELD IT FROM THE QUEEN. "This [is] the manor which Iudhael held from the Queen"; *hec st manŝ ą ten Iuhellus de regina*: the *st* is not quite like the normal abbreviation for *sunt* "there are" and has no abbreviation sign over it, but it is definitely not the abbreviation for *est* "is"; *hec* is probably nominative singular to agree with *mans(io)* rather than neuter plural; *ten* can abbreviate both the past or present tenses (cf. 23,1 note). |
| Ch. 2 | LAND OF THE BISHOP OF EXETER. Entered in Exon. under the heading of "Lands of the Church of St. Peter, Exeter, in Devonshire", but each entry begins either "The Bishop has" or "Bishop O(sbern) has". |
| 2,1 | 47 HOUSES PAY 10s 10d. "The Bishop has .... 48 houses and of these houses 10 of them pay 10s 10d in customary dues"; *xlvi* with *ii* interlined in addition. See General Notes here. |
| | 2½ ACRES .... [AND] BELONG. See General Notes here. |
| 2,2 | CREDITON. In the T.O. at 499 a 4 appear details of a manor within Crediton not mentioned either in Exchequer DB or in the main Exon. entry: "The Bishop of Exeter has a manor called Crediton. In it his canons hold a manor called Chaffcombe which a thane held jointly in 1066. Value 10s a year". See notes to 1,25 (last note). 1,66. 15,14. Ch. 44 and the last entry in these Notes for other instances of whole T.O. entries not in the main Exon. return. There does not seem to be anything illegal implied in this statement, so it is not clear why it was included in the T.O. See the section on the T.O. in the Introduction to these Notes and cf. notes to 1,11 ('½ hide .... 20s'). 2,15. 13a,2 and 42,10. |
| | VILLAGERS....PLOUGHS....HIDES. "Both men-at-arms and villagers have 9 hides and 172 ploughs"; however, the men-at-arms are not mentioned in the list of villagers, smallholders, slaves and pigmen. |
| | VALUE FORMERLY £21. "when the Bishop acquired it, it paid £21". |
| | THE BISHOP ALSO HOLDS.... "With this manor the Bishop has a manor called...."; *habet* "has" is interlined above *clamat* "claims" which is underlined for deletion, though Ellis fails to print the underlining. |
| | PAYS TAX. "paid tax"; however, the DB *geld* may abbreviate *geldabat* "paid", despite the present *tenet* at the beginning of the sentence. See General Notes here. |
| | ST. PETER'S CHURCH. "his church". |
| | IN ADDITION .... HE HAS PROVED BEFORE THE KING'S BARONS.... "further, he states that .... he has entered a plea about this land and has proved by the witness of the Frenchmen that it is his" (*adhuc dicit quod .... de hac terra placitauit et disraisnauit\* testimonio francigenarum esse suam*). There is no mention of this dispute in the T.O.; see the General Notes here for a possible reason for this and cf. 3,32 note below. On the 'Frenchmen' see last note under General Notes 2,2. |
| | \* *disraisnauit* is a latinization of an OFr compound *di(s)raisnier* (the simple form becoming Mod.Fr *raisonner* 'to reason'). This is itself derived from Latin *di(s)ratiocinare* |

|      | |
|------|---|
| | which, with the deponent *diratiocinari*, is the regular form used in DB (e.g. Wilts. 24,14; 19. Worcs. 2,24;63). The base is Latin *ratio* giving French *raison* "reason, cause". |
| 2,3 | 4 VILLAGERS AND 3 SMALLHOLDERS HAVE 2 PLOUGHS. "The Bishop has 3 villagers who have 2 ploughs. The Bishop has 3 smallholders"; see 1,9 note. |
| 2,4 | IN EXETER. "in the Borough of Exeter". |
| | 410(?) SHEEP. *cccc oues* 7 *x*; as numbers with *c, cc* etc. are very often split like this in Exon., it seems more likely that "410 sheep" are meant rather than "400 sheep and 10 [....] and 40 goats" or "400 sheep and 10 + 40 goats". VCH p. 415 translates '400 sheep; 10 and 40 goats'. See 12,1 note. |
| | VALUE FORMERLY OF THE WHOLE MANOR. "Value when the Bishop acquired it"; similarly for DB's past values of 2,5-6;9;12;15-17;23-24. |
| 2,6 | UNDERWOOD, 3 ACRES. "underwood, 4 acres"; the first *i* of the *iiii* is slightly paler and longer than the others, but is not erased, though the Exchequer scribe may have thought it had been. |
| 2,7 | STAVERTON. "which Bishop Leofric held in 1066". Leofric was ordained Bishop of Cornwall and Devon in 1046, but in 1050 he transferred his episcopal seat from Crediton to Exeter. He died in 1072. The Exchequer scribe omitted details of the 1066 holders of several church lands (2,7-8;14;16-23. 5,8. 6,1;7-12. 7,3-4; see notes to these below); a study of the Exon. MS yields no obvious reason for this, but it is possible that it was only felt necessary to include in DB details of lay TRE holders of church land (as in 2,9-10;15. 5,9. 10,2. 11,1-3. 12,1. 13,1), though this does not explain 5,11-14 and 10,1. Or perhaps the Exchequer scribe intended to write a cross-head at some point(s) in these chapters; like those in Ch. 1 (and cf. 32,10). See also General Notes 19,34. |
| 2,8 | ST. MARYCHURCH. "which Bishop Leofric held in 1066". |
| | THESE 4 VILLAGES .... SUPPLIES. Included in the accounts of the 4 manors. |
| 2,9-10 | HAXTON. BENTON. In the T.O. at 499 b 6: "The Bishop of Exeter has a manor called Haxton which Ordwulf held. A manor called Benton has been added to it, which a thane held jointly in 1066. Value 5s a year". |
| 2,10 | EDNOTH HELD IT FREELY. "which Ednoth held jointly; he could [go] to whichever lord he would"; *ire* is omitted in error after *potuit*. "jointly .... would" is interlined in slightly paler ink and with a thicker pen, but probably by the scribe of the main part of the entry. Cf. 13a,2 note. |
| | VILLAGE. "manor"; i.e. Haxton. |
| 2,11 | 3 OF THEM HAVE NEVER PAID TAX. "the Bishop had the remaining 3 in lordship and they never paid tax". Later the 3 hides are repeated with the ploughs in lordship. |
| 2,14 | TALATON. "which Bishop Leofric held in 1066". |
| | 20 VILLAGERS. So Exon. MS; Ellis misprints *xv uill'*. |
| | MILL WHICH PAYS. "mill which paid"; *reddit* may be a scribal error for *reddit* "pays", the abbreviation sign possibly being an attempt to make the *d* into a *t*. DB's *redd* could abbreviate *reddidit* "paid", however, although the present tense is more usual in this phrase. |
| | [VALUE] FORMERLY. "when he acquired it", most probably referring to the Bishop. In the great majority of entries where this formula occurs, the subject of *recepit* (when given, as it is more than half the time) is that of the tenant-in-chief and the value of the manor is that at the date of his acquisition of it from King William. However, see 16,88 note for exceptions. |
| 2,15 | SIDBURY. In the T.O. at 506 a 10: "The Bishop of Exeter has a manor called Sidbury which 2 thanes, namely Alwin and Godwin, held jointly. Value £6 a year; when the Bishop acquired it, as much". There is no obvious reason for the inclusion of this information in the T.O. as no illegality seems to have been practised. It is possible that because the TRE holders were thanes who held 'jointly' (= 'freely', see General Notes 1,15) the Bishop ought not to have acquired their land; the Bishop's other predecessors in his Devon lands (except 2,9-10 which had been exchanged) were Bishop Leofric either stated (see 2,7 note) or implied. It is unlikely that the fact that 2 thanes had held it implies that this entry is of the type mentioned in the T.O. section of the Introduction to these Notes where one manor has been added to another. See also notes to 1,11 ('½ hide .... 20s'). 2,2. 13a,2 and 42,10. |
| | ALWIN AND GODWIN HELD. "....jointly"; so also in 506 a 10. |
| | TAX FOR 5 HIDES. "tax for 3 hides", which agrees with the total of lordship and villagers' land. |
| | 30 PLOUGHS. "20 ploughs", with a gap after it, perhaps due to a very well executed erasure. |

Exon. 2 - 3

2,15 (cont'd.) 25 PLOUGHS. "18 ploughs", the *& xviii* being written over an erasure, though it cannot be seen what was originally written. These three discrepancies of hidage and ploughs suggest, according to Finn LE p. 53 and MDeD pp. 101-102, that the Exon. scribe wrote down the details for only one of the two former manors, but, if this were the case, it is odd that the other information for the manor is the same in DB as in Exon. Baring pp. 317-318 and note 23 states that the figures in Exon. were once those of DB, but were altered to their present ones. However, a close examination of the MS does not reveal this at all; although some of the figures are in darker ink, this is due to the parchment rather than to erasures, the only clear erasure being under the villagers' ploughs here.

2,16-22 SALCOMBE (REGIS). 'BRIGHTSTON'. PAIGNTON. ASHBURTON. (CHUDLEIGH) KNIGHTON. (BISHOPS) NYMPTON. BRANSCOMBE. "which Bishop Leofric held in 1066" for each of these manors.

2,20-21 VALUE FORMERLY. FORMERLY. "value when he acquired it" for each entry; see 2,14 last note.

2,22 IN LORDSHIP. "The canons have....in lordship". The canons (*C.*) similarly 'have' the villagers etc. On both occasions the *C.* presumably abbreviates *canonici*. In the other manors which were for the canons' supplies it is the Bishop who has land and ploughs in lordship and 'has' the villagers etc.

2,23 DITTISHAM. "which Bishop Leofric held in 1066".

2,24 BEFORE 1066 IT PAID TAX. "It paid tax"; see notes to 5,6 and 19,18 and cf. sixth note under 23,5 for similar omissions of the TRE phrase.
21 COTTAGERS. The *i* of *xxi coscetos* is in darker ink and appears to have been added later; it is interesting that in DB the number has been corrected from *xx* to *xxi*. See also 3,68 note below and General Notes 16,108. 28,10 and 32,10.

3,1 WERE IN KING EDWARD'S LORDSHIP. ".... in 1066".

3,2 THIS ENTRY appears also in full in the T.O. at 506 a 4.
THERE. "In Exeter", as also in 506 a 4.
4 OF THEM WERE EXEMPT .... 2 .... DUES. "4 of them were exempt from customary dues before 1066 and 2 paid customary dues .... that is 16d". Similarly in 506 a 4, but ".... 2 paid 16d", the 'customary dues' not being repeated.

3,4 VALUE FORMERLY. "value when the Bishop acquired it". Also for the past value of 3,5-7;9-10;13-14;16-21;24-32;35-53;55-68;71-72;74-77;79;81-86;88-89;91-92; 95-97.

3,8 MILL WHICH PAYS 10s. "mill which pays 5s".
TO THIS MANOR .... £10. So also, in abbreviated form, in the T.O. at 504 b 5.
LAND OF 15 THANES IN (LITTLE) BOVEY....PULLABROOK. "land of 15 thanes: one of these booklands (*bochelandis* interlined above *mans* which is dotted for deletion; see General Notes here) is called (Little) Bovey and 4 thanes lived there; another is called Warmhill and 1 thane lived there; another Scobitor and 2 thanes lived there; another *Brungarstone* and 3* thanes lived there; another Elsford and another Woolleigh − 1 thane held these two; with this thane was another thane in Woolleigh; another called Hawkmoor and 1 thane lived there; another Hatherleigh and 1 thane lived there; another Pullabrook and 1 thane lived there.... They held their land jointly before 1066".
* In the MS *iii*, although the last *i* is rather faint; Ellis reads *ii*, but *iii* fits in with the total of 15 thanes and is obviously what the Exchequer scribe took it to be.
In 504 b 5 the thanes were "so free that they could go with their lands to whichever lord they would in 1066".
TO BOVEY (TRACEY). "to the revenue of Bovey (Tracey)" in 504 b 5.

3,9 DROGO. Called Drogo son of Mauger for 3,9;13-14;16. 'Mauger' is *Malger(us)* for 3,9;13-14 and *matelgerius* for 3,16, representing OFr *Malger*, OG *Madalgar*.

3,10 1 PLOUGH THERE. "Drogo has 1 plough there...."; *in dominio* probably implied or omitted in error.

3,11 OSWULF. After the details of meadow and pasture is added "The said thane could go with this land to whichever lord he would". In the T.O. at 496 b 1 a thane is said to have held Horton "jointly" and at 505 a 1 Oswulf held Horton "jointly".
IT .... HORWOOD .... 1066. Also in the T.O. at 496 b 1 and 505 a 1. In the main Exon. entry "The Bishop holds it with the manor of Horwood....".

3,12 HENSCOTT. In the T.O. at 497 a 1: "The Bishop of Coutances has a manor called Henscott. Two manors have been added to it, which 2 thanes held jointly. They (manors) did not belong to the said manor in 1066. Value of them 10s a year; value when he acquired them, 15s".

Exon. 3

| | |
|---|---|
| 3,12 (cont'd.) | THREE THANES HELD IT AS A MANOR BEFORE 1066. "which three thanes — Cola, Edric and Godric — held in 1066 and which the Bishop now holds as one manor". The first letter of *Cola* is written *Ç*, the *ʒ* part being added; it is neither a *C* nor a *G* (cf. the *G* in *Godric*), though the man's name was undoubtedly *Cola*. See PNDB §§ 119, 128 on C/G interchange. |
| | FORMERLY. "when he acquired it", most probably referring to the Bishop (see notes to 2,14 and 16,88). Similarly for DB's past values in 3,69;78;93. |
| 3,14 | 3 PIGMEN; THEY PAY .... See 1,67 note. |
| 3,18 | FORMERLY 30s. "25s". |
| 3,19 | BARLINGTON. The details of this added manor are written in the left margin of the Exon. MS, level with the entry for Roborough by the same scribe as the next entry (124 b 3 = DB 3,20), who is different from the scribe of the main entry for 3,19. A capital *A* appears above the first word of 122 b 2 and a capital *B* above the marginal addition to indicate the order. See DB Somerset Exon. Notes 1,1 for a similar use of *a* and *b* to link separated parts of an entry; both these Devon and Somerset entries are by the same scribe. Details also appear in slightly abbreviated form in the T.O. at 500 a 2, where Drogo is given as the tenant of Barlington. |
| | ALFRED HELD IT FREELY. "Alfred held it....he could go to whichever lord he would". Similarly for 500 a 2 with the addition of "with this land". |
| 3,21 | VALUE....£4. In the Exon. MS *iii* with *i* interlined above in the same colour ink, probably correcting *iii* to *iiii* as there is no underlining for deletion. |
| 3,22 | TWO THANES HELD IT FREELY. "which 2 thanes held jointly". |
| | ENGELBALD .... 10s. In the T.O. at 498 a 4: "The Bishop of Coutances has a manor called Coldridge. 1 virgate of land has been added to it which a thane held jointly in 1066 and which did not belong to the said manor before 1066. Now Drogo holds it from the Bishop. Value 10s a year". |
| | ALGAR HELD IT FREELY. "Algar held it....; he could go with his land to whichever lord he would". |
| | FORMERLY 5s. "value when Drogo received it, 5s"; see 16,88 note. |
| 3,26 | TO THIS MANOR .... 20s. Also in abbreviated form in the T.O. at 499 a 7 where the 3 lands are called "3 manors". |
| | WHICH THEY HELD FREELY. "which 3 thanes held jointly....; they could go to whichever lord they would". In 499 a 7 "which 3 thanes held jointly" only. |
| | 3 VILLAGERS. "Drogo has 3 villagers". |
| 3,27 | 2 VILLAGERS .... 1 SMALLHOLDER. "Drogo has 2 villagers who have 2 ploughs and (he has) 1 smallholder"; see 1,9 note. |
| 3,28 | IN LORDSHIP 1 PLOUGH. "1½ ploughs in lordship". |
| 3,29 | 2 VILLAGERS HAVE IT THERE. "D(rogo) has 2 villagers who have 1 plough". |
| 3,30 | WHITEFIELD .... 10s. Details of this added manor also appear in the T.O. at 499 a 9 in abbreviated form. |
| | SAEWIN HELD IT AS A MANOR. "which a thane held jointly" .... 499 a 9. |
| 3,32 | BEFORE 1066 .... HAVE IT. This information is written in 2 lines, apparently by the same scribe, at right-angles down the length of the left margin of folio 126b (not on 126a as well, as Ellis prints). The first 3 letters of *Bristric'*, the first word, are missing, though there is room for them; likewise the *W* (presumably) before *aluilla* at the beginning of the second line which is hard up against the bottom edge of the folio. There are no transposition signs. There is no entry for this claim in the T.O., so it is possible that the information came to light after the main Exon. and the T.O. had been written, and was added only to the former, or perhaps the claim was settled before the T.O. were written. Cf. General Notes 2,2 on Newton St. Cyres and notes below to 5,5 (last entry). 16,33. 23,5 (fifth note). 23,6 and 52,33 on the possible reasons for the omission from the T.O. of other information one would expect to find therein. |
| | 1 VIRGATE OF LAND. ".... called Boode". |
| | WHICH HAD PREVIOUSLY BEEN IN.... "which....before King Edward's death had been acquired from....". |
| 3,34 | IT WAS WASTE. DB *Vasta fuit*, Exon. *erat uastata*; no real distinction between the adjective and the past participle was probably intended; see the General Notes for this entry and for C 3 (second note). |
| 3,36 | 9 PIGS. So the Exon. MS clearly; Ellis misprints '2 pigs'. |
| 3,40 | AYLESCOTT. In the T.O. at 500 a 5: "The Bishop of Coutances has a manor called Aylescott. 1 virgate of land has been added to it, which a thane held, who could go with |

# Exon. 3

| | |
|---|---|
| 3,40 (cont'd.) | his land to whichever lord he would in 1066. Value 10s a year. [Drogo] holds it from the Bishop (*hanc tenet de epo*; *Drogo* probably omitted in error)". |
| | TWO BROTHERS HELD IT FREELY. "which two brothers held jointly....; they could go to whichever lord they would". |
| 3,45 | IN BARNSTAPLE A GARDEN .... 4d. Interlined in the Exon. MS; it is interesting that the garden in 10,1 is also an addition (as also the details of the garden in Dorset 36,4; see Exon. Notes there). |
| 3,48 | 3 SMALLHOLDERS. So the Exon. MS; Ellis misprints *iiii bord'*. |
| 3,51 | LAND FOR 2 PLOUGHS. Omitted. The Exchequer scribe may have deduced the estimate from the number of actual teams recorded; this also occurs in 23,1 (see note below) and in DB Dorset 11,12. It is an unreliable method of determining the estimate, however, as in Devon the plough-teams detailed regularly do not total the estimate; see General Notes 1,3 (fourth note). For the other major additions in Devon by the Exchequer scribe, see notes to 3,54 and 23,1 and cf. notes to 3,70. 17,71. 34,11 and 36,9. There are only about 25 such additions in those parts of the five south-western counties for which Exon. survives; see last note under Dorset Exon. Notes B 4 for the Dorset 'additions'. |
| 3,54 | 1 VILLAGER AND 2 SLAVES. No mention is made in Exon. of the villager or 2 slaves, but after the lordship details appears the information "on another furlong (*ferlino*) lives a slave", the other furlong being 'needed' to make up to the tax total of ½ virgate. See 3,51 note. |
| 3,57 | 1 VILLAGER (WITH) 1 FURLONG. *uitt i ferlinū*; *uitt* could abbreviate either the singular *uillanus*, referring only to the 1 villager, or the plural *uillani*, referring to both the villager and the slave recorded after this statement. See notes to 16,145-146. 17,58. 19,9 and 35,5. |
| 3,59 | VALUE .... 5s. "Value 6s". |
| 3,63 | 2 SMALLHOLDERS WITH 1 PLOUGH AND ½ VIRGATE. The smallholders are termed *uillani* "villagers" when their plough and land are stated after the lordship details; see also for 15,31. 16,50;90;100. 17,26;38;40;77;79;90. 19,9. 20,5;17. 23,23. 25,17. 34,33;35;44. 35,8. 36,3. 40,1;3. 45,2. 50,5. 52,1;5. In the case of the entry for 45,2 the statement about the lordship and villagers' ploughs appears after, rather than in its usual place before, the inhabitants of the village are detailed, so there would be no excuse for the Exon. scribe to term them *uillani* in temporary ignorance of whether there were any villagers on the manor. In fact the term *uillani* is being used generically here, including the smallholders as well as the 'villagers' proper (see 1,26 note). However, in some entries where only smallholders — or smallholders and slaves — are recorded, the scribe has *bordarii* in place of *uillani* when their land and ploughs are given; see DB Dorset Exon. Notes 12,16 and the Introduction to the Exon. Notes in the Somerset volume (p. 310). See 20,6 note below for a different formula. |
| 3,64 | PASTURE, 20 ACRES. "Pasture, 30 acres". |
| 3,68 | VALUE NOW 20s. In the Exon. MS *.x. sol'* with a further *.x.* interlined above to make the value *.xx. sol'*. It is interesting that in the DB MS the present value has also been corrected from *x* to *xx solid'*. See also 2,24 note and General Notes 28,10 and 32,10. |
| 3,70 | IN LORDSHIP 1 PLOUGH. The plough is omitted from the lordship. The Exchequer scribe could not, as possibly in 3,51 (see note), have deduced its existence from the plough estimate. It is possible, however, that the Exchequer scribe may have included the lordship plough in error; see General Notes here. |
| 3,71 | 1 HIDE .... BEFORE 1066. "The Bishop has 1 hide of land which Wulfnoth held in 1066". Details of this hide appear on a separate line, preceded by a 'gallows' sign, so it is not clear whether the hide had anything to do with Up Exe in the preceding entry. |
| | VALUE OF THE WHOLE, 30s. "Value of this hide, 30s a year". |
| 3,72 | (LOWER) CREEDY. In the T.O. at 506 a 11: "The Bishop of Coutances has a manor called (Lower) Creedy which Goda held jointly in 1066. Value 5s". See the reference to this entry in the section on the T.O. in the Introduction to these Notes. |
| | (CRUWYS) MORCHARD. "The manor called (Cruwys) Morchard". |
| 3,73 | IN LORDSHIP 1 PLOUGH. The last 3 lines on folio 132b, which form 132 b 4 up as far as the lordship details, have had gall applied to them because the ink appears to have faded. Most of what Ellis read can still be deciphered. The lordship plough (and probably ½ virgate to make up to the total of 1 virgate and 1 furlong ('ferling') tax) cannot be read. |
| 3,76 | COOMBE. "a manor called Coombe". In the T.O. at 502 a 1: "The Bishop of Coutances |

Exon. 3 - 5

|         | has a manor called *Cheluerstesberia* which Alwin held. 1 virgate of land and 1 furlong (*ferdinus*) have been added to it. A thane held this land jointly in 1066. It lies waste"; Coombe is not named, see notes to 5,2 and 7,4 for similar omissions in the T.O. |
|---------|---|
| 3,78    | 1 PLOUGH, WHICH IS THERE. "He (Drogo) has 1 plough"; *in dominio* probably implied, or omitted in error. |
| 3,79    | 1 PLOUGH .... 1 VILLAGER AND 1 SLAVE. "The villagers (have) .... ½ plough. Drogo has 1 villager and 1 slave". (Drogo has the other ½ plough; see the Lordship and Villagers' Table.) By the use of the plural *uillani* the scribe may intentionally be including the slave with the villager as having a share in the land and the ½ plough (see General Notes 1,3 on the slave), using the term *uillani* generically. Or he may have used the plural inadvertently as a stock phrase (as apparently in the entry corresponding to DB Somerset 21,62; see Exon. Notes there). See notes to 5,9. 28,16 and 34,56 and cf. notes to 16,6. 16,145-146. 19,9 and 35,5. |
| 3,80    | MIDDLEWICK. Abbreviated details of the addition of this manor appear in the T.O. at 506 a 12, which also states that Middlewick does not belong (*pertinet*; perhaps a mistake for the past *pertinuit*) to the above manor. |
| 3,84    | 3 MEN (HAVE) ½.... After the lordship virgate and plough are given, is written 7 *uillani dim̄*; the *dim̄* probably refers to ½ plough, carr̄ being the last mentioned noun. The Exchequer scribe was obviously unsure what the *dim̄* described (*dim̄ hid'* − ½ hide − is a possibility and would add up to the 3 virgates tax), so omitted it altogether, although villagers' ploughs are normally given. No villagers are mentioned in the detail, only the 3 men. |
| 3,86    | VILLAGERS.... "14 villagers there....", rather than the usual formula "*X* (holder) has *y* villagers, *z* smallholders etc.". See 34,46;57. 52,9;48 notes for a similar, unusual formula. |
|         | 4 PLOUGHS. "4½ ploughs"; the 7 *dimid'* is on the next line, perhaps the reason for the discrepancy. Cf. notes to 17,69 and 34,25. |
| 3,87-88 | SHE ALSO.. ."Engelbald's wife", for each entry. |
| 3,90    | OSGOT. Exon. *Ansgottus* 'Ansgot'; see **General Notes** here. |
| 3,91    | IN LORDSHIP.... Unusually it is the Bishop, rather than his subtenant, who has the land and ploughs in lordship in this entry; possibly a scribal error, but see the similar tenure in DB Dorset Exon. Notes 55,32. Cf. 19,36 where the lordship of the manor is held by a villager and Dorset Exon. Notes 47,10 where it is held by the 1066 tenants. |
| 3,92    | FROM THIS HIDE .... 10s. Also in the T.O. at 500 a 1, an entry written almost entirely in the right margin and by a different scribe to those entries around it. The value is only given there, not in the main Exon. entry; cf. fourth and last notes under 1,4 and 42,12 note for other examples of the value of a sub-holding only being given in the T.O. entry. |
| 3,94    | ALWIN. "Alwin the Steward (*dapifer*) held it from Alwin; he could not be separated from him in 1066". Other examples of the Exchequer scribe 'pruning out' TRE subtenants occurs in Devon in 15,33 (see note below), 15,39 and 24,24 and cf. General Notes 17,33 and, for the excision of lower levels of 1086 subtenancies, General Notes 3,70 and 35,10. Cf. also General Notes 3,80. |
| 3,98    | SAEWIN HELD IT. "....he could go to whichever lord he would", added after the plough estimate, presumably referring to Saewin and briefly omitted, the misplacement perhaps accounting for its not being in DB. |
| Ch. 4   | LAND OF GLASTONBURY CHURCH. Entered in Exon. under the heading of "Land of the Abbot of Glastonbury in Devonshire". His lands in Somerset follow this one entry without a proper heading (only a marginal *In Sumerseta* level with the first line of the first Somerset entry, 161 a 2). Among the summaries of Glastonbury Abbey lands in Wiltshire, Dorset and Somerset appears an account of its one holding in Devon (527 b 7): "Glastonbury Church has one manor of 6 hides in Devonshire. On them 2 ploughs in lordship and 6 villagers and 4 smallholders and 4 slaves who have 5 ploughs. This land is assessed (*appreciata est*) at £4. This land is enough for 7 ploughs". The scribe of this summary is not the same as the scribe of the main entry. |
| 4,1     | GLASTONBURY CHURCH HOLDS. "The Abbot of Glastonbury has". He was called Thurstan; see Knowles HRH p. 51 and General Notes Ch. 4. |
|         | VALUE FORMERLY AND NOW £4. "Value £4 a year; value when he acquired it, as much". So Exon. MS; Ellis misprints *iii lib'*. |
| Ch. 5   | LAND OF THE CHURCH OF TAVISTOCK. Entered in Exon. under the heading of "Lands of the Abbot of Tavistock Church in Devonshire", with "The Abbot of Tavistock" for DB's "Tavistock Church" in 5,1-2 and "Abbot Geoffrey has" for 5,7, and elsewhere |

## Exon. 5

in the chapter "The Abbot has" for DB's "The Church holds". Geoffrey was abbot *c*. 1082-1088; Knowles HRH p. 72. The folio on which the Abbot of Tavistock's fief begins has for some reason two numbers, 176 and 177, written on it by Ralph Barnes in 1816. The next folio is numbered 178. Ellis printed only the number 177 and this edition follows his numbering.

5,1 SERVES THE COURT. "serves the Abbey".
OF THIS MANOR'S LAND.... "Of these 3½ hides six men-at-arms hold 1½ hides....". Details of the individual holdings are then given; see Details Table.
4 PLOUGHS. The details total 3 ploughs and 9 oxen. See General Notes 3,44.
VALUE OF THE WHOLE, TO THE ABBOT....TO THE MEN-AT-ARMS. "Value of this manor for the Abbot's use....for the men-at-arms' use".
VALUE FORMERLY £22, IN TOTAL. "Value when the Abbot acquired it £14; value when the men-at-arms acquired it £8".

5,2 FORMERLY. "when the Abbot acquired it" on both occasions and also for the past values of 5,3;6-7;12-14.
WITH THIS MANOR .... 60s. In the T.O. at 495 b 2: "The Abbot of Tavistock has ½ hide of land with the manor called Milton (Abbot), which did not belong to it before 1066, which two thanes held jointly. 15 ploughs can plough it. Value £6 a year". Rather surprisingly, the names of the added lands are not mentioned in the T.O.; cf. notes to 3,76 and 7,4.
TWO THANES HELD THEM....AS TWO MANORS. "two thanes held jointly"; so also in 495 b 2.
VALUE NOW 60s. "Value £6 a year" in 495 b 2.

5,3
5,4 GEOFFREY HOLDS LIDDATON. ".... and it is (part) of the Abbot's lordship".
OF THIS MANOR'S LAND. In this entry for some reason the details of the subtenancies are given after the lordship and villagers' land and ploughs and before the rest of the details of population and resources.
WALTER, 3 VIRGATES. "Walter has ½ hide and ½ virgate there"; this then adds up with the remainder of the subtenancies, the lordship and villagers' land, to 3 hides as in the tax.
4 SMALLHOLDERS. 6 smallholders; see the Details Table.
MILL .... ON GEOFFREY'S LAND. On Walter's land, a simple mistake by the Exchequer scribe: details of Geoffrey's holding succeed those of Walter.
VALUE....TO THE ABBOT....TO THE MEN-AT-ARMS. "Value for the Abbot's use....for the men-at-arms' use".
VALUE FORMERLY. "value when the Abbot acquired it £4; value when the Abbot acquired the land of the men-at-arms, 40s". This does not agree with the DB total of £9. In the Exon. MS the *iiii lib'* has an unusual dot between the first two minim strokes (perhaps *.iii.* corrected to *iiii* and the dot is the original one not erased), which at a quick glance could perhaps be taken for a *v*, making *vii lib'*, which could explain the discrepancy. Baring p. 316 states that that *vii* was corrected to *iiii*, but the first two minims were definitely never a *v*.

5,5 VALUE....LESS. As there is a dot after *min'* it would seem that the scribe did not intend later to fill in the amount by which the value of the manor had increased since the Abbot acquired it.
BETWEEN THE DETAILS of the manors of Thornbury (DB 5,5) and Abbotsham (DB 5,6) there appears in Exon. 178 b 2 details of another manor, Werrington, written by the same scribe as the preceding entry, but not included by the Exchequer scribe in DB, possibly because the Abbot had subsequently lost Werrington (see 1,50) or because the DB scribe intended to add the information at the end of the chapter where details of disputed manors often appear (e.g. in Cornwall 3,7). The entry runs:
"The Abbot of Tavistock was in possession of the manor called WERRINGTON on the day on which King William sent his barons to inquire into the lands of England; his predecessor before him had been in possession of it. He was dispossessed (*disaisit'* in the MS; Ellis misprints *desaisit'*) of it through the King's barons because the English testified that it did not belong to the Abbey in 1066".
The Abbot of Tavistock was Sihtric (*c*. 1043-1082; Knowles HRH p. 72) and his predecessor was Aldred (1027-1042/3; see General Notes 5,12). There is no record of this dispute over ownership in the T.O., perhaps because judgement had already been given in favour of the King before the T.O. were compiled; cf. 3,32 note and General Notes 2,2 on Newton St. Cyres. The Abbot of Tavistock appealed against the DB Commissioners' decision and in 1096 Werrington and its lands were restored to the Abbey; see Mon. Ang. ii p. 497 (= *Regesta* i no. 378 p. 97). See General Notes 1,50 on Werrington.

Exon. 5 -7

| | |
|---|---|
| 5,6 | BEFORE 1066 IT PAID TAX. "it paid tax" only; the usual formula "on the day on which King Edward was alive and dead" or, as often in this fief, "in King Edward's time" was probably omitted in error. See also notes to 2,24 and 19,18. |
| 5,8 | BURRINGTON. "which Abbot Sihtric held in 1066"; see two notes above. He is mentioned several times in DB Cornwall. |
| | TAX FOR 3 HIDES. So Exon. MS; Ellis misprints *iiii hidis*. |
| | WOODLAND, 60 ACRES. *lx agros nemoris & nemusculi*; the scribe may possibly have omitted the dimensions of the underwood in error or through lack of information, but it is far more likely that the 60 acres refer to both the woodland and the underwood (so VCH p. 431), as also in 17,21 (see note). Several times in Somerset the Exchequer scribe has combined details of underwood and woodland in Exon. under the one word 'woodland' (see Somerset Exon. Notes to 2,7. 5,54. 8,20 etc.). |
| | 9 CATTLE. So the Exon. MS clearly; Ellis misprints '8 cattle'. |
| | FORMERLY 100s; VALUE NOW £7. "It pays £7; value when he acquired it, 100s". |
| | TWO LANDS .... ABBOT. Abbreviated details of these 2 added manors also appear in the T.O. at 497 b 6 with the addition that they did not belong to the said manor (of Burrington) before 1066. |
| | WHICH TWO THANES HELD AS TWO MANORS. "land of two thanes who held jointly", as also in 497 b 6. |
| 5,9 | WILLIAM THE USHER. So 500 a 3; plain William in the main Exon. entry. Another part of Raddon is held by William the Usher among lands he has exchanged (51,6). |
| | RADDON. In the T.O. at 500 a 3: "The Abbot of Tavistock has a manor called Raddon, which a thane held jointly in 1066. It did not belong to the Abbey before 1066. William the Usher holds it from the Abbot. Value 10s a year". |
| | 1 VILLAGER WITH ½ PLOUGH AND 1 FURLONG AND 1 SLAVE. "The villagers (have) 1 furlong *(ferdinum)* and ½ plough"; *uillan[i]* is written in full (there is an erasure immediately after this, so that the last *i* is malformed), implying perhaps that the slave as well as the villager had the land and plough. See notes to 3,79. 28,16 and 34,56 and cf. notes to 3,57. 16,6;145-146. 17,58. 19,9 and 35,5 and General Notes 1,3 on slaves. |
| 5,10 | LAND FOR 1 PLOUGH. "10 ploughs can plough it". |
| | VILLAGERS....5 PLOUGHS. "3 ploughs"; see Details Table. |
| | WOODLAND, 38 ACRES. The details total 39 acres; see Details Table. |
| 5,15 | USED TO PAY THE KING 8d IN CUSTOMARY DUES. "used to pay the King's customary dues, that is 8d". In the T.O. at 506 a 7: "before 1066 it paid 8d in customary dues, which he keeps back". |
| Ch. 6 | LAND OF THE CHURCH OF BUCKFAST. Entered in Exon. under the heading of "Lands of the Abbot of Buckfast Church in Devonshire" with "The Abbot has" for DB's "Buckfast Church holds" and for "The Church holds" throughout the chapter. |
| 6,1 | PETROCKSTOWE. "which Abbot Alwin held in 1066". |
| | FORMERLY. "when he acquired it", most probably referring to the Abbot (see notes to 2,14 and 16,88), as also for the past value of 6,2;5; "when the Abbot acquired it" for the past value of 6,7;9-12. |
| 6,3 | LAND FOR 8 PLOUGHS. So the Exon. MS; Ellis misprints *vii carr̄*. |
| 6,4 | UNDERWOOD, 7 FURLONGS. "8 furlongs", possibly corrected from *vii*, though the ink is dark on the last minims and it is impossible to see an original dot under the last one. |
| 6,7-12 | '(ABBOTS) ASH'. HEATHFIELD. NORTON. CHARFORD. (SOUTH) BRENT. (SOUTH) BRENT. "which Abbot Alwin held in 1066" for each manor. |
| 6,12 | MEADOW, 2 ACRES. *ii agros* only, *prati* being omitted but probably intended as it is normally listed between the woodland and pasture. See 1,46 note. It is possible, though less likely, that the Exon. scribe meant the pasture to measure "2 acres and 1 league in length and ½ (league) in width". (But see 3,24 where pasture is measured in leagues and acres.) |
| 6,13 | BUCKFAST .... ABBEY. "The Abbot has a manor called Buckfast; it is the head of the Abbey". |
| Ch. 7 | LAND OF THE CHURCH OF HORTON. Entered in Exon. under the heading of "Land of the Abbot of Horton in Devonshire", with "The Abbot has" for DB's "Horton Church holds" and for "The Church holds" throughout the chapter. |
| 7,1 | IN LORDSHIP 1 VIRGATE. "½ virgate", written *dim̄ lurgam*; the unusual tall half of the *v*(?) of *virgam* — probably a scribal error — may have been the cause of the discrepancy. |
| 7,3-4 | SEATON. BEER. "which he (Abbot) held himself in 1066" for each entry. |

7,3 SALT-HOUSES. *salinarias*, accusative after "the Abbot has", from *salinaria* 'salt-house' (RMLWL s.v. *sal*). The Exchequer DB word for 'salt-house' is *salina*, which is the form used elsewhere in the Exon. for Devon, including in the next entry which is by the same scribe as this one. Finn in DGSW p. 271 and note 2 seems to have read *salinarios* 'salt-workers' here, unless he thought *salinaria* was a female salt-worker.

7,4 6 VILLAGERS. "7 villagers", the last minim stroke of the *vii* being written on greasy parchment and so not completely there, probably the reason for the discrepancy (cf. 15,23 second note and 31,1 first note). The Exchequer scribe may also have concentrated on the interlined *uitt* (which is in very pale ink) and not paid enough attention to the number.
VALUE 60s. "Value £4 a year". Finn ('Immediate Sources' p. 58 and MDeD p. 116) states that the last *i* of the *iiii* is obviously postscriptal; there is no sign of this in the Exon. MS, all the minims being in the same colour ink. It is just possible that *iii lib'* was corrected to *iiii lib'* by the addition of a first *i*, as there is no dot before the number (if corrected, it is probably under the first *i*), although this scribe regularly omits the first dot after *annum*.
FROM THIS MANOR .... MORTAIN. Also in the T.O. in full at 503 b 2, although the manor is not named as Beer, merely being called "a manor of the Abbot of Horton"; cf. notes to 3,76 and 5,2.

Chs. 8-13a THESE HOLDINGS appear in Exon. under the heading of "Lands of the Churches which have been given to the Saints in Alms", folios 194a-196 a 1 inclusive; 'Devon' is not mentioned, although 'Somerset' is included in the similar heading dealing with DB Somerset Chs. 11-13;15-16. The Exon. section is arranged by Hundreds, not by fiefs as in DB; see General Notes here. In Exon., with the exception of 13a,1;3, the King is not mentioned as the person from whom the lands were held, as on some occasions in these DB chapters. See 51,14 second note.

8,1 CRANBORNE CHURCH. "The Abbot of Cranborne Church". He was called Gerald; Knowles HRH p. 87.

9,1-2 CHURCH OF BATTLE. THE CHURCH ITSELF. "The Abbot of Battle", similarly in the T.O. entry (505 b 8) referring to 9,2. He came from Marmoutier (see General Notes Ch. 9), was called Gausbert and was abbot *c*. 1076-1095; Knowles HRH p. 29.

9,1 THE CHURCH OF CULLOMPTON. "1 church in Cullompton".

9,2 WHICH PAID 4s 8d. In the T.O. at 505 b 8: "which paid 4s 8d a year in customary dues before 1066" with "but he has kept them back" interlined (though not later nor by a different scribe).
1 HOUSE .... DUES. In 505 b 8: "1 house exempt (*quietam*)".

10,1 ST. MARY'S CHURCH, ROUEN....THE CHURCH ITSELF HELD. "The Canons of St. Mary's of Rouen....which they had themselves".
A GARDEN .... ST. MICHAEL'S LAND. This is added in the right margin of the Exon. MS with a sign beside it corresponding to one above *Otri*. The verb is *reddi* which normally abbreviates the plural *reddunt* but this would mean that the garden and the salt-house (both) paid 30d "in the land of St. Michael of Sidmouth (*in terram sancti michahelis de sedemuda*)". See 3,45 note.

10,2 THE CHURCH ITSELF HOLDS...TO ST. MARY'S. "The canons also hold....to the canons themselves".

11,1 CHURCH OF MONT ST. MICHEL. "The Abbot of Mont St. Michel" and "The Abbot of St. Michel's has" for DB's "The Church holds" in 11,2.

11,2 VALUE FORMERLY AND NOW 40s. "It paid 40s a year; when he acquired it, it paid as much".

11,3 THE CHURCH ITSELF HOLDS. "St. Michel's has", but "The Abbot of St. Michel's" as holder of the lordship land, etc.
11 PLOUGHS. "10 ploughs".
PIGMAN. In this entry he occurs after the mill render, rather than in the usual Exon. position after the villagers, smallholders and slaves.
MILL WHICH PAYS 6s. "mill whose value is 6s a year".
VALUE FORMERLY AND NOW 60s. "It paid 60s a year; when he acquired it, it paid as much".

12,1 ST. STEPHEN'S CHURCH, CAEN, HOLDS. "The Abbot of Caen has .... now the Abbot of St. Stephen's holds it in alms, by gift of the Queen".
345(?) SHEEP. *cccxl oues 7v*; see 2,4 note on the splitting of numbers with *c*, *cc*, etc. It is possible, however, that *capras* 'goats' is omitted in error after the *v*. OJR in VCH

| | |
|---|---|
| 12,1 (cont'd.) | p. 434 translates '345 sheep', though he translates differently the similar phrase in 117 a 3 (2,4, see note), an entry by the same scribe as this one.<br>VALUE FORMERLY AND NOW £12. "It pays £12 a year; value when the Abbot acquired it, as much". |
| 13,1 | HOLY TRINITY CHURCH, CAEN, HOLDS. "The Abbess of Holy Trinity, Caen, has". She was called Matilda and held that office until 1113 when she was succeeded by King William's daughter Cecilia; see Chibnall's edition of Orderic Vitalis vol. ii p. 130 note 1.<br>FORMERLY. "value when the Abbess acquired it". |
| 13a,1 | SOUTH MOLTON. "South Molton, the King's manor". |
| 13a,2 | SAEWIN THE PRIEST. "Saewin, the Queen's priest".<br>SWIMBRIDGE. In the T.O. at 498 a 7: "Saewin the priest has a manor called Swimbridge which an uncle of his held who could go with his land to whichever lord he would in 1066. Value 10s a year. Queen M(atilda) gave it to this priest in alms". The fact that this is in the T.O. implies that there was some illegality or dispute over the tenure. As it comes immediately after two entries in which the only hint of wrongdoing seems to lie in the fact that they had been held TRE by free men (see 24,28-29 notes), it might appear that Saewin ought not to have been in possession of the land, though one would have thought that the Queen's gift of it to him would have quelled any claims. Cf. notes to 1,11 ('½ hide .... 20s'). 2,2;15 and 42,10.<br>BRICTFERTH HIS UNCLE HELD IT. "....jointly; he could go to whichever lord he would", interlined in slightly paler ink but probably at the time of writing the rest of the entry; cf. the similar addition to 2,10, an entry by the same Exon. scribe (see note).<br>FORMERLY. "when S(aewin) acquired it".<br>QUEEN M(ATILDA) .... IN ALMS. So also in 498 a 7. |
| 13a,3 | BRAUNTON. "Braunton, the King's manor". |
| 14,1-4 | VALUE FORMERLY. "value when the Earl acquired it" for each entry. |
| 14,2 | ANSTEY. "another manor (aliam mansionem) called Anstey".<br>8 VILLAGERS .... 2 PLOUGHS. "The Earl has on it 8 villagers and they have 2 ploughs, and (he has) 1 smallholder and 2 slaves". See 1,9 note. |
| 14,3 | ALNOTH HELD IT. "which Ednoth held". The DB form Alnod(us) and the Exon. Ednod(us) probably represent different personal names, OE Alnoth and Eadnoth; but both might represent the same OE personal name Ealdnoth (see PNDB s.nn.). OE Eald- might drop l (PNDB §64) or d (PNDB §103) to produce spellings Al(d)-, Ad-, El(d)-, Ed-. So this man's name could well be Aldnoth. Cf. General Notes 15,12 on Edmer Ator. It is interesting that in DB Dorset both 'Alnoth' and 'Ednoth' are numbered among the predecessors of Earl Hugh in his lands in that county; see Dorset General Notes 27,1-2 and General Notes 14,1 here. |
| Ch. 15 | THE COUNT OF MORTAIN. He is called "Robert, Count of Mortain" for 15,39 and Comes R. for 15,40. |
| 15,3 | FORMERLY. "when the Count acquired it"; as also for the past value of 15,4-5;8-22; 26-30;32-33;35-45;47-52;54-57;59;64-77;79. |
| 15,4 | LAND FOR 4 PLOUGHS. "8 ploughs".<br>VILLAGERS....8 PLOUGHS. "villagers....4 ploughs". See the General Notes here for the probable reason for these two discrepancies. |
| 15,7 | FROM THE COUNT. de consule, an unusual term. Cf. 16,159;165 below where Baldwin the Sheriff, usually styled vicecomes, is called viceconsul. |
| 15,11 | CULLEIGH .... KIPPING HELD IT. "Culleigh which Kipping held jointly in 1066 and the men of the Count of Mortain hold it as of the Honour (tenent ad honorem) of Ordwulf, but that thane could go to whichever lord he would without Ordwulf's permission .... Now Erchenbald holds it from the Count". Abbreviated details of this manor also occur in the T.O. at 497 a 6 where Kipping is not named but called a thane who held jointly, and which states that before 1066 the virgate "did not belong to the lands of Ordwulf which the Count holds". Although Kipping was a free man, not bound to Ordwulf, his land nevertheless was passed to the Count as part of Ordwulf's holding which had been legally transferred to the Count; see General Notes 15,31 on this apparently wrongful method of acquiring lands.<br>4 SMALLHOLDERS. "3 smallholders". |
| 15,12 | BUCKLAND (BREWER). The Exon. extract at the front of this edition is of this entry.<br>3 PIGMEN. Probably omitted by the DB scribe because they were interlined before the slaves rather than in their usual place after them. The scribe appears to be the same as for the rest of the entry, so it is unlikely that the interlineation was done after the Exchequer scribe had seen and used Exon. Cf. General Notes 16,23. |

# Exon. 15

| | |
|---|---|
| 15,12 (cont'd.) | GALSWORTHY. Described as a manor; Ansger holds it too. In the T.O. at 497 a 8: "The Count of Mortain has a manor called Buckland (Brewer). ½ virgate of land has been joined to it, called Galsworthy .... it did not belong to the above (*predictae*) manor in 1066....". The Exon. extract given at the front of this edition gives the full T.O. entry. EDWY HELD IT AS ONE MANOR. "which Edwy held in 1066; he could go to whichever lord he would". In 497 a 8 "a thane held it jointly". |
| 15,14 | ANSGER THE BRETON. So 497 b 1; plain Ansger in the main Exon. entry. BULKWORTHY. In the T.O. at 497 b 1: "It did not belong in 1066 to Edmer Ator's lands which the Count holds, and to which this manor has been wrongfully added"; in the MS *iiuste*; Ellis misprints *iiuste*. ERIC HELD IT. "....and he could go with this land to whichever lord he would". In 497 b 1 "which Eric held jointly". IN LORDSHIP 1 PLOUGH. "7 oxen". IN THE T.O. at 506 a 9 is another reference to Bulkworthy: "Robert son of Ivo holds 1 virgate of land – in the manor called Bulkworthy (*Bochesurda*) [interlined] – from the Count of Mortain, which up till now has been concealed, from which he has kept back the tax". It appears after an entry also dealing with land that has been concealed, but, unlike with that entry (= DB 19,6), there is no mention of it either in DB or in the main Exon. The addition to the Exon. for 19,6 of the concealed virgate is a late one by a different scribe (see note there), so it is possible that an addition may have been planned for the main Exon. either for 15,10 or for 15,14 (see General Notes 15,10, second note). Cf. notes to 1,25 (last note);66 and 2,2 above, Ch. 44 note and the last entry in these Notes, on other complete T.O. entries whose information is not to be found either in the main Exon. or in DB. |
| 15,15 | ANSGER THE BRETON. So 497 b 2; plain Ansger in the main Exon. entry. SMYTHAM. In the T.O. at 497 b 2: "It has been wrongfully added to the lands of Edmer Ator, the Count's predecessor, (lands) which the Count holds". AELFRIC HELD IT. "....and he could go with this land to whichever lord he would". In 497 b 2 "which a thane held jointly". |
| 15,16 | LITTLE TORRINGTON. Abbreviated details of this manor, which has been "added to the lands of Edmer Ator", appear in the T.O. at 497 b 3. ALWARD RUFUS....HE COULD GO WHERE HE WOULD. "....he could go with this land to whichever lord he would". In 497 b 3 "which a thane held jointly in 1066", neither his name nor his freedom to choose a lord being mentioned. 1 VILLAGER, 1 SMALLHOLDER....1 PLOUGH. "Alfred has 1 villager who has 1 plough and Alfred has 1 smallholder....". See 1,9 note. |
| 15,17-19 | 'STOCKLEIGH'. 'STOCKLEIGH'. POUGHILL. Abbreviated details of these manors, which "the Count holds with Edmer Ator's lands", appear in the T.O. at 500 a 10, 500 b 2 and 500 b 1 respectively. |
| 15,17-18 | ORDGAR. HADEMAR. "and he was a man of Edmer Ator, but he could go with this land to whichever lord he would" for both Ordgar and Hademar. In 500 a 10 Ordgar "could go with his land to whichever lord he would", and in 500 b 2 Hademar held "jointly". |
| 15,18 | ALFRED THE BUTLER. So the main Exon. entry; plain Alfred in the T.O. entry (500 b 2). |
| 15,19 | ALFRED THE BUTLER ALSO HOLDS POUGHILL. "....as one manor" in the T.O. entry (500 b 1). TWO THANES HELD IT FREELY. "which two thanes held jointly in 1066; they were men of Edmer Ator, but they could go with this land to whichever lord they would". In 500 b 1 "which two thanes held jointly in 1066". |
| 15,20-22 | HOLBROOK. FARRINGDON. ROCKBEARE. Abbreviated details of these manors, which "the Count holds with the Honour of Edmer Ator", appear in the T.O. at 501 a 2, 501 a 1 and 501 a 3 respectively. |
| 15,20 | SAEMER HELD IT. "....jointly....he could go to whichever lord he would". In the T.O. entry (501 a 2): "which Saemer held who could go with his land to whichever lord he would". AT THE END OF THIS ENTRY in Exon. is written "The Count holds these said three manors with the Honour of Edmer Ator; the holders were men of Edmer Ator". The three manors are the 'double' manor of Farringdon (15,21) and Holbrook (15,20). See 15,31 note. |
| 15,21 | BRETEL ALSO. "Bretel", with no *idem*, so not necessarily the same man as the holder |

Exon. 15

| | |
|---|---|
| 15,21 (cont'd.) | of 15,20 which is what DB implies. Exchequer DB very often has *idem* after the 1086 subtenant in second and subsequent holdings by a person of the same name, whereas Exon. rarely does; in most cases this is probably because the Exchequer scribe rearranged lands in large fiefs under subtenants excerpting them from the Hundred order in which they appeared in Exon. It is to be assumed that before putting *idem* after a person's name the DB scribe had established that all mentions of the name were of the same person, i.e. that the Bretel who held this manor was the same as the Bretel who held 15,20. For other instances of the addition of *idem* in DB, see notes below to 15,27-30;60. 16,66. 17,72;84;92;98. 19,22. 22,2. 23,11. 36,4-6. 52,2;13;21;23 and cf. 15,40 note.<br>TWO BROTHERS HELD IT. "....jointly....they could go with this land to whichever lord they would". See 15,20 second note. In the T.O. entry (501 a 1): "which two brothers held jointly".<br>1 PLOUGH THERE. "Bretel has 1 plough"; *in dominio* probably implied or omitted in error. |
| 15,22 | ALWARD HOLDS.... "....from the Count"; cf. notes to 15,30;71. 16,127. 17,73-74. 34,57 and 35,25.<br>SAEWIN HELD IT. "....and he was a man of Edmer Ator, but he could go with this land to whichever lord he would". In the T.O. entry (501 a 3): "which Saewin held who could go with his land to whichever lord he would".<br>WOODLAND, 3 ACRES. "4 acres".<br>FORMERLY 12s. "Value when the Count acquired it, 12d". It is hard to tell whether the Exon. or the Exchequer value is the correct one here: there are other instances of dramatic increases in value between 1066 and 1086 (cf. the almost seven-fold increase for Alminstone, 42,3), but the other cases of even larger increases in value in Devon (16,172 and 48,1) are probably the result of scribal error (see General Notes to these). |
| 15,23-25 | HONITON. 'WOMBERFORD'. NORTHLEIGH. Abbreviated details of these manors, which have been added to Edmer Ator's lands, appear in the T.O. at 503 a 6, 503 a 7 and 503 a 8 respectively. |
| 15,23 | AELMER HELD IT. "which Aelmer held freely" in the T.O. entry (503 a 6).<br>MILL WHICH PAYS 6s 6d. "mill which pays 7½s", probably, although the last minim stroke of the *vii* is not completely there, possibly the reason for the discrepancy. Cf. 7,4 (first note) and 31,1 (first note).<br>2 SALT-WORKERS WHO PAY 5s. "....in revenue (*de firma*)". As in DB they are placed after the mill details, not in their usual place with the other 'villagers'.<br>VALUE FORMERLY. "value when he acquired it", probably referring to the Count (see notes to 2,14 and 16,88). Similarly for the past values of 15,24-25;31;34;46;58;60-63;78. |
| 15,24 | WULFWARD HELD IT. "which Wulfward held jointly" in the T.O. entry (503 a 7).<br>MEADOW, 3 ACRES. So Exon. MS; Ellis misprints *iiii agros*. |
| 15,25 | ALWARD HOLDS. In the T.O. entry (503 a 8) Drogo is said to hold "the above 3 manors" from the Count, referring to 15,23-25. Alward may be a subtenant of Drogo here or there may have been a change in subtenant between the compilation of Exon. and the T.O.<br>SAEWIN HELD IT. "which Saewin held jointly" in 503 a 8.<br>VALUE NOW 30s. "value 20s a year". So also in 503 a 8. |
| 15,26-28 | LUDBROOK. LUPRIDGE. HEWIS. Abbreviated details of these manors, which have been added to Edmer Ator's lands, appear in the T.O. at 505 a 4, 505 a 5 and 505 a 7 respectively. |
| 15,26 | COLBERT HELD IT FREELY. "Colbert held this land jointly".<br>MEADOW, 2 ACRES. "½ acre".<br>[VALUE] .... NOW 20s. "25s" in the T.O. entry (505 a 4). |
| 15,27-30 | REGINALD ALSO. "Reginald" with no *idem*, so not necessarily the same man as the 1086 holder of 15,26; see 15,21 note. Similarly plain Reginald for DB's "Reginald also" in 15,37;52-53;65;69-72;79 and 35,21-22. Cf. 15,51 note. |
| 15,27 | EDRIC HELD IT FREELY. "Edric held this land jointly". |
| 15,28 | EDRIC HELD IT. "....and he could go to whichever lord he would". |
| 15,29-31 | HARESTON. WINSTON. DENSHAM. Abbreviated details of these manors appear in the T.O. at 505 a 11, 505 a 12 and 501 a 6 respectively. Hareston "has been added to the lands of Edmer Ator"; Winston "has been added to the lands...." (of Edmer Ator, probably omitted in error because the entry is written partly on the other side of the folio), and the Count holds Densham "with the Honour of Edmer Ator". |

# Exon. 15

| | |
|---|---|
| 15,29-30 | EDRIC HELD....EDWIN HELD. "....jointly....he could go to whichever lord he would" for both Edric and Edwin. |
| 15,30 | REGINALD....HOLDS. "....from the Count"; see 15,22 note. |
| | VALUE NOW 8s. So main entry, but "Value 10s" in the T.O. entry (505 a 12). |
| 15,31 | AETHELMER HELD IT. "which Aethelmer held who could go with his land to whichever lord he would" in the T.O. entry (501 a 6). |
| | COUNT.... HOLDS THE ABOVE 17 LANDS WITH EDMER ATOR'S LANDS.... THANES HELD THEM FREELY. This information is given in Exon. under the individual manors, 18 of them not 17 (= DB 15,14-31 inclusive). At the end of each of the entries corresponding to 15,14-16;22;28 is written "The Count holds this land with the Honour of Edmer Ator (*cum honore Edmeratorii*)" and at the end of the entries for 15,19 and 15,20 is the statement "The Count holds these 3 manors with the Honour of Edmer Ator" referring to 15,17-19 and 15,20-21 respectively (see 15,20 note on the '3' manors). At the end of the entry for 15,23 is written "This manor was free in 1066; now it has been added to Edmer Ator's land" and after the entry for 15,25 "These 2 manors [15,24-25] were free (*fuerunt liberate**) in 1066; now they have been added to Edmer Ator's land". At the end of the entries for 15,26-27 is written "Now it has been added to Edmer Ator's Honour (which the Count holds)". For 15,29-31 the phrase "This (manor/land) has been joined with the Honour of Edmer Ator" appears, at the end except for 15,31. |

The 'freedom' of the thanes who held these lands TRE is also expressed in Exon. under the individual holdings; see notes to these TRE tenants in 15,14-22;28. In the entries for 15,26-27 they are said to have held 'jointly', but this seems to have meant more or less the same as 'freely' (see General Notes 1,15), and for 15,23-25 see the quotations above. See 15,14-31 notes above for the T.O. treatment of this statement. The fact that reference is made to all these manors in the T.O. is further proof that these 'additions' of lands were considered illegal; see General Notes 15,31. Cf. first note under 15,47 below.

\* The use of the past participle *liberate* 'freed' (agreeing with *mansiones*) is unusual: either it is a mistake for the adjective *liberae*, used by the same scribe for 15,23, or, like *uasta/uastata* (see General Notes C 3), there was no real difference in meaning between the two forms, or the scribe meant to convey that at some time in the past these manors were tied, but that they had been freed in 1066 (and were now illegally added to Edmer's lands). The fact that the scribe originally wrote *liba* (= *libera*) and corrected it to *liberate* by interlining *te* suggests that there was some significance in the use of the past participle.

| | |
|---|---|
| 15,33 | EDMER HELD IT. "Aelmer (*Almarus*) Rufus ['the red'] held from Edmer Ator; he could not separate (himself) from him with this land". Edmer and Aelmer are on the face of it different names – OE *Eadmaer* and *Almaer* (*AEthel-, Ealh-, Eald-*), perhaps kin-linked in -*maer*; but the complicated possibilities of *eald-, ald-* before *m* might yield one common personal name *Eald-maer*; cf. Alnoth/Ednoth in 14,3. (JMcND). It is possible, meanwhile, that the Exchequer scribe made a mistake in the name of the subtenant, getting the 'Edmer' from the 1066 tenant-in-chief. However, it is more likely either that it was decided that TRE subtenants were not worth mentioning and so not included in the Exchequer DB (cf. notes to 3,94 and 24,24 and see 15,39 and 17,33), or that it was discovered that Aelmer Rufus did not in fact hold from Edmer Ator. On the omission of Edmer's byname in DB, see the third note under General Notes 15,12. |
| | 2 PLOUGHS....THERE. 2 ploughs and 2 oxen; see Lordship and Villagers' Table. See General Notes to 3,37 and 3,44. |
| 15,36 | 8 SMALLHOLDERS. So Exon. MS; Ellis misprints *vii*, perhaps because the last minim stroke is very close to the edge of the parchment. |
| 15,37 | REGINALD ALSO. "Reginald"; see 15,27-30 note. |
| | ½ PLOUGH. "4 oxen". |
| 15,38 | BUCKLAND. Abbreviated details of this added manor appear in the T.O. at 505 a 6. |
| | EDEVA HELD IT FREELY. "which Edeva held jointly.... she could go to whichever lord she would". In 505 a 6 just "which Edeva held jointly". |
| | 1½ PLOUGHS, WHICH ARE THERE. Although the plough estimate is 1½ in both DB and Exon., only 1 plough is recorded in Exon. as actually on the land and that is had by the villagers and smallholders. The reason for the discrepancy can probably be found by looking at the Exchequer MS: the scribe originally wrote $Tra\ \bar{e}\ .i.\ ca\bar{r}\ \bar{q}\ ibi\ \bar{e}$, then, perhaps as a result of checking the Exon. MS, he interlined *7 dimid'*, but without altering |

Exon. 15

|       | the second half of the phrase. However, it is possible, though less likely, that he received other information on the number of ploughs on the land. |
|-------|---|
| 15,40 | HE ALSO. "Erchenbald", probably, but not necessarily, the same man as the subtenant of 15,39, as DB implies. Cf. 15,21 note. |
|       | THREE LANDS. Abbreviated details of these three manors appear in the T.O. at 499 a 3. |
|       | THREE THANES HELD FREELY. "which three thanes held jointly; they could go to whichever lord they would". In 499 a 3 just "which 3 thanes held jointly". |
|       | THEY PAID TAX.... "These three manors paid tax....". |
|       | 5 VILLAGERS AND 3 SLAVES HAVE 5 PLOUGHS. "E(rchenbald) has 5 villagers who have 5 ploughs there, and (he has) 3 slaves". DB implies that the slaves had a share in the ploughs; see General Notes 1,3 on the slave and cf. 15,59 note below. |
|       | VALUE 22s. "Value of these three manors 21s 8d". In 499 a 3 "Value 20s 8d a year". |
| 15,44 | A SALT-HOUSE WHICH PAYS 30d. "a salt-house whose value is 30d a year". |
| 15,47 | COUNT HOLDS .... WITH ORDWULF'S LAND. As with the lands added to Edmer Ator's Honour (see 15,31 note), Exon. gives the information on these added lands (15,47-53) generally at the end of each individual entry. For 15,47-48 the phrase is "The Count holds this (land) with the Honour of Ordwulf (*cum honore Ordulfi*)"; for 15,49 see the addition in small type to the translation; for 15,50-52 the phrase is "It has been joined with the Honour of Ordwulf". For 15,53 a fuller statement occurs, again at the end, see the addition in small type at the end of the translated entry. See the first entries under 15,47-53 notes below of the treatment of this statement in the T.O. and see General Notes 15,31 for its meaning. |
|       | HELE. Abbreviated details of this manor, which "has been added to Ordwulf's lands which the Count holds", appear in the T.O. at 497 b 4. |
|       | TWO THANES HELD IT FREELY (AND) JOINTLY. "which two thanes held jointly.... they could go with this land to whichever lord they would. Aelmer Eastry (*estrege*; OEB p. 125) held 3 furlongs (*ferlinos*) of it and Frawin held 1 furlong (*ferlinum*). In 497 b 4 "which 2 thanes held jointly". |
| 15,48 | STOCKLEIGH (ENGLISH). Abbreviated details of this manor, which "the Count holds with the Honour of Ordwulf", appear in the T.O. at 500 b 7. |
|       | SAEWULF HELD IT JOINTLY. "and he could go to whichever lord he would". In 500 b 7 "Saewulf who could go with his land to whichever lord he would in 1066". |
| 15,49-50 | MODBURY. TORRIDGE. Abbreviated details of these manors, which have been "added to Ordwulf's lands", appear in the T.O. at 505 a 8 and 505 a 9 respectively. |
|       | WADO HELD IT FREELY (AND) JOINTLY. "which Wado held jointly....he could go to whichever lord he would" for each entry. |
| 15,49 | THIS LAND. "this hide", presumably excluding the virgate. |
|       | VILLAGERS .... ½ HIDE AND 1 VIRGATE .... THERE ALSO .... 1 VIRGATE. "the villagers (have) ½ hide and 1 virgate, which virgate Wado held from Ordwulf; he could not separate (himself) with that virgate from Ordwulf, but with the above hide he could. The villagers have 3 ploughs". Details of the villagers, livestock, woodland and value of the hide follow, with the value of the 1 virgate being entered at the very end after the statement on the Count's wrongful tenure of the hide as part of Ordwulf's Honour (see 15,47 first note). The description of this additional virgate as part of the villagers' land, though held by the TRE tenant and then by the 1086 subtenant, is unusual, but cf. 1,70. |
| 15,50 | WOODLAND. "underwood (*nemusculi*)". |
| 15,51-52 | HARESTON. SPRIDDLESTONE. Abbreviated details of these manors which have been "added to Ordwulf's lands" appear in the T.O. at 505 a 10 and 505 b 1 respectively. |
| 15,51 | HE ALSO. "Reginald", probably, but not necessarily, the same man as the subtenant of 15,50, as no *idem* is used as it is in DB. Cf. 15,27-30 note. |
|       | SWEET HELD IT JOINTLY. ".... and he could go to whichever lord he would". |
| 15,52-53 | REGINALD ALSO. "Reginald", see 15,27-30 note. |
| 15,52 | FOUR THANES HELD IT FREELY (AND) JOINTLY. "which four thanes held jointly ....they could go to whichever lord they would. Each of them held 1 furlong (*ferlinum*)". |
| 15,53 | WEDERIGE. Abbreviated details of the manor called *Wedreriga*, which has been added to Ordwulf's lands, appear in the T.O. at 505 b 5. |
| 15,57 | 3 VIRGATES OF LAND AND ½ FURLONG. "3½ virgates and ½ furlong (*ferdino*, abl.)"; see General Notes here. |
|       | MILL WHICH PAYS 7s 6d. "mill whose value is 7s 6d a year". |
|       | ALWINESTONE. It is described as a manor "which did not belong to this manor before 1066"; Mauger also holds it from the Count. Abbreviated details of this added manor appear in the T.O. at 499 b 2. |

| | |
|---|---|
| 15,57 (cont'd.) | ALWIN HELD IT. "A thane held it jointly".... 499 b 2.<br>MILL WHICH PAYS 8d. "mill whose value is 8d a year". |
| 15,59 | 3 VILLAGERS WITH 1 SLAVE HAVE 1 PLOUGH. "Alfred has 3 villagers and they have 1 plough and (he has) 1 slave....". See General Notes 1,3 on the slave and cf. 15,40 note above. |
| 15,60 | ALFRED ALSO. "Alfred", with no *idem*, so not necessarily the same man as the subtenant of 15,59; see 15,21 note. |
| 15,62 | WOODLAND. "underwood (*nemusculi*)". |
| 15,64 | LAND FOR 23 PLOUGHS. In the Exon. MS the *xxiii* is written over an erasure, with space left between the *xx* and *iii* because part of the original number was (and is) still visible (apparently part of an *x*; not an added *i* to make *xxiiii* as Finn in 'Immediate Sources' p. 58 and in MDeD p. 116).<br>A PIGMAN. Although in Exon. he is listed between the livestock and the meadow and woodland details, he may be classed with the *uillani* who had the ploughs and hides; see 1,26 note. |
| 15,65 | REGINALD ALSO. "Reginald"; see 15,27–30 note.<br>SALT-HOUSE WHICH PAYS 5s. "salt-house whose value is 5s a year". |
| 15,67 | FROM THIS MANOR....STATE. "From this manor the Hundred men (*hundremani*) and the King's reeve claim 30d and the customary dues from the pleas for the benefit of the revenue of the King's manor of Ermington (*consuetudinem placitorum ad opus firme Erm̄tone mansione regis*; *mansione* a scribal error for *mansionis*)". The T.O. entry reads slightly differently: "The Count of Mortain has a manor called Fardel which Godfrey holds from him. Before 1066 it paid 30d in customary dues to the King's manor of Ermington, and other customary dues which belong to the Hundred, but after King William held England these said customary dues were taken away from the King's manor".... 504 a 7. |
| 15,69-72 | REGINALD ALSO. "Reginald", see 15,27–30 note. |
| 15,70 | 4 SMALLHOLDERS. "3 smallholders", an understandable mistake on the part of the Exchequer scribe because of the 4 villagers and 4 slaves. |
| 15,71 | REGINALD .... PEEK. ".... from the Count"; see 15,22 note. |
| 15,77 | OSGOT. Exon. *Ansgot(us)* 'Ansgot'; see General Notes 3,90. |
| 15,78 | WADO. Exon. *Wadel* 'Waddell'; see General Notes 15,49.<br>2 VILLAGERS AND 2 SLAVES (HAVE) 1 VIRGATE. It is the *uillani*, used generically, who have the virgate; the slaves may not be included among them. See General Notes 1,3 on slaves. |
| 15,79 | REGINALD ALSO. "Reginald", see 15,27–30 note.<br>LIPSON. Abbreviated details of this manor, added to Algar's lands, appear in the T.O. at 505 b 4.<br>GODWIN HELD IT FREELY (AND) JOINTLY. "Godwin held jointly" in the left margin; there is no mention of 'freely'. |
| 16,1 | HOLDS FROM THE KING. "has....by King William's gift".<br>WHICH WERE IN....WHICH BELONGED TO. "....in 1066" with both phrases. |
| 16,2 | THEY PAY.... "These burgesses and these destroyed houses pay....". |
| 16,3 | CASTLE....BURGESSES....MARKET. These details are given at the end of the entry, after the account of the rest of Okehampton but before the Value statement.<br>21 VILLAGERS. "31 villagers".<br>VALUE OF THE WHOLE. "Value of this manor with its dependencies (*appenditiis*; Ellis misprints *appenditus*)".<br>WHEN HE ACQUIRED IT. "value when B(aldwin) acquired it". |
| 16,4 | VALUE FORMERLY. "Value when *B*. (*B. uicecomes* for 16,65) acquired it". Similarly for the past values of 16,5–13; 15–17; 19–20; 43–71; 73–74; 76–79; 81–83; 86–87; 89–93; 95–140; 142–144; 152–157; 176. |
| 16,5 | THERE WERE .... 30s. In 495 a 1, the first of the *Terrae Occupatae* entries for Devon, "Baldwin the Sheriff has ½ virgate of land in the manor called Bratton (Clovelly) which 2 thanes .... 7½ ploughs can plough it (½ virgate) ....".<br>FREELY. "jointly; they could go to whichever lord they would with this land". So also in 495 a 1. |
| 16,6 | 7 SLAVES, WITH 1 PLOUGH. "The villagers hold the rest of the land and they have 1 plough. R(olf) has 7 slaves....". No other 'villagers' are mentioned. See General Notes here. |
| 16,7 | WITH THIS MANOR.... In the T.O. at 495 a 2: "Baldwin the Sheriff holds 6 manors in the manor called Bridestowe which 6 thanes held jointly in 1066....". The names of the manors are given; see last note. |

Exon. 16

| | |
|---|---|
| 16,7 (cont'd.) | IT PAID TAX FOR ½ HIDE AND 1½ FURLONGS. "....before 1066". VALUE NOW 60s LESS 20d. In 495 a 2 "£3". SAEWIN TUFT.... ABBOT SIHTRIC. Their lands are named both in the main Exon. entry and in the T.O.: Saewin Tuft held Kersford, Doda held Battishill, Doda held Combebowe, Godwin held Ebsworthy, Godwin held Fernworthy and Abbot Sihtric held Way. "These thanes could go with this land to whichever lord they would" (main entry only). |
| 16,8 | WOODLAND. "underwood (*nemusculi*)". |
| 16,9 | LEWTRENCHARD. In the T.O. at 495 a 3: "Baldwin has a manor in Lewtrenchard which did not belong to that manor in 1066. This is called *Wadelescota*....". The details of 1086 and TRE holders, tax, plough estimate and value that follow fit the description of Warson in 16,10 which was in Lewtrenchard parish (see General Notes). Neither the main Exon. nor the Exchequer DB records the link between the two manors; this also happens with Bradaford and Tillislow (17,11-12 note), Instaple and Bradworthy (19,3 note), *Tamerlande* and Peeke (35,5-6 note), Kimber and Rutleigh (35,7-8 note). It is interesting that these latter occur in a group of 496a,b of the T.O. and that for a manor in the middle of the group (496 b 1 = DB 3,11) the main Exon. and Exchequer DB do record the link. Cf. 16,79 note. |
| 16,10 | HE COULD....WOULD. Added at the end of the entry, referring to Waddell, as the T.O. entry (495 a 3, see 16,9 note) states with the addition of "with his land". |
| 16,12 | WOODLAND, 60 ACRES. "....160 acres". |
| 16,14 | FORMERLY. "when he acquired it", probably referring to Baldwin (see notes 2,14 and 16,88). Similarly for the past values of 16,18;21-24;26;28-36;39-42;80;84-85;94;141; 144-151;158-159;161-165;167-168;170-173;175. |
| 16,15 | IT PAID TAX FOR. "it answered for" *se defendit pro* (possibly being present rather than perfect tense, as the imperfect *defendebat* is the more usual past tense) in place of the usual *reddidit gildum pro*. Cf. 16,71 note and see General Notes 1,4 on this phrase. |
| 16,16 | 4 SMALLHOLDERS. "3 smallholders". |
| 16,24 | OSGOT. *Ansgot(us)* 'Ansgot'; see General Notes 3,90. |
| 16,29 | IN LORDSHIP 1 PLOUGH. "1½ ploughs". |
| 16,30 | VILLAGERS....1½ PLOUGHS. "villagers....½ plough". It seems likely that the DB scribe mistakenly added the lordship plough (which he failed to include, though it is his normal practice to do so) to the villagers' ½ plough. Cf. notes to 16,87 and 17,71. |
| 16,33 | BRICTMER HELD IT. "....in 1066". The information on Sedborough (MS *Sedeḃga*; Ellis misprints *Seteḃriga*) is written in the left margin of the MS. Unusually, it is not in the T.O., possibly because the information came to light later. See 52,33 note. |
| 16,36 | IT PAID TAX. "it pays tax"; *reddit* is probably a scribal error for *reddidit*. Cf. 17,2 note. 1 MARE(?). In the Exon. MS *i quá*, appearing between the slaves and the cattle, is perhaps a scribal error for *i equá*. However, VCH p. 451 reads *quat[arium]* and translates "1 cottager". Although *quo-* is sometimes the Exon. spelling for DB's *co-* (as *quo(s)cetos* for DB's *cocetos* in 3,86-87), one would expect *quotarius* not *quatarius* for *cotarius* (as for DB 1,4, an entry by the same scribe as this one; see note). Also, there is definitely no *t* at the end and the *ł* mark, though it can mean that several letters have been omitted, can, as in *reddit gildũ* and *p añú* in this entry, merely indicate that an *m* is to be added. |
| 16,37 | UNDERWOOD. "woodland (*nem*¹)"; see also notes to 16,42 and 17,77 and cf. 1,27 note for the reverse. |
| 16,42 | VILLAGERS....3 PLOUGHS. "2 ploughs". UNDERWOOD, 5 ACRES. "woodland (*nemor*̃), 3 acres". |
| 16,43 | 3 PIGMEN; THEY PAY. See 1,67 note. |
| 16,44 | WILLIAM SON OF WIMUND HOLDS. "Baldwin gave it to William son of Wimund with his daughter in marriage". IN LORDSHIP 2 PLOUGHS. "6 ploughs". 2 PIGMEN. "2 pigmen who pay 10 pigs a year", this time (and also for 42,16) added after the smallholders and before, rather than after, the slaves (who end the list of inhabitants, possibly the reason for the omission of the slaves by the Exchequer scribe in both these entries). See General Notes 1,6 on the usual place of pigmen in the list of population. |
| 16,48 | WADO. Exon. *Walo* which represents OG *Wadilo*, a diminutive and pet form of OG *Wado*; see General Notes 15,49. |
| 16,49 | 1½ PLOUGHS....THERE. According to the lordship and villagers' details (see Table) 1 plough and 5 oxen were there; see General notes 3,37 on the number of oxen to a team. |

# Exon. 16

| | |
|---|---|
| 16,52;56 | WADO. Exon. *Walo* 'Wadilo' for each entry; see **16,48** note. |
| 16,56 | VALUE NOW 10s. "Value of this part, 10s", referring to the half of the manor not attached to (North) Tawton.<br>HALF OF THIS LAND. "Half of the above ½ virgate". |
| 16,57 | IN LORDSHIP 2 PLOUGHS. "2½ ploughs". |
| 16,58 | 11 BURGESSES....THEY PAY 53d. "....they pay 4s 5d....they are in the above value" (*iiii sol'* 7 *v den*? *isti s(un)t i(n) sup(ra)dict[o] p(re)tio*, written in the right margin; the whole of this statement is in paler ink, probably added by a different scribe). The burgesses' payment was included in the manor's value; cf. 1,66 note and General Notes 21,2 and DB Somerset Exon. Notes 9,3. |
| 16,63 | VILLAGERS....5 PLOUGHS. "4 ploughs". |
| 16,65 | FROM BALDWIN. "from the Sheriff (*de vicecomite*)".<br>IN BARNSTAPLE. "In Barnstaple Borough". |
| 16,66 | ROBERT ALSO HOLDS. "Robert". Although there is no *idem* like in DB (so that this Robert is not necessarily the same as Robert of Beaumont of 16,65), it is likely that he is because of the descent of the holding (see General Notes here). Cf. 15,21 note above. |
| 16,69 | FISHERY WHICH PAYS. "fishery whose value is". |
| 16,72 | THIS (MANOR) SETTLED ITS TAX .... 2 VIRGATES OF LAND. "It paid tax with the above manor (Charles) for 1 virgate in such a way that (*ita quod*) these two manors settled the King's tax at a rate of / for 1 virgate (*adquietabant se ad Gildum regis pro i uirga*). Now it is accounted for as 2 virgates" (*cumputatur pro ii uirgis*, perhaps a scribal error for the plural *cumputantur* with the two manors as subject, unless the subject is the 1 virgate – i.e. the 1 virgate (that paid tax) is now accounted for as (or counted as) 2 virgates. The Exchequer scribe saw the confusion of the singular verb here and decided to make it plural, but in excising parts of the Exon. sentence he lost a subject for his plural verb). See General Notes here.<br>LAND HERE FOR 3 PLOUGHS. "3 ploughs can plough that virgate which lies in Mockham".<br>FORMERLY. "value when the Sheriff acquired it", referring to Baldwin. |
| 16,74 | IT PAID TAX. "It answered": *defendebat se* interlined (by the same scribe and in the same colour ink) above *reddidit Gildū*, which has 3 deletion dots under it not shown by Ellis. See General Notes 1,4 (second note).<br>THIS LAND .... STATE. "This virgate ....". See 1,5 note for the T.O. entry (498 b 6). |
| 16,75 | WOODLAND, 20 ACRES. *xx nemoris; agros* probably omitted in error, but likely as woodland is regularly measured in acres and, with the exception of in 2,7, that number of furlongs is not used in Devon. Omissions of part of a measurement such as this occur quite often in Exon. (see 1,3 note), but generally (as, for example, for 1,3) when the expected noun has already been given for other resources; here, on the other hand, the woodland entry heads the list. |
| 16,76 | SIWARD. In the Exon. MS *Seuuard'* is interlined above *Vlf'* which is underlined for deletion, though Ellis fails to print this underlining. The scribe is the same as for the rest of the entry. Cf. notes to 25,27 and 34,6.<br>5 SMALLHOLDERS. "6 smallholders". |
| 16,79 | RINGCOMBE. The main Exon. entry begins "To the above manor (of Anstey) has been added a manor called Ringcombe....". In the T.O. entry (499 b 7) Ringcombe is similarly described as having been added to Anstey. Cf. 16,9 note for examples of one manor being added to another and this fact only being recorded in the T.O.<br>KIPPING HELD IT. In 499 b 7 "a thane held it jointly". |
| 16,80 | A LAND CALLED LOBB....BRAUNTON. "A manor called Lobb"; Braunton is described as "the King's lordship manor". See 1,5 note for the details of the T.O. entry (498 b 6). |
| 16,81 | VALUE FORMERLY....10s. "Value when B(aldwin) acquired it...." with no amount and no dot after *ual'* and space for only 2-3 letters left at the end of the line; the scribe probably intended to add either *tantundem* "as much" (as the DB scribe presumably thought) or a different value to the 1086 one, if this proved necessary. |
| 16,82 | 1 PLOUGH THERE. 8 oxen total; see General Notes 3,37. |
| 16,83 | A LAND .... 10s. "A manor called Yard". The details of this added manor are written partly in the right margin of the Exon. MS. They also appear in abbreviated form in the T.O. at 499 b 10.<br>GODRIC HELD IT. "....jointly". In 499 b 10 "which a thane held jointly". |
| 16,87 | VILLAGERS....1½ PLOUGHS. "½ plough". It seems likely that the Exchequer scribe added the lordship and villagers' ploughs together; this also occurs in 16,30 (see note). |

Exon. 16

| | |
|---|---|
| 16,88 | FORMERLY. "value when G(ilbert) acquired it"; see DB Dorset Exon. Notes 55,29-30 for other examples of the past value of a manor being when it was acquired by the subtenant, rather than by the tenant-in-chief (as is usually the case; see 2,14 note). Cf. 3,22 note and the sub-holding in 35,10. |
| 16,89 | FOUR THANES HELD IT. "....jointly". |
| 16,91 | 2 PLOUGHS .... THERE. "The canons have 2 ploughs"; *in dominio* probably implied or omitted in error. |
| 16,92 | TAX FOR 2½ VIRGATES OF LAND. The only detail given is *i uirgā dim̄* in lordship, which is unclear, either 1½ virgates or ½ virgate being possible meanings. Cf. 50,3 note. FORMERLY 20s. "15s". FROM THIS MANOR .... 12d. Written in the right margin of the Exon. MS by a different scribe to the one who wrote the main part of 16,92. Also in the T.O. at 500 b 6. WHICH BELONGED THERE. "which rightly lay there"; "rightly" also in 500 b 6. |
| 16,93 | THE MONKS OF MONT ST. MICHEL. "The monks of St. Michel". Cf. General Notes 1,33 for a similar omission of 'Mont', though by the Exchequer scribe this time. |
| 16,94 | BEFORE 1066 ½ HIDE .... HOLDS IT. Also in the T.O. at 499 b 11. The ½ hide is said to belong rightly to Baldwin's manor of Whimple. See 39,10 note. AELMER. *Idem Almer'*: the same Aelmer as held the main manor of Whimple. |
| 16,97 | WILLIAM HOLDS FROM BALDWIN. "William Black (*niger*, interlined)" for 16,97 only; plain William for 16,98-103. On the byname *niger* see OEB pp. 292-293. A William Black (*blach*), the Bishop of Bayeux's man, appears in DB Herts. 42,11; possibly the same man. |
| 16,99 | ½ PLOUGH THERE. "W(illiam) has ½ plough"; *in dominio* probably implied or omitted in error. |
| 16,110 | AFTER THIS ENTRY in the MS 1½ lines have been left blank, possibly for some additional information on the manor to be added when and if available. The same scribe wrote the following entries. |
| 16,121 | TAX FOR 2 HIDES....LORDSHIP....1 HIDE....VILLAGERS....1 HIDE. In the Exon. MS the tax is *ii hidis & dim̂*, but the *& dim̂* is extremely faint and appears to have been erased. The lordship land is *i hidā & i virgā*, but the *& i virgā* is likewise very faint and probably erased. Similarly with the *& i virḡ* after the *i hida* in the villagers' land. Ellis prints all the faint parts, though he does not print the equally faint and obviously erased *x* under the interlined *viii* for the villagers and the *xl* under the interlined *xxxv* in the present value. See General Notes here. LAND FOR 6 PLOUGHS. In the MS *viii carr̄*, but the last *ii* of the *viii* are very faint and probably intended for deletion. Ellis prints *viii*. IN LORDSHIP 2 PLOUGHS. In the MS *iii carr̄*, but again the last *i* of the *iii* is extremely faint and appears to have been erased. Ellis, however, prints *iii*. |
| 16,122 | IN LORDSHIP 2 PLOUGHS. "2½ ploughs". |
| 16,125 | WOODLAND. "underwood (*nemusculi*)". |
| 16,127 | BERNARD HOLDS ROCOMBE. "....from Baldwin". See 15,22 note. |
| 16,131 | MODBERT. Merely *M.*, but no doubt standing for *Mo(d)bertus* as in the surrounding entries for 16,130 and 16,132. Cf. 16,175 for which the scribe likewise gives only the initial of the tenant (*W.*), though in that case the expanded form of the name is far from clear; see General Notes there. |
| 16,133 | PASTURE, 40 ACRES. Just *xl agros, pascu̧e* being omitted in error, but no doubt intended as pasture normally follows meadow in Exon. See 1,46 note. As this comes at the end of the list of resources, it would not be possible for the acres to be combined with the measurement of the next 'resource', as perhaps is the case with the 12 furlongs in 1,53 (see note). See also General Notes to 1,46 and 1,53. |
| 16,134 | 1 VILLAGER HAS IT THERE. "R(ainer) has 1 villager who has 1 plough". |
| 16,135 | 1½ PLOUGHS THERE. "R(ainer) has (1)½ ploughs"; *in dominio* probably implied or omitted in error. |
| 16,144 | ANSGER. Exon. *Ansgerid'*, probably = *Ansger idem* "the same Ansger", as an Ansger holds the two preceding entries (= DB 16,142-143), although Exon. rarely has the word *idem* (see 15,21 note) and where it does it is either written in full or as *Idē*, whereas the abbreviation *'* here regularly stands for an omitted *-us*, especially with personal names (as in *Ansger'* in the preceding entry). ADDED CREACOMBE. "Baldwin has another manor called Creacombe .... Ansger holds it from B(aldwin)". Abbreviated details of this added manor appear also in the T.O. at 506 b 2. |

# Exon. 16 – 17

| | |
|---|---|
| 16,144 (cont'd.) | LEOFGAR HELD FREELY (AND) JOINTLY. "Leofgar held jointly"; so also in 506 b 2. No mention of 'freely' in either entry.<br>1 VILLAGER, 1 SMALLHOLDER AND 1 SLAVE. "A(nsger) has 1 villager and he has with him ½ plough and 1 smallholder and 1 slave". Cf. 16,156 note. |
| 16,145- 146 | 1 VILLAGER AND 1 SLAVE (WITH) ½ VIRGATE. The wording in Exon. is *uitt dim uirḡ*, but unless *uitt* abbreviates *uillanus* singular, *uill(ani)* is being used here in its general sense and the slave may thus be included. Cf. notes to 3,57. 3,79. 5,9. 16,6. 17,58. 19,9. 28,16 and 35,5 and see General Notes 1,3 on slaves and on the difficulty of knowing from DB or Exon. whether they had ploughs and land. |
| 16,151 | O(SWY). In the Exon. MS *Oswicus* is abbreviated *O.* in its second occurrence in this entry; Ellis misprints *c*. |
| 16,156 | 1 PLOUGH, WHICH IS THERE .... SMALLHOLDERS. "She has 2 smallholders and has with them 1 plough and 1 slave". Cf. 16,144 note. |
| 16,158 | ROGO. Exon. *Rogro* which is unusual: it ought to represent *Rogero*, dative or ablative of the latinized form of the personal name *Roger* (i.e. *Rogerus, -i*, 2nd declension), but the name here is obviously nominative in each of its three occurrences in this entry. Meanwhile, DB *Rogo* (on which see General Notes 16,76), is latinized *Rogo, Rogonis* (3rd declension). It is interesting that the name obviously caused the Exon. scribe some problems because in its first occurrence in the entry he omitted, then interlined, the first *o* and likewise with the second *r* in the second occurrence. The Norman name *Roger* was adopted into the OE nominative form *Rogere* and it is possible that at some stage in the Domesday Inquest this was written *Rog'e*, where the ' represents an abbreviation for *er*: if the final *e* were miswritten or misread as *o* and if the abbreviation were inaccurately expanded to *r* instead of to *er*, then the form *Rogro* would appear. That the man *Rogro* was in fact *Roger* is lent some support by the fact that in 16,170 (where Exon. again has *Rogro* for DB's *Rogo*) his holding may be represented in the Tax Return for Colyton Hundred (xx) by the ½ hide which *Rogerus de Roerico*\* [holds] for which the King had no tax.<br>\* *de Roerico* would be "from Roric/Roderick (OG *Hrodric*)"; it would seem that Exon. and DB omitted a middle tenant of Baldwin's here. |
| 16,159 | BALDWIN. Called *B. uiceconsul*; also for 16,165. Cf. 15,7 note. |
| 16,163 | WOODLAND. "underwood (*nemusculi*)". |
| 16,164 | MILL....WOODLAND. The woodland details here precede rather than succeed the mill details, but in the Exon. MS two commas have been placed beneath the two &'s that begin the phrases to reverse their order. Ellis does not print these commas. |
| 16,167 | R(ANULF) HAS ½ PLOUGH. *in dominio* probably implied or omitted in error. Cf. notes to 20,9. 24,18. 42,21. 47,9 and cf. General Notes 1,34 on lordship ploughs in Exon. being omitted by the Exchequer scribe. |
| 16,168 | 1 PLOUGH....THERE. "R(oger) has 1 plough"; *in dominio* probably implied or omitted in error. |
| 16,170 | ROGO. Exon. *Rogro*; see 16,158 note. |
| 16,174 | ALWOLD. Exon. *Adeluuold(us)* 'Aethelwold'; see PNDB p. 188 and General Notes 16,28. |
| 16,176 | PASTURE, 64 ACRES. "pasture, 63 acres". |
| Ch. 17 | IUDHAEL OF TOTNES. Only called Iudhael (*Juhellus*), both in the main Exon. returns and in the T.O.; 'of Totnes' omitted, as also in the Cornwall section (334 b 2 = DB Cornwall 6,1). |
| 17,1 | WHICH KING EDWARD HELD IN LORDSHIP. "which King Edward held in 1066".<br>FORMERLY THEY PAID. "when I(udhael) acquired it (Totnes), they paid".<br>THIS BOROUGH .... PAYS 40d IN TAX. "This town (*uilla*) only pays tax when Exeter pays and when it was accustomed (*solebat*) to pay tax it paid (*reddebat*, in full) 40d". |
| 17,2 | WHICH BEFORE 1066 PAID. "which pays....before 1066"; *reddit* is a scribal error for the past *reddebat* or *reddidit*. Cf. 16,36 note. In the T.O. at 505 b 10: "which paid 8d .... but he has kept them back". |
| 17,3 | IT PAID TAX. "....before 1066".<br>FORMERLY. "when I(udhael) acquired it". Similarly for the past values of 17,4-15; 18-20; 22-50; 52-53; 55-57; 61-68; 70-90; 93-103; 106-107. |
| 17,4 | VALUE NOW 100s. "Value 105s a year"; 7 *v* is interlined, probably the reason for the Exchequer scribe's missing it. |
| 17,5 | BROADWOODWIDGER. See last note under 1,25 for an entry in the T.O. (496 a 3) which contains details which are neither in the main Exon. nor in DB. |

Exon. 17

17,5 (cont'd.) AT THE FOOT OF FOLIO 316a (in the middle of the entry corresponding to 17,5, though several lines below it), written up against the left, inner, edge of the Exon. MS, are the words *h̅* (or possibly *h'*) *sc̄psit Ricardus* "Richard wrote this/these/here". The scribe does not appear to be the same as for the entries on this folio or succeeding ones, though the hand is contemporary with the MS; the ink is paler than the rest of 316a ff. There is no mark beside the words or in the text indicating what Richard wrote. Ellis does not print this statement, nor a similar one at the bottom of 406b: *h̅ qd̄ Jordan sc̄psit* "what Jordan wrote" (with something written before it which is only partially legible: ...*ic...de..bet* [or *ber*] *se* ?). Although the writing is faint and the script small (the parchment is yellow and thick; see 19,28-46 note on the original position of this mostly blank folio and the damage to it), it seems like that on 316a. A third, similar piece of information, which Ellis does print (though not in the correct place), appears on 414a (see 35,19 note); the writing is larger than that of the other two.
    According to Finn 'Immediate Sources' pp. 48-49 these phrases (he makes no mention of the one at the foot of 406b), together with the words *consummatum est* (see below), were written by scribes involved in making a fair copy of Exon. (for Exchequer use). However, there is no proof that the person(s) writing these statements were Richard, Jordan or *R*; the statements could have been written, for example, by the chief clerk in the scriptorium (which would explain why the writing of two at least of the three seems to be the same and also why the script and ink colour are not the same as in the surrounding entries), possibly notes by him to be used as a record for the future payment of the scribes concerned. There may be more similar statements in the Exon. MS, which only a lengthy and close study of it will reveal.
    As to the phrase *consummatum est*, it occurs nine times on the reverse of an otherwise blank last folio of a booklet/quire: on 209b, 370b, 387b, 449b, 451b, 455b (perhaps erased), 467b (there is writing on 467a; Finn (op. cit.) misprints 476b), 474b and 494b; once on 155a (the first page of a booklet); and once, in the form *consummatum est usque huc*, in the middle of a booklet on 490a in the right margin level with the 3-line space between the end of the 'Lands of English Thanes in Devonshire' and the beginning of the section on the English thanes in Somerset. These phrases appear after folios dealing with Somerset lands, apart from the one on 209b which comes after Cornish lands. With the exception of the phrase on 490a which is definitely written in the same colour ink, and by the same scribe, as the last entries for the Devon thanes and perhaps even the first for the Somerset thanes, these *consummatum est* phrases are written in large lower-case letters or capitals, often in a 'square' hand. It seems likely, as Ker p. 804 thinks, that these phrases were meant to indicate that "all the matter for the quire had been gathered in and that the blank space was to remain blank". The fact that the phrase on 490a (if, as seems probable, it was written for the same purpose as the others) was clearly done by the scribe of the surrounding entries, argues against Finn's view that these phrases were the work of scribes involved in copying the MS: if this were the case the ink colour on 490a would not be the same.
    See the section on the relationship between Exon. and DB in the Introduction to these Notes for further views on the idea of a fair copy of the Exon. MS.

17,11-12 BRADAFORD. TILLISLOW. In the T.O. at 500 b 3: "Iudhael has a manor called Bradaford which Saewin held. Another manor called Tillislow has been added to it, which Saewin also held; he could go with his land to whichever lord he would in 1066. Nigel holds it from Iudhael. Value 10s a year; value when Iudhael acquired it, as much". Neither the main Exon. nor DB mentions the linking of these two manors (except by TRE tenant); see 16,9 note.

17,12 1½ PLOUGHS THERE. 1 plough and 3 oxen; see the Lordship and Villagers' Table. SAEWIN .... WOULD. "The thane who held the two said manors could go with his land to whichever lord he would in 1066".

17,13 TO THIS MANOR .... AS THREE MANORS. "With this manor Iudhael has the land of three thanes who did not belong to the above manor before 1066. One of these lands is called Warne which Aelfric held; another is called Burntown which Alwin held, and the third is called Wringworthy which Aldwulf held. These three thanes could go to whichever lord they would with this land". Abbreviated details of the three added lands are also in the T.O. at 495 a 5, but there it is the manors which are said not to have belonged to Mary Tavy before 1066; also the three thanes held them jointly.
½ PLOUGH THERE. "Nigel holds this (added land) in lordship from Iudhael and has ½ plough there".

# Exon. 17

|  |  |
|---|---|
| | VALUE OF THESE THREE LANDS. "Value of these three villages". |
| 17,14 | SYDENHAM (DAMEREL). In the T.O. at 495 b 1: "Iudhael has....Sydenham (Damerel) ....to it have been added 3 manors which did not belong to this manor in 1066. Three thanes held them jointly in 1066. They paid tax for 1 virgate and 2 furlongs (*ferdinis*). 4 ploughs can plough them. Value of them 20s a year". |
| | FOUR THANES HELD IT FREELY (AND) JOINTLY. "which 4 thanes held jointly"; no mention of 'freely'. |
| 17,15 | PASTURE, 1 LEAGUE; WOODLAND, 1 LEAGUE. "pasture, 1 league in length and width"; "woodland, 1 league in length and width". See General Notes 1,4 on the league used in this manner. |
| 17,16 | 2 PIGMEN(?). *ii porc̄*. The usual abbreviation for *porcarius* "pigman" is *porcaȓ* (but see 6 notes below where *porc̄* must abbreviate *porcarium* because of the plural *habent*). Here *porc̄* could abbreviate *porcos*, though pigs are normally listed after, not before, cattle. It is not unusual for there to be no pigs on a manor where pigmen are recorded; see General Notes 1,18. |
| | MEADOW, 1 LEAGUE; PASTURE, 1 LEAGUE. "meadow, 1 league in length and width; pasture, 1 league in length and width". |
| | FORMERLY. "when he acquired it", most probably referring to Iudhael (see notes to 2,14 and 16,88). Similarly for the past values of 17,17;21;51;54;58-60;69;91;104. |
| 17,17 | IN LORDSHIP 1 PLOUGH. "in lordship....1 plough and 2 oxen". |
| | TO THIS MANOR .... 10s. Abbreviated details of this added furlong ('ferling') also appear in the T.O. at 495 b 4. |
| | WHICH ALWIN HELD FREELY (AND) JOINTLY. "which Alwin held jointly....which did not belong to the said manor". In 495 b 4: "which a thane held jointly....and it did not belong to the said manor". No mention is made of 'freely' in either entry. |
| | 2 VILLAGERS HAVE IT THERE. "I(udhael) has 1 villager and 1 pigman (*porc̄*) and they have 1 plough". See General Notes 1,6 on pigmen. |
| 17,18 | LAND FOR 2 PLOUGHS, WHICH ARE THERE. "2½ ploughs can plough this ('ferling') and these ploughs are there". No mention is made as to whether the ploughs belonged to the lordship or to the villagers; see also the penultimate note under 1,11 and notes to 35,24. 45,3 and 52,9. Two different Exon. scribes wrote these entries, so it is likely that it was simply not known who had the ploughs on these manors, rather than a particular scribe's idiosyncrasy of formula. |
| | VALUE NOW 20s. "he (Aiulf) pays him (Iudhael) 20s a year for it (manor)". |
| 17,20 | 3 SMALLHOLDERS. "8 smallholders". |
| 17,21 | PASTURE, ½ LEAGUE. "pasture, ½ league in length and in width". |
| | WOODLAND 1 LEAGUE LONG AND 1 FURLONG WIDE. "woodland and underwood, 1 league in length and 1 furlong in width". See 5,8 note. |
| 17,28 | 2 PLOUGHS THERE. 1 plough and 6 cattle (*animalia*) in a plough; see Lordship and Villagers' Table and General Notes 17,26. |
| 17,29 | 15 VILLAGERS AND 12 SMALLHOLDERS. "5 cottagers (*cotarios*)" added after the villagers and smallholders and before the slaves. There seems no reason for their omission in DB; cf. 1,4 first note. |
| 17,30 | VALUE .... 60s. "Value 40s; when I(udhael) acquired it, as much". |
| 17,34 | OSBERN. "Osbert (*Osbertus*)"; see notes to 24,7 and Ch. 43 and cf. Dorset General Notes 44,1. |
| 17,37 | VALUE NOW 50s. "30s". |
| 17,39 | 1 PLOUGH THERE. 6 cattle in a plough; see Lordship and Villagers' Table and General Notes 17,26. |
| 17,41 | THESE SAID NINE .... IRISHMEN. This additional information is given in the right margin of the Exon. MS, in the same colour ink as the rest of the folio and apparently by the same scribe, so it is unlikely to have been added after the Exchequer scribe used the MS. Perhaps he merely missed it because it was in the margin, or perhaps he did not think the information worth recording. See General Notes here on these Irishmen. The *p irlandinos* is in slightly darker ink and clearer with the letters spaced more widely apart as if the scribe were unfamiliar with the word and it was spelt out to him. |
| 17,43 | LAND FOR 1 PLOUGH. "1½ ploughs". |
| 17,49 | 11 SLAVES. "12 slaves"; see General Notes here. |
| 17,51 | 40 SHEEP. In the Exon. MS *xl xl oues* in error; this entry is written by 2, possibly 3, scribes and the second (or third) scribe had just taken over; otherwise the entry is neat. Cf. first note under 1,50. |

Exon. 17

| | |
|---|---|
| 17,52 | 2 PLOUGHS .... THERE, IN LORDSHIP, AND ½ HIDE. The phrasing and order are unusual in Exon.: "W(illiam) has this ½ hide and 6 villagers and 4 smallholders and 1 slave and 2 ploughs in lordship". The phrase "2 ploughs in lordship" was originally omitted and then added out of place. |
| 17,53 | 2 PLOUGHS....THERE. 2 ploughs and, probably, 2 cattle; see Lordship and Villagers' Table. The *ii animl'* are given between the villagers' ploughs and the list of population, not in the usual place for livestock which is between the population and the resources (where the "50 sheep" appear). Before *animl'* is erased a *c* (perhaps for *carr* 'plough'). As there are several occurrences of cattle in ploughs (see General Notes to 1,3 and 17,26), it would seem likely that the DB scribe has just omitted the odd animals, as often happens (see General Notes 3,44), rather than that he did not believe the *animalia* were oxen. |
| 17,57 | 3 SMALLHOLDERS. "5 smallholders". |
| 17,58 | THE CLERGY OF ST. MARY'S HOLD. "I(udhael) gave this (manor) to St. Mary's for the Queen's soul". |
| | 1 VILLAGER (WITH) ½ VIRGATE. *uitt dim uirg*; it is not possible to tell whether the *uitt* abbreviates the singular *uittanus* (in which case only the villager would have the ½ virgate) or the plural *uillani* which would mean that the slave might be included with the villager. See notes to 3,57. 16,145-146. 19,9 and 35,5 and cf. 3,79 note. |
| 17,61 | 2 PLOUGHS THERE. 1½ ploughs and 6 oxen; see Lordship and Villagers' Table. |
| 17,66 | 3 PLOUGHS....THERE. 2 ploughs and 6 oxen; see Lordship and Villagers' Table. |
| 17,67 | MEADOW, 3 ACRES. "2 acres". |
| 17,68 | 3 SMALLHOLDERS. "4 smallholders". |
| 17,69 | TAX FOR 1 HIDE. "tax for 1½ hides"; the 7 *dim* begins a new line in the Exon. MS, probably the reason for its omission in DB (see also notes to 3,86 and 34,25 and cf. Dorset Exon. Notes 1,13 and 55,35). |
| 17,70 | 2 VILLAGERS HAVE IT THERE. "O(do) has 2 villagers who have 1 plough". |
| 17,71 | VILLAGER....½ PLOUGH. No villagers' plough is mentioned in Exon. It seems likely that the Exchequer scribe miscopied the lordship ½ plough as the villagers' one. A similar thing occurs in 48,1 and in DB Somerset Exon. Notes 5,7 and 21,57;59. Cf. notes to 3,70 and 16,30 above. |
| 17,72 | ODO ALSO HOLDS. "Odo holds" with no *idem* for any of the entries 17,72-77, so not necessarily the same man as the Odo of 17,71 (which is what DB implies). See 15,21 note. |
| 17,73-74 | WESTON (PEVERELL). BURRINGTON. Odo is said to hold both these manors "from I(udhael)"; cf. 15,22 note. |
| 17,73 | IN LORDSHIP 2 PLOUGHS. "2½ ploughs". |
| 17,77 | UNDERWOOD. "woodland (*nemor*)". |
| 17,79 | UNDERWOOD, ½ ACRE. "underwood, ½ league". Cf. 1,38 note. |
| 17,81 | PASTURE, ½ LEAGUE. "pasture, ½ league in length and width". |
| 17,84 | WILLIAM ALSO HOLDS. "William holds" with no *idem* for any of the entries 17,84-89, so not necessarily the same man as the William of 17,83 (which is implied in Exchequer DB). Similarly for 34,36-37. See 15,21 note. |
| 17,85 | 4 VILLAGERS. In the Exon. MS *iiii uill'* was originally written, but the last *i* has been erased, making "3 villagers"; the erasure may have been done later, after the MS had been used at Winchester, or the Exchequer scribe may not have realised that this last *i* was erased (cf. 23,15 second note). |
| | PASTURE, 2 FURLONGS. "pasture, 2 furlongs in length and width". |
| 17,89 | 1 PLOUGH THERE. ½ plough; see Lordship and Villagers' Table. |
| 17,92 | RALPH ALSO HOLDS. "Ralph", with no *idem* so he is not necessarily the same as the Ralph of 17,91 (which DB implies). Similarly for 17,103-104. See 15,21 note. |
| | VILLAGERS....1 PLOUGH. "2 ploughs". |
| | ANOTHER 'BACCAMOOR' HAS BEEN ADDED. "To this manor has been added another (manor) called 'Baccamoor' ". Similarly in the T.O. at 505 b 3. |
| | SIGERIC HELD IT. "which Sigeric held jointly" .... 505 b 3. |
| | THESE TWO LANDS TOGETHER. "These 2 manors". |
| | VALUE 20s. The value of the added manor is given as 10s in 505 b 3. |
| 17,94 | AUBREY AND ALGAR. Named and described as two thanes. |
| 17,98 | THORGILS ALSO HOLDS. "Thorgils holds" with no *idem* for any of the entries 17,98-101, so not necessarily the same man as the Thorgils of 17,97 (which DB implies). See 15,21 note. |

## Exon. 17 - 19

17,98 (cont'd.)    1 VILLAGER....PLOUGH. The villager's land holding is given in the usual place after the lordship land, but the plough detail is given after the villager.

17,103-104    RALPH ALSO HOLDS. "Ralph"; see 17,92 note.

17,105    ANOTHER WOODFORD HAS BEEN ADDED. "Another (manor) has been added called Woodford". Similarly in the T.O. entry (505 b 6).
VALUE OF THESE TWO LANDS. "manors"; the value of the added manor is given as 20s in 505 b 6.

17,106    LAND FOR 2 PLOUGHS. "2½ ploughs".

18,1    FORMERLY. "Value when W(illiam) acquired it".

19,1    2 HOUSES WHICH PAID 16d. "2 houses....paid 16d....which W(illiam) has kept back since he has had the houses" (505 b 9).

19,2    FORMERLY. "value when W(illiam) acquired it". Similarly for the past value of 19,3-6; 10;25-26;28;33-34;41;44.

19,3    INSTAPLE. In the T.O. at 496 b 2: "William Cheever has a manor called Instaple which he and his brother added to the manor called Bradworthy. A thane held it jointly in 1066. It did not belong to the said manor namely Bradworthy. Value 5s a year; when they acquired it, 7[s]". His brother was Ralph of Pomeroy (see Ch. 34 note) and Bradworthy was his manor (34,6); see 19,33 note for another manor held by both William and Ralph. See 16,9 note for another instance of neither the main Exon. nor DB recording the addition of one manor to another and cf. 16,79 note.

19,4    (WEST) PUTFORD. In the T.O. at 496 b 4: "William Cheever has a manor called (West) Putford, to which ½ virgate of land has been added, which a thane held jointly in 1066. It did not belong to the said manor. Ansketel holds it from W(illiam). Value 3s 9d a year; value when W(illiam) acquired it, 10s".
TWO THANES HELD IT JOINTLY. It is interesting that in the Exon. MS *parit(er)* is interlined, probably by the same scribe as the rest of the entry. The thanes are named as Godric and Rewruin and each had ½ virgate. For Rewruin (*Rewruin'*), see PNDB p. 348.

19,6    TO THIS MANOR .... FROM IT. Interlined in the Exon. MS by a different scribe to the rest of the entry, possibly later. This information also appears in the T.O. at 506 a 8.
THE KING HAS NO TAX FROM IT. "The King has not had his tax"; so also in 506 a 8. However, the Exchequer *hað* may abbreviate the perfect *habuit* rather than *habet*.

19,7    FORMERLY. "when he acquired it", probably referring to William Cheever (see notes to 2,14 and 16,88). Similarly for the past values of 19,8-9;11-15;17;19-24;29-31; 37-40;42;45-46.

19,8    MEADOW, 6 ACRES. The meadow details occur as the last words on folio 399b. The entry continues on folio 401a with the same scribe and in the same colour ink. The present foliation of the Exon. MS is incorrect here: the folio numbered 400 should have been numbered 401 and folios 401-402 should have been numbered 402, 400 respectively (not as OJR in VCH p. 376 states). Charles Lyttelton (Dean of Exeter 1748-1762) who had worked on the foliation of the Exon. MS, writing on the MS itself the order of many of the pages, gave the correct order of these folios: for example, he wrote in the bottom margin of 399b "go on to Page 497", this being the old numbering for the folio now numbered 401a, and in the top margin of 401a he wrote "This follows 2nd side of Page 495" (i.e. of 399b). For some reason Barnes did not follow his advice (which he seems to have done elsewhere), and so misfoliated these pages. See notes to 19,20;27.

19,9    1 SMALLHOLDER (WITH) ½ FURLONG. *uitt dim' ferd*. it is not possible to tell whether *uitt* should be extended to *uillanus*, referring only to the smallholder (see 3,63 note), or to *uillani* in which case the slave may also have had a share in the land (see General Notes 1,3 on the slave). See notes here to 3,57. 16,145-146 and 17,58 and cf. notes to 3,79. 5,9. 16,6. 28,16 and 35,5.

19,16    LYNTON AND ILKERTON. "William has a manor called Lynton which Alward son of Toki (*tochesone*) held in 1066. To this manor has been added another called Ilkerton which Algar held. W(illiam) holds these as one manor". Ilkerton is described as an added manor in the T.O. at 498 b 8, held by a thane (unnamed) jointly in 1066.
PASTURE 2 FURLONGS LONG.... "pasture, 2 leagues in length....".
FORMERLY 35s; VALUE NOW £7. "Value of Lynton £4 a year and of Ilkerton £3; when he acquired them, the value of Lynton was 20s and of Ilkerton 15s". These values of Ilkerton are also given in 498 b 8.

19,17-18    LYN. 'BADGWORTHY'. In the T.O. at 499 a 1: "William Cheever has a manor called Lyn. A manor called 'Badgworthy' has been added to it, which a thane held jointly in 1066. Fulcwy holds it from W(illiam). Value 10s a year; when he acquired it, it was waste (*deuastata erat*)".

Exon. 19

| | |
|---|---|
| 19,17 | 2 PIGMEN; THEY PAY. See 1,67 note. |
| 19,18 | FULCWOLD. "Fulcwy" (*Fulcoidus*, with *Fulcoius* in the T.O.: OG *Fulcwig* with loss of final *g* [PNDB §133]; *oi* for *wi* [PNDB §55] and substitution of final -*g* > -*c* > -*t* > -*d* [PNDB §133]). Fulcwold and Fulcwy may be related (kin-linked in *Fulc-w*). (JMcND) BEFORE 1066. Omitted, but the past *reddidit* is used. See notes to 2,24 and 5,6. |
| 19,20 | IN LORDSHIP. Folio 402b ends with the words "R(alph) has in lordship 3", and the entry continues with the same scribe and in the same colour ink with the words "virgates and 1½ ploughs" on folio 400a. See 19,8 note on the misfoliation here.<br>2 VILLAGERS WITH 1 PLOUGH. "1½ ploughs". After the number of villagers is added "3 smallholders". There is no reason for the omission in DB of the smallholders here or in 48,12. |
| 19,21 | 8 VILLAGERS. "7 villagers". |
| 19,22 | HAMO ALSO HOLDS. "Hamo holds", with no *idem*, so not necessarily the same man as the Hamo of 19,21. See 15,21 note. |
| 19,24 | 1 COB. Ellis omits the *i* before *runcin* in error. |
| 19,27 | WARIN HOLDS .... FROM WILLIAM. Folio 400b ends with these words and the entry continues with the same scribe and in the same colour ink on folio 403a. See 19,8 note.<br>VALUE WHEN W(ILLIAM).... Or perhaps the *W.* here abbreviates *Warinus*; see notes to 2,14 and 16,88. |
| 19,28-48 | THE INNER EDGES OF THE FOLIOS dealing with these entries (403a–405b) appear to have had water spilt down most of their length or to have got very damp at some stage: they are faint and blurred, as are letters/words which are erased with water. Gall has been applied in many places; no one knows exactly when, but perhaps by Dean Lyttelton (see 19,8 note). DGSW p. 396 note 7 errs in attributing this damage to ink blots. This faintness and blurring occurs in the same place on each folio, from the eighth line on 403a. Gall is applied at the beginning of the second and fourth lines of 403 a 2, every line end of 403 b 2-4, from the eighth line (inner edges) on 404a,b, from the eleventh line on 405a and the ninth on 405b. Most of what Ellis prints can still be deciphered, but attention is drawn to these cases in the notes below. According to Ker (pp. 803, 805) folios 403–406 [406 has only 6 lines on it and so is not affected by the water, the damage beginning below it] formed a 'booklet', which came at the end of one of the two volumes the manuscript was in before it was rebound in 1816. (There are worm-holes on these sheets, a couple of them reaching as far into the volume as f. 403, and the pinmark for the original binding is visible, clearly different from the worm-holes because of the pale greenish tinge round it from the metal pin used and the signs that the parchment was punctured.) This may be the reason for the damage.<br>The folios preceding 403–406 in the old binding (415–418 new foliation = DB Ch. 21) also show signs of dampness on their inner edges and the writing is faint (especially on 416a where the ink is now very pale), but almost every word can be deciphered (and where one cannot be, it is obvious what it was); Ellis prints them all correctly with the exception of the pasture acres and present value in 416 b 3 (= 21,13 see notes). The indentation of the pinmark can also be seen on these folios, gradually getting fainter. |
| 19,28 | VILLAGER....1 PLOUGH. "2 ploughs". |
| 19,29 | IN LORDSHIP .... ½ (FURLONG?). The beginning of the second and fourth lines of 403 a 2 are mostly illegible in the Exon. MS due to the water damage (see 19,28-48 note), but all can be read except for some such words as *ea die q̃ rex* on line 2 and, probably, *ferl'* "furlong" on line 4 here (which would then add up with the 1½ virgates and 1½ 'ferlings' to the ½ hide tax total). |
| 19,32 | 2 VILLAGERS HAVE 1 PLOUGH. See 19,28-46 note. Ellis prints *ht ibi* as the last words of line 1 of this entry and *i carr* at the beginning of the next. However, he does not print dots after the *ht ibi*, although there are several words still under the gall (see below) and although it is his practice to do so elsewhere in such cases (e.g. on folios 404–405, but see 19,34 note); he merely leaves a gap which could be construed as due to an erasure in the MS (as in 404 a 1; see first note under 19,35) and the sense is thus altered to William (not the villagers) having the plough. Meanwhile, it is just possible to read *ii uitt* under the gall after the *ht ibi* and some such words as *q̃ hnt* "who have" probably follow. |
| 19,33 | RALPH HOLDS YOWLESTONE .... 2 SLAVES. "William Cheever has a manor called Yowlestone (*Aeldestan* in the Exon. MS; Ellis misprints *Deidestan*, though the *A* is a normal one) which Edsi held in 1066. It paid tax for 1 hide. William Cheever has half of it and Ralph of Pomeroy the other half. 1 plough can plough William('s part: *& pa[rtem]* |

## Exon. 19

19,33 (cont'd.) is just visible under the gall). Ralph, a man-at-arms, holds it from W(illiam). R(alph) has 1 plough and 2 slaves....". A confused entry: it is not clear whether Ralph the man-at-arms is the subtenant of the whole manor or just of William's half, and it is uncertain which Ralph has the plough, slaves, livestock, meadow, etc. Cf. 19,43 note.
40 SHEEP. *xl ou*, then dark gall obscures the rest of the line, but there is room only for two or three letters (undoubtedly the *-es* of *oues*).

19,34 PASTURE 1 FURLONG. It is just possible to read *& i* under the gall at the end of the third line of this entry in Exon.; Ellis does not print it, nor dots to show that something has been omitted (see 19,32 note).

19,35 AELMER HELD IT. "....jointly", only in the T.O. entry (501 b 5). In the main entry there is an erasure after the statement that Aelmer held it in 1066; Ellis leaves a gap.
HE TOOK IT AWAY FROM ALWARD SON OF TOKI .... ENGLAND. "Alward son of Toki (*Aluuardus toquison[e?]*) took it away by force from him after King William held England". In 501 b 5: "Alward son of Toki (*Aluuardus filius Tochi*) took it away from Aelmer by force after King William held England"; *p uĩ* (= *per uim* "by force") in the MS; Ellis misprints *p iñ* which is meaningless. This statement precedes the tax statement. See General Notes here.
A SMITH. Unlike in DB, the smith is not definitely excluded in Exon. from a share in the ploughs; he occurs at the end of the list of 'villagers', but, as with the pigmen, salt-workers etc., it is not clear whether he is classed as one of the *uillani* when their ploughs and land are given; see 1,26 note.
MEADOW, 40 ACRES. The number of acres cannot be read in the Exon. MS.
[....] CATTLE. The number of cattle cannot certainly be deciphered under the gall, but judging from the space and what can be seen it might be either *xxii* or *xxiii* or *xvii* or *xviii*. VCH p. 505 reads *xxiiii*, although Ellis does not print the figure.
FORMERLY 40s; VALUE NOW £6. Only *vat p anñ vi ... sot* can be read under the gall, which covers sufficient line space for *l' 7 qñ recep ualeb xl* to have been written though rather abbreviated (*ualab xl* can just be made out).
WILLIAM HOLDS THIS WITH ALWARD'S LAND. "William holds it with the Honour of Alward"; so also in 501 b 5. It is probable that many of the other Alwards who are given as William's predecessors refer to Alward son of Toki and that, as he does not appear again in DB, all his lands passed to William and his brother Ralph of Pomeroy.

19,36 MUCH OF THE LEFT EDGE OF THIS ENTRY is illegible (see 19,28-46 note). All of what Ellis prints can still be deciphered, the most important part that he could not read being the name of the TRE tenant; VCH p. 505, however, has 'Almer', presumably by deduction from the Exchequer DB.
AELMER HELD IT. "....jointly", only in the T.O. entry (501 b 3).
THIS LAND .... AWLISCOMBE. In 501 b 3: "William Cheever has a manor called Awliscombe. A manor called Mackham has been added to it....".

19,37 IN LORDSHIP .... ½ HIDE. Under the gall (see 19,28-46 note) it is possible to decipher *W. dim̃* before *hid⁺*, with presumably *ten'* or *hŧ* ("holds" or "has") as the first word on the line. Ellis prints dots before *hid⁺*.
VILLAGERS....9 PLOUGHS. Ellis has *iiii carr*, but it is not now possible to decipher the number.
A MILL. Before *molendinũ* there is an *&* and then probably a small ink blot, partially hidden by the gall. Ellis prints dots.
[....] CATTLE. The number of cattle is obscured under the gall.
MILDON .... 10s. Abbreviated details of this added manor are also in the T.O. at 502 a 2.
EDITH HELD IT. "....jointly", in 502 a 2 only.
8 VILLAGERS HAVE 2 PLOUGHS. "W(illiam) has 8 villagers and 2 ploughs".

19,38 UNDERWOOD....VALUE NOW £6. Neither the details of the underwood nor the present value of the manor can be deciphered under the gall. VCH p. 506 gives the present value from Exchequer DB with dots for the obscured underwood, though this could also have been added from DB.

19,39 PARTS OF THIS ENTRY which are covered in gall and so cannot be checked against DB include the smallholders and the woodland's measurement. VCH p. 506 prints both dots and then the Exchequer version in brackets.

19,40 PARTS OF THIS ENTRY which are covered in gall and so cannot be checked against DB include the number of ploughs that can plough the land.
BEATRIX, WILLIAM'S SISTER. The fact that she is his sister is only given in the T.O. entry (502 a 7), but see the General Notes here.

Exon. 19 - 20

| | |
|---|---|
| 19,40 (cont'd.) | 5 VILLAGERS. So Exon. MS, the *v uill'* not being affected by the water damage and gall. Ellis misprints *vi uill'*. |
| | TOREDONE .... 40d. Abbreviated details of this added manor also appear in 502 a 7; Beatrix held *Toredone* as well as Bradford from her brother. |
| | AELFRIC COLLING HELD IT FREELY (AND) JOINTLY. "which Aelfric Colling held jointly"; the *pariter* is interlined in the Exon. MS, but appears to be by the scribe of the rest of the entry and is in the same colour ink. So also in 502 a 7, but *pariter* forms part of the text. There is no mention of 'freely' in either entry. |
| 19,41 | MUCH OF THIS ENTRY is illegible due to the gall (see 19,28-46 note), the more important parts being the name of the 1086 holder (*R.* only is given later on) and the villagers' land and ploughs and all but *sot* of the present value; see also next two notes. OJR in VCH p. 506 adds in brackets the 1086 holder and the present value from Exchequer DB, but he also gives in brackets the villagers' land and ploughs which are not in DB and then has dots for the word(s) before the sheep (next note). |
| | 3 .... ; Gall obscures some 8-9 letters' width of information; *animalia &* ("cattle and") could be the reading or possibly *porcarios &* ("pigmen and"). |
| | 30(?) SHEEP. Ellis reads *ix oues*, but the number is greater than that, probably *xxx*. |
| 19,42 | ILLEGIBLE PORTIONS OF THIS ENTRY include the tenant-in-chief, the slave (though part of *seruum* is just visible) and the present value. |
| | 1 PLOUGH THERE. "Warin has 1 plough"; *in dominio* probably implied or omitted in error. |
| 19,43 | RALPH .... IVEDON. "Ralph son of Payne (*pagani*) holds half this virgate from William". The name of the manor is illegible under the gall. See 34,27 note and cf. notes to 19,33 and 23,22. |
| | TAX FOR 1 VIRGATE. It is just possible to decipher $\bar{p}$ *i virg$^t$* under the gall here. Ellis prints dots. |
| | ½ VILLAGER HAS IT THERE. "Ralph has ½ villager who has ½ plough". |
| | THIS LAND .... AWLISCOMBE. "William added this manor to the manor called Awliscombe". In the T.O. at 502 b 7: "To William Cheever's manor of Ivedon has been added another manor called Awliscombe". |
| 19,44 | PASTURE. The word *pascu$_e$* is either omitted in error (as in 21,19, see note, and see 1,46 note) or misplaced (at the end of the measurements, rather than after $\bar{q}$*drag$^t$*) and so hidden under the gall (cf. 83 a 2 where *pascu$_e$* was originally written after the dimensions referring to it and then underlined for deletion and a new *pascu$_e$* interlined above its normal position). |
| | VALUE....NOW 10s. The present value is illegible under the gall. |
| 19,45 | PARTS OF THIS ENTRY which are illegible due to the gall (see 19,28-46 note) include the 1066 holder, the amount of land on which tax was paid, who holds the 1½ ploughs and the amount of the past value. However, in the blank in the middle of folio 406a is written in a 'modern' hand, probably that of Dean Lyttelton, *quam tenuit Wichinus ea die* with a X beside it corresponding to one beside *Alseministra* opposite. Presumably this could be read when the gall had been newly applied. |
| | EDWULF HOLDS....FROM WILLIAM. "Ulf (*Vlfus*) holds it from W(illiam) the Count/Earl". *W* is interlined above *comite* which may be underlined for deletion, though it is impossible to be certain because of the gall; Ellis does not underline it, but this is no proof that it was not underlined in the MS; see the section on Ellis' text in the Introduction to these Notes. There are several possible explanations for the apparent difference of subtenants, Edwulf and Ulf. The Exchequer scribe may have had access to other data informing him either that the Exon. *Vlfus* was a scribal error for *Eddulfus* or that the subtenant had changed. Or *Vlfus* may represent a short-form of the personal name *Eddulfus* or the basic name might be *Wulf, Ulf*, with a prefixed byname in one instance (OE *Edda*). It is also possible that the Exchequer scribe misread the Exon. *Et Vlfus* as one word (*Etulfus → Edulfus → Eddulfus*; Exon. regularly has *Et-* for *E(a)d-* names). Although the *V* of *Vlfus* in Exon. is slightly smaller than one would expect, there is the normal size gap after *Et* and the formula *Et A. tenet eam de B.* is a fairly common one in Exon. See General Notes 16,60 on the name Edwulf. |
| 19,46 | GALL OBSCURES half of the 1066 holder's name (only *El* there) and for the villagers' ploughs only *ii* remains, which might be part of *iii* as in DB. |
| 20,1 | BRICTRIC AND EDWY HELD IT FREELY (AND) JOINTLY. "jointly" only; "freely" omitted. Although William appears to have combined two manors for this holding, there is no mention of this in the T.O. which one would expect. See also notes to 24,21. 34,54 |

# Exon. 20 – 21

| | |
|---|---|
| 20,1 (cont'd.) | and 36,1, and for possible reasons for omissions from the T.O. of entries of a type normally included there, see 3,32 note.<br>VALUE FORMERLY. "value when *W.* ("William" in full for 20,3;6–9) acquired it". Similarly for the past values of 20,3–13;15–17. |
| 20,2 | IT IS WASTE. "It is completely waste (*est penitus uastata*)"; see the General Notes here. |
| 20,6 | 1 PLOUGH THERE .... 3 SMALLHOLDERS HAVE 1 FURLONG. "Peter has 3 furlongs (*fertinos*) in lordship and 1 plough and his 3 smallholders have 1 furlong (*fertinum*)". The second half of this statement is an unusual variation on the formula 'the villagers (have) so much land and so many ploughs'. Cf. 3,63 note on the Exon. treatment of this where only smallholders (or smallholders and slaves) are recorded for a manor. |
| 20,7 | WORLINGTON. In the T.O. at 501 b 2: "William of Falaise has a manor called Worlington. ½ furlong (*ferdinus*) of land has been added to it, which a thane held jointly in 1066. Value 5s".<br>TWO THANES HELD IT FREELY (AND) JOINTLY. "jointly" only; "freely" omitted.<br>2 VILLAGERS HAVE IT THERE. "His villagers have 1 plough on that land"; their number is given in the usual place after this statement. |
| 20,8 | 1 VILLAGER HAS IT THERE. "William has 1 villager and he has 1 plough"; the subject of the second "has" is not clear. |
| 20,9 | HE HAS ON IT 1 PLOUGH. The Englishman; *in dominio* probably implied or omitted in error. |
| 20,10 | OF THIS LAND ALRIC.... "Of the above 3 hides Alric also (*idem*) held a manor called 'Dewdon' in 1066. It paid tax for 1 virgate". Slightly abbreviated details of this added manor appear also in the T.O. at 502 b 1, where Alric (*idem Alric'*) is said to have held "jointly". |
| 20,11 | PASTURE, 1 LEAGUE; WOODLAND, 1 LEAGUE. "pasture, 1 league in both length and width"; "woodland, 1 league in length and another in width". |
| 20,14 | MEADOW....PASTURE. Details of these (but not of the livestock) are given under the holdings of the 2 men-at-arms; no meadow or pasture details are given for the main holding. The livestock on the men-at-arms' holding comprises 19 cattle, 12 pigs, 111 sheep and 40 goats.<br>AN ENGLISHMAN 1 VIRGATE OF LAND. No details of his holding are given, although he is said to have held the virgate in 1066, but he could not separate (himself) from the land.<br>IN LORDSHIP 2 PLOUGHS; 2 SLAVES; 8 VILLAGERS AND 7 SMALLHOLDERS. All these details appear under the holding of the 2 men-at-arms, not of the Englishman as well (see above note).<br>VALUE FORMERLY AND NOW £3 10s. The values are given separately for the holdings: the value of William's main holding is 40s in 1086 and the same when he acquired it; the value of the men-at-arms' holding is 20s in 1086 and the same when W(illiam) acquired it; the Englishman pays William 10s a year for his virgate (no 1066 value is given). |
| 20,15 | VILLAGERS....8 PLOUGHS. "8½ ploughs".<br>21 PIGS. "19 pigs" (x¦x).<br>BEFORE 1066 .... LUSCOMBE. "Of the above virgate a thane held a manor called Luscombe before 1066 .... but he could not separate from the lord". |
| 20,16 | LAND FOR 4 PLOUGHS. "3 ploughs". |
| 21,1 | FORMERLY. "value when W(illiam) acquired it". Similarly for the past values of 21,2–4;6;14;16–17;19–20. |
| 21,2 | OF THIS LAND. "Of the above 3 virgates". |
| 21,3 | 2 SMALLHOLDERS. "3 smallholders". |
| 21,5 | THE WHOLE OF IT IS WASTE. "It is completely waste (*est penitus uastata*)". See the General Notes here. |
| 21,7 | FORMERLY. "value when he acquired it", probably referring to William (see notes to 2,14 and 16,88). Similarly for the past values of 21,8–10;12–13;15;21. |
| 21,11 | LAND FOR ½ PLOUGH. "½ furlong (*ferd'*) can plough this (furlong: *hunc* in MS; Ellis misprints *hanc*)"; *ferd'* is no doubt a scribal error for *carr̃* "plough". VCH p. 514 has "This ½ plough can till" with no note on the scribal error.<br>THESE TWO LANDS .... 12s 6d. Details of these 2 added manors are written in the left margin of the Exon. MS, with transposition signs. In the T.O. at 502 a 5: "William of Poilley has a manor called Blagrove. Two manors have been added to it, Pedley and *Assacota*, which two thanes held jointly in 1066. Value of them 12s 6d a year". |

Exon. 21 - 23

21,13   WOODLAND, 3 ACRES. "4 acres"; the first *i* of the *iiii* is oddly shaped and is interlined before the *iii*; the Exchequer scribe could easily have missed it.
PASTURE, 20 ACRES. So Exon. MS, although the *xx* is rather faint, probably due to the MS being damp at some stage (see 19,28-46 note). Ellis misprints *ix*.
VALUE NOW 13s. In the Exon. MS *iii sol'* with the oblique stroke of a letter crossed out (possibly an *x*), or perhaps a blot, before the *iii*; definitely not *vii sol'* as Ellis prints.
21,18   VILLAGER....1VIRGATE. *uillani hñt d. i uirgā*; it is not clear what the *d* is — if meant for *dim̄* (= ½ virgate? cf. 16,92 first note) the detail would not total the tax. VCH p. 515 quotes the *d* without comment.
21,19   A FISHERY WHICH PAYS 5s. "A fishery whose value is 5s a year".
PASTURE. The word *pascuę* is omitted, but the measurements are there (cf. 19,44 note). The DB scribe probably correctly supplied the corresponding Exchequer word *pastura*, as this is the usual place for it in Exon. in the list of resources (see General Notes 1,53). However, it is just possible that the measurements refer to the meadow which precedes them, making it measure 14 acres and 1 league in length and 4 furlongs in width (though one would expect the word *prati* to have then come at the end of the whole measurement, not in the middle); see notes to 1,46 and 1,53 and cf. 42,15 note.
21,20   A FISHERY WHICH PAYS 10s. "A fishery whose value is 10s a year".
Ch. 22  LAND OF WILLIAM OF EU. His two holdings are entered in Exon. under the heading of "Lands of the French Men-at-Arms in Devonshire". Also under this heading, which covers folios 456a-462b inclusive, appear the fiefs of landholders in DB Chs. 26-27; 31-33;40-41;43;45-46, Morin's land at 51,14 and a manor of Flohere not recorded in DB (see below). See 40,1-2 note on the list. The lands are entered in Exon. in Hundred order not grouped by fief (see General Notes Ch. 22), and the Exchequer scribe obviously thought this removal of individual landholders' fiefs from the large Exon. section was useful and in keeping with the practice adopted elsewhere in DB. It is interesting that this practice was only carried out in DB Somerset with regard to the holdings of Ralph Pagnell and Ralph of Limesy (Somerset Chs. 31-32). The Exchequer scribe detailed the landholders, thus excerpted, in order of importance, not, as in his treatment of another composite Exon. section (Chs. 47-50, see note), in the order in which they first appeared in the Exon. (e.g. the first entry in the Exon. here is for Osbern of Sacey, but he was a relatively minor tenant, so he was placed well down the list at Ch. 43).
Placed between William of Eu's manor of Whitestone (DB 22,2) and Gerard's manor of Manley (DB 46,1) in this large Exon. section is Flohere's manor of *Sotrebroc* which the Exchequer scribe omitted, probably by accident during the excerpting:
459 a 3: "Flohere has a manor called *Sotrebroc* ['Shutbrook' or 'Floyers Hayes'; see General Notes Ch. 22] which Alfgeat held in 1066. It paid tax for ½ virgate, which 4 oxen can plough. Value 2s a year".
Cf. 49,7 for a similarly omitted entry in another composite section in Exon., though this was later discovered and entered in the margin of Exchequer DB (see General Notes there).
22,1    UNDERWOOD, 4 ACRES. After the livestock details is written "1 league and 4 acres of underwood". It is not clear whether the league refers to the underwood as well, is a scribal error (there are several corrections here), or *nemoris* "woodland" was omitted by mistake after it; details of the meadow and pasture follow, as in DB. See 1,46 note on the omission of *nemoris* and 1,53 note on furlongs and acres being combined in a measurement. The Exchequer scribe seems to have been perplexed about the phrase and omitted the first part, as probably at first in the similar phrase in 1,53 (see General Notes).
FORMERLY. "value when he acquired it", probably referring to William of Eu; see notes to 2,14 and 16,88.
22,2    RANULF ALSO HOLDS .... FROM WILLIAM. "Ranulf, who holds the land from W(illiam)"; an unusual formula. As there is no *idem* with Ranulf, he is not necessarily the same man as the Ranulf of 22,1 (which is what DB implies). See 15,21 note.
6 VILLAGERS HAVE IT THERE. "Ranulf has....6 villagers, who have on it 2 ploughs".
FORMERLY. "Value when William acquired it".
23,1    ALWIN HELD IT BEFORE 1066. IT PAID TAX. "which Alwin holds (*ten*') and it pays (*reddit*) tax"; *ten*' regularly abbreviates both the present *tenet* and the past *tenuit*, especially the latter in this position, though usually only with some reference to date (the usual phrase "on the day on which King Edward was alive and dead" is omitted) — cf. 1,71 note: *reddit* may also be a scribal error for *reddit* (= *reddidit* "paid"), as in

# Exon. 23

| | |
|---|---|
| 23,1 (cont'd.) | 17,2 (see note). VCH p. 485 translates 'held' and 'paid' with no comment. However, Alwin is the person who is stated to have the villager, slave, livestock etc. (and probably the lordship too), which would not be the case if he were only the 1066 holder (but see DB Dorset Exon. Notes 47,10). The statement about Alwin holding the manor occurs in Exon. where the TRE holder is normally given, and this may have misled the Exchequer scribe, especially as no TRE holder is given for this entry.<br>LAND FOR 1 PLOUGH. Omitted; the Exchequer scribe may have deduced it from the lordship plough stated. See 3,51 note and cf. Dorset Exon. Notes 11,12. |
| 23,2 | FORMERLY. "Value when *W. (Walscin(us)* for 23,5;12) acquired it". Similarly for the past values of 23,4-5;10;12-14;16-20;23;25-26. |
| 23,3 | HAGGINTON. In the T.O. at 498 b 7: "Walscin has a manor called Hagginton. A manor has been added to it, which a thane held jointly in 1066. Value 10s a year". From the value the thane would appear to be Godric; see next note.<br>FORMERLY 15s; VALUE NOW 30s. "Value (now) of the manor which Wulfmer held, 20s; value (now) of the other which Godric held, 10s; value when Walscin acquired them, 15s". |
| 23,4 | 2 SMALLHOLDERS AND 3 SLAVES. "A(rnold) has....2 villagers who have ½ plough and (he has) 2 smallholders and 3 slaves....". See 1,9 note. The formula here appears to have confused the Exchequer scribe into omitting the villagers altogether, as also happens in 49,3 (but cf. 48,4 note); see General Notes 3,27 (last note). |
| 23,5 | KING EDWARD HELD IT. In 1066.<br>THIS LAND HAS NEVER PAID TAX. "We do not know (*nescimus*) how many hides lie on this land because it has never paid tax". See the Exon. Notes for DB Somerset 36,7 and 40,2 and for Dorset 1,20 on the rare intrusion of the first person into the text. The scribe of this entry did not write the Somerset entries, but may have written the Dorset one.<br>IN LORDSHIP 2 PLOUGHS....LAND FOR 4 PLOUGHS. "W(alscin) has land for 4 ploughs in lordship; he has 2 ploughs there". It would appear that he had 4 carucates of land and 2 ploughs in lordship; see next note.<br>VILLAGERS....18 PLOUGHS. "The villagers have land for 18 ploughs", i.e. 18 carucates of land; no actual ploughs are mentioned. As the *Trā* is interlined (by the scribe of the rest of the entry and apparently at the same time), it could easily have been missed by the Exchequer scribe who assumed the *xviii carr'* was their actual plough holding rather than their land holding. A similar error occurs in 52,10 (see note).<br>TO THIS MANOR .... WILLIAM OF MOHUN .... WALSCIN. Unusually these added and removed lands do not appear in the T.O., perhaps because they were part of Bampton when the King held it and so the addition was known to be legal (so Finn LE p. 94), but this still leaves the detail of the ½ furlong ('ferling') – presumably wrongfully acquired by William of Mohun after the exchange – which one would expect to be noted in the T.O. Cf. 23,6 note.<br>BEFORE 1066. Omitted; cf. 2,24 note.<br>RADEMAR, RADEMAR. *Renuallus, Rademar(us)*. The first Exon. name should probably be rendered 'Reginwal' (OG *Ragin-, Reginwalch*, Förstemann 1238). In DB Somerset a frequent subtenant of Walter of Douai is a man called *Reneuualdus, Reneuuarus*, who would appear to be the same as this Reginwal in Devon (*-uualdus* by epenthesis and analogy with OG *Raginwald; -uarus* by AN l/r interchange); in the Somerset edition in this series the *-r-* spellings misled JMcND into adducing OG *Raginward*, whence 'Rainward' by JRM's anglicizing process. As Rademar is also a frequent subtenant of Walter's in both Devon and Somerset, the Exchequer scribe probably wrote two *Rademar*s by mistake for one *Renuallus* and one *Rademar* (unless he had received other information to correct Exon.); this can be seen also in Somerset 24,27 where DB has *Rademar* holding from Walter while Exon. has *Reineuualus*.<br>3 VILLAGERS. 10 villagers altogether; see Details Table. The DB scribe probably omitted Reginwal's 7 villagers – the (lordship) plough interlined above them may have been the cause. The DB scribe also omitted the woodland given in the same holding.<br>WITH ITS DEPENDENCIES. "with this land", referring to the added 1 hide. |
| 23,6 | DIPFORD....TWO THANES HELD IT JOINTLY AS TWO MANORS. "Walscin holds two manors called Dipford, which two thanes held jointly in 1066". No record of this combination appears in the T.O., probably because the King was involved in the tenure (see below and cf. 23,5 fifth note).<br>VILLAGERS....6 PLOUGHS. "3 ploughs". |

Exon. 23

| | |
|---|---|
| 23,6 (cont'd.) | FORMERLY. "value when he acquired it", probably referring to Walter/Walscin (see notes to 2,14 and 16,88). Similarly for the past values of 23,7;9;15;20-22. |
| | CALLS UPON THE KING (TO WARRANT) IT. "He calls on the King as his guarantor for this (*inde uocat rege͡ aduocatu͡*)". See the General Notes here. |
| 23,7 | W(ALSCIN) HOLDS HOCKWORTHY HIMSELF. "Walscin has....Hockworthy....and Gerard holds it from W(alscin)". See General Notes 47,2 and also General Notes 23,5 on Gerard. It is possible that since Exon. had been compiled Gerard had given up his subtenancy of Hockworthy. |
| 23,11 | ROLF ALSO. "Rolf" with no *idem*, so perhaps not the same man as the Rolf of 23,10. See 15,21 note. |
| 23,12-17 | THESE ENTRIES are on folio 347 which the transcriber Ralph Barnes noted in 1810 had been cut out and "no doubt stolen" (Exon. f. 541), but which was discovered soon afterwards and sent to him (see Ellis' note on p. 327* of DB3) and re-inserted among the MS folios. A transcription of it was prepared and printed for inclusion in subsequent bindings of DB3 as pp. 326*-327*. $q̄dra\bar{g}$ |
| 23,12 | WOODLAND, 10 ACRES. "woodland, 10 furlongs": x *agros nemoris*, the *agros* being underlined for deletion (though this is not shown by Ellis). The interlineation is in the same colour ink and by the same scribe, so is very unlikely to be a correction done after the MS was seen and used by the compiler of DB. See 1,38 for another example of DB having acres for Exon.'s furlongs, though there is no obvious reason there for the change. Cf. 17,79 note. |
| 23,13 | 1 PLOUGH, WHICH IS THERE. "L(udo) has 1 plough"; *in dominio* probably implied or omitted in error. |
| 23,15 | 11 VILLAGERS. "21 villagers". |
| | 61 PIGS. "60 pigs", the *lx* being written over the erasure of a longer figure (possibly *xviii*) of which a final *i* is still visible, hence, probably, the discrepancy with DB. |
| | PASTURE, 10 FURLONGS. "pasture, 10 furlongs in both length and width". |
| | VALUE.....£7. So Exon. MS; Ellis misprints *vm libras*. |
| 23,16 | ASGAR. Exon. *Ansgar(us)* 'Ansger'; see General Notes 1,23-24. |
| 23,20 | TO THIS MANOR .... 20s. Abbreviated details of this added manor, which is also held by Ludo, appear twice in the T.O.: in 503 b 3 and in 500 a 6, referring to 42,16 where Ludo is named and described as Walscin's man-at-arms and the value is stated to be "30s". See the General Notes here. |
| 23,22 | LUDO HOLDS STOKE (FLEMING). Ludo only holds 4 of the 5 hides in Stoke (Fleming), the remaining hide being held by Ralph and a woman. Cf. notes to 19,33;43 and 34,27. |
| | ASGAR. Exon. *Ansgar(us)* 'Ansger'; see General Notes 1,23-24. |
| | A MILL IN LORDSHIP WHICH RENDERS SERVICE. "A mill which only serves his house (*molendinum qui tantummodo* * *seruit domui suae*)", the meaning being that the mill provides grain only for the lord's residence, not for the villagers. Cf. 5,1 "a mill which serves the court". |
| | * In the Exon. MS *tantū m̊* with a slight space between, possibly intended as two words. Although *tantum* and *modo* each have several meanings, when brought together (whether as one word or two) they mean "only". VCH p. 488 is wrong to translate "only now". |
| | A WOMAN HOLDS ½ HIDE. "....which W(alscin) gave her in alms". The Exchequer scribe may have intentionally omitted this, because he thought it unimportant in a sub-holding. |
| 23,23 | BICCA HELD IT. "which Bicca held jointly", only in the T.O. entry (504 a 1); both Exon. and DB describe the manner of Bicca's tenure in the last sentence. |
| | ASGAR'S LANDS. "Ansger's Honour"; in 504 a 1: "Ansger's Honour which W(alscin) holds". On Asgar/Ansger representing the same name, see General Notes 1,23-24. |
| | THE HOLDER .... WOULD. "This manor belonged to a thane free to go where he would before 1066". Similarly for 23,24. The (extended) Latin for both these entries (*haec mansio fuit liberi tagni ad pergendum quocumque uoluit tempore regis Eduuardi*), though slightly contorted and involving an unusual use of the gerund, is clear: *liberi* is genitive and *ad pergendum* depends on it (= "free to go"). A different Exon. scribe to this one also attempted the use of the gerund in a similar phrase for DB 40,7, but his command of Latin was not good enough to carry it through; see 40,7 note. VCH p. 488 translates the *tempore regis Eduuardi* phrase as describing the date at which the manor belonged to the thane, which alters the meaning. Although this is how DB puts it, it is unlikely here because of the position of the phrase at the end of the sentence. |

## Exon. 23 – 24

| | |
|---|---|
| 23,24 | EDRIC HELD IT. "which Edric held jointly" only in the T.O. entry (504 a 2). 1½ PLOUGHS THERE. "Alric has 1½ ploughs"; *in dominio* probably implied or omitted in error. ASGAR'S LANDS. "Ansger's Honour"; in 504 a 2 "Ansger's Honour which W(alscin) holds". See General Notes 1,23-24 on Asgar/Ansger. THE HOLDER .... WOULD. See 23,23 note. |
| 23,25 | 1 PLOUGH, WHICH IS THERE. "Aelfeva has 1 plough"; *in dominio* probably implied or omitted in error. |
| 23,27 | ASGAR. Exon. *Ansger(us)* 'Ansger'; see General Notes 1,23-24. HE HAS ALSO .... KEPT BACK. Also in the T.O. at 506 b 1. CUSTOMARY DUES. "King's customary dues, that is 8d" in 506 b 1. |
| Chs. 24 -25 | WALTER OF CLAVILLE. GOTSHELM. In Exon. the holdings of Walter and Gotshelm are given under the heading of "Lands of Gotshelm and Walter in Devonshire", folios 388a-397a inclusive. According to Galbraith p. 107 the two fiefs were combined in Exon. because the first entry to be written there (= DB 24,32) was held jointly by the two men, so the scribe wrote the joint heading and then continued. However, it is more likely that the returns of Walter and Gotshelm (apparently brothers; see General Notes Ch. 25) came in together and were never separated, but retained in their original Hundred order; cf. General Notes Ch. 19. The lands of Walter are entered for one Hundred, then those of Gotshelm in the same Hundred, then for the next Hundred Gotshelm's holdings come first, Walter's second, and so on with only a couple of exceptions to this rule; see General Notes Chs. 24-25 for the order and cf. General Notes 24,8-16. The Exchequer scribe separated this Exon. section into two chapters, as he did with other composite Exon. sections (see notes to Ch. 22 and to Chs. 47-50). However, instead of beginning his excerpting of Walter's land at folio 388a, he began in the middle of the Exon. section at folio 392a which coincides with the beginning of the second of the three 'booklets' forming the section (4d; see Ker's list on p. 803). It would seem that the Exchequer scribe inadvertently mislaid the first 'booklet' and then came back to it when he had got to the end of the section; see General Notes 24,21-22 for the space in the DB MS probably caused by this. Having recovered the first 'booklet' he proceeded to excerpt Gotshelm's lands in the logical order, beginning with 25,1 on folio 388a. This is strong proof that the Exchequer scribe used Exon. in the form we have it now, rather than a copy: the odd order of excerpting Walter's lands can only be explained by the 'booklet' division of the Exon. at this point (in a copy it would be unlikely that the scribe would use identical size 'booklets' to his original; almost certainly he would use uniform 'booklets' throughout with no blanks). To explain this contradiction of the 'copy' view Finn (MDeD p. 116) stated that some of the 'booklets' in the copy were apparently constructed in the same way as their originals. |
| Ch. 24 | WALTER OF CLAVILLE. See note above. He is only called Walter of Claville for 24,1;3. |
| 24,1 | VALUE FORMERLY. "value when W. ('Walter' in full for 24,22) acquired it". Similarly for the past values of 24,2-4;6-7;19;21-22;31. |
| 24,3 | 3 VILLAGERS. "8 villagers". |
| 24,5 | FORMERLY. "value when he acquired it", probably referring to Walter (see notes to 2,14 and 16,88). Similarly for the past values of 24,8-10;13-17;23-30. TO THIS MANOR .... 3s. Also in the T.O. at 501 b 6, where a thane is said to have held the added furlong (*ferdinus*) jointly in 1066. |
| 24,7 | OSBERN HOLDS. "Osbert holds". See notes to 17,34 and Ch. 43 on Osbern/Osbert. |
| 24,8 | 'KIDWELL' .... 10s. Abbreviated details of this added manor also appear in the T.O. at 502 b 3. ALFRUN HELD IT FREELY. "which Alfrun held"; "freely" omitted. In 502 b 3: "which Alfrun held jointly", with again no mention of "freely". |
| 24,9 | WOODLAND, 8 ACRES. "9 acres". |
| 24,10 | 3 PLOUGHS, WHICH ARE THERE. 3½ ploughs; see the Lordship and Villagers' Table. |
| 24,11 | 4 SMALLHOLDERS HAVE IT THERE. "W(alter) has 4 smallholders"; no mention is made of their plough. It is possible that the *hanc* of Exchequer DB refers to the land (see General Notes here), but Exon. does not mention the smallholders as having that either. |
| 24,14 | WULFWY. 'Wulfgeat': *OlWiet* (for *Oluuiet*), which is OE *Wulfgeat*. The DB form is *Vluui* (OE *Wulfwig*). It is possible that a mistake in the name of the TRE tenant of Appledore was discovered after Exon. was written and the Exchequer scribe is recording |

Exon. 24

24,14     the correction, but it is equally likely that an error in transcription took place, the
(cont'd.) endings *-wiet* (= *-geat*) and *-uui* (= *-wig*) being easily confused (see PNDB p. 412 note 2).
As a Wulfgeat (DB *Vluiet*, Exon. *Oluietus*) was the TRE tenant of Burlescombe (24,30) in which Appledore lies, and had also held Fenacre in Burlescombe tithing (25,12, held in 1086 by Walter's brother), it is very probable that the DB scribe was the one guilty of mistranscription, as he was with several personal names (see 28,1 note and General Notes 52,1) and place-names (see General Notes 3,24-25 and 16,42).
THIS THANE .... WOULD. "He could go to whichever lord he would"; 'thane' is not mentioned.

24,16     3 VILLAGERS AND 3 SMALLHOLDERS HAVE 1 PLOUGH. "W(alter) has 3 villagers who hold 1 plough and (he has) 3 smallholders". See 1,9 note.

24,17     TAX FOR ½ HIDE. In the MS *gildū p iti* "tax for 3(?)...." with an erasure of 3-4 letters after the *iti*, if that is in fact what it is (so Ellis prints it). The last two minims of the *iti* are close together and the abbreviation sign is out of place over a number; it is possible that the scribe wrote *dim' hida*, for which there is room, erasing only the *d* and the last minim of the *m* for some reason and *hida*; a dot at the end of the erasure, before *Hanc*, is visible. In any case it would seem that the Exchequer scribe either had access to other information on the taxability of this manor, or deduced it from the lordship and villagers' land, though this is not a foolproof method because of the number of discrepancies in Devon between the detail and tax total; see General Notes 1,4 on the hide. VCH p. 500 has 'it paid geld for 3 virgates', with no comment on the lack of *virgis*.

24,18     WOODMAN HELD IT. "which Woodman held jointly", only in the T.O. entry (504 a 5). W(ALTER) HAS 1½ PLOUGHS. *in dominio* probably implied or omitted in error.
THIS LAND HAS BEEN ADDED TO BRICTRIC'S LANDS. In 504 a 5 the manor is said to have been added "wrongfully".

24,19     IN LORDSHIP 1 PLOUGH. "1½ ploughs".
24,20     PASTURE, 1 FURLONG. "Pasture, 1 furlong in length and width".
24,21     TWO THANES HELD IT FROM BRICTRIC SON OF ALGAR. "....they could not be separated from him". There is no entry in the T.O., although the manor was combined (see last statement in the translation), perhaps because the two thanes held it from Brictric, rather than from the King (so Whale in TDA 37 p. 272). But see 20,1 note on other omissions from the T.O. of information one would expect to find there.

24,22     SEPARATED FROM THE KING'S MANOR. "separated from the manor", no mention of 'King's', but this is probably implied from the previous description of Iddesleigh.
3 PLOUGHS .... THERE. "William has 1 plough in lordship" (see Lordship and Villagers' Table for the villagers' ploughs): presumably *Willelm(us)* is a scribal error for *Walter(us)*, as there is no mention elsewhere in the entry of a subtenant of Walter.
2 SMALLHOLDERS. So Ellis; but in the Exon. MS *iii bord'* appears; the last *i* is faint and obviously the Exchequer scribe and Ralph Barnes thought it had been erased, though there is no sign of erasure by water and the top part of the minim is quite dark: possibly the parchment was greasy here and not all of the ink 'took'.

24,23     HE COULD GO WHERE HE WOULD. "This Alward could go with his land to whichever lord he would".

24,24     LOOSEDON. In the T.O. at 498 a 1: "Walter of Claville has a manor called Loosedon which was (part) of Brictric's land. A manor called Dowland has been added to it, which 2 thanes held jointly. It did not belong to the said manor in 1066. Value 12s 6d a year; value when W(alter) acquired it, as much". See 24,25 note and General Notes here.
BRICTRIC HELD IT. "which Alward Mart (*merta*) held from Brictric"; see notes to 3,94 and 15,33.
VILLAGERS....2½ PLOUGHS. "W(alter) has 5 villagers and 3 smallholders and 2½ ploughs". Because of the position of the 2½ ploughs it is unlikely that they were in lordship. Cf. 25,10 note.
2 SMALLHOLDERS. "3 smallholders".

24,25     IN DOWLAND 1 VIRGATE OF LAND. "in the above manor called Dowland [= DB 24,23] Walter has 1 virgate of land". In the T.O. at 498 a 2: "In the above Dowland Walter has 1 virgate of land which 2 thanes held jointly in 1066 [and] which did not belong to this said manor. Value 12s 6d; value when he acquired it, as much". It will be noticed that the second half of this entry is virtually the same as for the preceding entry 498 a 1 (see first note under 24,24) and that the "above (*supradicta*) Dowland" must be the Dowland of 498 a 1, not the main holding at Dowland, 24,23, which the main Exon. entry implies, but which is not mentioned in the T.O. Moreover, "this said manor" to which the virgate did not belong, must be Loosedon, not Dowland. The scribe and ink colour of 498 a 1-2 are the same, though the pen used for 498 a 2 is slightly thinner and the writing smaller and neater. It is interesting that in both 498 a 1 and 498 a 2 the value was originally written *xii sol'* and then the *& vi den'* was interlined, probably at the same time to both entries; also that in 498 a 1 the scribe originally wrote "1 thane" (which would fit in with the TRE holder of 24,23) and corrected it to "2 thanes" to agree with 498 a 2.

24,28    WALTER HOLDS WOLFIN. "Walter holds it from W(alter)". No subtenant of Walter of Claville is mentioned in the corresponding T.O. entry, 498 a 5, which merely states that "Walter of Claville has a manor called Wolfin, which Alward a thane held who could go with his land to whichever lord he would in 1066" and gives the two values. The fact that this is included in the T.O. implies that some illegality was being practised and this is strengthened by the statement that Alward was a thane and he and his holding were not bound to anyone. The same is probably true of the next entry in the T.O. (= DB 24,29, see note).

ALWARD MART, A FREE MAN. "This Alward could go with his land to whichever lord he would", added at the end of the entry. Similarly in 498 a 5.

24,29    SHOBROOKE. Also held in 1086 by a Walter from Walter. No subtenant of Walter of Claville is mentioned in the corresponding T.O. entry, 498 a 6, which, like the preceding entry (= DB 24,28, see note), merely states that Walter has a manor called Shobrooke which Brictric held who could go to whichever lord he would with his land in 1066, and gives the value. It would seem that Walter's claim to the manor was not watertight.

BRICTRIC, A FREE MAN. "Brictric could go with his land where he would", added at the end of the entry. So also in 498 a 6.

24,30    BURLESCOMBE. No subtenant of Walter's is mentioned.

4 SMALLHOLDERS. In the MS $v\ bordar^{iiii}$; as the $v$ is not underlined for deletion, the number would appear to be *viiii*: the scribe of this entry elsewhere writes "9" as *viiii* rather than as *ix* (e.g. *xviiii* "19" in 110 b 2 = DB 1,35). VCH p. 497 translates "4 bordars".

24,31    CICLET. "Walter the Wild (*siluestris*) holds it from W(alter)".
4 VILLAGERS AND 3 SMALLHOLDERS HAVE 2 PLOUGHS. "W(alter) has 4 villagers who have 2 ploughs and (he has) 3 smallholders". See 1,9 note.

24,32    FORMERLY. "value when they acquired it", referring to Walter and Gotshelm.
Ch. 25    LAND OF GOTSHELM. See notes to Chs. 24-25 and to 25,28.
25,1    PASTURE, ½ LEAGUE. "pasture, ½ league in length and width".
FORMERLY 100s. "When G(otshelm) acquired it". Similarly "when G. acquired it" ('Gotshelm' in full for 25,27) for the past values of 25,3-4;11-15;23-24;27.

25,2    VALUE FORMERLY. "value when he acquired it", probably referring to Gotshelm (see notes to 2,14 and 16,88). Similarly for the past values of 25,5-10;16-22.

25,3    COLSWEIN. In the Exon. MS *Colsuen'* clearly corrected from *Golsuen'*; Ellis misprints *Golsuen'*.

WHICH WAS ATTACHED TO IT.... "which belonged to the village before 1066 and after King William had [England?] Gotshelm had it undisturbed for 5 years": the (extended) Latin is *quae pertinebat uillae tempore regis Eduuardi et postquam Willelmus rex habuit .... -licam(?) habuit eam Goscelmus quietam\* per v annos*. The whole of this statement on the removal of the common pasture has been added in 1½ lines in the space between the penultimate and last lines of the entry, extending from one edge of the parchment to the other; the ink is paler than that of the rest of the entry, but the scribe is the same, so it is unlikely to be a late addition to the Exon. MS. The second line begins with *lıcā* which would seem to be part of *Anglicā* ("English" with *terram* "land" presumably understood), the first 3 letters apparently being cut or torn off at some stage (*de* may also have disappeared before the *hac mansione* in the line above, though the preposition is not absolutely necessary); cf. 36,18 note, although the MS there shows definite signs of being cut. The first visible letters in both lines are faint. Although the end of the word on the second line is probably *cā*, the letters are joined together so that they rather resemble an *m̄* (making *-lim̄* ?) and there is an odd dot immediately to the left of the *cā* (or *m̄*) which may or may not be relevant. Ellis prints *-dicā* but there is definitely not a *d* visible, though part of a letter can be seen before the *licā* which might be part of the *g* of *Anglicā*; anyway it is hard to see what word could end *-dicā* which would fit the context. Both VCH p. 495 and DGSW p. 268 have

Exon. 25 - 28

*Anglicam* with no comment and VCH translates it as "England". There is no record in the T.O. of this removal of pasture, though this may have been intentional as being unworthy of note in such a document.
\* "undisturbed, peaceful" is the normal meaning of *quietam*, but in DB it regularly means "exempt (from dues)", though it is more likely that the meaning here is that no one interfered with, or made a claim on, Gotshelm's tenure of the pasture. See General Notes 3,2 on *quietus*.

25,10    2 VILLAGERS HAVE ½ PLOUGH. "O(smund) has 2 villagers and ½ plough"; it is unlikely that the ½ plough is in lordship. Cf. 24,24 note.

25,18    1 VILLAGER HAS ½ PLOUGH. "Gotshelm has in lordship 1 villager and ½ plough"; the explicit inclusion of the villager in the lordship is most unusual.

25,19    HE HELD IT HIMSELF. It is not absolutely clear whether Aelmer the priest is the TRE tenant: *Elmerus* appears first in the Exon. entry as the 1066 holder with *Almerus presbiter* as the 1086 tenant. *Elmerus/Almerus* represent the OE personal name *Aelfmaer/ Aethelmaer*; see General Notes 3,47 on 'Aelmer'.
VALUE 4s. So Exon. MS; Ellis misprints *iii sol'*.

25,20    ASH (THOMAS). In the T.O. at 502 b 6: "Gotshelm holds ½ hide of land which has been added to Brictric's lands. A woman held this ½ hide freely in 1066. Value 10s a year". The ½ hide apparently refers to Ash (Thomas). See the General Notes here on the odd initial letter of the place-name in the main Exon. entry.

25,25    AELFRIC HELD IT. In the T.O. entry (504 a 4): "which Aelfric held jointly".
ADDED TO BRICTRIC'S LANDS. In 504 a 4: "....wrongfully".
THE HOLDER....FREE MAN. "a thane held this manor as free".

25,26    1 PLOUGH THERE. "In it (manor) B(aldwin) has 1 plough"; *in dominio* probably implied or omitted in error.
WOODLAND. "underwood (*nemusculi*)"; see General Notes here.

25,27    WULFSTAN HELD IT. Originally *bristri'* (– 'Brictric'), but it is underlined (not shown by Ellis) and *Vlestan'* is interlined in correction, an early correction done by the scribe of the rest of the entry in the same colour ink. Cf. notes to 16,76 and 34,6.
THE HOLDER BEFORE 1066 .... BRICTRIC. "This thane held his land freely from Brictric before 1066 (*tempore regis*; the scribe omitted *Eduuardi*); he could not be separated from Brictric's lands".

25,28    THIS ENTRY is the only one on folio 398a and is separated from the holdings of Gotshelm and Walter by Gotshelm's land in Cornwall (on folio 397b) though in the same 'booklet' (Ker pp. 803, 805). It appears under the heading of "Land of Gotshelm of Exeter". See General Notes here.
HE COULD GO WHERE HE WOULD. "he could go to whichever lord he would".
6 VILLAGERS HAVE THEM THERE. "G(otshelm) has 6 villagers who have these 1½ hides and 3 ploughs at a revenue (*ad firmam*)". A clear example of villagers 'farming' the land; see General Notes 6,6.
AFTER THIS ENTRY there appears in the MS, in very pale ink and small script and by a different scribe to 398 a 1, the words *Eduuard' tenet iii hidas tr̄ę*, preceded by a gallows sign. They are not printed by Ellis, no doubt because begun in the wrong place. The only 1086 holding of 3 hides by an Edward in the south-west counties is that of Witherington in DB Wilts. 67,54 by Edward a thane, although that of Shrewton in Wilts. 24,7 held by Edward of Salisbury is a possibility. (In two other instances in Wilts. – 15,2 and 41,10 – an Edward holds 3 hides but he is a subtenant and the Exon. scribe would not have begun the entry thus with him.) The Exon. folios for Wiltshire have not survived, so it cannot be checked where the full entry occurs there.

Ch. 26    LAND OF RICHARD SON OF COUNT GILBERT. His holding appears in Exon. under the heading of "Lands of the French Men-at-Arms in Devonshire"; see Ch. 22 note.

26,1    10 VILLAGERS .... £8. "10 villagers, 6 smallholders and 2 slaves pay from this (manor) £8 to William in revenue (*ad firmam Willelmo*) and when Richard [acquired] this manor the value was £10". See General Notes 6,6 on villagers 'farming' land. It is noteworthy that the slaves are included here in the transaction.
FORMERLY £10. "When Richard [acquired] this manor, the value was £10".

Ch. 27    LAND OF ROGER OF BULLY also appears in Exon. under the heading of "Lands of the French Men-at-Arms in Devonshire"; see Ch. 22 note.

27,1    9 PLOUGHS. So Exon. MS; Ellis misprints '8'.
FORMERLY 100s. "When he acquired it, it paid 100s".

28,1    WULFEVA. Exon. *Wlwena*, probably *n* for *u* by scribal error (so PNDB p. 174 note 3

# Exon. 28

| | |
|---|---|
| 28,1 (cont'd.) | and cf. 37,1 note). A Wulfwen (*Vlwena, Oluuena*) occurs twice in Devon as a TRE holder, so it is possible it was the Exchequer scribe who made the error in transcription (as also probably in 24,14; see note).<br>IN LORDSHIP 1 PLOUGH. "2 ploughs".<br>7 SLAVES. "7 smallholders"; *bordarios* repeated in error, the *xi bordarios* being written immediately before.<br>[VALUE] FORMERLY. "value when *R*. (*Rotbertus* in full for 28,3–5;15 and with his byname for 28,10) acquired it". Similarly for the past values of 28,3–15. |
| 28,2 | OTTERY. In the T.O. at 495 a 4: "Robert of Aumale has a manor calld Ottery. To this manor have been added three other manors which 2 thanes held jointly in 1066. Value of them 50s a year".<br>ROBERT HOLDS OTTERY, COLLACOMBE AND WILLESTREW .... THREE THANES .... FOUR MANORS. "Robert has land in 3 villages which 3 thanes held as 4 manors"; then at the end of the entry the manors and thanes are named: Oslac and Burgred held "one of these manors called Ottery; Oslac held "the third called Collacombe" and Burgred held "the fourth manor called Willestrew". There were, however, two manors in Ottery and the *Una* is obviously a mistake for *Duae* because of the *tertius* (for *tertia*) and *quarta* following (it is perhaps relevant that the *a* and possibly the *n* of *Una* are squashed in). There seems to be some confusion as to the number of thanes holding the 4 manors in 1066: the T.O. entry gives 2 thanes (presumably Oslac and Burgred) for part of Ottery and all of Collacombe and Willestrew, whereas the main Exon. entry by mentioning 3 thanes for the 3 villages suggests there were either two Burgreds or two Oslacs. The first four lines of the main entry are written over an erasure, but the *iii tagni* are clear enough, though possibly a scribal error for *ii* (because of the *iii* in *iii uillis* before it) which Exchequer DB perpetuates.<br>WOODLAND .... *iiii q̃drag̃* & *xx agros nemoris in long̃* & *ii in lat̃*, followed by the details of the meadow and pasture. It may be that *nemusculi* was omitted in error after the *iiii q̃drag̃* (= "underwood, 4 furlongs; woodland, 20 acres in length and 2 in width") though details of underwood in Exon. usually succeed rather than precede those of woodland; see 1,46 note for other entries where the Exon. scribe has omitted to state what is being measured. Woodland and underwood occur together in several entries in DB and Exon. (e.g. 1,3. 3,81. 12,1 etc.). Or the meaning may be "woodland, 4 furlongs and 20 acres in length and 2 in width"; see 1,53 note on the combining of furlongs and acres in one measurement. However, it is more probable that there were two stretches of woodland, one of 4 furlongs (by 4 furlongs) and the other measuring 20 acres by 2 acres (see General Notes to 1,35 and 1,53). The Exchequer scribe may have been unsure of the meaning, so omitted all reference to the *iiii q̃drag̃*, although he included similar phrases that are equally ambiguous in Exon. (e.g. 1,35).<br>VALUE 60s. "Value of two of the manors, 20s; value of the other two, 40s"; the names of the manors are not mentioned. The T.O. entry (see first note here) states that the value of the 3 manors added to Ottery (i.e. the other manor in Ottery, and Collacombe and Willestrew) is 50s. So, as 2 manors in a village that have been combined in 1086 regularly (according to the T.O.) have the same value (e.g. 17,92;105. 47,14, but cf. 23,3 second note), it seems likely that the 20s refers to the two manors in Ottery (10s each) and the 40s to those in Collacombe and Willestrew. |
| 28,3 | WULFRUN, A FREE WOMAN. "A woman, Wulfrun; she could go to whichever lord she would". |
| 28,4 | WOODLAND. "underwood (*nemusculi*)". |
| 28,5 | IN LORDSHIP 1 PLOUGH. "Gilbert has 1 plough"; *in dominio* probably implied or omitted in error.<br>2 SLAVES; 2 VILLAGERS WITH 1 PLOUGH. "(Gilbert has) 2 villagers and 2 slaves who have another plough". See 28,16 note and General Notes 1,3 on slaves; cf. 34,13 note below. |
| 28,6 | 3 SLAVES. "4 slaves". |
| 28,10 | VILLAGERS....½ PLOUGH. "4 oxen for a plough (*ad carrucam*)". |
| 28,11 | WOODLAND. "underwood (*nemusculi*)". |
| 28,14 | 1 VILLAGER WHO PAYS 30d. VALUE FORMERLY 5s. "R(obert) has 1 villager who pays 30d a year and when R(obert) acquired it, it (or possibly 'he' referring to the villager) paid 5s". |
| 28,16 | 3 SLAVES, WITH 1 VILLAGER HAVE ½ PLOUGH .... "The villagers (*uillani*, in full) have .... ½ plough. Oswulf has 1 villager and 3 slaves". Here it would seem that the slaves |

| | |
|---|---|
| 28,16 (cont'd.) | were counted as 'villagers' with a share in their land and plough, unless the scribe used the term *uillani* when giving their land and plough without checking whether there was more than one 'villager'. See notes to 3,79. 5,9 and 34,56 and cf. notes to 3,57. 16,6. 16,145-146. 17,58. 19,9 and 35,5.<br>WOODLAND....4 FURLONGS WIDE. "woodland....3 furlongs wide".<br>WHITLEIGH.... 10s. No mention is made of this added manor in the main Exon.: folio 421b ends with the value of the main manor of Widey. It would seem that the folios containing the details of Whitleigh (and also 28,17 and Chs. 29, 30; see notes to these) have not survived; some of these folios may have formed the 'missing 3 leaves' of the 6-leaf quire ('booklet') that began on folio 419 (see Ker pp. 803, 806). Abbreviated details of Whitleigh's addition to Widey appear in the T.O. at 505 a 3, as would be expected.<br>WADDELL HELD IT FREELY (AND) JOINTLY. "which Waddell held jointly" in 505 a 3; no mention of 'freely'. |
| 28,17 | NO EXON. survives for this entry. See third note under 28,16. |
| Chs. 29 -30 | NO EXON. survives for these two chapters, with the exception of one T.O. entry, 506 a 13, referring to 30,4, which is virtually identical to DB. Richard is given the byname *filius turulfi*. |
| Chs. 31 -33 | THE HOLDINGS of Ralph of Limesy, Ralph Pagnell and Ralph of Feugères appear in Exon. under the heading of "Lands of the French Men-at-Arms in Devonshire"; see Ch. 22 note. |
| 31,1 | 10 SLAVES. In the Exon. MS *ix*, but only part of the *i* is there, either because it was written on greasy parchment or, as the Exchequer scribe may have thought, an attempt had been made to erase it. Cf. 7,4 first note and 15,23 second note.<br>VALUE FORMERLY. "when R(alph) acquired it". Similarly for the past value of 31,2;4. |
| 31,3 | VALUE 31d(?). "30d"; the *xxx* is clearly written in a neat entry. |
| 32,1 | FORMERLY. "value when R. ('Ralph' in full for 32,8) acquired it". Similarly for the past values of 32,5;7-10. |
| 32,2-3 | FORMERLY. "value when he acquired it" for each entry, probably referring to Ralph; see notes to 2,14 and 16,88. |
| 32,6 | PASTURE....WIDTH. "2 leagues of pasture and 8 furlongs in both length and width", that is, the *pascue* is written immediately after the *ii leugas*, rather than after the furlongs. Although the 8 furlongs are probably both measurements of the pasture (which is how the Exchequer scribe took them), it is possible that the Exon. scribe omitted 'underwood' after the furlongs (though the underwood would then be out of place; see General Notes 1,53) and that the reading should be "pasture, 2 leagues; underwood, 8 furlongs in both length and width". See 1,46 note and also General Notes 1,35.<br>1 HOUSE WHICH PAYS 10s. See the General Notes here. |
| 32,10 | MERLESWEIN.... 1066. Added in the usual place in each of the entries corresponding to 32,2-10. |
| 33,1 | UNDERWOOD, ½ LEAGUE. "underwood, ½ league in length and width". |
| 33,2 | VILLAGERS....5½ PLOUGHS. "....5 ploughs and 4 oxen". |
| 34,1 | FORMERLY. "value when R. ('Ralph' in full for 34,2;18) acquired it". Similarly for the past values of 34,2;8-9;12-13;18;23-24;31-33;35-40;44;48-52. |
| 34,2 | IN LORDSHIP.... VILLAGERS.... MEADOW.... GOATS. These details only refer to the 2 virgates left in Dunsdon.<br>VALUE 100s. "Value of this manor, 100s a year with the exception of the virgate which the Count of Mortain has". The value of the removed virgate is given as 30s in the T.O. entry (496 b 5). It is not clear whether the former value (when Ralph acquired the manor) was for all 3 virgates.<br>FROM THESE 3 VIRGATES.... PLOUGHS. Also in 496 b 5 in abbreviated form. |
| 34,4 | FORMERLY. "value when he acquired ", probably referring to Ralph (see notes to 2,14 and 16,88). Similarly for the past values of 34,5-7;10;14-16;19-20;22;25-30;41;43; 54-55. |
| 34,5 | RALPH SEIZED IT. In the T.O. at 497 a 3: "Ralph also appropriated (*occupauit*) a manor called Ash which a thane held jointly in 1066. Value 10s a year; value when he appropriated it, 20s".<br>LEDMER WAS A FREE MAN. Omitted in that exact form, but "he could go to whichever lord he would". |
| 34,6 | TOVI. In the Exon. MS *Tovi* is written, probably by a different scribe, above *Aluuard'* (= Alward) which is underlined for deletion, though Ellis omits to show this. Cf. notes to 16,76 and 25,27. |

## Exon. 34

| | |
|---|---|
| 34,7 | (WEST) PUTFORD. See 1,37 note for a customary due Ralph did not pay from this manor to the King's manor of (Black) Torrington. |
| 34,9 | 1 PLOUGH, WHICH IS THERE. "Roger and his men have 1 plough"; only Roger 'has' the smallholders and slave. |
| 34,10 | ASHCOMBE. Abbreviated details of the three added manors appear in the T.O. at 498 a 9, which states that they did not belong to Ashcombe before 1066 and that their (1086) value is £7 10s.<br>WHICH THREE THANES HELD FREELY (AND) JOINTLY. "freely" omitted; likewise omitted in 498 a 9.<br>FOUR LANDS. "four manors". |
| 34,11 | HOLCOMBE....IT PAID TAX FOR 1 VIRGATE. "Ralph has 1 virgate of land called Holcombe"; no mention is made of tax. The Exchequer scribe probably thought it was implied in the Exon. statement, as land regularly paid tax on its full extent in Devon (see General Notes 1,4 on the hide), or he could have had access to other information. See the note to 36,9, an entry perhaps by the same scribe as this one; also DB Dorset Exon. Notes 55,7 and Somerset Exon. Notes 19,84 and 24,16. Cf. General Notes here to 24,25 and 34,32. |
| 34,13 | RI(CHARD) HAS.... In the MS *Ri* for *Ricardus*; Ellis misprints *R. i.*<br>2 SMALLHOLDERS. "2 slaves"; no smallholders mentioned. Exon. is explicit in stating that the slaves as well as the villagers have the furlong ('ferling'). Cf. 28,5 note. |
| 34,14 | 'LANK COMBE' .... 3s. Also in the T.O. at 499 a 2 in abbreviated form.<br>1 VILLAGER WHO PAYS 3s. "There is a villager who pays 3s a year". But in 499 a 2 the value of 'Lank Combe' is given as 3s, no mention being made of the villager's payment (villagers are not usually mentioned in the T.O., though see 1,11 note ('Deneworthy' .... said manor) for the few examples of population recorded there). |
| 34,16 | (CAFFYNS) HEANTON. Helgot holds it from Ralph. |
| 34,24 | 1 PLOUGH THERE AND 1½ VIRGATES. "R(ozelin) has 1½ virgates and 1 plough"; *in dominio* probably implied or omitted in error. |
| 34,25 | TAX FOR 1½ HIDES. "tax for 1½ hides and 1 virgate", which agrees with the details; the *& i virg*' is on the next line in the Exon. MS, probably the reason for its omission in DB; cf. notes to 3,86 and 17,69.<br>3 SLAVES....11 VILLAGERS. Unusually given after the livestock, rather than before. |
| 34,27 | WILLIAM OF POITOU HOLDS OGWELL. Two subtenants are mentioned: William of Poitou who has 2 virgates and Robert who has 1 virgate and of whom there is no mention in DB. The details of villagers, resources and value given in DB do not tally exactly with either of the two holdings, though they are closer to William's; see Details Table. See 19,43 note and the Exon. Notes to DB Dorset 47,7 and Somerset 36,7 for similar examples of the Exchequer scribe giving as 1086 holder of the whole of a manor someone who held only a part of it according to Exon. Cf. notes to 19,33 and 23,22. |
| 34,29 | A MILL WHICH PAYS 6s. "A mill whose value is 5s a year". |
| 34,32 | ½ PLOUGH. "3 oxen in a plough". |
| 34,33 | VALUE....30s. "Value....20s". |
| 34,34 | RALPH .... AUNK. In the T.O. at 501 a 5: "Ralph has a manor called Aunk. A manor called *Heppasteba* has been added to it, which a thane held who could go with his land to whichever lord he would in 1066. Value 5s a year". |
| 34,35 | 2 PLOUGHS THERE. 2 ploughs and 7 oxen; see Lordship and Villagers' Table. See General Notes to 3,37 and 3,44. |
| 34,36-37 | WILLIAM ALSO HOLDS. "William holds"; see 17,84 note. |
| 34,37 | VALUE 2s. "The rest of the land (*alia terra*) is so wasted that (*ita uastata quod*) the value is only 2s". This sentence comes immediately after the 1 acre of meadow, implying that the *alia terra* is the whole of the furlong ('ferling') apart from the 1 acre. On *uastata/uasta* see General Notes C 3 (second note). |
| 34,42 | ½ PLOUGH, WHICH IS THERE. "W(illiam) has ½ plough"; *in dominio* probably implied or omitted in error. |
| 34,43 | UPLOWMAN .... RALPH. Slightly abbreviated details of this added manor also appear in the T.O. at 502 b 2.<br>ALWIN HELD IT. "....jointly" in 502 b 2 only. |
| 34,44 | GAPPAH. In the T.O. at 502 b 4: "Ralph of Pomeroy has a manor called Gappah. The lands of 4 thanes have been added to it, who held them jointly in 1066. Value of them, 24s a year".<br>FIVE THANES HELD IT JOINTLY. "and they could go to whichever lord they would". |

Exon. 34

| | |
|---|---|
| 34,45 | 1 PLOUGH, WHICH IS THERE, WITH ½ VILLAGER. "Ralph has ½ villager who has 1 plough". After this in the Exon. MS is written *Et hanc mans' addidit Radulf' ad mans q uocat'* with *Otria* interlined; the words have been scored through for deletion, with the exception of *Otria* (which should have been also). After the value — which comes next — is written "Ralph added this manor to the manor called Awliscombe"; *holescōba* is interlined over another *Otria* which has been erased but is still visible. VALUE 30d. RALPH.... AWLISCOMBE. In the T.O. at 502 b 8: "To the manor called Ivedon Ralph of Pomeroy has added a manor called Awliscombe; it pays 30d a year". |
| 34,46 | ROGER HOLDS....FROM RALPH. In the Exon. MS *hanc tenet Rogerius Radulfus*; *Radulfus* is probably a scribal error for *de Radulfo* "from Ralph" (which is otherwise omitted), as a Roger is given as Ralph's subtenant some eleven times, rather than a byname (= "Roger Ralph holds it"). However, a Roger son of Ralph is a subtenant of the Bishop of Coutances in DB Somerset and a tenant-in-chief in DB Glos. and it is possible that this person was intended (see DB Glos. G 4, col. 162a, and note and Herefords. 1,8 note, on the accidental omission of *filius*). 'BLACKSLADE' HAS BEEN ADDED TO THIS MANOR. "With this manor Ralph has a manor called 'Blackslade' ". Abbreviated details of this added manor also appear in the T.O. at 502 b 9. EDWIN HELD IT. "....jointly"; only in 502 b 9. 2 VILLAGERS AND 3 SMALLHOLDERS. "On it (virgate) are 2 villagers and 3 smallholders"; an unusual variation on the normal Exon. formula "*B* (1086 tenant) has....". It also occurs in Devon for 34,57. 52,9 and 52,48 and it is interesting that these four entries are all by the same scribe. Cf. 3,86 note on a similar variation, though this is by a different scribe. |
| 34,47 | 1 PLOUGH, WHICH IS THERE. "R(ozelin) has 1 plough"; *in dominio* probably implied or omitted in error. |
| 34,49 | VILLAGERS....1½ VIRGATES. Exon. actually says "the villagers (have) as much"; as this statement comes as usual straight after the 1½ virgates in lordship the meaning is clear there, but would be less so in the position dictated by this edition. 1 VIRGATE .... 5s. Abbreviated details of this added land also appear in the T.O. at 503 b 5. A WOMAN HELD IT FREELY (AND) JOINTLY BEFORE 1066. "which a woman held jointly in 1066; she could go to whichever lord she would". In 503 b 5 she is said to have held "jointly", but no mention is made of "freely". A VILLAGER. "R(alph) has 1 villager". |
| 34,54 | THESE THREE MANORS .... 1 VIRGATE. See 35,4 and note. It is odd that there is no T.O. entry on the fact that there were two manors in Radish in 1066 which were combined in 1086. See 20,1 note. |
| 34,55 | POOL .... 10s. Abbreviated details of this added manor also appear in the T.O. at 504 a 6. In both the main entry and in the T.O. Roger is said to hold the added manor from Ralph. The same scribe wrote both the main entry and the T.O. entry. EDWY HELD IT FREELY (AND) JOINTLY. "which Edwy also (*idem*) held jointly" as also in 504 a 6; "freely" omitted in both entries. |
| 34,56 | 2 CARUCATES .... 2 PLOUGHS THERE. "On it (manor) are 2 carucates of land and 2 ploughs; 1 is (part) of R(oger)'s lordship, the other is the villagers' (.... *ii carrucatę Trę 7 ii carr̃ .i. dnīca ē R. 7 alia uillanoŗ* .)". It is not clear whether it is the carucates or the ploughs which are divided thus. The use of the plural *uillanorum* is noteworthy, apparently implying that the slaves, as well as the villager, had a share in either the carucates or ploughs. See notes to 3,79. 5,9 and 28,16. |
| 34,57 | ROGER HAS ½ VIRGATE. "....from R(alph)"; cf. 15,22 note. 1 VILLAGER. A MILL WHICH PAYS 30d. "On it (½ virgate) is a villager and a mill; value 30d a year". See 34,46 note on the formula. As in the Exchequer DB, it is not absolutely clear whether the value of the mill or of the whole ½ virgate is 30d. However, in the T.O. entry (505 b 2) "....½ virgate of land whose value is (*ualet*) 30d a year". Ellis prints *xx· den'* for the value in the T.O. entry, but the parchment of the MS is merely rubbed between the last *x* of *xxx* and the dot, possibly when an ink blot was erased there. IT HAS BEEN ADDED TO WEYCROFT. "It has been added to Ralph's manor called Weycroft". So also in 505 b 2. |
| 34,58 | FROM WHICH HE HAS KEPT BACK. "....since he has had them (houses)" in the T.O. entry (506 a 1). |

Exon. 35

| | |
|---|---|
| 35,1 | FORMERLY. "value when *R*. ('Roald' in full for 35,23-24) acquired it". Similarly for the past values of 35,2-15;19-21;23-24. |
| 35,3 | PASTURE, 2 FURLONGS. "pasture, 2 furlongs in length and width". |
| 35,4 | ROALD HOLDS .... 'RADISH'. In the T.O. at 497 a 2: "Ralph of Pomeroy appropriated (*occupauit*) a manor called Panson and gave it to Roald in exchange for Bruckland and 'Radish' (DB 34,53-54). Value 20s a year; value when R(oald) acquired it, 30s". |
| 35,5-6 | *TAMERLANDE*. PEEKE. In the T.O. at 496 a 4: "Roald has a manor called *Tamerlanda*. Another manor called Peeke has been added to it, which did not belong to this manor in 1066. Value 5s a year; value when R(oald) acquired it, 10[s]". Neither the main Exon. nor DB mentions the linking of these two manors; see 16,9 note. |
| 35,5 | 1 VILLAGER; 1 PLOUGH AND 3 FURLONGS. *uitt iii ferdiñ & i carr̃*; it is not clear whether *uitt* abbreviates *uillanus* and refers only to the 1 villager or abbreviates the more usual *uillani*, in which case the slave might have had a share in the plough and land. Cf. notes to 3,57;79. 5,9. 16,6;145-146. 17,58. 19,9. 28,16 and 34,56 and see General Notes 1,3 on slaves. |
| 35,6 | ½ VIRGATE OF LAND. .... It is very likely that the Exon. scribe mistakenly omitted to give details of how many ploughs could plough the ½ virgate (and the Exchequer scribe was forced also to omit them). It is interesting that in the next entry (= DB 35,7) the scribe also originally omitted these details, but then interlined them; perhaps he had intended to interline them for this entry too. Both entries have much interlined material. |
| 35,7-8 | KIMBER. RUTLEIGH. In the T.O. at 496 a 6: "Roald has a manor called Kimber. A manor called Rutleigh has been added to it, which a thane held jointly in 1066. It did not belong to the said manor. Value 5s a year". Neither the main Exon. nor DB records the link between these two manors; see 16,9 note. |
| 35,7 | 1 PLOUGH THERE. 1 plough and 3 oxen; see Lordship and Villagers' Table. |
| 35,8 | ALRIC HELD IT FREELY (AND) JOINTLY. "which Alric held jointly"; no mention of "freely". |
| 35,9 | (WEST) PUTFORD. In the T.O. at 496 b 3: "Roald has a manor called (West) Putford. ½ virgate of land has been added to it, which a thane held jointly in 1066. It did not belong to the said manor. Reginald holds it from Roald. Value 10s a year; value when he acquired it, 5[s]". |
| | TWO THANES HELD. "....One of them, Alwold, had ½ hide; the other, Leofwin, ½ virgate". |
| 35,10 | VILLAGERS....5½ PLOUGHS AND 2½(?) VIRGATES. In the Exon. MS *uill' ii uirḡ & v carr̃* with *& dimid̃* interlined midway between the *uirḡ* and *v*, with no indication as to which it was to add to. The DB scribe obviously thought that 5½ ploughs were meant, but 2½ virgates adds up with the 1 virgate lordship and ½ virgate held by the Count of Mortain to the 1 hide tax. |
| | ½ FISHERY WHICH PAYS 40d. "½ fishery whose value is 40d a year". |
| | THE COUNT OF MORTAIN .... 5s. Abbreviated details of this ½ virgate also appear in the T.O. at 505 b 7. |
| 35,14 | 4 SLAVES. "3 slaves". |
| 35,16-18 | FORMERLY. "value when he acquired it" for each of these entries, presumably referring to Roald as there are no subtenants; see 2,14 note. |
| 35,19 | HANKFORD. "Roald has a manor called Hankford. R. wrote up to this point". Ellis prints *Ruald' hl̃ i. mans̄ q̄ uocat' usq; huc scripsit R: Hanecheforda*, but in the Exon. MS the *usq; huc scripsit R.* [not *R:* as in Ellis] is clearly written in the right margin level with the first line of the entry. It does not appear to be written by the scribe of the main entry and is in paler ink and with a sign in the same colour ink before *Hanecheforda* indicating presumably how far the scribe *R.* had written. However, the scribe of the entry does not appear to change after this sign, nor does the colour of the ink. See 17,5 note for two similar statements and their possible implication. |
| | 1 VILLAGER HAS IT THERE, WITH 1 SMALLHOLDER. "R(eginald) has 1 villager and 1 smallholder who have 1 plough". |
| 35,20 | 4 VILLAGERS. "3 villagers". |
| 35,21-22 | REGINALD ALSO. "Reginald" in both entries, with no *idem*, so perhaps not the same man as the Reginald of 35,20 (which DB implies); cf. 15,27-30 note. |
| 35,22 | TWO THANES HELD IT FREELY (AND) JOINTLY. "which 2 thanes held jointly"; no mention of "freely". |
| | THIS (LAND) .... 3s. This confused statement is almost identically phrased in the main Exon. entry, but is clarified in the T.O. (499 b 1) where the ½ virgate called Praunsley is |

Exon. 35 – 36

said to have been added to Roald's manor of Pulham. A thane held the land jointly in 1066 and Reginald holds it from Roald. However, the scribe of the T.O. also seems to have had problems with his source, because both the phrases "this (land) is called Praunsley" and "½ virgate" are interlined above the phrase "to it has been added the land of 1 thane", apparently at the same time because of the ink colour. See the General Notes here.

35,23   ½ PLOUGH THERE. "On it (manor) Solomon has 4 oxen"; *in dominio* perhaps omitted in error. The oxen may possibly form part of the livestock list which succeeds this statement, though oxen are not normally included in this list.

35,24   LAND FOR 2 PLOUGHS, WHICH ARE THERE. "2 ploughs can plough it (the manor). On it are the ploughs"; the actual number of teams there is not given nor whether they were lordship or villagers' ploughs. Cf. notes to 17,18. 45,3 and 52,9.

35,25   WALTER HOLDS DOCKWORTHY. "....from him (Roald)"; cf. 15,22 note.
THIS ENTRY, which occurs at the foot of folio 414b in Exon., breaks off after 3½ lines with the words "W(alter) has 1 furlong (*ferlinum*) and 1", presumably referring to 1 plough and 1 furlong in lordship. It would appear that at least one folio is missing here, which contained the rest of this entry and those corresponding to DB 35,26–31. At the bottom of folio 414b Charles Lyttelton (see 19,8 note) wrote 'These lands are imperfect'. Folio 415a begins the land of William of Poilley in Devon (DB Ch. 21).

35,31   THIS ENTRY occurs in the T.O. at 506 a 2: "Roald Dubbed has a house in Exeter which paid 8d in customary dues before 1066, which King William has never had".

36,1   TWO THANES HELD IT JOINTLY. "....and they could go with their land to whichever lord they would". There is no mention of this manor in the T.O., unusually for a combined manor, though there is for the almost identical 1066 tenure of 36,2. See 20,1 note.
8 VILLAGERS. In the Exon. MS *ſiii*, the first figure being neither *v* (as the DB scribe presumably read it) nor an *l* (Ellis prints *liii* '53') nor an added *i* to make the figure *iiii*.
FORMERLY. "value when he acquired it", probably referring to Theobald; see notes to 2,14 and 16,88. Similarly for the past values of 36,10;12–16;21.

36,2   BUCKS (CROSS). In the T.O. at 497 a 5: "Theobald has a manor called Bucks (Cross). 1 virgate of land has been added to it, which 2 thanes held jointly in 1066. It did not belong to the said manor. Value 6s 3d a year".
THREE THANES HELD IT JOINTLY. "....and they could go with their land to whichever lord they would".
FORMERLY. "value when Theobald acquired it". Similarly for the past values of 36,3–9;17–20;22;24;26.

36,4-6   GOSBERT ALSO. "Gosbert" for each entry; no *idem* so not necessarily the same man as the Gosbert of 36,3 which DB implies. See 15,21 note.

36,8   1 PLOUGH THERE. "Bernard has 1 plough"; *in dominio* probably implied or omitted in error.

36,9   HOLLOWCOMBE....TAX FOR 1 VIRGATE. "Theobald has 1 virgate of land called Hollowcombe"; no mention is made of the tax payment. See 34,11 note.

36,14   FORMERLY 20s. "15s".

36,18   WITH THIS MANOR .... 10s. Details of this added manor are written in the right margin of the Exon. MS, probably by a different scribe to the main Culm (Davy) entry. Several letters are missing from the right hand edge, the parchment of this folio being cut in a wavy line at some stage (which is not clear in Ellis' edition), but the content appears to be the same as in DB, although the name of Gorwell is missing in it. Colbran is the same man as the TRE holder of the main manor of Culm (Davy). Slightly abbreviated details also appear in the T.O. at 500 b 4 which confirms the statement, partly legible in the main entry, that Gorwell did not belong to Culm (Davy) in 1066. Ellis misprints *tedehat* for the MS's *tenebat*.

36,19   WOODLAND, 6 ACRES. *vi agro* only remains on the edge of the parchment, the *-s* and possibly *nemoris* too having been cut off (see preceding note). Even if the Exchequer scribe saw the Exon. MS in the same state here as it is now, he could have deduced that the "6 acres" referred to woodland, as the woodland details invariably precede those for the meadow (and pasture) in Exon.; see General Notes 1,53. It is very unlikely that the Exon. scribe intended the meaning to be "6 + 3 acres of meadow".

36,21   2 VILLAGERS AND 2 SMALLHOLDERS HAVE ½ PLOUGH. "Theobald has 2 villagers who have ½ plough on it (manor) and (he has) 2 smallholders". See 1,9 note.

36,22   1 PLOUGH THERE. "T(heobald) has 1 plough"; *in dominio* probably implied or omitted in error.

Exon. 36 – 39

| | |
|---|---|
| 36,23 | THEOBALD HOLDS THESE THREE MANORS AS ONE MANOR. In the T.O. at 501 b 4: "Theobald has a manor called Washford Pyne (DB 36,21) which Colbert held. Another manor called Washford Pyne (DB 36,22) has been added to it, which 4 thanes held jointly in 1066; value 5s. With this above-mentioned Washford Pyne Theobald has a manor likewise called Washford Pyne which Wulfmer held jointly in 1066; Alwold (*Aluuardus*; see General Notes here) holds it from Theobald; value 12s 6d a year. T(heobald) holds these as one manor". SIX THANES HELD THEM FREELY. "six thanes held them jointly before 1066"; no mention is made of "freely". |
| 36,24 | ALWOLD ALSO HOLDS. *Predictus Aluuardus*; see General Notes here. |
| 36,25 | TO THIS MANOR .... 4s. Details of this added virgate also appear in full in the T.O. at 501 b 7. WHICH A THANE HELD FREELY BEFORE 1066. "which a thane held who could go with his land to whichever lord he would". In 501 b 7: "which a thane held jointly in 1066". |
| 36,26 | A MILL WHICH PAYS 5s. "A mill at 5s (*molendinum v. solidorum*)". WOODLAND, 160 ACRES. "155 acres". WILMINGTON....5s. Details of this added manor also appear, slightly abbreviated, in the T.O. at 503 a 5. ALWARD HELD IT. In 503 a 5: "which Alward held jointly". |
| 36,27 | WHICH PAYS 8d TO THE KING IN CUSTOMARY DUES. "which before 1066 paid 8d a year in customary dues". Similarly in the T.O. at 506 a 6 with the addition of "which (8d) he keeps back". |
| 37,1 | AELFEVA HELD IT. Exon. *Alwena*, probably *n* for *u* by scribal error (PNDB p. 174 note 3). Cf. 28,1 note. FORMERLY. "value when T(hurstan) acquired it". |
| 38,1 | PASTURE, ½ LEAGUE. "pasture, ½ league in length and width". FORMERLY. "when A(lfred) acquired it". TWITCHEN. Abbreviated details of this added manor also appear in the T.O. at 499 a 8. BRICTWOLD HELD IT FREELY. "which Brictwold held". In 499 a 8: "which a thane held jointly". No mention of "freely" in either entry. |
| 38,2 | VALUE FORMERLY. "value when he acquired it", presumably referring to Alfred, as there is no subtenant (see 2,14 note). |
| Ch. 39 | LAND OF ALFRED THE BRETON. The folios in the main Exon. Book containing details of this fief have not survived. A few entries, however, appear in abbreviated form in the T.O. |
| 39,6 | CURWORTHY. In the T.O. at 496 a 5: "Alfred the Breton has a manor called Curworthy. Two other manors have been added to it, which did not belong to this manor in 1066. One of them is called Curworthy and the other is called Widefield (*Witefelda*). Value of them 7s 6d a year. Two thanes held them jointly". Widefield is not mentioned by name in the Exchequer DB, but is presumably one of the original "three manors" that comprised the 1086 manor of Curworthy. |
| 39,10 | TO THIS MANOR .... 5s. In the T.O. at 499 b 11: "Alfred the Breton holds ½ hide of land called Larkbeare, which rightly belongs to Baldwin's manor called Whimple. Value 5s". See 16,94 note. |
| 39,14 | CREACOMBE .... 10s. In the T.O. at 504 b 4: "Alfred the Breton has a manor called Battisborough which Aelmer held. Another manor called Creacombe has been added to it, which Aelmer held jointly in 1066. Alfred has these as one manor. Value of this (manor) 10s a year". |
| 39,15 | (SOUTH) MILTON. In the T.O. at 504 b 7: "To* Alfred the Breton's manor called (South) Milton have been added ½ hide and ½ virgate which a thane held jointly in 1066. Alfred now holds these two as one manor. Value 20s a year; when Alfred acquired them, as much". *Valet*, singular, refers just to the added land, as usual. * *Cum mansione .... addita est*; the scribe has mixed his Latin constructions: he should either have written *cum mansione .... iuncta est* ("with this manor has been joined") or *ad mansionem .... addita est*, the construction he used in the preceding entry (see next note). Cf. last note under 42,21. Throughout the T.O. there is much evidence that the scribes liked to ring the changes in formulae and sometimes, as here, their enthusiasm for this did not match their command of Latin grammar. |
| 39,16 | THIS LAND .... GRIMPSTONLEIGH. In the T.O. at 504 b 6: "To Alfred the Breton's manor called Moreleigh has been added another manor called Grimpstonleigh, which |

Alwold held jointly in 1066; it paid tax for ½ hide; value 20s a year": *ad mansionem aluuredi britonis quae uocatur Morleia est addita est alia mansio quae uocatur lega quam tenuit aluualdus pariter ea die ... et reddidit gildum pro dimidia hida et ualet per annum xx solidos.* The subject of *reddidit gildum* ought grammatically to be *alia mansio .... lega*, i.e. Grimpstonleigh (39,13), but in fact it is Moreleigh that paid tax for ½ hide. However, the TRE tenant mentioned (Alwold) is different from that given in DB for Moreleigh (Aelfric). This could merely be a result of scribal error or of a discrepancy between DB and the main Exon. (from which it is possible that the T.O. were compiled) due to newer information being available to the Exchequer scribe. However, it is possible that the T.O. *Aluuald(us)* is the result of a series of scribal errors for Alnoth, the TRE tenant of Grimpstonleigh (*Alnodus → Aluodus → Aluuodus → Aluuoldus → Aluualdus*), and that the phrase *quam tenuit Aluualdus* correctly refers to Grimpstonleigh. (It is very probable that the TRE holder given by the DB scribe for 39,13 (Alnoth) is the correct one, because of the link between that manor and Grimpstonleigh, 39,12, which was also held by Alnoth; see General Notes 39,13.) The rest of the sentence then seems to be loosely constructed, the 7s before the tax and value not joining statements that are governed by the *alia mansio* phrase. Cf. 502 b 9 (= DB 34,46) where the 7 *ualet* phrase is, however, governed by the *addita est alia mansio* phrase.

    It is interesting that the T.O. states that Grimpstonleigh has been added to Moreleigh, whereas DB (and probably the main Exon.) has Moreleigh being added to Grimpstonleigh; this also happens with the addition of Ivedon to Awliscombe (see both Exon. and General Notes to 19,43 and 34,45 and cf. 34,34 note).

39,22    ALFRED .... DUES. In the T.O. at 505 b 11: "Alfred the Breton has a house in Exeter which before 1066 paid 8d a year in customary dues. Since he has had it, he has kept back these (pence)".

Chs. 40-41    ANSGER. AIULF. Their holdings appear in Exon. under the heading of "Lands of the French Men-at-Arms in Devonshire"; see Ch. 22 note.

40,1-2    ANSGER OF MONTACUTE....ANSGER. Called plain Ansger in the main Exon. entries, but in the T.O. he is called both plain Ansger and Ansger of Senarpont (for 40,4-7; see notes). He is also Ansger of Senarpont in the Tax Return for Tawton Hundred (ix, in which Hundred lie the manors of 40,1;3;7).

    At the foot of folio 456a in the Exon. MS is written, in one line in paler, browner ink than the rest of 456a but apparently contemporary with the entries, a partial list of the men-at-arms "in Devonshire" dealt with in the section; Ellis does not print it. After 'Osbern', 'Gerald', 'R(alph) Pagnell' and 'William of Eu' is written as the last name *Ansger(us) de monte acuto*. The Exchequer scribe probably got Ansger's title from this list, though he may have known it already.

    FORMERLY. "value when *A*. ("Ansger" in full for 40,2) acquired it" for each entry.

40,1    STAFFORD. In the T.O. at 498 b 3: "Ansger has a manor called Stafford which did not belong before 1066 to Brictric's lands which he holds. A thane held it jointly in 1066. Value 12s 6d a year; value when A(nsger) acquired it, 7s 6d".

    AELFRIC HELD IT. "....and he could go with this land to whichever lord he would".

    LAND FOR 1 PLOUGH. "1½ ploughs".

40,3    BRIMBLECOMBE. In the T.O. at 498 b 4: "Ansger also (*idem*) has a manor called Brimblecombe which before 1066 did not belong to Brictric's lands which he holds. A thane held it jointly in 1066. Value 7s 6d a year".

    ALCHERE HELD IT. "....and he could go with his land to whichever lord he would".

    3 SMALLHOLDERS. The parchment of the Exon. MS here is torn almost completely down its left hand edge and has been stitched together. It is not possible to tell whether Ansger had 3 smallholders on the manor, as only *ii* with no dot before the number survives; Ellis reads *ii* but includes a dot in error.

40,3;5-6    FORMERLY. "value when he acquired it" for each entry, presumably referring to Ansger as there are no subtenants (see 2,14 note).

40,4    TO THIS MANOR .... AS A MANOR. Slightly abbreviated details of this added manor also appear in the T.O. at 502 a 8, where Ansger is called Ansger of Senarpont (*de Senarpont*; see OEB p. 114) and the value of the added land is given as 25s. Both in the main entry and in the T.O. the added manor is called Cheldon and the tax is on ½ virgate and ½ furlong.

    BRICTMER HELD THEM. In 502 a 8: "which Brictmer held jointly".

    THESE TWO LANDS PAY 50s. "And they pay 50s a year", added immediately after the details of the added land. However, the plural *reddunt* cannot refer only to the

# Exon. 40 - 42

|  |  |
|---|---|
|  | added ½ virgate and ½ furlong ('ferling'), as they are only described in Exon. by the singular *mansio*. The T.O. (see note above) gives the value of the added land as 25s. |
| 40,5 | MUXBERE. In the T.O. at 502 b 10: "Ansger of Senarpont (*de Senarpont*) holds the lands of 5 thanes in a manor called Muxbere; value 30s a year". FIVE THANES HELD IT FREELY (AND) JOINTLY FROM BRICTRIC. "which 5 thanes held jointly from Brictric; they could not be separated from him". ANSGER HOLDS IT.... "Ansger holds these lands of the said 5 thanes....". |
| 40,6 | SUTTON. In the T.O. at 503 a 1: "Ansger of Senarpont (*de Senarpōt* in the MS; Ellis misprints *de Senarpot̄*) has a manor called Sutton which 2 thanes held jointly in 1066. This manor has been wrongfully added to Brictric's lands. Value 10s a year". GODRIC HELD IT. "which Godric held", then "Godric held the said land jointly and his brother" added after the value statement, though in the same colour ink and by the same scribe. It would seem from the two thanes mentioned as TRE holders in the T.O. entry that Godric and his brother were joint holders (cf. DB Glos. 53,10 where Godric and his brother Edric held 'Sheriffs' Haresfield in 1066), and that the Exchequer scribe somehow missed the statement, though he included the information about the land being wrongfully added to Brictric's lands, which comes immediately afterwards (there is no gap such as Ellis prints). |
| 40,7 | DOLTON. In the T.O. at 503 b 4: "Ansger of Senarpont (*de Senardi ponte*) has a manor called Dolton which Brictric (not Edric) held in 1066; it has been added to Brictric's lands. Value 50s a year". The first Brictric (*Bristritius*) is most probably a scribal error for *Edric*; it is just possible that a different Brictric to the second one is intended, but the manor was called 'Edric's *cote*' in the early 13th century (see General Notes here). WRONGFULLY ADDED.* "wrongfully" omitted, as also in 503 b 4. See General Notes to 40,6-7 and 15,31. THE HOLDER .... WHERE HE WOULD. "which a thane held, able to go to whichever lord he would": the Latin (extended) is *quam tenuit quidam tegnus potens eundi ad quem[c]umque* uoluisset dominum*. The meaning is clear, but a clear expression of it in Latin seems to have been beyond the ability of the scribe: *potens eundi* "powerful of going", "master of going", is a strange dependence of a gerund on *potens* which is scarcely ever used as the present participle of the verb *possum* ("I am able"); the phrase is meant to be equivalent to *qui potuit ire* ("who could go"). Cf. 23,23 note for a similar unusual phrase in 23,23-24, though these entries are by a different scribe. * In the Exon. MS *ad quemou͘ q*; which is a scribal error for *ad quemcu͘q*;(although the ᵻ abbreviation sign for an *m* omitted is unusual; see 16,36 note). |
| 41,1-2 | VALUE FORMERLY. "value when he acquired it", presumably referring to Aiulf (see notes to 2,14 and 16,88). |
| 42,1 | FORMERLY. "value when O. ("Odo" in full for 42,11) acquired it". Similarly for the past values of 42,2-3;6;10-11;13;20;22. |
| 42,2 | 4 PLOUGHS THERE. 4 ploughs and 3 oxen; see Lordship and Villagers' Table. |
| 42,4 | FORMERLY. "value when Ralph (interlined) acquired it". A THANE HELD 1 FURLONG .... WOULD. "A thane held the said furlong (*fertinum*) in 1066; he could be separated with the said furlong from Saewin". In the T.O. at 497 a 7: "Odo has a manor called Huish; his father-in-law Theobald appropriated 1 furlong of land which a thane held jointly in 1066. Value 15s a year; value when T(heobald) appropriated it, 10[s]": the Latin (*Odo habet i mansionem .... cum qua Tebaldus socer eius occupauit i ferdinum terrae*....) is compressed; the scribe should have written either *cum qua .... iunxit i ferdinum quem occupauit* ("(manor) with which ... (he) joined 1 furlong which he appropriated") or *cum qua ... i ferdinum occupatum iunxit* ("(manor) with which .... (he) joined 1 furlong (he had) appropriated"). For a possible identification of this Theobald, see General Notes Ch. 36. |
| 42,5 | 3 SMALLHOLDERS. "2 smallholders". VALUE FORMERLY. "value when he acquired it", probably referring to Odo (see notes to 2,14 and 16,88). Similarly for the past values of 42,7-8;16-19;21;23-24. |
| 42,6 | VALUE NOW £20. "Value £15"; *xx* appears to have been written originally, but corrected to *xv*. The Exchequer scribe may have misread the correction as in 20,15 and 21,13; according to Finn (MDeD p. 116) the correction to *xv* came after the 'copy' of Exon. had been made for Exchequer use, though there is no sign in the MS that this was a late correction. THREE FRENCHMEN .... 45s. Their names, holding and its value are given: "Gotshelm holds 1 virgate; value 15s a year. Walter has another virgate; value 15s. Ansger has a third |

virgate; value 15s a year". Their holdings are "of the above 3½ hides". See General Notes here.

42,7   AELMER HOLDS. "Alfgeat (*Aluietus*) holds".

42,10  (GEORGE) NYMPTON. In the T.O. at 499 b 5: "Odo son of Gamelin has a manor called (George) Nympton which 4 thanes held jointly in 1066. Value 40s a year". Although there is no obvious sign of illegality in this statement, it is possible, as in the entry referring to DB 2,15 (see note), that Odo's holding consisted of several manors in 1066 which he had combined. See also notes to 1,11 ('½ hide .... 20s'). 2,2 and 13a,2.
FOUR THANES HELD IT FREELY (AND) JOINTLY. "which 4 thanes held jointly"; so also in 499 b 5. There is no mention of "freely" in either entry.

42,12  EDDA .... WOULD. In the T.O. at 499 b 8 this furlong (*ferdinus*) is stated to have been added to Aller and "a certain woman held (it) jointly".
GO WHERE SHE WOULD. "go with her land to whichever lord she would".
VALUE 12d A YEAR. Only in 499 b 8.

42,15  MEADOW, 2 ACRES. *prati* omitted, but likely because of the position in the list of resources; see 1,46 note. It is possible, however, that the Exon. scribe meant the *ii agros* to go with the ½ league of pasture which succeeds it; see 1,53 note on the combining of acres and furlongs/leagues in measurements. Cf. 21,19 note.

42,16  LAND FOR 14 PLOUGHS. In the Exon. MS *x\iii*, the second figure being either half an *x* (making *xxiii*) or half a *v* (making *xviii*, which is what Ellis prints) or a badly written *i* (making *xiiii*, as the Exchequer scribe presumably read).
PIGMEN....SLAVES. See 16,44 note on the order.
1 HIDE IN SHAPCOMBE .... 30s. In the T.O. at 500 a 6: "Ludo, a man-at-arms of Walscin's, has 1 hide of land called Shapcombe which rightly belongs to Odo son of Gamelin's manor called Broadhembury. Value 30s a year". This information is duplicated (though with several different details) in 23,20 and also appears a second time in the T.O. at 503 b 9 where the value is said to be 20s a year.

42,18  1 PLOUGH THERE AND 1 VIRGATE. "R(eginald) has 1 virgate and 1 plough"; *in dominio* probably omitted in error or implied.

42,19  ½ PLOUGH, WHICH IS THERE. "H(ubert) has ½ plough"; *in dominio* probably implied or omitted in error.

42,21  A(LWY) HAS ½ PLOUGH. *in dominio* probably implied or omitted in error.
TO THIS MANOR HAS BEEN ADDED THE LAND OF NINE THANES WHICH THEY HELD FREELY (AND) JOINTLY.... "Nine thanes, who held their land jointly in 1066, have been added to this manor". In the T.O. at 501 a 4: "....The lands of 9 thanes have been added to it; they could go with their lands to whichever lord they would in 1066...." (*potant* "could" in the Exon. MS; Ellis misprints *potant* "they drink").
ALWY HAS 3½ PLOUGHS THERE. The total of the (lordship) and villagers' ploughs is 3½; see Lordship and Villagers' Table.
UNDERWOOD, 5 ACRES. In the Exon. MS *ii* with a dot under the second *i* (which Ellis does not print) and *v* interlined; either there should have been a deletion dot under both minim strokes or the intended measurement is *iv ag*ʰ or possibly *vi ag*ʰ. VCH p. 494 translates the number as '7'.
2 VIRGATES .... TWO MANORS. "With these have been joined 2 other manors which 2 thanes held jointly in 1066; they paid tax for 2 virgates". In the T.O. at 501 a 4: "To* these have been added 2 other manors which 2 thanes held who could go with their lands to whichever lord they would in 1066".
* *cum istis sunt additae*, a mixed construction: the scribe should either have written *cum istis sunt (con)iunctae* (as the scribe of the main Exon. entry did) or *ad istas sunt additae* or omitted the preposition altogether and used the dative *istis*. Cf. 39,15 note (though the scribe is not the same).

42,24  MEADOW. "meadows": *pratorum*, genitive plural, possibly a scribal error for *prati*, genitive singular, but the plural also occurs in a similar phrase in the Exon. for Dorset 48,1, an entry written by a different scribe (see Exon. note there).

Ch. 43  OSBERN OF SACEY. His holding appears in Exon. under the heading of "Lands of the French Men-at-Arms in Devonshire"; see Ch. 22 note. He is called Osbern of Sacey for 43,1;3;6, Osbert of Sacey for 43,4-5 and in the T.O. for 43,3, plain Osbern for 43,2 and plain Osbert in the value of 43,3. What may have happened here (as also in 17,34 and 24,7 and cf. DB Dorset General Notes 44,1 and Cambs. 14,41) is the result of the Norman tendency to drop the final *n* and *t* after *r* (PNDB §§ 78, 100), causing confusion of *Osber(t)* (OE *Osbeorht*) and *Osber(n)* (OE *Osbeorn* (< ON *Ásbiorn*) or OG *Osbern*). The DB scribe probably corrected the Exon. 'Osbert' forms in each case.

Exon. 43 - 45

43,1      GODRIC HELD IT. In the T.O. entry (496 a 1): "which a thane held jointly".
VALUE FORMERLY. "value when O(sbern) acquired it". Similarly with *Osbertus* in full for 43,3 and *O(sbert*'?) for the past values of 43,4–5 (see Ch. 43 note).
OWES. "it paid....but since Osbern has had it, the King has not had his customary due" in the T.O. at 496 a 1.
KING'S MANOR. "King's lordship manor"; so also in 496 a 1.
43,2      VILLAGERS....6 PLOUGHS. "3 ploughs".
FORMERLY. "value when he acquired it", presumably referring to Osbern (see 2,14 note).
43,3      1 VIRGATE .... 3s. Also in the T.O. at 500 a 8 in abbreviated form.
2 VILLAGERS THERE. "2 villagers live (*manent*) on it".
43,5      3 SMALLHOLDERS. "4 smallholders".
43,6      FROM WHICH .... 8d. "which paid 8d a year in customary dues before 1066; Osbern keeps it back". Similarly in the T.O. at 506 a 5.
Ch. 44      THE FOLIOS IN THE MAIN PART OF EXON., containing the holding of Hervey of Helléan, have not survived. There are 3 entries in the T.O.: one dealing with the added manors of 44,1 (see below) and two for other manors not in DB (so apparently not in the main Exon. returns) which run as follows:
     501 b 1: "Hervey's wife has a manor called *Esseorda*. From this manor has been taken away ½ furlong (*ferdinus*) of land which has been put in 1066; it has been added to the King's manor called Silverton. Value 5s a year". Silverton appears as 1,7 in DB, but no mention is made there of the added ½ furlong ('ferling'). See General Notes here for *Esseorda*.
     503 a 9: "Hervey's wife has a manor called Whitley (*Witeleia*) to which ½ hide of land has been added, which Edmer held jointly in 1066. Value 7s a year".
The Tax Return for Colyton Hundred (xx) states that Emma a widow\* has ½ hide and ½ virgate lordship there which probably corresponds to this T.O. entry.
\* *ima uidua*; the *ima* is probably a miscopying of *im̄a* (= *Imma*, an alternative form of *Emma*, PNDB p. 247; in the Exminster Hundred Tax Return quoted in the General Notes here the same scribe wrote *Imma* first then corrected the first letter to an E), as Emma was apparently the name of Hervey's wife (see General Notes here), rather than a scribal error for *una* used as the indefinite article (= "a widow") due to a misreading of the minims in the original.
A reason for there being no mention of these two manors in DB may be that information on them did not come to light until after the main Exon. had been written (and copied by the Exchequer scribe). Cf. the other entries in the T.O. which record information not in the main Exon.: see notes to 1,25 (last note),66. 2,2. 15,14 and the end of these notes for whole entries, and penultimate notes to 1,25;41 for part entries, notes to 16,9. 17,11-12. 19,3. 35,5-6;7-8 on the linking of manors, notes to 1,4. 3,92 and 42,12 on the value of sub-holdings and notes to 5,9 and 19,40 on bynames supplied.
44,1      ASHTON .... TWO THANES .... TWO MANORS ... 10s. In the T.O. at 498 b 2: "Hervey's wife has a manor called Ashton. Two other manors, which did not belong to the said manor before 1066, have been added to it. Two thanes held them jointly in 1066. Value of them 20s a year".
Chs. 45      GERALD THE CHAPLAIN. GERARD. Their holdings appear in Exon. under the
-46      heading of "Lands of the French Men-at-Arms in Devonshire"; see Ch. 22 note. Gerald is called Gerald the Chaplain for 45,1-2, but plain Gerald for 45,3.
A THANE HELD IT BEFORE 1066....THIS LAND OWES. In the T.O. at 496 a 2: "which a thane held jointly in 1066; however, it (or perhaps "he") paid 10s a year.... since G(erald) has had it the King has not had his customary due from it". The *sed tamen* (literally "but however") is unusual; cf. DB Somerset Exon. Notes 1,27 where 2 thanes held 2 of the 3 hides added to Martock "jointly....but (*sed tamen*) they paid 40d in customary dues to Martock". The implication might be that if a land was held jointly, it should not have to pay dues, or perhaps that a thane did not normally have to pay customary dues. It is possible, however, in this entry anyway, that the *sed tamen* is pointing up the payment to South Tawton rather than the fact of payment itself.
KING'S MANOR. "King's lordship manor"; so also in 496 a 2.
45,3      CANONS OF THIS PLACE. "canons of this manor"; there were 12 of them. The canons of Hartland Abbey which had St. Nectan as its patron saint (Stoke was earlier called Stoke St. Nectan). Hartland was a college of secular canons, perhaps founded by Countess Gytha, mother of 'Earl' Harold; Oliver *Mon*. p. 204.

Exon. 45 - 48

| | |
|---|---|
| 45,3 (cont'd.) | 12 PLOUGHS; AS MANY THERE. "12 ploughs which are there"; unusually Exon. does not detail how many were in lordship and how many the villagers hold. See 17,18 note. VALUE TO GERALD. "They pay to G(erald) himself". |
| 46,1-2 | FORMERLY. "when he acquired it" for each entry, presumably referring to Gerard (see 2,14 note). |
| Chs. 47 - 50 | GODBOLD. NICHOLAS THE BOWMAN. FULCHERE. HAIMERIC. Their holdings appear in Exon. under the heading of "Land of Nicholas the Bowman in Devonshire", folios 468a-473a inclusive; see also 51,1 note. As with the large section French Men-at-Arms (see Ch. 22 note) and the combined holdings of Walter and Gotshelm (see Chs. 24-25) this Exon. section is arranged by Hundred, not tenant. The Exchequer scribe worked through the Exon. here excerpting the individual holdings and listed the tenants in the order in which they first occurred. See General Notes Ch. 47 for the order of entries in the Exon. Godbold is called Godbold the Bowman (*archibalistari(us)*) in the T.O. entry for 47,14, *arbalestari(us)* for 47,2 and *arbalistari(us)* in the T.O. for 47,15), but plain Godbold for 47,1;3;5-15 and *Idem Godbold* "the same Godbold" for 47,4. See General Notes Ch. 48 on the meaning of *archibalistarius* etc. A possible reason why Godbold is only described as "Bowman" for the one entry in the main Exon. may be that that entry succeeded one in which Nicholas is also called "the Bowman" (48,1) though it is by a different scribe, whereas the entries preceding the other mentions of Godbold only have simple names (although the entry for 47,13 is preceded by Fulchere the Bowman's manor of 49,7, it is on the reverse of the folio and by a different scribe). Cf. the similar naming in Ch. 49 (see note). |
| 47,2 | FORMERLY. "value when G. ('Godbold' in full for 47,7) acquired it". Similarly for the past values of 47,3-4;7;14. |
| 47,5 | ALSI. In the MS *Alsius*; Ellis misprints *Alstus*, possibly because the *i* curves slightly to the right, though it does not in the least resemble this scribe's *t*. FORMERLY. "value when he acquired it", probably referring to Godbold (see notes to 2,14 and 16,88). Similarly for the past values of 47,6;8;11-13. |
| 47,7 | A THANE.... In the T.O. at 498 b 5: "Godbold has a manor called Mullacott. 1 furlong (*ferdinus*) has been added to it, which did not belong to the said manor in 1066. A thane held it jointly. It is completely waste (*penitus uastata est*)". OF THIS LAND. "Of the above ½ hide". |
| 47,9 | G(ODBOLD) HAS ½ PLOUGH. *in dominio* probably implied or omitted in error. |
| 47,10 | YARD. "Richard holds it from G(odbold)". 2 VILLAGERS HAVE IT THERE. "R(ichard) has 2 villagers who have ½ plough". |
| 47,13 | 4 SMALLHOLDERS. "3 smallholders". |
| 47,14 | LOWTON. In the T.O. at 502 a 6: "Godbold the Bowman has a manor called Lowton. 1 virgate of land has been added to it, which a thane held jointly in 1066. Rainer holds it from G(odbold). Value 5s a year". |
| 47,15 | WHICH PAID 16d IN CUSTOMARY DUES BEFORE 1066. "which were among King Edward's customary dues in 1066, paying 16d a year".* In the T.O. at 506 a 3: "which paid 16d a year in customary dues before 1066, which King William has never had". * The (extended) Latin for this is (*ii domus in Essecestra*) *quae fuerunt in consuetudine Eduuardi regis ea die qua ipse fuit uiuus et mortuus reddentes xvi denarios per annum*; the *reddentes* is interlined above an erasure. The beginning of this sentence is either careless or compressed; if the latter, it should be expanded to some such phrase as (*ii domus in Essecestra*) *quarum redditus fuerunt in consuetudine Eduuardi regis*.... ("2 houses in Exeter whose revenues were in/part of / belonged to King Edward's customary dues...."). The sentence became further complicated when the scribe decided to include the actual revenue, which necessitated his linking it with what he had previously written by a rather loose *reddentes* "paying". |
| Ch. 48 | NICHOLAS THE BOWMAN. See Chs. 47-50 note. He is called *Archibalistarius* for 48,1;4-7; *arbalestari(us)* for the heading and for 48,8;11 and plain Nicholas for 48,2-3; 9-10. See General Notes here. |
| 48,1 | 4 SMALLHOLDERS HAVE 1 PLOUGH. Their plough is not mentioned in Exon. It seems likely that the DB scribe transferred the lordship plough to the smallholders by mistake; this also occurs in 17,71 (see note). FORMERLY. "value when N. ('Nicholas' in full for 48,3;6-7) acquired it". Similarly for the past values of 48,3-4;6-11. ROGER GOAD .... NICHOLAS. This is interlined, possibly the reason for its being missed by the DB scribe. The Exon. scribe obviously wrote the whole entry, then added the subtenant, because *Nicholaus* is corrected to *R.* (for Roger) when his lordship land and plough are given, but *N.* is not similarly so corrected in the phrase *Ibi ht̃ N. ı̈ı̈ı̈*. |

|  |  |
|---|---|
|  | *bordarios*..... . However, the DB scribe includes the details of subtenant, similarly interlined and by the same scribe, for 48,4;6–7. |
| 48,2 | TAX FOR 3 VIRGATES. "2 virgates", but the detail (see Lordship and Villagers' Table) totals 3 virgates, so *ii* is probably a scribal error for *iii*. |
| 48,2;5 | FORMERLY. "value when he acquired it" for each entry, presumably referring to Nicholas (see 2,14 note). |
| 48,4 | 3 SMALLHOLDERS. "2 villagers" added before them. There is no obvious reason here for the omission of the villagers in DB, as there seems to be for their omission on the two other instances in Devon (see notes to 23,4 and 49,3). |
| 48,6 | MEADOW, 1 ACRE; WOODLAND, 10 ACRES. "woodland, 10 acres; woodland, 1 acre", the second *nemoris* no doubt being a scribal error for *prati* "meadow", which normally follows the woodland details; the Exchequer scribe probably corrected it. |
| 48,9 | VILLAGERS....½ PLOUGH. "villagers....3 oxen in a plough". |
| 48,10 | 3½ PLOUGHS THERE. 2½ ploughs; see Lordship and Villagers' Table. |
|  | OF THIS LAND....1 VIRGATE. "Of this land" is omitted; the 1 virgate appears from Exon. to be additional to the 3 virgates which are accounted for in the detail (see Lordship and Villagers' Table), making 1 hide total for Buckland. |
| 48,11 | ALLER. John holds it from Nicholas. |
|  | 2 OXEN. "2 oxen in a plough". |
| 48,12 | MEADOW, 2 [ACRES]. "meadow, 1½ acres". |
| Ch. 49 | LAND OF FULCHERE. See note to Chs. 47–50. He is called plain Fulchere except for the entry for 49,7 where he is Fulchere the Bowman (*archibalistarius*) both in the main entry and in the T.O. The Tax Return for Cliston Hundred (xii) states that Fulchere the Bowman (*archibalistarius* also) has ½ hide 1 furlong (*fertinum*) lordship there, which more or less corresponds to his holdings in 49,2–3. On the term *archibalistarius*, see General Notes Ch. 48. A possible reason why Fulchere is only styled "the Bowman" in this one entry in the main Exon. may be that the preceding 4 entries were concerned with Nicholas the Bowman, whereas in the entries preceding the details of his other manors in Devon, the tenants-in-chief are not given their occupations (although Haimeric is styled 'of Arques' in the entry preceding 49,6, it is not an occupation and in any case is on a different folio). It is unlikely, in view of the T.O. and Tax Return evidence, that the Exon. scribe made a mistake in including a title for Fulchere. Cf. Chs. 47–50 note on the similar naming of Godbold as the Bowman in just one entry. |
| 49,1–3; 5–6 | FORMERLY. "value when he acquired it" for each of these entries, probably referring to Fulchere, as in 49,7; see notes to 2,14 and 16,88. |
| 49,3 | 1 PLOUGH, WHICH IS THERE, WITH 3 SMALLHOLDERS. "Fulchere has 2 villagers who have 1 plough, and (he has) 3 smallholders". This separation of the villagers who had the plough is probably the reason for their omission in DB, as also happens in 23,4. See 1,9 note. |
| 49,4 | 1 VILLAGER WHO PAYS 10s. "1 villager who pays him 10s a year". See General Notes 6,6. |
| 49,7 | HUISH. "Helgot holds it now from Fulchere". In the T.O. at 500 a 9: "Fulchere the Bowman has a manor called Huish. 1 virgate and 1 furlong (*ferdinus*) have been added to it, which a thane held jointly in 1066. Helgot holds it now from F(ulchere). Value 15s a year". |
|  | 3 SMALLHOLDERS. "4 smallholders". |
|  | [VALUE] FORMERLY. "value when Fulchere acquired it". |
| Ch. 50 | HAIMERIC. See note to Chs. 47–50. He is called Haimeric of Arques for 50,1–2 (*de arcis*);5 (*de archa*), but plain Haimeric for 50,3–4. The Tax Return for Tiverton Hundred (xi) states that Haimeric of Arques (*de arcis*) has ½ virgate lordship there, which points to 50,5. See OEB pp. 68–69 on the byname. |
| 50,1 | POLTIMORE. In the T.O. at 500 a 7: "Haimeric of Arques (*de arcis*) has a manor called Poltimore. 1½ hides and 3 furlongs (*fertini*) have been added to it; value of them, 30s a year". |
|  | FORMERLY. "value when he acquired it", presumably referring to Haimeric, as in 50,5; see 2,14 note. |
| 50,2 | 1 PLOUGH, WHICH IS THERE. "Haimeric has 1 plough"; *in dominio* probably implied or omitted in error. |
| 50,3 | TAX FOR ½ FURLONG. In the Exon. MS *dim⁹ .i. ferdino*; it is not absolutely clear whether 1½ furlongs ('ferlings') or one ½ furlong is meant. Cf. 16,92 first note. The |

| | |
|---|---|
| 50,3 (cont'd.) | comma below the *i* rather suggests the former as it is often used as an omission sign; also there is no underlining for deletion which one would expect if the *dim*⁺ were to replace the *i*, as the Exchequer scribe apparently took it.<br>½ PLOUGH THERE. "H(aimeric) has ½ plough"; *in dominio* probably implied or omitted in error. Similarly for 50,4. |
| 50,5 | FORMERLY. "when Ha(imeric) acquired it". |
| 51,1 | WILLIAM THE PORTER. In Exon. his holding does not appear with 51,2-13 under the heading of "Lands of the King's Servants in Devonshire" (folios 475a–476b inclusive), but under the heading of "Land of Nicholas the Bowman in Devonshire" (see Chs. 47-50 note), appearing between entries corresponding to DB 49,5 and 48,8. The DB scribe may have included William's land here because the single entry did not justify a separate chapter, as apparently did those of Godbold, Nicholas, Fulchere and Haimeric (Chs. 47-50). Moreover, William's byname suggests, like those of 51,2-13, that he held this manor as a 'reward' for a particular local service (see General Notes here), rather than for performing general military service. The Exon. scribe may simply have misplaced his holding and the Exchequer scribe corrected this.<br>FORMERLY. "when W(illiam) acquired it". |
| 51,2 | GODRIC HELD IT. In the T.O. at 495 b 5: "which a thane held jointly".<br>FORMERLY. "value when W(illiam) acquired it". Similarly for the past value of 51,9;12.<br>THIS MANOR .... KING'S MANOR. "This manor paid to the King's lordship manor called (South) Tawton either 1 ox or 30d a year in customary dues". Similarly in 495 b 5 with the addition of "and since W(illiam) the Usher has held it, the King has not had this customary due from it". |
| 51,3 | FORMERLY. "when he acquired it", probably referring to William, as in 51,2 (see notes to 2,14 and 16,88). Similarly for the past values of 51,5-8;10-11. |
| 51,5 | TWO THANES HELD IT FREELY (AND) JOINTLY. "which two thanes held jointly"; no mention of "freely". |
| 51,10 | THE ABOVE MANORS .... EXCHANGE. This information is added at the end of each entry corresponding to 51,4-10 in the form *(hec mansio) est de escangiis/escanbiis/ excambio W(illelmi)*. The Latin form *escangiis* is affected by the spelling and pronunciation of OFr *esc(h)ange* (Mod. Fr *échange*) which is itself derived from ML *escambium*. |
| 51,11 | PASTURE, 25 ACRES. "30 acres". |
| 51,13 | FORMERLY. "value when Ansger acquired it". |
| 51,14 | MORIN'S holding appears in Exon. under the heading of "Lands of the French Men-at-Arms in Devonshire"; see Ch. 22 note. He probably came from Caen; see General Notes here.<br>MORIN HOLDS .... FROM THE KING. "Now Morin holds this (manor) from the King" added at the end of the entry. It is unusual for Exon. to state that the 1086 tenant held "from the King", but see notes to 52,5;40, also Chs. 8-13a note and 1,11 note on 'Edward son of Edric holds it'.<br>1 PLOUGH THERE. "M(orin) has on it 1 plough"; *in dominio* probably implied or omitted in error.<br>[VALUE] FORMERLY. "value when he acquired it", presumably referring to Morin, as there is no subtenant (see 2,14 note). |
| 51,15-16 | THESE HOLDINGS appear in Exon. under the heading of "Lands of English Thanes in Devonshire"; see Ch. 52 note. |
| Ch. 52 | LANDS OF THE KING'S THANES. Entered in Exon. under the heading of "Lands of English Thanes in Devonshire", folios 481a-490 a 3 inclusive; this section also contains entries corresponding to DB 51,15-16. The Exchequer scribe worked through the Exon. section excerpting the lands of individuals and put these together; see General Notes here. |
| 52,2 | COLWIN ALSO HOLDS. "Colwin has", with no *idem* as DB has, though no doubt the same man as the Colwin of 52,1 is intended. See 15,21 note. |
| 52,3 | THE THIRD PART OF 1 FURLONG. "The third part of another furlong *(alio ferdino)*". |
| 52,4 | FORMERLY. "value when C(olwin) acquired it". |
| 52,5 | DUNSBEARE. "Colwin holds it from the King". See 51,14 note. |
| 52,5-6 | FORMERLY. "when he acquired it" for each entry, presumably referring to Colwin, as there is no subtenant (see 2,14 note). |
| 52,9 | 2 PLOUGHS, WHICH ARE THERE. "On it (manor) are 2 ploughs, 2 villagers....". See 17,18 note on the lack of detail given on the ploughs and 34,46 note on the unusual formula. |

# Exon. 52

| | |
|---|---|
| 52,10 | IN LORDSHIP 5 PLOUGHS. "3 ploughs"; the Exchequer scribe probably mistook the *v carrucatas* for the ploughs, which are on the next line. Cf. fourth note under 23,5 for a similar mistake.<br>VILLAGERS WITH 10 PLOUGHS. *x carr̄* probably abbreviates *carrucas*, rather than *carrucatas*, the villagers' land holding being omitted as for 52,11-14 and on numerous occasions in Exon. for Devon when the lordship land is nevertheless given; see General Notes 1,4 on the hide. |
| 52,11 | FORMERLY. "value when he acquired it", presumably referring to Godwin, as in 52,12 (see 2,14 note).<br>20s; VALUE NOW 10s. In the Exon. MS, before the *xx* of the past value, a *v* is visible, erased badly, and the present value appears as *xiii* with the *iii* apparently erased, even less well, with water. |
| 52,12-16 | FORMERLY. "when G(odwin) acquired it" for each entry. |
| 52,13 | GODWIN ALSO HOLDS. "Godwin has", with no *idem* as in DB, but probably the same man as the Godwin of the preceding DB entries. See 15,21 note. |
| 52,15 | 1 PLOUGH THERE. "Godwin has 1 plough on it"; *in dominio* probably implied or omitted in error. |
| 52,17 | FORMERLY. "when [he acquired it]"; *recepit* omitted in error. |
| 52,19 | WOODLAND. "underwood (*nemusculi*)". |
| 52,20 | GALL has been applied over all of this entry in Exon. (except for the first line) because it is faint, but most of what Ellis printed can still be deciphered; see notes below.<br>LAND FOR 3 PLOUGHS. Ellis prints "2 ploughs", but *iii* can just be made out under the gall and the dots at the beginning and end of the figure are clearly visible, thus determining its length.<br>3 SLAVES. Ellis prints "2 slaves"; it is impossible to tell as the *ii* comes right on the inner edge of the parchment and is covered in gall.<br>WOODLAND, 1 ACRE. "underwood (*nemusculi*)" with no room for *una ac̄* before it, but the gall prevents the words being checked.<br>24(?) SHEEP. So Ellis prints, but it may be "34 sheep", as there seems to be too much room under the gall for *xxiiii*. |
| 52,20-21 | FORMERLY. "value when he acquired it" for each entry, presumably referring to Godric (see 2,14 note). |
| 52,21 | GODRIC ALSO HOLDS. "Godric has", but no doubt the same man as the Godric of 52,20. See General Notes here for Godric and 15,21 note above. |
| 52,22-25 | VALUE FORMERLY. "value when he acquired it" for each entry, presumably referring to Odo (see 2,14 note). |
| 52,23 | ODO ALSO HOLDS. "Odo has" with no *idem*, but probably the same man as the Odo of 52,22 (see General Notes 52,22-25). See 15,21 note. |
| 52,24 | 1 PLOUGH, WHICH IS THERE. "Odo has 1 plough"; *in dominio* probably implied or omitted in error. |
| 52,26 | TAX FOR 1 VIRGATE. "½ virgate", which agrees with the total of 2 furlongs ('ferlings') for lordship and villagers' land. |
| 52,29 | VALUE 5s. "Value 10s a year". |
| 52,33 | SEDBOROUGH BELONGED TO. "Sedborough lay (in)". There is no entry in the T.O. on this, possibly because, as can be seen from the corresponding entry under Baldwin's fief (16,33 note), details of this former attachment of Sedborough to Parkham came in late, though they are not added late under the other details of Sedborough in the main Exon. for 52,33. |
| 52,36 | PASTURE ½ LEAGUE LONG .... *dīm leugā pascuę* ...; the scribe omitted *in longitudine* "in length" in error.<br>WOODLAND 3 FURLONGS LONG AND 1 FURLONG WIDE. In the Exon. MS *xii quadragenarias nemoris ī lonḡ*; the first figure is not an *x* as Ellis prints (*xii*), but an oddly written *i* (probably crossed through, 2 furlongs being intended for the length). The width in Exon. is 1½ furlongs. |
| 52,37 | 1 PLOUGH, WHICH IS THERE. "Alwin has on it 1 plough"; *in dominio* probably implied or omitted in error.<br>UNDERWOOD, 2 ACRES. "3 acres". |
| 52,40 | ULF HOLDS WADHAM. "Ulf has....Wadham....now he holds it from the King". See 51,14 note. |
| 52,43 | GALL has been applied over all this entry in Exon., but most of what Ellis printed can be deciphered now (see notes below) and where he prints dots nothing more can be made out in the MS.<br>3 SMALLHOLDERS. Ellis prints "2 smallholders", but the gall is too dark here to be able to check this. |

Exon. 52

| | |
|---|---|
| 52,43 (cont'd.) | WOODLAND, 6 ACRES. It is only possible to read *vi ag* under the gall, but *nemoris* fits the space and usually comes in this position. |
| | .... SHEEP. The number cannot be made out; Ellis prints dots. |
| | VALUE FORMERLY. "value when he acquired it", presumably referring to Alric (see 2,14 note). |
| | VALUE.....NOW 20s. None of the 1086 value statement can be deciphered under the gall; Ellis prints dots. |
| 52,46 | VILLAGERS....½ PLOUGH. "villagers....3 oxen in a plough". |
| | VALUE 20d. "Value 30d". |
| 52,48-49 | HE ALSO. "Saewulf" for each entry. |
| 52,48 | 1 VILLAGER. "On it (manor) is 1 villager"; see 34,46 note on this unusual formula. |
| 52,50 | 1 PLOUGH, WHICH IS THERE. "Aelfeva has 1 plough on it"; *in dominio* probably implied or omitted in error. |
| 52,51 | ½ PLOUGH THERE. "Alfhild has ½ plough"; *in dominio* probably implied or omitted in error. |

ANOTHER ITEM OF INFORMATION, not in the main Exon. nor in DB, occurs in the T.O. between details of the Abbot of Tavistock's newly acquired manor of Raddon (5,9 note; it is interesting that it also records an item of information not in the main Exon. nor in DB) and the Bishop of Coutances' combined manor of Aylescott (3,40 note):
   **500 a 4**: "In the Hundred of Molton is 1 furlong (*ferdinus*) of land which 1 plough can plough. It lies completely waste (*penitus uastatus iacet*). No man claims it".
It is not clear whether this is North or South Molton Hundred; see the Appendix below on the Devonshire Hundreds. Because the furlong ('ferling') could not be assigned to anyone's fief (unlike the virgate attached TRE to Shilstone, DB 43,3, which "no one holds", though there are 2 villagers on it), it does not appear in the main Exon. returns and thus not in DB. It is unlikely that the reason for its non-appearance was due to details of it arriving after the main Exon. had been written. For other whole T.O. entries not in the main Exon. nor in DB, see notes to 1,25 (last note). 1,66. 2,2. 15,14 and Ch. 44, and, for those T.O. entries which add significant information to DB, see Ch. 44 note also.

## DETAILS OF LORDSHIP AND VILLAGERS' LAND AND PLOUGHS OMITTED IN DB AND GIVEN IN EXON.

The details below are for the main holding at the place named, unless the place is marked with an asterisk. Exon. folio references are given on the translation pages.

Rest = rest of the land (*aliam* or *aliam terram*). h. = hide; v. = virgate; f. = furlong

| DB ref. | Place | In lordship land | In lordship ploughs | The villagers have land | The villagers have ploughs |
|---|---|---|---|---|---|
| 1,72 | ?Down St. Mary | 1 v. | 1 | 2 f. | 1 |
| 2,8 | St. Marychurch | 1 v. | 1 | 1 v. | 2 |
| 2,20 | Chudleigh Knighton | 1½ v. | 2 | ½ v. | 1 |
| 3,17 | Horwood | 1 v. | 1 | 2 v. | ½ |
| 3,48 | Trentishoe | 2 v. | ½ | 2 v. | ½ |
| 3,51 | Warcombe | ½ v. | 1 | ½ v. | 1 |
| 3,55 | East Buckland | ½ f. | — | ½ f. | 1 |
| 3,75 | Coombe | 1 v. | 1 | 1 v. | 1 |
| 3,79 | Bradley | 1 v. | ½ | 1 v. | ½ |
| 3,89 | Kimworthy | ½ v. | 1 | ½ v. | 1 |
| 3,94 | Crealy | 2 f. | 1 | 2 f. | 1 |
| 3,95 | Ruston | ½ f. | ½ | ½ f. | ½ |
| 5,3 | Liddaton | ½ v. | 1 | ½ v. | 2 |
| 15,2 | *Stochelie* | ½ v. | ½ | ½ v. | ½ |
| 15,3 | Wyke | ½ h. | 2 | ½ h. | 2 |
| 15,12 | Galsworthy* | — | — | — | 1 |
| 15,15 | Smytham | — | — | — | 1 |
| 15,24 | 'Womberford' | 1 f. | 1 | 3 f. | 2 |
| 15,25 | Northleigh | 1 f. | 2 | 3 f. | 3 |
| 15,29 | Hareston | 1 v. | ½ | 1 v. | 4 oxen in a plough |
| 15,30 | Winston | 1 v. | ½ | 1 v. | ½ |
| 15,31 | Densham | 1 f. | — | 1 v. | 3 |
| 15,33 | Wedfield | ½ v. | 1 | ½ v. | 1 + 2 oxen |
| 15,52 | Spriddlestone | ½ v. | ½ | ½ v. | ½ |
| 15,54 | Stockleigh | 1 f. | 1 | 2 f. | 1 |
| 15,55 | Matford | 1 f. | 1 | 1 f. | ½ |
| 15,60 | Chitterley | 1½ v. | 1 | 1½ v. | 3 |
| 15,63 | Cheriton | 3 v. 1 f. | ½ | 3 f. | ½ |
| 15,65 | Orcheton | ½ h. | 1 | ½ h. | 1 |
| 15,79 | Lipson | 1 v. | — | 1 v. | 1 |
| 16,16 | Dunsland | 1 f. | 1 | 1 f. | 3 |
| 16,28 | Middlecott | 1 f. | 1 | 2 f. | 1 |
| 16,41 | Woolleigh | 1 f. | 1 | 3 f. | 3 |
| 16,46 | Leigh | 1 v. | 2 | 2 v. | 4 |
| 16,49 | Appledore | ½ v. | 5 oxen | ½ v. | 1 |
| 16,52 | Walson | ½ v. | 1½ | ½ v. | 1½ |
| 16,53 | Brushford | 1 v. | ½ | 1 v. | ½ |
| 16,54 | Brushford | 1 v. | ½ | 1 v. | ½ |
| 16,58 | Kenn | 3 h. | — | 3 h. | 25 |
| 16,59 | George Teign | ½ v. | 1 | 2½ v. | 3 |

| DB ref. | Place | In lordship land | ploughs | The villagers have land | ploughs |
|---|---|---|---|---|---|
| 16,60 | Beetor | 1 f. | 1 | 3 f. | 2 |
| 16,61 | Shapley | ½ v. | 1 | ½ v. | 1 |
| 16,64 | Shapley | ½ v. | — | ½ v. | 1½ |
| 16,66 | Ashford | 1 v. | 1 | 1 v. | 1 |
| 16,67 | Loxhore | 1 v. | 1 | 1 v. | 1 |
| 16,68 | Loxhore | 1 v. | 1 | 1 v. | 2 |
| 16,72 | Mockham | 1 f. | 1 | — | 2 |
| 16,74 | Blakewell | 1 f. | 1 | — | 1 |
| 16,82 | Whitstone | 1 f. | 6 oxen | 1 f. | 2 oxen |
| 16,88 | Snydles | 1 f. | 1 | 3 f. | 1 |
| 16,92 | West Clyst | 1½ v.(?)† | 1 | — | 2½ |
| 16,97 | Ponsford | 1 v. | 1 | 1 v. | 1 |
| 16,102 | Kentisbeare | 1 v. | 2 | 1 v. | 2 |
| 16,104 | 'Monk Culm' | 2½ v. | 1 | 1½ v. | 1 |
| 16,105 | 'Bernardsmoor' | 1 v. | 1 | 1 v. | 2 |
| 16,115 | Martin | 2 f. | 1 | 2 f. | ½ |
| 16,116 | Melhuish | 1 v. | 1 | 1 v. | 6 |
| 16,117 | Teignharvey | 1 v. | 2 | 1 v. | 1 |
| 16,120 | Tedburn St. Mary | 1 f. | 1 | 3 f. | 2 |
| 16,123 | Bramford Speke | 1 v. | 1 | 1 v. | ½ |
| 16,124 | Hole | 1 v. | 1 | 1 v. | 1 |
| 16,125 | Whitestone | 1 v. | ½ | 1 v. | 1 |
| 16,126 | Maidencombe | 1 v. | ½ | 1 v. ½ f. | ½ |
| 16,127 | Rocombe | 1 v. | ½ | 1 v. | ½ |
| 16,132 | Great Fulford | ½ v. | 1 | — | 2 |
| 16,137 | Whitestone | ½ v. | 1 | — | 1 |
| 16,144 | Creacombe | 3 parts of 1 f. | 1 | 2 f. | 1 |
| 16,154 | Langstone | 1 f. | 1 | 3 f. | 1 |
| 16,157 | Whiteway | 1 v. | 1 | 1 v. | 1 |
| 16,158 | Chevithorne | ½ v. | 1 | ½ v. | ½ |
| 16,161 | Sellake | 1 v. 3 f. | 1 | 1 f. | ½ |
| 17,12 | Tillislow | 1 f. | 1 | (1) f.†† | 3 oxen |
| 17,20 | Henford | ½ v. | 1 | ½ v. | 1 |
| 17,23 | Combe Fishacre | 1 v. | ½ | 1 v. | 1 |
| 17,24 | Combe Fishacre | ½ v. | ½ | ½ v. | ½ |
| 17,27 | Shiphay Collaton | ½ v. | 1 | ½ v. | 1 |
| 17,28 | Lupton | ½ v. | 1 | ½ v. | 6 cattle in a plough |
| 17,31 | Coleton | 1 v. | 1 | 1 v. | 1 |
| 17,34 | Bagton | 1 v. | 1 | 1 v. | 1 |
| 17,35 | Collaton | 1 v. | ½ | 1 v. | ½ |

† See Exon. Notes for this entry.
†† *alium ferlinum*.

L

| DB ref. | Place | In lordship land | In lordship ploughs | The villagers have land | The villagers have ploughs |
|---|---|---|---|---|---|
| 17,39 | Ilton | 1 v. | — | 1 v. | 6 cattle in a plough |
| 17,40 | Alston | 1 v. | 1 | 1 v. | ½ |
| 17,43 | Poulston | ½ v. | 1 | ½ v. | ½ |
| 17,44 | Curtisknowle | 1 v. | 1 | 1 v. | ½ |
| 17,47 | Woolston | ½ v. | 1 | 1½ v. | 2 |
| 17,53 | South Allington | ½ h. | 1 | ½ h. | 1 + 2 cattle† |
| 17,54 | Stancombe | 1 v. | 1 | 1 v. | 1 |
| 17,55 | Malston | ½ h. | 1 | ½ h. | 3 |
| 17,57 | Chivelstone | ½ h. | 1 | ½ h. | 2 |
| 17,61 | Butterford | 1 v. | 6 oxen | 1 v. | 1½ |
| 17,63 | Stadbury | ½ v. | 1 | ½ v. | 2 |
| 17,65 | Okenbury | 1 v. | 1 | 1 v. | 2 |
| 17,66 | Blachford | ½ v. | 6 oxen | ½ v. | 2 |
| 17,68 | Membland | ½ h. | 1 | ½ h. | 1½ |
| 17,72 | *Leuricestone* | ½ v. | 1 | ½ v. | 1 |
| 17,74 | Burrington | ½ f. | 1 | ½ f. | 1 |
| 17,75 | Manadon | 1 v. | 1 | 1 v. | 1 |
| 17,76 | Whitleigh | 1 v. | ½ | 1 v. | ½ |
| 17,78 | Compton Gifford | 3 v. | 2 | 2 v. | 2 |
| 17,80 | Meavy | ½ v. | — | ½ v. | 1 |
| 17,82 | Meavy | ½ v. | — | ½ v. | ½ |
| 17,83 | Sherford | 1 v. | 1 | 1 v. | 1 |
| 17,86 | Brixton | 1 v. | 1 | 1 v. | 1 |
| 17,88 | Down Thomas | 1½ f. | 1 | 1½ f. | 1 |
| 17,89 | Staddiscombe | ½ v. | ½ | ½ v. | — |
| 17,91 | Brixton | ½ v. | 1 | ½ v. | 1 |
| 17,95 | Langdon | 1 v. | 1 | 1 v. | 1 |
| 17,97 | Coldstone | 1 v. | 1 | 1 v. | 1 |
| 17,102 | Torridge | ½ v. | 1 | ½ v. | ½ |
| 17,103 | Loughtor | ½ v. | 1 | ½ v. | ½ |
| 17,106 | Hooe | ½ v. | 1 | ½ v. | 1 |
| 19,13 | Buckland | ½ v. | 1 | ½ v. | 2 |
| 19,14 | Ash | ½ v. | 2 | ½ v. | 1 |
| 19,18 | 'Badgworthy' | ½ v. | 1 | ½ v. | 1 |
| 19,19 | Radworthy | ½ v. | 2 | ½ v. | 1 |
| 19,23 | Colebrook | 1½ v. | 1 | ½ v. | ½ |
| 19,24 | Cadeleigh | 2 v. | 2 | 1 v. | 1 |
| 19,27 | Weston | 1½ v. | 1 | ½ v. | ½ |
| 19,41 | Buckland | ½ v. | 1 | [ ]† | [ ]† |
| 20,5 | 'Beare' | ½ v. | ½ | ½ v. | ½ |

† See Exon. Notes.

# L

| DB ref. | Place | In lordship land | ploughs | The villagers have land | ploughs |
|---|---|---|---|---|---|
| 20,15 | Luscombe* | ½ f. | 1 | ½ f. | 1½ |
| 20,17 | Englebourne | 1 v. 3 f. | 2 | 1 f. | ½ |
| 21,8 | Bowley | 1 v. | 1 | 1 v. | 1 |
| 23,1 | Hollacombe | 1 f. | ½ | 1 f. | ½ |
| 23,4 | ?Stoodleigh | – | 1‡ | – | ½ |
| 23,23 | Coleridge | 1 f. | ½ | 1 f. | ½ |
| 23,26 | Townstall | 1 f. | 1 | 3 f. | 1 |
| 24,2 | Bramford Speke | 1 v. | 1 | – | 1 |
| 24,7 | Sydeham | ½ v. | 1 | – | 1 |
| 24,9 | Murley | 1 v. 1 f. | 1 | ½ v. 1 f. | 1 |
| 24,10 | Coombe | 1 v. 1 f. | 1 | ½ v. 1 f. | 2½ |
| 24,13 | Ayshford | ½ h. | 1 | ½ h. | 2 |
| 24,22 | Iddesleigh | – | 1 | – | 2 |
| 24,25 | Dowland | 3 f. | 1 | 1 f. | 1 |
| 24,27 | *Chetelescote* | ½ v. | 1 | ½ v. | ½ |
| 24,28 | Wolfin | 3 f. | 1 | 1 f. | 1 |
| 24,32 | Virworthy | ½ f. | 1 | 3 f. | 2 |
| 25,7 | Brushford | 1½ f. | 1 | 2½ f. | 1 |
| 25,8 | Hampson | ½ v. | 1 | ½ v. ½ f. | 1 |
| 25,11 | Goodcott | ½ v. | 1 | ½ v. | 1 |
| 25,12 | Fenacre | ½ h. | 1 | ½ v. | 1 |
| 25,21 | East Manley | 1 v. | 1 | 1½ v. | 2 |
| 25,25 | Buckland Tout Saints | 1 f. | 1 | 1 f. | 1 |
| 28,12 | Beenleigh | 1 v. | ½ | 1 v. | 1½ |
| 31,4 | Mortehoe | 1 v. | 1 | – | 1†† |
| 34,4 | *Alwineclancavele* | – | 1 | – | 1 |
| 34,7 | West Putford | 1 f. | 1 | 1 f. | 1 |
| 34,15 | Cheriton | 1 f. | 1 | 1 f. | 1 |
| 34,20 | Blackborough | 1 v. | 1 | 1 v. | 1 |
| 34,26 | Awliscombe | 1½ v. | 1 | 1 v. | 2 |
| 34,33 | Dunscombe | 1 v. | 2 | 1 v. | 1 |
| 34,35 | Lower Creedy | ½ v. | 1 | ½ v. | 1 + 7 oxen in a plough |
| 34,38 | Strete Ralegh | 1 v. | 1½ | 1 v. | ½ |
| 35,3 | Wonford | 1 f. | 1 | 1 f. | 1 |
| 35,7 | Kimber | 1 f. | – | 1 f. | 1 + 3 oxen |
| 35,12 | Hollam | ½ f. | 1 | ½ f. | ½ |
| 35,13 | Peters Marland | 1 v. | 1 | 2 v. | 5 |
| 35,14 | Twigbeare | ½ v. | 2 | ½ v. | 1 |
| 35,15 | Winscott | ½ v. | 1 | ½ v. | 1 |
| 35,16 | Winswell | ½ v. | 1 | ½ v. | 1 |

‡ *In dominio* omitted, probably in error.
†† in the MS *i ararr̄*, a scribal error for *i carr̄*.

L

| DB ref. | Place | In lordship land | In lordship ploughs | The villagers have land | The villagers have ploughs |
|---|---|---|---|---|---|
| 35,21 | Crockernwell | ½ v. | 1 | ½ v. | 1 |
| 36,3 | South Hole | (1) h. | 1 | 1 v. | ½ |
| 36,4 | Milford | 1 v. | 1½ | 1 v.†† | 1 |
| 36,7 | Owlacombe | 1 v. | 1 | 1 v.†† | 2 |
| 36,12 | Georgeham | 1½ v. | 1 | 1½ v. | 2 |
| 36,13 | Spreacombe | ½ v. | 1 | ½ v. | 1½ |
| 36,14 | Ossaborough | ½ v. | — | ½ v. | 1 |
| 36,15 | Woolacombe | ½ v. | 1 | ½ v. | ½ |
| 36,16 | Marwood | ½ v. | 1 | ½ v. | 1 |
| 36,18 | Culm Davy | ½ h. less 1 f. | 2 | 2 v. 1 f. | 1 |
| 36,23 | Washford Pyne | 1 v. | 1 | — | 1 |
| 36,24 | 'Dart' | ½ v. | 1 | — | ½ |
| 36,25 | Rifton | 1 v. | 1 | — | ½ |
| 36,26 | Widworthy | ½ h. | 1 | ½ h. | 1 |
| 40,1 | Stafford | 1 f. | ½ | 1 f. | ½ |
| 40,2 | Great Torrington | 1 f. | 1 | 3 f. | 1 |
| 40,3 | Brimblecombe | 1 f. | ½ | 1 f. | ½ |
| 40,6 | Sutton | 1½ v. | 1 | ½ v. | 1 |
| 41,2 | Westleigh | 1 v. 1 f. | 1 | 1 v. 1 f. | 1 |
| 42,2 | Stowford | ½ v. | 2 | Rest | 2 + 3 oxen |
| 42,3 | Alminstone | 1 f. | 1 | 3 f. | 2 |
| 42,4 | Huish | 1 v. | 3 | 2 v. | 2 |
| 42,7 | Buckland | — | 2 | — | 1½ |
| 42,8 | Whiddon | ½ v. | 1 | ½ v. | ½ |
| 42,9 | Shirwell | ½ v. | ½ | ½ v. | ½ |
| 42,11 | Honiton | — | 1 | — | 1 |
| 42,12 | Aller | — | 2‡ | — | 1 |
| 42,13 | Hacche | 1 v. | 2 | — | 1 |
| 42,14 | Stallenge Thorne | ½ h. | 1 | ½ h. | 1 |
| 42,15 | Brayley | ½ v. | 1 | ½ v. | ½ |
| 42,21 | Worlington* | 1 v. ½ f.‡ | 2 | 2 v. less ½ f. | 1½ |
| 42,22 | Chilton | 1 f. | 1 | 1 f. | 1 |
| 42,24 | Willand | 1 v. | 1 | 3 v. | 1 |
| 45,2 | Abbots Bickington | — | 1 | — | 2 |
| 46,1 | West Manley | ½ v. | 1 | ½ v. | 1 |
| 47,6 | Lowley | 1 f. | 1 | ½ v. | 1½ |
| 47,7 | Mullacott | 1 v. | 1 | 1 v. | 1 |
| 47,8 | Satterleigh | ½ v. | 2 | ½ v. | 1 |
| 47,12 | Halstow | 1 v. | 1 | 1 v. | 1 |
| 47,13 | West Whitnole | 1 v. | 1 | ½ v. | 2 |

†† *aliam virgam.*
‡ *In dominio* omitted, probably in error.

| DB ref. | Place | In lordship land | In lordship ploughs | The villagers have land | The villagers have ploughs |
|---|---|---|---|---|---|
| 48,2 | Greenslinch | 1 v. | 1 | 2 v. | 2 |
| 48,3 | Stokeinteignhead | 1 v. | 2 | — | 2 |
| 48,4 | Rocombe | ½ h. | 2 | — | 1 |
| 48,6 | Holbeam | — | 1 | — | 1 |
| 48,10 | Buckland in the Moor | 1 v. | 1½ | 2 v. | 1 |
| 49,5 | Farringdon | 1 f. | 1 | 3 f. | 2 |
| 49,6 | Leigh | 1 v. 1 f. | 2 | 2 v. less 1 f. | 1 |
| 49,7 | Huish | 1 v. | 1 | — | 4 |
| 51,1 | Bicton | ½ h. | 2 | ½ h. | 3 |
| 51,6 | Raddon | 1 v. | 1 | 1½ v. | 2 |
| 51,9 | Ilsham | ½ h. | 1 | ½ h. | ½ |
| 51,15 | Hollacombe | — | 1 | — | 2 |
| 52,1 | Chilsworthy | third part of ½ v. | 1 | 2 parts of that land** | 2 |
| 52,4 | Woolfardisworthy | 1 f. | 1 | 3 f. | 3 |
| 52,5 | Dunsbeare | 1 f. | 1 | 3 f. | 3 |
| 52,6 | Allisland | ½ v. | 1 | 1 v. | 3 |
| 52,11 | Cheriton Bishop | 2 f. | 1 | — | 1 |
| 52,12 | Lambert | 2 f. | 1 | — | 5 |
| 52,14 | Ogwell | 1 v. | 1 | — | 1 |
| 52,16 | Wray | 1 v. | 2 | 3 v. | 4 |
| 52,17 | 'Combe Sackville' | 1 v. | 1 | 3 v. | 2 |
| 52,19 | 'Down Umfraville' | ½ h. | 2 | ½ h. | 1 |
| 52,20 | Bulworthy | 1 f. | 1 | 1 v. | 1 |
| 52,21 | Calverleigh | ½ v. | 1 | 1½ v. | 1½ |
| 52,22 | Payhembury | 3 v. | 1 | 1 v. | 1 |
| 52,23 | Coddiford | 3 f. | ½ | 1 f. | ½ |
| 52,25 | Rousdon | ½ v. | 1 | ½ v. | 1 |
| 52,26 | ?Week | 1 f. | 1 | 1 f. | 1 |
| 52,27 | Manaton | ½ v. | 1 | ½ v. | 1 |
| 52,28 | Bickford | ½ f. | ½ | ½ f.†† | ½ |
| 52,29 | Colscott | 1 f. | 1 | 1 f. | 1 |
| 52,31 | Meddon | ½ v. | 1 | 1½ v. | 1½ |
| 52,35 | Nutwell | 1 h. | 1 | ½ h. | 2 |
| 52,36 | Bray | ½ v. | 1 | — | 3 |
| 52,38 | Butterleigh | ½ v. | 1 | ½ v. | 2 |
| 52,40 | Wadham | 1 f. | 1 | — | 2 |
| 52,41 | Knowstone | ½ v. | 1 | ½ v. | 1 |
| 52,42 | Dunstone | 1 v. | 1 | 1 v. | 1 |
| 52,43 | Waspley | ½ v. | 1 | 3 f. | 2 |
| 52,44 | Shapley | 1 f. | 1 | 1 f. | 1 |
| 52,45 | Skerraton | 1 f. | 1 | 3 f. | 1 |

** A hole in the MS has obliterated the $t$ of $\bar{tre}$, 'that land' presumably being the ½ virgate.
†† Literally 'as much' (as the lordship land).

# D

## DETAILS OF HOLDINGS OMITTED IN DB AND GIVEN IN EXON.

ac. = acre   f. = furlong   v. = virgate   h. = hide

| DB ref. | PLACE | Sub-tenant | Holding | Land for ploughs | LORDSHIP | | VILLAGERS HAVE | | Villagers | Small-holders | Cottagers (*coceti*) | Slaves |
|---|---|---|---|---|---|---|---|---|---|---|---|---|
| | | | | | land | ploughs | land | ploughs | | | | |
| 5,1 | Tavistock | Ermenald | ½ v. | — | — | 1* | — | 1** | — | — | — | — |
| | | Ralph | ½ v. | — | — | — | — | ½ | (1)*** | — | 3 | — |
| | | Hugh | ½ h. & third part of 1 v. & 1 f. | — | — | 2 | — | 7 oxen for a plough | 1 | 6 | — | 2 |
| | | Robert | 1 v. & 2 f. | — | — | (1)½ | — | (1)½ | 3 | 6 | — | 2 |
| | | Ralph of Tilly | 3 parts of 1 v. | — | — | 1* | — | 2 oxen | 1 | 4 | — | — |
| | | Geoffrey | 1 f. | — | — | 1* | — | — | — | 1 | — | — |
| 5,4 | Hatherleigh | Nigel, a French man-at-arms | ½ v. less ½ f. | — | — | 1 | — | 1 | — | — | 5 | 1 |
| | | Walter | ½ h. & ½ v. | — | ½ v. | 1 | ½ h. | 4 | 7 | 2 | — | 1 |
| | | Geoffrey | ½ v. & ½ f. | — | — | 1* | — | 1 | 4 | — | — | 1 |
| | | Ralph | ½ v. | — | — | 1* | — | — | 1 | 4 | — | — |

\* *In dominio* omitted, but probably implied.
\*\* No villagers are detailed, however, for Ermenald's holding.
\*\*\* In the MS *uillanū*; Ellis misprints *uillani*.

| DB ref. | PLACE | Sub-tenant | Cattle | Cows | Pigs | Sheep | Goats | Woodland | Underwood | Meadow | Pasture | VALUE when 1086 acquired |
|---|---|---|---|---|---|---|---|---|---|---|---|---|
| 5,1 | Tavistock | Ermenald | 7 | – | – | 40 | – | – | – | – | ⎫ | See Exon. Notes |
|  |  | Ralph | – | – | – | – | – | – | – | – | ⎬ |  |
|  |  | Hugh | 10 | – | 12 | 60 | – | – | – | – | ⎬ |  |
|  |  | Robert | 12 | – | – | 60 | 20 | – | – | – | ⎬ |  |
|  |  | Ralph of Tilly | 7 | – | – | 30 | 10 | – | – | – | ⎬ |  |
|  |  | Geoffrey | 6 | – | – | 30 | – | – | – | – | ⎭ |  |
| 5,4 | Hatherleigh | Nigel, a French man-at-arms | 6 | – | 4 | 40 | – | – | – | – | ⎫ | See Exon. Notes |
|  |  | Walter | 12 | – | 10 | 50 | – | – | – | – | ⎬ |  |
|  |  | Geoffrey | – | 1 | – | – | 5 | – | – | – | ⎬ |  |
|  |  | Ralph | 7 | – | 3 | 12 | 6 | – | – | – | ⎭ |  |

# D

| DB ref. | PLACE | Sub-tenant | Holding | Land for ploughs | LORDSHIP land | LORDSHIP ploughs | VILLAGERS HAVE land | VILLAGERS HAVE ploughs | Villagers | Small-holders | Cottagers (coceti) | Slaves |
|---|---|---|---|---|---|---|---|---|---|---|---|---|
| 5,8 | Burrington | William Cheever | 1½ v. | 6 | — | 1½* | — | — | 3 | 1 | — | — |
|  |  | Geoffrey | 1 v. | 5 | — | 3* | — | — | 3 | 3 | — | — |
| 5,10 | Romansleigh | Nigel | — | — | 2½ f. | 2 | 2 v. less third part of 1 f. | 3 | 7 | 6 | — | 4 |
|  |  | Robert | — | — | 1 f. & third part of 1 f. | 1 | — | — | 3 | 4 | — | 3 |
| 23,5 | Bampton | Reginwal | 2½ v. | — | — | 1* | — | 2 | 7 | 3 | — | 2 |
|  |  | Rademar | 1 v. | — | — | 1 | — | — | 3 | — | — | — |
|  |  | Gerard | ½ f. | — | — | — | — | — | — | — | — | — |
| 34,27 | Ogwell | William of Poitou | 2 v. | — | 1 v. | 1 | 1 v. | 1 | 2 | 3 | — | 1 |
|  |  | Robert | 1 v. | — | — | — | — | — | 4 | 3 | — | — |

\* *In dominio* omitted, but probably implied.

D

| DB ref. | PLACE | Sub-tenant | Cattle | Cows | Pigs | Sheep | Goats | Woodland | Underwood | Meadow | Pasture | VALUE 1086 | VALUE when acquired |
|---|---|---|---|---|---|---|---|---|---|---|---|---|---|
| 5,8 | Burrington | William Cheever | — | — | — | — | — | — | — | — | — | 20s | 30s |
|  |  | Geoffrey | — | — | — | — | — | — | 6 ac. | 3 ac. | common pasture | 15s | 30s |
| 5,10 | Romansleigh | Nigel | 6 | — | 10 | 60 | 17 | 26 ac. | — | 20 ac. | 40 ac. | 25s | — |
|  |  | Robert | 6 | — | 6 | 40 | 10 | 13 ac. | — | 10 ac. | 20 ac. | 15s | 12s |
| 23,5 | Bampton | Reginwal | 1 | — | 1 | — | — | 2 ac. | — | 3 ac. | — | — | — |
|  |  | Rademar | — | — | — | — | — | — | — | 1½ ac. | 10 ac. | — | — |
|  |  | Gerard | — | — | — | — | — | — | — | — | — | — | — |
| 34,27 | Ogwell | William of Poitou | 6 | — | — | 30 | — | — | 12 ac. | 1 ac. | 12 ac. | 20s | 10s |
|  |  | Robert | — | — | — | — | — | — | — | — | — | 10s | 10s |

# Appendix

## APPENDIX — THE DEVONSHIRE HUNDREDS

This Appendix describes the probable Hundredal organisation of Devonshire in 1086 and surveys the main differences between that pattern and the medieval Hundreds (as shown by the Feudal Aids, the Lay Subsidy Rolls and the *Nomina Villarum*) which survived into the 19th century.

With the exception of the five south-western counties, Exchequer Domesday Book usually indicates, at the end of the first line of each entry, or group of entries (or, sometimes, in the space left after the 'Value' statement of the preceding entry), the Hundred in which the place or places lay. In many counties it can be shown that the Hundredal groups of places are entered in the same or very similar order within each individual fief; see Sawyer (2). In DB Devon there is no Hundredal rubrication, although a few Hundreds are mentioned incidentally in the text: thus Molland (1,41) is said to receive the third penny of the Hundreds of North Molton, Bampton and Braunton; Moretonhampstead (1,45) receives the third penny of Teignbridge Hundred, and 2½ virgates belonging to Iddesleigh (1,63) lie in (North) Tawton Hundred; moreover one furlong (*ferdinus*) of waste which "no man claims" lay in 'Molton' Hundred according to the Exon. *Terrae Occupatae* (500 a 4) — see the last entry under the Exon. Notes.

Despite the absence of any systematic reference within individual fiefs to Hundreds, places appear to be entered in the Exon. Book in a series of exclusive geographical groupings, that is in a largely consistent order of Hundreds, or groups of Hundreds, as can be seen from the detailed introductory note to most chapters in the General Notes. In itself, this allows some conception of the 1086 Hundreds to be formed which can be amplified from a study of the Tax Returns for Devonshire (Exon. folios 65a-71a) covering thirty-one Hundreds. As is explained in Introductory Note 1 on Places, these record the total hidage for each Hundred, the amount of lordship land for each holder and details of holdings on which tax is owed. From these Returns, valuable evidence for the identification of places can be obtained when the names of landholders or the lordship hidage or the land stated to be owing tax are compared with DB entries, even though the Tax Returns rarely contain place-names.

The names of the late 11th-century Hundreds can also be seen from two lists of Devonshire Hundreds which are bound up with the Exon. Domesday (folio 63a). As can be seen from the table below there are many similarities between these Lists and the Hundred names of the Tax Returns and of the later period. Tabulated below are the names of the Tax Return Hundreds (in the nominative case, whereas in the Exon. MS they occur in the genitive, ending in -*e* or -*ę* (for -*ae*) in phrases such as "In the Hundred of Lifton"), with their folio references in Exon. and with the modern derivative of the name (in brackets) where this name differs from that of the 'modern' Hundred. These are followed by the hidage of each Hundred as given in the Tax Return, then by the equivalent names from the two Exon. Lists and, in the last column, the name of the later Hundred which each formed, or into which it was incorporated. The numbering of the Tax Returns and of the Exon. Hundred lists is that of the present editors, following their order in Exon.; of the 'modern' Hundreds, the numbering is that of the Maps and Map Keys in this edition. In the first three columns royal manors have been starred and an 'M' indicates that the 'Hundred' was only a manor with few or no members.

# Appendix

## TABLE OF HUNDRED NAMES

h. = hides    v. = virgates

| Exon. Ref. | | | Tax Return | Exon. List I (folio 63a) | Exon. List II (folio 63a) | 'Modern' Hundred |
|---|---|---|---|---|---|---|
| 65 a 1 | | i | *Liftona | 20 h. | 18 *Lifetona | 1 *Listona | 18 Lifton / – Tavistock |
| 65 a 2 | | ii | *Hertilanda | 20 h. | 1 *Hertilanda | 3 *Hertilanda | 3 Hartland |
| 65 a 3 | | iii | *Toritona | 34½ h. | 4 *Toritona | 2 *Toritona | 11 Black Torrington |
| 65 a 4 | | iv | *Framintona | 20 h. | 5 *Framintona | 5 *Framintona | 5 Fremington |
| 65 b 1 | | v | Mertona (Merton) | 48 h. | 2 Mertona | 4 Mertona | 4 Shebbear |
| 66 a 1 | | vi | *Brantona and Scireuuella | 50 h. | 23 *Brantona / 22 Scireuuella | 11 *Brantona / 12 Scireuuella | 1 Braunton / 2 Shirwell |
| 66 a 2 | | vii | *Sut Moltona | 22 h. | 24 *Moltona | 13 *Sut Moltona | 6 South Molton |
| 66 b 1 | | viii | *Chridiatona | 20 h. | 25 *Chridiatona | 7 Crediatona | 13 Crediton |
| 66 b 2 | | ix | *Tauuentona | 42 h. | 6 *Tautona | 6 *Tauuuetona | 12 North Tawton |
| 66 b 3 | | x | *Witric | 30 h. | 20 *Witric | 17 *Wetriga | 7 Witheridge |
| 67 a 1 | | xi | *Tuuuertona | 20 h. | 19 *Tueruetona | 18 *Tuluertona | 9 Tiverton |
| 67 a 2 | | xii | *Clistona | 27 h. | 12 *Clistona | 9 *Clistona | 20 Cliston |
| 67 a 3 | | xiii | *Sulfertona (Silverton) | 52 h. | 17 *Sulfertona | — | 15 Hayridge |
| 67 b 1 | | xiv | *Hamiohc | 24 h. | — | 16 *Hamioth | 16 Hemyock |
| 67 b 2 | M | xv | Offecolum (Uffculme) | 14 h. | — | 31 Ofecolum | 8 Bampton (part) |
| 67 b 3 | | xvi | *Budeleia | 72 h. | 27 *Budeleies | 15 *Budeleia | 14 Budleigh |
| 68 a 1 | | xvii | *Hasbertona | 18½ h. | 31 *Halsbretona | 20 *Halbretona | 10 Halberton |
| 68 a 2 | M | xviii | Otri[1] | 25 h. | 32 Otric Sanctę Marię[2] | 19 Otric[3] | 21 Ottery St. Mary |
| 68 a 3 | | xix | *Axemenistre | 50 h. | 30 *Axaministres | 21 *Axeministra | 17 Axminster |
| 68 b 1 | | xx | *Culintona | 25 h. / 3 v. | 28 *Cullinctona | 23 *Culintona | 22 Colyton |

# Appendix

| Exon. Ref. | | Tax Return | | Exon. List I (folio 63a) | | Exon. List II (folio 63a) | | 'Modern' Hundred |
|---|---|---|---|---|---|---|---|---|
| 68 b 2 | xxi | *Axemuda (Axmouth) | 9 h. 1 v. | 29 *Axamudes | | 24 *Alsemuda | | 17 Axminster (part) |
| 68 b 3 | xxii | Badentona | 25 h. | 21 Badentona[4] | | 10 Badentona[5] | | 8 Bampton |
| 69 a 1 | xxiii | *Æsseministra[6] | 50 h. | 11 *Esseministra | | 8 *Esseministra | | 24 Exminster |
| 69 a 2 | xxiv | *Taintona (Teignton) | 30 h. | 9 *Taintona | | 30 Tainebruga | | 23 Teignbridge |
| 69 b 1 | xxv | *Carsewilla (Kerswell) | 50 h. | 8 *Chersuuelles[7] | | 22 *Carsuella | | 29 Haytor |
| 69 b 2 | xxvi | *Dippeforda (Diptford) | 39 h. | 7 *Dippesforda | | 29 *Dippeforda | | 28 Stanborough |
| 69 b 3 | xxvii | *Cadelintona (Chillington) | 46 h. | 16 *Caedelintona | | 25 *Cadelintona | | 30 Coleridge |
| 70 a 1 | xxviii | *Plintona | 25 h. | 15 *Plintona | | 28 *Plintona | | 26 Plympton |
| 70 a 2 | xxix | *Walchentona (Walkhampton) | 25 h. | 14 *Walchentona | | 27 *Rueberga | | 25 Roborough |
| 70 a 3 | xxx | Aleriga (——) | 40 h. | 13 *Hernintona[8] | | 26 Aleriga | | 27 Ermington |
| 70 b 1 | xxxi | *Wenfort | 54 h. | 10 *Wenforda | | 14 *Wenforda | | 19 Wonford |
| — | M | | | 3 *Mollanda (Molland) | | ———— | | 6 South Molton (part) |
| — | M | | | 26 Hertesberia (Berrynarbor) | | ———— | | 1 Braunton (part) |

**Textual Notes on the Table**

1. In the Exon. MS *Otri* is a correction from *Odtri*; the *d*, though erased, is still partially visible.
2. In the Exon. MS *Otric* with *Scę̄ Marię* interlined; Ellis misprints *Otrie* with *scę̄ marie*.
3. *Otric* in the Exon. MS; Ellis misprints *Otrie*.
4. In the Exon. MS *Badentone hund̄* is interlined (in paler ink and by a different scribe) above *Clauuetonae* which is underlined for deletion. Ellis omits the underlining and prints *Clauueton&*
5. *Badentonę* in the Exon. MS; Ellis misprints *Badentone*.
6. *aesseministrę* in the Exon. MS, a diphthong squiggle being added to an original *a*; Ellis misprints *Esseministrę*.
7. *Cerṣ̌uelles* in the Exon. MS; Ellis misprints *Cersuelles*.
8. *Hermitonę hud̄ret* in the Exon. MS; Ellis misprints *hermtone hud̄ret*.

# Appendix

It will be seen that the discrepancies between the various lists are few: Exon. List II omits Silverton (Hayridge) Hundred, but otherwise corresponds to the Hundreds of the Tax Returns; List I, while omitting a number of Tax Return Hundreds, includes Molland and Berrynarbor that are not in the Tax Returns. Moreover, the correspondence between the Tax Return Hundreds and the 'modern' Hundreds is strikingly close, except that Uffculme was treated as a separate Hundred and Braunton and Shirwell as a single Hundred, places belonging to these latter Hundreds being intermixed in the order of the Exon. Book.

It will be noted also that no Devon Hundred in the Tax Returns contains 100 hides or even an approximation (if that was the original total), but the hide can also be a measure of tax liability and is not always a measure of area (see General Notes 1,4 on the hide). Many of the King's manors have a low tax-value but a large number of ploughs that suggests a larger areal hidage.

The first Exon. List contains a Hundred of *Clauuuetona* [Clawton], the name being deleted and Bampton inserted. It is not certain that in deleting the name the scribe was intending to substitute another name for the same Hundred. There is a Clawton in (Black) Torrington Hundred (17,15), which in later surveys occurs as a complex manor accounting for a number of places (17,15-18) separately mentioned in DB and covering the modern parishes of Clawton, Pyworthy and Tetcott. Moreover, all these lands had the same 1086 holder and the lands of no other magnate intruded upon them. It may be that at some stage in the DB enquiry a manorial return was mistaken for a Hundredal one.

The differences between the two Exon. Lists and the Hundreds of the Tax Returns must lie in their different purposes. Some 'Hundreds' may well have been temporary, artificial creations by a particular landholder or for the needs of a particular survey. Sometimes isolated royal manors might be treated as a Hundred, their manorial details forming a separate return for some purposes, but if they were exempt from tax, they would not appear among the Tax Returns. The Hundredal organisation that produced the Tax Returns may not have been identical to that which produced DB, and may well have differed from the Hundreds which under the Anglo-Saxon kings had particular administrative and judicial functions.

In the case of the adjacent Somerset, many manors (usually royal or ecclesiastical) had by 1086 been withdrawn from the Hundreds in which geographically they lay and had either become small self-contained administrative units, also called 'Hundreds', or were treated as remote outliers of their holder's chief manor (see DB Somerset Appendix I); for the purposes of the Tax Returns, however, these separate 'manorial Hundreds' are sometimes grouped with other manors.

To a lesser degree, the same seems to have been true of Devon. Berrynarbor (*Hertesberia*) of the first Exon. List, held by Walscin of Douai in 1086, seems to have been a separate unit when the List was completed, yet it can be identified in the Tax Return for Braunton and Shirwell Hundred (23,2 note); Berrynarbor may once have been a royal or church manor-Hundred, a fact not mentioned in DB. Uffculme (Tax Return xv), another single-manor Hundred, had belonged to Glastonbury Church (Ch. 4 and 23,9 notes) and was probably a small ecclesiastical 'Hundred' like several in Somerset. Molland (1,41), also included in the first Exon. List, was a royal manor and was probably separately administered like several royal manors that appear in the corresponding Exon. Hundred Lists for Somerset (folios 63b-64b). The details for Molland, however, seem to appear in the Tax Return for South Molton Hundred (vii).

The list of manors that were 'manorial Hundreds', though grouped with larger units in the Tax Returns, should probably be extended: a Hundred of North Molton is mentioned in connection with Molland (1,41) and probably represents only the royal manor of North Molton (1,37) treated as a Hundred. South Tawton was also probably a manorial Hundred, since in the Exon. order of Chapter 1, otherwise consistent, it is entered in the wrong place for a member of Wonford Hundred, where it later lay. Moreover, it received a number of customary dues from places that later formed part of Wonford Hundred, but which, each in their particular fief, occupy a place at the beginning of the schedule (1,29 note and OJR in TDA 44 pp. 343-365). On the other hand, the fact that these dues gain a special mention in DB does not necessarily suggest that South Tawton was the *caput* of a full Hundred with a number of tenants-in-chief, although there was a Hundred of South Tawton (first evidenced in 1170; Anderson p. 99) in later times. The alleged members of the 1086 Hundred of South Tawton are in fact found in the Tax Return for Wonford Hundred. The existence

# Appendix

of a Domesday Hundred or Hundred-manor of Winkleigh should be treated with even more reserve. Winkleigh (1,64) appears in the correct place in the schedule for a North Tawton Hundred place and is in the Tax Return for that Hundred (ix); but a medieval Hundred of Winkleigh (first attested in 1238; Anderson p. 85) enjoyed a brief existence.

The advance of feudalism, with its stress on the stratification of tenure and the lordship of the Hundred, is reflected in the names used for the Hundreds in the Exon. Lists and in the Tax Returns. In other counties the Anglo-Saxon names, from which most Domesday Hundreds were named, were derived from the meeting places of the Hundred, often a prominent tree, hill-ridge or barrow, but in the case of Devonshire, the Lists and the Tax Returns refer to Hundreds by the names of their chief manors in every case except *Alleriga*, and possibly Merton which was named from a manor held in 1086 by the Bishop of Coutances. *Alleriga* is now (as in the first List) called after its chief royal manor, Ermington (1,23), and Merton has become Shebbear (first noted in 1168; see Anderson p. 87) after the royal holding (1,39). But in many cases the medieval and later name of a Hundred is probably the restoration of its moot-name: Roborough (25) for Walkhampton; Stanborough (28) for Diptford; Coleridge (30) for Chillington; Haytor (29) for Kerswell; Hayridge (15) for Silverton and possibly Teignbridge (23) for Teignton. Roborough is called from Roborough or Roborough House in Bickleigh parish (SX 5062) or from Roborough Down in Buckland Monachorum (southwards from SX 5069; Anderson p. 91). *Alleriga* is unidentified, but is perhaps near Modbury (from OE *gemōt-beorg* 'moot-hill'; Anderson p. 92). Stanborough's meeting-place was perhaps the 'camp' or 'fort' marked on the OS map at the former junction of the parishes of Moreleigh, Halwell, Blackawton, East Allington and of several roads (SX 7551). This site now lies in Halwell parish, Coleridge Hundred, the parish and Hundred boundaries having moved to the west. Coleridge (30) is both an OE moot-name and a DB place (23,23). Haytor (29) can scarcely be connected with Haytor rock in Ilsington parish, which is not in Haytor Hundred: it was possibly near the place called Moothill Cross near Staverton (GR SX 7964). Hayridge (15) is unidentified; although it is tempting to connect it with Whorridge in Bradninch (so Finberg in DCNQ vol. 25 p. 38), the derivation is philologically unlikely (see Anderson p. 84 and EPNS ii p. 554). Teignbridge (23) is so called from the bridge over the river in Kingsteignton parish (Anderson p. 98; see the article by Davidson).

Not only are the Hundreds of the Exon. Lists and the Tax Returns named after the chief manor; the great majority of these are manors belonging to the crown or to the King himself. The only clear exceptions are Crediton and Ottery St. Mary Hundreds which were in the hands of churches. Most of the other Hundred-names have some connections with the King. *Alleriga* changed its name to Ermington when the King acquired the latter manor (and Blackawton) by exchange for Bampton (see 1,23-24), which as a royal manor had named Bampton Hundred. Shirwell was not named after a royal manor, but may have been administered by Braunton (1,5) with which it shares a Tax Return (vi). Fremington was not royal land in 1086 (3,6 note) but had been held by Earl Harold before 1066; Merton (3,5) may have been in a similar position.

The purpose of the first Exon. List of Hundreds is unclear, as is the corresponding list for Somerset. But the second List (as also in the case of Somerset) is a key to the order of the Exon. Book. This List, with the names modernised and the corresponding 'modern' Hundred numbers in brackets, is: Lifton (18), (Black) Torrington (11), Hartland (3), Merton (4), Fremington (5), (North) Tawton (12), Crediton (13), Exminster (24), Cliston (20), Bampton (8), Braunton (1), Shirwell (2), South Molton (6), Wonford (19), Budleigh (14), Hemyock (16), Witheridge (7), Tiverton (9), Ottery (St. Mary) (21), Halberton (10), Axminster (17), Kerswell (29), Colyton (22), Axmouth (17), Chillington (30), *Alleriga* (27), Roborough (25), Plympton (26), Diptford (28), Teignbridge (23), Uffculme (8). If allowance is made for the omission of a return for the manors contributing to South Tawton and for one for Hayridge (Silverton) Hundred, and for the fact that the last two, Teignbridge and Uffculme, may have been passed over and then added to the List at the end, this order is very close to that in which Hundreds are entered in individual chapters of the Exon. Book and can illuminatingly be compared with the order as shown in the introductory note to most chapters in the General Notes above.

It seems that this second List (in a variety of hands) was a schedule made of the Hundreds in which the Domesday material had been arranged (possibly for checking before the Hundred

# Appendix

courts) as they were entered fief by fief in the Exon. folios. In comparing this List with the Hundred order of individual fiefs, it must be allowed that a scribe, faced with the task of looking through each Hundred return for the manors of a particular tenant-in-chief, sometimes missed one or more manors and so entered them in the schedule partly or wholly later than the normal position for the Hundred group; or that because of the pressure of time two or more scribes were working simultaneously on the gatherings of parchment or 'booklets' that formed each individual fief list and exchanged the returns as they finished them. Even without such allowances made, some fiefs are entered Hundredally in exactly the order of the second Exon. list (although no fief actually contains a manor in every Hundred). Other fiefs appear to show a greater variation in order for the reasons suggested above or because some information was entered not Hundred by Hundred, but in groups of Hundreds: Braunton and Shirwell Hundred places (1 and 2) for example, are not only entered together but often mingled with places from South Molton (6) and Cliston (20). On the other hand, Lifton places (18) are always entered before those of (Black) Torrington (11), (Black) Torrington before Hartland (3) and Hartland before Shebbear (4) and so on.

The list of Exon. order standing as the second note for most chapters in the General Notes will illustrate the order of individual fiefs and it will be seen that the pattern is often striking: the third to sixteenth entries in the Count of Mortain's fief (Ch. 15) in Exon. are all in Shebbear Hundred, the first eleven of Baldwin's fief (Ch. 16) are in Lifton, the next seventeen in (Black) Torrington and so on. A study of the Exon. returns for Devon suggests the following patterns which, allowing for the grouping of some Hundreds, is almost identical to Exon. List II (the names are modernised, with the number of the corresponding 'modern' Hundred in brackets):

      Manors paying dues to South Tawton;
      Lifton (18);
      (Black) Torrington (11);
      Hartland (3);
      Merton (4);
      Fremington (5);
      (North) Tawton (12);
      Crediton (13);
      Exminster (24);
Braunton (1), Shirwell (2), Bampton and Uffculme (8), South Molton (6) and Cliston (20); Silverton (15), Wonford (19), Hemyock (16), Budleigh (14), Witheridge (7), Teignbridge (23) and Tiverton (9);
      Ottery (St. Mary) (21);
      Halberton (10);
Axminster (17), Kerswell (29), Colyton (22) and Axmouth (17);
Chillington (30), *Alleriga* (27), Diptford (28), Roborough (25) and Plympton (26).
(Reichel proposes a similar order in TDA 33 pp. 583-584; see TDA 28 p. 391, VCH p. 378 and Finn MDeD pp. 103-108.)

The differences between the 1086 Hundreds and those of later times is not great. North Molton and Molland, both of uncertain status in 1086, were later combined with South Molton (6); Uffculme was amalgamated with Bampton (8); South Tawton was absorbed by Wonford (19), and Axmouth by Axminster (17). Some of these survived separately beyond the 11th century, South Tawton, North Molton and Molland still being found in the *Nomina Villarum* of 1316 (in FA; see Anderson pp. 77-78, 99), Uffculme as late as 1428 (Anderson p. 80). Axmouth (17) is often treated separately in the Middle Ages, while Tiverton (9) and Halberton (10) were frequently combined. These last two may have been close in earlier times since parts of a parish in one are sometimes tithings of the other Hundred; it is interesting that a duplicate entry for Tiverton (1,35; see Exon. Notes) occurs next to Halberton (1,70) in the order of the Exon. Book.

New Hundreds were also created. A Hundred of Winkleigh (dates of 1238-1428 are quoted in Anderson p. 85) has already been mentioned. West Budleigh, earlier a detachment of (East) Budleigh, was given separate status in the 14th century (Anderson p. 100) and Tavistock Hundred, grouping some of the possessions of the Abbey, was created out of Lifton (18) in 1114 (Anderson p. 89, TDA 46 p. 222 ff., Oliver *Mon.* p. 95 and EPNS i p. 213).

# Appendix

In a few cases, a hamlet, village or vill is shown by the Tax Returns or the order of the Exon. Book to have lain in one Hundred in 1086, but is later found in the returns for another (usually adjacent) Hundred.
Since the Tax Return Hundreds are very largely those of later times, it is not necessary to give all the members of each Hundred as deduced from them, but differences evidenced, or presumed, are given below. Unidentified places are included in the Map Keys under their 1086 Hundred where this can be deduced from the Tax Returns or from Exon. order.

LIFTON HUNDRED (i) in 1086 included Willsworthy (39,1 note) which lay here also in 1316 (though later in Roborough, 25), as well as those lands — Liddaton, Milton Abbot, Leigh and Tavistock — which later lay in Tavistock Hundred.

TORRINGTON HUNDRED (iii) contained Kigbeare (16,22 note), a tithing of the Hundred in 1334, later in Lifton Hundred (18).

FREMINGTON HUNDRED (iv) counted Little Weare (42,5 note) among its lands, later in Shebbear Hundred (4).

MERTON HUNDRED (v) was affected by later boundary changes. Wedfield (15,33 note) was here in 1086, though later transferred to (Black) Torrington Hundred (11), while three places now in Roborough parish, Fremington Hundred (Barlington, Villavin and Owlacombe; see notes to 3,15. 25,1. 36,7), were in this Hundred in 1086 and in the Middle Ages. See also 36,2 and 42,4 notes.

BRAUNTON AND SHIRWELL HUNDREDS (vi) are treated as a unity by the Tax Returns and this masks any evidence that Pickwell, Spreacombe, Woolacombe, Bridwick and Hole (3,39;47. 19,11. 36,11-13;15 notes), which in the 14th century were a detached part of Shirwell within Braunton, were so in 1086. Snydles (16,88 note) and Swimbridge (13a,2 note) seem to have lain in these Hundreds in 1086, rather than in South Molton.

CREDITON HUNDRED (viii) included part of Down St. Mary (6,4) (the rest of the parish lying in (North) Tawton Hundred), also Chaffcombe (2,2 note) and possibly Bury (2,3 note), both the latter being parts of (North) Tawton Hundred later.

TAWTON HUNDRED (ix) on the other hand included the main holding of what was later Morchard Bishop in Crediton Hundred (1,68 note), as well as Shobrooke (24,29 note). On the border with Shebbear Hundred, part of Iddesleigh was here in 1086 (1,63 note) and Brimblecombe (40,3 note). Irishcombe (1,66 note) and Affeton (1,3 note) were outliers of Tawton Hundred manors lying within Witheridge Hundred (7). Emlett (in Woolfardisworthy) was a similar case in the Middle Ages, although it is not mentioned in DB.

WITHERIDGE HUNDRED (x) contained Dockworthy (35,25 note) which later lay in (North) Tawton Hundred (12).

TIVERTON HUNDRED (xi) was closely related to Halberton (xvii). Sampford Peverell (27,1 note) lay in both Hundreds, while it would appear from the order of Exon. that Uplowman, Combe, Murley and Kidwell (all later parts of Uplowman parish, Halberton Hundred) lay here in 1086 (24,8-10. 25,19. 34,43 notes). Chieflowman, also in Uplowman parish, appears to have been a part of Halberton manor in 1086, but probably lay in Tiverton Hundred, where the Tax Return records a portion of the royal manor of Halberton (1,70 note). The Hundred also had, as evidenced in DB and in the Middle Ages, an outlying portion at Ivedon (19,42-43. 34,45;47 notes) now in Awliscombe parish, Hemyock Hundred (16), and another at Nutcott (46,2 note) and at Batsworthy (42,21 note). Both the latter are now in Witheridge Hundred (7).

CLISTON HUNDRED (xii) contained Larkbeare (16,94. 39,10 notes), that was later in Hayridge (15).

SILVERTON HUNDRED (xiii), afterwards known as Hayridge, had Up Exe (3,70 note) in 1086 and the Middle Ages (though it was afterwards in Wonford Hundred, 19) and possibly Coddiford (52,23 note) as an outlier.

BUDLEIGH HUNDRED (xvi) was not yet divided between East and West in 1086. The order of Exon. suggests that Strete Ralegh (34,38) was in this Hundred in 1086, as in the Middle Ages, although later in Cliston (20). In the outlying part that later became West Budleigh were included Yeadbury (34,36 note) and Yowlestone (19,33 note), later in Witheridge, and this

# Appendix

area seems to have included Langley (1,9 note) now in Cadeleigh, Hayridge Hundred (15), and Thongsleigh (36,20 note) now in Cruwys Morchard, Witheridge Hundred (7), neither being directly mentioned by DB.

HALBERTON HUNDRED (xvii) was involved with Tiverton (see xi above). While much of Uplowman parish was in Tiverton Hundred, Whitnage (25,22), another part of the parish, lay in Halberton Hundred; as did Canonsleigh which was in that part of Burlescombe parish that was not in Bampton Hundred (see xxii below).

AXMINSTER HUNDRED (xix) had not yet been enlarged by amalgamation with Axmouth (xxi). Smallicombe (16,168 note) may have counted as an outlier, dependent on Trill in 1086 as later.

AXMOUTH HUNDRED (xxi) contained in the Middle Ages, before its incorporation in Axminster, the DB places of Axmouth, Bruckland, Combpyne, 'Down Umfraville', Musbury, Rousdon and Stedcombe (see Anderson p. 103; FA i pp. 318, 384). The Domesday Hundred, as it can be reconstructed from the Tax Return, was of the same extent except that Musbury (16,164) was divided between both Axminster and Axmouth Hundreds.

BAMPTON HUNDRED (xxii). The Tax Return indicates that Burlescombe parish was divided in 1086, as later, between Bampton and Halberton (xvii) Hundreds. Burlescombe itself, the unidentified *Ciclet* and Fenacre (24,30-31. 25,12) lay in Bampton Hundred. It is probable that the boundary between this Hundred and Witheridge (7) was adjusted soon after 1086, since in the Tax Return for Bampton Hundred Bishop G(eoffrey) has 1 hide and 3½ furlongs (*fertinos*) of lordship land, which it seems can only be accounted for by most or all of Spurway, Coombe, *Celvertesberie* and Stoodleigh (3,74-78 notes) which later lay in Witheridge Hundred. OJR in TDA 30 pp. 453-455 would go further: see notes to 16,150-151. 19,37. 34,40-41. 36,25. 47,13 and 52,43.

EXMINSTER HUNDRED (xxiii) seems to have included in 1086 and later a detached moorland portion at Beetor and Shapley, Venn and Jurston (16,60-62;64 notes), as well as 'South Teign' (1,26 note). A part of Manaton (52,27 note) and Netherton (in Haccombe, south of the river Teign, 19,10 note) also lay here in 1086, as in the *Nomina Villarum* of 1316 (FA i p. 377).

TEIGNTON HUNDRED (xxiv) appears from the Tax Return to have included a part of Ashton (6,6 note), the rest lying in Exminster Hundred (24). From Exon. order it seems to have embraced Canonteign (3,97 note) which was here in the Middle Ages, though later in Wonford Hundred (19), as well as Buckland in the Moor (48,4 note) later in the detachment of Haytor (29), and also Buckland Barton and Haccombe (19,41. 16,152 notes). These last two were later tithings of Haytor Hundred within a detached part of Wonford.

KERSWELL HUNDRED (xxv), later Haytor, had a detached moorland portion in 1086 and later; it may have originated in moorland pasture that formed outlying parts of Kerswell Hundred manors, such as 'Dewdon' which was a member of Cockington (20,10) and Blackaton (16,163 note) attached to one of Baldwin's manors.

DIPTFORD HUNDRED (xxvi), later Stanborough, encompassed, according to Exon. order, Hazard (29,2 note), Poulston (1,34 and 17,43 notes) and East Allington (30,3 note), all found here in the 14th century, though later in Coleridge Hundred (30), and possibly Englebourne (20,17 note), also subsequently in Coleridge.

CHILLINGTON HUNDRED (xxvii), subsequently called Coleridge, had Grimpstonleigh (39,13) as an outlier of Grimpstone in 1086 and later, as well as Dodbrooke (52,53 note). Both were afterwards in Stanborough Hundred (28).

*ALLERIGA* HUNDRED (xxx), later named Ermington, included Dunstone (29,4 and 52,42 notes) in 1086 and the Middle Ages; it was later in Plympton Hundred (26). Lupridge and Butterford (15,27. 24,20 and 17,61-62 notes), both ultimately in Stanborough Hundred (28), were here in 1086.

WONFORD HUNDRED (xxxi) contained West Clyst (16,92 note) both in 1086 and in the 14th century; it was later in Cliston Hundred (20). In 1086 and later Wonford Hundred had a detached portion in three parts: (a) an area south of the river Teign, known as 'Teignhead' and corresponding to the modern parishes of Haccombe with Coombe, St. Nicholas and Stokeinteignhead; (b) the parish of Ogwell (including East Ogwell, West Ogwell and Holbeam) lying to the west; finally (c) a part lying in Ilsington parish (itself in Teignbridge Hundred, 23)

# Appendix

and consisting of Bagtor (48,7 note), Sigford (35,23 note), as well as a part of Horridge (19,29 note, but see 32,6-7 note). Staplehill (48,9) which was in Teignton (Teignbridge) Hundred in 1086 was added to this last area in the Middle Ages. 'Teignhead' is a corruption of 'Ten Hides', influenced by the river-name 'Teign' (EPNS ii p. 459). The sum total of the DB manors in the three parts of this detachment (including Buckland (19,41), Netherton (19,10 note) and Haccombe (16,152) which though they form a natural part of this detachment seem to have been assessed in other Hundreds in 1086) is just short of ten hides.

Although it is possible in the case of Devon to form a good general picture of the 1086 Hundreds, fuller details about boundaries and the exact location of villages in particular Hundreds can only be found by studying the late-medieval Hundreds as they survived into the 19th century. It is these which (as is the practice in the other south-western counties' volumes in this series) have been used as the basis for the maps and the indices of this edition, as they were for the EPNS volumes. These latter map Hundreds according to parishes, tithings of another Hundred being included in the Hundred to which the parish belongs. The composition of Hundreds here differs, however, in two respects from that of the EPNS volumes: East Allington parish is mapped in Stanborough (28) rather than Coleridge (30) (it appears in both Hundreds in later documents and maps); Uplowman parish, which was partly in Tiverton (9) and partly in Halberton (10), is included in Tiverton where the major part lay (EPNS puts it in Halberton where Whitnage tithing was). Following EPNS, Burlescombe parish is wholly included in Halberton (10), although part of the parish (including Burlescombe village) was in Bampton Hundred (8).

## Tithings

As will have been understood above, a number of places while locally situated in one Hundred, because that is where their parish lies, are actually tithings of another. These tithings have different origins and differ from one list to another, but a list of major tithings is given below, since in many cases the tithing recalls the Hundred in which the place lay in 1086:

| Place | Tithing in | Actually in |
|---|---|---|
| Snydles (16,88) | Braunton Hundred (1) | Chittlehamholt parish, South Molton Hundred (6) |
| Pickwell (3,39) | Shirwell Hundred (2) | Georgeham parish, Braunton Hundred (1) |
| Spreacombe (36,13) | Shirwell Hundred (2) | Mortehoe parish, Braunton Hundred (1) |
| Woolacombe (19,11. 36,15) | Shirwell Hundred (2) | Mortehoe parish, Braunton Hundred (1) |
| Burlescombe (24,30) | Bampton Hundred (8) | Halberton Hundred (10) — rest of parish of Burlescombe |
| Ivedon (19,42-43. 34,45;47) | Tiverton Hundred (9) | Awliscombe parish, Hemyock Hundred (16) |
| Nutcott (46,2) | Tiverton Hundred (9) | Rackenford parish, Witheridge Hundred (7) |
| Uplowman (25,16;19. 34,43) | Tiverton Hundred (9) | Halberton Hundred (10) — rest of parish of Uplowman |
| Appledore (24,14) | Halberton Hundred (10) | Burlescombe parish, Bampton Hundred (8) |
| Canonsleigh (24,15) | Halberton Hundred (10) | Burlescombe parish, Bampton Hundred (8) |
| Ayshford (24,13) | Halberton Hundred (10) | Burlescombe parish, Bampton Hundred (8) |
| Kigbeare (16,22) | (Black) Torrington Hundred (11) | Okehampton parish, Lifton Hundred (18) |

# Appendix

| Place | Tithing in | Actually in |
|---|---|---|
| Yeadbury (34,36) | (West) Budleigh Hundred (14) | Cruwys Morchard parish, Witheridge Hundred (7) |
| Strete Ralegh (34,38) | (East) Budleigh Hundred (14) | Whimple parish, Cliston Hundred (20) |
| Up Exe (3,70) | Hayridge Hundred (15) | Rewe parish, Wonford Hundred (19) |
| Bagtor (48,7) | Wonford Hundred (19) | Ilsington parish, Teignbridge Hundred (23) |
| Sigford (35,23) | Wonford Hundred (19) | Ilsington parish, Teignbridge Hundred (23) |
| Staplehill (48,9) | Wonford Hundred (19) | Ilsington parish, Teignbridge Hundred (23) |
| West Clyst (16,92) | Wonford Hundred (19) | Broad Clyst parish, Cliston Hundred (20) |
| Canonteign (3,97) | Teignbridge Hundred (23) | Christow parish, Wonford Hundred (19) |
| Shapley (16,61-62;64. 45,1) | Exminster Hundred (24) | Chagford parish, Wonford Hundred (19) |
| Butterford (17,61-62) | Ermington Hundred (27) | North Huish parish, Stanborough Hundred (28) |
| Dunstone (29,4. 52,42) | Ermington Hundred (27) | Yealmpton parish, Plympton Hundred (26) |
| Lupridge (15,27. 24,20. 25,26) | Ermington Hundred (27) | North Huish parish, Stanborough Hundred (28) |
| Buckland (19,41) | Haytor Hundred (29) | Haccombe parish, Wonford Hundred (19) |
| Haccombe (16,152. 19,10) | Haytor Hundred (29) | Wonford Hundred (19) — rest of parish of Haccombe |
| Grimpstonleigh (39,13) | Coleridge Hundred (30) | Woodleigh parish, Stanborough Hundred (28) |

The composition of the medieval Hundreds can best be studied in the volumes of the Book of Fees, the Feudal Aids (FA) which contains the important *Nomina Villarum* of 1316, also in the *Rotuli Hundredorum* (RH) and the Lay Subsidy Rolls (LSR). The 19th century Hundredal organisation is reproduced in the earliest censuses and in Directories and Gazetteers such as those by White and Kelly, as well as on the large-scale maps of Cary and Greenwood. The works of the earliest antiquarians, such as Hooker, Pole, Polwhele and Risdon, still have value as do the various studies by Whale and Reichel. The best study of the names and composition of the Hundreds is Anderson's work.

# INDEX OF PERSONS

Familiar modern spellings are given when they exist. Unfamiliar names are usually given in an approximate late 11th century form, avoiding variants that were already obsolescent or pedantic. Spellings that mislead the modern eye are avoided where possible. Two, however, cannot be avoided: they are combined in the name of 'Leofgeat', pronounced 'Leffyet' or 'Levyet'. It should be noted that in the Devon volumes, as in Dorset, certain personal names have been treated differently: thus the Alfward of previous volumes in this series has been changed to Alward; Alfwold to Alwold; Alfsi to Alsi; Alfwy to Alwy; attention is drawn to the notes at the first occurrence of these names. The definite article is omitted before bynames, except where there is reason to suppose that these described the individual's occupation rather than that of a predecessor (as at 51,1 and see General Notes 1,64).

The chapter numbers of listed tenants-in-chief are printed in bold type at the beginning of the list of references and are the numbers of the text, not the Landholders' List (but see General Notes Ch. 40). Names in italics indicate that persons or bynames occur only in Exon.; likewise references in italics indicate that the name, or a fuller form of it, is to be found only in Exon. In this edition such information is found either in small type in the translation or in the Exon. Notes.

It should be emphasized that this is essentially an index of personal names, not of persons; it is probable that in the case of some entries of simple names more than one person bearing the same name has been included. Likewise, a person who bears a title or byname may be represented under the single name, e.g. in Devon many of the references to plain Baldwin are undoubtedly to Baldwin the Sheriff (as in 39,10) and 'Brictric' is probably 'Brictric son of Algar' on several occasions (see General Notes 24,21).

Where there is a cross-head in the translation (e.g., 'William also holds') referring to several succeeding entries, the reference in this Index is to the first entry only, above which the cross-head occurs, so that an individual might hold more manors than would appear from the Index. Similarly, when a phrase such as 'Brictric held all these lands before 1066' occurs, usually extended in the translation or in capitals and referring to several preceding entries, the reference here is to the last entry only, before which the statement occurs; likewise with a phrase such as 'Queen Edith held the undermentioned lands'.

| | |
|---|---|
| Abbot | 3,95 |
| Adolf | 1,72 |
| Aeleva | 17,19 |
| Aelfeva Thief | 24,22 |
| Aelfeva | 16,40;166. 23,25. 24, 2-4. 25,20. 34,31. 36,7. 37,1. 52,50. |
| Aelfled | 35,25 |
| Aelfric *Colling* | 19,40 |
| Aelfric *Pig* | 34,10 |
| Aelfric Pike | 28,13 |
| Aelfric | 3,35;38. 15,15;75. 16,91;117. 17,13;24;27; 57-58;85;87;97;107. 19,21;28. 25,6;25. 29,1-3. 31,4. 34,27;57. 39,16. 40,1-2. 42,21. 47,3-4. 52,44-45 |
| Aelfric (Aubrey?) | 17,88-89 |
| *Aelmer Eastry* | *15,47* |
| *Aelmer Rufus* | *15,33* |
| Aelmer *the priest* | 25,19 |
| Aelmer | 3,47;49;60;85. 15,23. 16,18;50;66;75;84;94; 105-106;119;121;131;136;142;145;147;149; 158;164;170. 17,91;105. 19,15;23;35-36;40; 46. 21,11. 28,10. 34,9;11;25;38;40;43. 36,9; 19-20;25-26. 39,14. 42,7;22. 44,1. 50,2. 52,20-21 |
| Aethelhard *the monk* | 34,53 |
| Aethelmer | 15,31 |

| | |
|---|---|
| Aethelred, see Aldred | |
| Aethelric | 16,132 |
| *Aethelwold* | *16,174* |
| Aiulf | **41.** 17,18. 35,7. 39,8 |
| Alchere | 39,2. 40,3. 47,7 |
| Aldchurl | 3,41;62. 15,59;71. 16,72. 20,2 |
| Aldhild | 19,44 |
| Archbishop Aldred | 5,12-13 |
| Aldred | 16,61;151;156. 17,10;17. 47,11-12. 51,11. 52,26-28 |
| Aldwulf | 17,13 |
| *Alfgeat* | *42,7* |
| Alfhere | 35,15 |
| Alfhild | 52,51 |
| Alfred of 'Spain' | **38** |
| Alfred the Breton | **39.** 16,94. *35,4* |
| Alfred *the Butler* | 15,16-19;32-33;55 |
| Alfred | 3,19. 15,9;31;59-60. 16,141. 17,15-16. Also in T.O. 496 a 3 (see Exon. Notes 1,25) |
| Alfrun | 24,6-8;15 |
| Alfsi, see Alsi | |
| Alfward, see Alward | |
| Alfwold, see Alwold | |
| Alfwy, see Alwy | |
| Algar *Long* | 16,20-21 |
| Algar the priest | 13a,3. *34,17* |
| Algar | 3,22;26;37;62;73-74;82-84. 15,79. 16,33;63. 17,25;34;36;39;41-42;51;94. 19,16-17. 20,9. 23,4;10. 25,5;24. 52,41-42 |
| Algar, see Brictric | |
| Alnoth | 14,1;3-4. 16,25;39;47;73;95;155. 24,9. 25,16-17. 34,20-21. 39,12-13. 52,36 |
| Alric *the priest* | 34,50. 42,14;23 |
| Alric | 1,11. 3,66. 16,45-46. 17,52;61;84. 19,41. 20,10; 16-17. 21,1;3;6. 23,23-24. 34,19;48. 35,8;13. 49,5. 51,12. 52,43 |
| Alsi (for Aelfsige or Aethelsige) | 15,54. 16,41. 23,12;17-21. 34,49. 35,14. 47,5-6. 48,10. 51,1 |
| Alstan *Tilley* | 46,1-2 |
| Alstan | 52,9;11-17 |
| Alward Mart | *24,23-24;28.* 52,30 |
| Alward *Rufus* | 15,16 |
| Alward son of Toki | 19,*16;19*;35;*39. 34,14* |
| Alward (for Aelfward or Aethelward) | 1,41. 3,10;15;45;64;75. 15,6;22;25;58;61. 16,103. 17,31;37;79. 19,5-6;14;24-25. 24,26. 25,3;9;21. 28,12;14. 34,1;8. 35,11;18. 36,26. 51,3. 52,29 |
| Alware *Pet* | 1,63 |
| Abbot *Alwin* | *6,1;7-12* |
| Alwin *Black* | 16,27 |
| *Alwin the Steward* | *3,94* |
| Alwin | 2,15. 3,4;9;20-21;30;76-77;86-87;94;99. 15,57; 72. 16,87. 17,13;17;21;40;44-46;59-60;66;71; 74;80;90;98. 20,11;13-15. 21,17. 23,1. 28,9. 29,5-10. 34,26;43. 35,16. 39,17-18. 52,37;39 |
| Alwold (for Aelfwold or Aethelwold) | 16,28;30;81;139;174. 17,23. 25,8. *35,9.* 36,23-24. *39,16.* 42,11 |
| Alwy Tabb | 15,55 |
| Alwy (for Aelfwig or Aethelwig) | 25,2. 29,4. 38,1-2. 42,13;21 |
| Ansfrid | 24,19 |
| Anger of Montacute | 40,1 |

| | |
|---|---|
| *Ansger of Senarpont* | *40,4–7* |
| Ansger *the Breton* | 15,12–15 |
| Ansger *the King's servant* | 51,13 |
| Ansger (Asgar) | **40**. 3,99. 16,60;73;78–79;81–82;142–144;159. 23,15;26. *42,6* |
| Ansgot (Osgot) | 52,31–33 |
| Ansketel | 16,145. 19,3–4;6. 20,15 |
| Arnold | 23,4 |
| Asgar (Ansger) *the Cramped* | 1,23–24 |
| Asgar (Ansger) | 23,15–16;22–24;27 |
| Ator, see Edmer | |
| Aubrey | 16,36–38;150. 17,68;83;93–94;99–106. 36,25 see Aelfric (Aubrey?) |
| Baldwin the Sheriff | **16**. C 2. 1,5;*30;36–38;40. 2,24*. 52,33 |
| *Baldwin the Sheriff's daughter* | *16,44* |
| Baldwin (the Sheriff)'s wife | 16,94;128. See also under Emma |
| Baldwin | *1,4;8–12;15–18;29*;33–34;*45–48;54–55*. 2,23. 25,25–26. 39,10. See also in Exon. 97 b 2 (in Exon. Notes after 1,55) |
| Bastard, see Robert | |
| Bear | 51,9 |
| Beatrix, *sister of William (Cheever)* | 19,40;46 |
| Beatrix | 34,43 |
| Bernard Nap(e)less (?) | 16,125 |
| Bernard | 16,25;39;126–127. 36,8;17 |
| Berner, see Theobald | |
| Bernwin, see Jocelyn | |
| Bicca | 23,23 |
| Black, see Alwin, William | |
| Boia | 1,72 |
| Botin, see Ralph | |
| Bretel | 15,20–21;63 |
| Bricteva | 52,8 |
| Brictferth, *uncle of Saewin the priest* | 13a,2 |
| Brictith | 36,15 |
| Brictmer | 3,80. 16,4;12;19;31;33;58;65;69;71;83;85;96; 104;110;116;140;161;175. 19,37. 21,19–21. 28,15. 34,41. 40,4. 49,1–3. 52,33 |
| Brictric *son of Algar* | 24,21 |
| Brictric *son of Camm* | 3,32. 19,12 |
| Brictric, *Godiva's man* | 52,52 |
| Brictric | 1,*40*;57;63. 3,28–29;31;34;51. 12,1. 13,1. 16,5–6;9;13;112;128;162. 17,6;8;55. 19,27;*34*. 20,1. 23,20. 24,18–19;24;29. 25,20;25;27. 27,1. 28,14. 35,23. 36,16. 40,*1*;*3*;5–7. 42,1;5–6;16–17;20. 50,1. 51,8. 52,24;53 |
| Brictsi | 3,47 |
| Brictwin | 25,10 |
| Brictwold | 3,53;58–59. 17,43. 19,31. 20,3–5. 28,4;11. 38,1. 48,9 |
| Brictwy *son of Camm* | 17,13 |
| Broder | 17,20 |
| Brungar | 3,78. 16,123. 20,8 |
| Burgred | 16,86;172. 19,30. 28,2. 34,18;22. 51,13 |
| *(another?) Burgred* | *28,2* |
| Cadio | 16,16 |
| Camm, see Brictric, Brictwy | |
| Cheever, see William | |
| Cola | *3,12*. 17,35. 24,20 |
| Colbert | 15,26. 17,47;75. 36,21 |
| Colbran | 16,77. 36,18 |

Colling, see Aelfric
Colswein, a man of the Bishop of Coutances'  25,3
Colwin  C 2. *1,25*. 16,13;37;41. 42,3. 52,1-2
Cott, see Wulfmer
Cynegar  20,6
Cynestan  17,5;7
Doda *the priest*  16,135
Doda  3,18;23;25;43;65. 16,7;114;118;120. 25,4. 36,10
(another) Doda  16,7
Doleswif  16,67
*Drogo son of Mauger*  *3,9;13-14;16*
Drogo  *1,11*. 3,2;9-*10;12;22;26-27;41-42;50;64;68;70;* 85. 7,4. 15,23-24;*25*; 34;62

Dubbed, see Roald
Dunn  15,67;70;77. 52,32;34-35
Dunning  15,57
Eastry, see Aelmer
Eccha the *King's* reeve  1,4
Edda  42,12
Edeva  15,38. 23,9. 25,1
Edhild  3,95
Queen Edith  C 2. 1,25
Edith  19,37. 23,2
Edlufu Thief  25,1
Edmer Ator  15,*12-*13;*14-30*;31;*32-33*. See Hademar, Ordgar, Saemer, Saewin
Edmer  3,24;52;56-57;94. 15,33-38. 16,7;34;82;133; 173. 17,77. 19,7. 34,23. 35,3;12;19;24. 36,11-12. 41,2. 42,19;24. 48,11. 50,3-5. See also in Exon. T.O. 503 a 9 (in Exon. Notes to Ch. 44)
Ednoth  2,10. 3,36. *14,3*. 16,8. 23,7
Edric the Cripple  1,11. See Edward
Edric  3,8;*12*;41;91;93;96-97. 15,27-29;56;69. 16,42; 88;137. 19,29. 23,24. 31,1-4. 34,28. 40,7. 41,1. 43,3. 44,2. 52,22-23
Edsi  16,99. 19,33
Edward *the priest*  51,6
Edward son of Edric (the Cripple)  1,11
Edward  16,165. 17,81. 30,2
Edwin  3,89. 15,30. 16,35;97. 19,11. 24,32. 34,14;37; 46. 35,6. 52,38-39
Edwulf  16,60;93;115;124. 19,45
Edwy  3,44. 15,12. 16,62;100;113;154;160. 20,1. 34,55
Elaf  36,5
Engelbald  3,22
wife of Engelbald  3,86-88
*Emma*, wife of Baldwin (the Sheriff)  16,128
Erchenbald  15,11;39-41;47;54. 35,10
Eric  15,14
Ermenald  5,1
Everwacer  16,109
*Flohere*  *41,1*. See also in Exon. T.O. 459 a 3 (in Exon. Notes Ch. 22)
Frank  28,4
Frawin  *15,4*7. 35,2. 43,5. 51,14
Fulchere *the Bowman*  49,7
Fulchere (the Bowman)  **49**
Fulcwold  19,18
*Fulcwy*  *19,18*
Fulk  17,38-40;42. 39,3
Gamelin, see Odo, Theobald

| | |
|---|---|
| *Abbot Geoffrey* | *5,7* |
| Geoffrey *of Trelly* | 3,97 |
| Geoffrey | 3,93. 5,1;3-4;8. 34,53-54 |
| Gerald the Chaplain | **45** |
| Gerard | **46.** 23,5;7-8;12. 32,8-9 |
| Gero | 37,1 |
| Count Gilbert, see Richard | |
| Gilbert | 16,31;88;141. 28,5;12. 35,12. 42,9 |
| Goad, see Roger | |
| Goda *the priest* | 45,2 |
| Goda | 3,72. 17,53;96. 33,1-2. 34,35;39. 35,28. 42,7 |
| Godbold *the Bowman* | 47,2;14-15 |
| Godbold (the Bowman) | **47** |
| Godfrey *the Chamberlain* | 16,53-54 |
| Godfrey | *1,23. 15,67.* 19,13. 25,7;13;20 |
| Godiva | 25,11. 42,12. 52,52-53. See Brictric |
| Godman *the priest* | 16,51;129 |
| Godman | 16,171 |
| Godric | *3,12.* 16,83;101. 19,2-3;*4.* 23,3;13. 34,24;32. 39,4;9. 40,6. 43,1. 51,2. 52,4-7;20-21 |
| *Godric's brother* | *40,6* |
| Godwin *the priest* | 15,7 |
| Godwin | 2,15. 15,79. 16,7;32;64;78;111;122;168. 17,70; 76. 36,8. 49,6. 52,9;13;19 |
| (another) Godwin | 16,7 |
| Gosbert | 36,3-6 |
| Gotshelm of Exeter | 25,28 |
| Gotshelm | 25. 1,*57-59;61;64-65*;70. 16,138;161. 24,32. 36,7. *42,6* |
| Grento *a man-at-arms* | 5,13 |
| Grim | 17,3;9 |
| Gunhard | 24,10 |
| Gunnar | 24,31 |
| Gunter | 32,2 |
| Countess Gytha | 11,1. See also under next entry |
| Gytha, mother of Earl Harold | 1,29;*50.* See also under previous entry |
| Haca | 21,9-10 |
| Hademar, *Edmer Ator's man* | 15,18 |
| Hademar | 15,2;18;60 |
| Haimeric *of Arques* | 50,1-2;5 |
| Haimeric (of Arques) | **50** |
| ?Halewise | 25,7 |
| Hamelin | 15,8;43 |
| Hamo | 19,21-22;26;36 |
| Hardwulf | 3,79 |
| Earl Harold | 1,36. 3,6. 11,2-3. See Gytha |
| Heca *the Sheriff* | 17,38 |
| Heca | 17,32;49;64;69;95. 21,18 |
| Helgot | 34,*16*;26. *49,7* |
| ?Heloise | 17,92 |
| Herbert | 21,15 |
| Hermer | 23,14. 25,8;24 |
| Hervey of Helléan('s wife) | **44** |
| wife of Hervey of Helléan | 44,1-2. See also in Exon. T.O. 501 b 1 and 503 a 9 (see Exon. Notes to Ch. 44) |
| wife of Hervey | 16,156 |
| Hildwine | 21,11 |
| Hubert | 23,21. 42,19 |
| Earl Hugh | **14** |
| Hugh *of Dol* | 20,7 |
| Hugh *of Rennes* | 16,116 |

| | |
|---|---|
| Hugh | 5,1. 15,38;74. 16,117;154 |
| *Humphrey* | *3,70* |
| Ifing | 16,167 |
| Ingvar | 15,62. 16,23. 21,7. 39,19-20 |
| Iudhael of Totnes | 17 |
| Iudhael | 1,55;71 |
| Ivo, see Robert | |
| Jagelin | 36,20. 47,13 |
| Jocelyn *Bernwin* | 16,118 |
| Jocelyn | 16,148. 36,15. See also in Exon. 97 b 3 (see Exon. Notes after 1,55) |
| John | 17,22;33. *48,11* |
| Kenias | 25,14-15;23 |
| Ketel | 24,27. 34,15 |
| Kipping | 15,11. 16,79. 47,9-10;13 |
| Knight | 16,125-126. 25,28 |
| Lambert, see Modbert | |
| Ledmer | 34,5;7 |
| Ledwin | 34,4 |
| Leofgar | 3,50. 15,66. 16,130;144. 21,13. 34,13. 35,4. 36,6. 42,3. 43,4 |
| Leofmer | 21,15 |
| Leofnoth | 16,49 |
| Leofred | 24,12 |
| *Bishop Leofric* | *2,7-8;14;16-23* |
| Leofric | 3,98. 16,26;53-54;57. 21,4. 34,47. 39,7. 52,46 |
| Earl Leofwin | 1,51 |
| Leofwin *Sock* | 51,7 |
| Leofwin | 23,11. *35,9* |
| Long, see Algar | |
| Ludo, *a man-at-arms of Walscin's* | 42,16 |
| Ludo | 23,13;17;*20*;22. 25,23 |
| Lufa | 35,17 |
| Manfred | 19,23 |
| Mart, see Alward | |
| Queen Matilda | 1,57. *13a,2. 27,1* |
| Matilda | 24,1. 40,4. 52,25 |
| Mauger *of Carteret* | 15,57 |
| Mauger, see Drogo | |
| Merleswein | 32,1;10 |
| Modbert *son of Lambert* | 16,50 |
| Modbert | 16,11;26;130-132 |
| Morin | 16,169;173-174. 51,14 |
| Count of Mortain, see under Count Robert of Mortain | |
| Nap(e)less(?), see Bernard | |
| Nicholas the Bowman | **48** |
| Nigel, *a French man-at-arms* | 5,4 |
| Nigel | 5,10. 17,4-5;10;82 |
| Norman *Parker* | 1,64 |
| Norman | 14,2. 15,65;68. 16,14;102. 20,4. 36,17. 42,8 |
| Odo son of Gamelin | 42. See Theobald |
| Odo | 16,92;171. 17,41;70-72;77. 52,22-25 |
| Oliver | 36,16;18;26 |
| Ordgar, *Edmer Ator's man* | 15,17 |
| Ordric | 15,64. 23,8. 48,1;3-8 |
| Ordwulf | 1,56. 2,9. 15,3-5;8-10;39-47;*48-49*;*50-53*. 30,1. 35,1;10. See also Exon. 97 b 4 (in Exon. Notes after 1,55) |
| Ordwulf's sister | 15,41 |
| Bishop Osbern | 2. 2,2 |
| Osbern of Sacey | **43** |

| | |
|---|---|
| *Osbert of Sacey* | *43,3-5* (see Exon. Notes to Ch. 43) |
| Osbern | 3,92. 17,34. 24,7. 29,3 |
| *Osbert* | *17,34. 24,7* |
| Oseva | 52,1 |
| Osferth | 16,3;11;15;55;80;107-108;157;176. 21,16. 35,27 |
| Osgot (Ansgot) | 3,90. 15,77. 16,24 |
| *Oslac* | *28,2* |
| *(another?) Oslac* | *28,2* |
| Osmer | 16,127. 17,50 |
| Osmund | 25,9-10;12 |
| Oswulf | 3,11;17. 17,4;78;82. 28,16 |
| Oswy | 16,151 |
| Otelin | 16,23;55;86;111;121-122;124;176 |
| Othere | 15,53. 17,26;28;56. 19,10 |
| Pagnell, see Ralph | |
| Parker, see Norman | |
| Payne, see Ralph, Roger | |
| Pet, see Alware | |
| Peter | 20,6 |
| Pig, see Aelfric | |
| Pike, see Aelfric | |
| Rademar | 23,5 |
| (another) Rademar | 23,5 |
| Rainer *the Steward* | 16,56 |
| Rainer | 16,8;22;95-96;119;133-135. 47,14 |
| Ralph *Botin* | 51,7 |
| Ralph Pagnell | 32 |
| Ralph *Vitalis* | 42,2;4 |
| Ralph *of Bruyère* | 16,12;35;48-49;153;163 |
| Ralph of Feugères | 33 |
| Ralph of Limesy | 31 |
| Ralph of Pomeroy | 34. 1,11. *15,66.* 16,7;*51-52;63;114;120. 17,20; 23;25;44. 19,33. 35,4.* See also under William Cheever's brother |
| Ralph *of Tilly* | 5,1 |
| Ralph *son of Payne* | 19,43 |
| Ralph *a man-at-arms* | *19,33.* 23,16 |
| Ralph | *1,37.* 5,1;4-5. 17,9;24;36-37;45-46;55-57;63; 91-92;94;102-105. 19,9;14;20;25;33;39. 21,6; 10;13-14. 23,22;26. 42,8. 48,4. 51,4 |
| Ralph, see Roger | |
| Ranulf | 16,28;157;166-167. 22,1-2. 29,4 |
| Reginald *of Vautortes* | 15,44 |
| Reginald | *1,23.* 5,11. 15,26-30;36-37;45-46;48;50-53; 64-65;67-72;75;78-79. 16,149;172. 20,16-17. 21,1. 35,9;13;19-22;27;30. 42,15;18. See also in Exon. 97 b 4 (in Exon. Notes after 1,55) |
| *Reginwal* | 23,5 |
| *Rewruin* | *19,4* |
| Richard *of Néville* | 16,57 |
| Richard son of Count Gilbert | 26 |
| Richard son of Thorold(?), see General Notes Ch. 30 | |
| Richard son of Thorulf | *15,42. 16,115.* 30,1 |
| Richard | 15,35;49;73;76. 16,15;24;29-30;33-34;162. 34,13. *47,10.* 51,10 |
| Riculf | 24,27;32 |
| Roald Dubbed | 35 |
| Count *Robert* of Mortain | **15.** 1,11;*23*;25;50. 2,10. 7,4. 34,2. 35,10 |
| Robert Bastard | 29 |
| Robert of Aumale | 28 |

| | |
|---|---|
| Robert *of Beaumont* | 16,65;67-68;137 |
| Robert of *'Hereford'* | 28,10 |
| Robert of Pont-Chardon | 1,5. *16,69;72;74* |
| Robert *son of Ivo* | 15,10. See also in Exon. T.O. 506 a 9 (in Exon. Notes 15,14) |
| Robert | 2,14. 3,96. 5,1;10. 16,32;40;61-62;66;70-71; 83-85;87. 17,43. 18,1. 19,10;41. 21,18;21. 34,27;40. *51,2* |
| Roger *Goad* | 48,*1*;6 |
| Roger *Ralph* (?) | *34,46* (see Exon. Notes here) |
| Roger of Bully | 27 |
| Roger *of Flanders* | 35,7-8 |
| Roger of Meulles | 16,9-*10;59;139* |
| Roger *son of Payne* | 16,155. 34,12 |
| Roger *a man-at-arms* | 48,10 |
| Roger | 2,20. 3,92. 16,4;18-20;168. 20,5. 34,3;7;9; 29-30;44;46;52;55-57. 48,7. 49,6 |
| Rogo | 16,76-77;104-105;150;158;170 |
| Rolf | 16,6. 23,10-11 |
| Rolf, see Thurstan | |
| Rozelin | 34,24;32;47 |
| Rufus, see Aelmer, Alward | |
| Saegar | 34,33 |
| Saemer, *Edmer Ator's man* | 15,20 |
| Saemer | 15,63. 19,43. 24,16. 34,45 |
| Saeric | 34,36;42 |
| Saeward | 21,14. 26,1 |
| Saewin *Tuft* | 16,7 |
| Saewin the *Queen's* priest | 13a,2. See Brictferth |
| Saewin, *Edmer Ator's man* | 15,22 |
| Saewin | 3,30;88;98. 15,25. 16,22;38;134. 17,11-12. 35,26;29-30. 36,3-4. 39,3. 42,2;4 |
| Saewulf | 15,48. 17,72. 39,11. 52,47;*48-49* |
| Sheerwold | 42,18. 50,1 |
| Sidwin | 16,98. 17,86. 35,5 |
| Sigeric | 17,92 |
| Abbot Sihtric | 5,*8*;11;*14*. 16,7 |
| Siward | 16,43;76;143-144;148;163. 39,1;21 |
| Snot | 17,54 |
| Snotta | 25,26 |
| Sock, see Leofwin | |
| Solomon | 35,23 |
| Sotman | 25,18 |
| Stephen | 16,110;112;152. 17,78;106 |
| Summerled | 48,12 |
| Sweet | 15,51 |
| Tabb, see Alwy | |
| Theobald son of Berner | 36 |
| *Theobald, father-in-law of Odo son of Gamelin* | 42,4 |
| Thief, see Aelfeva, Edlufu | |
| Thorbert | 9,1 |
| Thorgils | 17,22;35;53-54;61-62;80-81;97-98;*99-101* |
| Thorkell | 3,5 |
| Thorold(?), see Richard | |
| Thorulf, see Richard | |
| Thurs | 22,1 |
| Thurstan son of Rolf | 37 |
| Thurstan | 34,38 |
| Tilley, see Alstan | |
| Toki, see Alward | |
| Toli | 22,2 |

| | |
|---|---|
| Topi | 16,146 |
| Tovi | 17,62-63;65;67. 34,2;6. 39,15 |
| Tuft, see Saewin | |
| Uhtred | 16,59. 17,47. 18,1. 19,20. 43,2 |
| Ulf | 3,39;46;55. 16,36;44;70;152-153;169. 17,29-30; 48. 19,13;*45*. 34,16. 35,20-21. 39,10. 47,1-2. 52,40 |
| Viking | 19,8-9;22;26;38;45. 34,12;29-30;52;56 |
| Vitalis *of Colyton* | 16,129 |
| Vitalis | 36,13. 42,9;13;24 |
| Vitalis, see Ralph | |
| W.... | 16,175 |
| Waddell | *15,78*. 16,10. 34,3. 36,14 |
| Wadilo | *16,48;52;56*. 28,16 |
| Wado | 15,49-50;73;76;78. 16,48;52;56 |
| Waldin | 17,7;68;95-96 |
| Walscin (of Douai), see Walter of Douai, Ludo | |
| Walter *(of) Burgundy* | 25,*1*;3-4 |
| Walter of Claville | 24. *1,66*. Also in Exon. T.O. 497 b 5 (in Exon. Notes 1,66) |
| Walter (*alias* Walscin) of Douai | 23 |
| Walter *of Omonville* | 35,3;5-6 |
| Walter *the Steward* | 24,4;13 |
| Walter *the Wild* | 24,9-10;*31* |
| Walter | 1,63. 5,4. 16,27;45-47;123;147. 24,5;*28-29*. 35,25;28. 42,*6*;16 |
| Warin | 17,31. 19,27;34;42;44 |
| Weland | 3,76 |
| Wigot *the priest* | 3,7 |
| Wihenoc | 39,2;7-8 |
| *William Black* | *16,97* |
| William Cheever | 19. 1,11. 5,8. *26,1*. See Beatrix |
| *William Cheever's brother* | *19,3*, see also under Ralph of Pomeroy |
| William of Eu | 22. 1,4 |
| William of Falaise | **20** |
| William *of Lestre* | 15,56 |
| William of Mohun | **18**. 23,5 |
| William of Poilley | **21** |
| William *of Poitou* | 34,27-28 |
| William of Vauville | 1,15. 3,32 |
| William *son of Wimund* | 16,44 |
| *William son of Wimund's wife* | *16,44* |
| William the Porter | 51,1 |
| William the Usher | *5,9*. 51,2;*6-12* |
| William | 16,42;97;146. 17,6;8;19;50-52;79;83-84;*85;87*; 90;93;107. *24,22*(?). 34,33;35-37;42. 39,9; 11-13;16. 41,2. 51,3-5 |
| Wimund, see William | |
| Winemar | 20,12. 25,13 |
| Woodman | 24,18 |
| Wordrou | 24,17 |
| Wulfeva | 3,13-14;16;19;80-81;92. 10,2. 16,92. 20,12. 28,1 |
| Wulffrith | 3,27 |
| Wulfgeat | 24,*14*;30. 25,12 |
| Wulfmer *Cott* | 16,90 |
| Wulfmer | 3,33;54. 5,9. 16,138;159. 21,8. 23,3. 25,22. 36,23 |
| Wulfnoth | 3,67-71. 16,17;29. 17,73. 19,42. 21,5;12. 30,3. 34,51. 39,5. 47,8 |
| Wulfric | 1,29. 15,74. 16,16;64. 23,3;6;14 |

| | | |
|---|---|---|
| Wulfrun, a free woman | | 28,3 |
| Wulfrun | | 3,90. 24,11 |
| Wulfstan | | 25,27 |
| Wulfward | | 15,24. 16,68. 21,2. 24,13. 28,5-8. 34,34 |
| Wulfwen | | 3,61. 42,15 |
| Wulfwin | | 51,10. 52,36 |
| Wulfwy | | 24,14 |

## CHURCHES AND CLERGY

| | | |
|---|---|---|
| **Abbess of:** | *Holy Trinity, Caen* | *13,1* |
| **Abbeys of:** | Battle | 1,52 |
| | Buckfast | 6,13 |
| **Abbots of:** | Battle | 1,34;*52. 9,1-2* |
| | Buckfast | 6 |
| | *Caen* | *12,1* |
| | *Cranborne* | *8,1* |
| | *Glastonbury* | *4* |
| | *Horton* | *7* |
| | Mont St. Michel | *1,33.* 11,1;*2-3* |
| | *Tavistock Church* | *5* |
| | see Alwin, Geoffrey, Sihtric | |
| **Archbishop:** | see Aldred | |
| **Bishops of:** | Coutances | 3. 1,1;11 |
| | Coutances' niece | 3,89 |
| | Coutances, see Colswein | |
| | Exeter | 2 |
| | see Leofric, Osbern | |
| **Canons of:** | Exeter(?) | 2,2;8;22 |
| | St. Mary's (of Exeter) | 16,89;*90-92* |
| | (Hartland Abbey; see note) | 45,3 |
| | *St. Peter's of Plympton* | 1,17 |
| | *St. Mary's, Rouen* | *1,11. 10,1-2* |
| **Chaplain:** | see Gerald | |
| **Churches of:** | Battle | 9 |
| | Buckfast | 6 |
| | Holy Trinity, Caen | 13 |
| | St. Stephen's, Caen | 12 |
| | Cranborne | 8 |
| | St. Olaf, (Exeter) | 9,2 |
| | St. Peter, (Exeter) | 2,2 |
| | Glastonbury | 4 |
| | Horton | 7 |
| | Mont St. Michel | 11. 1,33 |
| | St. Mary, Rouen | 10 |
| | Tavistock | 5 |
| **Clergy of:** | St. Mary's (of Totnes) | 17,58 |
| | Yealmpton | 1,18 |
| | see Ch. 13a | |
| **Monks of:** | Battle | 1,4 |
| | Mont St. Michel | 16,93 |
| | see Aethelhard | |

| Priests: | of Bodmin | 51,15-*16* |
| | see 1,4. 13a,1. 24,26 | |
| | see Aelmer, Algar, Alric, Doda, Edward, | |
| | Goda, Godman, Godric, Godwin, | |
| | Saewin, Wigot | |
| Saint: | Stephen's of Caen | 12 |
| | Michael's (land in Sidmouth) | 10,1 |
| | *Michel's* | *11,3* |
| | Mary's of Rouen | 1,11 |
| | Peter's of Plympton | 29,10 |
| | *Mary's* | *17,58* |
| | see also under Churches | |

## SECULAR TITLES AND OCCUPATIONAL NAMES

Bowman (*arbalestarius, arbalistarius, archibalistarius*) ... Fulchere, Godbold, Nicholas
Butler (*pincerna*) ... Alfred
Chamberlain (*camerarius*) ... Godfrey
Count (*comes*) ... Gilbert, Robert
Countess (*comitissa*) ... Gytha
Earl (*comes*) ... Harold, Hugh, Leofwin
Queen (*regina*) ... Edith, Matilda
Porter (*portitor*) ... William
Reeve (*prepositus*) ... Eccha
Servant (*serviens*) ... Ansger
Sheriff (*vicecomes*) ... Baldwin, Heca
Steward (*dapifer*) ... Alwin, Rainer, Walter
Usher (*hostiarius*) ... William

## INDICES OF PLACES

There are four Indices of places. Index 1 lists all places named in Exchequer DB, together with any additional names given in the Tax Returns, the *Terrae Occupatae* and in the main returns in Exon. Book. Index 2 lists those cases where a place-name has been omitted from a main DB section within a chapter. Index 3 gives places mentioned in DB that are not in Devon, while Index 4 sets out place-names given in the Notes that are identifiable as probable constituents of DB holdings.

In Index 1, the name of each place is followed by (i) the number of its Hundred and its numbered location on the Maps in this volume; (ii) its National Grid reference; (iii) chapter and section reference in DB, in which bracketed figures denote mention in sections dealing with a different place. Unless otherwise stated in the notes, the identifications of VCH and DG and the spellings of the Ordnance Survey are followed for places in England, of OEB for places abroad. Places that occur only in the Exon. Book are bracketed and indexed plain Exon., or Exon. Tax Return, or Exon. T.O. with the folio references. Other Exon. references and those to the Tax Returns are given beside the translation and in the notes. Inverted commas mark (a) lost places with known modern spelling, some no longer on modern maps, others now represented not by a building but by a wood, field or road name; (b) places such as 'Stockleigh' whose basic name can be identified and located, but where the actual holding among several of the same name cannot be determined. Unidentifiable places are given in DB spelling, in italics. The National Grid reference system is explained on all Ordnance Survey maps, and in the Automobile Association Handbooks: the figures reading from left to right are given before those reading from bottom to top of the map. Devon lies partly in four 100-kilometre Grid squares; their reference letters, SS, ST, SX and SY are given in each case before the reference numbers. Places with bracketed Grid references are not found on modern 1:50,000 (1¼ inch) maps; unless their names are within inverted commas they are to be found on larger-scale maps. A few places that were in Devon in 1086 are now in adjacent (pre-1974) counties, whose names appear after them in Index 1. The Devon Hundreds are numbered from west to east working southwards on the Maps; their names and numbers are listed at the head of the Map Keys. Places that lay in Cornwall or Dorset in 1086, but were later transferred into Devon are prefixed C or D respectively in place of the Hundred number in Index 1 and in the Map Keys. Because there is insufficient evidence to reconstruct the 1086 Hundreds fully, the 'modern' (early 19th century) Hundreds are followed, as in the EPNS volume, but with certain adjustments that are detailed in the Appendix. Place-names sharing certain elements, especially river names, e.g., 'Nymet', 'Otter', 'Clyst', are grouped together in Index 1; the problems of their identification are discussed in Introductory Note 2 at the head of the General Notes. A name in brackets following a place-name is that of its parish or an adjacent major settlement, given to distinguish this place from others of the same name. A star beside a place-name in Index 1 indicates that there is a further entry in Index 4 below.

### 1. PLACES NAMED IN DB

|  | Map | Grid | Text |
|---|---|---|---|
| Abbotsham | 4-2 | SS 42 26 | 5,6 |
| Abbotskerswell, see Kerswell |  |  |  |
| Adworthy | 7-30 | SS 77 15 | 34,42 |
| Afton | 29b-21 | SX 84 62 | 34,49 |
| Aller (in Abbotskerswell) | 29b-4 | SX 87 68 | 48,11 |
| Aller (in Kentisbeare) | 15-13 | ST 05 06 | 16,103. 32,3 |
| Aller (in South Molton) | 6-11 | SS 69 27 | 3,57. 42,12 |
| East Allington | 28-24 | SX 77 48 | 30,3 |
| South Allington | 30-29 | SX 79 38 | 17,53 |
| Allisland | 4-38 | SS 48 11 | 52,6 |
| Alminstone | 3a-8 | SS 34 20 | 42,3 |
| Alphington | 19a-50 | SX 91 89 | 1,43 |
| *Alreford* | 17a- — | — — — | 16,167 |
| Alston (in Malborough) | 28-37 | SX 71 40 | 17,40 |
| Alverdiscott | 5-14 | SS 51 25 | 15,39 |
| West Alvington | 28-30 | SX 72 43 | 1,16 |

# Places 1

| | Map | Grid | Text |
|---|---|---|---|
| Alwineclancavele | 11- – | – – – | 34,4 |
| Alwinestone | 8a- – | – – – | 15,57 |
| Alwington | 4-5 | SS 40 23 | 15,8 |
| Anstey: | | | |
| East Anstey | 6-13b | SS 86 26) | |
| West Anstey | 6-13a | SS 85 27) | 3,62. 14,1–2. 16,78 |
| Appledore (in Burlescombe) | 10-7 | ST 06 14 | 24,14 |
| Appledore (in Clannaborough) | 12-34 | SS 74 01 | 16,49 |
| Arlington | 2-17 | SS 61 40 | 38,1 |
| 'Abbots Ash' | 27- – | – – – | 6,7 |
| Rose Ash | 7-8 | SS 78 21 | 16,143 |
| Ash (in Bradworthy) | 11-2 | SS 32 16 | 34,5 |
| Ash (in Braunton) | 1a-43 | SS 51 37 | 19,14 |
| Ash (in Petrockstow) | 4-50 | SS 51 08 | 6,2 |
| Ash (in South Tawton) | 19a-34 | SX 68 91 | 1,29 |
| Ash Thomas | 10-13 | ST 00 10 | 25,20 |
| Ashburton | 23-32 | SX 76 79 | 2,19 |
| Ashbury | 11-55 | SX 50 97 | 39,7 |
| Ashclyst, see River Clyst | | | |
| Ashcombe | 24-17 | SX 91 79 | 34,10 |
| Ashford (near Barnstaple) | 1a-52 | SS 53 35 | 16,66;85 |
| Ashleigh | 18-31 | SX 39 83 | 17,9 |
| Ashmansworthy | 3a-11 | SS 33 18 | 16,31 |
| Ashprington | 30-5 | SX 81 57 | 1,71 |
| Ashreigney | 12-6 | SS 62 13 | 1,65 |
| Ashton | 24-10 | SX 85 84 | 6,6. 44,1 |
| Ashwater | 11-60 | SX 38 95 | 3,4 |
| Assecote | 7- – | – – – | 21,11 |
| Aunk | 20b-3 | ST 04 00 | 34,18; (34) |
| Aveton Gifford | 27-29 | SX 69 47 | 35,26 |
| Awliscombe | 16-13 | ST 13 01 | 19,25–26;32;(36;43). 25,14. 34,23;26;(45) |
| Axminster | 17a-15 | SY 29 98 | 1,11. 19,45 |
| Axmouth | 17c-5 | SY 25 91 | 1,14 |
| Aylesbeare | 14c-6 | SY 03 91 | 16,136 |
| Aylescott | 1a-25 | SS 52 41 | 3,40 |
| Ayshford | 10-6 | ST 04 15 | 24,13 |
| 'Baccamoor' | 26-6 | (SX 58 59) | 17,92 |
| Backstone | 7-16 | SS 83 19 | 29,1 |
| 'Badgworthy' | 2-14 | SS 79 43 | 19,18 |
| Bagton | 28-34 | SX 70 41 | 17,34 |
| Bagtor | 23-25 | SX 76 75 | 48,7 |
| Bampton | 8a-4 | SS 95 22 | (1,24). 23,5 |
| Barlington | 5-19 | SS 56 16 | 3,15;19 |
| Barnstaple | 1a-57 | SS 55 33 | (C 6). 1,1;(2). 3,3;(6;45). 16,2;(65. 17,1). 28,17 |
| Batson | 28-39 | SX 73 39 | 15,74 |
| *Battisborough | 27-26 | SX 59 48 | 39,14 |
| Battisford | 26-17 | (SX 57 54) | 21,17 |
| (Battishill) | 18-29 | SX 50 85 | Exon. 288 b 2 (= 16,7) |
| Battleford | 29b-16 | (SX 83 64) | 39,11 |
| Beaford | 4-29 | SS 55 14 | 1,51 |
| Beara Charter | 1a-38 | SS 52 38 | 3,31 |
| 'Beare' (? in Worlington) | 7- – | – – – | 20,5 |
| Beaworthy | 11-49 | SX 46 99 | 21,4 |
| Beenleigh | 28-15 | SX 75 76 | 28,12 |
| 'Beer' (in Offwell) | 22-8 | (SY 20 98) | 16,174 |
| Beer (near Seaton) | 22-19 | SY 22 89 | 7,4 |
| Great Beere | 12-28 | SS 69 03 | 16,47 |
| Beetor | 23-3 | SX 71 84 | 16,60 |

# Places 1

| | Map | Grid | Text |
|---|---|---|---|
| Belstone | 11-64 | SX 61 93 | 16,15 |
| Benton | 1a-50 | SS 65 36 | 2,10 |
| *Bere* | 22- – | – – – | 24,17 |
| Bere Ferrers | 25-9 | SX 45 63 | 15,46 |
| 'Bernardsmoor' | 15- – | – – – | 16,105 |
| Berry Pomeroy | 29b-23 | SX 82 61 | 34,48 |
| Berrynarbor | 1a-5 | SS 56 46 | 23,2 |
| Bickford | 26-8 | (SX 57 58) | 29,8. 52,28 |
| Bickham | 7-12 | SS 86 20 | 28,10 |
| Abbots Bickington | 11-10 | SS 38 13 | 45,2 |
| High Bickington | 12-2 | SS 59 20 | 1,(40);67 |
| Bickleigh (near Plymouth) | 25-11 | SX 52 62 | 21,19 |
| Bickleigh (near Silverton) | 15-8 | SS 94 07 | 15,61 |
| Bickleton | 5-3 | SS 50 31 | 36,8 |
| Bicton | 14c-18 | SY 07 85 | 51,1 |
| Bideford | 4-3 | SS 45 26 | 1,60 |
| Bigbury | 27-30 | SX 66 46 | 15,44 |
| Bishopsteignton, see Teignton | | | |
| Bittadon | 1a-26 | SS 54 41 | 3,60 |
| Blachford | 27-1 | SX 61 60 | 17,66. 29,5 |
| Blackawton | 30-13 | SX 80 50 | 1,24 |
| Blackborough | 15-2 | ST 09 09 | 16,101. 34,20. 51,7 |
| Blackpool | 6-18 | SS 68 25 | 1,41 |
| 'Blackslade' | 29a-3 | SX 73 75 | 34,46 |
| Blagrove | 7-28 | SS 77 16 | 21,9;(11) |
| Blakewell | 1a-48 | SS 55 36 | 16,74 |
| Blaxton | 25-10 | SX 47 62 | 39,20 |
| Boasley | 18-10 | SX 49 92 | 16,6 |
| Boehill | 10-5 | ST 03 15 | 24,11–12 |
| Bolberry | 28-40 | SX 69 39 | 15,38;73 |
| Bolham (in Tiverton) | 9-10 | SS 95 14 | 51,8 |
| Bolham Water (in Clayhidon) | 16-7 | ST 16 12 | 16,121 |
| Bondleigh | 12-24 | SS 65 04 | 3,20 |
| (Boode) | 1a-37 | SS 50 38 | Exon. 126 b marginal (= 3,32) |
| Borough (in Bridgerule) | C-1 | SS 26 02 | EC 1 |
| Little Bovey | 23-23 | SX 83 76 | 3,8 |
| North Bovey | 23-5 | SX 73 83 | 17,22 |
| Bovey Tracey | 23-8 | SX 82 78 | 3,8 |
| Bowcombe | 27-10 | SX 66 55 | 15,75 |
| *Bowley | 15-17 | SS 90 04 | 21,8 |
| Bradaford | 18-4 | SX 39 94 | 17,11 |
| Bradford (near Cookbury) | 11-24 | SS 42 07 | 16,21 |
| Bradford (in Pyworthy) | 11-44 | SS 28 01 | 17,19 |
| Bradford (in Witheridge) | 7-29 | SS 82 16 | 19,40. 20,8 |
| Bradley | 9-15 | SS 90 13 | 3,79;82. 50,5 |
| Bradninch | 15-20 | SS 99 04 | 19,31 |
| Bradstone | 18-36 | SX 38 80 | 1,36 |
| Bradwell | 1a-18 | SS 49 42 | 31,2 |
| Bradworthy | 11-5 | SS 32 14 | 34,6. Exon. T.O. 496 b2 (see Exon. Notes 19,3) |
| Bramford Speke | 19a-3 | SX 92 98 | 3,67. 16,123;129. 24,2 |
| Branscombe | 22-20 | SY 19 88 | 2,22 |
| Bratton Clovelly | 18-11 | SX 46 91 | 16,5 |
| Bratton Fleming | 1a-45 | SS 65 37 | (2,9;10). 15,40 |
| Braunton | 1a-46 | SS 48 36 | 1,5. (3,31). 13a,3. (16,74; 80) |
| High Bray | 2-29 | SS 69 34 | 3,30 |
| *Bray (in South Molton) | 6-15 | (SS 67 26) | 3,45. 52,36 |
| Brayley | 1b-5 | SS 68 30 | 42,15 |

# Places 1

|  | Map | Grid | Text |
|---|---|---|---|
| Bremridge | 6-6 | SS 69 29 | 3,56 |
| Brendon | 2-6 | SS 76 48 | 34,14 |
| South Brent | 28-10 | SX 69 60 | 6,11-12 |
| *Brexworthy | 11-7 | SS 28 13 | 52,2 |
| Bridestowe | 18-17 | SX 51 89 | 16,7 |
| Bridford | 19a-56 | SX 81 86 | 16,128. 17,21 |
| Bridgerule | 11-37 | SS 27 02 | 35,2 |
| Bridwick | 1a-23 | SS 64 42 | 3,47 |
| 'Brightston' | 14c- — | — — — | 2,17 |
| Brimblecombe | 4-47 | SS 56 09 | 40,3 |
| Brixham | 29b-28 | SX 92 56 | 17,29 |
| Brixton (in Broadwood Kelly) | 11-32 | SS 60 05 | 16,29 |
| Brixton (in Shaugh Prior) | 26-4 | SX 55 52 | 17,91 |
| Brixton (near Yealmpton) | 26-26 | SX 54 60 | 17,86-87 |
| Broadaford | 27-9 | (SX 65 55) | (1,23). 15,69 |
| Broadclyst, see Clyst | | | |
| Broadhembury, see Hembury | | | |
| Broadhempston, see Hempston | | | |
| Broadnymett, see River 'Nymet' | | | |
| Broadley | 28-16 | SX 72 54 | 17,45 |
| Broadwood Kelly | 11-33 | SS 61 05 | 16,26 |
| Broadwoodwidger | 18-15 | SX 41 89 | 17,5. Exon. T.O. 496 a 3 (see Exon. Notes to 1,25) |
| *Bruckland | 17c-2 | SY 28 93 | 34,53. (35,4) |
| *Brungurstone* | 23- — | — — — | 3,8 |
| Brushford | 12-19 | SS 67 07 | 16,53-54. 25,7. 47,3 |
| Buckfast | 28-3 | SX 74 67 | 6,13 |
| East Buckland | 1b-4 | SS 67 31 | 3,54-55;63 |
| North Buckland | 1a-29 | SS 47 40 | 19,12 |
| West Buckland | 1b-3 | SS 65 31 | 16,73 |
| Buckland (in Braunton) | 1a-42 | SS 48 37 | 19,13 |
| Buckland (in Dolton) | 12-4 | SS 56 13 | 42,7 |
| Buckland (in Haccombe) | 19c-1 | SX 88 71 | 19,41 |
| *Buckland (in Thurlestone) | 28-29 | SX 67 43 | 15,38 |
| Buckland Brewer | 4-13 | SS 41 20 | 15,12 |
| Buckland Filleigh | 4-43 | SS 46 09 | 3,13 |
| Buckland in the Moor | 29a-5 | SX 72 73 | 48,10 |
| Buckland Monachorum | 25-7 | SX 49 68 | 21,20 |
| Buckland Tout Saints | 30-15 | SX 75 46 | 24,18. 25,25 |
| Bucks Cross | 3a-4 | SS 34 23 | 36,2 |
| East Budleigh | 14c-20 | SY 06 84 | 1,9 |
| Budshead | 25-13 | (SX 45 60) | 39,18 |
| Bulkworthy | 4-26 | SS 39 14 | 15,14. Exon. T.O. 506 a 9 (see Exon. Notes 15,14) |
| Bulworthy | 7-26 | SS 86 17 | 52,20 |
| Burlescombe | 10-4 | ST 07 16 | 24,30 |
| Burn (in Silverton) | 15-15 | ST 94 05 | 47,9 |
| (Burntown) | 18-42 | (SX 50 78) | Exon. 317 b 3 (= 17,13) |
| Burrington (near Chulmleigh) | 12-3 | SS 63 16 | 5,8 |
| Burrington (in Weston Peverell) | 25-22 | (SX 47 57) | 17,74 |
| Burston, see River 'Nymet' | | | |
| Bury | 12-21 | SS 73 07 | 2,3 |
| Buscombe | 2-20 | SS 68 39 | 3,35 |
| Butterford | 28-12 | SX 70 56 | 17,61-62 |
| Butterleigh | 20a-1 | SS 97 08 | 52,38 |
| Bywood | 16-11 | ST 16 08 | 24,1 |
| Cadbury (near Thorverton) | 15-18 | SS 91 04 | 21,7 |
| Cadeleigh | 15-3 | SS 91 07 | 19,24. 51,5 |
| Calverleigh | 9-9 | SS 92 14 | 52,21 |
| Canonsleigh | 10-2 | ST 06 17 | 24,15 |

# Places 1

|  | Map | Grid | Text |
|---|---|---|---|
| Canonteign | 19a-58 | SX 83 82 | 3,97 |
| *Celvertesberie* | 7- — | — — — | 3,76 |
| (Chaffcombe) | 12-30 | SS 75 03 | Exon. T.O. 494 a 4 (see 2,2 General and Exon. Notes) |
| Chagford | 19a-54 | SX 70 87 | 3,65. 32,5 |
| Challacombe | 2-19 | SS 69 40 | 3,33 |
| Challonsleigh | 26-16 | SX 59 55 | 21,16 |
| Chardstock | D-2 | ST 30 04 | ED 1 |
| Charford | 28-11 | SX 72 58 | 6,10 |
| Charles | 2-30 | SS 68 32 | 16,71 |
| Charleton | 30-23 | SX 75 42 | 17,49 |
| 'Charlton' | 17a- — | — — — | (1,11). 3,96 |
| Chawleigh | 12-11 | SS 71 12 | 16,43 |
| Cheldon | 7-37 | SS 73 13 | 16,147. 40,4 |
| Cheriton (in Brendon) | 2-9 | SS 73 46 | 34,15 |
| Cheriton (in Payhembury) | 15-33 | ST 10 01 | 15,63 |
| Cheriton Bishop | 19a-19 | SX 77 93 | 52,11 |
| Cheriton Fitzpaine | 14b-5 | SS 86 06 | 36,19 |
| *Chetelescote* | 12- — | — — — | 24,27 |
| Chettiscombe | 9-11 | SS 96 14 | 16,159 |
| Chevithorne | 9-5 | SS 97 15 | 16,158. 34,43 |
| Chichacott | 18-2 | SX 60 96 | 16,4 |
| Chillington | 30-24 | SX 79 42 | 1,34 |
| Chilsworthy | 11-22 | SS 32 06 | 52,1 |
| Chilton (in Cheriton Fitzpaine) | 14b-7 | SS 86 04 | 42,22. (44,2) |
| Chitterley | 15-19 | SS 94 04 | 15,60 |
| Chittleburn | 26-24 | SX 54 52 | 17,84 |
| Chittlehampton | 6-16 | SS 63 25 | 52,10 |
| Chivelstone | 30-28 | SX 78 38 | 17,57 |
| Chudleigh Knighton, see Knighton |  |  |  |
| Chulmleigh | 7-34 | SS 68 14 | 16,140 |
| Churchill | 1a-30 | SS 59 40 | 20,4 |
| Churchstanton (SOMERSET) | 16-4 | ST 19 14 | 37,1 |
| Churston Ferrers | 29b-27 | SX 90 56 | 17,30 |
| *Ciclet* | 8- — | — — — | 24,31 |
| Clannaborough | 12-33 | SS 74 02 | 16,51 |
| Clawton | 11-47 | SX 34 99 | 17,15 |
| Clayhanger | 8a-5 | ST 02 22 | 18,1 |
| Clayhidon | 16-2 | ST 16 15 | 16,111 |
| Clifford | 19a-44 | SX 78 90 | 16,110. 47,11 |
| Clovelly | 3a-3 | SS 31 24 | 1,59 |
| **River Clyst** |  |  |  |
|   Ashclyst | 20b-6 | SY 01 98 | 16,89 |
|   Broadclyst | 20b-7 | SX 98 97 | 1,56 |
|   West Clyst | 20b-10 | SX 97 95 | 16,92 |
|   Clyst Gerred | 20b-5 | (SY 02 98) | 43,2 |
|   Clyst Hydon | 20b-1 | ST 03 01 | 16,86 |
|   Clyst St. George | 14c-10 | SY 98 88 | 34,30 |
|   Clyst St. Lawrence | 20b-2 | ST 02 00 | 15,58 |
|   *Clyst St. Mary | 14c-8 | SX 97 90 | 3,7 |
|   Clyst William | 15-29 | ST 06 02 | 52,39 |
|   Sowton (*formerly* Clyst Fomison) | 19a-33 | SX 97 92 | 3,93 |
| Cockington | 29b-18 | SX 89 63 | 20,10 |
| Coddiford | 14b-3 | SS 86 07 | 52,23 |
| Coffinswell | 29b-5 | SX 89 68 | 5,13 |
| Colaton Raleigh | 14c-15 | SY 07 87 | 1,46 |
| Coldridge | 12-20 | SS 69 07 | 3,22 |
| Coldstone | 26-2 | SX 55 61 | 17,97 |
| *Colebrook (in Cullompton) | 15-16 | ST 00 05 | 19,23 |
| Coleridge (in Eggbuckland) | 25-15 | (SX 49 58) | 17,77 |

# Places 1

|  | Map | Grid | Text |
|---|---|---|---|
| Coleridge (in Stokenham) | 30-22 | SX 79 43 | 23,23;25 |
| Coleton | 29b-31 | SX 90 51 | 17,31 |
| Collacombe | 18-47 | SX 43 76 | 28,2 |
| Shiphay Collaton | 29b-13 | (SX 89 65) | 17,27 |
| Collaton (in Malborough) | 28-42 | SX 71 39 | 17,35 |
| Colscott | 11-6 | SS 36 14 | 52,29 |
| Columbjohn | 20b-4 | SX 95 99 | 49,2 |
| Colwell | 22-6 | SY 19 98 | 16,170 |
| Colyton | 22-14 | SY 24 94 | 1,13 |
| 'Lank Combe' | 2-11 | SS 78 45 | 34,14 |
| Combe (in South Pool) | 30-25 | SX 76 40 | 17,52 |
| Combe Fishacre | 29b-12 | SX 84 65 | 17,23–24 |
| Combe Martin | 1a-6 | SS 58 46 | 20,1 |
| Combe Raleigh, see River Otter |  |  |  |
| Combe Royal | 28-27 | SX 72 45 | 29,3 |
| 'Combe Sackville' | 15-26 | (SS 97 02) | 52,17 |
| (Combebowe) | 18-19 | SX 48 87 | Exon. 288 b 2 (= 16,7) |
| Combeinteignhead | 19c-2 | SX 90 71 | 19,28 |
| Combpyne | 17c-3 | SY 29 92 | 16,171 |
| Compton Gifford | 25-23 | SX 49 56 | 17,78 |
| Cookbury Wick, see Wick |  |  |  |
| Coombe (in Cheriton Fitzpaine) | 14b-2 | SS 89 08 | 36,20 |
| Coombe (in Cruwys Morchard) | 7-45 | SS 85 11 | 50,4 |
| Coombe (in Drewsteignton) | 19a-35 | SX 76 91 | 52,15 |
| Coombe (in Templeton) | 7-33 | SS 88 15 | 3,75–76;78 |
| Coombe (in Uplowman) | 9-2 | ST 00 17 | 24,10. 25,17 |
| Cornwood | 27-2 | SX 60 59 | 15,36 |
| Cornworthy | 30-7 | SX 82 55 | 17,48 |
| Coryton | 18-33 | SX 45 83 | 3,9 |
| Cotleigh | 22-1 | ST 20 02 | 15,35 |
| Countisbury | 2-2 | SS 74 49 | 19,15 |
| Cowick | 19a-39 | (SX 90 91) | 16,106 |
| Creacombe (in Newton Ferrers) | 27-22 | SX 59 49 | 39,14 |
| Creacombe (near Witheridge) | 7-15 | SS 81 19 | 16,144 |
| Crealy | 14c-9 | SY 00 90 | 3,94 |
| Crediton | 13-3 | SS 83 00 | 2,2 |
| *Lower Creedy | 14b-9 | SS 84 02 | 3,72. 34,35;37 |
| Crockernwell | 19a-28 | SX 75 92 | 35,21 |
| Crooke Burnell | 12-39 | SS 68 00 | 51,3 |
| Cross, see Bucks Cross |  |  |  |
| Croyde | 1a-31 | SS 44 39 | 15,41 |
| Culleigh | 4-15 | SS 45 19 | 15,11 |
| *Cullompton | 15-11 | ST 02 07 | 9,1 |
| 'Monk Culm' | 15- — | — — — | 16,104 |
| Culm Davy | 16-1 | ST 12 15 | 36,18 |
| Culm Pyne | 16-3 | ST 13 14 | 16,122 |
| Culm Vale | 19a-5 | SX 93 97 | 49,4 |
| Culmstock | 16-5 | ST 10 13 | 2,12 |
| Culsworthy | 11-9 | (SS 36 12) | 52,3 |
| Curscombe | 15-34 | ST 11 01 | 15,62 |
| Curtisknowle | 28-18 | SX 73 53 | 17,44 |
| Curworthy | 11-56 | SX 55 97 | 39,6 |
| 'Dart' | 7- — | — — — | 36,24. 42,20 |
| Dart (in Cadeleigh) | 15-4 | (SS 92 08) | 21,6 |
| Dart Raffe | 7-31 | SS 79 15 | 21,13 |
| Dartington | 28-8 | SX 78 62 | 20,15 |
| Dawlish | 24-18 | SX 96 76 | 2,5 |
| Dean Prior | 28-5 | SX 73 63 | 20,13 |
| Delley | 3b-1 | SS 54 24 | 42,1 |
| Denbury | 29b-2 | SX 82 68 | 5,12 |

# Places 1

|  | Map | Grid | Text |
|---|---|---|---|
| 'Deneworthy' | 17a- — | — — — | 1,11 |
| Dennington (in Yarcombe) | 17a-1 | ST 23 11 | 11,2 |
| Densham | 7-51 | SS 81 09 | 15,31. 20,9 |
| 'Dewdon' | 29a- — | — — — | 20,10 |
| Dinnaton (in Cornwood) | 27-6 | SX 62 57 | (1,23). 15,70 |
| Dipford | 8a-2 | (SS 97 23) | 23,6 |
| Diptford | 28-14 | SX 72 56 | 1,15 |
| Dittisham | 30-8 | SX 86 55 | 2,23 |
| Dockworthy | 12-9 | (SS 72 13) | 35,25 |
| Dodbrooke | 30-18 | SX 74 44 | 52,53 |
| Doddiscombsleigh | 24-8 | SX 85 86 | 47,5 |
| *Dodscott | 5-17 | SS 54 19 | 25,4 |
| Dolton | 12-10 | SS 57 12 | 16,44. 40,7 |
| Donningstone | 8a-3 | (ST 00 23) | 15,57 |
| Dotton, see River Otter |  |  |  |
| Dowland | 12-13 | SS 56 10 | 24,23;25. Exon. T.O. 498 a 1 (see Exon. Notes 24,24) |
| East Down | 1a-27 | SS 60 41 | 31,1 |
| West Down (near Ilfracombe) | 1a-19 | SS 51 42 | 3,26 |
| Down Ralph, see Rousdon |  |  |  |
| Down St. Mary | 12-26 | SS 74 04 | 1,72. 6,4 |
| Down Thomas | 26-33 | SX 50 50 | 17,88 |
| 'Down Umfraville' | 17c- — | — — — | 52,19 |
| Downicary | 18-12 | SX 37 90 | 17,7 |
| Drayford | 7-39 | SS 78 13 | 24,6 |
| Drewsteignton | 19a-43 | SX 73 90 | 16,107 |
| Dunchideock | 24-5 | SX 88 87 | 32,1 |
| Dunkeswell | 16-12 | ST 14 07 | 34,25 |
| Dunsbeare | 4-32 | SS 51 13 | 52,5 |
| Dunscombe | 14b-6 | (SS 88 05) | 34,33 |
| Dunsdon | 11-18 | SS 30 08 | 34,2 |
| Dunsford | 19a-49 | SX 81 89 | 23,12. 52,47 |
| Dunsland | 11-41 | SS 40 03 | 16,16 |
| Dunstone (in Widecombe in the Moor) | 29a-2 | SX 71 75 | 34,46 |
| Dunstone (in Yealmpton) | 26-32 | SX 59 51 | 29,4. 52,42 |
| Dunterton | 18-37 | SX 37 79 | 16,12 |
| Eastleigh | 5-10 | SS 48 27 | 19,6 |
| (Ebsworthy) | 18-13 | SX 50 90 | Exon. 288 b 2 (= 16,7) |
| Edginswell | 29b-10 | SX 88 66 | 32,10 |
| Efford | 25-24 | SX 50 56 | 29,6 |
| Eggbeer | 19a-36 | SX 77 91 | 16,130 |
| Eggbuckland | 25-20 | SX 49 57 | 17,69 |
| Elfordleigh | 26-7 | SX 54 58 | 17,104 |
| Elsford | 23-7 | SX 79 83 | 3,8 |
| *Eltemetone* | 7- — | — — — | 16,149 |
| Englebourne | 30-6 | SX 77 56 | 16,175. 20,17 |
| Ermington | 27-15 | SX 63 53 | 1,23. (15,67) |
| Essebeare | 7-32 | SS 80 15 | 42,19 |
| (*Esseorda*) | — — | — — — | Exon. T.O. 501 b 1 (see Ch. 44 Exon. Notes) |
| 'Eveleigh' | 20b — | — — — | 49,3 |
| Exbourne | 11-42 | SS 60 02 | 16,18. 39,5 |
| Nether Exe | 15-35 | SS 93 00 | 3,69 |
| Up Exe | 19a-1 | SS 94 02 | 3,70 |
| Exeter | 19a-31 | SX 92 92 | C 1-7. (1,40). 2,1;(4). 3,1-2. 5,15. 9,2. 15,1. 16,1;(58). 17,(1);2. 19,1. 23,27. 30,4. (32,6). 34,58. 35,31. 36,27. 39,22. 43,6. 47,15 |

**Places 1**

|  | Map | Grid | Text |
|---|---|---|---|
| Exminster | 24-7 | SX 94 87 | 1,4. 19,8. (22,1) |
| Exwick | 19a-15 | SX 90 94 | 16,109 |
| Fardel | 27-5 | SX 61 57 | (1,23). 15,67 |
| Farleigh | 28-19 | SX 75 53 | 1,15 |
| Farringdon | 14c-5 | SY 01 91 | 15,21. 49,5 |
| Farway | 22-11 | SX 18 95 | 3,85. 25,23 |
| *Farwood | 22-12 | SY 20 95 | 21,15 |
| Fenacre | 10-1 | ST 06 17 | 25,12 |
| Feniton | 15-37 | SY 10 99 | 15,34 |
| *Ferding* | — — | — — — | 39,3 |
| Fernhill (in Shaugh) | 26-5 | SX 56 60 | 17,98 |
| (Fernworthy) | 18-20 | SX 51 87 | Exon. 288 b 2 (= 16,7) |
| Filleigh | 1b-6 | SS 66 28 | (1,5). 16,80 |
| Flete | 27-20 | SX 62 51 | 28,11 |
| 'Floyers Hayes', see Hayes |  |  |  |
| Follaton | 30-1 | SX 78 60 | 17,58 |
| Ford (in Chivelstone) | 30-27 | SX 78 40 | 17,56 |
| 'Ford' (in Musbury) | 17a- — | — — — | 16,166 |
| Fremington | 5-1 | SS 51 32 | 3,6 |
| Frithelstock | 4-16 | SS 46 19 | 15,10 |
| Frizenham | 4-17 | SS 47 18 | 15,32 |
| Great Fulford | 19a-37 | SX 79 91 | 16,132 |
| Fursham | 19a-18 | SX 71 93 | 16,93 |
| Furze (in West Buckland) | 1b-1 | SS 64 33 | 20,2 |
| Galmpton (in Churston Ferrers) | 29b-26 | SX 88 56 | 33,2 |
| Galmpton (in South Huish) | 28-36 | SX 69 40 | 17,37 |
| Galsworthy | 4-19 | SS 39 16 | 15,12 |
| Gappah | 23-20 | SX 86 77 | 34,44 |
| Gatcombe | 22-17 | SY 22 91 | 51,13 |
| Georgeham | 1a-33 | SS 46 39 | 36,12 |
| Germansweek, see Week |  |  |  |
| Gidcott | 11-17 | SS 40 09 | 28,5 |
| Gidleigh | 19a-51 | SX 67 88 | 15,7 |
| Gittisham | 14c-1 | SY 13 98 | 25,15 |
| Goodcott | 12-7 | (SS 63 13) | 25,11 |
| Goodleigh | 1a-56 | SS 59 34 | 28,7 |
| Goodrington | 29b-25 | SX 88 58 | 23,16 |
| Goosewell | 26-22 | SX 52 52 | 21,18 |
| Gorhuish | 11-54 | SX 53 98 | 16,25 |
| Gorwell | 16-10 | ST 16 09 | 36,18 |
| Gratton (in High Bray) | 2-25 | SS 68 37 | 3,42 |
| Greenslade | 12-37 | SS 64 00 | 16,56 |
| Greenslinch | 15-23 | SS 96 03 | 48,2 |
| Greenway | 17a-6 | ST 16 05 | 23,20 |
| Grimpstone | 30-11 | SX 79 52 | 39,12 |
| Grimpstonleigh | 28-21 | SX 75 49 | 39,13;(16) |
| 'Guscott' | 18- — | — — — | 16,13 |
| Hacche | 6-12 | SS 71 27 | 42,13 |
| Haccombe | 19c-5 | SX 89 70 | 16,152. 19,10 |
| Hackworthy | 19a-20 | SX 80 93 | 44,2 |
| Hagginton | 1a-4 | SS 55 47 | 3,27. 16,70. 23,3 |
| Halberton | 10-10 | ST 00 12 | 1,70. Exon. Tax Return 67 a1 (= 1,70) |
| Halse | 12-38 | SS 67 00 | 16,50 |
| Halstow (in Dunsford) | 19a-30 | SX 82 92 | 47,12 |
| 'Halstow' (in Woodleigh) | 28- — | — — — | 28,14 |
| Halwell | 26-23 | SX 53 52 | 17,107 |
| Halwill | 11-48 | SX 42 99 | 1,58 |
| *Hame* | 4- — | — — — | 52,7 |
| Hampson, see River 'Nymet' |  |  |  |

# Places 1

|  | Map | Grid | Text |
|---|---|---|---|
| *Hamsworthy | 11-19 | SS 31 08 | 3,10 |
| Hankford | 4-24 | SS 38 15 | 35,19 |
| Harbourneford | 28-7 | SX 71 62 | 20,16 |
| Hareston | 26-20 | SX 56 53 | 15,29;51 |
| Harford (near Cornwood) | 27-3 | SX 63 59 | 15,45 |
| Hartland | 3a-2 | SS 26 24 | 1,30 |
| Hartleigh | 4-49 | SS 50 08 | 3,14 |
| Hatherleigh (in Bovey Tracey) | 23-11 | (SX 79 80) | 3,8 |
| Hatherleigh (near Okehampton) | 11-36 | SS 54 04 | 5,4 |
| Hawkmoor | 23-12 | (SX 80 80) | 3,8 |
| Haxton | 1a-49 | SS 64 36 | 2,9 |
| ('Floyers Hayes') | 19a-45 | (SX 91 91) | Exon. 459 a 3 (see Ch. 22 General and Exon. Notes) |
| Hazard | 30-3 | SX 75 59 | 29,2 |
| Caffyns Heanton | 2-4 | SS 69 48 | 34,16 |
| West Heanton | 4-44 | SS 47 09 | 52,8 |
| Heanton Punchardon | 1a-51 | SS 50 35 | 16,69 |
| Heanton Satchville | 4-39 | SS 53 11 | 16,35 |
| Heathfield | 27-21 | SX 68 50 | 6,8 |
| Heavitree | 19a-32 | SX 93 92 | 34,56 |
| Hele (in Ilfracombe) | 1a-3 | SS 53 47 | 3,44 |
| Hele (in Meeth) | 4-54b | SS 52 06) | 15,47. 39,8. 47,1 |
| Hele (in Petrockstowe) | 4-54a | SS 51 06) |  |
| *Helescane* | 4- — | — — — | 16,42 |
| Hembury: |  |  |  |
| Broadhembury | 15-22 | ST 10 04 | (23,20). 42,16 |
| Payhembury | 15-32 | ST 08 01 | 16,95. 52,22 |
| Hemerdon | 26-10 | SX 56 57 | 35,28 |
| Hempston: |  |  |  |
| Broadhempston | 29b-7 | SX 80 66 | 15,43 |
| Littlehempston | 29b-20 | SX 81 62 | 1,47. 17,25 |
| Hemyock | 16-6 | ST 13 13 | 1,8 |
| Henford | 11-61 | SX 37 94 | 17,20 |
| Hennock | 23-14 | SX 82 80 | 16,155 |
| Henscott | 11-21 | SS 40 08 | 3,12 |
| *Heppastebe* | 14- — | — — — | 34,34 |
| *Herstanhaia* | 20b- — | — — — | 25,28 |
| *Hetfelle* | 17- — | — — — | 23,17 |
| *Hewis* | — — | — — — | 15,28 |
| *Hewise* | 15- — | — — — | 19,22 |
| Highampton | 11-34 | SS 48 04 | 16,19 |
| Highleigh | 7-4 | SS 91 23 | 34,41 |
| Hill (in Cruwys Morchard) | 7-49 | SS 85 10 | 50,3 |
| Hillersdon | 15-9 | SS 99 07 | 42,18 |
| Hittisleigh | 19a-11 | SX 73 95 | 16,114 |
| Hockworthy | 8a-8 | ST 03 19 | 16,77. 23,7 |
| Holbeam | 19b-1 | SX 82 71 | 48,6 |
| Holbrook | 14c-4 | SX 99 91 | 15,20. 52,18 |
| Holcombe (in Dawlish) | 24-19 | SX 95 74 | 34,11 |
| Holcombe Burnell | 19a-38 | SX 85 91 | 1,69 |
| Holcombe Rogus | 8a-9 | ST 05 18 | 16,76 |
| Hole (in Clayhidon) | 16-8 | ST 16 10 | 16,124 |
| Hole (in Georgeham) | 1a-32 | SS 45 39 | 36,11 |
| South Hole (in Hartland) | 3a-7 | SS 22 20 | 36,3 |
| Hollacombe (near Holsworthy) | 11-40 | SS 37 03 | 51,15 |
| Hollacombe (in Kentisbury) | 1a-16 | SS 64 43 | 23,1 |
| Hollam | 4-22 | SS 50 16 | 35,12 |
| Holland | 26-14 | (SX 56 56) | 17,94 |
| Hollowcombe (in Ermington) | 27-17 | SX 62 52 | 15,66 |
| Hollowcombe (in Fremington) | 5-2 | SS 53 33 | 36,9 |

**Places 1**

|  | Map | Grid | Text |
|---|---|---|---|
| *Holne | 28-2 | SX 70 69 | 20,11 |
| Holsworthy | 11-39 | SS 34 03 | 1,38 |
| Honeychurch | 11-43 | SS 62 02 | 16,27 |
| Honicknowle | 25-17 | SX 46 58 | 15,78 |
| Honiton (near Axminster) | 17a-12 | ST 16 00 | (1,11). 15,23 |
| Honiton (in South Molton) | 6-20 | SS 68 24 | 42,11 |
| Hooe | 26-21 | SX 50 52 | 17,106 |
| Hook (in Ashreigney) | 12-8 | SS 64 14 | 47,2 |
| Horton | 11-1 | SS 30 17 | 3,11 |
| Horwood | 5-11 | SS 50 27 | 3,(11);17. 34,8 |
| Houndtor | 23-16 | SX 75 79 | 5,11 |
| North Huish | 28-13 | SX 71 56 | 17,46 |
| South Huish | 28-33 | SX 69 41 | 17,36 |
| Huish (near Dolton) | 4-40 | SS 53 11 | 25,2. 42,4 |
| Huish (in Instow) | 5-6 | SS 48 29 | 3,16 |
| Huish (in Tedburn St. Mary) | 19a-22 | SX 82 93 | 49,7 |
| Huntsham | 9-1 | ST 00 20 | 42,(14);23 |
| Huntshaw | 5-15 | SS 50 22 | 19,5 |
| Huxham | 19a-6 | SX 94 97 | 34,29 |
| Huxhill | 4-9 | SS 49 23 | 35,11 |
| Iddesleigh | 4-52 | SS 56 08 | 1,63. 24,22 |
| Ide | 24-1 | SX 89 90 | 2,6 |
| Ideford | 23-21 | SX 89 77 | 48,8 |
| Ilfracombe | 1a-2 | SS 51 47 | 16,84 |
| Ilkerton | 2-8 | SS 70 46 | 19,16 |
| Ilsham | 29b-19 | SX 93 64 | 51,9 |
| Ilsington | 23-22 | SX 78 76 | 32,6 |
| Ilton | 28-38 | SX 72 40 | 17,39 |
| Ingleigh | 11-25 | SS 60 07 | 39,4 |
| Ingsdon | 23-28 | SX 81 73 | 32,7. 43,5 |
| Instaple | 11-11 | SS 32 11 | 19,3 |
| Instow | 5-4 | SS 47 30 | 24,26 |
| Inwardleigh | 11-52 | SX 56 99 | 16,23 |
| Ipplepen | 29b-9 | SX 83 66 | 33,1 |
| Irishcombe | 7-24 | SS 78 17 | 1,66 |
| Ivedon, see River Otter |  |  |  |
| Kelly | 18-35 | SX 39 81 | 16,11 |
| Kenn | 24-9 | SX 92 85 | 16,(1);58 |
| Kentisbeare | 15-6 | ST 06 08 | 16,100;102 |
| Kentisbury | 1a-15 | SS 62 43 | 16,75 |
| Kenton | 24-13 | SX 95 83 | 1,26 |
| (Kersford) | 18-24 | SX 49 86 | Exon. 288 b 2 (= 16,7) |
| Kerswell (in Broadhembury) | 15-14 | ST 08 06 | 32,2 |
| Kerswell (in Hockworthy) | 8a-6 | ST 01 20 | 23,8 |
| Kerswell (near Newton Abbot): |  |  |  |
|   Abbotskerswell | 29b-3 | SX 85 68 | 7,2 |
|   Kingskerswell | 29b-6 | SX 88 67 | 1,12 |
| Keynedon | 30-21 | SX 77 43 | 34,55 |
| 'Kidwell' | 9-14 | (ST 01 14) | 24,8 |
| Kigbeare | 18-1 | SX 54 96 | 16,22 |
| Killington | 2-7 | SS 66 46 | 3,37 |
| Kilmington | 17a-16 | SY 27 97 | 1,53 |
| Kimber | 11-53 | SX 49 98 | 35,7 |
| Kimworthy | 11-8 | SS 31 12 | 3,89 |
| Kingsford | 15-5 | ST 04 08 | 16,99 |
| Kingskerswell, see Kerswell |  |  |  |
| Kingsteignton, see Teignton |  |  |  |
| Chudleigh Knighton | 23-19 | SX 84 77 | 2,20 |
| Knowstone | 6-22 | SS 82 23 | 23,10-11. 52,41;51 |
| Lambert | 19a-27 | SX 75 92 | 43,4. 52,12 |

# Places 1

|  | Map | Grid | Text |
|---|---|---|---|
| Lambside | 27-27 | SX 57 47 | 17,67 |
| Lamerton | 18-44 | SX 45 77 | 35,1 |
| Landcross | 4-7 | SS 46 24 | 16,40 |
| *Landeshers* | 14- – | – – – | 14,4 |
| Landinner (CORNWALL) | – – | – – – | (1,25) |
| Langage | 26-15 | SX 67 56 | 3,98 |
| Langdon | 26-35 | (SX 51 49) | 17,95–96 |
| Langford (in Cullompton) | 15-27 | ST 02 02 | 16,96 |
| Langford (in Ugborough) | 27-8 | SX 69 56 | 1,55 |
| Langley (in Yarnscombe and Atherington) | 3b-2 | SS 56 24 | 1,40;(67) |
| Langstone | 23-8 | SX 74 82 | 16,154 |
| Langtree | 4-25 | SS 45 15 | 1,62 |
| 'Lank Combe', see Combe | | | |
| Lapford | 12-18 | SS 73 08 | 1,66 |
| Larkbeare | 20b-9 | SY 06 97 | 16,94. 39,10 |
| Lashbrook | 11-29 | SS 43 05 | 16,20 |
| Leigh (in Churchstow) | 28-25 | SX 72 46 | 24,21 |
| Leigh (in Coldridge) | 12-22 | SS 69 05 | 16,46 |
| Leigh (in Harberton) | 30-4 | SX 76 58 | 17,50 |
| Leigh (in Loxbeare) | 9-8 | SS 91 14 | 49,6 |
| Leigh (in Milton Abbot) | 18-43 | SX 39 77 | 5,2 |
| Leigh (in Modbury) | 27-19 | SX 68 52 | 17,60 |
| Leigh, see also Canonsleigh, Challonsleigh, Eastleigh, Grimpstonleigh, Inwardleigh, Monkleigh, Northleigh, Romansleigh, Southleigh, Westleigh | | | |
| Leonard | 10-15 | ST 00 09 | 24,16. 51,14 |
| *Leuricestone* | 25- – | – – – | 17,72 |
| Lewtrenchard | 18-23 | SX 45 86 | 16,9 |
| Liddaton | 18-34 | SX 45 82 | 5,2–3 |
| *Lidemore* | 11- – | – – – | 17,18 |
| Lifton | 18-25 | SX 38 85 | 1,25. Exon. T.O. 496 a 3 (see Exon. Notes 1,25) |
| Lincombe | 1a-11 | SS 50 45 | 16,83 |
| Lipson | 25-25 | (SX 48 55) | 15,79 |
| Littleham (near Bideford) | 4-6 | SS 44 23 | 1,61 |
| Littleham (near Exmouth) | 14c-23 | SY 02 81 | 7,1 |
| Littlehempston, see Hempston | | | |
| Lobb | 1a-41 | SS 47 37 | (16,80). 35,20 |
| Loddiswell | 28-22 | SX 72 48 | 17,32 |
| Loosebeare | 12-23 | SS 71 05 | 8,1 |
| Loosedon | 12-15 | SS 60 08 | 24,24. 25,6 |
| *Loteland* | 9- – | – – – | 25,18 |
| Loughtor | 26-9 | (SX 55 57) | 17,103 |
| Lovacott (in Shebbear) | 4-48 | SS 45 08 | 35,17 |
| *Loventor | 29b-22 | SX 84 62 | 17,26 |
| Lowley | 24-4 | SX 83 87 | 47,6 |
| **River Lowman** | | | |
|   Craze Lowman | 9-13 | SS 98 14 | 24,8 |
|   Uplowman | 9-6 | ST 01 15 | 25,16;19. 34,43 |
| Lowton | 23-2 | SX 74 85 | 47,14 |
| Loxbeare | 9-4 | SS 91 16 | 3,83 |
| Loxhore | 2-22 | SS 61 38 | 16,67–68 |
| Ludbrook | 27-13 | SX 65 54 | (1,23). 15,26;72 |
| Luppitt | 17a-4 | ST 16 06 | 23,19 |
| Lupridge | 28-17 | SX 71 53 | 15,27. 24,20. 25,26 |
| Lupton | 29b-29 | SX 90 55 | 17,28 |
| Luscombe (in Rattery) | 28-6 | SX 74 63 | 20,15 |
| Lydford | 18-30 | SX 50 84 | (C 6). 1,2. (17,1). 34,3 |
| Up Lyme, see Uplyme | | | |
| Lympstone | 14c-19 | SX 99 84 | 26,1 |
| Lyn | 2-5 | SS 72 48 | 19,17;(18) |

# Places 1

|  | Map | Grid | Text |
|---|---|---|---|
| Lynton | 2-1 | SS 71 49 | 19,16 |
| Mackham | 16-9 | ST 15 09 | 19,36 |
| Maidencombe | 19c-8 | SX 92 68 | 16,126 |
| Maker (CORNWALL) | 25-30 | SX 44 52 | 1,22 |
| Malston | 30-16 | SX 77 45 | 17,55 |
| Mamhead | 24-15 | SX 93 81 | 16,63. 52,48 |
| Manadon | 25-18 | SX 48 58 | 17,75 |
| Manaton | 23-9 | SX 75 81 | 16,160. 52,27 |
| East Manley | 10-11 | SS 98 11 | 25,21 |
| West Manley | 9-17 | (SS 98 12) | 46,1 |
| Mariansleigh | 7-5 | SS 74 22 | 51,11 |
| Little Marland | 4-36 | SS 49 12 | 36,6 |
| Peters Marland | 4-30 | SS 47 13 | 35,13 |
| Martin | 19a-26 | SX 68 92 | 16,115 |
| Martinhoe | 2-3 | SS 66 48 | 3,23 |
| Marwood | 1a-44 | SS 54 37 | 16,87. 28,8. 36,16 |
| Marytavy, see Tavy | | | |
| *Matford | 24-2 | (SX 92 89) | 15,55. 19,9 |
| Meavy | 25-8 | SX 54 67 | 17,79–82. 29,9 |
| Meddon | 3a-10 | SS 27 17 | 52,31 |
| Medland | 19a-12 | SX 77 95 | 52,13 |
| Meeth | 4-51 | SS 54 08 | 16,39 |
| Melbury | 11-58 | (SX 49 96) | 21,5 |
| Melhuish | 19a-29 | SX 79 92 | 16,116 |
| Membland | 27-25 | SX 56 48 | 17,68 |
| *Membury | 17a-9 | ST 27 03 | (1,11). 19,44 |
| Merton | 4-37 | SS 52 12 | 3,5 |
| Meshaw | 7-14 | SS 75 19 | 16,141 |
| Metcombe | 1a-34 | SS 53 39 | 3,29 |
| Middlecott (in Broadwood Kelly) | 11-26 | SS 61 06 | 16,28;30 |
| Middlecott (in Chagford) | 19a-55 | SX 71 86 | 52,37 |
| Middleton | 2-10 | SS 64 45 | 3,52 |
| Middlewick | 7-36 | SS 82 14 | 3,80 |
| Mildon | 7-6 | SS 88 22 | 19,37 |
| Milford (in Hartland) | 3a-5 | SS 23 22 | 36,4 |
| Milford (in Stowford) | 18-21 | SX 40 86 | 3,87 |
| South Milton | 28-32 | SX 69 42 | 39,15 |
| Milton Abbot | 18-38 | SX 40 79 | 5,2 |
| Milton Damerel | 11-13 | SS 37 11 | 28,1 |
| Mockham | 2-28 | SS 67 35 | 16,72 |
| Modbury | 27-18 | SX 65 51 | 15,49;64 |
| Molland (in North Molton) | 6-2 | SS 70 33 | 36,17 |
| Molland (near West Anstey) | 6-9 | SS 80 28 | 1,41. 3,61 |
| North Molton | 6-7 | SS 73 29 | 1,27 |
| South Molton | 6-19 | SS 71 25 | 1,6. 13a,1 |
| Monkleigh | 4-14 | SS 45 20 | 15,9 |
| Monkokehampton | 11-31 | SS 58 05 | 16,17 |
| Monkswell | 25-5 | (SX 52 71) | 35,30 |
| Moor (in Broadwoodwidger) | 18-5 | SX 42 94 | 17,10 |
| Cruwys Morchard | 7-43 | SS 87 12 | 3,(72);73. 19,35 |
| Morchard Bishop | 13-1 | SS 77 07 | 1,68 |
| Morebath | 8a-1 | SS 95 24 | 1,42 |
| Moreleigh | 28-20 | SX 76 52 | 39,16 |
| Moretonhampstead | 23-1 | SX 75 86 | 1,45 |
| Mortehoe | 1a-8 | SS 45 45 | 31,4 |
| Mowlish | 24-16 | SX 95 81 | 34,13. 52,49 |
| Mullacott | 1a-12 | SS 51 45 | 47,7 |
| Murley | 9-3 | ST 02 16 | 24,9 |
| Musbury | 17c-1 | SY 27 94 | 16,164 |
| Mutley | 25-27 | SX 48 55 | 17,70–71 |

# Places 1

|  | Map | Grid | Text |
|---|---|---|---|
| Muxbere | 10-12 | (ST 03 11) | 40,5 |
| Natson, see River 'Nymet' | | | |
| Natsworthy | 29a-1 | SX 72 79 | 30,2 |
| Neadon | 23-10 | SX 75 81 | 16,156 |
| Newton (in Chittlehampton) | 6-17 | (SS 66 25) | 16,81 |
| Newton (in Zeal Monachorum) | 12-25 | SS 69 04 | 25,10. 47,4 |
| Newton Ferrers | 27-24 | SX 54 48 | 15,37 |
| Newton St. Cyres | 13-4 | SX 88 98 | 2,2. 52,34 |
| Newton St. Petrock | 4-33 | SS 41 12 | 51,16 |
| Newton Tracey | 5-13 | SS 52 26 | 25,3 |
| *Nimete* | 6- — | — — — | 1,41 |
| Northam | 4-1 | SS 44 29 | 12,1 |
| Northcote (in East Down) | 1a-21 | SS 60 42 | 3,46;49 |
| Northleigh | 22-10 | SY 19 95 | 15,25. 48,12 |
| Northlew | 11-50 | SX 50 99 | 1,57. Exon. Tax Return 65 a 3 (= 1,57) |
| Norton (in Broadwoodwidger) | 18-9 | SX 40 92 | 17,6 |
| Norton (in Churchstow) | 28-28 | SX 72 45 | 6,9 |
| Nutcott | 7-19a | SS 84 18 | 46,2 |
| Nutwell | 14c-17 | SX 98 85 | 52,35 |
| **River 'Nymet'** | | | |
| Broadnymett | 12-40 | SS 70 00 | 16,48 |
| Burston | 12-32 | SS 71 02 | 16,55 |
| Hampson | 12-36 | SS 70 01 | 25,8 |
| Natson | 12-41 | SS 71 00 | 52,9 |
| Nichols Nymet | 12-31 | SS 69 02 | 25,9 |
| Nymet Rowland | 12-17 | SS 71 08 | 16,45 |
| Nymet Tracey (*alias* Bow) | 12-42 | SS 72 00 | 3,21 |
| Walson | 12-43 | SS 73 00 | 16,52 |
| Wolfin | 12-27 | SS 75 04 | 24,28 |
| Zeal Monachorum | 12-29 | SS 71 03 | 6,3 |
| Bishops Nympton | 7-1 | SS 75 23 | 2,21 |
| George Nympton | 6-24 | SS 70 22 | 42,10 |
| Kings Nympton | 7-13 | SS 68 19 | 1,49 |
| Oak | 11-51 | SX 53 99 | 16,24 |
| Oakford | 7-10 | SS 91 21 | 19,37 |
| Offwell | 22-2 | SY 19 99 | 16,172 |
| Ogwell: | | | |
| East Ogwell | 19b-2b | SX 83 70) | 34,27–28. 48,5. 52,14 |
| West Ogwell | 19b-2a | SX 81 70) | |
| Monk Okehampton, see Monkokehampton | | | |
| Okehampton | 18-3 | SX 58 95 | 16,3 |
| Okenbury | 27-28 | SX 64 47 | 17,65 |
| Oldridge | 19a-10 | SX 82 96 | 16,118 |
| Orcheton | 27-23 | SX 63 49 | 15,65 |
| *Orway | 15-12 | ST 08 07 | 38,2 |
| Ossaborough | 1a-14 | SS 48 43 | 36,14 |
| **River Otter** | | | |
| Combe Raleigh | 17a-10 | ST 15 02 | 23,21 |
| Dotton | 14c-11 | SY 08 88 | 16,135 |
| Ivedon | 16-14 | ST 14 01 | 19,42–43. 34,45;47 |
| Otterton | 14c-21 | SY 08 85 | 11,1 |
| Mohuns Ottery | 17a-7 | ST 18 05 | 23,18 |
| Ottery St. Mary | 21-1 | SY 09 95 | 10,1 |
| *Rapshays | 14c-2 | (SY 14 98) | 19,34. 34,32 |
| Upottery | 17a-3 | ST 20 07 | 34,50 |
| Weston | 16-15 | ST 14 00 | 19,27 |
| Ottery (in Lamerton) | 18-48 | SX 44 75 | 28,2 |
| Owlacombe | 5-20 | SS 57 16 | 36,7 |
| Paignton | 29b-24 | SX 88 60 | 2,18 |

**Places 1**

|  | Map | Grid | Text |
|---|---|---|---|
| *Panson | 11-63 | SX 36 92 | 35,4 |
| Parford | 19a-48 | SX 71 89 | 43,1 |
| Parkham | 4-12 | SS 38 21 | 16,33. (52,33) |
| Parracombe | 2-12 | SS 66 44 | 20,3 |
| Patchole | 1a-22 | SS 61 42 | 3,36 |
| Payhembury, see Hembury | | | |
| Peadhill | 9-12 | SS 97 14 | 3,84 |
| Peamore | 24-3 | SX 91 88 | 34,12 |
| Pedley | 7-41 | SS 77 12 | 21,10;(11) |
| Peek (in Ugborough) | 27-4 | (SX 68 58) | 15,71 |
| Peeke (in Luffincott) | 11-62 | SX 34 93 | 35,6 |
| *Petecote* | — — | — — — | 16,139 |
| Pethill | 26-3 | SX 53 60 | 17,99 |
| Petrockstowe | 4-45 | SS 51 09 | 6,1 |
| Pickwell | 1a-28 | SS 45 40 | 3,39 |
| Pilland | 1a-53 | SS 54 35 | 3,24;38 |
| Pilton | 1a-54 | SS 55 34 | 3,25 |
| Pinhoe | 19a-16 | SX 96 94 | 1,52 |
| Pirzwell | 15-1 | ST 07 09 | 19,21 |
| Plaistow | 2-21 | SS 57 38 | 3,58 |
| Plympton | 26-12 | SX 53 56 | 1,17 |
| Plymstock | 26-18 | SX 51 53 | 5,14 |
| Plymtree | 15-28 | ST 05 02 | 42,17 |
| Polsloe | 19a-24 | SX 93 93 | 3,99. 16,91 |
| Poltimore | 19a-7 | SX 96 96 | 16,90;(92). 50,1 |
| Ponsford | 15-10 | ST 00 07 | 16,97–98 |
| Pool (near Kingsbridge) | 30 26 | SX 77 40 | 17,51. 21,19. 34,55 |
| West Portlemouth | 28-41 | SX 71 39 | 17,38 |
| Potheridge | 4-28 | SS 51 14 | 16,36 |
| Poughill | 14b-1 | SS 85 08 | 15,19. 35,24 |
| *Poulston | 30-9 | SX 77 54 | 17,43 |
| Powderham | 24-11 | SX 96 84 | 22,1 |
| Praunsley | 6-4 | SS 76 30 | 35,22 |
| West Prawle | 30-30 | SX 76 37 | 16,176 |
| Puddington | 7-47 | SS 83 10 | 19,39 |
| Pulham | 6-8 | SS 77 29 | 35,22 |
| Pullabrook | 23-17 | SX 79 79 | 3,8 |
| East Putford | 4-18 | SS 36 16 | 15,13 |
| West Putford | 11-4 | SS 35 15 | (1,37). 19,4. 34,7. 35,9 |
| Pyworthy | 11-38 | SS 31 02 | 17,16 |
| Little Rackenford | 7-21 | SS 86 18 | 23,13 |
| Rackenford | 7-20 | SS 85 18 | 16,148 |
| West Raddon | 14b-10 | SS 89 02 | 15,5. 24,4 |
| Raddon (in Marystowe) | 18-28 | SX 45 85 | 17,4 |
| Raddon (in Thorverton) | 15-24 | SS 90 02 | 5,9. 51,6 |
| 'Radish' | 22-16 | SY 18 91 | 34,54. (35,4) |
| 'Radworthy' (in Challacombe) | 2-15 | SS 69 42 | 21,1 |
| 'Radworthy' (in North Molton) | 6-1 | SS 75 34 | 19,19 |
| Raleigh | 1a-55 | SS 56 34 | 3,28 |
| Rapshays, see River Otter | | | |
| Rattery | 28-9 | SX 74 61 | 20,14 |
| Rawridge | 17a-5 | ST 20 06 | (1,11). 10,2 |
| Rewe | 19a-2 | SX 94 99 | 3,68 |
| Riddlecombe | 12-5 | SS 60 13 | 25,5 |
| Rifton | 7-27 | SS 89 17 | 36,25 |
| Ringcombe | 6-10 | SS 83 28 | 16,79 |
| *Ringedone* | 6- — | — — — | 1,6 |
| Ringmore (near Bigbury) | 27-31 | SX 65 46 | 17,64 |
| Ringmore (in St. Nicholas) | 19c-4 | SX 92 71 | 16,112 |
| Roadway | 1a-17 | SS 47 42 | 31,3. 39,9 |

#  Places 1

|  | Map | Grid | Text |
|---|---|---|---|
| *Roborough (near Great Torrington) | 5-18 | SS 57 17 | 3,19 |
| Rockbeare | 14c-3 | SY 02 95 | 15,22. 16,133–134;138 |
| Rocombe | 19c-7 | SX 90 69 | 16,127. 19,29. 48,4 |
| Romansleigh | 7-11 | SS 72 20 | 5,10 |
| Rousdon (*alias* Down Ralph) | 17c-6 | SY 29 90 | 52,25 |
| Rowley | 2-13 | SS 65 43 | 3,64 |
| Ruckham | 7-46 | SS 87 11 | 50,2 |
| Rushford | 19a-47 | SX 70 89 | 16,113 |
| Ruston | 7-40 | SS 76 12 | 3,95 |
| Rutleigh | 11-45 | SS 51 01 | 35,8 |
| St. James Church | 19a-46 | (SX 93 90) | 52,50 |
| St. Marychurch | 29b-14 | SX 91 65 | 2,8. 15,42 |
| Salcombe Regis | 14c-12 | SY 14 88 | 2,16 |
| Sampford Courtenay | 11-46 | SS 63 01 | 16,14 |
| Sampford Peverell | 10-9 | ST 03 14 | 27,1 |
| Sampford Spiney | 25-4 | SX 53 72 | 21,21 |
| Satterleigh | 6-23 | SS 66 22 | 47,8 |
| Saunton | 1a-40 | SS 45 37 | 36,10 |
| Scobitor | 29a-4 | SX 72 75 | 3,8 |
| Seaton | 22-18 | SY 24 96 | 7,3 |
| Sedborough | 4-11 | SS 36 21 | 16,33. 52,33 |
| Sellake | 10-8 | ST 00 14 | 16,161 |
| Shapcombe | 17a-8 | (ST 15 04) | 23,20. 42,16 |
| Shapley (in Chagford) | 19a-57 | SX 68 84 | 16,61–62;64. 45,1 |
| Shapley (in North Bovey) | 23-6 | SX 71 83 | 52,44 |
| Shaugh Prior | 26-1 | SX 54 63 | 17,100–101 |
| Shebbear | 4-42 | SS 44 09 | 1,39 |
| Sheldon | 15-7 | ST 12 08 | 34,19 |
| Sherford (in Brixton) | 26-19 | SX 54 53 | 17,83 |
| Sherford (near Kingsbridge) | 30-19 | SX 77 44 | 1,34 |
| Shillingford | 24-6 | SX 90 87 | 19,7. 49,1 |
| Shilston | 27-16 | SX 67 53 | 15,76 |
| *Shilstone | 19a-42 | SX 70 90 | 43,3 |
| Shiphay Collaton, see Collaton |  |  |  |
| Shirwell | 2-24 | SS 59 37 | 16,65. 21,2. 42,9 |
| Shobrooke (near Crediton) | 14b-11 | SS 86 01 | 15,4 |
| Shobrooke (in Morchard Bishop) | 13-2 | SS 75 04 | 24,29 |
| 'Shutbrook', see 'Floyers Hayes' |  |  |  |
| Sidbury | 14c-7 | SY 13 91 | 2,15 |
| *Sidmouth | 14c-16 | SY 12 87 | (10,1) |
| Sigford | 23-27 | SY 77 73 | 35,23 |
| *Silverton | 15-25 | SS 95 02 | 1,7. Exon. T.O. 501 b 1 (see Exon. Notes Ch. 44) |
| Skerraton | 28-4 | SX 70 64 | 52,45 |
| Slapton | 30-20 | SX 82 44 | 2,24 |
| Smallicombe | 22-9 | SY 20 97 | 16,168 |
| Smallridge | 17a-13 | ST 30 00 | (1,11). 34,51 |
| Smytham | 4-20 | SS 48 16 | 15,15 |
| Snydles | 6-25 | SS 66 19 | 16,88 |
| Soar | 28-43 | SX 70 37 | 17,41 |
| Sorley | 28-26 | SX 72 46 | 17,42 |
| Sourton | 18-14 | SX 53 90 | 3,86 |
| Southleigh | 22-15 | SY 20 93 | 19,46 |
| Southweek, see Week |  |  |  |
| Sowton, see Clyst Fomison (River Clyst) |  |  |  |
| *Sparkwell | 29b-11 | SX 78 65 | 16,162 |
| Speccott | 4-27 | SS 50 14 | 36,5 |
| Spitchwick | 29a-6 | SX 70 72 | 1,48 |
| Spreacombe | 1a-24 | SS 48 41 | 36,13 |
| Spreyton | 19a-9 | SX 69 96 | 16,108 |

**Places 1**

|  | Map | Grid | Text |
|---|---|---|---|
| Spriddlescombe | 27-14 | SX 68 54 | 15,77 |
| Spriddlestone | 26-29 | SX 53 51 | 15,52 |
| Sprytown | 18-26 | SX 41 85 | 39,2 |
| Spurway | 7-9 | SS 89 21 | 3,74. 23,14 |
| Stadbury | 27-32 | SX 68 45 | 17,63 |
| Staddiscombe | 26-28 | SX 51 51 | 17,89 |
| Staddon (in Plymstock) | 26-27 | SX 49 51 | 17,90 |
| Stafford | 12-12 | SS 58 11 | 40,1 |
| Stallenge Thorne | 8a-7 | ST 02 20 | 42,14 |
| Stancombe (in Sherford) | 30-17 | SX 78 45 | 17,54 |
| *Standone* | 2- — | — — — | 34,17 |
| Staplehill | 23-29 | SX 82 73 | 48,9 |
| Staverton | 29b-15 | SX 79 64 | 2,7 |
| Stedcombe | 17c-4 | SY 26 91 | 16,169 |
| *Stochelie* | 15- — | — — — | 15,2 |
| Stockland | D-1 | ST 24 04 | ED 2 |
| Stockleigh (in Highampton) | 11-35 | SS 51 04 | 15,6 |
| Stockleigh (in Meeth) | 4-46 | SS 54 09 | 15,54. 16,37 |
| Stockleigh: |  |  |  |
|   'Stockleigh' | 14b- — | — — — | 15,17–18 |
|   Stockleigh English | 14b- — | SS 85 06 | 15,48 |
|   Stockleigh Pomeroy | 14b- — | SS 87 03 | 34,31 |
| Stoke (in Devonport) | 25-26 | SX 46 55 | 28,15 |
| Stoke (in Hartland) | 3a-1 | SS 23 24 | 45,3 |
| Stoke (in Holne) | 28-1 | SX 69 70 | 20,12 |
| Stoke Canon | 19a-4 | SX 93 98 | 2,13 |
| Stoke Fleming | 30-14 | SX 86 48 | 23,22 |
| Stoke Rivers | 2-27 | SS 63 35 | 21,3 |
| Stokeinteignhead | 19c-6 | SX 91 70 | 48,3 |
| Stonehouse | 25-28 | SX 46 54 | 29,7 |
| Stoodleigh (in West Buckland) | 1b-2 | SS 65 32 | 3,53. 23,4 |
| Stoodleigh (near Oakford) | 7-23 | SS 92 18 | 3,77. 34,40 |
| Stowford (in Colaton Raleigh) | 14c-14 | SY 06 87 | 14,3 |
| Stowford (near Lifton) | 18-22 | SX 43 86 | 42,2 |
| Stowford (in West Down) | 1a-20 | SS 53 42 | 3,41 |
| Strete Ralegh | 20b-11 | SY 05 95 | 34,38 |
| Sutcombe | 11-12 | SS 34 11 | 3,91 |
| *Sutreworde* | 23- — | — — — | 23,15 |
| Sutton (in Halberton) | 10-16 | ST 01 09 | 40,6. 41,1 |
| Sutton (in Plymouth) | 25-29 | (SX 48 54) | 1,20 |
| Sutton (in Widworthy) | 22-5 | SY 20 98 | 51,10 |
| Swimbridge | 6-5 | SS 62 29 | 13a,2 |
| Sydeham | 7-18 | SS 87 19 | 24,7 |
| Sydenham (in Marystowe) | 18-32 | SX 42 83 | 17,8 |
| Sydenham Damerel | 18-46 | SX 40 76 | 17,14 |
| Tackbear | C-2 | SS 25 01 | EC 2 |
| Talaton | 15-36 | SY 06 99 | 2,14 |
| Tale | 15-31 | ST 06 01 | 34,21–22 |
| *Tamerlande* | 11- — | — — — | 35,5 |
| Kings Tamerton | 25-16 | SX 45 58 | 1,21 |
| Tamerton Foliot | 25-12 | SX 47 60 | 39,19 |
| Tapeley | 5-7 | SS 47 29 | 3,92 |
| Tapps | 7-3 | SS 89 23 | 16,150 |
| Tattiscombe | 1a-7 | SS 63 46 | 15,56 |
| Mary Tavy | 18-40 | SX 50 79 | 17,13 |
| Peter Tavy | 25-2 | SX 51 77 | 39,21 |
| Tavistock | 18-49 | SX 48 74 | 5,1 |
| Taw Green | 19a-8 | SX 63 56 | 51,2 |
| Tawstock | 5-7 | SS 55 29 | 1,40;(67) |
| Bishops Tawton | 6-3 | SS 56 30 | 2,11 |

# Places 1

| | Map | Grid | Text |
|---|---|---|---|
| North Tawton | 12-35 | SS 66 01 | 1,3. (16,56) |
| South Tawton | 19a-13 | SX 65 94 | 1,29. (43,1. 45,1. 51,2) |
| Tedburn St. Mary | 19a-14 | SX 81 94 | 16,119-120. 19,30 |
| George Teign | 24-12 | SX 85 83 | 16,59 |
| Teigncombe | 19a-53 | SX 67 87 | 3,66 |
| Teigngrace | 23-30 | SX 84 73 | 16,153 |
| Teignharvey | 19c-3 | (SX 91 72) | 16,117 |
| Teignton: | | | |
|   Bishopsteignton | 24-20 | SX 91 73 | 2,4 |
|   Kingsteignton | 23-31 | SX 87 73 | 1,10 |
| Tetcott | 11-57 | SX 33 96 | 17,17 |
| Thelbridge | 7-42 | SS 78 12 | 3,80 |
| Thornbury (in Drewsteignton) | 19a-17 | SX 70 93 | 15,59 |
| Thornbury (near Holsworthy) | 11-20 | SS 40 08 | 5,5 |
| Thorncombe (DORSET) | 17b-1 | ST 37 03 | 16,165 |
| Thorne, see Stallenge Thorne | | | |
| Thorne (in Holsworthy Hamlets) | 11-27 | SS 30 05 | 3,88 |
| Throwleigh | 19a-41 | SX 66 90 | 32,4 |
| Thrushelton | 18-18 | SX 44 87 | 17,3 |
| Thuborough | 11-15 | SS 34 10 | 28,4 |
| Thurlestone | 28-31 | SX 67 42 | 17,33 |
| Tillislow | 18-7 | SX 38 93 | 17,12 |
| Tiverton | 9-16 | SS 95 12 | 1,35. 32,8 |
| Topsham | 19a-52 | SX 96 88 | 1,44 |
| Torbryan | 29b-8 | SX 82 66 | 52,52 |
| *Toredone* | 7- — | — — — | 19,40 |
| Tormoham | 29b-17 | (SX 92 64) | 51,12 |
| Torridge | 26-13 | (SX 54 56) | 15,50. 17,102 |
| Black Torrington | 11-30 | SS 46 05 | 1,37 |
| Great Torrington | 5-18 | SS 49 19 | 34,9. 40,2. 42,(5)-6 |
| Little Torrington | 4-21 | SS 49 16 | 1,31. 15,16. 16,34 |
| Totnes | 30-2 | SX 80 60 | (C 6. 1,2;55). 17,1 |
| Townstall | 30-12 | (SX 86 51) | 23,26 |
| Train | 26-34 | (SX 52 50) | 35,27 |
| Trebeigh (CORNWALL) | — — | — — — | (1,25) |
| Trentishoe | 1a-1 | SS 64 48 | 3,48 |
| Trusham | 24-14 | SX 85 82 | 6,5 |
| Twigbeare | 4-34 | SS 47 12 | 35,14;18 |
| Twinyeo | 23-24 | SX 84 76 | 52,46 |
| Twitchen (in Arlington) | 2-18 | SS 64 40 | 38,1 |
| Uffculme | 8b-1 | ST 06 12 | 23,9 |
| Ugborough | 27-11 | SX 67 55 | 39,17 |
| *Ulestanecote* | — — | — — — | 25,27 |
| Umberleigh | 12-1 | SS 60 23 | 13,1 |
| Undercleave | 17a-11 | ST 29 01 | 1,11 |
| Uplowman, see Lowman | | | |
| Uplyme | 17a-18 | SY 32 93 | 4,1 |
| Upottery, see River Otter | | | |
| Uppacott (in Tedburn St. Mary) | 19a-21 | SX 81 93 | 16,131 |
| Varley (in Marwood) | 1a-47 | SS 54 36 | 3,59 |
| Varleys (in Petrockstowe) | 4-41 | (SS 50 10) | 52,32 |
| Venn (in Ugborough) | 27-7 | SX 68 56 | 15,68 |
| Villavin | 5-21 | SS 58 16 | 25,1 |
| Virworthy | 11-14 | SS 31 10 | 19,2. 24,32 |
| Wadham | 6-21 | SS 81 23 | 52,40 |
| 'Walford' | 26- — | — — — | 17,93 |
| Walkhampton | 25-6 | SX 53 69 | 1,19;22 |
| Wallover | 2-23 | SS 68 38 | 3,50 |
| Walson, see River 'Nymet' | | | |
| Warcombe | 1a-10 | SS 47 45 | 3,51 |

# Places 1

|  | Map | Grid | Text |
|---|---|---|---|
| Waringstone *alias* Weston, see River Otter | | | |
| Warmhill | 23-15 | SX 83 80 | 3,8 |
| (Warne) | 18-39 | (SX 50 79) | Exon. 317 b 3 (= 17,13) |
| Warson | 18-28 | SX 48 85 | 16,10 |
| *Washbourne | 30-10 | SX 79 54 | 25,24 |
| Washfield | 14a-1 | SS 93 15 | 34,39 |
| 'Little Washfield' | 7- — | — — — | 32,9 |
| Washford Pyne | 7-44 | SS 81 11 | 20,6. 24,5. 36,21–23 |
| *Waspley | 7-19 | SS 88 19 | 52,43 |
| (Way) | 18-16 | SX 49 89 | Exon. 288 b 2 (= 16,7) |
| *Little Weare | 4-8 | SS 48 23 | 42,5 |
| Weare Giffard | 4-10 | SS 47 21 | 35,10 |
| Webbery | 5-12 | SS 49 26 | 48,1 |
| *Wederige* | — — | — — — | 15,53 |
| Wedfield | 11-3 | SS 35 17 | 15,33 |
| Week (in Thornbury) | 11-23 | SS 38 07 | 52,26 |
| Week: | | | |
|   Germansweek | 18-6 | SX 43 94 | 16,8 |
|   Southweek | 18-8 | SX 43 93 | 34,1 |
| Welcombe | 3a-9 | SS 22 18 | 3,90 |
| Well, see Edginswell, Coffinswell | | | |
| Wembworthy | 12-14 | SS 66 09 | 16,57 |
| Werrington (CORNWALL) | 11-65 | SX 32 87 | 1,50. Exon. 178 b 2 (see Ch. 5 note and Exon. Notes after 5,5 note). Exon. Tax Return 65 a 3 (= 1,50) |
| Westleigh (near Bideford) | 5-9 | SS 47 28 | 28,6 |
| Westleigh (near Burlescombe) | 10-3 | ST 06 17 | 41,2 |
| Weston *alias* Waringstone, see River Otter | | | |
| Weston Peverell | 25-21 | SX 45 57 | 17,73 |
| Weycroft | 17a-14 | SY 30 99 | 34,52;(57) |
| Whiddon | 1a-39 | SS 55 38 | 42,8 |
| Whimple | 20b-8 | SY 04 97 | 16,94. 19,20. 39,10 |
| Whipton | 19a-25 | SX 95 93 | 19,38 |
| Whitchurch | 25-3 | SX 49 72 | 35,29 |
| Whitefield (in Challacombe) | 2-16 | SS 67 41 | 3,34 |
| Whitefield (in High Bray) | 2-26 | SS 70 36 | 3,30 |
| Whitefield (in Marwood) | 1a-35 | SS 55 39 | 28,9 |
| Whitestone (near Exeter) | 19a-23 | SX 86 93 | 16,125;137. 22,2 |
| Whiteway | 23-26 | SX 88 75 | 16,157 |
| Whitford | 22-13 | SY 25 95 | 1,54 |
| Whitleigh | 25-14 | SX 47 59 | 17,76. 28,16 |
| (Whitley) | 22-7 | SY 17 97 | Exon. T.O. 503 a 9 (see Exon. Notes Ch. 44) |
| Whitnage | 9-7 | ST 02 15 | 25,22 |
| West Whitnole | 7-22 | SS 88 18 | 47,13 |
| Whitstone | 6-14 | SS 65 26 | 16,82 |
| Cookbury Wick | 11-28 | SS 38 05 | 28,3 |
| (Widefield) (in Inwardleigh) | 11-59 | SX 55 96 | Exon. T.O. 496 a 5 (= 39,6) |
| Widey | 25-19 | (SX 48 58) | 28,16 |
| Widworthy | 22-4 | SY 21 99 | 36,26 |
| Willand | 10-14 | ST 03 10 | 42,24 |
| Willestrew | 18-41 | SX 43 78 | 28,2 |
| Willsworthy | 25-1 | SX 53 81 | 39,1 |
| Wilmington | 22-3 | SY 21 99 | 16,173. 36,26 |
| Wilson (in Witheridge) | 7-25 | SS 83 17 | 16,146 |
| Winkleigh | 12-16 | SS 63 08 | 1,64. Exon. Tax Return 66 b 2 (= 1,64) |
| Winscott (in Peters Marland) | 4-35 | (SS 49 12) | 35,15 |

|  | Map | Grid | Text |
|---|---|---|---|
| Winsham | 1a-36 | SS 49 38 | 3,43 |
| Winston | 26-30 | SX 55 51 | 15,30 |
| Winswell | 4-31 | SS 49 13 | 35,16 |
| Witheridge | 7-35 | SS 80 14 | 1,32 |
| Withycombe Raleigh | 14c-22 | SY 02 82 | 24,3 |
| Wolborough | 29b-1 | SX 85 70 | 16,163 |
| Wolfin, see River 'Nymet' | | | |
| Wollaton | 26-25 | SX 55 52 | 17,85 |
| 'Womberford' | 22- — | — — — | 15,24 |
| Wonford (in Heavitree) | 19a-40 | SX 94 91 | 1,28 |
| Wonford (in Thornbury) | 11-16 | SS 37 09 | 35,3 |
| Woodbeare | 15-21 | ST 05 04 | 25,13 |
| Woodburn | 7-2 | SS 86 23 | 16,151 |
| Woodbury | 14c-13 | SY 00 87 | 1,33 |
| Woodcombe | 30-31 | SX 78 37 | 23,24 |
| Woodford | 26-11 | SX 52 56 | 17,105 |
| Woodhuish | 29b-30 | SX 91 52 | 30,1 |
| Woodleigh | 28-23 | SX 73 48 | 28,13 |
| Woolacombe | 1a-13 | SS 45 43 | 19,11. 36,15 |
| Woolfardisworthy (in Hartland) | 3a-6 | SS 33 21 | 52,4 |
| Woolfardisworthy (near Witheridge) | 7-52 | SS 82 08 | 21,12 |
| Woolladon | 4-53 | SS 52 07 | 16,38 |
| Woolleigh (in Beaford) | 4-23 | SS 53 16 | 16,41 |
| Woolleigh (in Bovey Tracey) | 23-13 | SX 80 80 | 3,8 |
| *Woolston | 28-35 | SX 71 41 | 17,47 |
| Worlington (in Instow) | 5-5 | SS 48 30 | 3,18 |
| Worlington (near Witheridge) | 7-38 | SS 77 13 | 3,81. 20,7. 42,21 |
| Worth | 14a-2 | SS 94 14 | 21,14 |
| Worthele | 27-12 | SX 62 54 | 17,59 |
| Worthy (? in Rackenford) | 7-17 | SS 84 19 | 16,145 |
| Worthygate | 4-4 | (SS 36 23) | 5,7 |
| Wray | 23-4 | SX 77 84 | 52,16 |
| (Wringworthy) | 18-45 | SX 50 77 | Exon. 317 b 3 (= 17,13) |
| Wyke Green (in Axminster) | 17a-17 | SY 29 96 | 52,24 |
| Wyke (in Shobrooke) | 14b-12 | SX 87 99 | 15,3 |
| Yarcombe | 17a-2 | ST 24 08 | 11,3 |
| Yard (in Ilfracombe) | 1a-9 | (SS 46 45) | 16,83 |
| Yard (in Rose Ash) | 7-7 | SS 77 21 | 16,142 |
| Yard (in Silverton) | 15-30 | (ST 97 01) | 47,10 |
| Yarnscombe | 3b-3 | SS 56 23 | 16,32. 36,1 |
| Yeadbury | 7-50 | SS 86 10 | 34,36 |
| Yealmpton | 26-31 | SX 57 51 | 1,18 |
| Yowlestone | 7-48 | SS 84 10 | 19,33 |
| Zeal Monachorum, see River 'Nymet' | | | |

## 2. PLACES NOT NAMED IN DOMESDAY BOOK
(Main entries only are included, not subdivisions of a named holding)
- 3,32  1 virgate which lay in Braunton (1,5) before and after 1066, claimed by the Bishop of Coutances. [Exon. names this as Boode]
- 3,71  1 hide held by Drogo from the Bishop of Coutances.
- 24,22  1 virgate belonging to Iddesleigh (1,63), held by Walter of Claville.
- 29,10  2 villagers on the land of St. Peter's of Plympton, held by Robert Bastard.
- 34,57  ½ virgate added to Weycroft (34,52), held by Roger from Ralph of Pomeroy.
- 51,4  1 virgate held by Ralph from William (the Usher).
- 52,30  ½ virgate held by Alward Mart.

## 3. PLACES NOT IN DEVON
Names starred are in Index 1 above; others are in the indices of Persons or of Churches and Clergy. Words in italics refer to people found only in Exon.

*Elsewhere in Britain*
| | |
|---|---|
| CORNWALL | Bodmin ... Priests; Landinner*; Maker*; Trebeigh*; Werrington*. |
| DORSET | Cranborne ... *Abbot*, Church; Horton ... *Abbot*, Church; Thorncombe*. |
| HAMPSHIRE | Winchester C 4. |
| HEREFORDSHIRE | *Hereford ... Robert.* |
| MIDDLESEX | London C 4. |
| SOMERSET | Churchstanton*; Glastonbury ... *Abbot*, Church; Montacute ... Ansger. |
| SUSSEX | Battle ... Abbey, Abbot, Church, Monks. |
| YORKSHIRE | York C 4. |

*Outside Britain*
The départements to which French places belong are given under the first occurrence of the name either in the Exon. or in the General Notes.

Arques ... *Haimeric*
Aumale ... Robert
Beaumont ... *Robert*
Bruyère ... *Ralph*
Bully ... Roger
Burgundy ... *Walter*
Caen ... *Abbess, Abbot*, Churches
Carteret ... *Mauger*
Claville ... Walter
Coutances ... Bishop
Dol ... *Hugh*
Douai ... Walter/Walscin
Épaignes ... see 'Spain'
Eu ... William
Falaise ... William
Feugères ... Ralph
Flanders ... *Roger*
Helléan ... Hervey, his wife
Lestre ... *William*
Limesy ... Ralph

Meulles ... Roger
Mohun (Moyon) ... William
Mont St. Michel ... Abbot, Church, Monks
Mortain ... Count
Néville ... *Richard*
Omonville ... *Walter*
Poilley ... William
Poitou ... *William*
Pomeroy ... Ralph
Pont-Chardon ... Robert
Rennes ... *Hugh*
Rouen ... *Canons*, Church
Sacey ... Osbern, *Osbert*
Senarpont ... *Ansger*
'Spain' (Épaignes) ... Alfred
Tilly ... *Ralph*
Trelly ... *Geoffrey*
Vautortes ... *Reginald*
Vauville ... William

## 4. IDENTITIES OF UNNAMED DB HOLDINGS OR OF UNNAMED SUBDIVISIONS OF NAMED DB HOLDINGS

Index 1 lists the identifications of DB places as printed in the Translation. The present index contains two categories of place-names found in the General Notes: (a) the identification of main holdings that DB does not name or for which another name was later used; (b) the names of subdivisions of DB holdings. Many DB entries refer to a large number of hides by a single place-name, although these hides must have contained many separate named settlements: this index lists the place-names that later evidence shows were included in the DB holding. In both cases the evidence is of varying certainty.

Places starred are also found in Place Index 1 above, since a named main DB holding also lay there in 1086.

In place-names beginning with the French feminine definite article, such as *La Fenne*, the article is disregarded in indexing.

| | | | |
|---|---|---|---|
| Accott | 2,11 note | Bickington (near Ashburton) | 2,19 note |
| Addiscott | 1,29 note | Birch | 1,64 note |
| Affeton | 1,3. 21,9-12 notes | Bishopsleigh | 2,2 note |
| Alfardisworthy | 19,2 note | Blackaton | 16,163 note |
| Alfordon | 16,3 note | Blackberry | 1,9 note |
| Allaleigh | 17,48 note | Blagdon | 17,15 note |
| 'Allen Wood' | 14,3-4 note | Blatchworthy | 47,13 note |
| North Aller | 42,12-13 note | Blinsham | 36,7 note |
| Allerford | 17,4 note | Bolealler | 32,3 note |
| Allhallows | 34,20 note | Boohay | 23,16 note |
| *Als* | 40,2 note | Borcombe | 34,54 note |
| Alscott | 15,39 note | Boringdon | 1,17 note |
| Alston (in Holbeton) | 17,67 note | Borough (in Chivelstone) | 17,53 note |
| Annery | Ch. 5. 5,6 notes | Borough (in Mortehoe) | 31,3-4 note |
| Applethorn Slade | 1,7 note | Bosomzeal | 1,34 note |
| Seven Ash | 3,36 note | Bottreaux Mill | 1,41 note |
| Ash (in Iddesleigh) | 1,63 note | *Bovystok* | 2,11 note |
| 'Ash' (? in Cullompton) | 9,1 note | Bowden (in Cheriton Bishop) | 16,130 note |
| Chapel Ashe | 16,164 note | Bowden (in Totnes) | 1,34 note |
| 'Ashford' (in Mamhead) | 52,48 note | Bowerhayes | 34,25 note |
| *Ashforde* (? in Kentisbeare) | 51,7 note | *Bowley | 9,1 note |
| Ashridge | 12,1 note | Bradham | 1,9. Ch. 9 notes |
| Ashwell | 1,15 note | Bradiford | 24,28 note |
| *Asselonde* | 16,140 note | *Bray (in South Molton) | 1,41 note |
| *Assh*, see *Choldasshe* | | Little Bray (in Charles) | 3,30 note |
| *Assh* | 40,2 note | South Bray (in Chittlehampton) | 1,41 note |
| Atworthy | 34,6 note | Brenton | 1,4 note |
| *Ayneshill* | 15,44 note | *Brexworthy | 34,6 note |
| 'Azores' | 5,1 note | Bridge (in North Tawton) | 16,56 note |
| Babcombe | 34,44 note | Brightlycott | 16,65 note |
| East Barton (in Horwood) | 34,8 note | 'Brightston' | 1,56. 43,2 notes |
| West Barton (in Horwood) | 3,17 note | Brisworthy | 17,79-82 note |
| Batshorne | 15,23 note | Broadridge | 1,9. 35,24 notes |
| Batsworthy | 42,21 note | Brockhill | 1,56 note |
| *Battisborough | 6,7-8 note | Broomford | 5,4 note |
| Bealy | 16,140 note | Broomscott | 2,11 note |
| Beaples Barton | 23,10-11 note | Brownstone (in Brixham) | 23,16 note |
| Beara (in Rose Ash) | 16,142 note | Brownstone (? in Newton Ferrers) | 15,37 note |
| Beardon | 39,1 note | *Bruckland | 16,164 note |
| Beare (in Broad Clyst) | 1,56 note | *La Brunthuchene* | 34,16 note |
| Bearscombe | 24,18 note | Buckerell | 34,23 note |
| Beckett | 17,12 note | | |
| *Beden* | 25,16 note | | |
| Bellamarsh | 34,44 note | | |
| Benley | 16,140 note | | |

## Places 4

| | | | |
|---|---|---|---|
| Buckfastleigh | 6,13 note | Colleton | 16,140 note |
| *Buckland (in Thurlestone) | 17,36 note | Colley | 16,119-120 note |
| Budbrooke | 1,28 note | Colmer | 24,20 note |
| Budleigh Salterton | 1,9 note | Colston | 3,73 note |
| Bunson | 16,140 note | Colyford | 1,13 note |
| Burdon | 16,19 note | Challons Combe | 35,26 note |
| Burrough | 52,15 note | Combe (in Aveton Giffard) | 35,26 note |
| Buskin | 16,18 note | Combe (in Bigbury) | 15,44 note |
| Buston, see Buskin | | Combe (in Cornwood) | 15,36 note |
| Bystock | 1,46 note | Combe Lancey | 2,2 note |
| Cadbury (in Chulmleigh) | 16,140 note | Combe Pafford | 2,7-8 note |
| Cadover | 17,79-82 note | Comberoy | 49,3 note |
| *Calchurch* | 16,137 note | Compton Pool | 2,18 note |
| Campscott | 3,46 note | Cookbury | 28,3 note |
| Canworthy | 16,148 note | Coombe (in Puddington) | 19,39. 50,4 notes |
| Carey | 1,50 note | Coombe (in Witheridge) | 50,4 note |
| Casehayes | 1,11 note | Coombeland | 36,20 note |
| Catshayes | 16,97-100;102 note | Corscombe | 16,14 note |
| Caulston | 17,68 note | Corstone | 16,26;28;30 note |
| Champson | 3,61 note | Countess Wear, see Wear | |
| Chapner | 3,80 note | Cove | 1,35 note |
| Charlecombe | 48,4;10 notes | Cowley | 3,67. 24,2 notes |
| Chawleigh Week, see Week | | Coxleigh | 16,65 note |
| | | Coxwell | 39,5 note |
| 'Chawlmoor' | 3,74 note | Crackaway | 3,40-41 note |
| Chelsdon | 52,5-6 note | Crannaford | 1,56 note |
| Chenson | 16,43 note | Crebor | 5,1;4 notes |
| Chieflowman | 1,70 note | *Lower Creedy | Ch. 44 note |
| Chillaton | 5,2 note | Crockadon | 1,34 note |
| Chilton (in Thorverton) | 1,7. 44,2 notes | 'Crossworthy' | 17,15 note |
| Chittlehamholt | 52,10 note | Cruft | 16,22 note |
| *Chochele* | 15,44 note | Cudliptown | 5,1 note |
| *Choldasshe* | 25,8-9 note | *Cullompton | 1,7 note |
| Chollaton | 35,9 note | Cutland | 16,140 note |
| Christow | 16,106;128 notes | Cutton | 16,90 note |
| Churchstowe | 6,9 note | Daccombe | Ch. 5. 5,12-13 notes |
| Cleeve | 1,23 note | Dainton | 7,2. 33,1 notes |
| Clifton | 23,22 note | Dalditch | 1,9 note |
| Clotworthy | 3,56-57 note | Dartmoor | 1,2 note |
| Bishops Clyst | 3,7 note | Dartmouth | 23,22 note |
| Clyst Honiton | 2,15-17 note | Dene (in West Down) | 3,26 note |
| *Clyst St. Mary | Ch. 44 note | Deptford (in Hartland) | 52,31 note |
| *La Clyve* | 1,44 note | Deptford (in Cruwys Morchard) | 36,21-23 note |
| Cobden | 19,20 note | | |
| Cockesputt | 16,95 note | Dennington (in Swimbridge) | 2,11 note |
| Cocktree | 51,2 note | | |
| Cofflete | 1,18 note | Dexbeer | 34,2 note |
| Colbrook | 9,1 note | Dimworthy | 34,6 note |
| Colcombe | 1,13 note | Dinnaton (in Swimbridge) | 2,11 note |
| Coldethorn | 52,20 note | Doddiscombe | 23,5 note |
| Colebrook (in Plympton St. Mary) | 1,17 note | *Dodscott | 42,6 note |
| | | Dornaford | 16,18 note |
| Colebrooke (near Crediton) | 2,2 note | Dorsley | 1,34 note |
| | | Dorweeke | 47,9 note |
| *Colebrooke (in Cullompton) | Ch. 5 note | *Doune*, see *Stevenedon* | |
| | | West Down (in Bradworthy) | 34,6 note |
| *Colewilhilt* | 15,44 note | | |
| Colhays | 25,14;21 notes | Dowrich | 2,2 note |
| Collacott | 1,64 note | Drascombe | 1,28 note |
| Collaton (in Halwell) | 1,34 note | Duvale | 23,5 note |
| Collaton St. Mary | 2,18 note | Earlscombe | 15,75 note |

## Places 4

| | | | |
|---|---|---|---|
| Eastacombe | 16,23 note | Hardingsleigh | 16,43 note |
| Eastbrook | 24,30 note | Hardisworthy | 36,3-4 note |
| Eastdown | 17,15 note | 'Hardness' | 23,22 note |
| Easton | 52,11 note | Harford (in Landkey) | 2,11 note |
| Ebberly | 3,19 note | Harpford | 1,9. 11,1. 52,35 notes |
| Mount Edgecumbe | 1,20-22 note | | |
| Edmeston | 15,26;28;64 notes | Harrowbeer | Ch. 21 note |
| Eggesford | 16,57 note | Haske | 3,72 note |
| Ernsborough, see Irishborough | | Hatch | 17,32 note |
| *Estelleia* | 11,1 note | Haukadon | 1,50 note |
| *Estwere* | 3,39. 36,11 notes | Hawkerland | 23,5 note |
| Exbridge | 23,5 note | Hawson | 1,34 note |
| Exton | 34,34 note | Haylake | 16,130 note |
| Fair Oak, see Oak | | Moss Hayne | 16,92 note |
| Great Fairwood | 19,30 note | Hayne (in Bishops Nympton) | 2,21 note |
| *Farwood | 3,85 note | | |
| *La Fenne* | 19,18 note | Hayne (in Brushford) | 16,53-54 note |
| Fernhill (in Clawton) | 17,15 note | Hayne (in Whitestone) | 16,125 note |
| Fishleigh | 5,4 note | Heath Barton | 16,137 note |
| Fludda | 16,155 note | Heazille | 3,68 note |
| Foghangar | 5,2 note | *La Heghland* | 15,22 note |
| Foldhay | 47,2-4 note | Hele (in Bickleigh) | 21,21 note |
| Ford (in Coryton) | 3,9 note | Hele (in Bradninch) | 16,104 note |
| Ford (in Crediton Hamlets) | 2,2 note | Hele (in Clayhanger) | 23,5 note |
| Forde | 16,165 note | Henceford | 1,32 note |
| *Forde* | 15,31 note | Henland | 9,1 note |
| *La Forsen* | 15,52 note | Henstill | 2,2 note |
| France | 16,101 note | Hernaford | 20,17 note |
| 'Freemancott' | 24,6 note | 'Hetherland' | 11,1 note |
| *Frieland* | 32,3 note | Highweek | 1,10 note |
| *Frodetone* | 16,78 note | 'Hill' (? in Colyton) | 21,15. 51,10 notes |
| Fursdon | 19,24 note | Hill (in Farringdon) | 34,34 note |
| Furze (in Shobrooke) | 36,19 note | Hill (in Iddesleigh) | 1,63 note |
| Furzehill | 19,16 note | 'Hill' (? in Merton) | 24,6 note |
| *Fytelecoth'* | 42,9 note | Hill (in Withycombe Raleigh) | 1,9 note |
| Gabwell | 16,117. 48,3 notes | | |
| Garland | 16,140 note | 'Hinton' | 1,44 note |
| Godford | 19,26;32 notes | Hiscott | 1,40. 25,3. 40,2 notes |
| *Godwynescoth* | 52,9 note | | |
| Goodameavy | 17,79-82 note | Hockford Waters | 23,7 note |
| Gorlofen | 17,86-87 note | Holbeton | 1,23 note |
| Gratton (in Meavy) | 17,79-82 note | Holcombe (in Dawlish) | Ch. 2. 2,4-6. 16,131 notes |
| Greendale | 1,33 note | | |
| Greendown (in Warkleigh) | 1,41 note | Holditch | 23,17 note |
| | | *Holleham* | 1,4 note |
| Greendown (in Northlew) | 35,7 note | Hollocombe | 1,64 note |
| Grendon | 42,19 note | *Holne | 1,34. Ch. 5 notes |
| Grilstone | 2,21 note | Holwell | 15,44 note |
| Grindle Brook | 1,33 note | Nether Holwells | 1,56 note |
| Halford | 16,14 note | Clyst Honiton, see Clyst | |
| Halmpstone | 2,11 note | Hoo Meavy, see Meavy | |
| Halsdon (in Cookbury) | 28,3 note | Hood | 20,15 note |
| Halsdon (in Dolton) | 42,7 note | Hoodown | 17,29 note |
| Halsford | 1,28 note | Hook (in Okehampton) | 16,3 note |
| 'Halswill' | 1,23 note | Hookedrise | 19,27 note |
| *Hamsworthy | 34,2 note | Hookney | 52,44 note |
| Handsford (in Bondleigh) | 3,20 note | Hookway | 2,2 note |
| Handsford (in Chawleigh) | 16,140 note | Horner | 1,15 note |
| Hannaborough | 5,4 note | Horridge | 19,29. 32,6-7 notes |
| Harberton | 1,34 note | Horswell | 39,15 note |
| Harbertonford | 1,34 note | Houghton | 15,44 note |

# Places 4

| | | | |
|---|---|---|---|
| Houndbeare | 14,3-4. 16,136 notes | Luton | 2,4-6 note |
| Howton | 1,45 note | Lutton | 15,36 note |
| Hudson | 34,2 note | Lydcott | 16,14 note |
| Hurdwick | 5,1 note | Lymbury | 1,56 note |
| Iddlecott | 40,7 note | Lymscott | 34,6 note |
| *Ieclescombe* | 15,44 note | Lyneham | 1,18 note |
| Incledon | 3,43.19,12-13 notes | Maddaford | 16,22 note |
| Irishborough | 2,11 note | Madford | 1,8. 19,36 notes |
| Jacobstowe | Ch. 4. 5,4 notes | 'Magdalene' | 34,9 note |
| Jewelscombe | 15,44 note | Maidenford | 3,3 note |
| Julian | 35,9 note | Mansley | 36,3-4 notes |
| Jurston | 16,61-62;64 note | Marlcombe | 25,14;16 note |
| Kempthorne | 17,15 note | Marley | 20,14 note |
| Kenbury | 1,4 note | Marshall | Ch. 2. 2,4-6 notes |
| Kendon | 52,44 note | Marshford | 5,4 note |
| Kennerleigh | 2,2 note | Marwell | 17,65 note |
| Kennicott | 17,15 note | Maristow | 39,19-20 note |
| Kerscott | 2,21 note | *Matford | 1,43 note |
| Kerswell (in Hatherleigh) | 5,4 note | Meadwell | 16,11 note |
| Kilbury | 1,23. 6,13 notes | Hoo Meavy | 17,79-82 note |
| Killatree | 17,15 note | Meldon | 16,3 note |
| Killerton | 1,56 note | *Membury | 1,11 note |
| Kingsbridge | 6,9 note | Mere | 1,35 note |
| Kingsford | 1,69 note | 'Metherell' | 2,7-8 note |
| Kingston | 1,23 note | Middlecott (in Virginstow) | 17,5 note |
| Kingswear | 23,22 note | | |
| Kingswell | 1,69 note | 'Mill' | 52,11 note |
| Kipscott | 2,21 note | Millsome | 47,2-4 note |
| Kismeldon | 28,4 note | Minchingdown | 20,8-9 note |
| South Knighton | 2,20 note | Monkerton | 1,52 note |
| Knightstone | 2,2 note | Monkton (near Honiton) | 1,13 note |
| Knowle | 2,2 note | 'Monkton' (in Shobrooke and in Thorverton) | 2,2 note |
| *Kynetete* | 34,16 note | | |
| '*Kynewardesbergh*' | 1,56 note | Monyeston | 16,78 note |
| *Lamsede* | 52,53 note | 'Moor' (? in Clyst Honiton) | 15,20 note |
| Landkey | 2,11 note | Moor (? in Pyworthy) | 17,15;18 notes |
| Lane | 36,2. 42,3 notes | Moorstone | 51,14 note |
| Langabeare | 5,4 note | Morwell | 5,1 note |
| Langham | 15,70 note | Morwellham | 5,1 note |
| Langley (in Cadeleigh) | 1,9 note | Narracott | 5,10 note |
| Langston | 17,65 note | 'Nethercote' | 19,10 note |
| Lapland | 1,15;55 notes | Netherton (in Farway) | 24,17 note |
| Larcombe | 28,12 note | Netherton (in Haccombe with Combe) | 19,10 note |
| Lea | 23,5;7 notes | | |
| Lee | 16,83 note | Newcott | 16,124 note |
| Leigham | 17,69;75 notes | Newenham | 1,11 note |
| Leworthy | 17,15 note | Newland (in Bradworthy) | 3,86-87;89 notes |
| Ley (in Bere Ferrers) | 15,46 note | Newland (in Cullompton) | 1,7 note |
| Ley (in North Huish) | 15,27 note | Newland (in Landkey and in Swimbridge) | 2,11 note |
| 'Littlecombe' | 15,36 note | | |
| 'Longacre' | 1,56 note | Newland (in North Tawton) | 16,56 note |
| Lovacott (in Fremington) | 34,8 note | | |
| Lovaton | 29,9 note | Newnham | 16,140 note |
| *Loventor | 2,18 note | Osborne Newton | 39,15 note |
| Lovistone | 25,2 note | Newton (in Zeal Monachorum) | 16,48-49 note |
| Luffincott | 35,5 note | | |
| 'Lurcombe' | 2,19 note | Newton Abbot | 1,10. 16,163 notes |
| Lurley | 1,35 note | Newton Poppleford | 16,136 note |
| Luscombe (in Harberton) | 20,17 note | Noddon | 15,44 note |
| Lustleigh | 23,15 note | Northcombe | 16,5 note |

# Places 4

| | | | |
|---|---|---|---|
| Northcote (in Burrington) | 5,8 note | *Rapshays | 25,15 note |
| Northcote (in Cruwys Morchard) | 3,73. 19,35 notes | Rawstone | 2,21 note |
| | | Reddaway | 16,14 note |
| Northcott (in Ashreigney) | 25,5 note | Ridgeway | 1,17 note |
| Northcott (in Luffincott) | 35,5 note | Ringmoor | 21,21 note |
| *Northwill* | 48,2 note | Ringwell | 19,38 note |
| Norton (in Dartmouth) | 23,22 note | Lower Rixtail | 2,4-6 note |
| Norton (in Newton St. Cyres) | Ch. 2. 2,2 notes | 'Roborough' (near Tavistock) | Ch. 5. 5,1 notes |
| Nutley | 5,1 note | *Roborough (near Great Torrington) | 5,8 note |
| Fair Oak | 34,50 note | | |
| Oar Stone, see Stone | | Rocknell | 24,30 note |
| Oburnford | 1,70 note | *Rokewrth*' | 16,14 note |
| Odham | 5,10 note | Rollstone | 16,129 note |
| Ogbere | 5,1 note | Rolstone | 2,2 note |
| 'Orchard' | 16,9-10 note | Rosamondford | 49,5 note |
| Orleigh | Ch. 5. 5,6 notes | Rowden | 42,19 note |
| *Orway | 19,21 note | Rowhorne | 1,44 note |
| Osborne Newton, see Newton | | Rudge (in Crediton Hamlets) | 2,2 note |
| Venn Ottery | 1,9 note | | |
| *Ottery (in Lamerton) | Ch. 5. 5,3 notes | Rudge (in Morchard Bishop) | 2,2 note |
| Oxen, see White Oxen | | North Russell | 3,86-87 note |
| Padbrook | 1,7 note | St. Giles in the Heath | 1,50 note |
| Pafford, see Combe Pafford | | St. Sidwells | Ch. 2 note |
| Palstone | 6,11-12 note | Saint Hill | 16,101 note |
| Pancrasweek | 34,2 note | *Sakynton* | 2,2 note |
| *Panson | 1,50. Ch. 5 notes | Salcombe | 15,74 note |
| Partridge | 52,11 note | Sandford | 2,2 note |
| Partridge Walls | 16,53-54 note | Sandridge | 2,18 note |
| Paschoe | 2,2 note | Scobchester | 39,7 note |
| Patsford | 36,16 note | Scorriton | 1,34 note |
| Penhorwood | 34,8 note | 'Scotworthy' | 19,2 note |
| Penson | 15,27 note | 'Sedge' | 1,44 note |
| Penstone | 2,2 note | Sepscott | 16,65 note |
| Peterhayes | 11,2-3 note | Sessacott | 19,2 note |
| North Petherwin | 1,50 note | Shaftsboro | 31,3-4 note |
| Petton | 15,57 note | Sharpham | 1,34 note |
| Pidsley | 2,2 note | Sheafhayne | 11,3 note |
| Pippacott | 3,31 note | Sheepsbyre | 16,140 note |
| Poflet | 5,2 note | Sheepstor | 21,21 note |
| Pomeroy | 34,32 note | Sheepwash (in Bishops Nympton) | 2,21 note |
| 'Pool' (? in Stokeinteignhead) | 16,126 note | | |
| Pool Anthony | 1,35. 46,1 notes | Sheepwash (near Shebbear) | 1,39 note |
| Port | 2,21 note | | |
| East Portlemouth | 52,53 note | *Shilstone | 1,26 note |
| *Poulston | 1,34 note | Shute | 16,139 note |
| Preston | 1,41 note | *Sidmouth | 11,1 note |
| Priorton | 2,2 note | Silkland | 15,12 note |
| Pugsley | 1,41 note | *Silverton | 3,68 note |
| Pulworthy | 5,4. 16,19 notes | Slade | 1,3 note |
| Puslinch | 15,37 note | Slade, see Applethorn Slade | |
| Pynamead | 16,140 note | Smallbrook | 2,2 note |
| Pynes | 16,129 note | Smythapark | 16,67-68 note |
| Quither | 5,2 note | *Somerton* | 52,11 note |
| Raddicombe | 30,1-2 note | Southbrook | 1,56 note |
| Radford | 1,17 note | 'Southcombe' | 16,5 note |
| Radsbury | 19,16 note | Southcott (in Morchard Bishop) | 2,2 note |
| 'Radway' | 11,1 note | | |
| Rake | 17,40;42 notes | Southcott (in Winkleigh) | 1,64 note |

# Places 4

| | | | |
|---|---|---|---|
| 'Southteign' | 1,26 note | Titwell | 35,26 note |
| 'Southwood' | 1,7 note | *Tongeslond* | 15,79 note |
| Southwood (in Dawlish) | 1,4. Ch. 2. 2,4-6 notes | 'Torkridge' | 2,21 note |
| | | Torpeek | 15,71 note |
| Sowden | 26,1 note | *Tortysfenne* | 17,48 note |
| Sowton (in Dunsford) | 23,12. 52,47 notes | Tower | 1,30 note |
| Sparhanger | 19,17 note | West Town | 16,125 note |
| *Sparkwell | 2,7-8 note | Towsington | 19,8 note |
| Spittle | 16,140 note | Treable | 52,11 note |
| Staddon (in Cheriton Bishop) | 52,11 note | Treasbeare | 2,15-17 note |
| | | *Trilbehegh* | 34,24 note |
| Staddon (in North Tawton) | 1,3 note | Trill | 16,168 note |
| | | Trobridge | 2,2 note |
| Stancombe (in Harberton) | 1,34 note | Turnham | 16,77 note |
| Standon | 39,1 note | Tythecott | 15,12 note |
| Stantor | 2,18 note | Uggaton | 52,22 note |
| Stapledon | 28,3 note | Upcott (in Cheriton Fitzpaine) | 15,17-18 note |
| Stenhill | 23,9 note | | |
| Stentwood | 34,35 note | Upcott (in Cookbury) | 28,3 note |
| *Stevenedon* | 1,41 note | Upcott (in Dowland) | 1,63 note |
| Stevenstone (in St. Giles in the Wood) | 40,2 note | Upcott (in Thelbridge) | 36,21-23 note |
| | | Uppacott (in Mariansleigh) | 2,21 note |
| Stevenstone (in Upton Pyne) | 24,2 note | | |
| | | Upton (in Cullompton) | 9,1 note |
| Stock | 19,16 note | Upton (in South Milton) | 17,36 note |
| Stokenham | 1,24;34 notes | North Upton (in Thurlestone) | 17,36 note |
| Stockey | 16,39 note | | |
| Stockley | 16,3 note | Upton Pyne | 16,129 note |
| Oar Stone | 15,42 note | Uton | 2,2 note |
| Stone | 16,140 note | Vaglefield | 28,3 note |
| *Stone*, see *Stevenedon* | | Valeridge | 3,74 note |
| Storridge | 39,16 note | Venn (in Brixton) | 15,52 note |
| Stourton | 3,39. 36,11-13; 21-23 notes | Venn (in Chagford) | 16,61-62;64 note |
| | | Venn (in Morchard Bishop) | 2,2 note |
| Stowford (in Bradworthy) | 34,6 note | Venn (in Teignmouth) | 2,4-6 note |
| Stowford (in Swimbridge) | 2,11 note | Venn Channing | Ch. 44 note |
| Stretch | 36,21-23 note | Venn Ottery, see Ottery | |
| Stroxworthy | 16,31 note | Venny Tedburn, see Tedburn | |
| Sutton (in Stockleigh English) | 15,17-18 note | Venton | 20,15 note |
| | | Veraby | 2,21 note |
| Swainstone | 1,23 note | Waddeton | 2,18 note |
| Taddiport | 1,31 note | Waddon | 2,2;4-6 note |
| *Tare* | 25,13 note | Wagland | 1,15;55 notes |
| Taviton | 5,1 note | Waldons | 42,4 note |
| Venny Tedburn | 2,2 note | Wallaford | Ch. 5. 20,13 notes |
| Teignmouth | 2,4-6 note | Walland | 42,3-4 notes |
| 'Teignwick', see Highweek | | Wallon | 16,110 note |
| Tennaton | 1,15 note | Wansley | 3,19 note |
| Thongsleigh | 36,20 note | *Wardeslegh'* | 28,10-11 note |
| *Thoredoghes* | 15,12 note | Warkleigh | 1,41 note |
| Thorn (? in St. Budeaux) | 17,76 note | *Washbourne | 1,34 note |
| Thorndon | 17,12 note | *Waspley | 28,10-11 note |
| North Thorne (in Broadwoodwidger) | 17,12 note | Watercombe | 15,36 note |
| | | Waterhouse | 1,11 note |
| Thorne (in Clannaborough) | 16,52 note | Countess Wear | 1,44 note |
| Thornworthy | 19,16 note | *Little Weare | 15,39 note |
| Thorverton | 1,7 note | Weaver | 9,1 note |
| Tideford | 17,48 note | Week (in Chillaton) | 5,2 note |
| Tinacre | 17,15 note | Week (in Chulmleigh) | 16,140 note |
| 'Titterton' | 1,64. 25,7;13 notes | Week (in North Tawton) | 1,3 note |

## Places 4

| | | | |
|---|---|---|---|
| Chawleigh Week | 16,43 note | Wiscombe | 11,1 note |
| East Week (in South Tawton) | 1,29 note | Within | 49,5 note |
| | | Within Furze | 49,5 note |
| Great Weeke | 1,26 note | Withymore | 17,10;36 notes |
| Welsbeare | 44,2 note | Wolfgar | 52,11 note |
| Wembury | 1,17 note | Wolverstone | 25,14 note |
| Westacombe (in Dunsford) | 16,110 note | 'Wood' | 42,7 note |
| Westacombe (in Inwardleigh) | 16,23;24 notes | Woodbury Salterton | 1,33. 11,1 notes |
| | | Woodcourt | 20,17 note |
| Westacott (in Inwardleigh) | 16,23 note | Woodington | 1,32 note |
| Westacott (in Landkey) | 2,11 note | Woodland (in Crediton Hamlets) | 2,2 note |
| Westacott (in Sampford Courtenay) | 16,14 note | Woodland (in Swimbridge) | 2,11 note |
| Westcott (in Marwood) | 36,16 note | 'Woodmanstone' | 24,18 note |
| Westcott (in Thelbridge) | 36,21-23 note | Woodscombe | 50,4 note |
| *Westecot* | 16,78 note | Woolhanger | 19,16 note |
| Weston (? in Staverton) | 52,52 note | *Woolston | Ch. 5 note |
| Whelmstone | 2,2 note | Worden | 34,6 note |
| South Whimple | 1,56 note | *La Worth* | 34,16 note |
| Whitechapel | 2,21 note | 'Worthy' (? in Chulmleigh) | 16,140 note |
| Whiteheathfield | 32,3. 49,4 notes | Wrangaton | 1,15;55 notes |
| Higher Whiteleigh | 1,37 note | *Wryngoldon* | 15,44 note |
| White Oxen | 20,14 note | West Wyke (in South Tawton) | 1,29 note |
| Whitham | 5,1 note | | |
| Whitsleigh | 40,2 note | *Wyneslegh* | 35,15 note |
| Whitwell | 1,13 note | *Wytefeld* | 40,2 note |
| Whympston | 15,64 note | Yalberton | 2,18 note |
| Widcombe | Ch. 44. 48,12 notes | *Yales* | 3,65-66 note |
| Widecombe in the Moor | 34,46 note | Yarde | 17,40 note |
| Willeswell | 35,16 note | 'Yarnscombe' | 34,55 note |
| Willey | 16,14 note | Yendacott | 24,2;4 notes |
| Wilson (in Cheriton Bishop) | 52,11 note | Yenne Park | 39,4 note |
| | | 'Yeo' | 2,2 note |
| Wilson (in East Worlington) | 42,21 note | Yeoford | 2,2 note |
| | | Yettington | 1,9 note |
| Windbow | 11,1 note | Yondercott | 23,9 note |
| Winscott (in Pyworthy) | 17,15 note | Youngcott | 5,2 note |

# THE MAPS
# AND
# THE MAP KEYS

# MAPS AND MAP KEYS

For reasons explained at the end of the Appendix, Devon places are mapped in the 'modern' Hundreds that survived into the nineteenth century. On the Maps and in the Map Keys, detached portions of Hundreds are distinguished by letters (a, b, c, etc.) after the figure for the Hundred. Where possible on the Maps, single detached places are directed by an arrow to the main body of their Hundred and numbered with it.

The Devon Hundreds with the modern names and the number of the corresponding Tax Return Hundreds (see the Appendix) are as follows:

| | *'Modern' Hundred* | *Tax Return Hundred* |
|---|---|---|
| 1 | Braunton | ⎫ vi Braunton and Shirwell |
| 2 | Shirwell | ⎭ |
| 3 | Hartland | ii Hartland |
| 4 | Shebbear | v Merton |
| 5 | Fremington | iv Fremington |
| 6 | South Molton | vii South Molton |
| 7 | Witheridge | x Witheridge |
| 8 | Bampton | xxii Bampton and xv Uffculme |
| 9 | Tiverton | xi Tiverton |
| 10 | Halberton | xvii Halberton |
| 11 | Black Torrington | iii Torrington |
| 12 | North Tawton | ix Tawton |
| 13 | Crediton | viii Crediton |
| 14 | Budleigh | xvi Budleigh |
| 15 | Hayridge | xiii Silverton |
| 16 | Hemyock | xiv Hemyock |
| 17 | Axminster | xix Axminster and xxi Axmouth |
| 18 | Lifton (and Tavistock) | i Lifton |
| 19 | Wonford | xxxi Wonford |
| 20 | Cliston | xii Cliston |
| 21 | Ottery St. Mary | xviii Ottery |
| 22 | Colyton | xx Colyton |
| 23 | Teignbridge | xxiv Teignton |
| 24 | Exminster | xxiii Exminster |
| 25 | Roborough | xxix Walkhampton |
| 26 | Plympton | xxviii Plympton |
| 27 | Ermington | xxx *Alleriga* |
| 28 | Stanborough | xxvi Diptford |
| 29 | Haytor | xxv Kerswell |
| 30 | Coleridge | xxvii Chillington |

Apart from dots, the following symbols indicate places on the Maps:

- ○    A place in another county in 1086, all being later transferred into Devon (see Introductory Note 4 on the County Boundary).
- +    Places that are members of a Hundred (Tavistock) created after 1086. They are mapped here in their 1086 Hundred (Lifton 18), marked with a cross in the Map Keys and discussed in the Appendix.
- □    Places only mentioned in the Exon. Book. The symbol is repeated beside the entry in the Map Keys below.

Places starred in the Map Keys are tithings of another Hundred (see Tithings note in the Appendix). The bracketed figure is that of their actual Hundred, although they are mapped in the Hundred in which they lie geographically. (T) here stands for Tavistock Hundred.

The County Boundary is marked on the Maps by thick lines, continuous for 1086, broken where uncertain, dotted for the modern (pre-1974) boundary. Hundred boundaries are marked by thin lines, broken where uncertain.

National Grid 10-kilometre squares are shown on the map borders. Each four-figure square covers 1 square kilometre or 247 acres, approximately 2 hides at 120 acres to the hide.

County Names in brackets after a place-name in the Map Keys are those of the modern (pre-April 1974) counties to which places that were in Devon in 1086 were subsequently transferred.

The Devon Hundreds are numbered from West to East working Southwards on the Maps; within each Hundred, places are numbered in the same manner, but listed alphabetically in the Keys.

In 1086 Devon had isolated outlying portions at Maker (within Cornwall) and Thorncombe (within Dorset). Both were transferred away from Devon in the last century.

# DEVON NORTHERN HUNDREDS

DEVON EASTERN HUNDREDS

DEVON WEST CENTRAL HUNDREDS

DEVON SOUTHERN HUNDREDS

# DEVON HUNDREDS AND MAP KEYS

## 1 Braunton
- 1a 43 Ash
- 52 Aylescott
- 25 Ashford
- 57 Barnstaple
- 38 Beara Charter
- 50 Benton
- 5 Berrynarbor
- 26 Bittadon
- 48 Blakewell
- 37 Boode □
- 18 Bradwell
- 45 Bratton Fleming
- 46 Braunton
- 23 Bridwick
- 29 North Buckland
- 42 Buckland
- 30 Churchill
- 6 Combe Martin
- 31 Croyde
- 27 East Down
- 19 West Down
- 33 Georgeham
- 56 Goodleigh
- 4 Hagginton
- 49 Haxton
- 51 Heanton Punchardon
- 3 Hele
- 32 Hole
- 16 Hollacombe
- 2 Ilfracombe
- 15 Kentisbury
- 11 Lincombe
- 41 Lobb
- 44 Marwood
- 34 Metcombe
- 8 Mortehoe
- 12 Mullacott
- 21 Northcote
- 14 Ossaborough
- 22 Patchole
- 28 *Pickwell (2)
- 53 Pilland
- 54 Pilton
- 55 Raleigh
- 17 Roadway
- 40 Saunton
- 24 *Spreacombe (2)
- 20 Stowford
- 7 Tattiscombe
- 1 Trentishoe
- 47 Varley
- 10 Warcombe
- 39 Whiddon
- 35 Whitefield
- 36 Winsham
- 13 *Woolacombe (2)
- 9 Yard

### 1b
- 5 Brayley
- 4 East Buckland
- 3 West Buckland
- 6 Filleigh
- 1 Furze
- 2 Stoodleigh

## 2 Shirwell
- 17 Arlington
- 14 'Badgworthy'
- 29 High Bray
- 6 Brendon
- 20 Buscombe
- 19 Challacombe
- 30 Charles
- 9 Cheriton
- 11 'Lank Combe'
- 2 Countisbury
- 25 Gratton
- 4 Caffyns Heanton
- 8 Ilkerton
- 7 Killington
- 22 Loxhore
- 5 Lyn
- 1 Lynton
- 3 Martinhoe
- 10 Middleton
- 28 Mockham
- 12 Parracombe
- 21 Plaistow
- 15 'Radworthy'
  *Standone*
- 13 Rowley
- 24 Shirwell
- 27 Stoke Rivers
- 18 Twitchen
- 23 Wallover
- 16 Whitefield
  (in Challacombe)
- 26 Whitefield
  (in High Bray)

## 3 Hartland
- 3a 8 Alminstone
- 11 Ashmansworthy
- 4 Bucks Cross
- 3 Clovelly
- 2 Hartland
- 7 South Hole
- 10 Meddon
- 5 Milford
- 1 Stoke
- 9 Welcombe
- 6 Woolfardisworthy

### 3b
- 1 Delley
- 2 Langley
- 3 Yarnscombe

## 4 Shebbear
- 2 Abbotsham
- 38 Allisland
- 5 Alwington
- 50 Ash
- 29 Beaford
- 3 Bideford
- 47 Brimblecombe
- 13 Buckland Brewer
- 43 Buckland Filleigh
- 26 Bulkworthy
- 15 Culleigh
- 32 Dunsbeare
- 16 Frithelstock
- 17 Frizenham
- 19 Galsworthy
  *Hame*
- 24 Hankford
- 49 Hartleigh
- 44 West Heanton
- 39 Heanton Satchville
- 54a Hele (in Petrockstowe)
- 54b Hele (in Meeth)
  *Helescane*

## DEVON HUNDREDS AND MAP KEYS

**4 Shebbear** (cont'd.)
22 Hollam
40 Huish
9 Huxhill
52 Iddesleigh
7 Landcross
25 Langtree
6 Littleham
48 Lovacott
36 Little Marland
30 Peters Marland
51 Meeth
37 Merton
14 Monkleigh
33 Newton St. Petrock
1 Northam
12 Parkham
45 Petrockstowe
28 Potheridge
18 East Putford
11 Sedborough
42 Shebbear
20 Smytham
27 Speccott
46 Stockleigh
21 Little Torrington
34 Twigbeare
41 Varleys
8 Little Weare
10 Weare Giffard
35 Winscott
31 Winswell
53 Woolladon
23 Woolleigh
4 Worthygate

**5 Fremington**
14 Alverdiscott
19 Barlington
3 Bickleton
17 Dodscott
10 Eastleigh
1 Fremington
2 Hollowcombe
11 Horwood
5 Huish
15 Huntshaw
4 Instow
13 Newton Tracey
20 Owlacombe
18 Roborough
7 Tapeley
8 Tawstock
15 Great Torrington
21 Villavin
12 Webbery
9 Westleigh
5 Worlington

**6 South Molton**
11 Aller
13b East Anstey
13a West Anstey
18 Blackpool
15 Bray
6 Bremridge
16 Chittlehampton
12 Hacche
20 Honiton
22 Knowstone
9 Molland (near West Anstey)
2 Molland
  (in North Molton)
7 North Molton
19 South Molton
17 Newton
  *Nimete*
24 George Nympton
4 Praunsley
8 Pulham
1 Radworthy
10 Ringcombe
  *Ringedone*
23 Satterleigh
25 *Snydles (1)
5 Swimbridge
3 B;shops Tawton
21 Wadham
14 Whitstone

**7 Witheridge**
30 Adworthy
8 Rose Ash
  *Asecote*
16 Backstone
  'Beare'
12 Bickham
28 Blagrove
29 Bradford
26 Bulworthy
  *Celvertesberie*
37 Cheldon
34 Chulmleigh
45 Coombe
  (in Cruwys Morchard)
33 Coombe (in Templeton)
15 Creacombe
  'Dart'
31 Dart Raffe
51 Densham
39 Drayford
  *Eltemetone*
32 Essebeare
4 Highleigh
49 Hill
24 Irishcombe
5 Mariansleigh
14 Meshaw
36 Middlewick
6 Mildon
43 Cruwys Morchard
19a *Nutcott (9)
1 Bishops Nympton
13 Kings Nympton
10 Oakford
41 Pedley
47 Puddington
21 Little Rackenford
20 Rackenford
27 Rifton
11 Romansleigh
46 Ruckham
40 Ruston
9 Spurway
23 Stoodleigh
18 Sydeham
3 Tapps
42 Thelbridge
  *Toredone*
  'Little Washfield'
44 Washford Pyne

## DEVON HUNDREDS AND MAP KEYS

**7 Witheridge** (cont'd.)
19 Waspley
22 West Whitnole
25 Wilson
35 Witheridge
2 Woodburn
52 Woolfardisworthy
38 Worlington
17 Worthy
7 Yard
50 *Yeadbury (14)
48 Yowlestone

**8 Bampton**
8a *Alwinestone*
4 Bampton
*Ciclet*
5 Clayhanger
2 Dipford
3 Donningstone
8 Hockworthy
9 Holcombe Rogus
6 Kerswell
1 Morebath
7 Stallenge Thorne
8b 1 Uffculme

**9 Tiverton**
10 Bolham
15 Bradley
9 Calverleigh
11 Chettiscombe
5 Chevithorne
2 Coombe
1 Huntsham

14 'Kidwell'
8 Leigh
*Loteland*
13 Craze Lowman
4 Loxbeare
17 West Manley
3 Murley
12 Peadhill
16 Tiverton
6 Uplowman
7 *Whitnage (10)

**10 Halberton**
7 Appledore
13 Ash Thomas
6 Ayshford
5 Boehill
4 *Burlescombe (8)
2 Canonsleigh
1 Fenacre
10 Halberton
15 Leonard
11 East Manley
12 Muxbere
8 Sellake
9 Sampford Peverell
16 Sutton
3 Westleigh
14 Willand

**11 Black Torrington**
*Alwineclancavele*
2 Ash
55 Ashbury
60 Ashwater

49 Beaworthy
64 Belstone
10 Abbots Bickington
24 Bradford
  (near Cookbury)
44 Bradford (in Pyworthy)
5 Bradworthy
7 Brexworthy
37 Bridgerule
32 Brixton
33 Broadwood Kelly
22 Chilsworthy
47 Clawton
6 Colscott
9 Culsworthy
56 Curworthy
18 Dunsdon
41 Dunsland
42 Exbourne
17 Gidcott
54 Gorhuish
48 Halwill
19 Hamsworthy
36 Hatherleigh
61 Henford
21 Henscott
34 Highampton
40 Hollacombe
39 Holsworthy
43 Honeychurch
1 Horton
25 Ingleigh
11 Instaple
52 Inwardleigh
53 Kimber

8 Kimworthy
29 Lashbrook
  *Lidemore*
58 Melbury
26 Middlecott
13 Milton Damerel
31 Monkokehampton
50 Northlew
51 Oak
63 Panson
62 Peeke
4 West Putford
38 Pyworthy
45 Rutleigh
46 Sampford Courtenay
35 Stockleigh
12 Sutcombe
  *Tamerlande*
57 Tetcott
20 Thornbury
27 Thorne
15 Thuborough
30 Black Torrington
14 Virworthy
3 Wedfield
23 Week
65 Werrington
  (CORNWALL)
28 Cookbury Wick
59 Widefield□
16 Wonford

**12 North Tawton**
34 Appledore
6 Ashreigney

## DEVON HUNDREDS AND MAP KEYS

12 **North Tawton** (cont'd.)
28 Great Beere
2 High Bickington
24 Bondleigh
40 Broadnymett
19 Brushford
4 Buckland
3 Burrington
32 Burston
21 Bury
30 Chaffcombe□
11 Chawleigh
 *Chetelescote*
33 Clannaborough
20 Coldridge
39 Crooke Burnell
9 Dockworthy
10 Dolton
13 Dowland
26 Down St. Mary
7 Goodcott
37 Greenslade
38 Halse
36 Hampson
8 Hook
18 Lapford
22 Leigh
23 Loosebeare
15 Loosedon
41 Natson
25 Newton
31 Nichols Nymet
17 Nymet Rowland
42 Nymet Tracey
5 Riddlecombe

12 Stafford
35 North Tawton
1 Umberleigh
43 Walson
14 Wembworthy
16 Winkleigh
27 Wolfin
29 Zeal Monachorum

13 **Crediton**
3 Crediton
1 Morchard Bishop
4 Newton St. Cyres
2 Shobrooke

14 **Budleigh**
14a (**West Budleigh**)
1 Washfield
2 Worth
14b (**West Budleigh**)
5 Cheriton Fitzpaine
7 Chilton
3 Coddiford
2 Coombe
9 Lower Creedy
6 Dunscombe
1 Poughill
10 West Raddon
11 Shobrooke
 'Stockleigh'
4 Stockleigh English
8 Stockleigh Pomeroy
12 Wyke
14c (**East Budleigh**)
6 Aylesbeare

18 Bicton
 'Brightston'
20 East Budleigh
10 Clyst St. George
8 Clyst St. Mary
15 Colaton Raleigh
9 Crealy
11 Dotton
5 Farringdon
1 Gittisham
4 Holbrook
23 Littleham
19 Lympstone
17 Nutwell
21 Otterton
2 Rapshays
3 Rockbeare
12 Salcombe Regis
7 Sidbury
16 Sidmouth
14 Stowford
22 Withycombe Raleigh
13 Woodbury
(**In East or West Budleigh**)
 *Heppastebe*
 *Landeshers*

15 **Hayridge**
13 Aller
 'Bernardsmoor'
8 Bickleigh
2 Blackborough
17 Bowley
20 Bradninch
22 Broadhembury

15 Burn
18 Cadbury
3 Cadeleigh
33 Cheriton
19 Chitterley
29 Clyst William
16 Colebrook
26 'Combe Sackville'
11 Cullompton
 'Monk Culm'
34 Curscombe
4 Dart
35 Nether Exe
37 Feniton
23 Greenslinch
 *Hewise*
9 Hillersdon
6 Kentisbeare
14 Kerswell
5 Kingsford
27 Langford
12 Orway
32 Payhembury
1 Pirzwell
28 Plymtree
10 Ponsford
24 Raddon
7 Sheldon
25 Silverton
 *Stochelie*
36 Talaton
31 Tale
21 Woodbeare
30 Yard

# DEVON HUNDREDS AND MAP KEYS

## 16 Hemyock
13 Awliscombe
7 Bolham Water
11 Bywood
4 Churchstanton (SOMERSET)
2 Clayhidon
1 Culm Davy
3 Culm Pyne
5 Culmstock
12 Dunkeswell
10 Gorwell
6 Hemyock
8 Hole
14 *Ivedon (9)
9 Mackham
15 Weston

## 17 Axminster and Axmouth
### 17a (Axminster) Alfreford
15 Axminster 'Charlton'
10 Combe Raleigh 'Deneworthy'
1 Dennington 'Ford'
6 Greenway Hetfelle
12 Honiton
16 Kilmington
4 Luppitt
9 Membury
7 Mohuns Ottery
5 Rawridge
8 Shapcombe
13 Smallridge
11 Undercleave
18 Uplyme
3 Upottery
14 Weycroft
17 Wyke Green
2 Yarcombe

### 17b (Axminster) (DORSET)
1 Thorncombe

### 17c (Axminster)
5 Axmouth
2 Bruckland
3 Combpyne 'Down Umfraville'
1 Musbury
6 Rousdon
4 Stedcombe

## 18 Lifton
31 Ashleigh
29 Battishill□
10 Boasley
4 Bradaford
36 Bradstone
11 Bratton Clovelly
17 Bridestowe
15 Broadwoodwidger
42 Burntown□
2 Chichacott
47 Collacombe
19 Combebowe□
33 Coryton
12 Downicary
37 Dunterton
13 Ebsworthy□
20 Fernworthy□
6 Germansweek 'Guscott'
35 Kelly
24 Kersford□
1 *Kigbeare (11)
44 Lamerton
43 Leigh+
23 Lewtrenchard
34 Liddaton+
25 Lifton
30 Lydford
21 Milford
38 Milton Abbot+
5 Moor
9 Norton
3 Okehampton
48 Ottery
28 Raddon
14 Sourton
8 Southweek
26 Sprytown
22 Stowford
32 Sydenham
46 Sydenham Damerel
49 Tavistock+
40 Mary Tavy
18 Thrushelton
7 Tillislow
39 Warne□
28 Warson
16 Way□
41 Willestrew
45 Wringworthy□

## 19 Wonford
19a 50 Alphington
34 Ash
3 Bramford Speke
56 Bridford
58 *Canonteign (23)
54 *Chagford (24)
19 Cheriton Bishop
44 Clifford
35 Coombe
39 Cowick
28 Crockernwell
5 Culm Vale
43 Drewsteignton
49 Dunsford
36 Eggbear
1 *Up Exe (15)
31 Exeter
15 Exwick
45 'Floyers Hayes'□
37 Great Fulford
18 Fursham
51 Gidleigh
20 Hackworthy
30 Halstow
32 Heavitree
11 Hittisleigh
38 Holcombe Burnell
22 Huish
6 Huxham
27 Lambert
26 Martin

# DEVON HUNDREDS AND MAP KEYS

**19 Wonford** (cont'd.)
- 12 Medland
- 29 Melhuish
- 55 Middlecott
- 10 Oldridge
- 48 Parford
- 16 Pinhoe
- 24 Polsloe
- 7 Poltimore
- 2 Rewe
- 47 Rushford
- 46 St. James Church
- 57 Shapley
- 42 Shilstone
- 'Shutbrook'
  (see 'Floyers Hayes')
- 33 Sowton
- 9 Spreyton
- 4 Stoke Canon
- 8 Taw Green
- 13 South Tawton
- 14 Tedburn St. Mary
- 53 Teigncombe
- 17 Thornbury
- 41 Throwleigh
- 52 Topsham
- 21 Uppacott
- 25 Whipton
- 23 Whitestone
- 40 Wonford
- 19b 1 Holbeam
- 2b East Ogwell
- 2a West Ogwell
- 19c 1 *Buckland (29)
- 2 Combeinteignhead
- 5 *Haccombe (29)
- 8 Maidencombe
- 4 Ringmore
- 7 Rocombe
- 6 Stokeinteignhead
- 3 Teignharvey

**20 Cliston**
- 20a 1 Butterleigh
- 20b 6 Ashclyst
- 3 Aunk
- 7 Broadclyst
- 10 *West Clyst (19)
- 5 Clyst Gerred
- 1 Clyst Hydon
- 2 Clyst St. Lawrence
- 4 Columbjohn
  'Eveleigh'
  *Herstanhaia*
- 9 Larkbeare
- 11 *Strete Ralegh (14)
- 3 Whimple

**21 Ottery St. Mary**
- 1 Ottery St. Mary

**22 Colyton**
- 19 Beer
- 3 'Beer'
  *Bere*
- 20 Branscombe
- 6 Colwell
- 14 Colyton
- 1 Cotleigh
- 11 Farway
- 12 Farwood
- 17 Gatcombe
- 10 Northleigh
- 2 Offwell
- 16 'Radish'
- 18 Seaton
- 9 Smallicombe
- 15 Southleigh
- 5 Sutton
- 13 Whitford
- 7 Whitley□
- 4 Widworthy
- 3 Wilmington
  'Womberford'

**23 Teignbridge**
- 32 Ashburton
- 25 *Bagtor (19)
- 3 Beetor
- 23 Little Bovey
- 5 North Bovey
- 18 Bovey Tracey
  *Brungarstone*
- 7 Elsford
- 20 Gappah
- 11 Hatherleigh
- 12 Hawkmoor
- 14 Hennock
- 16 Houndtor
- 21 Ideford
- 22 Ilsington
- 28 Ingsdon
- 31 Kingsteignton
- 19 Chudleigh Knighton
- 8 Langstone
- 2 Lowton
- 9 Manaton
- 1 Moretonhampstead
- 10 Neadon
- 17 Pullabrook
- 6 Shapley
- 27 *Sigford (19)
- 29 *Staplehill (19)
  *Sutreworde*
- 30 Teigngrace
- 24 Twinyeo
- 15 Warmhill
- 26 Whiteway
- 13 Woolleigh
- 4 Wray

**24 Exminster**
- 17 Ashcombe
- 10 Ashton
- 20 Bishopsteignton
- 18 Dawlish
- 8 Doddiscombsleigh
- 5 Dunchideock
- 7 Exminster
- 19 Holcombe
- 1 Ide
- 9 Kenn
- 13 Kenton
- 4 Lowley
- 15 Mamhead
- 2 Matford
- 16 Mowlish
- 3 Peamore
- 11 Powderham
- 6 Shillingford
- 12 George Teign

# DEVON HUNDREDS AND MAP KEYS

**24 Exminster** (cont'd.)
14 Trusham

**25 Roborough**
9 Bere Ferrers
11 Bickleigh
10 Blaxton
7 Buckland Monachorum
13 Budshead
22 Burrington
15 Coleridge
23 Compton Gifford
24 Efford
20 Eggbuckland
17 Honicknowle
*Leuricestone*
25 Lipson
30 Maker (CORNWALL)
18 Manadon
8 Meavy
5 Monkswell
27 Mutley
4 Sampford Spiney
26 Stoke
28 Stonehouse
29 Sutton
16 Kings Tamerton
12 Tamerton Foliot
2 Peter Tavy
6 Walkhampton
21 Weston Peverell
3 Whitchurch
19 Widey
1 Willsworthy

**26 Plympton**
6 'Baccamoor'
17 Battisford
8 Bickford
4 Brixton
    (in Shaugh Prior)
26 Brixton
    (near Yealmpton)
16 Challonsleigh
24 Chittleburn
2 Coldstone
33 Down Thomas
32 *Dunstone (27)
7 Elfordleigh
5 Fernhill
22 Goosewell
23 Halwell
20 Hareston
10 Hemerdon
14 Holland
21 Hooe
15 Langage
35 Langdon
9 Loughtor
3 Pethill
12 Plympton
18 Plymstock
1 Shaugh Prior
19 Sherford
29 Spriddlestone
28 Staddiscombe
27 Staddon
13 Torridge
34 Train
    'Walford'
30 Winston
25 Wollaton
11 Woodford
31 Yealmpton

**27 Ermington**
    'Abbots Ash'
29 Aveton Gifford
26 Battisborough
30 Bigbury
1 Blachford
10 Bowcombe
9 Broadaford
2 Cornwood
22 Creacombe
6 Dinnaton
15 Ermington
5 Fardel
20 Flete
3 Harford
21 Heathfield
17 Hollowcombe
27 Lambside
8 Langford
19 Leigh
13 Ludbrook
25 Membland
18 Modbury
24 Newton Ferrers
28 Okenbury
23 Orcheton
4 Peek
31 Ringmore
16 Shilston
14 Spriddlescombe
32 Stadbury
11 Ugborough
7 Venn
12 Worthele

**28 Stanborough**
24 East Allington
37 Alston
30 West Alvington
34 Bagton
39 Batson
15 Beenleigh
40 Bolberry
10 South Brent
16 Broadley
3 Buckfast
29 Buckland
12 *Butterford (30)
11 Charford
42 Collaton
27 Combe Royal
18 Curtisknowle
8 Dartington
5 Dean Prior
14 Diptford
19 Farleigh
36 Galmpton
21 *Grimpstonleigh (30)
    'Halstow'
7 Harbourneford
2 Holne
13 North Huish
33 South Huish
38 Ilton
25 Leigh

# DEVON HUNDREDS AND MAP KEYS

**28 Stanborough** (cont'd.)
22 Loddiswell
17 *Lupridge (30)
6 Luscombe
32 South Milton
20 Moreleigh
28 Norton
41 West Portlemouth
9 Rattery
4 Skerraton
43 Soar
26 Sorley
1 Stoke
31 Thurlestone
23 Woodleigh
35 Woolston

**29 Haytor**
29a 3 'Blackslade'
5 Buckland in the Moor
 'Dewdon'
2 Dunstone
1 Natsworthy
4 Scobitor
6 Spitchwick
29b 3 Abbotskerswell
21 Afton
4 Aller
16 Battleford
23 Berry Pomeroy
28 Brixham
7 Broadhempston
27 Churston Ferrers

18 Cockington
5 Coffinswell
31 Coleton
13 Shiphay Collaton
12 Combe Fishacre
2 Denbury
10 Edginswell
26 Galmpton
25 Goodrington
19 Ilsham
9 Ipplepen
6 Kingskerswell
20 Littlehempston
22 Loventor
29 Lupton
24 Paignton
14 St. Marychurch
11 Sparkwell
15 Staverton
8 Torbryan
17 Tormoham
1 Wolborough
30 Woodhuish

**30 Coleridge**
29 South Allington
5 Ashprington
13 Blackawton
15 Buckland Tout Saints
23 Charleton
24 Chillington
28 Chivelstone

22 Coleridge
25 Combe
7 Cornworthy
8 Dittisham
18 Dodbrooke
6 Englebourne
1 Follaton
27 Ford
11 Grimpstone
3 Hazard
21 Keynedon
4 Leigh
16 Malston
26 Pool
9 Poulston
30 West Prawle
19 Sherford
20 Slapton
17 Stancombe
14 Stoke Fleming
2 Totnes
12 Townstall
10 Washbourne
31 Woodcombe

**C In Cornwall in 1086**
1 Borough
2 Tackbear

**D In Dorset in 1086**
2 Chardstock
1 Stockland

**PLACES UNIDENTIFIED, NOT MAPPED, NOT ASSIGNED TO ANY HUNDRED**
*Esseorda* (Ch. 44 note)
*Ferding* (39,3 note)
*Hewis* (15,28 note)
*Petecota* (16,139 note)
*Vlestamecote* (25,27 note)
*Wederige* (15,53 note)

# TECHNICAL TERMS

Many words meaning measurements have to be transliterated. But translation may not dodge other problems by the use of obsolete or made-up words which do not exist in modern English. The translations here used are given in italics. They cannot be exact; they aim at the nearest modern equivalent. The Latin forms used in the Exon. DB, where divergent from those used in the Exchequer DB, are given after the semi-colon.

ACRA; AGRA, AGER. A unit of land measurement, usually square, mostly used in Devon as a measurement of meadow, woodland and pasture, though once used in the tax assessment (General notes 6,6). On the number of acres to a hide, see General Notes 1,3. *a c r e*

BORDARIUS. Cultivator of inferior status, usually with a little land; see General Notes 1,3. *s m a l l h o l d e r*

BURUS. A cultivator, similar to the OE *(ge)bur*, though probably of slightly lower status and on three occasions in DB equated with the *colibertus*. See General Notes 5,8. *b o o r*

c. Marginal abbreviation for *canonicis* 'for (the supplies of) the canons'; see General Notes 2,8.

CARUCA; CARRUCA. A plough, with the oxen that pulled it, usually reckoned as 8; see General Notes 3,37. *p l o u g h*

CARUCATA; CARRUCATA. Normally the equivalent of a *hide* in former Danish areas, but elsewhere, especially in the south-west counties, the equivalent of 'land for *y* ploughs'; see General Notes 1,2. *c a r u c a t e*

COLIBERTUS; QUOLIBERTUS. A continental term, rendering OE *(ge)bur*; a former slave, sometimes holding land and ploughs and rendering dues; see General Notes 1,50. *f r e e d m a n*

CONSUETUDO. Latin 'custom' or 'habit'; in DB generally used as a fixed rent or service payable at regular intervals. *c u s t o m a r y   d u e*

COSCET (sing.), COSCEZ (pl.); COCETUS (sing.), COTSETI, COCETI (pl.). A cultivator who lived in a cottage; see General Notes 2,24. *C o t t a g e r*

COTARIUS; QUOTARIUS. Inhabitant of a *cote*, cottage, often without land; see General Notes 15,21. *c o t t a g e r*

DOMINICUS. Belonging to a lord or lordship. *l o r d s h i p* or *h o u s e h o l d* (adjs.)

DOMINIUM. The mastery or dominion of a lord *(dominus)*, including ploughs, land, men, villages, etc., reserved for the lord's use; often concentrated in a *home farm* or *demesne*, a 'Manor Farm' or 'Lordship Farm'. *l o r d s h i p*

FERLING; FERLINUS, FERDINUS, FERTINUS. A 'fourth', regularly used as a measurement, a quarter (of a virgate); used in Devon in recording the tax assessment and the lordship and villagers' land and, once, in measuring underwood; a 'ferling'. See General Notes 1,4 and 47,6. *f u r l o n g*

FEUDUM. Continental variant of *feuum*, not used in England before 1086; either a landholder's holding or land held by a special grant. *H o l d i n g*

FIRMA. Old English *feorm*, provisions due to the King or lord; a fixed sum paid in place of these and of other miscellaneous dues. See General Notes 1,5 (second and fourth notes) and to 1,21. *r e v e n u e*

FIRMARIUS. Someone who agreed to pay the King, the Sheriff or the lord of a manor a fixed sum of money in return for administering and receiving the rents, dues and profits from a manor. See General Notes 1,5 (second note). *' f a r m e r '*

GABLUM. Old English *gafol*, tribute or tax to the King or lord. *t r i b u t e*

GELDUM. The principal royal tax, originally levied during the Danish wars, normally at an equal number of pence on each *hide* of land. *t a x*

HIDA. A unit of land measurement, generally reckoned at 120 acres, but often different in practice; a measure of tax liability, often differing in number from the hides actually cultivated see General Notes 1,4. *h i d e*

HONOR. Equivalent to *feudum*, Holding. *H o n o u r*

HUNDREDUM. A district within a Shire, whose assembly of notables and village representatives usually met about once a month. *H u n d r e d*

LEUGA. A measure of length, usually of woodland and pasture, generally reckoned at a mile and a half, possibly shorter; see General Notes 1,2. *l e a g u e*

MANERIUM; MANSIO. A territorial and jurisdictional holding. *m a n o r*

MARKA. A coin; a silver mark was worth 13s 4d, a gold mark, £6. *m a r k*

ORA. An 'ounce'; a unit of currency reckoned at either 16d or 20d; see General Notes 1,28. *o r a*

PERTICA, PERCA; PERCATA, PERTIQUA. A measure of length 5½ yards, a 40th of a furlong; see General Notes 16,172. *p e r c h*

PREPOSITUS. Old English *gerefa*, a royal officer. See General Notes 1,4. *r e e v e*
QUARENTINA; QUADRAGENARIA. A subdivision of the league; see General Notes 1,4. *f u r l o n g*
r. Marginal abbreviation for *require*, 'enquire', occurring when the scribe has omitted some information. See General Notes 11,1.
SEXTARIUM; SEXTARIA. A liquid or dry measure of uncertain size, reckoned at 32 oz. for honey; see General Notes 23,15. *s e s t e r*
SUMMA. A dry measure, mainly of salt, corn and fish; see General Notes 15,66. *p a c k l o a d*
TAINUS, TEGNUS; TAGNUS. Person holding land from the King by special grant; formerly used of the King's ministers and military companions. See General Notes 1,32. *t h a n e*
T.R.E. *tempore regis Edwardi*, in King Edward's time. *b e f o r e 1 0 6 6*
T.R.W. *tempore regis Willelmi*, in King Edward's time. *b e f o r e 1 0 6 6*
VILLA. Translating Old English *tun*, 'town'. The later distinction between a small *village* and a large *town* was not yet in use in 1086. *v i l l a g e* or *t o w n*
VILLANUS. Member of a *villa*, usually with more land than a *bordarius*. See the section on Exon. and Exchequer Formillae in the Introduction to the Exon. Notes on Exon.'s use of *villani* as a comprehensive term to cover most classes of population in a village. *v i l l a g e r*
VIRGA. A measure of uncertain length; see General Notes 11,6. *' r o d '*
VIRGATA; VIRGA. An areal measure, a fraction of a hide, usually a quarter, notionally 30 acres. *v i r g a t e*

## SYSTEMS OF REFERENCE TO DOMESDAY BOOK

The manuscript is divided into numbered chapters, and the chapters into sections, usually marked by large initials and red ink. Farley did not number the sections and later historians, using his edition, have referred to the text of DB by folio numbers, which cannot be closer than an entire page or column. Moreover, several different ways of referring to the same column have been devised. In 1816 Ellis used three separate systems in his indices: (i) on pages i-cvii, 435-518, 537-570; (ii) on pages 1-144; (iii) on pages 145-433 and 519-535. Other systems have since come into use, notably that used by Vinogradoff, here followed. The present edition numbers the sections, the normal practicable form of close reference; but since all discussion of DB for two hundred years has been obliged to refer to folio or column, a comparative table will help to locate references given. The five columns below give Vinogradoff's notation, Ellis's three systems, and that used by Welldon Finn and others. Maitland, Stenton, Darby, and others, have usually followed Ellis (i).

| Vinogradoff | Ellis (i) | Ellis (ii) | Ellis (iii) | Finn |
|---|---|---|---|---|
| 152 a | 152 | 152 a | 152 | 152 ai |
| 152 b | 152 | 152 a | 152.2 | 152 a2 |
| 152 c | 152 b | 152 b | 152 b | 152 bi |
| 152 d | 152 b | 152 b | 152 b2 | 152 b2 |

In Devon the relation between the Vinogradoff column notation, here followed, and the chapters and sections is:

| | | | | | | | | | |
|---|---|---|---|---|---|---|---|---|---|
| 100a | C 1-7. Landholders | | 107a | 16,74 | − 16,88 | 114a | 34,2 | − | 34,17 |
| b | 1,1 | − 1,11 | b | 16,89 | − 16,104 | b | 34,18 | − | 34,32 |
| c | 1,11 | − 1,23 | c | 16,105 | − 16,120 | c | 34,33 | − | 34,49 |
| d | 1,23 | − 1,35 | d | 16,120 | − 16,135 | d | 34,49 | − | 35,5 |
| 101a | 1,35 | − 1,47 | 108a | 16,136 | − 16,149 | 115a | 35,5 | − | 35,19 |
| b | 1,48 | − 1,62 | b | 16,150 | − 16,166 | b | 35,20 | − | 36,5 |
| c | 1,62 | − 1,72 | c | 16,167 | − 17,5 | c | 36,6 | − | 36,21 |
| d | 2,1 | − 2,13 | d | 17,5 | − 17,17 | d | 36,22 | − | 39,3 |
| 102a | 2,14 | − 3,4 | 109a | 17,18 | − 17,34 | 116a | 39,4 | − | 39,17 |
| b | 3,5 | − 3,20 | b | 17,35 | − 17,53 | b | 39,18 | − | [41],2 |
| c | 3,21 | − 3,37 | c | 17,53 | − 17,70 | c | [42],1 | − | [42],14 |
| d | 3,38 | − 3,54;56-59;55 | d | 17,71 | − 17,89 | d | [42],15 | − | [43],3 |
| 103a | 3,59 | − 3,74;76;75 | 110a | 17,89 | − 17,105 | 117a | [43],3 | − | [47],5 |
| b | 3,77 | − 3,94 | b | 17,105 | − 19,12 | b | [47],5 | − | [48],8 |
| c | 3,95 | − 5,5 | c | 19,13 | − 19,28 | c | [48],8 | − | [49],6. [50],1−[51],2. [49],7 |
| d | 5,5 | − 6,4 | d | 19,29 | − 19,44 | d | [51],2 | − | [51],16 |
| 104a | 6,4 | − 9,1 | 111a | 19,44 | − 20,14 | 118a | [52],1 | − | [52],19 |
| b | 9,2 | − [13a],3 | b | 20,14 | − 21,11 | b | [52],20 | − | [52],36 |
| c | 14,1 | − 15,14 | c | 21,12 | − 23,2 | c | [52],37 | − | [52],53 |
| d | 15,15 | − 15,31 | d | 23,2 | − 23,15 | d | Blank | | |
| 105a | 15,32 | − 15,44 | 112a | 23,16 | − 24,2 | | | | |
| b | 15,44 | − 15,58 | b | 24,3 | − 24,18 | | | | |
| c | 15,59 | − 15,74 | c | 24,19 | − 25,3 | | | | |
| d | 15,75 | − 16,7 | d | 25,3 | − 25,20 | | | | |
| 106a | 16,8 | − 16,22 | 113a | 25,21 | − 28,4 | | | | |
| b | 16,23 | − 16,38 | b | 28,4 | − 29,2 | | | | |
| c | 16,39 | − 16,56 | c | 29,2 | − 31,4 | | | | |
| d | 16,56 | − 16,73 | d | 32,1 | − 34,1 | | | | |